Homo Migrans

THE INSTITUTE FOR EUROPEAN AND MEDITERRANEAN ARCHAEOLOGY
DISTINGUISHED MONOGRAPH SERIES

Peter F. Biehl, editor-in-chief
Sarunas Milisauskas and Stephen L. Dyson, editors

The Magdalenian Household: Unraveling Domesticity
Ezra Zubrow, Françoise Audouze, and James G. Enloe, editors

Eventful Archaeologies: New Approaches to Social Transformation in the Archaeological Record
Douglas J. Bolender, editor

The Archaeology of Violence: Interdisciplinary Approaches
Sarah Ralph, editor

Approaching Monumentality in Archaeology
James. F. Osborne, editor

The Archaeology of Childhood: Interdisciplinary Perspectives on an Archaeological Enigma
Güner Coşkunsu, editor

Diversity of Sacrifice: Form and Function of Sacrificial Practices in the Ancient World and Beyond
Carrie Ann Murray, editor

Climate and Cultural Change in Prehistoric Europe and the Near East
Peter F. Biehl and Olivier P. Nieuwenhuyse, editors

Water and Power in Past Societies
Emily Holt, editor

Coming Together: Comparative Approaches to Population Aggregation and Early Urbanization
Attila Gyucha, editor

The Early Bronze Age in Western Anatolia
Laura K. Harrison, A. Nejat Bilgen, and Asuman Kapuci, editors

The Archaeology of Inequality
Orlando Cerasuolo, editor

Homo Migrans: Modeling Mobility and Migration in Human History
Megan J. Daniels, editor

HOMO MIGRANS

Modeling Mobility and Migration in Human History

IEMA Proceedings,
Volume 11

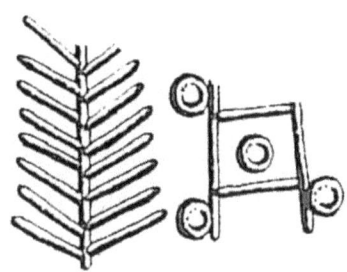

EDITED BY
Megan J. Daniels

STATE UNIVERSITY OF
NEW YORK PRESS

Logo and cover/interior art: A vessel with wagon motifs from Bronocice, Poland, 3400 B.C. Courtesy of Sarunas Milisauskas and Janusz Kruk, 1982, Die Wagendarstellung auf einem Trichterbecher aus Bronocice, Polen, *Archäologisches Korrespondenzblatt* 12: 141–144.

Published by
State University of New York Press, Albany

© 2022 State University of New York

All rights reserved

Printed in the United States of America

No part of this book may be used or reproduced in any manner whatsoever without written permission. No part of this book may be stored in a retrieval system or transmitted in any form or by any means including electronic, electrostatic, magnetic tape, mechanical, photocopying, recording, or otherwise without the prior permission in writing of the publisher.

For information, contact
State University of New York Press, Albany, NY
www.sunypress.edu

Library of Congress Cataloging-in-Publication Data

Name: Daniels, Megan J., editor
Title: Homo migrans : modeling mobility and migration in human history / Megan J. Daniels, editor.
Description: Albany : State University of New York Press, [2022] | Series: SUNY series, The Institute for European and Mediterranean Archaeology Distinguished Monograph Series | Includes bibliographical references and index.
Identifiers: ISBN 9781438488011 (hardcover : alk. paper) | ISBN 9781438488028 (ebook) | ISBN 9781438488004 (pbk. : alk. paper)
Further information is available at the Library of Congress.

10 9 8 7 6 5 4 3 2 1

Contents

ILLUSTRATIONS ix

CHAPTER ONE *Megan J. Daniels*
Movement as a Constant? Envisioning a Migration-Centered
Worldview of Human History 1

PART I
NEW DATA AND NEW NARRATIVES

CHAPTER TWO *Kristian Kristiansen*
Toward a New Prehistory: Re-Theorizing Genes, Culture, and
Migratory Expansions 31

CHAPTER THREE *David W. Anthony*
Migration, Ancient DNA, and Bronze Age Pastoralists from
the Eurasian Steppes 55

CHAPTER FOUR *Omer Gokcumen*
The Conceptual Impacts of Genomics to the Archaeology
of Movement 79

PART II
MIGRATIONS, VISIBLE AND INVISIBLE: TOWARD MORE INCLUSIVE HISTORIES

CHAPTER FIVE *Franco De Angelis*
New Data and Old Narratives: Migrants and the Conjoining of
the Cultures and Economies of the pre-Roman Western Mediterranean 95

CHAPTER SIX *Catherine M. Cameron*
Captives: The Invisible Migrant 111

CHAPTER SEVEN
The In/Visiblity of Migration
Elena Isayev
133

CHAPTER EIGHT
A Harbor Scene: Reassessing Mobility in the Bronze Age Eastern Mediterranean Following the Archaeological Science Revolution
Assaf Yasur-Landau
147

Part III
Computational Models of Migration

CHAPTER NINE
Surfing with the Alien: Simulating and Testing the Spread of Early Farming across the Adriatic Basin
Marc Vander Linden, Cornelis Drost, Jane Gaastra, Ivana Jovanović, Sébastien Manem, Anne de Vareilles
165

CHAPTER TEN
The Settlement Record, Paleodemography, and Evidence for Migrations in Eneolithic Ukraine
Thomas K. Harper
183

CHAPTER ELEVEN
N Site Continuous Model for Migration: Parameter and Prehistoric Tests
Ezra B. W. Zubrow, Aleksandr Diachenko, Jay Leavitt
201

Part IV
Sociohistorical Models of Migration

CHAPTER TWELVE
Toward A Social Archaeology of Forced Migration: Rebuilding Landscapes of Memory in Medieval Armenian Cilicia
Aurora E. Camaño
229

CHAPTER THIRTEEN
Macro- and Micro-Mobilities and the Creation of Identity in the Ancient Near East
Anne Porter
249

CHAPTER FOURTEEN
Wandering Ports on the Datça Peninsula: Exploring Regional Mobility in a Maritime Landscape
Elizabeth S. Greene and Justin Leidwanger
269

Part V
Migration and Complexity

CHAPTER FIFTEEN
Assessing the Possibility of Trans-Maritime Mobility in Archaic Hominins: Does Afro-Eurasian Coastal Palaeogeography Support Sweepstakes Dispersal in *Homo*?
Thomas P. Leppard
293

CHAPTER SIXTEEN *Homo mobilis*: Interactions, Consciousness, and the Anthropocene	*Hans Barnard* 317	
CONTRIBUTORS	345	
INDEX	347	

Illustrations

FIGURES

Figure 2.1   The three science revolutions in archaeology and the accumulating conversion from relative to absolute knowledge in tandem with the accumulation of archaeological data.   32

Figure 2.2   Model of the basic organizing categories of society and their dynamics.   34

Figure 2.3   Conceptual model of forces of power in human societies that integrates micro- and macrodynamics.   35

Figure 2.4   Cyclical swings of discourse between humanistic- and science-based interpretations of the world.   43

Figure 3.1   M. Gimbutas (1963: Figure 2) map of Kurgan Culture migrations. Reproduced by permission of the American Anthropological Association, from *American Anthropologist* 65, no. 4 (1963): 815–36. https://doi.org/10.1525/aa.1963.65.4.02a00030. Not for sale or further reproduction.   58

Figure 3.2   A processual model of long-distance migration, from Anthony 1990.   59

Figure 3.3   Yamnaya kurgan cemeteries in the Danube valley, 3100–2800 B.C., from Anthony 2007.   64

Figure 3.4   The nine regional groups (I–IX) of the Yamnaya culture defined by N. Y. Merpert (1974: Figure 1). In his legend, a = documented border of a culture region; b = supposed border of region; and c = direction of invasion of other culture areas.   67

Figure 6.1	A Northwest Coast Village. Men are returning from a raid, with bound captives and trophy heads. By François Girard, courtesy Canadian Museum of History, 1-a-42, s95–23505. 115
Figure 6.2	Guaraní women and children captured by slave hunters. Image by French artist Jean-Baptiste Debret, who lived in Brazil during the early decades of the nineteenth century. From *Voyage pittoresque et historique au Brésil* [A picturesque and historic voyage to Brazil], Imprimerie Nationale Éditions (Arles: Actes Sud, 2014) (Public Domain). 118
Figure 8.1	Overlapping interaction ranges; after Yasur-Landau 2010: Figure 1.1. 150
Figure 8.2	Interactions in a harbor scene, tomb of Kenamun (after Davies and Faulkner 1947: pl. 8, additions by Yasur-Landau). (Public Domain) 151
Figure 9.1	Top left: behavior of the unmodified CDM model at steps 5 k, 100 k, 500 k, and 1,500 k. Top right: Behavior of the wave toy model for corresponding steps. The red dotted lines indicate the eight vertical slices used to calculate Shannon's diversity index values (after Drost and Vander Linden 2018: Figure 5). 169
Figure 9.2	Plot of Shannon's diversity values for all vertical blocks (after Drost and Vander Linden 2018: Figure 5). 169
Figure 9.3	Interpolated dates for the dispersal of early farming across Europe. 171
Figure 9.4	Plot of absolute population growth rate for the Adriatic Neolithic, as inferred from the analysis of the ^{14}C record. 172
Figure 9.5	Taxonomic representation of sites by region for initial and secondary phases of Neolithic settlement expressed via correspondence analysis (after Gaastra and Vander Linden 2018: Figure 8). 174
Figure 9.6	Violin plots of eigenvalues for Dimension 1 for first and second Adriatic Neolithic zooarchaeological assemblages. 176
Figure 9.7	Violin plots of eigenvalues for Dimension 2 for both first and second Adriatic Neolithic zooarchaeological assemblages. 177
Figure 10.1	The study area, overlaid with the distribution of Cucuteni-Tripolye sites and the positions of cemeteries discussed in the text. 186
Figure 10.2	Population expansion and movement over the course of the Neo-Eneolithic period in Romania, Moldova, and Ukraine, expressed as a stacked percentage (simplified to five regions for clarity). 188

Figure 10.3   Comparison of observed values of q_x (probability of death for a given age cohort) with a generalized model life table drawn from global ethnographic observations of traditional societies (data from Weiss 1973).   192

Figure 10.4   Percentage distribution of deaths for a given age cohort x (d_x).   193

Figure 10.5   The spatio-temporal distribution of population growth episodes probably outstripping PNI.   195

Figure 11.1   A comparison between a population growing at a faster and slower rate to an available resource limit (expressed in population).   206

Figure 11.2   A growing population with nonrenewable resources: 2a—as population increases resources decrease to an equilibrium point; 2b—the dynamic process of reaching equilibrium.   207

Figure 11.3   A growing population with nonrenewable resources—as population grows resources decline appropriately reflecting consumption.   208

Figure 11.4   Surplus population migrating sequentially from areas of higher resources to areas of lower resources.   208

Figure 11.5   User interface for the N Site Migration Model.   217

Figure 11.6   Flowchart for the N Site Migration Model.   217

Figure 11.7   Location of sites concerned in this study: 1—Stena I, IV, 2—Chechelnik, 3—Belyj Kamen, 4—Dobrovody, 5—Talianki, 6—Romanovka, 7—Maidanetske, 8—Chichirkozovka, 9—Vasilkov.   219

Figure 11.8   Model of Migration combined with growth.   220

Figure 12.1   Church of T'oros at Anavarza, taken c. 1905 (Gertrude Bell Archive, Newcastle University, Image: C-198).   242

Figure 13.1   Map of the Near East showing key sites of the Upper Kingdom of Samsi-Addu and the Assyrian trading system, with the location of Elam and Emutbal territories.   251

Figure 13.2   Map of the Near East showing core distribution of sites with Uruk and Uruk-related materials.   254

Figure 13.3   Map of the Near East showing main clusters of settlements with Kura-Araxes/Khirbet Kerak materials.   255

Figure 14.1   Map of the eastern Mediterranean and Aegean, with detail of the southeast Aegean, showing locations of major sites of interest (J. Leidwanger).   271

Figure 14.2   General plan of Burgaz showing locations of the settlement, harbors, and other features (J. Leidwanger and N. Riddick).   273

Figure 14.3   Map of 56 sites on the Datça peninsula recorded by Tuna (1983) and Sevimli (2016) ranging in date from the Archaic through the Late Roman period: 1. Bağharımı; 2. Barkaz; 3. Batıraltı; 4. Billiktepe; 5. Bükceğiz; 6. Çeşmeköy; 7. Datça Kalesi; 8. Döşeme Kalesi; 9. Emecik; 10. Gavurdere; 11. Gerenci; 12. Germe; 13. Gökçedere/Kabakkoyu; 14. Göktaş; 15. Gölyeri; 16. Göztepe/Yanıkharman; 17. Gümüş-Ülüklü; 18. Güznetepe; 19. Harıplık; 20. Karaincir; 21. Karfitepe; 22. Kargı; 23. Katıyalı; 24. Kepçemel Burnu; 25. Kiliseyanı; 26. Killik; 27. Killiktepe/Karakuştepe; 28. Kislebükü; 29. Kisletepe; 30. Kisleyanı; 31. Kızılağaç; 32. Kızılağaç kezi; 33. Kızılbükü; 34. Kızılkilise/Karıncalı; 35. Körmen; 36. Kumyer; 37. Maltepe; 38. Mersincik; 39. Mersincik Adası; 40. Mesudiye; 41. Muhaltepe; 42. Murdala; 43. Olgun Boğazı; 44. Palamutbükü Adası; 45. Sakızyakası; 46. Sarılimanı; 47. Sındı/Asartepe; 48. Tekirlikyolu; 49. Yağtaşı-Devtaşı; 50. Yarıkdağ; 51. Yassıdağaltı; 52. Yazıköy Kalesi; 53. Yelimli; 54. Yollucu Adası   274

Figure 14.4   Boundary stone, perhaps of the harbor at Körmen, inscribed *horos limenos*, in its contemporary context, built sideways into a mosque at Karaköy, about 2 km inland (E. S. Greene).   277

Figure 14.5   Network visualization (ForceAtlas2 layout) of connections across the Datça Peninsula during the Archaic/Early Classical period.   280

Figure 14.6   Network visualization (ForceAtlas2 layout) of connections across the Datça Peninsula during the Late Classical/Early Hellenistic period.   282

Figure 14.7   Network visualization (ForceAtlas2 layout) of connections across the Datça Peninsula during the Late Hellenistic /Early Roman period.   284

Figure 14.8   Network visualization (ForceAtlas2 layout) of connections across the Datça Peninsula during the Mid-/Late Roman period.   285

Figure 15.1   Contexts of possible over-water hominin dispersal in Northwest Eurasia, with sites and locations mentioned in the text and modern sea level depicted. Note that, because Lefkada/Leukas has definitely been connected to the mainland during glacials, Middle Palaeolithic sites on it are not depicted. Sites on the other Ionian Islands after Ferentinos et al. 2012.   296

Figure 15.2   Contexts of possible over-water hominin dispersal in ISEA, with sites and locations mentioned in the text and modern sea level depicted. Biogeographic regions (Sahul, etc.) in italic boldface, and biogeographic boundaries as dashed lines.   299

Figure 15.3　Reconstruction of the palaeogeography of ISEA during a moderate glacial. After Voris 2000 and Hall 2011. Stars indicate Lower and Middle Palaeolithic sites (on Flores, Sulawesi, and Luzon) noted in Fig. 15.2.　304

Figure 15.4　Reconstruction of the palaeogeography of the Balkan and Aegean during a severe glacial (e.g., MIS 12). After Lykousis 2009. Note that reconstructed rivers (dashed lines) are fully hypothetical. Dashed box indicates the Ionian Islands, whose insularity during severe glacials is debated. Stars indicate possible Lower and Middle Palaeolithic sites (at Plakias and in the Ionian archipelago) noted in Fig. 15.1.　305

Figure 16.1　Left column (a-d): The deconstruction of the boundaries we experience between brain, body, and the world around us. Right column (a-d): The emergence of sentience, consciousness, agency, and ownership out of our systems for motor control.　323

Figure 16.2　The interconnections between our body, environment, and culture. The grey background symbolizes our sentience or consciousness that arises from the interactions within this system as a whole.　324

Figure 16.3　The development of bilateral symmetric organisms and sentience (in grey) from the transition between the Neoproterozoic and the Cambrian Periods, around 541 million years ago, onward.　326

Figure 16.4　The hand of the author moves a piece of an alternative chess set. Our ability to initiate and control such movements (grasp in the most literal sense) may be more relevant to our being in the world than our ability to appreciate and compute where to place the piece (grasp in a more figurative sense).　328

Tables

Table 8.1　The use of interaction parameters to analyze the various interactions in the Kenamun harbor scene.　152

Table 10.1　Mean adult age-at-death from selected studies throughout the Near East and southeastern Europe.　189

Table 10.2　Life table for Neo-Eneolithic inhabitants of Ukraine and Moldova (both sexes; n = 562).　191

Table 10.3　Life table for Neo-Eneolithic inhabitants of Ukraine and Moldova (females; n = 135, plus ~56 assigned children and indeterminates).　191

Table 10.4　Life table for Neo-Eneolithic inhabitants of Ukraine and Moldova (males; n = 258, plus ~113 assigned children and indeterminates).　192

Table 11.1   Migration researchers by country.   203

Table 11.2   The decision table for migrants and local populations.   211

CHAPTER ONE

Movement as a Constant?

Envisioning a Migration-Centered Worldview of Human History

Megan J. Daniels

Abstract *Migration is, paradoxically, one of the great constants throughout human history: our story is one of continuous movement and exchange, despite our attempts to draw neat geographical and conceptual boundaries around particular groups and regions past and present. This emerging axiom has come about via several means: fast developing methodologies such as aDNA and isotope analyses have truly changed the very questions that we can ask about our data. Combined with new sociohistorical models of the ancient world, these integrated approaches push for a migration-centered view of human history, one that sees mobility and migration as fundamental, constant features of human development and adaptation over the long term. This model, while releasing us from past paradigms that used migration almost solely as an explanation for cultural change, presents new challenges to archaeologists, historians, anthropologists, and geneticists, not least those that involve teasing out the entangled causes, processes, and consequences of human movement to build broader theoretical paradigms. This introductory paper will present the objectives of the volume against archaeology's fraught history with migration as an analytical concept as well as our modern entanglements with migration. It lays the groundwork for the subsequent papers in this volume by highlighting the opportunities and challenges of a migration-centered paradigm of human history, and the promises of integrative, interdisciplinary, theoretically informed, and multiscalar research.*

Movement, through Space and Time

> The news in those days was full of war and migrants and nativists, and it was full of fracturing too, of regions pulling away from nations, and cities pulling away from hinterlands, and it seemed that as everyone was coming together everyone was also moving apart.
>
> —Mohsin Hamid, *Exit West*

The inspiration for this volume—and the conference from which it stems—comes, in large part, from where we find ourselves today: in a world rocked by global movement and by our whirlwind experiences of these displacements, so poignantly captured by novelist Mohsin Hamid. It is increasingly common to characterize the twenty-first century through its mass movements of people. For instance, the tellingly named textbook by Stephen Castles, Hein de Haas, and Mark J. Miller, *The Age of Migration*, ascribes its title to the fact that "[m]igration has gained increasing political salience over the past decades" (Castles et al. 2013:5). While the authors acknowledge that human movement is nothing new, they argue that migration has taken on a distinctly novel character with the beginnings of European expansion in the sixteenth century and especially with the mass rural to urban movement in wake of the Industrial Revolution. The *International Organization for Migration's* (IOM) 2018 World Migration Report now estimates that in 2015 there were 244 million international migrants (3.3% of the world's population), and the most recent reports lift that number to 272 million for 2019, an increase of 51 million since 2010 according to the *UN International Migrant Stock 2019*. This number is projected to grow in the coming years due to various factors including climate change and conflict (e.g., Laczko and Aghazarm 2009).

Humans today are constantly on the move, and we are just as frequently trying to get our minds around what to do about being on the move, or else how to deal with other humans on the move. Yet, while the idea of migration is often framed as an event or, most recently, a crisis of the modern world, we must understand these moments as surges in a much longer continuum of human movement, one that has its roots in our evolution. The recent migrations of people from the Middle East and North Africa into the Mediterranean and Europe, undoubtedly as a result of dire situations only a decade or so old, have been framed as an event or crisis. Yet if we asked how long populations have dispersed around the Mediterranean, Europe, and the Middle East, pushed by war, scarcity, and disaster, and pulled by promises and possibilities of social and political stability and economic abundance, how far back in time would we have to go? This is not to deny the importance of understanding and addressing particular causes and consequences of migration by labeling it as "natural" (Castaneda 2017); but two points need emphasizing from the start: (1) migration is not something peculiar to our age, and (2) it is more our definitions of and attitudes toward migration that have changed in recent times than migratory behavior itself (see Isayev, this volume and 2017:11–12; also Greenblatt 2010; van Dommelen 2014:480). Furthermore, while global movement might seem a product of our modern era of hyper-connection fueled especially by the wide availability of air travel, technology merely amplifies what humans have been doing since we first emerged as a species. To quote Russell King (2007:16), "In a sense, humans are born migrants: our evolution is fundamentally linked to the act of migration, to moving from one place to another and adapting to that environment." In her recent book, *The Next Great Migration* (2020), Sonia Shah takes this claim even farther: migration is not merely a human cultural tendency, but a biological imperative of all life on earth, and, in opposition to modern-day framings of migration as some crisis to be averted, it is *the* key answer to the survival and flourishing of all forms of life.

The earliest phases of migrations include those of extinct members of the genus *Homo* out of Africa after 2.5 million years ago (Hertler et al. 2013), followed by anatomically modern humans between 120,000 and 10,000 years ago, and then the migrations of farmers, herders, and boat builders across the globe from 10,000 years ago onward (Bellwood 2013a; see papers in Bellwood 2013b). Timothy Earle and Clive Gamble, in their chapter on migration in Shryock and Smail's edited volume *Deep History*, capture the complexity, the interconnectedness, and the cloudiness of this relentless human movement in a single sentence:

> Even with the first settlement of regions, new migrations continued often at even greater rates, displacing earlier settlers, forcing removals and relocations, creating regional movements of marriage partners and workers, funnelling vast populations through colonial and postcolonial global economies, and creating diverse, intermingled diasporas. [Shryock and Smail 2011:192]

This explanation, encompassing prehistory to modern-day, captures the blurriness not only of migrations themselves, but also their concomitant causes and effects. The complexities of this process have afforded migration a troubled place in archaeological studies over the course of the twentieth century, from undertheorized "catch-all" explanation for cultural change, to racist narratives of dominance, to a subject largely avoided in archaeology in the second half of the century (Anthony, this volume). Since the 1990s, however, in wake of disciplinary turns within archaeology and history responding to intensifying postcolonial narratives and a growing awareness of modern-day globalization, migration has reemerged as a subject of study for understanding the human past. Revolutionary advances in genetics, isotopes, and data manipulation have further bolstered its significance. Given our current global experiences with human movement—and the troubled responses by individuals and governments to this movement—interdisciplinary and nuanced perspectives of migration and its role in driving human development are now more conceivable—and more necessary—than ever before.

This volume, therefore, seeks to take a sharp lens to various parts of this long history of movement, integrating new models and explanations built using diverse methodologies and case studies into a much longer history—and ultimately a much greater understanding—of human migration. It seeks to capitalize on what Kristian Kristiansen has called the "Third Science Revolution" (2014, with responses; also this volume), which has emerged in response to unparalleled advances in the sciences in areas such as genetics and Big Data, and coincides with current theoretical and methodological reorientations in archaeology (Kristiansen 2014:14). This volume also aims to engage these revolutionary changes in archaeology with ongoing shifts in historical models of the ancient world, chiefly paradigms such as connectivity, networks, and globalization, which continue to influence research agendas and offer their own steep challenges in characterization and application. I will elaborate on these developments further below, but in the following section I take a closer look at migration's appearance, disappearance, and subsequent reemergence in archaeology to frame the rest of this volume.

Migration and Archaeology: A Fraught History

How and why humans move, and the resultant effects of those movements on sociocultural configurations, are the piloting questions behind historical, archaeological, anthropological, and genetic research into migration. But the place of migration in archaeological research has had a fascinating and, at times, fraught history. Its emergence as a driving factor in the story of human evolution seems to have been motivated by two seemingly simple yet groundbreaking realizations from the Renaissance onward: first, that humans were very diverse across space and time and second, that human history was very long—at least compared to the biblical worldview that held sway over Medieval Europe and persisted well into the nineteenth century. This outlook, emerging from the studies of Archbishop James Ussher and John Lightfoot, encompassed human history in a mere 6,000 years (Ussher 1658; Murray-Wallace 1996), and saw humans originating from the Garden of Eden somewhere in the Middle East (see Delumeau 2000, especially chapter 3). Humans were seen to have changed over time due to the influence of geography and climate on individuals and bodily humors, ideas that came both from Greco-Roman theories (e.g., Aristotle, *Politics* 7.1327b) and Medieval characterizations (Harvey 2016). In the biblical view, however, human diversity was a mark of moral degeneration: humans were said to be "made of one blood" (*Acts* 17:26), and their linguistic and physical variety, along with their dispersion across the globe, found explanation in stories of divine punishment for human transgressions such as the Deluge (*Genesis* 6:5–7) and Tower of Babel (*Genesis* 11:1–9) (cf. Randsborg 2000:212–213).

How this worldview eroded over time is due to compounding causes too numerous and complex to capture accurately in this brief space, but I will mention a few major factors related to the study of migration. The rise of antiquarian tradition and methodology, founded in critical study of history using documentary, topographical, and physical sources, influenced new approaches to the study and interpretation of sacred scriptures, and coincided with a number of religious shifts in northern Europe (Backus 2003). Moreover, the emergence of new types of scientific enquiries in the early seventeenth century, such as evidence-based autopsy and philosophical skepticism, set the stage for novel approaches to history and science that transformed both the antiquarian and biblical traditions (Acciarino 2018:13–14). The Enlightenment turn toward ideals of evolution and progress only furthered this process, although antiquarian approaches continued to spread far and wide, despite experiencing increasing marginalization in the eighteenth and nineteenth centuries (Miller and Louis 2012:2, 4–5), and biblical models of history persisted doggedly into the nineteenth century, and still survive today.

The concept of migration as an explanatory device materialized from a number of avenues during this time. Certain antiquarian writers put forth theories about human migration to account for common origins of variegated peoples. The royal historiographer for the Hapsburgs, Wolfgang Lazius, for instance, wrote *De Aliquot Gentium Migrationibus* (1557), which stressed the migration of Germanic tribes (*migratio gentium*, later *Völkerwanderung*) as a way to offer narrative coherence to the history of the diverse subjects of the Hapsburgs (Goffart 1989:122, note 42).[1] This concept of the *Völkerwanderung* would carry particular valence into the eighteenth and nineteenth centuries in the process of German nation building, with the strength and vigor of the Germanic people envisioned as a culmination of previous conquests under the Huns and Vandals in the so-called Migration Period.[2] The concept of German nationality as based on blood and not residence in a particular territory would continue to influence archaeological thought in the German-speaking world well into the twentieth century (Härke 1997:63; Sherratt 1990).

Undoubtedly, the European experiences in the New World prompted theories and arguments about the origins of the indigenous peoples present throughout the Americas. Many accounts from the fifteenth to eighteenth centuries argued for indigenous peoples coming across the Atlantic or Pacific, and biblical views tended to position these peoples as descended from the Canaanites, who had fled from the Hebrews and their Levantine homeland (Trigger 2006:115–116). Yet as early as the late sixteenth century, the recognition of physical similarities between American Indigenous peoples and those from East Asia prompted a Jesuit priest, José de Acosta, to write *Historia natural y moral de las Indias* (1589). In this work, Acosta argued that the Indigenous peoples of the Americas must have traveled from the Middle East, by way of a land bridge from Siberia. But even de Acosta's account, as prescient as it may have been, nonetheless depicted these peoples as having lost all knowledge of, not only sedentary life, but also of their divine origins, thus remaining in line with dominant biblical narratives of the day. Even so, a realization was slowly but steadily emerging of the diversity of human life that covered the globe, and it set the stage for continuing inquiry into human origins.[3]

These converging intellectual developments were augmented further by another great discovery—one with roots in the late eighteenth century and that came to fruition in the mid-nineteenth century: that of deep time, a realization that led to the First Science Revolution (Kristiansen 2014:14–15) and the birth of archaeology, anthropology, and paleontology as scientific disciplines. The rise of nationalism and romanticism across Europe in this same period also spurred interests in chronological ordering and stylistic classification of vast collections of artifacts to characterize and celebrate national identities of emerging European nations.[4] This collection frenzy led to the uncovering of the European Stone, Bronze, and Iron Ages and the diversities of human cultural configurations these periods encompassed (Diaz-Andreu 2008:326–327). But alongside these nationalist tendencies there was emerging a realization, starting with James Hutton's *Theory of the Earth* (1788), that the planet and its inhabitants had a history that stretched well beyond the biblical 6,000 years, involving many processes of change and adaptation over this span of time. Hutton's discoveries were furthered by geologists such as Charles Lyell, who popularized the idea of deep geological time in *Principles of Geology*, thus setting the stage for the elaboration of biological evolution by Charles Darwin and Alfred Russel Wallace. Deep time opened up the door to concepts of evolutionism and diffusionism as the driving factors of human change, particularly for European prehistory (Adams et al. 1978:497). Yet, with the application of Darwinian theory to sociocultural evolution by individuals such as Herbert Spencer, migration also emerged as a viable explanatory device for cultural phenomena in the archaeological record. Both migration and the diffusion had been employed as explanations for culture change by Scandinavian archaeologists like C. J. Thomsen and his successors to articulate the shifts from Stone to Bronze to Iron Ages (Trigger 2006:128–129; Hakenbeck 2008:10). These endeavors were largely fueled by the rise of nationalist identities and nation-states in Europe that emphasized common cultural histories stretching back into prehistoric times, and set the stage for the rise of the culture history approach in archaeology, which would dominate the first half of the twentieth century (Eisenmann et al. 2018:7; see below). The overriding model to arise, however, by the late nineteenth century, was that of unilinear evolutionism, which drew from earlier Enlightenment models of progress and especially social Darwinism. This model propagated the belief that all humans were on a single line of social, cultural, and technological development, with white industrialized European societies at the top, and most other societies more or less falling short of this "ideal." The resulting syntheses of decades' worth of archaeological and anthropological studies came in the form of publications such as John Lubbock's *Prehistoric Times*. These narratives tended to assume Indigenous societies to be static and unable to advance culturally, and any change in the archaeological record was explained via migrations of more "advanced" peoples into a given area.

The racist underpinnings of this scholarship in various parts of the world adopted migrationist explanations to account for what were seen to be cultural "peculiarities" in the archaeological landscape. European archaeologists and colonizers in Africa tended to regard its peoples as "a living museum of the human past" (Trigger 2006:196). Any mark of cultural sophistication, such as Great Zimbabwe or Namibian rock art, was explained via prehistoric European and Near Eastern colonization into the area, which reinforced the idea of European migrants as superior carriers of culture and civilization into a region (Fagan 1981; Härke 1997:64–65, 1998:22; Chirikure 2020:8–11). The same sentiments were applied in North America, for instance to the "Mound Builder" culture (Adams et al. 1978:497–498; Fagan 1981:43–44). In fact, migrationist explanations in this period, as they were applied to the emerging fields of prehistoric archaeology, comparative linguistics, and comparative racial studies, fell largely in line with both evolutionary and biblical models of change, lending biblical models in particular "a broadened scope and a new guise of empirical respectability" (Adams et al. 1978:484). In reality, however, little attempt was made to infer human behavior from artifacts and their respective contexts, or offer any real demonstration of how specific artifacts related to specific stages of cultural and technological advancement (Trigger 2006:209).

As mentioned above, there was also emerging in this period a growing tendency to equate specific classes of artifacts with cultural groups, a tendency that emerged from growing nationalist identities coupled with broader interests in cultural diffusion in the social sciences, and that aided archaeologists in explaining variation in time and space across Europe (Kroeber and Kluckhohn 1952; Eisenman et al. 2018:6). These new orientations resulted in a type of historical particularism known as the culture history paradigm in archaeology, which took precedence in the first half of the twentieth century, although unilinear evolutionary schemes still persisted in archaeological accounts that increasingly attempted to map out zones of archaeological "cultures" across continents (e.g., Holmes 1914). Culture history, which still pervades archaeological thought today (see below), equates groupings of material remains with actual cultural and ethnic groups. Vere Gordon Childe characterized these associations in *The Danube in Prehistory*: "We find certain types of remains—pots, implements, ornaments, burial rites, house forms—constantly recurring together. Such a complex of regularly associated traits we shall term a 'cultural group' or just a 'culture'" (1929:vi). Yet, like unilinear evolutionism, culture history still utilized migration to explain changes observed in an assemblage of artifacts, particularly changes that appeared to be sudden (Adams et al. 1978:483, 498–499). The grand syntheses produced, from Oscar Montelius (1843–1921) to Childe (1892–1957), argued that cultural and technological developments moved via diffusion and migration from the Near East into Europe, a model that came to be known as *ex oriente lux* ("light from the east").[5] Like earlier racist ideas about human development, this paradigm, which tended to view certain areas and groups as founts of innovation, fueled belief in European superiority in wake of the colonization of Africa, the Middle East, and the Americas (Blaut 1987:30). In Childe's view especially, with his clear equation of archaeological cultures with ethnic groups (1925 and especially 1929:vi-viii; see Meheux 2017), Europeans were seen to have adopted technological ideas from the East only to adapt them into heightened innovative forms (1925:xiii), a sentiment shared with the earlier accounts of Montelius. Other European archaeologists, particularly from the German-speaking regions, were determined to see the *lux* as coming from Europe itself, and so promulgated the notion of Aryan peoples descending from the north as culture carriers into the rest of Europe, rooting the genetic basis of culture in blood and not territory (Kossinna 1911; Schuchhardt 1919; see Trigger 2006:228–229; Härke 1997:63–64). The use of archaeology to bolster claims to cultural superiority was brought to extremes under the Nazi use of Gustaf Kossinna's *Siedlungsarchäologie* (Kossinna 1911), a paradigm that also influenced Childe's concept of archaeological cultures, although Childe later moved away from Kossinna's "Nordic myth."[6]

World War II brought several changes to Anglophone and broader European archaeological thought. The Second Science Revolution in the 1950s and '60s largely retreated from culture history approaches and their stress on diffusion and migration, at least for British and American archaeology. The post–World War II revolutions in scientific dating and the rise of the New Archaeology, or processualism, in the Anglophone world resulted, over the 1950s, '60s, and '70s, in turns to more internal processes of adaptation to generate universal laws concerning the operation of human societies (e.g., Renfrew 1972). The higher chronologies of European prehistory afforded by new scientific dating in the 1950s and '60s, and the general amassment of archaeological data, allowed more room to argue for slower processes of internal evolution (Hakenbeck 2008:14). Migration, often simplistically modeled as quick, sweeping waves (or invasions) of peoples into a given territory, could be not so much refuted as ignored as a historical explanation that did nothing to explain adaptive or evolutionary processes (Clark 1966:173; Cabana 2011:20; Härke 1997; Anthony, this volume). Culture history's tendency to present archaeological cultures as monolithic, bounded, and univariate was criticized as descriptive and simplistic (Binford 1965; Rowe 1966).[7] Furthermore, the rise of cultural ecology was seen as the most secure model for explaining development and change through a cultural system's (multilinear) evolutionary adaptations to environments (Steward 1955).[8] Processualism's influence continues to be pervasive, especially in the wariness toward assuming large movements of people, which has persisted into the 1990s and 2000s, even as migration has come back into focus (Härke 1997:62).

Conversely, in Central Europe, archaeology turned to more antiquarian tendencies of collecting and classifying material remains. In the German-speaking world in particular, archaeology's post–World War II retreat from political and nationalist discourses tended to sustain abstract and undertheorized equations of artifact assemblages with ethnicity, but from a more neutral sense than earlier hyper-nationalist perspectives (Rieckhoff 2007:9; Burmeister 2013; Hofmann and Stockhammer 2017:6–7; Eisenmann et al. 2018:7). In German-speaking archaeology, therefore, migration continued to be invoked uncritically as an explanation for culture change into the 1990s, when new conversations surrounding acculturation emerged.[9] Indeed, even despite the continuing impact of processualism and the countermovement, post-processualism, on the Anglophone world, culture history remains pervasive into the twenty-first century in archaeological thought and continues to influence scientific and interpretative frameworks, as will be discussed below.

With the countermovement known as post-processualism beginning in the 1980s and its focus on individual agency and subjective experience, migration was slow to reemerge within archaeological agendas (van Dommelen 2014:479). A number of studies before and during this period, however, focused on articulating the spread of farming (Ammerman and Cavalli-Sforza 1971, 1973—see Anthony, this volume) and the links between farming and the movement of Indo-European speakers (Renfrew 1987, 1989, 1992) kept migration in the picture.[10] These large studies also began to incorporate genetics data into their models, although there were significant drawbacks in early attempts to properly extract and authenticate aDNA from human remains (e.g., Ammerman and Cavalli-Sforza 1984; Renfrew 1992; Boyle and Renfrew 2001; see Eisenmann et al. 2018:2). The diversity of interpretative viewpoints in post-processual archaeology, which stressed multivocality and multiple levels of explanation (Hodder 1987), widened the scope for migration to reemerge (Cabana 2011:11)—this time as a subject of study in its own right. Kristian Kristiansen (1989, 1998) and David Anthony (1990) called for a return to migration as a systematic and predictable component of human behavior (Anthony 1990:908), which could be studied within broader social structures and historical and evolutionary contexts (Kristiansen 1989:212; Anthony 1997). Migration thus rematerialized within scholarly agendas over the 1990s (e.g., Champion 1990; Anthony 1992; Cameron 1995; Chapman and Hamerow

1997; Bellwood and Renfrew 2002; Kristiansen and Larson 2005). While the conversation has often focused on the use of explicit methods to identify migrations in the archaeological record (Burmeister 2000; Yasur-Landau 2010, 2011; van Dommelen 2014:479), the rise of multiple types of stable isotope analysis, new data analysis techniques, and, most recently whole genome sequencing (Anthony and Brown 2017; Kristiansen et al. 2017), have expanded our methodologies enormously. As Kristiansen argues (this volume), science revolutions have turned relative knowledge into absolute knowledge, freeing up archaeology to ask new questions about data. As such, the role of social identity in archaeological migration studies (see Cabana 2011:22–23 and Camaño, Porter, this volume) and the positioning of migration as a part of much broader and long-term social and evolutionary processes is coming more into focus. I will return to these advances at the end of this chapter. In the next section, I consider new models of Mediterranean history, and how they might integrate with and strengthen the archaeological study of migration.

Migration and Mediterranean Connectivity

In the 1980s, scholars such as Colin Renfrew (1980), Stephen Dyson (1981), and Anthony Snodgrass (1985) articulated the disparities between Classical Archaeology and New Archaeology (processualism)—a disparity Renfrew termed the "Great Divide" (Renfrew 1980). I will not belabor this point, but suffice to say, as the New Archaeology emerged in the 1960s, so did the disciplinary divides between what came to be known as anthropological archaeology, usually housed under anthropology in university departments, and classical archaeology, traditionally the domain of departments of classics, and closely associated with art history and the study of the Greek and Latin texts. Yet, as the New Archaeology was in full swing in the 1970s, a new paradigm was evolving within classics, often attributed to the great economic historian Moses Finley, who wrote his groundbreaking work *The Ancient Economy* in 1973. Finley, very much influenced by Max Weber and Karl Polanyi, stressed, in this work, the "cellular self-sufficiency" of the Greco-Roman worlds (Hopkins 1983:xi); in other words, he painted a picture of a world that saw little interregional movement or trade, where each farm, town, and region was largely self-sufficient and produced everything that it needed. Although Finley was certainly not solely responsible for this, his work served to further isolate the Greeks and Romans from their neighbors to the north, south, east, and west, drawing sharp, defined boundaries around particular cultural groups. This approach was reminiscent of the tradition of culture history, demonstrating the persistence of this paradigm across many sects of archaeology.

The "Great Divide" of course was not as clean-cut as the metaphor suggests: both anthropological archaeology and classical archaeology were and continue to be vastly diverse fields; nor can we assume a simple elision between "classical" and "Mediterranean" archaeologies when this diversity is taken into account. The recent shifts within classics and Mediterranean archaeology and history, indeed, have much to offer when it comes to building innovative theoretical paradigms of migration and mobility. Since the 1990s in particular, new models of Mediterranean history have taken form, signified in Nicholas Purcell and

Peregrine Horden's *The Corrupting Sea* (2000). These approaches stressed the cultural fluidity and rampant economic, social, and ecological interconnectivity of humans across the Mediterranean basin. *The Corrupting Sea* defied fixed boundaries, chronological and cultural barriers, and any conception of human groups as cellular, self-sufficient entities with their own destinies. Although it drew from the much earlier work of Fernand Braudel (1949), Horden and Purcell's work was nothing short of a paradigm shift in classics, one that opened the door to new interests in human mobility and migration in the Mediterranean world. This paradigm has of course seen its share of second-wave criticisms, particularly those that critique the paradoxically "static" and "timeless" nature of this interconnectivity (Morris 2003; Broodbank 2013; Concannon and Mazurek 2016:8–9; Manning 2018:87–88), which in some instances continued to be plagued by simplistic and unidirectional movements of people and innovations (van Dommelen and Knapp 2010:3; De Angelis 2016, this volume). Most of all, these critiques call for more precise analytical categories and clearer understandings of the processes that produce, sustain, and alter these mobilities and interconnections, as well as the role of institutions, states, and economies in these processes.

The early twenty-first century has indeed seen new techniques emerge within this paradigm, in particular the ever-intensifying interest in network approaches for conceptualizing and modeling human connectivity (Malkin 2011; Knappett 2011, 2013; Tartaron 2013; Collar 2013; Brughmans et al. 2016; Leidwanger and Knappett 2018; Greene and Leidwanger, this volume). These approaches have helped to move us past earlier critiques of interconnectivity's "static" and "timeless" nature and envision more dynamic, multidirectional processes of interaction, which shaped the growth and trajectories of societies (Greene and Leidwanger 2019). Along with the interest in networks and the movement of innovations they allow through human actors (Collar 2013), a renewed focus on objects has emerged. In particular, scholars have stressed the agency of objects in structuring human interaction over long distances into "affiliation networks" and "communities of practice" (e.g., Lave and Wenger 1991; Gamble 1998; Knappett 2011; although see caveats in Kristiansen, this volume). Material culture is no longer solely used to identify human movement (e.g., van Dommelen and Knapp 2010), but to articulate the social processes and—increasingly—the social experiences behind that movement (Camaño, this volume). Within these shifts, other concepts and characterizations are being reconfigured, in particular modern ideas of ancient "colonization," which in earlier decades tended to sustain simplistic models of cultural transfer and contact (De Angelis 2020; Kotsonas and Mokrišová 2019; Wallace 2018).[11] Mediterranean historians and archaeologists are thus moving toward more sophisticated and integrative ways of accounting for both structure and agency within the paradigm of interconnectivity, which mirrors reorientations in the discipline of archaeology more broadly (discussed below).

I will not go so far as to say that the study of migration and mobility can heroically bridge any remaining "Great Divide," but I will highlight the similar turning points in both anthropological and classical archaeology toward migration and mobility—namely, the period of the 1990s. I will also relate these developments to forces that stretch well beyond these two disciplines, namely, globalization, which has heavily influenced scholarly agendas in the study of the past (Morris 2003; Hodos 2014, 2017). And, in a related sense, we might look back on the 1990s as a time of critical self-reflection of both disciplines and their colonial underpinnings as the interest in postcolonial studies intensified (Knapp and van Dommelen 2010:1; van Dommelen 2012:402–403), interests that were in many ways responding to the often-insidious effects of globalization (During 2000). The colonial substructures of the discipline have come into clearer focus in the twenty-first century as researchers grapple with the continuing use of the past to both bolster and challenge modern ideological stances, including in the arenas of migration and immigration (Padilla Peralta 2015a, 2015b, 2017). The renewed interests in migration and mobility also bring new light to peoples previously marginalized in scholarship (e.g., Kennedy 2014; Cameron, this volume). The reemergence of migration studies, once the explanatory device used by the researcher to deny certain groups any notion of agency or evolution, thus offers ways to move beyond static and one-sided ideas of cultural transmission and dominance, given the proper use of reflexive, ethical, and data-driven models.

A Migration-Centered Worldview: Caveats and Opportunities

If the earlier scientific revolutions of the mid-twentieth century strained the interest in large-scale human movements, the current scientific revolutions—in aDNA, isotope, and data analysis—are doing the opposite. Since the 1990s we have been moving, more and more, to a migration-centered worldview of human history, a view that sees mobility and migration as fundamental, constant features of human development and adaptation over the long term. This model, while releasing us from past paradigms that used migration almost solely as an explanation for culture change, presents new challenges to archaeologists, historians, anthropologists, and geneticists, not least those that involve teasing out, magnifying, and modeling the entangled causes, processes, and consequences of human movement and developing new interdisciplinary frameworks to characterize the realities of migration and mobility.

Culture history, and the use of archaeological cultures as a heuristic device for characterizing past societies in general, still looms large, for instance (Roberts and Vander Linden 2011:2; Furholt 2018:160; Crellin and Harris 2020:38; Cameron, this volume). The culture history paradigm and its influence over archaeological understandings of migrations has been a persistent and pervasive shaper of emerging discourses (Hakenbeck 2008:13) Many recent approaches to migration still fall into the trap of equating ethnicity with languages and material culture and reducing complex migration processes to "arrows on maps" (Hakenbeck 2008:16). The culture history approach thus persists in simplistically characterizing migrations as mass movements of people that replace the host population in a given territory, defined and proven through changes in material culture (e.g., Brace et al. 2018—see Crellin and Harris 2020:39–40 and Anthony, this volume). Cabana (2011:23) emphasizes the continuing knotty issue of equating migrations with cultural change: "A presumed tie between migration and culture change is usually the default starting point for archaeological migration studies. . . . We assume to know the nature of the relationships among migration, material remains, and the archaeological record. In reality, however, we do not know that any of these relationships exist" (also Harper, this volume).

aDNA, especially whole genome sequencing, has certainly revealed important correctives to previous assumptions (e.g., Allentoft et al. 2015; Haak et al. 2015; Mathieson et al. 2015; see also Vander Linden 2016; Krause and Haak 2017; Furholt 2018, with responses; Gokcumen 2018). Has genome sequencing, however, "surpassed the toolkit of archaeology" (Reich 2018:xx) in terms of what it reveals about cultural and social change in the deep past? Omer Gokcumen (this volume; Taskent and Gokcumen 2017) offers the insightful reminder that, as with the relationships between human groups and material culture, there are no clear "across-the-board" correlations between genetics and cultures, whether we define cultures through human groups or assemblages of artifacts. Or, as Marc Vander Linden (2018:187, this volume) sums up, "The difficulty lies when one attempts to translate biological relatedness in social terms, materialized by archaeological artefacts." Genomic studies indeed have been criticized for lacking archaeological rigor, for assuming an equation between biological groups, material culture, and complex identities, and, consequently, for treating migrations in the same, simplistic manner as the culture history paradigm. Furholt (2018:165) has noted the continued treatment of human movement in genomic studies as univariate, bounded phenomena, "reduced to a binary choice between migration and diffusion," and thus our ignorance of the wide range of mobilities, social processes, and other contributing factors subsumed under the concepts of migration and diffusion continues (see Leppard, this volume). The identification of genetic changes in the archaeological record has also been catapulted into catch-all explanations for intricate social and technological changes such as the spread of farming, such that Crellin and Harris have recently asserted that aDNA papers in archaeology "presage a return to older forms of thinking," namely, culture history (2020:41). Furthermore, the politicizing of aDNA in recent months and years (Gannon 2019; Hakenbeck 2019; Frieman and Hofmann 2019) has demonstrated that scientific methods are no safer than older culture-historical techniques when it comes to appropriation and misrepresentation of ancient data via modern ideologies of ethnicity and identity (Furholt 2018:171). The consensus from scholars working with diverse geographical regions and populations is uniform. We need to apply social theory and proper archaeological and anthropological agendas to understand the myriad complex social and cultural processes behind migration and avoid positivistic and oversimplified interpretations of our data (Müller 2013; Hofmann 2015; Burmeister 2017; Furholt 2018, 2019; Anthony, Barnard, De Angelis, Camaño, Cameron, Gokcumen, Kristiansen, Vander Linden, Yasur-Landau, this volume).

Yet, as Eisenmann et al. have noted, the mass accrual of new genetic data "has not been matched by the development of a theoretical framework for the discussion of ancient DNA results" (2018:1)—in other words, method is outstripping theory. Crellin and Harris (2020) suggest one of the main sources of tension is the binaries drawn between nature (DNA) and culture (material remains) and the supposed need to map one cleanly onto the other, especially by testing archaeological models against seemingly solid, unambiguous, and verifiable genetic evidence. In reality, such binaries between nature and culture do not exist either now or in the past, just as one human group or identity cannot be cleanly separated from another; nor can scientific approaches remain tidily detached from interpretative ones (McCoskey 2018). Crellin and Harris call for relational, multiscalar, and posthumanist approaches that can grasp the messiness and complexities of information about the past from interdisciplinary perspectives. This relational importance is key, and if we are to better conceptualize and model human movements, we cannot divorce these from things and environments. Hans Barnard (this volume), quotes Woolford and Dunn (2014:125), who state: "The boundaries between bodies, tools, and the environment are fluid and dependent upon relationships more than materials." The challenge of integrating new techniques and evidence into archaeological work is coming into clearer focus, and indeed requires the redrafting of paradigms that stretch far beyond the discipline of archaeology. The characterization of migration must be understood as part of an endlessly intricate web of relations between human, things, identities, and environments: aDNA is but one of many tools to grasp these complexities.

Zubrow et al. (this volume) suggest that we are working on the "transition line between processual and post-processual archaeology." Yet, this transition line must bring us back not to old frameworks but toward paradigms that more accurately characterize the reality of human movement, entangled as it is within broader social processes (Yasur-Landau, this volume). In Kristiansen's words (this volume), "The third science revolution allows the reintroduction of a new interdisciplinary social, science-based theory of history and human behavior based on the material conditions of life." Given the criticisms of "first-wave" interpretations of genomic data discussed above, Kristiansen's argument positions us to build frameworks that incorporate micro- and macrodynamics of the organizing forces of society understood through material culture and language. We are now better able to study and conceptualize human movement as a fundamental part of these social strategies and institutional structures, not some outside force or event (Anthony, this volume). In sum, culture history's tendencies to incorporate migrations into historical models and processualism's reasons for excluding them are both no longer valid.

We are also no longer simply looking at cultural (or genetic) change, but also continuity, as advocated by Cabana (2011) and earlier post-processual models (e.g., Hodder 1987). Continuity in particular encompasses the broader environmental, social, and cultural dynamics that direct the trajectories of human development and change over the long term:

> The problem here has been the failure to identify continuity with change as social-symbolic processes. . . . An alternative approach is to examine the ways in which similarity and difference, continuity and change, are constructed through material culture, and to interpret the way in which these constructions play a role in the dialectical relationship between structure and event. [Hodder 1987:8]

Paradoxically, continuity does not entail predictive evolutionary models à la processualism that erase human agency. Instead, continuity requires us to incorporate both structure and agency into our analyses of human movement, subsumed under models such as complexity theory, which can combine unpredictable (individual and group) variability with enduring constraints, or "attractors," such as cultural and ethnic affiliation, that direct societies' adaptations over the long term (Bintliff 2006:187). Evolutionary models, just as they were a part of the First and Second Science Revolutions, also have their role to play this time around (see Kristiansen, this volume, Figure 2.1). When used properly they can, in John Bintliff's words (2006:187), "nullify the supposed incompatibility of processual and post-processual approaches to the human past," and allow us to characterize the complex social processes that direct and result from human movement, from the individual to society. Migration is a part of human adaptive strategies (Leppard 2014; Weninger and Harper 2015) yet can be a catalyst for new sociocultural formulations and even higher cognitive complexity (Barnard, this volume). As these new scientific techniques free up archaeologists to ask new and better questions about their data, the evolutionary role of migration in social complexity will certainly come more into focus (see Vander Linden et al., this volume).

The Scope of the Volume

The papers in the first section of this volume, "New Data and New Narratives," synthesize scientific, social scientific, and humanistic data and evaluate the new models of historical and social development that we need to consider in light of new evidence. As is clear from this section, all of these papers focus on European prehistory, and in particular the Final Neolithic and Early Bronze Age groups from the Pontic steppes, the Yamnaya people, which were shown through recent genetic studies (Haack et al. 2015; Allentoft et al. 2015) to have migrated into northern Europe. These 2015 studies using whole genome sequencing from these regions were revolutionary in their findings, yet also subject to "first wave" criticisms, as noted above (e.g., Furholt 2018; Crellin and Harris 2020), and the chapters that deal with these phenomena answer to these criticisms in different ways. Both Kristian Kristiansen and David Anthony, who were a part of the research teams that analyzed the genomes that demonstrated the Yamnaya steppe origin for much of the European Corded Ware culture, reveal the complex social processes involved in these movements. While earlier reactions to these findings justifiably included concern and caution toward being overly simplistic and positivistic with this new genomic data (e.g., Furholt 2018), Kristiansen and Anthony demonstrate how genomic, isotopic, and archaeological evidence can be synthesized to tease out the multiple processes that arise out of and drive human movement. Anthony frames his paper largely around countering the continuing ideas of migrations as singular events or invasions (a characterizing stemming largely from the work of Gimbutas), while Kristiansen builds on these findings to suggest new theoretical models of migratory expansions applied to European and Mediterranean prehistory as a whole. Omer Gokcumen's paper in this same section helpfully introduces the tools of genomics to archaeologists and historians, highlighting its impact on research into human origins and providing further caveats on how we correlate genetic signatures with concepts such as nationality, culture, and ancestry. Gokcumen emphasizes especially that genetic research, rather than providing clean definitive answers, often demonstrates that our original questions and assumptions—e.g., the "spread" of farming—were too simplistic.

The next section, "Migrations: Visible and Invisible" analyzes ancient migration studies from a different angle, that of the individuals and groups that we miss if we continue to employ inadequate narratives, methodologies, and interpretations. Franco De Angelis's paper in this section cautions that we risk perpetuating one-dimensional narratives of movement and transfer if we do not take data-driven interdisciplinary approaches that assess not only the processes but also the outcomes of ancient migrations and the role of host populations. De Angelis investigates the polarizing historical narratives and methodologies that have been applied to the sociocultural developments of the pre-Roman western Mediterranean. These narratives largely mirror the earlier culture history-versus-processualism standoff, with one side arguing for cultural stimuli from outsiders, the other arguing for local, internal processes of development. De Angelis argues for deeper nuancing of our narratives driven by emerging data to capture the role of migration in cultural transfer and change. Catherine Cameron's chapter, "Captives: The Invisible Migrant," challenges our generalizing view of population movement as an intentional process linked to economic concerns through ethnohistoric and ethnographic accounts of captives, particularly their roles in cultural networks. Forced migration is garnering more attention in archaeological studies (Cameron 2016; Hamilakis 2017; Driessen 2018), and Cameron reveals a remarkable variety of social processes and strategies in the forced movement of peoples across different societies, and importantly their influences and roles within those societies, all of which further textures our archaeological interpretations and nuances new data emerging form isotope and genetic studies. Ultimately, Cameron's work moves us past migrations as faceless "events" and into the lived experiences of captives and their influences on past societies.

The next chapter, by Elena Isayev, asks the important question: "At what point does one's presence as an outsider become visible?" Using a number of case studies from the Roman-period Mediterranean, Isayev demonstrates the significant gaps in our knowledge of the shape and scale of movement when we rely on traditional methods for studying migration (e.g., inscriptions and material culture), arguing that social factors such as status played a key role in the (in)visibility of migration. Both Cameron and Isayev emphasize the undeniable importance that aDNA and isotope analyses will have on our interpretations of the processes of migration as they are employed with increasing frequency (see Killgrove and Montgomery 2016). Likewise, the final chapter in this section, by Assaf Yasur-Landau, comprehensively assesses the scientific revolution's impact on the archaeology of the Levant. Taking a harbor scene from a New Kingdom Egyptian tomb as his point of departure in signaling previously ignored manners and scales of human movement, Yasur-Landau's chapter calls for a "unified model of interaction" that incorporates the whole range of mobility "events" within a "wider interaction continuum," allowing for more inclusive models of human movement.

The section entitled "Computational Models of Migration" presents several new statistical and mathematical methods of identifying and characterizing migrations. The first chapter in this section, by Marc Vander Linden et al., presents an agent-based model to predict the effects of migrating populations on cultural diversity through a series of simulations. The authors test the predictions of their simulations through analysis of archaeological and zooarchaeological data from the western Balkans and Adriatic basin. Their model is not only widely applicable to a number of archaeological scenarios (and thus testable), but, importantly, demonstrates a method of characterizing the complex interrelationships between migration and cultural variability, revealing the multiphase characteristics of both of these phenomena. Thomas K. Harper's paper, "The Settlement Record, Paleodemography, and Evidence for Migrations in Eneolithic Ukraine," introduces a mathematical model using paleodemographic data to chart the maximum possible limits of population growth in a given region to identify a means of pinpointing when migrations likely have or have not occurred. Harper's model is a good example of a method that looks beyond changes in cultural (or genetic) components to characterize the shape of migrations in prehistory. The final chapter, by Zubrow, Diachenko, and Leavitt, presents a simulation model based on neo-Malthusian population dynamics to predict migrations. This model takes into account not only top-down population-level dynamics, but also builds in human cognition (through perception of resource availability at both the origin and targeted area of migration). The models introduced in this section of the volume are applicable to a wide variety of case studies, and aid us in characterizing migration as a social and cognitive process and not simply as an external, unpredictable event.

The volume's next section, "Sociohistorical Models of Migration," elaborates on human-generated socioeconomic structures and identities that both constrain and enable human migration. The first paper in this section, by Aurora Camaño, combines the theoretical and methodological orientations within social anthropology with studies of the physical and cultural landscapes of migrants in Armenian Cilicia. Camaño calls for a social archaeology of forced migration, "which ultimately seeks to reconstruct past migrant narratives and the often-overlooked societal impacts of mass displacement and resettlement." Anne Porter's chapter also considers the practice of identity in structuring human movements in the late Chalcolithic/Bronze Age Near East. Using several case studies including the Uruk expansion, Porter argues that specific aspects of identity could be reified and expressed materially to overcome the social fragmentation brought about by mobility, thus demonstrating the dynamic ways in which groups used material culture to reproduce social bonds over long distances. Finally, Elizabeth Greene and Justin Leidwanger's chapter broadens the discussion to examine how geographies of routine, small-scale mobility operated diachronically among various types of settlement on a single peninsula. Their paper is an important example of how recent interests in networks—in particular their ability to demonstrate how constant, local mobilities configured broader social, economic, and political development—will necessarily shape conversations moving forward. The chapters in this section show a fascinating dialectic between human perception and action (reflecting the computational models described above), yet also weave in larger social structures and environmental constraints that shaped human movement and the social experiences of movement.

The final section is entitled "Migration and Complexity," and looks forward (as it looks back in time) to the future of migration studies. "Assessing the Possibility of Trans-Maritime

Mobility in Archaic Hominins" by Thomas Leppard, interestingly, focuses on non–*Homo Sapiens* movements across waters in both the eastern Mediterranean and regions around Southeast Asia. Tackling the question of whether over-water mobility in archaic *Homo* indeed signified "complex, strategic, technologically advanced plans for maritime mobility," Leppard synthesizes and nuances interpretations of a number of data sets to argue that hominin mobility might have taken many forms quite distinct from the behavioral complexity we tend to associate with *Homo Sapiens*, which calls us to rethink assumptions between movement and complexity. Hans Barnard, in his chapter, "*Homo mobilis*: Interactions, Consciousness, and the Anthropocene," examines how the study of human sentience, evolving from sensory input and associated motor responses, can help analogize the complex cognitive and physical abilities that migration induces in individuals and groups. Arguing for a need to synthesize new scientific data in broader interpretative structures, Barnard takes the nature of sentience as his framework for interpreting the outcomes of human movements across the globe, which amounted to "rapid and fundamental developments in human material and immaterial culture, their mental and physical abilities, as well as the world around them." Barnard's chapter presses us to recognize the evolution of human complexity as not located solely in neurological developments, but in individual and group movements that feed back into consciousness and intelligence, emphasizing migration's fundamental role in human adaptation through time.

There are other aspects not captured in this introduction, which the volume either explicitly or implicitly addresses. Many papers explicitly utilize isotope data, yet no paper focuses solely on this topic (see Knudson 2011; Killgrove and Montgomery 2016). Isotopes, before whole genome sequencing became more accessible, were already demonstrating the amount of mobility in early European populations, and continue to contribute remarkably fine-tuned analyses of individual and group movements (e.g., Frei et al. 2017). The concept of "mobility" over "migration" is another issue. Under older conceptualizations, migration might be considered a large-scale "event," while mobility might signify a more generalized "background noise" of everyday movement, or at the very least, denote the latent possibilities of movement. Often, mobility might be applied to certain types of populations (e.g., pastoralists) to distinguish them from sedentary ones, although this distinction has been problematized in recent years (Potts 2014; Porter 2016; see also Wendrich and Barnard 2008). Hakenbeck proposes adopting mobility over migration as a more encompassing, "bottom-up" concept that can subsume migration alongside other forms of movement (2008:19); this configuration may also work well within the paradigm of Mediterranean interconnectivity (see Kotsonas and Mokrišová 2019:218–219). Several papers in this volume stress this background "noise" of mobility as a constant backdrop to human societies (Greene and Leidwanger, this volume), sometimes termed "micro-mobility" (Porter, this volume), and underscoring a much broader interaction "continuum" of movement, from the micro to the macro scales (Yasur-Landau, this volume). Greene and Leidwanger consider whether we can even separate out migration "events" from the backdrop of routine movements, and pose the question of whether migrations themselves should actually be considered as "large-scale extensions of micro-mobilities." Unceasing mobility is thus coming into focus as the hidden hallmark of all human cultures (Greenblatt 2009). Given the various scales and periods encompassed in this volume, no strict separation of migration and mobility is offered—the focus is on, rather, the proper interdisciplinary and interpretative frameworks that can move us toward more balanced treatment of human movement as a fundamental component of our development—physical, cultural, and otherwise.

Finally, the term *modeling* in the volume title deserves some comment. The current science revolution incorporates not only advances in genetics and isotopes but also in data manipulation, and these methodological leaps are certainly reflected in the computational models section of this volume, which brings various forms of archaeological data into new means of hypothesis testing on migrations. Yet "modeling" insinuates much more than incorporating computational techniques, extending to sociohistorical understandings of how humans move and interact, to the human migrants that we have missed with older models, and finally to our very ontological understandings of human-thing-environment relations (Crellin and Harris 2020). To this end, the sections in this volume on inclusive histories, sociohistorical models, and migration and complexity all push us to conceive of more encompassing research agendas to characterize and understand movement. Migration might be conceived of as physical movements of humans from one place to another, but on a deeper level it should press us to recognize movement and mobility as basic organizing forces of human and all earthly reality, as hidden as it often seems within that reality (or denied by certain members of that reality). As Stephen Greenblatt puts it (2009:250), "Indeed one of the characteristic powers of a culture is its ability to hide the mobility that is its enabling condition." If new scientific techniques and historical models can accomplish anything in regard to ancient migration studies it should be to undermine any residual notions of purity and boundedness that society attempts to perpetuate, and to build migratory processes into the very biological and cultural scaffolding that comprises human societies (Shah 2020). This is not to do away with large-scale narratives or discussions of identity, which are ongoing cultural forces with very real consequences, but rather to base those narratives and identities on candid recognitions of flux, heterogeneity, and complexity.[12] This candid recognition must be at the heart of modeling migration and mobility and of cultivating a migration-centered worldview of the human past and present.

"NO VESTIGE OF A BEGINNING, NO PROSPECT OF AN END"

It seems apt to end by quoting the concluding words of chapter 1 of *Theory of the Earth* by James Hutton, a work that set in motion the First Science Revolution.[13] Our history begins with movement, and, despite the steep changes our planet faces in the coming decades, human movement will remain a constant. What will not remain constant are our illusions of cultural and ethnic boundedness and uniformity: these will shift, for better or for worse. Renowned anthropologist Michael Herzfeld (2007), for instance, has written on the idea of a European cultural identity that threatens to become ever more divisive, parochial, and implosive as long as it attempts to carve out a purist cultural agenda against the inevitable waves of transformation that are continually emerging. He has also suggested that, within this crisis of identity, anthropology can self-reflexively rise as a counterweight to these damaging notions or it can remain invisible in these debates (Herzfeld 2016; 2018). I would extend this responsibility to archaeologists as well, as other have done. Martin Furholt, for instance, cautions against the blurring of genetic descent and cultural identity (2018:171): "By integrating such residues of Kossinna-like ethno-essentialism and biologism, whether intentional or not, into models of population history that are combined with cutting-edge scientific methods, we run into the danger of providing supposedly scientific support for political forces who build their demagogies on exactly those assumptions about the nature of societies, ethnic identities, and biologic relatedness." Furholt's warnings hearken ominously back to characterizations of nineteenth-century migrationist arguments that lent the entanglement of unilinear evolutionism and biblical models of society "a broadened scope and a new guise of empirical respectability" (see also Hakenbeck 2019; Crellin and Harris 2020). The emergence of new methodologies and paradigms has indeed been nothing short of disruptive for archaeology; likewise, migration itself works as a disruptive force to our ideas of clear-cut borders, well-defined identities, and static ways of being (Tsuda and Baker 2015; Lightfoot 2015). Yet such disruptions contain opportunities for truer, more reflexive, and realist models of the human past and present. Above, all, they undermine narratives of exclusion, and illuminate a very basic truth of human existence: that we evolve not as neatly defined groups, but through constant movement and adaptation to new environments, whether physical or cultural.

Acknowledgments

I would like to thank the *Institute for European and Mediterranean Archaeology* for generously hosting the eleventh annual international visiting scholars conference on the topic of this volume, and especially Peter Biehl and Stephen L. Dyson for their mentorship and guidance. I would also like to thank the graduate student volunteers at the 2018 conference and of course all of the contributors to this volume for their tireless efforts in bringing it to fruition. Strong thanks go to the three anonymous volume reviewers for their helpful critiques and suggestions. Finally, I thank Jonathan Monk for his support throughout this process.

Notes

1. See also Annius of Viterbo's spurious *Antiquitates Variae* (1498), which positioned biblical and Near Eastern peoples as colonizers of Italy, specifically the Etruscans (Stephens 2013). I thank Damiano Acciarino for drawing my attention to these antiquarian sources.
2. For instance, as witness in Friedrich Schiller's *Allgemeine Sammlung historischer Memoires*, XXIX. See Burmeister 2016:48–49 and note 32.
3. The "origins" of various indigenous groups would continue to be a concern for non-Indigenous researchers for centuries: S. Percy Smith, for instance, argued in the early twentieth century from oral accounts that the Maori peoples of New Zealand migrated across the Pacific from India. Following their migration to New Zealand, Smith portrayed their culture has having essentially remained static for centuries (Trigger 2006:193–194), an assertion reminiscent of broader European colonialist mentalities toward Indigenous peoples around the world.

4. E.g., Warsae and Thomsen in Denmark (see Randsborg 2000).
5. On the distinctions between diffusion and migration, see Adams, Van Gerven, and Levy 1978:484–486 (also Hakenbeck 2008:11).
6. In addition to rejecting Kossinna's model as a "Nordic myth," Childe would come, in the Fourth Edition of *The Dawn of European Civilization*, to abandon certain assumptions about migration's role in technological change in favor of Soviet ideas of internal development, although he never completely relinquished diffusionism (Meheux 2017:98).
7. Although in certain functionalist interpretations diffusionism was still allowed for, albeit with certain limitations, and it could not compete with the comprehensive explanatory power of cultural materialism and systems theory (Haas 1977).
8. See also Härke (1997; 1998:23–24) and Kristiansen (1989) on the "immobilist" views of mid-twentieth-century Soviet and British archaeology. Note also that Processualists such as Lewis Binford built human mobility into their evolutionary models, particularly as part of the adaptive tactics of hunter-gatherers (e.g., Binford 1980; 2001; also Kelly 1983). I thank Christopher Troskosky for drawing my attention to this point.
9. See Härke 1997, who traces the historical and political reasons for the persistence of migration as an explanation for culture change in twentieth-century German-speaking archaeology. Härke contrasts Germany's history of displacement, immigration, and constantly changing borders with Britain's island status and increasing turn toward immobilism and acculturation (the "elite dominance model") as explanations for culture change. Cf. Burmeister 2013:230: "Der Grund hierfür ist weniger in der Migrationserfahrung der nationalen Gesellschaften zu suchen . . . als in den interpretationsleitenden Forschungsparadigmen der jeweiligen Archäologien."
10. See also Bellwood 1984–1985 and 1991 for the south Pacific. See discussion in Hakenbeck 2008:15–16.
11. See De Angelis 2020 on the application of migration, mobility, and diaspora studies to the ancient Mediterranean world, particularly in French-speaking scholarship.
12. These models relate to assemblage thinking (Jervis 2018), outlined in relation to aDNA studies by Crellin and Harris (2020), yet derive from the philosophical school known as Process Philosophy. This school, dating back to the sixth-century BCE philosopher Heraclitus and championed in the twentieth century most explicitly by the mathematician and philosopher Alfred North Whitehead, sees reality in a perpetual and dynamic state of becoming.
13. This work was originally published in 1788 in *Transactions of the Royal Society of Edinburgh*. An expanded version, in two volumes, later appeared in 1795.

References Cited

Acciarino, D. 2018 Nature of Renaissance Antiquarianism: History, Methodology, Definition. *Acta Antiqua* 57(4):1–18. DOI:10.1556/068.2017.57.4.9.

Adams, W. Y., D. P. Van Gerven, and R. S. Levy 1978 The Retreat from Migrationism. *Annual Review of Anthropology* 7:483–532.

Allentoft, M. E., M. Sikora, K.-G. Sjögren, S. Rasmussen, M. Rasmussen, J. Stenderup, P. B. Damgaard, H. Schroeder, T. Ahlström, L. Vinner, A.-S. Malaspinas, A. Margaryan, T.

Higham, D. Chivall, N. Lynnerup, L. Harvig, J. Baron, P. Della Casa, P. Dąbrowski, P. R. Duffy, A. V. Ebel, A. Epimakhov, K. Frei, M. Furmanek, T. Gralak, A. Gromov, S. Gronkiewicz, G. Grupe, T. Hajdu, R. Jarysz, V. Khartanovich, A. Khokhlov, V. Kiss, J. Kolář, A. Kriiska, I. Lasak, C. Longhi, G. McGlynn, A. Merkevicius, I. Merkyte, M. Metspalu, R. Mkrtchyan, V. Moiseyev, L. Paja, G. Pálfi, D. Pokutta, Ł. Pospieszny, T. D. Price, L. Saag, M. Sablin, N. Shishlina, V. Smrčka, V. I. Soenov, V. Szeverényi, G. Tóth, S. V. Trifanova, L.Varul, M. Vicze, L. Yepiskoposyan, V. Zhitenev, L. Orlando, T. Sicheritz-Pontén, S. Brunak, R. Nielsen, K. Kristiansen, and E. Willerslev 2015 Population Genomics of Bronze Age Eurasia. *Nature* 522:167–172.

Ammerman A. J., and L. L. Cavalli-Sforza 1971 Measuring the Rage of Spread of Early Farming in Europe. *Man: New Series* 6(4):674–688.

Ammerman A. J., and L. L. Cavalli-Sforza 1973 A Population Model for the Diffusion of Early Farming in Europe. In *The Explanation of Culture Change: Models in Prehistory*, edited by C. Renfrew, pp. 345–357. Duckworth, London.

Ammerman A. J., and L. L. Cavalli-Sforza 1984 *The Neolithic Transition and the Genetics of Population in Europe*. Princeton University Press, Princeton.

Anthony, D. W. 1990 Migration in Archaeology: The Baby and the Bathwater. *American Anthropologist* 92(4):895–914.

Anthony, D. W. 1992 The Bath Refilled: Migration in Archaeology Again. *American Anthropologist* 94(1):174–176.

Anthony, D. W. 1997 Prehistoric Migration as Social Process. In *Migrations and Invasions in Archaeological Explanation*, edited by J. Chapman and H. Hamerow, pp. 21–32. BAR International Series no. 664. Archaeopress, Oxford.

Anthony, D. W., and D. R. Brown 2017 Molecular Archaeology and Indo-European Linguistics: Impressions from New Data. In *Usque ad Radices: Indo-European Studies in Honour of Birgit Anette Olsen*, edited by B. S. S. Hansen, A. Hyllested, A. R. Jørgensen, G. Kroonen, J. H. Larsson, B. N. Whitehead, T. Olander, and T. M. Søborg, pp. 25–54. Copenhagen Studies in Indo-European 8. Museum Tusculanum Press, Copenhagen.

Backus, I. D. 2003 *Historical Method and Confessional Identity in the Era of the Reformation (1378–1615)*. Brill, Leiden.

Bellwood, P. 1984–1985 A Hypothesis for Austronesian Origins. *Asian Perspectives* 26:107–117.

Bellwood, P. 1991 The Austronesian Dispersal and the Origins of Languages. *Scientific American* 265:88–93. 2013a *First Migrants: Ancient Migration in Global Perspective*. Wiley-Blackwell, Chichester.

Bellwood, P. (editor) 2013b *The Global Prehistory of Human Migration*. Wiley-Blackwell, Chichester.

Bellwood, P., and C. Renfrew (editors) 2002 *Examining the Farming/Language Dispersal Hypothesis*. McDonald Institute for Archaeological Research, Cambridge.

Binford, L. R. 1965 Archaeological Systematics and the Study of Culture Process. *American Antiquity* 31(2):203–210.

Binford, L. R. 1980 Willow Smoke and Dogs' Tails: Hunter-Gatherer Settlement Systems and Archaeological Site Formation. *American Antiquity* 45(1):4–20.

Binford, L. R. 2001 *Constructing Frames of Reference: An Analytical Method for Archaeological Theory Building Using Ethnographic and Environmental Data Sets*. University of California Press, Berkeley and Los Angeles.

Bintliff, J. 2006 Time, Structure, and Agency: The *Annales*, Emergent Complexity, and Archaeology. In *A Companion to Archaeology*, edited by J. Bintliff, pp. 174–194. Blackwell, Malden.

Blaut, J. M. 1987 Diffusionism: A Uniformitarian Critique. *Annals of the Association of American Geographers* 77(1):30–47.

Boyle, K., and C. Renfrew (editors) 2001 *Archaeogenetics: DNA and the Population Prehistory of Europe*. Mcdonald Institute for Archaeological Research, Cambridge.

Brace, S., Y. Diekmann, T. J. Booth, Z. Faltyskova, N. Rohland, S. Mallick, M. Ferry, M. Michel, J. Oppenheimer, N. Broomandkhoshbacht, K. Stewardson, S. Walsh, M. Kayser, R. Schulting, O. E. Craig, A. Sheridan, M. P. Pearson, C. Stringer, D. Reich, M. G. Thomas, and I. Barnes 2018 Population Replacement in Early Neolithic Britain. Preprint at *bioRxiv*. DOI:10.1101/267443.

Braudel, F. 1949 *La Méditerranée et le monde méditerranéen à l'époque de Philippe II*. Librairie Armand Colin, Paris.

Broodbank, C. 2013 *The Making of the Middle Sea: A History of the Mediterranean from the Beginning to the Emergence of the Classical World*. Oxford University Press, Oxford.

Burmeister, S. 2000 Archaeology and Migration: Approaches to an Archaeological Proof of Migration. *Current Anthropology* 41(4):539–567.

Burmeister, S. 2013 Migration und Ethnizität. Zur Konzeptualisierung von Mobilität und Identität. In *Theorie in der Archäologie. Zur jüngeren Diskussion in Deutschland*, edited by M. K. H. Eggert and U. Veit, pp. 229–267. TAT 10. Waxmann, Münster.

Burmeister, S. 2017 The Archaeology of Migration: What Can and Should It Accomplish? In *Migration and Integration from Prehistory to the Middle Ages*, edited by H. Meller, F. Daim, J. Krause, and R. Risch, pp. 57–68. Landesmuseum für Vorgeschichte, Halle (Saale).

Cabana, G. S. 2011 The Problematic Relationship between Migration and Culture Change. In *Rethinking Anthropological Perspectives on Migration*, edited by G. S. Cabana and J. J. Clark, pp. 16–28. University Press of Florida, Gainesville.

Callaway, E. 2018 Divided by DNA: The Uneasy Relationship between Archaeology and Ancient Genomics. *Nature* 555:573–576.

Cameron, C. M. 1995 Migration and the Movement of Southwestern Peoples. *Journal of Anthropological Archaeology* 14:104–124. 2013 How People Moved among Ancient Societies: Broadening the View. *American Anthropologist* 115(2):218–231.

Cameron, C. M. 2016 *Captives: How Stolen People Changed the World*. University of Nebraska Press, Lincoln.

Castaneda, H. 2017 Migration Is Part of the Human Experience but It Is Far from Natural. *Nature Human Behaviour* 1. DOI:10.1038/s41562-017-0147.

Castles, S., H. de Haas, and M. J. Miller 2013 *The Age of Migration*. 5th Edition. The Guilford Press, New York.

Champion, T. 1990 Migration Revived. *Journal of Danish Archaeology* 9:214–218.

Chapman, J., and H. Hamerow (editors) 1997 *Migrations and Invasions in Archaeological Explanation*. BAR International Series no. 664. Archaeopress, Oxford.

Childe, V. G. 1925 *The Dawn of European Civilization*. 1st Edition. Routledge and Kegan Paul, London.

Childe, V. G. 1929 *The Danube in Prehistory*. Clarendon Press, Oxford.

Chirikure, S. 2020 *Great Zimbabwe: Reclaiming a "Confiscated" Past*. Routledge, London.

Clark, G. 1966 The Invasion Hypothesis in British Archaeology. *Antiquity* 40(159):172–189.

Collar, A. 2013 *Religious Networks in the Roman Empire: The Spread of New Ideas*. Oxford University Press, Oxford.

Concannon, C., and L. Mazurek 2016 Introduction: A New Connectivity for the Twenty-first Century. In *Across the Corrupting Sea: Post-Braudelian Approaches to the Ancient Eastern Mediterranean*, edited by C. Concannon and L. Mazurek, pp. 1–16. Routledge, London.

Crellin, R. J., and O. J. T. Harris 2020 Beyond Binaries. Interrogating Ancient DNA. *Archaeological Dialogues* 27:37–56.

Delumeau, J. 2000 *History of Paradise: The Garden of Eden in Myth and Tradition*. Translated by M. O'Connell. University of Illinois Press, Urbana-Champaign.

Diaz-Andreu, M. 2008 *A World History of Nineteenth-Century Archaeology*. Oxford University Press, Oxford.

De Angelis, F. 2016 *E pluribus unum*: The Multiplicity of Models. In *Conceptualising Early Colonisation (=Contextualising Early Colonisation)*, Vol. 2, edited by L. Donnellan, V. Nizzo, and G.-J. Burger, pp. 97–104. Brepols, Turnhout.

De Angelis, F. 2020 Introduction: Greeks across the Ancient World. In *A Companion to the Greeks across the Ancient World*, edited by F. De Angelis, pp. 1–10. Wiley-Blackwell, Hoboken.

Driessen, J. (editor) 2018 *An Archaeology of Forced Migration: Crisis-induced mobility and the Collapse of the 13th c. BCE Eastern Mediterranean*. Presses universitaires de Louvain, Louvain-la-Neuve.

During, S. 2000 Postcolonialism and Globalization: Towards a Historicization of Their Interrelation. *Cultural Studies* 14(3/4):385–404.

Dyson, S. 1981 A Classical Archaeologist's Response to the "New Archaeology." *Bulletin of the American Schools of Oriental Research* 242:7–13.

Earle, T., and C. Gamble. 2011 Migration. In *Deep History*, edited by A. Shryock and D. L. Smail, pp. 191–218. University of California Press, Berkeley, Los Angeles, and London.

Eisenmann, S., E. Bánffy, P. van Dommelen, K. P. Hofmann, J. Maran, I. Lazaridis, A. Mittnik, M. McCormick, J. Krause, D. Reich, and P. W. Stockhammer 2018 Reconciling Material Cultures in Archaeology with Genetic Data: The Nomenclature of Clusters Emerging from Archaeogenomic Analysis. *Nature Scientific Reports* 8(13003). DOI:10.1038/s41598-018-31123-z.

Fagan, B. 1981 Two Hundred and Four Years of African Archaeology. In *Antiquity and Man: Essays in Honour of Glyn Daniel*, edited by J. D. Evans, B. Cunliffe, and C. Renfrew, pp. 42–51. Thames and Hudson, London.

Finley, M. I. 1973 *The Ancient Economy*. University of California Press, Berkeley and Los Angeles.

Frei, K. M., C. Villa, M. L. Jørkov, M. E. Allentoft, F. Kaul, P. Ethelberg, S. S. Reiter, A. S. Wilson, M. Taube, J. Olsen, N. Lynnerup, E. Willerslev, K. Kristiansen, and R. Frei 2017 A Matter of Months: High Precision Migration Chronology of a Bronze Age Female. *PLOS ONE* 12(6). DOI:10.1371/journal.pone.0178834.

Frieman, C. J., and D. Hofmann 2019 Present Pasts in the Archaeology of Genetics, Identity, And Migration in Europe: a Critical Essay. *World Archaeology* 51(4):528–545.

Furholt, M. 2018 Massive Migrations? The Impact of Recent aDNA Studies on our View of Third Millennium Europe. *European Journal of Archaeology* 21(2):159–191.

Furholt, M. 2019 Re-Integrating Archaeology. A Contribution to aDNA Studies and the Migration Discourse on the 3rd Millennium BC in Europe. *Proceedings of the Prehistoric Society* 85:115–129. DOI:10.1017/ppr.2019.4.

Gamble, C. 1998 Palaeolithic Society and the Release from Proximity: A Network Approach to Intimate Relations. *World Archaeology* 29(3):426–449.

Gannon, M. 2019 When Ancient DNA Gets Politicized. Electronic document. *Smithsonian.com*: https://www.smithsonianmag.com/history/when-ancient-dna-gets-politicized-180972639/, accessed July 2, 2019.

Goffart, W. 1989 *Rome's Fall and After*. The Hambledon Press, London and Ronceverte.

Gokcumen, O. 2018 The Year in Genetic Anthropology: New Lands, New Technologies, New Questions. *American Anthropologist* 120(2):266–277.

Greenblatt, S. (editor) 2010 *Cultural Mobility: A Manifesto*. Cambridge University Press, Cambridge.

Greene, E. S., and J. Leidwanger 2019 Knidian "Anyports": a Model of Coastal Adaptation and Socioeconomic Connectivity from Southwest Turkey. *Mediterranean Historical Review* 34:9–25.

Haak, W., I. Lazaridis, N. Patterson, N. Rohland, S. Mallick, B. Llamas, G. Brandt, S. Nordenfelt, E. Harney, K Stewardson, Q. Fu, A. Mittnik, E. Bánffy, C. Economou, M. Francken, S. Friederich, R. Garrido Pena, F. Hallgren, V. Khartanovich, A. Khokhlov, M. Kunst, P. Kuznetsov, H. Meller, O. Mochalov, V. Moiseyev, N. Nicklisch, S. L. Pichler, R. Risch, M. A. Rojo Guerra, C. Roth, A. Szécsényi-Nagy, J. Wahl, M. Meyer, J. Krause, D. Brown, D. Anthony, A. Cooper, K. Werner Alt, and D. Reich 2015 Massive Migration from the Steppe was a Source for Indo-European Languages in Europe. *Nature* 522(7555):207–211. DOI:10.1038/nature14317.

Haas, J. 1977 On Diffusion, Diffusionism, and Cultural Materialism. *American Anthropologist* 79(3):649–652.

Hakenbeck, S. 2008 Migration in Archaeology: Are We Nearly There Yet? *Archaeological Review from Cambridge* 23(2):9–26.

Hakenbeck, S. 2019 Genetics, Archaeology, and the Far Right: An Unholy Trinity. *World Archaeology* 51(4):517–527. DOI:10.1080/00438243.2019.1617189.

Hamid, M. 2017 *Exit West*. Riverhead Books, New York.

Hamilakis, Y. 2017 Archaeologies of Forced and Undocumented Migration. *Journal of Contemporary Archaeology* 3(2):121–139.

Härke, H. 1997 Wanderungsthematik, Archäologen und politisches Umfeld. *Archäologische Informationen* 20:61–71.

Härke, H. 1998 Archaeologists and Migrations: A Problem of Attitude? *Current Anthropology* 39(1):19–45.

Harvey, S. P. 2016 Ideas of Race in Early America. *Oxford Research Encyclopedia of American History*. DOI: 10.1093/acrefore/9780199329175.013.262.

Hertler, C. A. Bruch, and M. Märker 2013 The Earliest Stages of Hominin Dispersal in Africa and Eurasia. In *The Global Prehistory of Human Migration*, edited by P. Bellwood, pp. 9–17. Wiley-Blackwell, Chichester.

Herzfeld, M. 2007 Small-Mindedness Writ Large: On the Migrations and Manners of Prejudice. *Journal of Ethnic and Migration Studies* 33(2):255–274.

Herzfeld, M. 2016 The Hypocrisy of European Moralism: Greece and the Politics of Cultural Aggression—part 2. *Anthropology Today* 32(2):10–13.

Herzfeld, M. 2018 Anthropological Realism in a Scientific Age. *Anthropological Theory* 18(1):129–150.

Hodder, I. 1987 The Contribution of the Long Term. In *Archaeology as Long-Term History*, edited by I. Hodder, pp. 1–8. Cambridge University Press, Cambridge.

Hodos T. 2014 Stage Settings for a Connected Scene. Globalization and Material-Culture Studies in The Early 1st Millennium B.C.E. Mediterranean. *Archaeological Dialogues* 21:24–30.

Hodos, T. (editor) 2017 *The Routledge Handbook of Globalization and Archaeology*. Routledge, London and New York.

Hofmann, D. 2015 What Have Genetics Ever Done for Us? The Implications of aDNA Data for Interpreting Identity in Early Neolithic Central Europe. *European Journal of Archaeology* 18(3):454–476.

Hofmann, K. P., and P. W. Stockhammer 2017 Beyond Antiquarianism: Current Theoretical Issues in German-speaking Archaeology. *Archaeological Dialogues* 24:1–65.

Holmes, W. H. 1914 Areas of American Culture Characterization Tentatively Outlined as an Aid in the Study of the Antiquities. *American Anthropologist, New Series* 16(3):413–446.

Hopkins, K. 1983 Introduction. In *Trade in the Ancient Economy*, edited by P. Garnsey, K. Hopkins, and C. R. Whittaker, pp. ix–xxv. University of California Press, Berkeley and Los Angeles.

Horden, P., and N. Purcell 2000 *The Corrupting Sea: A Study of Mediterranean History*. Blackwell, Malden.

Hutton, J. 1788 Theory of the Earth; Or an Investigation of the Laws Observable in the Composition, Dissolution, and Restoration of Land upon the Globe. *Transactions of the Royal Society of Edinburgh* 1:209–304.

International Organization for Migration *2018 World Migration Report* 2018. Electronic document. https://www.iom.int/wmr/world-migration-report-2018, accessed January 21, 2019.

Isayev, E. 2017 *Migration, Mobility, and Place in Ancient Italy*. Cambridge University Press, Cambridge.

Jervis, B. 2018 *Assemblage Thought and Archaeology*. Routledge, London.

Kelly, R. L. 1983 Hunter-Gatherer Mobility Strategies. *Journal of Anthropological Research* 39(3):277–306.

Kennedy, R. F. 2014 *Immigrant Women in Athens: Gender, Ethnicity, and Citizenship in the Classical City*. Routledge, London.

Killgrove, K., and J. Montgomery 2016 All Roads Lead to Rome: Exploring Human Migration to the Eternal City through Biochemistry of Skeletons from Two Imperial-Era Cemeteries (1st–3rd c AD). *PLOS ONE* 11(2): e0147585. DOI:10.1371/journal.pone.0147585.

King, R. (editor) 2007 *An Atlas of Human Migration*. Firefly Books, Buffalo.

Knapp, A. B., and P. van Dommelen 2010 Material Connections: Mobility, Materiality, and Mediterranean Identities. In *Material Connections in the Ancient Mediterranean: Mobility, Materiality, and Identity*, edited by A. B. Knapp and P. van Dommelen, pp. 1–18. Routledge, London and New York.

Knappett, C. 2011 *An Archaeology of Interaction: Network Perspectives on Material Culture and Society*. Oxford University Press, Oxford.

Knappett, C. (editor) 2013 *Network Analysis in Archaeology: New Approaches to Regional Interaction*. Oxford University Press, Oxford.

Knappett, C., and J. Leidwanger 2018 Maritime Networks, Connectivity, and Mobility in the Ancient Mediterranean. In *Maritime Networks in the Ancient Mediterranean World*, edited by C. Knappett and J. Leidwanger, pp. 1–21. Cambridge University Press, Cambridge.

Knudson, K. J. 2011 Identifying Archaeological Human Migration Using Biogeochemistry: Case Studies from the South-Central Andes. In *Rethinking Anthropological Perspectives on Migra-

tion, edited by G. S. Cabana and J. J. Clark, pp. 231–247. University Press of Florida, Gainesville.

Kossinna, G. 1911 *Die Herkunft der Germanen: Zur Methode der Siedlungsarchäologie*. Kabitzsch, Würzburg.

Kotsonas, A., and J. Mokrišová 2020 Mobility, Migration, and Colonization. In *The Wiley Companion to the Archaeology of Early Greece and the Mediterranean*, edited by I. Lemos and A. Kotsonas, pp. 217–246. Blackwell, Malden.

Krause, J., and W. Haak 2017 Neue Erkenntnisse zur genetischen Geschichte Europas. In *Migration and Integration from Prehistory to the Middle Ages*, edited by H. Meller, F. Daim, J. Krause, and R. Risch, pp. 21–38. Landesmuseum für Vorgeschichte, Halle (Saale).

Kristiansen, K. 1989 Prehistoric Migrations: The Case of the Single Grave and Corded Ware Cultures. *Journal of Danish Archaeology* 8:211–225.

Kristiansen, K. 1998 *Europe Before History*. Cambridge University Press, Cambridge.

Kristiansen, K. 2014 Towards a New Paradigm? The Third Science Revolution and its Possible Consequences in Archaeology. *Current Swedish Archaeology* 22:11–34.

Kristiansen, K., M. E. Allentoft, K. M. Frei, R. Iversen, N. N. Johannsen, G. Kroonen, Ł. Pospieszny, T. D. Price, S. Rasmussen, K.-G. Sjögren, M. Sikora, and E. Willerslev 2017 Re-theorising mobility and the formation of culture and language among the Corded Ware Culture in Europe. *Antiquity* 91(356):334–347.

Kristiansen, K., and T.B. Larsson 2005 *The Rise of Bronze Age Society: Travels, Transmissions and Transformations*. Cambridge University Press, Cambridge.

Kroeber, A. L., and C. Kluckhohn 1952 *Culture: A Critical Review of Concepts and Definitions*. Peabody Museum of American Archaeology and Ethnology, Harvard University, Cambridge.

Laczko, F., and C. Aghazarm (editors) 2009 *Migration, Environment and Climate Change: Assessing the Evidence*. International Organization for Migration, Geneva.

Lave, J., and E. Wenger 1991 *Situated Learning: Legitimate Peripheral Participation*. Cambridge University Press, Cambridge.

Leppard, T. 2014 Mobility and Migration in the Early Neolithic of the Mediterranean: Questions of Motivation and Mechanism *World Archaeology* 46(4):484–501.

Lightfoot, K. 2015 Dynamics of Change in Multiethnic Societies: An Archaeological Perspective from Colonial North America. *PNAS* 112(30):9216–9223.

Manning, J. G. 2018 *The Open Sea: The Economic Life of the Ancient Mediterranean World from the Iron Age to the Rise of Rome*. Princeton University Press, Princeton.

Malkin, I. 2011 *A Small Greek World: Networks in the Ancient Mediterranean*. Oxford University Press, Oxford.

Mathieson, I., J. Lazaridis, N. Rohland, S. Mallick, N. Patterson, S. A. Roodenberg, E. Harney, K. Stewardson, D. Fernandes, M. Novak, K. Sirak, C. Gamba, E. R. Jones, Bastien Llamas, Stanislav Dryomov, J. Pickrell, J. L. Arsuaga, J. M. Bermúdez de Castro, E. Carbonell, F. Gerritsen, A. Khokhlov, P. Kuznetsov, M. Lozano, H. Meller, O. Mochalov, V. Moiseyev, M. A. Rojo Guerra, J. Roodenberg, J. M. Vergès, J. Krause, A. Cooper, K. W. Alt, D. Brown, D. Anthony, C. Lalueza-Fox, W. Haak, R. Pinhasi, and D. Reich 2015 Genome-wide Patterns of Selection in 230 Ancient Eurasians. *Nature* 528(7583):499–503. DOI:10.1038/ nature16152.

McCoskey, D. I. 2018 Bad to the Bone the Racist Application of DNA Science to Classical Antiquity. Electronic document. *Eidolon*: https://eidolon.pub/bad-to-the-bone-617ca3e37347, accessed June 30, 2020.

Meheux, K. 2017 Digitising and Re-examining Vere Gordon Childe's "Dawn of European Civilization": A Celebration of the UCL Institute of Archaeology's 80th Anniversary. *Archaeology International* 20:91–105. DOI:10.5334/ai-357.

Miller, P. N., and F. Louis 2012 Introduction: Antiquarianism and Intellectual Life in Europe and China. In *Antiquarianism and Intellectual Life in Europe and China, 1500–1800*, edited by P. N. Miller and F. Louis, pp. 1–26. The University of Michigan Press, Ann Arbor.

Morris, I. 2003 Mediterraneanization. *Mediterranean Historical Review* 18(2):30–55.

Müller, J. 2013 Kossinna, Childe, and aDNA. *Current Swedish Archaeology* 21:35–38.

Murray-Wallace, C. V. 1996 Understanding "Deep" Time—Advances since Archbishop Ussher? *Archaeology in Oceania* 31(3):173–177.

Padilla Peralta, D. 2015a Barbarians Inside the Gate, Part I: Fears of Immigration in Ancient Rome and Today. Electronic document. *Eidolon*: https://eidolon.pub/barbarians-inside-the-gate-part-i-c175057b340f, accessed June 30, 2020.

Padilla Peralta, D. 2015b Barbarians Inside the Gate, Part II: Immigrant Labor and Its Discontents. Electronic document. *Eidolon*: https://eidolon.pub/barbarians-inside-the-gate-part-ii-c22c5becd228, accessed June 30, 2020.

Padilla Peralta, D. 2017 Classics Beyond the Pale. Electronic document. *Eidolon*: https://eidolon.pub/classics-beyond-the-pale-534bdbb3601b, accessed June 30, 2020.

Porter, A. 2016 *Mobile Pastoralism and the Formation of Near Eastern Civilizations: Weaving Together Society*. Cambridge University Press, Cambridge.

Potts, D. 2014 *Nomadism in Iran: From Antiquity to the Modern Era*. Oxford University Press, Oxford.

Randsborg, K. 2000 National History, Non-National Archaeology: The Case of Denmark. *Oxford Journal of Archaeology* 19(2):211–222.

Reich, D. 2018 *Who We Are and How We Got Here: Ancient DNA and the New Science of the Human Past*. Oxford University Press, Oxford.

Renfrew, C. 1972 *The Emergence of Civilization: The Cyclades and the Aegean in the Third Millennium BC*. Methuen, London.

Renfrew, C. 1980 The Great Tradition versus the Great Divide: Archaeology as Anthropology? *American Journal of Archaeology* 84(3):287–298.

Renfrew, C. 1987 *Archaeology and Language: The Puzzle of Indo-European Origins*. Cambridge University Press, Cambridge.

Renfrew, C. 1989 Models of Change in Language and Archaeology. *Transactions of the Philological Society* 87(2):103–155.

Renfrew, C. 1992 Archaeology, Genetics, and Linguistic Diversity. *Man (New Series)* 27:445–478.

Rieckhoff, S. 2007 Geschichte als Baustelle. In *Auf der Suche nach Identitäten. Volk—Stamm—Kultur—Ethnos*, edited by S. Rieckhoff and U. Sommer, pp. 7–16. BAR International Series 1705. Archaeopress, Oxford.

Roberts, B. W., and M. Vander Linden 2011 Investigating Archaeological Cultures: Material Culture, Variability, and Transmission. In *Investigating Archaeological Cultures: Material Culture, Variability, and Transmission*, edited by B. W. Roberts and M. Vander Linden, pp. 1–22. Springer, New York.

Rowe, J. H. 1966 Diffusionism and Archaeology. *American Antiquity* 31(3):334–337.

Schuchhardt, C. 1919 *Alteuropa in seiner Kultur- und Stilentwicklung*. Strassbourg and Berlin: de Gruyter.

Shah, S. 2020 *The Next Great Migration: The Beauty and Terror of Life on the Move.* London: Bloomsbury.

Sherratt, A. 1990 Gordon Childe: Paradigms and Patterns in Prehistory. *Australian Archaeology* 30:3–13.

Snodgrass, A. 1985 The New Archaeology and the Classical Archaeologist. *American Journal of Archaeology* 89:31–37.

Stephens, W. 2013 From Berossos to Berosus Chaldaeus: The Forgeries of Annius of Viterbo and Their Fortune. In *The World of Berossos: Proceedings of the 4th International Colloquium on "The Ancient Near East between Classical and Ancient Oriental Traditions,"* edited by J. Haubold, G. B. Lanfranchi, R. Rollinger, and J. Steele, pp. 277–289. Harrassowitz Verlag, Wiesbaden.

Steward, J. H. 1955 *Theory of Culture Change: The Methodology of Multilinear Evolution.* University of Illinois Press, Urbana-Champaign.

Taskent, R. O., and O. Gokcumen 2017 The Multiple Histories of Western Asia: Perspectives from Ancient and Modern Genomes. *Human Biology* 89(2):107–117.

Trigger, B. 2006 *A History of Archaeological Thought.* 2nd Edition. Cambridge University Press, Cambridge.

Tsuda, T., and B. J. Baker 2015 Conclusion: Migration and Disruptions from Prehistory to the Present. In *Migrations and Disruptions: Toward a Unifying Theory of Ancient and Modern Migrations*, edited by B. J. Baker and T. Tsuda, pp. 297–332. University Press of Florida, Gainesville.

United Nations, Department of Economic and Social Affairs 2019 *International Migrant Stock 2019.* Electronic document. United Nations, New York, https://www.un.org/en/development/desa/population/migration/index.asp, accessed September 12, 2019.

Ussher, J. 1658 *The Annals of the World.* Printed by E. Taylor for J. Crook and G. Bedell, London.

van Dommelen, P. 2012 Colonialism and Migration in the Ancient Mediterranean. *Annual Review of Anthropology* 41:393–409.

van Dommelen, P. 2014 Moving On: Archaeological Perspectives on Mobility and Migration. *World Archaeology* 46(4):477–483.

Vander Linden, M. 2016 Population History in Third-Millennium BC Europe: Assessing the Contribution of Genetics. *World Archaeology* 48(5):714–728.

Vander Linden, M. 2018 Touching the Void (reply to Martin Furholt). *European Journal of Archaeology* 22(2):186–189.

Wallace, S. 2018 *Travellers in Time: Imagining Movement in the Ancient Aegean World.* Routledge, London and New York.

Wendrich, W., and H. Barnard (editors) 2008 *The Archaeology of Mobility: Old World and New World Nomadism.* University of California Press, Los Angeles and Berkeley.

Weninger, B., and T. Harper 2015 The Geographic Corridor for Rapid Climate Change in Southeast Europe and Ukraine. In *Neolithic and Copper Age between the Carpathians and the Aegean*, edited by E. Schultze, pp. 475–505. Archäologie in Eurasien 31. DAI, Berlin.

Yasur-Landau, A. 2010 *The Philistines and Aegean Migration at the End of the Late Bronze Age.* Cambridge University Press, Cambridge.

Yasur-Landau, A. 2011 Deep Change in Domestic Behavioural Patterns and Theoretical Aspects of Interregional Interactions in the 12th Century Levant. In *On Cooking Pots, Drinking Cups, Loomweights and Ethnicity in Bronze Age Cyprus and Neighbouring Regions*, edited by V. Karageorghis and O. Kouka, pp. 245–255. The A. G. Leventis Foundation, Nicosia.

PART I

New Data and New Narratives

CHAPTER TWO

Toward a New Prehistory

Re-Theorizing Genes, Culture, and Migratory Expansions

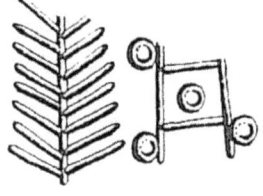

Kristian Kristiansen

Abstract *This paper introduces a theoretical framework for explaining different forms of migratory expansions and how they relate to the genetic, cultural, and environmental changes during the fifth–first millennium BCE. Three forms of migratory expansions are proposed: community-based farming colonization, pastoral male-dominated migrations, and finally, conquest migrations for new land. Forces of change, as well as mechanisms of cultural inclusion and exclusion are outlined. Finally, the future of the third science revolution and its effects is discussed.*

THE THIRD SCIENCE REVOLUTION IN ARCHAEOLOGY

Right now archaeology is experiencing its third science revolution (Kristiansen 2014).[1] Common to all three revolutions—the Darwinian revolution introducing to archaeology principles of stratification, deep time, and evolution (1850–1860), the C14 revolution introducing absolute dating (1950–1960), and now the DNA revolution introducing to archaeology prehistoric population genomics and migrations (2010–2020)—is the transformation of previous relative knowledge to absolute knowledge.[2] In doing so they freed intellectual resources to be spent on explaining change rather than describing and debating it (Figure 2.1). Thus, prior to the C14 revolution, most archaeological resources were poured into the classification and relative dating of prehistoric cultures. Beyond the safe dates of written sources one had to project back in time the supposed length of time periods, based on stratigraphy and typology. As we now know all prehistoric periods earlier than the Bronze Age were much older than anticipated. Once the C14 revolution unfolded and thousands of dates established safe chronologies, intellectual resources could instead be spent on explaining change, leading on to New Archaeology and what followed. Thus, these

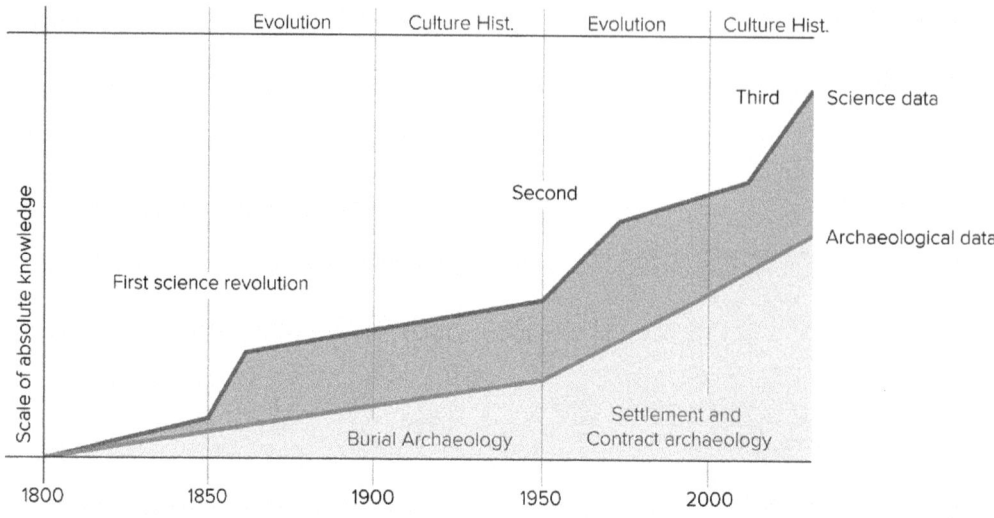

Figure 2.1. The three science revolutions in archaeology and the accumulating conversion from relative to absolute knowledge in tandem with the accumulation of archaeological data.

science revolutions were also intellectual revolutions propelling archaeological theory and interpretation forward.

Now once again, with the breakthrough of modern next-generation sequencing of prehistoric genomes since 2010, it has turned out that our understanding of cultural changes prior to the Iron Age was basically wrong. Major migrations were responsible for large-scale cultural changes in Neolithic and Bronze Age Eurasia (Allentoft et al. 2015; Haak et al. 2015; Olalde et al. 2018). We were thus ill prepared for the DNA revolution, even if ten years of strontium isotopic tracing of mobility had warned us that prehistoric societies were more mobile than we had thought. Some, such as David Anthony and myself (Anthony 1990; Kristiansen 1989), and, later, Burmeister (Burmeister 2000), made attempts to reintroduce a theoretical framework for migrations. Also, a series of dissertations were devoted to the question of migration in the German-speaking world, without coming to clear conclusions (Andresen 2004; Prien 2005). In our 2005 book, "The Rise of Bronze Age Society," Thomas B. Larsson and myself presented a theoretical framework for understanding the role of travels during the Bronze Age, much inspired by the works of Mary Helms (Kristiansen and Larsson 2005:chapters 1–2). Thus, mobility was increasingly accepted as an important factor in prehistoric societies, especially during the Bronze Age. However, mainstream archaeology had not yet taken onboard the theoretical and interpretative implications of migrations playing a major role in prehistory—that is, until now. Migrations and mobility can now be scientifically documented. They have been converted from relative to absolute knowledge. But knowledge and interpretation are not the same thing.

The Challenge in Front of Us

Therefore, the challenge in front of us is to develop better theoretical frameworks for understanding the relationship between genetic and cultural change, and in addition develop better frameworks for the collaboration between archaeology and genetics. This has been pointed out in several recent debate papers (Callaway 2018; Eisenmann et al. 2018; Furholt 2018; Ion 2017; Kristiansen 2019; Sørensen 2017a). A theoretical reorientation should aim at combining the micro and the macro perspective; things, humans, and societies—as genetics and strontium analysis allows this kind of resolution (Frei et al. 2015 and 2017; Kristiansen et al. 2017)—as well as large-scale C14 dating programs of individual sites (Whittle 2018). However, I wish to reintroduce humans, their social institutions, technologies, and cultural environments as driving or constraining factors, rather than mystifying things as agents. A materialist Marxist perspective allows us to understand that things are not what humans envision them to be. This perspective refers to Marx's concept of fetishism. A fetish is an object believed to have supernatural powers. Marx coined the concept to characterize money and markets in early capitalism as fetishism, since liberal economists ascribed to them an inherent supernatural, or self-regulating power that according to Marx was demonstratively derived from human actions based on the relationship between production, distribution, and consumption (Marx 1953/1974:introduction). By not including the value of labor in the equation, profits seemed magically to arise from market demands and price differences rather than from labor (Marx 1953/1974). Marx spent much of his later life in a partly failed attempt to demonstrate scientifically how this economic system worked, in order to unfold its laws (Liedman 2018). The point I wish to make here is that in much the same way we can attribute fetishism to modern thing theory and posthuman theories (Hornborg 2016). According to Hornborg, fetishism in this wider definition represents a false attribution of power—"the displacement of responsibility—to objects within networks of social relations where the political agency of humans is not apparent" (Hornborg 2016:172, note 13).

Thus, when critically compared with Marxist materialism, the so-called New Materialism in archaeology (Witmore 2014), anthropology, and cultural theory (Coole and Frost 2010) is rather a nonhuman-based pseudo materialism, trapped in fetishism, and therefore unable to explain historical processes. In *Global Magic* Hornborg (2016:7) referred to this phenomenon as the abandonment of relationism, and thus the abandonment of human power and responsibility, effectively leaving explanations of global environmental problems to natural science. The third science revolution allows the reintroduction of a new interdisciplinary social, science-based theory of history and human behavior based on the material conditions of life.

Basic to such a reinvigoration of social theory is an understanding of the primary role of institutions in organizing society and its power relations (Kristiansen and Larsson 2005:chapter 1.2). Material culture and language make institutions possible; as they provide social identity and behavioral norms to groups, they provide a blueprint for action. Thus, by institutionalizing technology and economy through material culture imbued with symbolic power (fetishism) social and religious networks organize production/distribution and allow for the manipulation of power. In Figure 2.2 I have summarized these relationships. All relations originate in the social organization of the political economy through the manipulation of things infusing them with symbolic power, well explained by Alfred Gell (1998), thereby transferring power over things through prestige goods and sacred objects to power over people. This basic dynamic has been at work from the beginning of modern humans in the Paleolithic to the Industrial Age. Therefore, we can apply a general Marxist/materialist theory for all human history since the Paleolithic, one that encapsulates the human condition from the individual to emerging World Systems (Figure 2.3).

Following from this, political economies and their Modes of Production (Kristiansen and Earle in press) are always to be understood as exploitive, whether of environments or humans, and thus deeply embedded in contested social relationships. Modes of production specify how individuals access the economy to mobilize revenues to support and institutionalize political power. Institutions thus organize production, circulation, and consumption, which form relations of production. A crucial theoretical concern is to describe how surplus labor and surplus wealth are generated and distributed, as this entails the dynamics behind

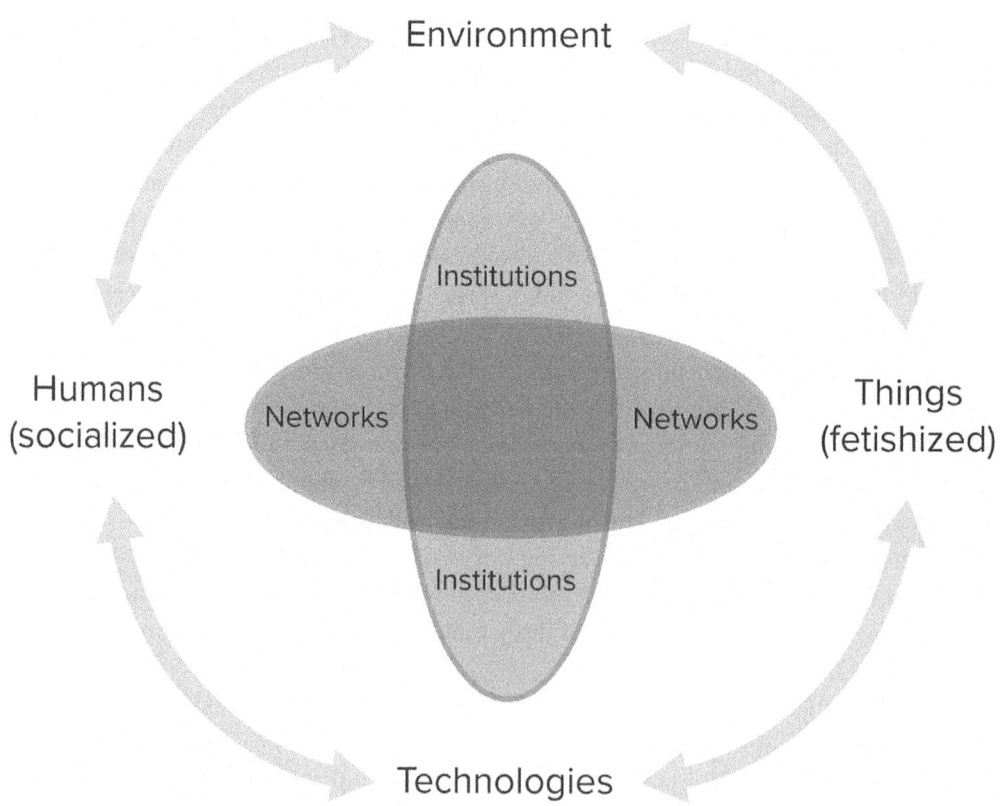

FIGURE 2.2. Model of the basic organizing categories of society and their dynamics.

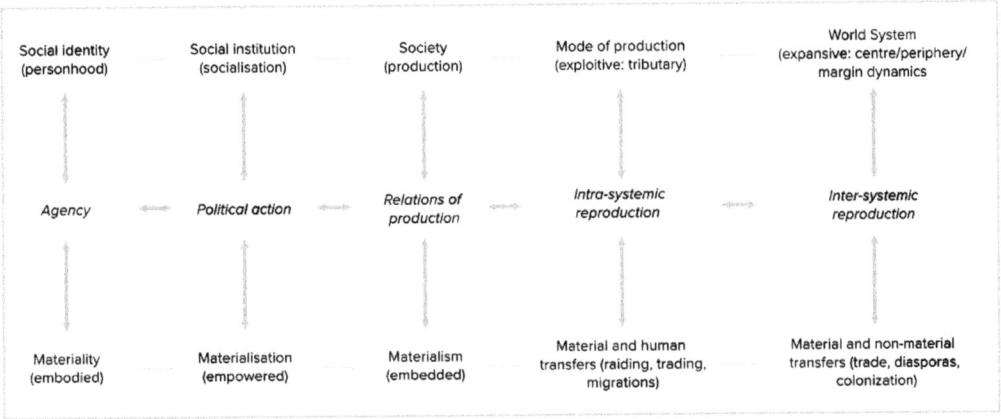

FIGURE 2.3. Conceptual model of forces of power in human societies that integrates micro- and macrodynamics.

both migratory processes and processes of hierarchization. They are dialectically related, as we shall demonstrate below and unfold according to a set of recurring circumstances through prehistory.

With this as my starting point I shall look more closely into the nature of migrations, their organization, and driving forces.[3]

Forms of Migratory Expansion and Mobility

Recent genetic and strontium evidence allows us to characterize different forms of expansion more precisely, not least their genetic and demographic impact, as well as their social organization and interaction with local groups and communities over time (Amorin et al. 2018; Knipper et al. 2017; Mittnik et al. 2019; Sjögren et al. 2020; Veeramah 2018). However, to distill various types of expansion and colonization demands a comparative analysis of archaeological/anthropological cases. Here, I base myself primarily on the works of David Anthony (1997), Gosden (2004), Kristinsson (2012), and my own work, especially in *Europe before History* (Kristiansen 1998). In the following I delineate different forms of mobility and their genetic and archaeological relationship. Such relationships can take many forms and therefore need to be inferred case by case, and then theorized. Likewise, migration is a covering concept for a variety of expansion types (Kristinsson 2010 and 2012).

Colonizing Expansions/Community Colonization

"The simplest kind of expansion cycle is colonizing expansion. This is triggered when new land becomes available by some historical chance or process such as finding new land that was previously unknown, had become empty for some reason (e.g., previous outmigration) or if new

methods were developed that made previously unproductive land suitable for farming. The prime mover here is newly available land" (Kristinsson 2012:378).

One might also add land occupied by small groups of people, such as hunter-gatherers, who cannot withstand the colonists in numbers, and which would have been the case with the Neolithic expansion into Europe. Whole family groups/communities moving *en bloc*: this is the Neolithic farming colonization of Europe. Recent genetic evidence demonstrates that the Linear Bandkeramik (LBK) groups were full family groups/communities, who were able to mobilize enough labor to clear forests and create new settlements (Shennan 2018). They were genetically the offspring of the original Anatolian farming colonization into Greece and the Balkans (Mathieson et al. 2018), and when they reached Hungary, they could no longer sustain large tell communities, but split up into smaller communities which became the LBK (Bánffy 2004, 2013, 2019). During the initial colonizing phase, they did not mix with existing hunter-gatherer groups (Szecsenyi-Nagy et al. 2014), and then only male hunter-gatherers, it seems (Nikitin et al. 2019). Such behavior corresponds to well-studied ethnographic cases for farmer/hunter-gatherer interaction (Nicolaisen 1976). As has been demonstrated, these colonizing farmers exhibited a remarkable demographic expansion until they reached the economic limits of the system, when warfare and massacres took over.[4] This led to increasing genetic admixture with hunter-gatherers and a new colonizing expansion toward western and northern Europe (Chylénski et al. 2017; Fernandes et al. 2018; Lipson et al. 2017).

The second type of expansion is quite unlike the community-based farming colonization.

Conquest Colonization/System Expansion

This type of expansion does not necessarily depend on access to new land, but rather represents social systems in constant competition, promoting centrifugal movements of populations into new lands. It is well described among the segmentary Tiv in Africa (Sahlins 1961), but covers most pastoral societies. According to Kristinsson: "*System expansions have their origins in competitive systems. These are cultures that show significant levels of conformity and usually, though not always, share a single language. However, they are politically divided which leads to constant and escalating competition between the polities*" (2012:380). Here we also find the Urnfield expansion of the Late Bronze Age, most Iron Age migratory expansion, such as the Celtic migrations, and later Germanic and Viking migrations. They were the results of an internal development toward increasing militarization, which had to find an outlet:

Even if these societies were originally based on social stratification and had elite armies they will sooner or later be forced to mobilize the common people in their conflicts. With such militarization comes democratization since the elite cannot effectively subdue or control a populace that is armed and seasoned in war (see Andreski 1954/1968). The common people in such societies are normally a farming population and their greatest political demand is usually the demand for land. (Kristinsson 2012:380) This is what Engels called The Germanic Mode of Production, but which rather represents a stage in a cyclical historical process from the Bronze Age into the Iron Age.

We should divide this type of expansion into two: pastoral conquest expansion and farming conquest expansions. They are both in search of new land for grazing and farming or a mix, and thus they differ in their economies and in their level of social organization. Pastoral conquest migrations are based on controlling clients, whether other pastoral groups, traders, or farmers, whereas the farming conquest expansion are more typically linked to need for new land and the control over subdued clients who are often made into slaves. In both these cases we witness a strong male-dominated militarization of society.

Pastoral expansions/conquests are well described in historical and ethnographic literature (Kradin et al. 2003). The later history of the Eurasian steppe typifies such pastoral or nomadic conquest colonization, which over time would lead to gradual linguistic and genetic admixtures or even replacements by new dominant groups (Damgaard et al. 2018). However, they are preceded by a more simple yet also male-dominated warrior-based type of migration during the third millennium B.C. in western Eurasia, typified by the Yamnaya, Corded Ware, and Bell Beaker migrations (Allentoft et al. 2015; Haak et al. 2015; Kristiansen et al. 2017; Olalde et al. 2018).

To minimize risks in a pastoral economy and to exchange for some products, cattle would have been lent out to networks of partners. We hypothesize that women were exchanged in the opposite direction from animals, and foster sons could become placed with their uncle, a common Indo-European practice, and now also demonstrated archaeologically in third-millennium Europe (Sjögren et al. 2020; Knipper et al. 2017). Strontium isotopic analyses of several large Corded Ware cemeteries confirm that males remained local, while women were mostly of nonlocal origin, and often had a Neolithic diet during childhood (Sjögren et al. 2016).

To conclude, the Yamnaya and Corded Ware cultures had a dominant Pastoral Mode of Production resulting in rapidly expanding, mobile, and low-density populations dependent on animals. This economy continued to dominate into the Bronze Age, and resulted in a long-term increase of a protein-rich diet (Münster et al. 2018:Figure 7), leading to a rapid population increase across Europe, especially after 2000 B.C. (Müller 2015).

Time and Transformation: The Forces of Initial Farming Colonization, Pastoral Migration and Conquest Migrations

Economic Drivers and Constraints

Here, I summarize some basic observations about constraints and drivers, which are dialectically related. Thus, constraints may become drivers if societies transform themselves to adapt to new circumstances. We observe this dynamic unfold when a social and economic system reached its limits of expansion, and then either had to stop or transform to continue expansion into a new social and economic environment. This is also when material culture changes, as social institutions and their cultural markers/identities changed. It is exemplified by the transformation of the tell cultures of the Balkan Neolithic (Starcevo-Vinca) into the farmhouse culture of the Linear Band Ceramic Culture of Central Europe (LBK). Eszter Bánffy has located and explained the transformative process in Hungary, when a tell culture of "clayscapes" (houses built with clay useful in a hot and dry environment) was transformed into a house culture of "timberscapes" (timber-built houses useful in a temperate environment with much forest and rain). The adaptation to a new forest environment was also followed by increasing genetic admixture with hunters over time, even if the initial expansion was marked by less admixture (Bánffy 2019)

A similar transformation took place when the Yamnaya pastoralists shortly after 3000 B.C. reached the western limit of the steppe in Hungary, and had to stop expanding or adapt to a new economy combining mixed farming with pastoralism, in order to cope with a more forested environment. To facilitate this transformation they would choose flat landscapes with less dense forest, such as the sandy soils of northwestern Europe that could more easily be transformed into open steppe–like grazing lands which happened on a broad scale after 2900–2850 B.C. However, to expand territories, they displaced or interacted with Neolithic farmers across broad regions of Europe. In central and northern Europe, they interacted through exogamy and female abduction with Neolithic societies (Muhl et al. 2010), and Neolithic women brought with them new material culture and farming practices, including linguistic terminology of crops, which helped reformulate economic strategies and material culture, becoming the Corded Ware Culture (Juras et al. 2018; Kristiansen et al. 2017).

Finally, conquest migrations of the second and first millennia B.C. and during the first millennium A.D. were all based on a militarized society where warriors were recruited into chiefly retinues that under certain conditions could be mobilized temporarily into larger armies in connection with conquest migrations. Here, constraints and drivers are internal contradictions between increasing hierarchies and a rising male population without access to land and farms. The same forces that fostered expansion in the Pastoral Mode of Production where sons that could not inherit were sent off as migrating warring colonists, would now lead to more organized raiding and trading expansions, and later conquest and colonization. This might unfold either through maritime forces of raiding and trading as during the Viking period and during the Nordic Bronze Age (Ling et al. 2018), later leading to more massive conquest colonization, or through land-based conquest migrations, as during the Celtic and later Iron Age migrations after the fall of the Roman Empire.

Common to the various forms of expansion after 3000 B.C. is that they share the same social structure based on exogamy in combination with patrilocal and patrilineal kinship systems. In combination with primogeniture it fostered strong male-driven expansionist forces, supported from the beginning by shared Indo-European languages, as local continuity, whether matri- or patrilocal, determine which language will dominate as demonstrated in comparative studies (Lansing et al. 2017). We may thus observe a *longue durée* in the basic forces of expansion originating in an Indo-European pastoral social organization of society that prevailed through time, even if the nature and organization of expansion changed.

We can now summarize three types of expansions, involving migration and colonization:

1. Farming colonizing groups of the sixth-fifth millennium B.C., where family groups and whole communities moved into new land, occupied by hunter-gatherers, with whom they had little interaction, either culturally or genetically (Mathieson et al. 2018). During initial colonization, fast demographic expansion is possible, doubling in each generation (Shennan 2018:6–9). This is reflected in curves of thousands of C14 dates (Hinz et al. 2012; Shennan et al. 2013). When reaching the ecological/economic ceiling we witness declining health/diet (Downey et al. 2016; Larsen 2014), and endemic warfare, before new migrations and admixing with hunter-gatherers created a new form of colonization into new unsettled lands of northern and western Europe during the later fifth to fourth millennium B.C.

2. Pastoral expansions of the early third millennium B.C. of young male warrior groups (Goldberg et al. 2017; Kristiansen et al. 2017): This represented a very different type of expansion that involved abduction of Neolithic women and probably killing off the Neolithic male population, or other ways of preventing their reproduction, as they left no or very few surviving genetic lineages. The original steppe groups expanded and transformed from Yamnaya to Corded Ware to Bell Beakers until reaching their geographical and demographic limits by the end of the third millennium B.C. After 2000 B.C. a more hierarchical and militarized Bronze Age society emerged, leading to a new type of expansion and colonization (Kristiansen 2018).

3. Farming expansion for new land characterized Bronze Age, Urnfield, La Tène, Germanic, and Viking expansions. They followed a pattern that started with raiding and trading, which later spurred colonization. They represented internal forces of expansion, creating an outlet for competing chiefly groups to mobilize warriors for raiding and conquest migrations (Kristiansen 1998:312–320). The site of Tollense in Mecklenburg seems to represent a battlefield resulting from a conquest migration to take over the fertile landscape of Mecklenburg by a Central European army between 1250–1200 B.C. (Price et al. 2017). Such migrations were often linked to maritime economies of trade and raids (Ling et al. 2018)

The Role of Captives and Unfree

Basic to all tribal and chiefdom societies is a constant need for human labor to allow the free part of the population to maintain their control of property and production. Impressive comparative and historical evidence for this has been summarized by Catherine Cameron (2016, this volume), which demonstrates that captives in most societies would provide between 10–30% of the population. In pre-state societies before regular slave trade, males would be killed as they were too dangerous. Women and children were taken for labor and reproduction, some entering into marriage and thus changing their status. Another consequence of this practice was intercultural exchange between competing populations. We clearly see this pattern documented from the third millennium onward (Mittnik et al. 2019). Abduction of Neolithic women by Corded Ware males was probably customary, while the killing of males represented ethnic cleansing. This would explain the extraordinary genetic fact that only two dominant male genetic lines are documented from Yamanaya to Bell Beaker communities, and these lines still dominate today's male population. Neolithic male lines thus became extinct already during the third millennium B.C. In contrast, multiple female lines existed, many of which show Neolithic origins. As the evidence stands, we can envisage a rather massive, if long-drawn out, genocide of Neolithic males that eliminated their reproductive contributions throughout temperate Europe. However, in that process exogamy combined with abduction lead to the transformation of the original pastoral Yamanaya economy into a mixed farming/herding economy, and the formation of a new material culture, Corded Ware. Thus, it is in the meeting between different social formations that new cultures and economies are formed in a process of ethnogenesis and economic transformation (for comparative evidence see Cameron 2016:chapter 5). It happened when Iberian maritime Bell Beaker people, moving north along the Atlantic seaboard and along the Rhone-Rhine corridor, met with Corded Ware people, who adopted their metallurgical and maritime know-how. From this meeting emerged the Beaker Culture (Case 2004), a cultural transmission without genetic admixture (Olalde et al. 2018). Thus, different scenarios for cultural and genetic admixture processes were at work, some more peaceful, others more violent.

During the second millennium when the pastoral and tribal migrations had come to an end and a more ranked Bronze Age society with a militarized warrior elite had emerged (Horn and Kristiansen 2018), the evidence is even more clear about the role of unfree and commoners. Only free chiefly lineages were buried in the barrows of the Nordic Culture, amounting to around 20% of the population; they were the owners of farms, cattle, and land, and they organized the trading and raiding supported by warrior retinues (Holst et al. 2013). Comparative studies suggest that such warrior groups were linked together in ritually organized sodalities (Hayden 2018). In Denmark, the missing part of the population can now be demonstrated to have been buried outside barrows in flat graves and gallery graves, with few or no burial goods. Here, we find women and children, who are underrepresented in elite barrow burials (Bergerbrant et al. 2017). It is in accordance with the evidence of the captured that those buried in flat graves—whether commoners or unfree—were commonly of nonlocal origin. In central Europe the groups of unfree were mostly buried in pits without much ritual or grave goods, but they still shared the same diet as those buried in ordinary graves (Knipper et al. 2015b), whereas high elites would from now on distinguish themselves through special diets (Knipper et al. 2015a; Knipper et al. 2014).

With the emergence of city-states in the Mediterranean the demand for slaves increased, not least after the formation of the Roman Empire. Beginning in the later Bronze Age and during the Iron Age the slave trade became an organized commercial venture, and unfree people continued to form a large proportion of the population. In the Celtic world, slave taking and trading took on large proportions, when slaves were traded for wine (Kristiansen 1998:346), and we should probably envisage conquest migrations as means also to secure slaves from the conquered populations.

Mechanisms of Cultural Exclusion/Inclusion during Expansion

Another frontier of new knowledge and need of retheorizing is the formation and function of cultural and ethnic identities during and after expansion, and how such categories relate to genetic admixture—or non-admixture (Kristiansen et al. 2017). Our knowledge of these transformative processes advances only in tandem with new genetic evidence, and therefore the use of old archeological/cultural classifications has raised critical discussion (Eisenmann et al. 2018). What have we learned thus far?

Across broad areas of western Eurasia, correspondences existed between migratory expansions and colonization of the Yamanaya, Corded Ware, and Bell Beaker groups when we consider the institution of burial rituals (Furholt 2019). These groups stood in some contrast to the cultural localism of Neolithic farmers, who kept rich soil areas cut out of the forest, improved by careful tending, and defended against others. They were the target of continuous raids to capture women by Corded Ware and later Bell Beaker warrior groups. As a result of these tensions sharp cultural and ethnic borders were sustained, a practice well documented from ethnohistorical sources (Cameron 2016:chapter 5). The cultural identities of the Corded Ware groups were supported by warrior sodalities (Vandkilde 2018), materialized in widespread similarities in male burials (Bourgeois 2017), and perhaps linked to the practice of raising foster sons from distant families networked by kinship and marriage (Knipper et al. 2017). Martin Furholt (2017) has proposed that the fluidity of social groups was behind the formation and maintenance of a homogenous material culture, at least for a few hundred years, which represented strong spatial mobility despite being settled. Later migrations during the La Tène and Migration periods documented that migrating groups often share symbolic elements fundamental to their identity, while exhibiting local cultural variation (Kristiansen 1998: 399–411; Hedeager 2011). A set of recurring patterns of strong material and cultural identities linked to societies in expansion can thus be observed.

The symbolic and ritual world, reinforced by language, provided a cultural and ethnic identity in periods of mobility and social tensions (see also Porter, this volume). When confronting hostile groups, such collective identities were crucial to form alliances in a segmentary system. Others outside these groups were despised, demonized, and sometimes exterminated. Archaeology documents massacred bodies thrown into pits like garbage, as at Pömmelte (2300–2000 B.C.) where 27 individuals, mostly juvenile and adult males, were thrown into pits around a circular ritual structure (Spatzier 2017).[5] Similar is the site of Pepkin in Russia, where several of the males had been decapitated (Mednikova and Lebedinskaya 2000). Thus, small-scale recurring violence was probably much more common than large-scale organized warfare in prehistory.

Language change and continuity has been broadly studied in processes of migration and political economies (Hornborg 2014). In comparative ethnographic cases (Lansing et al. 2017), the dominant language is the one spoken by the social groups, into which spouses found residence after marriage. Thus, whether matrilineal or patrilineal, the language of the receiving group dominates. Copper Age and Bronze Age societies were typically patrilineal with patrilocal residence following marriage, leading to language adoption, which is in line with the dominance of Indo-European languages across western Eurasia. I thus propose that the expansive patrilineal, patrilocal warrior-based societies of the third millennium B.C. supported the global expansion of Indo-European languages. Should the Neolithic Corporate Mode of Production have been dominant, we would in all probability have seen a much more diverse linguistic history across Europe.

During the second millennium B.C., the formation of new regional identities, in part linked to transregional networks of trade routes, raiding, and confederation, probably led to the formation of regional dialects and later languages, such as Germanic, Celtic, Italic, and Greek. They could well have their roots in the regional identities, political economies, and networks of mobility and trade formed during the second millennium B.C. (Kristiansen 2017; Reher and Fernandez-Götz 2015). Complex parallel identities evolved during the Bronze Age that allowed traders and warriors to form international sodalities or "secret societies" (Hayden 2017), while other chiefly institutions formed more closed regional identities (Kristiansen 2017). Membership in warrior sodalities allowed them to travel and cross regional and local ethnicities, carried by the institution of free farmers and household chiefs, which were able to form temporary confederacies to facilitate trade and travels. This is reflected in more varied geographic origins of nonlocal individuals in Denmark (Frei et al. 2019). Much of this was carried on during the Iron Age. Here, we can again observe the formation of new cultural and ethnic identities in periods of expansion and colonization. Irad Malkin (2011) demonstrated through his study of the Archaic Greek expansion throughout the Mediterranean, which created a network of small and independent Greek coastal communities and city-states, how a maritime network of traders and migrant populations developed a shared Greek culture of common narratives, language, and material culture without any central government or coordination. "The emergence of all of those commonalities was a process of convergence through divergence" (Malkin 2011:5). It is worth noticing that this process simultaneously stimulated economic growth and increasing wealth among Greek city-states and their households (Morris 2005).

We can thus profitably use the Greek—and the Phoenician—network model to interpret some earlier cultural expansions, as the Greek evidence seems to conform with our evidence of the third and second millennium in several aspects. We may conclude, therefore, that population expansions from the Neolithic through the Bronze Age into the Iron Age share some basic similarities, among which the maintenance of a strong cultural and cosmological ethos is perhaps the most prominent.

The Two Cultures: Where Now?

Archaeology is the lovechild of an impossible romance between Enlightenment and Romanticism, a hybrid discipline combining science and human material history. Ever since the Enlightenment, when science started on its journey to transform the world, science and history/humanities have fought for supremacy, creating a cyclical research history of opposing discourses (Figure 2.4). This has been well described by Wolf in his last book: "*Tracing out a history of our concepts can also make us aware of the extent to which they incorporate intellectual and political efforts that still reverberate in the present*" (1999:22). He sees the original debate between the Enlightenment and its enemies to have formed all subsequent debates. Or in his own words:

> *Each encounter provoked reactions that later informed the position taken during the next turn. The issue of Reason against Custom and Tradition was raised by the protagonists of the Enlightenment against their adversaries, the advocates of what Isaiah Berlin called the Counter-Enlightenment. In the wake of this debate Marx and Engels transformed the arguments advanced by both sides into a revolutionary critique of the society that had given rise to both positions. The arguments put forward by this succession of critics in turn unleashed a reaction against all universalizing schemes, schemes that envisioned a general movement of transcendence for humankind. This particularism was directed against Newtonian physics, Darwinian biology, Hegelian megahistory, and Marxian critique, on the debatable premise that they all subjugated the human world to some ultimate teleological goal.* (Wolf 1999:22)

This brief reference to the nineteenth-century debate entails all the major ingredients of later debates, including processual and post-processual archaeology. Will this end now? Or are we witnessing just another cyclical swing, and how long will it last? I suggest we are crossing the line toward a science paradigm right now, and this is perhaps the most exciting phase in the establishment of the new paradigm. Right now we know the main results of

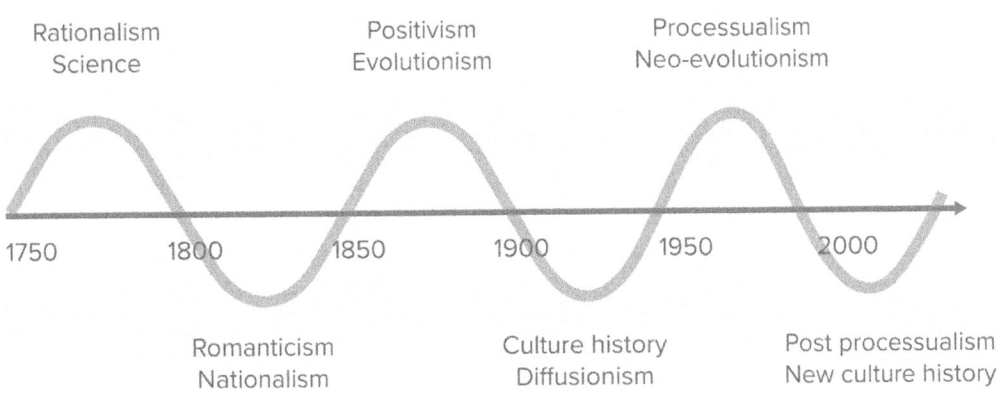

FIGURE 2.4. Cyclical swings of discourse between humanistic- and science-based interpretations of the world.

the genetic revolution, which allows us to start developing new theoretical frameworks of interpretations as proposed in the preceding sections. This paper is a small contribution toward such a goal, which will take time to accomplish. In that process we must be aware of the huge popular interest in the new genetic results, and the need to constantly and critically debate their dissemination, also in the public domain (Kristiansen 2014:25), when complex knowledge can sometimes be transformed into dangerous stereotypes (Frieman and Hoffman 2019; Heyd 2017). The past has always been exploited for political purposes, for good and bad (Díaz-Andreu 2007), and while some researchers right now are mostly concerned with the darker side of potential misuse (Hakenbeck 2019),[6] this should not lead us to introduce politically motivated restrictions on research and on academic freedom. Rather, we need to participate in the ways new results are disseminated, whether in writing popular books, articles, or engaging with science journalists, as their articles reach a wide readership. As archaeologists we are experiencing one of the most exciting times in the history of the discipline, but it also puts high demands on all parties to engage in the whole process from research questions and interpretation to popular dissemination.

Acknowledgments

I wish to thank Timothy Earle for inspiring discussions about Modes of Production, reflected in our paper in print, as well as Volker Heyd for inspiring collaboration on Bell Beaker social organization, also reflected in our paper in press. Finally, I wish to thank the research team led by Eske Willerslev at the Lundbech Centre for Geogenetic research in Copenhagen for our stimulating and generous collaboration since 2011. The manuscript was finalized in 2019.

Notes

1. See also Lucas 2015; Neustupny 2012; and Sørensen 2017b for discussions of paradigms.
2. This does not imply that there is no debate possible about interpretation or improvement of methodologies. A good historical example is the calibration curve of C14. Similarly, one can also discuss the way aDNA data are analyzed using different statistical methods (see Kristiansen 2019 for a discussion of archaeology and science). However, the baseline is that certain types of questions can be answered with a high degree of probability, and that genetically-based data are correct, if correctly sequenced. Importantly, both C14 dates and genetic data are stored and made accessible for further reanalysis and testing in global public databases. To match this archaeological data still has some way to go.
3. In this paper, I have excluded the role of diseases and epidemics, such as the early spread of plague (Rascovan et al. 2019). This might undoubtedly have influenced migration processes and their outcome. However, epidemics need to be understood in relation to the social and economic organization of society, which at least in part defines their impact.
4. During the Neolithic, we can observe a temporal trend in which deathly violence and massacres prevail during periods of population pressure and competition over resources (Downey et al. 2016), such as the late LBK before its collapse (Meyer et al. 2018), and

also during the following expansion period of the Late Neolithic societies, when competition for land increased (Chenal et al. 2015). Thus, during the late LBK enclosures become more numerous and grow in size during the crisis period (Shennan 2018:Figure 4.9). Massacres are of two kinds: execution of whole local communities to take over their territory or selective execution of males, where it is assumed that women are taken as captives, a normal practice well documented ethnographically and historically in pre-state societies (Cameron 2016, this volume). The same pattern continues during the later Neolithic period (Chenal et al. 2015), and prevailed during periods of internal stress and/or expansion of new groups into already occupied territories (Schroeder et al. 2019).

5. During the last 30 years an increasing body of evidence for massacres has turned up, due to the expansion of large-scale rescue archaeology. This has allowed for the uncovering of large areas, as such more informal burials, which are mostly found outside ordinary cemeteries, sometimes linked to fortifications, sometimes inside settlement, and sometimes found randomly where a raid or combat took place. Such small-scale violence and combat was therefore in all probability much more common than large-scale warfare, and conforms well with an increased understanding of raiding for captives and competition for land in certain periods (Armit 2010; Harding 2013).

6. One of the most destructive political misuses of the past has been for constructing nationalist narratives of exclusion (Kohl and Fawcett 1995). According to aDNA all Europeans have been subject to the same genetic admixture processes and thus there is no genetic support for such narratives. On the contrary, all Europeans belong to the same genetic stock or "family" (Bojs 2017).

References Cited

Allentoft, M. E., M. Sikora, K.-G. Sjögren, S. Rasmussen, M. Rasmussen, J. Stenderup, P. B.Damgaard, H. Schroeder, T. Ahlström, L. Vinner, A.-S. Malaspinas, A. Margaryan, T. Higham, D. Chivall, N. Lynnerup, L. Harvig, J. Baron, P. Della Casa, P. Dąbrowski, P. R. Duffy, A. V. Ebel, A. Epimakhov, K. Frei, M. Furmanek, T. Gralak, A. Gromov, S. Gronkiewicz, G. Grupe, T. Hajdu, R. Jarysz, V. Khartanovich, A. Khokhlov, V. Kiss, J. Kolář, A. Kriiska, I. Lasak, C. Longhi, G. McGlynn, A. Merkevicius, I. Merkyte, M. Metspalu, R. Mkrtchyan, V. Moiseyev, L. Paja, G. Pálfi, D. Pokutta, Ł. Pospieszny, T. D. Price, L. Saag, M. Sablin, N. Shishlina, V. Smrčka, V. I. Soenov, V. Szeverényi, G. Tóth, S. V. Trifanova, L.Varul, M. Vicze, L. Yepiskoposyan, V. Zhitenev, L. Orlando, T. Sicheritz-Pontén, S. Brunak, R. Nielsen, K. Kristiansen, and E. Willerslev 2015 Population Genomics of Bronze Age Eurasia. *Nature* 522:167–172. DOI:10.1038/nature14507.

Amorin, C. E. G. S. Vai, C. Posth, A. Modi, I. Koncz, S. Hakenbeck, M. C. La Rocca, B. Mende, D. Bobo, W. Pohl, L. P. Baricco, E. Bedini, P. Francalacci, C. Giostra, T. Vida, D. Winger, U. von Freeden, S. Ghirotto, M. Lari, G. Barbujani, J. Krause, D. Caramelli, P. J. Geary, and K. R. Veeramah 2018 Understanding 6th-Century Barbarian Social Organization and Migration through Paleogenomics. *Nature Communications* 9(3547). DOI:10.1038/s41467-018-06024-4.

Andresen, M. 2004 *Studien zur Geschichte und Methodik der archäologischen Migrationsforschung*. Waxman, Münster, New York, München, and Berlin.

Anthony, D. W. 1990 Migration in Archaeology: The Baby and the Bathwater. *American Anthropologist* 92:895–914.

Anthony, D. W. 1997 Prehistoric Migration as Social Process. In *Migrations and Invasions in Archaeological Explanation*, edited by John Chapman and Helena Hamerow, pp. 21–32. British Archaeological Reports International Series 664. Archaeopress, Oxford.

Anthony, David W. 2007 *The Horse, the Wheel, and Language: How Bronze Age Riders from the Eurasian Steppes Shaped the Modern World*. Princeton University Press, Princeton.

Armit, I. 2010 Violence and Society in the Deep Human Past. *British Journal of Criminology Advance Access*:1–19. DOI:10.1093/bjc/azq076.

Bánffy, E. 2004 *The 6th Millennium BC Boundary in Western Transdanubia and Its Role in the Central European Neolithic Transition. The Szentgyörgyvölgyi-Pityerdomb settlement*. Archaeological Institute of the HAS, Budapest.

Bánffy, E. 2013 Tracing the Beginnings of Sedentary Life in the Carpathian Basin: On the Formation of the LBK House. In *Tracking the Neolithic House in Europe*, edited by D. Hofmann and J. Smyth, pp. 117–149. Springer, New York. DOI:10.1007/978-1-4614-5289-8_6.

Bánffy, E. 2019 *First Farmers of the Carpathian Basin: Changing Patterns in Subsistence, Ritual and Monumental Figurines*. Prehistoric Society Research Paper 8. Oxbow Books, Oxford and Philadephia.

Bergerbrant S, K. Kristiansen, M. E. Allentoft, K. M. Frei, T. D. Price, K.-G. Sjögren, and A. Tornberg 2017 Identifying Commoners in the Early Bronze Age: Burials Outside Barrows. In *New Perspectives on the Bronze Age*, edited by S. Bergerbrant and A. Wessman, pp. 37–64. Archaeopress, Oxford.

Bojs, K. 2017 *My European Family. The First 54.000 Years*. Bloomsbury, London.

Bourgeois, Q. 2017 The Impact of Male Burials on the Construction of Corded Ware Identity: Reconstructing Networks of Information in the 3rd Millennium BC. *PLOS ONE* 12(10):e0185971. DOI:10.1371/journal. pone.0185971.

Burmeister, S. 2000 Archaeology and Migration: Approaches to an Archaeological Proof of Migration. *Current Anthropology* 41:539–567. DOI:10.1086/317383.

Callaway, H. 2018 The Battle for Common Ground. *Nature* 555:574–576.

Cameron, C. 2016 *Captives: How Stolen People Changed the World*. University of Nebraska Press, Lincoln.

Case, H. 2004 Beakers and the Beaker Culture. In *Similar but Different: Bell Beakers in Europe*, edited by J. Czebreszuk, pp. 11–34. Adam Mickiewicz University, Poznan.

Chenal. F., B. Perrin, and H. Barrand-Emam 2015 A Farewell to Arms: A Deposit of Human Limbs and Bodies at Bergheim, France, c. 4000 BC. *Antiquity* 89(348):1313–1330.

Chyleński, M., A. Juras, E. Ehler, H. Malmström, J. Piontek, M. Jakobsson, A. Marciniak, and M. Dabert 2017 Late Danubian Mitochondrial Genomes Shed Light into the Neolithisation of Central Europe in the 5th Millennium BC. *BMC Evolutionary Biology* 17:80. DOI:10.1186/s12862-017-0924-0.

Coole, D. H., and S. Frost 2010 *New Materialisms: Ontology, Agency, and Politics*. Duke University Press, Durham. DOI:10.1215/9780822392996.

Damgaard, P. de Barros, N. Marchi, S. Rasmussen, M. Peyrot, G. Renaud, T. Korneliussen, J. V. Moreno-Mayar, M. W. Pedersen, A. Goldberg, E. Usmanova, N. Baimukhanov, V. Loman, L. Hedeager, A. G. Pedersen, K. Nielsen, G. Afanasiev, K. Akmatov, A. Aldashev, A. Alpaslan, G. Baimbetov, Vladimir I. Bazaliiskii, A. Beisenov, B. Boldbaatar, B. Boldgiv,

C. Dorzhu, S. Ellingvag, D. Erdenebaatar, R. Dajani, E. Dmitriev, V. Evdokimov, K. M. Frei, A. Gromov, A. Goryachev, H. Hakonarson, T. Hegay, Z. Khachatryan, R. Khaskhanov, E. Kitov, A. Kolbina, T. Kubatbek, A. Kukushkin, I. Kukushkin, N. Lau, A. Margaryan, I. Merkyte, I. V. Mertz, V. K. Mertz, E. Mijiddorj, V. Moiyesev, G. Mukhtarova, B. Nurmukhanbetov, Z. Orozbekova, I. Panyushkina, K. Pieta, V. Smrčka, I. Shevnina, A. Logvin, K. G. Sjögren, T. Štolcová, K. Tashbaeva, A. Tkachev, T. Tulegenov, D. Voyakin, L. Yepiskoposyan, S. Undrakhbold, V. Varfolomeev, A. Weber, N. Kradin, M. E. Allentoft, L. Orlando, R. Nielsen, M. Sikora, E. Heyer, K. Kristiansen, and E. Willerslev 2018 137 Ancient Human Genomes from Across the Eurasian Steppes. *Nature* 557 (7705):369–374. DOI:10.1038/s41586-018-0094-2.

Díaz-Andreu García, M. 2007 *A World History of Nineteenth-Century Archaeology: Nationalism, Colonialism, and the Past*. Oxford University Press, Oxford.

Downey, S. S., W. R. Haas, and S. Shennan 2016 European Neolithic Societies Showed Early Warning Signals of Population Collapse. *PNAS* 113(35):9751–9756. DOI:10.1073/pnas.1602504113.

Eisenmann, S., E. Bánffy, P. van Dommelen, K. P. Hofmann, J. Maran, I. Lazaridis, A. Mittnik, M. McCormick, J. Krause1, D. Reich, and P. W. Stockhammer 2018 Reconciling Material Cultures in Archaeology with Genetic Data: The Nomenclature of Clusters Emerging from Archaeogenomic Analysis. *Nature Scientific Reports* 8(13003). DOI:10.1038/s41598-018-31123-z, DOI:10.1038/s41598-018-31123-z.

Fernandes, D. M., D. Strapagiel, P. Barówka, B. Marciniak, E. Ż Żądzińska, K. Sirak, V. Siska, R. Grygiel, J. Carlsson, A. Manica, W. Lorkiewicz, and R. Pinhasi 2018 A Genomic Neolithic Time Transect of Hunter-Farmer Admixture in Central Poland. *Nature Scientific Reports* 8(14879). DOI:10.1038/s41598-018-33067-w.

Frei, K. M., U. Mannering, K. Kristiansen, M. E. Allentoft, A. S. Wilson, I. Skals, S. Tridico, M. L. Nosch, E. Willerslev, L. Clarke, and R. Frei. 2015 Tracing the Life Story of a Bronze Age Girl with High Societal Status. *Nature Scientific Reports* 5(10431): DOI:10.1038/srep10431.

Frei, K. M., C. Villa, M.-L. Jørkov, M. E. Allentoft, F. Kaul, P. Ethelberg, S. S. Reiter, A. S. Wilson, M. Taube, J. Olsen, N. Lynnerup, E. Willerslev, K. Kristiansen, and R. Frei 2017 A Matter of Months: High Precision Migration Chronology of a Bronze Age Female. *PLOS ONE* 12(6):e0178834.

Frei K. M., S. Bergerbrant, K.-G. Sjögren, M. L. Jørkov, N. Lynnerup, L. Harvig, M. E. Allentoft, M. Sikora, T. D. Price, R. Frei, K. Kristiansen 2019 Mapping Human Mobility during the Third and Second Millennia BC in Present-Day Denmark. *PLOS ONE* 14(8):e0219850. DOI:10.1371/journal.pone.0219850.

Frieman, C. J., and D. Hofmann 2019 Present Pasts in the Archaeology of Genetics, Identity, and Migration in Europe: A Critical Essay. *World Archaeology* 51(4):528–545. DOI:10.1080/00438243.2019.1627907.

Furholt, M. 2017 Translocal Communities—Exploring Mobility and Migration in Sedentary Societies of the European Neolithic and Early Bronze Age. *Praehistorische Zeitschrift* 92(2):04–321.

Furholt, M. 2018 Massive Migrations? The Impact of Recent aDNA Studies on our View of Third Millennium Europe. *European Journal of Archaeology* 21(2):159–191.

Furholt, M. 2019 Re-integrating Archaeology: A Contribution to aDNA Studies and the Migration Discourse on the 3rd Millennium BC in Europe. *Proceedings of the Prehistoric Society* 85:115–129. DOI:10.1017/ppr.2019.4.

Gell, A. 1998 *Art and Agency: An Anthropological Theory*. Oxford University Press, Oxford.

Goldberg, A., T. Günther, N. A. Rosenberg, and M. Jakobsson 2017 Ancient X-chromosomes Reveal Contrasting Sex Bias in Neolithic and Bronze Age Eurasian Migrations. *PNAS* 114(10):2657–2662. DOI:10.1073/pnas.1616392114/DCSupplemental.

Gosden, C. 2004 *Archaeology and Colonialism: Cultural Contact from 5000 BC to the Present*. Cambridge University Press, Cambridge.

Haak, W., I. Lazaridis, N. Patterson, N. Rohland, S. Mallick, B. Llamas, G. Brandt, S. Nordenfelt, E. Harney, K Stewardson, Q. Fu, A. Mittnik, E. Bánffy, C. Economou, M. Francken, S. Friederich, R. Garrido Pena, F. Hallgren, V. Khartanovich, A. Khokhlov, M. Kunst, P. Kuznetsov, H. Meller, O. Mochalov, V. Moiseyev, N. Nicklisch, S. L. Pichler, R. Risch, M. A. Rojo Guerra, C. Roth, A. Szécsényi-Nagy, J. Wahl, M. Meyer, J. Krause, D. Brown, D. Anthony, A. Cooper, K. Werner Alt, and D. Reich 2015 Massive Migration from the Steppe was a Source for Indo-European Languages in Europe. *Nature* 522(7555):207–211. DOI:10.1038/nature14317.

Hakenbeck, S. 2019. Genetics, Archaeology, and the Far Right: An Unholy Trinity, *World Archaeology* 51:517–527. DOI:10.1080/00438243.2019.1617189.

Harding, A. 2013 Velim and Violence. *CPAG* 23:165–182.

Hayden, B. 2018 *The Power of Ritual in Prehistory. Secret Societies and Origins of Social Complexity*. Cambridge University Press, Cambridge.

Hedeager, L. 2011 *Iron Age Myth and Materiality*. Routledge, London.

Heyd, V. 2016 Das Zeitalter der Ideologien: Migration, Interaktion und Expansion im prähistorischen Europa des 4. und 3. Jahrtausends v.Chr. In *Transitional Landscapes? The 3rd Millennium BC in Europe*, edited by M. Furholt, R. Großmann, and M. Szmyt, pp. 53–85. Kommission bei Verlag Dr. Rudolf Habelt GmbH, Bonn.

Heyd, V. 2017 Kossinna's Smile. *Antiquity* 91(356):348–359.

Hinz, M., I. Feeser, K.-G. Sjögren, and J. Müller 2012 Demography and the Intensity of Cultural Activities: An Evaluation of Funnel Beaker Societies (4200–2800 ca BC). *Journal of Archaeological Science* 39:3331–3340.

Holst, M.K., M. Rasmussen, J.-H. Bech, and K. Kristiansen 2013 Bronze Age "Herostrats": Ritual, Political, and Domestic Economies in Early Bronze Age Denmark. *Proceedings of the Prehistoric Society* 79:1–32.

Horn, C., and K. Kristiansen (editors) 2018 *Warfare in Bronze Age Society*. Cambridge University Press, Cambridge.

Hornborg, A. 2014 Political Economy, Ethnogenesis, and Language Dispersals in the Prehispanic Andes: A World-System Perspective. *American Anthropologist* 116(4):810–823.

Hornborg, A. 2016 *Global Magic. Technologies of Appropriation from Ancient Times to Wall Street*. Palgrave Macmillan, New York.

Ion, A. 2017 How Interdisciplinary Is Interdisciplinarity? Revisiting the Impact of aDNA Research for the Archaeology of Human Remains. *Current Swedish Archaeology* 25:177–198.

Juras, A., M. Chyleński, E. Ehler, H. Malmström, D. Żurkiewicz, P. Włodarczak, S. Wilk, J. Peška, P. Fojtík, M. Králík, J. Libera, J. Bagińska, K. Tunia, V. I. Klochko, M. Dabert, M. Jakobsson, and A. Kośko 2018 Mitochondrial Genomes Reveal an East to West Cline of Steppe Ancestry in Corded Ware Populations. *Nature Scientific Reports* 8(11603). DOI:10.1038/s41598-018-29914-5.

Knipper, C., C. Meyer, F. Jacobi, C. Roth, M. Fecher, E. Stephan, K. Schatz, L. Hansen, A. Posluschny, B. Höppner, M. Maus, C. F. E. Pare, and K. W. Alt 2014 Social Differentiation and Land use at an Early Iron Age "Princely Seat": Bioarchaeological Investigations at the Glauberg (Germany). *Journal of Archaeologial Science* 41:818–835.

Knipper, C., P. Held, M. Fecher, N. Nicklisch, C. Meyer, H. Schreiber, B. Zich, C. Metzner-Nebelsick, V. Hubensack, L. Hansen, E. Nieveler, and K. W. Alt 2015a Superior in Life—Superior in Death: Dietary Distinction of Central European Prehistoric and Medieval Elites. *Current Anthropology* 56(4):579–589.

Knipper, C., M. Fragata, N. Nicklisch, A. Siebert, A. Szécsényi-Nagy, V. Hubensack, C. Metzner-Nebelsick, H. Meller, and K. W. Alt 2015b A Distinct Section of the Early Bronze Age Society? Stable Isotope Investigations of Burials in Settlement Pits and Multiple Inhumations of the Unetice Culture in Central Germany. *American Journal of Physical Anthropology* 159(3):496–516.

Knipper, C., A. Mittnik, K. Massy, C. Kociumaka, I. Kucukkalipci, M. Maus, F. Wittenborn, S. E. Metz, A. Staskiewicz, J. Krause, and P. W. Stockhammer 2017 Female Exogamy and Gene Pool Diversification at the Transition from the Final Neolithic to the Early Bronze Age in Central Europe. *PNAS* 114(38):10083–10088.

Kohl, P. L., and C. Fawcett 1995 *Nationalism, Politics, and the Practice of Archaeology*. Cambridge University Press, Cambridge.

Kradin, Nikolay N., D. Bondarenko, and T. Barfield (editors) 2003 *Nomadic Pathways in Social Evolution*. Center for Civilizational and Regional Studies of the Russian Academy of Sciences, Moscow.

Kristiansen, K. 1989 Prehistoric Migrations—The Case of the Single Grave and Corded Ware Cultures. *Journal of Danish Archaeology* 8:211–225.

Kristiansen, K. 1998 *Europe before History*. Cambridge University Press, Cambridge. 2014 Towards a New Paradigm? The Third Science Revolution and Its Possible Consequences in Archaeology. *Current Swedish Archaeology*, 22:11–34.

Kristiansen, K. 2017 Bronze Age Identities. From Social to Cultural and Ethnic Identity. In *A Companion to Ethnicity in the Ancient Mediterranean*, edited by J. McInery, pp. 82–96. Wiley Blackwell, Malden, Oxford, and Chichester.

Kristiansen, K. 2018 Warfare and the Political Economy: Europe 1500-1100 BC. In *Warfare in Bronze Age Society*, edited by C. Horn and K. Kristiansen, pp. 23–46. Cambridge University Press, Cambridge.

Kristiansen, K. 2019 Who Is Deterministic? On the Nature of Interdisciplinary Research in Archaeology. *Archaeological Dialogues* 26(1):12–14. DOI:10.1017/S1380203819000060.

Kristiansen, K., and T. B. Larsson 2005. *The Rise of Bronze Age Society: Travels, Transmissions, and Transformations*. Cambridge University Press, Cambridge.

Kristiansen, K., and T. Earle in press Modelling Modes of Production: European 3rd and 2nd Millennium BC Economies. In *Ancient Economies in Comparative Perspective*, edited by Poettinger, Fragipane, and Schefold.

Kristiansen, K., M. E. Allentoft, K. M. Frei, R. Iversen, N. N. Johannsen, G. Kroonen, Ł. Pospieszny, T. D. Price, S. Rasmussen, K.-G. Sjögren, M. Sikora, and E. Willerslev 2017 Re-Theorising Mobility and the Formation of Culture and Language among the Corded Ware Culture in Europe. *Antiquity* 91(356):334–347.

Kristinsson, A. 2010 *Expansions: Competition and Conquest in Europe Since the Bronze Age.* Reykjavíkur Akademían, Reykjavík.

Kristinsson, A. 2012 Indo-European Expansion Cycles. *The Journal of Indo-European Studies* 40(3–4):365–433.

Lansing, J. S., C. Abundo, G. S. Jacobs, E. G. Guillot, S. Thurner, S. S. Downey, L. Y. Chew, T. Bhattacharya, N. N. Chung, H. Sudoyo, and M. P. Cox 2017 Kinship Structures Create Persistent Channels for Language Transmission, *PNAS* 114(49):12910–12915.

Larsen, C. S. 2014 Life Conditions and Health in Early Farmers. A Global Perspective and Consequences of a Fundamental Transition. In *Early Farmers. The View from Archaeology and Science*, edited by A. Whittle and P. Bickle, pp. 215–232. Proceedings of the British Academy 198. Oxford University Press, Oxford.

Liedman, S.-E. 2018 *A World to Win: The Life and Works of Karl Marx.* Translated by J. N. Skinner. Verso, London and New York.

Lincoln, B. 198 *Priests, Warriors, and Cattle, A Study in the Ecology of Religion.* University of California Press, Los Angeles, London, and Berkley.

Ling, J., T. Earle, and K. Kristiansen 2018 Maritime Mode of Production. Raiding and Trading in Seafaring Chiefdoms. *Current Anthopology*, Volume 59(5). DOI:10.1086/699613.

Lipson, M., A. Szécsényi-Nagy, S. Mallick, A. Pósa, B. Stégmár, V. Keerl, N. Rohland, K. Stewardson, M. Ferry, M. Michel, J. Oppenheimer, N. Broomandkhoshbacht, E. Harney, S. Nordenfelt, B. Llamas, B. Gusztáv Mende, K. Köhler, K. Oross, M. Bondár, T. Marton, A. Osztás, J. Jakucs, T. Paluch, F. Horváth, P. Csengeri, J. Koós, K. Sebők, A. Anders, P. Raczky, J. Regenye, J. P. Barna, S. Fábián, G. Serlegi, Z. Toldi, E. Gyöngyvér Nagy, J. Dani, E. Molnár, G. Pálfi, L. Márk, B. Melegh, Z. Bánfai, L. Domboróczki, J. Fernández-Eraso, J. A. Mujika-Alustiza, C. Alonso Fernández, J. Jiménez Echevarría, R. Bollongino, J. Orschiedt, K. Schierhold, H. Meller, A. Cooper, J. Burger, E. Bánffy, K. W. Alt, C. Lalueza-Fox, W. Haak, and D. Reich 2017 Parallel Palaeogenomic Transects Reveal Complex Genetic History of Early European Farmers. *Nature* 551:368–372. DOI:10.1038/nature24476.

Lucas. G. 2015 The Mobility of Theory *Current Swedish Archaeology* 23:13–31.

Malkin, I. 2011 *A Small Greek World: Networks in the Ancient Mediterranean.* Oxford University Press, Oxford.

Marx, K. 1974 *Grundrisse. Foundations of the Critique of Political Economy (Rough Draft).* Penguin Books, in association with New Left Review. London.

Marx, K. 1953 *Grundrisse der Kritik der politischen Ökonomie: (Rohentwurf)* 1857–1858: Anhang 1850–1859. Dietz, Berlin.

Mathiesson, I., S. Alpaslan-Roodenberg, C. Posth, A. Szécsényi-Nagy, N. Rohland, S. Mallick, I. Olalde, N. Broomandkhoshbacht, F. Candilio, O. Cheronet, D. Fernandes, M. Ferry, B. Gamarra, G. González Fortes, W. Haak, E. Harney, E. Jones, D.Keating, B. Krause-Kyora, I. Kucukkalipci, M. Michel, A. Mittnik, K. Nägele, M. Novak, J. Oppenheimer, N. Patterson, S. Pfrengle, K. Sirak, K. Stewardson, S. Vai, S. Alexandrov, K. W. Alt, R. Andreescu, D. Antonović, A. Ash, N. Atanassova, K. Bacvarov, M. B. Gusztáv, H. Bocherens, M. Bolus, A. Boroneanț, Y.Boyadzhiev, A. Budnik, J. Burmaz, S. Chohadzhiev, N. J. Conard, R. Cottiaux, M. Čuka, C. Cupillard, D. G. Drucker, N. Elenski, M. Francken, B. Galabova, G. Ganetsovski, B. Gély, Tamás Hajdu, V. Handzhyiska, K. Harvati, T. Higham, S. Iliev, I. Janković, I. Karavanić, D. J. Kennett, D. Komšo, A. Kozak, D. Labuda, M. Lari, C. Lazar, M. Leppek, K. Leshtakov, D. Lo Vetro, D. Los, I. Lozanov, M. Malina, F. Martini, K.

McSweeney, H. Meller, M. Menđušić, P. Mirea, V. Moiseyev, V. Petrova, T. D. Price, A. Simalcsik, L. Sineo, M. Šlaus, V. Slavchev, P. Stanev, A. Starović, T. Szeniczey, S. Talamo, M. Teschler-Nicola, C. Thevenet, I. Valchev, F. Valentin, S. Vasilyev, F. Veljanovska, S. Venelinova, E. Veselovskaya, B. Viola, C. Virag, J. Zaninović, S. Zäuner, P. W. Stockhammer, G. Catalano, R. Krauß, D. Caramelli, G. Zariņa, B. Gaydarska, M. Lillie, A. G. Nikitin, I. Potekhina, A. Papathanasiou, D. Borić, C. Bonsall, J. Krause, R. Pinhasi, and D. Reich 2018 The Genomic History of Southeastern Europe. *Nature* 555(7695):197–203. DOI:10.1038/nature25778.

Mednikova M., and G. Lebedinskaya 2000 A Bronze Age Battle in European Russia: The Palaeopathological Evidence. In *Paleopathology Association: Papers and Posters Presented at the Thirteenth Biennale European Members Meeting*, p. 20. Palaeopathology Association.

Meyer, C., C. Knipper, N. Nicklisch, A. Münster, O. Kürbis, V. Dresely, H. Meller, and K. W. Alt 2018 Early Neolithic Executions Indicated by Clustered Cranial Trauma in the Mass Grave of Halberstadt. *Nature Communications* 9(2472). DOI:10.1038/s41467-018-04773-w.

Meyer, C., O. Kürbis, V. Dresely, and K. W. Alt 2018 Patterns of Collective Violence in the Early Neolithic of Central Europe. In *Prehistoric Warfare and Violence. Quantitative and Qualitative Approaches*, edited by A. Dolfini, R. J. Crellin, C. Horn and M. Uckelmann, pp. 21–38. Springer, Cham.

Meyer, C., R. Ganslmeier, V. Dresely, and K. W. Alt 2012 New Approaches to the Reconstruction of Kinship and Social Structure based on Bioarchaeological Analysis of Neolithic Multiple and Collective Graves. In *Theoretical and Methodological Considerations in Central European Neolithic Archaeology*, edited by J. Kolář and F. Trampota, pp. 11–23. British Archaeological Reports international series 2325. Archaeopress, Oxford.

Mittnik A., K. Massy, C. Knipper, F. Wittenborn, R. Friedrich, S. Pfrengle, M. Burri, N. Carlichi-Witjes, H. Deeg, A. Furtwängler, M. Harbeck, K. von Heyking, C. Kociumaka, I. Kucukkalipci, S. Lindauer, S. Met, An. Staskiewicz, A. Thiel, J. Wahl, View W. Haak, E. Pernicka, S. Schiffels, P. W. Stockhammer, and J. Krause 2019 Kinship-based Social Inequality in Bronze Age Europe. *Science* 366(6466):731–734. DOI:10.1126/science.aax6219.

Morris, I. 2005 Archaeology, Standards of Living and Greek Economic History. In *The Ancient Economy. Evidence and Models*, edited by J. G. Manning and I. Morris, pp. 91–126. Stanford University Press. Stanford.

Muhl, A., H. Meller, and K. Heckenhahn 2010 *Tatort Eulau. Ein 4500 Jahre altes Verbrechen wird Aufgeklärt*. Theiss, Stuttgart.

Müller, J. 2015 Eight Million Neolithic Europeans: Social Demography and Social Archaeology on the Scope of Change—from the Near East to Scandinavia. In *Paradigm Found. Archaeological Theory Present, Past, and Future: Essays in Honour of Evzen Neustupny*, edited by K. Kristiansen, L. Smedja, and J. Turek, pp. 200–215. Oxbow Books, Oxford.

Münster A., C. Knipper, V. M. Oelze, N. Nicklisch, M. Steche, B. Schlenker, R. Ganslmeier, M. Fragata, S. Friederich, V. Dresely, V. Hubensack, G. Brandt, H.-J. Döhle, W. Vach, R. Schwarz, C. Metzner-Nebelsick, H. Meller, and K. W. Alt 2018 4000 Years of Human Dietary Evolution in Central Germany, from the First Farmers to the First Elites. *PLOS ONE* 13(3):e0194862. DOI:10.1371/journal.pone.0194862.

Neustupny, E. 2012 Towards a New Paradigm. In *Rytm przemian kulturowych w pradziejach i sredniowieczu*, edited by B. Gediga, A. Grossman, and W. Piotrowski, pp. 1–26. Prace Komisji Archeologicznej Vol. 19. Muzeum Archeologiczne w Biskupinie, Biskupin–Wrocław.

Nicolaisen, I. 1976 The Penan of the Seventh Division of Sarawak: Past, Present and Future. *Sarawak Museum Journal* (New Series) 24(45):35–61.

Nikitin, A. G., P. Stadler, N. Kotova, M. Teschler-Nicola, T. D. Price, J. Hoover, D. J. Kennett, I. Lazaridis, N. Rohland, M. Lipson, and D. Reich 2019 Interactions between Earliest *Linearbandkeramik* Farmers and Central European Hunter Gatherers at the Dawn of European Neolithization. *Nature Scientific Reports* 9(19544). DOI:10.1101/741900.

Olalde, I., S. Brace, M. E. Allentoft, I. Armit, K. Kristiansen, T. Booth, N. Rohland, S. Mallick, A. Szécsényi-Nagy, A. Mittnik, E. Altena, M. Lipson, I. Lazaridis, T. K. Harper, N. Patterson, N. Broomandkhoshbacht, Y. Diekmann, Z. Faltyskova, D.Fernandes, M. Ferry, E. Harney, P. de Knijff, M. Michel, J. Oppenheimer, K. Stewardson, A. Barclay, K. W. Alt, C. Liesau, P. Ríos, C. Blasco, J. V. Miguel, R. M. García, A. A. Fernández, E. Bánffy, M. Bernabò-Brea, D. Billoin, C. Bonsall, L. Bonsall, T. Allen, L. Büster, S. Carver, L. C. Navarro, O. E. Craig, Gordon T. Cook, B. Cunliffe, A. Denaire, K. E. Dinwiddy, N. Dodwell, M. Ernée, C. Evans, M. Kuchařík, J. F. Farré, C. Fowler, M. Gazenbeek, R. G. Pena, M. Haber-Uriarte, E. Haduch, G. Hey, N. Jowett, T. Knowles, K. Massy, S. Pfrengle, P. Lefranc, O. Lemercier, A. Lefebvre, C. Heras Martínez, V. G. Olmo, A. B. Ramírez, J. L. Maurandi, T. Majó, J. I. McKinley, K. McSweeney, B. G. Mende, A. Modi, G. Kulcsár, V. Kiss, A. Czene, R. Patay, A. Endrődi, K. Köhler, T. Hajdu, T. Szeniczey, J. Dani, Z. Bernert, M. Hoole, O. Cheronet, D. Keating, P. Velemínský, M. Dobeš, F. Candilio, F. Brown, R. F. Fernández, A.-M. Herrero-Corral, S. Tusa, E. Carnieri, L. Lentini, A. Valenti, A. Zanini, C. Waddington, G. Delibes, E. Guerra-Doce, B. Neil, M. Brittain, M. Luke, R. Mortimer, J. Desideri, M. Besse, G. Brücken, M. Furmanek, A. Hałuszko, M. Mackiewicz, A. Rapiński, S. Leach, I. Soriano, K. T. Lillios, J. L. Cardoso, M. P. Pearson, P. Włodarczak, T. D. Price, P. Prieto, P.-J. Rey, R. Risch, M. A. Rojo Guerra, A. Schmitt, J. Serralongue, A. M. Silva, V. Smrčka, L. Vergnaud, J. Zilhão, D. Caramelli, T. Higham, M. G. Thomas, D. J. Kennett, H. Fokkens, V. Heyd, A. Sheridan, K.-G. Sjögren, P. W. Stockhammer, J. Krause, R. Pinhasi, W. Haak, I. Barnes, C. Lalueza-Fox, and D. Reich 2018 The Beaker Phenomenon and the Genomic Transformation of Northwest Europe. *Nature* 555(7695):190–196. DOI:10.1038/nature25738.

Price, D. T., R. Frei, U. Brinker, G. Lidke, T. Terberger, K. Margarita Frei, and D. Jantzen 2017 Multi-Isotope Proveniencing of Human Remains from a Bronze Age Battlefield in the Tollense Valley in Northeast Germany. *Archaeological and Anthropological Sciences 11:33–49*. DOI:10.1007/s12520-017-0529-y.

Prien, R. 2005 *Archäologie und Migration. Vergleichende Studien zur archäologischen Nachweisbarkeit von Wanderungsbewegungen*. Universitätsforschungen zur Prähistorischen Archäologie 120. Habelt, Bonn.

Rascovan, N., K.-G. Sjögren, K. Kristiansen, R. Nielsen, E. Willerslev, C. Desnues, and S. Rasmussen 2019 Emergence and Spread of Basal Lineages of Yersinia Pestis during the Neolithic Decline. *Cell* 176(1–2):295–305. DOI:10.1016/j.cell.2018.11.005.

Racimo, F., M. Sikora, H. Schroeder, and C. Lalueza-Fox 2019 Beyond Broad Strokes: Sociocultural Insights from the Study of Ancient Genomes. *arXiv preprint arXiv:1911.00755*.

Reher, G. S., and M. Fernandez-Götz 2015 Archaeological Narratives in Ethnicity Studies. *Archeologické rozhledy* LXVII:400–416.

Sahlins, M. D. 1961 The Segmentary Lineage: An Organisation of Predatory Expansion. *American Anthropologist* 63(2):332–345. [HV]

Schroeder H., A. Margaryan, M. Szmyt, Bertrand Theulot, P. Włodarczak, S. Rasmussen, S. Gopalakrishnan, A. Szczepanek, T. Konopka, T. Z. T. Jensen, B. Witkowska, S. Wilk, M. M. Przybyła, Ł. Pospieszny, K.-G. Sjögren, Z. Belka, J. Olsen, K. Kristiansen, E. Willerslev, K. M. Frei, M. Sikora, N. N. Johannsen, and M. E. Allentoft 2019 Blood Ties: Unravelling Ancestry and Kinship in a Late Neolithic Mass Grave. *PNAS* 116(22):10705–10710. DOI:10.1073/pnas.1820210116.

Shennan, S. 2018 *The First Farmers of Europe. An Evolutionary Perspective*. Cambridge University Press. Cambridge.

Shennan, S., S. S. Downey, A. Timpson, K. Edinborough, S. Colledge, T. Kerig, K. Manning, and M. G. Thomas 2013 Regional Population Collapse Followed Initial Agriculture Booms in Mid-Holocene Europe. *Nature Communications* 4(2486). DOI:10.1038/ncomms3486.

Sjögren, K.-G., I. Olalde, S. Carver, M. E. Allentoft, T. Knowles, G. Kroonen, A. W. G. Pike, P. Schröter, K. A. Brown, K. Robson-Brown, R. J. Harrison, F. Bertemes, D. Reich, K. Kristiansen, and V. Heyd. 2020 Kinship and Social Organization in Copper Age Europe. A Cross-Disciplinary Analysis of Archaeology, DNA, Isotopes, and Anthropology from Two Bell Beaker Cemeteries. *PLOS ONE*. DOI:10.1101/863944.

Sjögren, K.-G., T. D. Price, and K. Kristiansen 2016 Diet and Mobility in the Corded Ware of Central Europe. *PLOS ONE*, 11(5):e0155083. DOI:10.1371/journal.pone.0155083.

Spatzier, A. 2017 The Honoured and the Sacrificed? Gender and Violence at a Sanctuary of the Late 3rd Millennium BC in Central Germany (with anthropological analyses by Marcus Stecher and Kurt Alt). In *Archaeologies of Gender Violence*, edited by U. Mattic and B. Jensen, pp. 45–76. Oxbow Books, Oxford.

Szécsényi-Nagy, A, V. Keerl, J. Jakucs, G. Brandt, E. Bánffy, and K. Alt 2014 Ancient DNA Evidence for a Homogeneous Maternal Gene Pool in Sixth Millennium cal BC Hungary and the Central European LBK. In *Early Farmers. The View from Archaeology and Science*, edited by A. Whittle and P. Bickle, 71–93. Proceedings of the British Academy 198. Oxford University Press, Oxford.

Sørensen, T. F. 2017a The Two Cultures and a World Apart: Archaeology and Science at a New Crossroads. *Norwegian Archaeological Review* 50(2). DOI:10.1080/00293652.2017.1367031.

Sørensen, T. F. 2017b Archaeological Paradigms: Pendulum or Wrecking Ball? (a response to commentators). *Norwegian Archaeological Review*, 50(2). DOI:10.1080/00293652.2017.1388274.

Vandkilde, H. 2018 Body Aesthetics, Fraternity, and Warfare in the Long European Bronze Age. In *Warfare in Bronze Age Society*, edited by C. Horn and K. Kristiansen, pp. 229–243. Cambridge University Press, Cambridge.

Veeramah, K.R. 2018 The Importance of Fine-Scale Studies for Integrating Paleogenomics and Archaeology. *Current Opinion in Genetics & Development* 53:83–89.

Whittle, A. 2018 *The Times of Their Lives. Hunting History in the Archaeology of Neolithic Europe*. Oxbow Books, Oxford and Philadelphia.

Witmore, T. 2014 Archaeology and the New Materialisms. *Journal of Contemporary Archaeology* 1(2):203–246.

Wolf, E. 1999 *Envisioning Power. Ideologies of Dominance and Crisis*. University of California Press, Berkeley, Los Angeles, and London.

CHAPTER THREE

Migration, Ancient DNA, and Bronze Age Pastoralists from the Eurasian Steppes

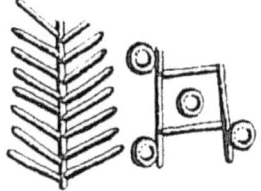

David W. Anthony

Abstract *In Europe the specter of nomads from the steppes invokes an image of mass migration by a faceless horde of savage warriors. Western archaeologists abandoned the faceless migrating horde decades ago as a usually imaginary and substantively worthless explanation for culture change, but Marija Gimbutas's conception of the Kurgan Culture kept this image alive in archaeological debates about Late Neolithic cultural shifts long after it had disappeared in other contexts. Recent studies of ancient DNA revealed large-scale, long-distance migrations from the steppes in the Late Neolithic/Early Bronze Age that have prompted some to ask the uneasy question of whether Gimbutas was right. This essay places the recent DNA discoveries and the debate about nomads from the steppes in its historical context, and pleads for a processual approach to migration quite different from the single-event, conquest model of Gimbutas.*

Nomads from the East

As is well known, before 1960 archaeologists often relied on migration as a default explanation for the changes between cultural "blocks" that constituted developmental phases in the "culture-history," or more accurately "history-of-cultures" approach to the past (reviews in Hakenbeck 2008; Fernández-Götz 2016; Burmeister 2017). But in the 1960s the widespread adoption of explicitly scientific theories of human behavior (e.g., Watson 1971; Clarke 1968) shifted attention to the myriad internal causes of social and material culture transformation, and these replaced long-distance migration as the preferred agents of cultural change. A change in material culture types was no longer equated with the arrival of a new population, so migration became reserved for situations of rapid turnover in customs and material culture with no apparent local source (Haury 1958). At the same time the methodological barriers to distinguishing the archaeological signals of migrants from other causes of change, even when there was an episode of rapid turnover, cast a pall of methodological uncertainty over any claim of migration, anywhere (Trigger 1968). Archaeologists discarded the faceless migrating horde as a usually imaginary and substantively worthless explanation.

However, many Western Euro-American archaeologists still thought of long-distance migrations and the arrows that illustrated them as single events—invasions and conquests—rather than the extended, long-term, shifting processes that long-distance migration streams usually are. While turning away from migration, Western archaeologists retained the faceless horde as a negative image, as if migration could be conceptualized only in this way. We have been slow to recognize that long-distance migrations are complex, multigenerational human processes that take different forms based on different causes and different pre-migration social relations between the local people in the destination and the pre-migration population in the home region (Clark et al. 2018). We failed to see that long-distance migrations created new social dynamics both at home and in the destination, and that some outcomes could be regarded as regular and predictable, including the creation of new kinds of sociopolitical hierarchy (Anthony 1990). Instead, too often we dismissed long-distance migration as an "always simplistic and usually groundless supposition" (Halsall 1995, quoted in Heather 2009:19). I argue that this was because many of us retained the "invasion" theory of migration as a foil for alternate theories of culture change that in themselves were worthy and useful. But they were Othered from a version of migration that left it no explanatory power. Another reason for retaining this simplistic view of migration was that the single-event "invasion" theory continued to be discussed and promoted by archaeologists who worked largely or wholly outside the sphere of Western Euro-American archaeological theory.

In Central Europe, a few steps were taken toward recognizing long-distance migrations as extended processes, using the language of "infiltration" (Neustupny 1982), which is what most modern migrations resemble. But in Eastern Europe archaeologists continued to use the essentialist language of whole-culture replacement and the concept of migration as a brief event or invasion, and many still do so today. After the 1960s, one of the most prominent defenders of migration in Western Euro-American archaeology was an Eastern European archaeologist, Marija Gimbutas of Harvard and UCLA. Gimbutas was widely respected for her masterful knowledge of museum collections across Europe and her well-published excavations in Greece and Bosnia, while her proposed Kurgan Culture migrations were largely dismissed by her Western peers (Elster 2015). In Eastern Europe her migration theories were taken more seriously because similar interpretations, although not necessarily connected with the "Kurgan Culture," were widely held among regional Eneolithic and Bronze Age archaeologists (Merpert 1974; Ecsedy 1979; Bökönyi 1987; Dergachev 2007).

For Gimbutas, the Kurgan Culture migrations explained the spread of the Indo-European languages. Reducing her broad narrative to a single sentence does her a disservice, so I am about to simplify greatly, but in brief, she proposed that Indo-European speakers originated as pasture-hungry horse-riding pastoral nomads (the Pit-Grave or Yamnaya culture) who originally occupied the steppes north of the Black and Caspian Seas (the Pontic-Caspian steppes), and who then surged westward out of the steppes in three "waves" of conquest, imposing patricentered, warlike Indo-European institutions, myths, and social organization on a matricentered Neolithic world of beauty and peace. She defended this explanatory frame until her death in 1994 (Gimbutas 1963, 1977, 1993).

The word Gimbutas used for her three Kurgan Culture migrations, *wave*, is instructive. The word *wave* and the others cited below are taken from Gimbutas 1977, where she introduced the theory of three waves of Kurgan Culture migrations. A wave sweeps across the beach as a brief event and randomly washes over non-ocean space, "invading" the space of terrestrial life but without knowledge, planning, goals, or direction—a purely mechanical motion. The other words she used for the Kurgan Culture migrations included *invasion* and *conquest* for the behavior of the nomadic migrants and *subjugated, wiped out, exterminated,* and *ceaseless flight* for the role of the local agriculturalists. She also used *infiltration* but reserved that word for exceptional regions where the local culture continued to coexist with the migrant culture after the nomads arrived. This choice of words shows that her conception of migration was an event in which one more or less homogenous culture invaded, subjugated, and replaced another: an essentialist approach to identity and a simplistic approach to migration. In 1963, Gimbutas published a map of Kurgan Culture migrations (Figure 3.1), illustrated with swarms of migration arrows penetrating Europe, probably the last such map published in *American Anthropologist*. Her arrows of invasion did not convey a useful theory about how and why migrations happened or how migrants and locals interacted. The question of *if* these suggested invasions happened at all, and if so how to *prove* that they did methodologically, was unresolved. After 1963, the Kurgan Culture migrations were regularly criticized in print (Anthony 1986; Renfrew 1987; Robb 1993; Häusler 2003).

But in Eastern Europe, N. Merpert, who was a friend and correspondent of Gimbutas and became the director of the Russian Institute of Archaeology, used the language of "invasion" in reference to Yamnaya culture migrations into the Danube valley in his foundational synthesis of Yamnaya origins and spread (Merpert 1974), and did not alter that concept later. The language of "invasion" was used also by other archaeologists in the region who studied the Yamnaya culture and its apparent spread up the Danube valley to Hungary about 3000–2600 B.C. (Ecsedy 1979; Bökönyi 1987; Dergachev 2007), with the same absence of attention to the different forms and dynamics that migrations can take. Gimbutas's approach therefore maintained her interpretive connection with her Eastern European colleagues who were the sources of much of her archaeological data, and the resulting maintenance of the "invasion" theory in the East kept the faceless horde alive as the face of migration theory in Western universities.

Recently, the surprising results of ancient DNA (aDNA) studies have confirmed that many of the migrations Gimbutas illustrated probably occurred. She made mistakes—she identified the Baden and Globular Amphorae cultures as steppe migrants, and aDNA shows

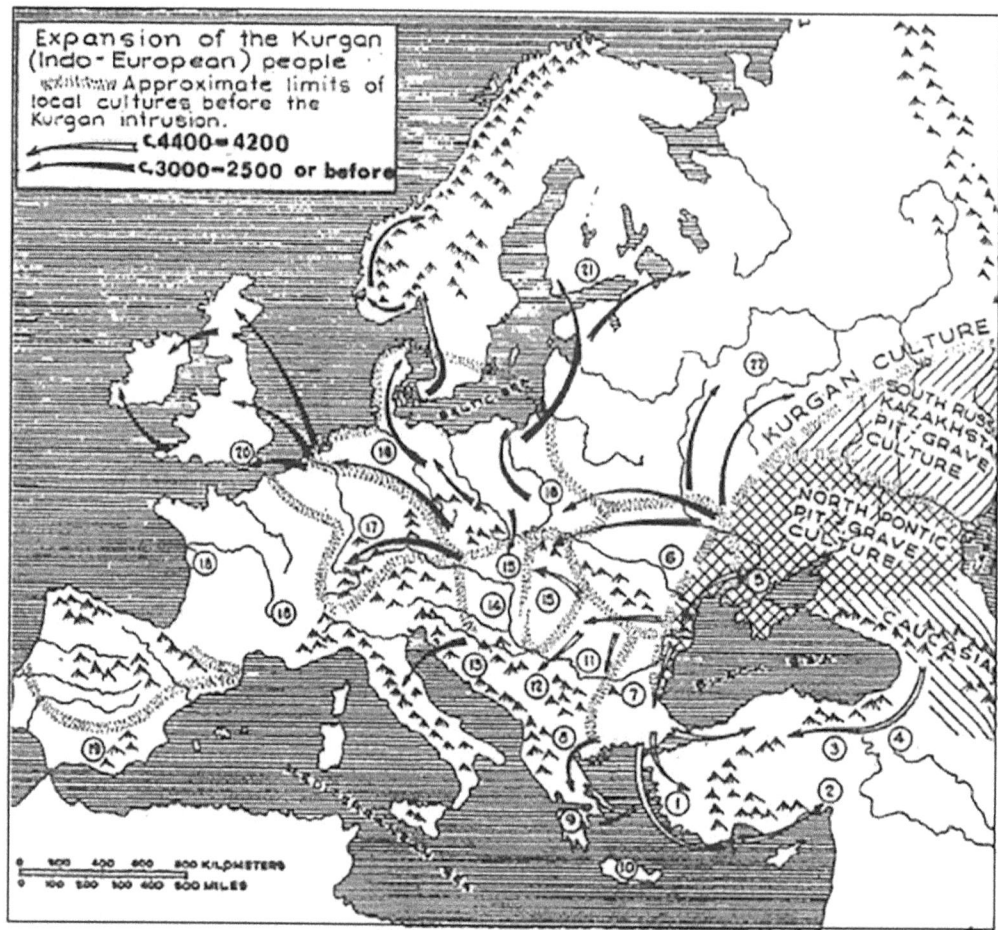

FIGURE 3.1. M. Gimbutas (1963:Figure 2) map of Kurgan Culture migrations. Reproduced by permission of the American Anthropological Association from *American Anthropologist* 65, no. 4 (1963): 815–836. https://doi.org/10.1525/aa.1963.65.4.02a00030. Not for sale or further reproduction.

that most of the people in graves assigned to those material culture types were descended genetically almost entirely from local farmers, so some of her migrations were disproved. But the fact that the centrally important Corded Ware culture was shown to have 70% or more ancestry from the Yamnaya population of the steppes (Haak et al. 2015; Allentoft et al. 2015; Olalde et al. 2018) confirmed a large and important migration that was central to Gimbutas's argument. The Corded Ware culture seemed from archaeological evidence to have evolved locally, without migration (Furholt 2014), but aDNA showed that the Corded Ware people were descended largely from steppe-derived migrant ancestors. As a result, at archaeological conferences in Europe and the United States I have heard the nervous question: Was Marija right? This essay is my attempt to answer that question. I begin by contrasting her approach to long-distance migration with mine.

The Baby and the Bathwater

By 1990, long-distance migration was so thoroughly excluded from archaeological discourse that I felt compelled to defend it in another essay published by the *American Anthropologist*, 27 years after Gimbutas's essay (Anthony 1990). I suggested that archaeologists should separate the useful baby of processual migration analysis from the properly discarded invasion-theory bathwater. I argued that in the social sciences outside archaeology, migration was regarded as a structured, predictable behavior, often understood through quantified push-pull models; but also that modern migration was often undertaken actively as a social strategy (reemphasized in Anthony 1997), not passively as a stimulus response to mechanical pushes; that it was not a rare or externally motivated event, but a central part of most human cultures, amenable to processual analysis and explanation; and I pointed to studies of the spatial structure and social organization of long-distance migrations, emphasizing recurring features such as first-comers positioned early in a migration stream, who could become "apex" families by giving loans and advice to later arrivals (Figure 3.2). The internal

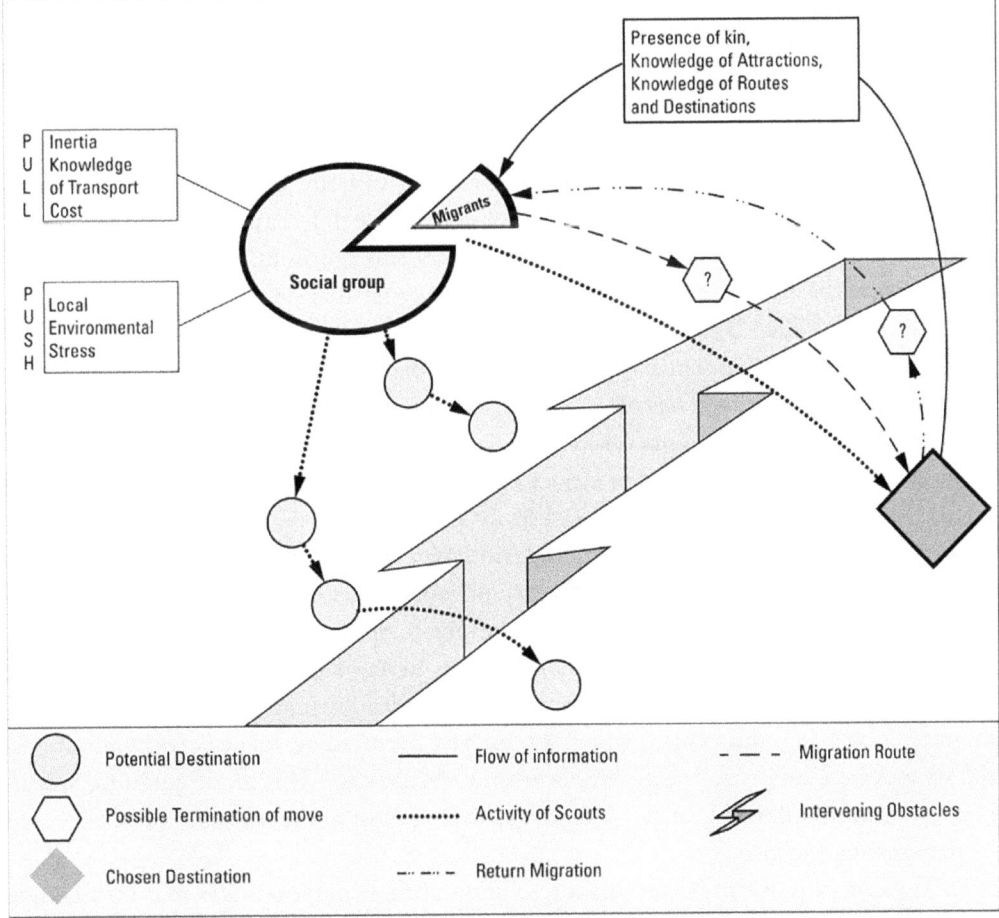

FIGURE 3.2. A processual model of long-distance migration, from Anthony 1990.

dynamics of long-distance migration therefore contained the seeds of social segmentation and possibly hierarchy, among many other structure-encouraging processes. These patterned behaviors within migration streams seemed applicable to the past, but they required new language. We should use the language of migration "streams" (continuous, targeted), not "waves" (momentary, washing over everything randomly). Also, "cultures" do not migrate; social segments with access to information about destinations migrate. Conduits of information might be marked by artifact exchanges that identify the social groups in the home region that had information about specific destinations. With new processual concepts and language, we might redefine migration as a complex cultural process with explanatory power rather than an externally caused event that lacked it.

The 1990 "Baby and Bathwater" article took as its case study a reexamination of Gimbutas's (and others') archaeological evidence for Kurgan Culture migrations out of the steppes and into central Europe. The methodological difficulties in recognizing migration might, I hoped, decrease if a processual theory of migration pointed toward the right *kinds* of evidence, rather than beginning automatically by comparing artifact types. Regional archaeologists in the countries around the Black Sea recognized two distinct periods of *increased contact and exchange* (the fundamental archaeological signal that could conceivably mask a migration) between the steppes and neighboring agricultural societies in southeastern Europe, centered on the lower Danube valley. The first period of contact and exchange happened during the Eneolithic period, about 4500–4200 B.C. (Gimbutas's Kurgan Culture Wave 1), and the second happened a millennium later, about 3100–2600 B.C. (Gimbutas's Kurgan Culture Waves 2 and 3). I had earlier (Anthony 1986) rejected the Kurgan Culture label for both periods because they unfolded quite differently, had different effects, and involved distinct steppe archaeological cultures and processes; and I had noted that Gimbutas's Wave 2 was not widely recognized by regional archaeologists.

Gimbutas's Wave 3 (Gimbutas 1977) began with the pastoral Yamnaya (or Pit-Grave) culture in the Pontic-Caspian steppes north of the Black and Caspian Seas. About 3000–2500 B.C., kurgan cemeteries that retained distinctive steppe Yamnaya–culture traits seemed to spread from the steppes into Bulgaria, Romania, Serbia, and Hungary, an archaeological intrusion that continued to attract attention later (Harrison and Heyd 2007; Heyd 2012). Reorganizing her evidence, I looked for explicit antecedent conditions that might define pushes and pulls between the home and target regions, tried to identify early-phase "scouts" who should have conveyed information about target destinations, tried to identify migration streams that flowed from home regions to specific target destinations, briefly considered the presentation of archaeological traits in Yamnaya graves in the steppes and in the target areas in the Danube valley, and searched for artifactual evidence for return migrations back into the steppes, which should have occurred unless negative conditions in the steppes were very bad, which did not seem to be the case. This set of questions was an improvement over drawing an arrow on a map even if most of them could not be answered by the existing evidence.

The central problem preventing a resolution of these questions was that no scientific method could reliably identify migrants within cemetery populations or isolate the effects of migration on material culture. We taught our students that pots did not equal people, but many archaeologists (myself included) continued to explore pot types, technological practices, and other material culture indicators (such as kurgans) as awkward proxies for migrant identity, even while recognizing that neither archaeological cultures nor types had a clearly defined social referent (Roberts and Vander Linden 2011). Archaeologists in the American Southwest invented a complex multidisciplinary approach to identify migrants and migrations (Clark 2001; Ortman 2012; Clark et al. 2018) but it required rich, well-controlled data on ceramic typological-chronological phases, human skeletal measurements, architectural plans and materials, ritual structures, grave types, linguistics, and oral histories, a foundation that archaeologists have built up in few other places. Cranio-facial shapes in some circumstances can indicate shared biological descent (von Cramon-Taubadel and Pinhasi 2011), but they are also partly determined by diet, so a change in skull shapes can reflect changing diet habits (Paschetta et al. 2010). In the absence of a clear method to identify migrants archaeologically it was difficult to determine if steppe people had migrated into the Danube valley or not. There the matter of Yamnaya migrations rested until just a few years ago.

Better Methods and Theories: Ancient DNA, Isotopes, and Neolithic Migrations

Luigi Cavalli-Sforza and his colleagues (1994) collected classical genetic markers—blood types and enzyme polymorphisms—from modern humans around the world, an enormous and controversial undertaking. Gene sequencing was not yet developed, but with such a large database of classical markers Cavalli-Sforza hoped to reconstruct the genetic origins and migrations of human populations by computing genetic distances between them. Working with archaeologist Al Ammerman, Cavalli-Sforza plotted *modern* genetic distances in these few "marker" genes against radiocarbon dates for the Neolithic advance of farming across Europe, and found that the modern genetic gradients seemed to retain the shape of a gradual demographic wave-of-advance (the mechanical, random wave analogy again) attributed to the first Neolithic farmers from Anatolia and the Near East (Ammerman and Cavalli-Sforza 1984). Grain-fed population growth and Brownian movements (random, short-distance) at the wave edge were said to explain the spread of agricultural populations and their genes. Agency and intentionality were still missing, but the quantification of migration and its correlation with genetics held the promise of testable migration hypotheses.

Many aspects of the wave-of-advance model were later proved wrong. The most important mistake was the acceptance of genetic continuity between Neolithic and modern populations in Europe, based on a few modern genetic markers and genetic models that inaccurately calculated time depth to a shared ancestor. This continuity model was conclusively discredited by Haak et al. (2005), who showed that modern Europeans were descended largely from a "ghost" population, then still unidentified, that arrived after the Neolithic, and had only a little ancestry from the Neolithic farmers of Europe. Another error was the random-movement model of the migration process, which described the migrant farmers as blind units responding to a simple set of mechanical rules, rather than people carrying out strategies or responding to push-pull factors that directed migration *streams* to socially and economically attractive targets.

Colin Renfrew (1987) boldly built on the wave-of-advance model to propose that gradually expanding Anatolian farmers, not migrating steppe nomads, had been responsible for the spread of the Indo-European languages. Anthony (1990) was partly a reply to Ammerman and Cavalli-Sforza (1984) and Renfrew (1987), in that I argued for long-distance, targeted "leap-frog" migrations to specific places rather than random short-distance movements. The "leap-frog" hypothesis was first developed in a graduate school paper with Fiedel, updated and published later (Fiedel and Anthony 2003). After Ammerman and Cavalli-Sforza (1984), many archaeologists began to discuss migration models in relation to the expansion of Neolithic farming and farmers, gradually making the archaeology of Neolithic migrations a focus of study in itself (Van Andel and Runnels 1995; Zilhao 2001; Perlès 2001; Zvelebil and Lillie 2000; Bellwood and Renfrew 2002; Fiedel and Anthony 2003; Bánffy 2004). A few hotspots of migration theory, mostly about how to identify migrations in the archaeological record, began to glow here and there in the previously frozen theoretical landscape (Kristiansen 1989; Mallory 1992; Härke 1998; Burmeister 2000). By around the year 2000 migration had returned to serious discussions of culture change in Europe, mostly in connection with the spread of agriculture, where a demographic argument for migration was based on agriculturally fueled population growth (Bellwood and Renfrew 2002).

The next big advance in archaeological migration studies was the development of methods to recover geographically sensitive stable isotopes of oxygen and strontium taken from human teeth (Price et al. 2001; Bickle and Hofmann 2007; Hofmann 2016). Strontium and oxygen isotopes were relatively simple to recover, but to interpret them, analysts needed extensive geographic background studies to accurately plot geographic isotopic variability. Applied to samples from the Early Neolithic Linear Pottery culture, oxygen and strontium isotopes showed that many Neolithic people died far from where they were born—they had migrated. Isotopic studies showed a surprising degree of mobility among European Neolithic farmers previously thought to have lived within small, self-sufficient communities.

After about 2005, at the same time that geographic isotope studies were beginning to identify migrants in cemetery populations, the direct analysis of sequenced ancient DNA (aDNA) replaced models, such as the wave-of-advance, that were derived from modern genetic markers. After the first aDNA studies it became clear that models derived from modern DNA could not be projected very far into the past, because human mobility in the past had been too great—the farther back in time, the greater the difference from modern geographic distributions of genetic traits (Pickrell and Reich 2014). Ancient DNA for the first time directly documented ancient mating networks—who was mating with whom. When individuals from one mating network migrated into a region previously occupied by people in a distinct mating network, the distinctive genetic traits of migrants and locals could easily be converted into genetic distances on a principal component plot, as Cavalli-Sforza had attempted with modern data, and migrants who were clear outliers from the local population could easily be recognized. This was a revolutionary development in the history of archaeology. For the first time, genetically distinct migrants could be identified in ancient cemeteries, or the absence of migrants could be confirmed. Material culture and biological descent could now be examined as completely independent variables.

The first studies of aDNA focused largely on two parental haplogroup indicators, mtDNA (tracing maternal ancestry only) and Y-DNA (paternal ancestry only), because these single traits were the first ones that could be recovered from the jumble of broken DNA fragments that genetic archaeologists had to examine. Whole genomes were at first so painstakingly slow to reassemble that they were practically unrecoverable. But these single parental genetic traits were sufficient to distinguish between migrant parental ancestry and local parental ancestry. They showed that most of the Early Neolithic farmers were migrants whose maternal and paternal ancestors came from Anatolia and the Near East (Haak et al. 2005). Indigenous European Mesolithic foragers had quite different maternal and paternal haplogroups and maintained them in the face of pioneer farmer immigration (Bramanti et al. 2009). Surprisingly, in northern and central Europe most of the farmers remained genetically distinct from the local European foragers for many centuries or even millennia, while in western Europe and Iberia these exclusionary customs were relaxed, and Neolithic farmers and foragers were more admixed. The spread of agricultural economies in Europe now appeared to have been achieved largely by migrating farmers from the Near East/Anatolia who leapfrogged over large unpopulated regions to arrive at targeted destinations such as the Thessalian Plain, a predictable behavior among long-distance migrants (Fiedel and Anthony 2003).

Although aDNA was not yet deployed in the Yamnaya migration debate, traditional archaeological surveys and excavations in Bulgaria and Hungary directed by Volker Heyd began to strengthen the archaeological evidence for Yamnaya migrations into the Danube valley (Harrison and Heyd 2007; Heyd 2012; Frînculeasa et al. 2015). I gathered evidence from Russian and Ukrainian sources (Anthony 2007) to suggest the possible routes of the Yamnaya migrations (Figure 3.3). In 2012, Heyd and Gerling began to publish stable isotopes from Yamnaya kurgans in Hungary, but the initial results were unclear (Gerling et al. 2012).

In the same year, 2012, Anthony and Brown began to cooperate with David Reich, who was establishing a new aDNA laboratory at Harvard Medical School that specialized in the recovery of genetic data from across the whole human genome, not limited to single parental markers. Human bones from 66 individuals ranging in age from the Mesolithic to the Late Bronze Age were recovered by us and our Russian colleagues in the middle Volga steppes during the Samara Valley Project (1995–2001) and were brought to the United States for isotope testing and radiocarbon dating (Anthony et al. 2016). Among them were 15 Yamnaya individuals from kurgan cemeteries in the Volga-Ural steppes. Nine Yamnaya individuals from five kurgan cemeteries passed screening and were accepted by Reich's team for deeper whole-genome analysis. The Yamnaya and western European samples would soon reveal a shocking surprise.

FIGURE 3.3. Yamnaya kurgan cemeteries in the Danube Valley, 3100–2800 B.C., from Anthony 2007.

The aDNA Revolution of 2015: Massive Migrations from the Steppes

In 2015, the Reich laboratory at Harvard Medical School and the Copenhagen National Museum laboratory led by Eske Willerslev described two large samples (69 individuals in the Reich study, including 28 from our Samara Valley Project and 101 in the Willerslev study) of prehistoric individuals from graves across Prehistoric Europe, analyzed at the whole-genome scale and published simultaneously in the June issue of *Nature* (Haak et al. 2015; Allentoft et al. 2015). This was the first significant application of new methods that permitted large numbers of individuals to be analyzed rapidly at the whole-genome scale, an enormous improvement over examining single genetic traits. Harvard's method was a sampling procedure called "capture," which was very fast but examined only the parts of the human genome known to vary significantly between modern humans, while Copenhagen's approach, known as "shotgun," was a slower but more complete count that sequenced all 3.3 billion base-pairs in the average human genome. Either way, with data taken from whole genomes, it was now possible to identify who was genetically related to whom in cemetery populations, and how closely they were related, and whether it was on the mother's or father's side, or both. Because each person carries a genetic record of descent from hundreds of recognizable individual ancestors (up to ten generations back) and many more broadly defined ancestral groups, the whole genomes of a few individuals could reveal the histories of substantial populations. Applied to large samples of individuals, statistical characterizations of genetic relationships could identify migrations, reveal their demographic structure, and delineate ancient mating networks—people who shared largely similar genetic ancestries—a new category of measurable human relationships (Anthony 2019; Anthony and Brown 2017a).

The two initial studies of whole genomes came to almost the same broad conclusions. Both agreed that there were massive migrations between 3000–2500 B.C. out of the Pontic-Caspian steppes into central and northern Europe by Yamnaya pastoralists who became the biological foundation of the Corded Ware culture. More than 70% of the genetic ancestry of Corded Ware individuals buried in Corded Ware graves with classic Corded Ware artifact assemblages and Corded Ware radiocarbon dates (2900–2400 B.C.) came from Yamnaya populations similar to those of the Volga and North Caucasus steppes. Even as far west as Germany and as late as 2400 B.C., centuries after the Corded Ware migrations began, Corded Ware individuals still exhibited more than 70% Yamnaya steppe ancestry. The resulting population, admixed between steppe immigrants and the local Late Neolithic farmers, was directly ancestral to most modern Europeans and perhaps to their languages. It was not exactly what Gimbutas (1963, 1977) had suggested, but it was close enough to stun most archaeologists (including me), who generally had regarded the Corded Ware culture as a local northern European development (Furholt 2014).

Radiocarbon dates show that there was an initial phase of migration from the steppes into the lower Danube valley and sporadically into the middle Danube valley, to the Hungarian plain, about 3100 B.C. (the "scouts" in a processual model), followed by a massive migration about 3000 B.C. into targeted regions in both the lower and middle Danube valleys (Frînculeasa et al. 2017). These more numerous migrants after 3000 B.C. created hundreds of kurgans in the Hungarian plain south of the Carpathian Mountains. The oldest Corded Ware sites seem just from proximity to have been derived from this Hungarian group, and appeared ca. 2900–2700 B.C. in the Czech Republic and Slovakia within the mountain environment and also just north of the Carpathians in southern and central Poland. Yamnaya ancestry of the Corded Ware type then rapidly expanded across northern Europe, largely replacing the genetic lineages of the Neolithic population.

Rather than drawing arrows on a map, or turning to artifact typology, we can now ask useful questions about the migration process and its manifestation in material remains.

1. Were the Yamnaya migrants genetically homogeneous or diverse?

Furholt (2018) raised important questions about how migrating populations that were partly derived genetically from steppe ancestors can be equated with a unitary, homogeneous "Yamnaya culture." But the Yamnaya culture was never defined as a unitary, homogeneous phenomenon in the steppes, before the migrations began. I can now cite 20 published Yamnaya individuals with whole-genome data from the Pontic-Caspian steppes, sometimes divided into two groups, eastern and western (Juras et al. 2018); and sometimes divided into three groups, Ukrainian, Volga-Don, and North Caucasus steppe (Wang et al. 2019). Merpert (1974) defined nine archaeological subregions within the Yamnaya "cultural-historical community" based on small differences in grave rituals and artifacts across the Pontic-Caspian steppes (Figure 3.4). We need data from many more Yamnaya individuals and regions in order to determine where the migration process began, or whether migrants came from all regions. That much-needed data collection and analysis is now under way.

The single fact that stands out now is the surprising homogeneity of Yamnaya genomes across the sampled regions. Almost all sampled Yamnaya individuals in the Pontic-Caspian steppes exhibit very similar genetic ancestries, derived primarily from older Eneolithic steppe populations, with the additional admixture of 5–15% ancestry from Danubian farmers (Wang et al. 2018). Almost all sampled Yamnaya males were members of Y-chromosome haplogroup R1b1a. Older Eneolithic cemeteries had yielded a more diverse set of patrilines (R1b, R1a, Q1a, J, Ia2a). Later Corded Ware populations, although derived from Yamnaya ancestry, were largely Y-chromosome haplogroup R1a, which had been present in the steppes during the Eneolithic and might have remained present but been excluded from kurgans through the Yamnaya era, reemerging as a dominant male lineage in in the Corded Ware population. This shifting of male lineages within a broadly related set of steppe-derived populations could indicate a succession of restricted male-defined clans gaining access to political power and to memorialization under prominent burial mounds while excluding other males from such positions. The regionally suppressed patrilines such as those that inherited the R1a haplotype would in this case have become almost invisible archaeologically in the steppes because of their exclusion from Yamnaya kurgan graves,

FIGURE 3.4. The nine regional groups (I–IX) of the Yamnaya culture defined by N. Y. Merpert (1974:Figure 1). In his legend, a = documented border of a culture region; b = supposed border of region; and c = direction of invasion of other culture areas.

but then emerged as migrants in central Europe. Social and political competition between patrilines might have encouraged migration to new regions. But if burial under a kurgan was restricted in this way, then aDNA is sampling only the dominant elite, not the whole population. Many questions about variability within Yamnaya sites, and the sources and causes of variability, remain to be answered.

2. WHO WERE THE SCOUTS? HOW WERE THEY CONNECTED TO THE POPULATIONS IN THE DESTINATION REGION?

The activities of the scouts are critical in any model of long-distance migration, as the scouts selected the destinations and conveyed information about them back to specific social segments (Figure 3.2). Brown and I argued (Anthony and Brown 2017b) that Bronze Age ritual canid sacrifices discovered at Krasnosamarskoe, Russia, during the Samara Valley Project in the Volga steppes closely paralleled Indo-European myths that described an Indo-European institution of initiatory male war bands composed of adolescent males who were expelled, migrated to a cultural frontier, and raided cultural Others. They were called the *luperci* or *suodales* in Latin, *kouros* or *ephebes* in Greek, *fian* in Celtic, *männerbünde* or *jungmannschaft* in Germanic, and *vrātyas* or *Maruts* in Indic, but all behaved this way, and all were described as dressed in wolf or dog skins, or were named after dogs, or they became like wolves. These shared tropes are evidence of a shared, Proto-Indo-European institution of male initiation connected with dog and wolf symbols. At Krasnosamarskoe on the Samara River in the middle Volga steppes, occupied between 1900–1700 B.C., at least 51 dogs and 7 wolves were roasted, fileted, and presumably eaten during a recurring, institutionalized winter-season ceremony, in a reversal and inversion of normal behavior in this region, where dogs were *not* eaten. Inversion of normal behavior is typical in a rite of passage but occurs in almost no other kind of institutionalized ritual. Canid DNA showed that 90% of the sacrificed and consumed dogs were males. Taken together, the archaeological evidence indicates a repeated rite of passage for males in which they became dogs and wolves through the consumption of dog and wolf flesh, an obvious parallel to the Indo-European myths.

War bands might act as scouts, who explore new territories and return with information about them. Scouts can be anyone, traders or missionaries or mercenaries or seasonal workers, and all of these should be considered in a processual explanation of migration. But the institution of initiatory male war bands is an intriguing possibility, supported by comparative mythology and some archaeology, that could have encouraged continuous small exploratory migrations by raiding groups composed primarily of adolescent boys. These probing raids might then have been followed by adult migrants who were related to the boys and received the boys' information about suitable destinations. In this case, migration streams should have flowed from the places that launched the initial adolescent raiding bands to the places they raided.

In the southwest of the United States, large migrations occurred between pueblos in the thirteenth and fourteenth centuries. Recent archaeological studies of these migrations (Clark et al. 2018) showed that relations between the migrants and the local communities at the destination depended very much on whether relations prior to the migration had been peaceful and inclusive or hostile and oppositional. Hostile prior relations like those proposed here were found to have resulted in maintaining both geographic distance and artifactual typological contrasts between migrants and local communities at the destination, while more peaceful prior relations resulted in more integrated migrant/local communities, socially and materially.

One of the remarkable aspects of the Yamnaya migrations into central Europe was that people of the largely immigrant-descended Corded Ware and mostly local Globular Amphorae cultures remained genetically quite distinct for centuries (Wang et al. 2018) while occupying different parts of the same landscape (Czebreszuk and Szmyt 2011; Machnik 1999). This reluctance to marry across the migrant/local social divide would be consistent with hostile relations. But as we will see, artifactual and stylistic sharing points toward a modicum of integration. Political alliances might have operated between the two groups, particularly during the brief period when the Corded Ware package was formed. The recombination of material cultural types and customs that happened at that moment of transformation created a material culture and set of funerary practices sufficiently distinctive so that archaeologists could not detect the underlying genetic connections between the

Corded Ware and Yamnaya populations, or perceive the migration processes that connected them, until whole genomes became available for study.

3. Why did the migrants create a new material culture in central Europe?

The shift from Yamnaya to Corded Ware material cultures probably occurred within a century (3000–2900 B.C.) at the beginning of an enormous expansion of range. Corded Ware grave mounds were generally smaller than Yamnaya kurgans, and often featured stone fences that were reminiscent of northern European Middle Neolithic megalithic graves but usually were absent from Yamnaya mounds. Corded Ware and Yamnaya both distinguished males from females in graves, but Yamnaya kurgans excluded most females, exhibiting a marked overrepresentation of adult males, while Corded Ware funerals often posed males and females differently under kurgans. Both had weapons, but the most frequent Yamnaya weapon types (cast copper flat axe or vertical-edged "sleeved" axe, cast copper tanged dagger, flint triangular arrowheads) differed from the common Corded Ware weapon types (stone "battle-axe," flint triangular arrowheads). Corded Ware material culture incorporated specific artifact types (globular amphorae, polished stone hammer-axes) copied from indigenous Middle Neolithic cultures in northern Europe (Globular Amphorae and Trichterbecker Culture or TRB), a material signal of integration not matched by intermarriage on a significant scale. These new artifact types could be seen as a material advertisement by the Corded Ware migrants directed at their Yamnaya parents and grandparents, warning of new political alliances with local Middle Neolithic (Globular Amphorae Culture) populations—an active material statement of political separation that contained pointed references to new allies, at the same time that the dominant male patriline switched from R1b to R1a.

The Corded Ware phenomenon was not just the spread of a new burial rite with a new set of weapons and ornaments. A new economy also was imported by the migrants. In the Kujavia region in Poland, where large surface areas were stripped by archaeologists in connection with highway and pipeline construction, the Corded Ware economy introduced a higher level of settlement mobility than had existed before (Czebreszuk and Szmyt 2011: Fig.11). Settlement stability was measured by counting three classes of material culture: pit features, animal bones, and pottery sherds. Ephemeral Corded Ware settlement sites had fewer pit features, fewer animal bones, and markedly fewer pottery sherds per square meter than any previous or succeeding archaeological culture, including the contemporary and genetically distinct Globular Amphorae culture, which shared the Kujavia landscape with the Corded Ware pastoralists. Corded Ware people had a higher protein diet than the earlier populations, probably derived from a higher proportion of dairy and meat foods and a lower proportion of cultivated grain (Sjögren, Price, and Kristiansen 2016). But their pastoral economy was anomalous in central Europe. In the succeeding Bell Beaker period, settlements reappeared and mobility decreased (Czebreszuk and Szmyt 2011). The Globular Amphorae people practiced localized mobility. Their seasonal settlements were centered around a fixed ancestral cemetery, usually located in a well-watered lowland or valley bottom suitable for agriculture. The earliest Corded Ware kurgans were often isolated monuments located on high ridge tops (Czebreszuk and Szmyt 2011:261). The Corded Ware population was genetically distinct, it introduced a new level of pastoral mobility to this region of Poland, it claimed a different part of the topography, and it remained largely separate from most of the local communities for centuries during the early third millennium B.C., all indicators that might suggest sustained hostility and opposition between migrants and locals. Mass graves containing families killed by blows to the head, found at Eulau (Meyer et al. 2009) and Koszyce (Schroeder et al. 2019), are testimony to such violent relations between Corded Ware and Globular Amphorae populations.

The creation of the Corded Ware package was an active and creative use of material culture to both represent and actively forge a new cultural identity among mobile, pastoral migrants. They separated geographically from their Yamnaya parent group by migrating into the mountains of Slovakia and the Czech Republic north of the Carpathian basin, where they quickly created a new package of customs that borrowed from local practices more than their Yamnaya parents in Hungary had done. Whole genomes testify that immigrant Corded Ware and local Globular Amphorae mating networks remained largely distinct and separate for 500 years while they shared the same landscapes. So, the integration of local Middle Neolithic weapon and pottery styles into Corded Ware migrant material culture was not equated with an equivalent level of integration in mating behaviors or kin-based networks. One important methodological lesson we should take from this fascinating case of prehistoric ethnogenesis is that migrants can create a new migrant material culture very rapidly during the migration process, such that the material and typological linkage to the parent culture and region is quickly obscured by innovation and a desire to form a separate identity, with a new social or kin group (R1a) at the top of the hierarchy.

4. Who migrated? Was it entire Yamnaya social groups, or mainly males?

We do not really have enough published aDNA to answer this question in a comprehensive way. Goldberg et al. (2017), who had earlier estimated an excess of steppe-derived males over steppe-derived females in the range of 5–14 males per female, in 2017 revised that estimate to 4–7 males per female, still a significant sex bias in the migration stream of steppe-derived people flowing into central Europe. But this 4–7/1 ratio later was shown to differ regionally. Juras et al. (2018) showed that both Yamnaya males and females formed the Corded Ware population in southern Poland, in what might be called a mass migration. Corded Ware individuals here had both fathers and mothers with strong steppe ancestry, easily explaining the dominance of steppe ancestry and its maintenance through time in a geographic setting where genetically quite different Globular Amphorae populations lived not far away. But mostly males made it as far west as Germany, where Yamnaya males who practiced Corded Ware customs mated with females from local agriculturalist ancestry. The western aspect of Corded Ware seems to have been created by a more specialized, male-biased migration process probably driven by prestige-seeking behavior. Corded Ware individuals here still had steppe ancestry that was dominant, but it was admixed more with female-mediated local farmer ancestry, more like the Bell Beaker pattern. Future aDNA research will focus on the variability between regions in sex bias. We also hope to investigate accompanying animal migrations: whether they brought steppe dogs and horses with them, or if they adopted local central European dogs and horses.

Was Gimbutas Right?

Gimbutas's mistake was not that she was a migrationist. We should all be migrationists, in the sense that we should accept migration as an important and recurring behavior in human history and prehistory. Many regional archaeologists had seen the kurgans that appeared in the Danube valley during the late Cotsofeni and Baden periods as evidence for Yamnaya migrations, and as it turns out they were correct, as was their colleague Marija Gimbutas who included their views in her conception of the Kurgan Culture. That part of her Kurgan Culture hypothesis was on ground as solid as any migration theory could be in the 1970s.

Her shortcomings were in theory and interpretation rather than in dates or artifact types. When she described migrations, Gimbutas painted an image of a wave of faceless warriors, an invasion, illustrated by arrows that marked the path they followed, which began in one unitary culture and subjugated another unitary culture. This is not an informative model of culture, or of migration, or of its causes and effects. The stated cause of her Kurgan Culture migrations was a shortage of pastures in the steppes, exacerbated by climate change. This is not an adequate analysis of the preceding pushes and pulls, or of the preceding relationships between steppe populations and the people who lived in the regions that became targets of Yamnaya migrations. Finally, she included in her expanded definition of the Kurgan Culture other archaeological cultures, importantly Globular Amphorae and Baden, now known to be genetically Neolithic farmers who had adopted the new technology of wheeled vehicles and a more mobile economy before the Yamnaya migrations began.

So, it is an exaggeration to say that she was right. We need to move beyond the single-event, invasion model of migration and accept the much more complex models that historians and demographers use to model migrations (for example, Moch 1992 and Clark et al. 2018). But she was quite correct that the Yamnaya migration up the Danube valley about 3000 B.C. had massive effects that were felt across most of Europe. She organized and synthesized large bodies of archaeological evidence from across eastern Europe and she presented these syntheses in monographs that opened the door to this region's prehistory for many grateful followers, including me. Today, although new methods permit us to recognize the Yamnaya–Corded Ware expansion, theory still lags in understanding why and how it happened. We have just begun to examine the Yamnaya migrations through the lens of processual models.

Acknowledgments

For their help guiding my thinking on migration I would like to thank Stuart Fiedel, who wrestled with migration concepts with me in graduate school at the University of Pennsylvania; Bernard Wailes, my advisor who encouraged me to read and write about migration; my partner Dory Brown, who co-directed my field projects and introduced me to the ethnohistorical literature on European migrations and material cultures in Colonial eastern North America; and Jeffery Clark, whom I have met only once or twice, but whose publications introduced me to the literature on late prehistoric migrations in the U.S. Southwest. For organizing and supporting the conference that produced this volume, I thank the State University at Buffalo, Peter Biehl, and Megan Daniels.

REFERENCES CITED

Allentoft, M. E., M. Sikora, K. G. Sjögren, S. Rasmussen, M. Rasmussen, J. Stenderup, P. B. Damgaard, H. Schroeder, T. Ahlström, L. Vinner, A.-S. Malaspinas, A. Margaryan, T. Higham, D. Chivall, N. Lynnerup, L. Harvig, J. Baron, P. Della Casa, P. Dąbrowski, P. R. Duffy, A. V. Ebel, A. Epimakhov, K. Frei, M. Furmanek, T. Gralak, A. Gromov, S. Gronkiewicz, G. Grupe, T. Hajdu, R. Jarysz, V. Khartanovich, A. Khokhlov, V. Kiss, J. Kolář, A. Kriiska, I. Lasak, C. Longhi, G. McGlynn, A. Merkevicius, I. Merkyte, M. Metspalu, R. Mkrtchyan, V. Moiseyev, L. Paja, G. Pálfi, D. Pokutta, Ł. Pospieszny, T. D. Price, L. Saag, M. Sablin, N. Shishlina, V. Smrčka, V. I. Soenov, V. Szeverényi, G. Tóth, S. V. Trifanova, L. Varul, M. Vicze, L. Yepiskoposyan, V. Zhitenev, L. Orlando, T. Sicheritz-Pontén, S. Brunak, R. Nielsen, K. Kristiansen, and E. Willerslev 2015 Population Genomics of Bronze Age Eurasia. *Nature* 522:167–172.

Ammerman, A. J., and L. L. Cavalli-Sforza 1984 *The Neolithic Transition and the Genetics of Population in Europe.* Princeton University Press, Princeton.

Anthony, D. W. 2019 Archaeology, Genetics, and Language in The Steppes: A Comment on Bomhard. *Journal of Indo-European Studies* 47(1 and 2):1–2.

Anthony, D. W. 2007 *The Horse, the Wheel, and Language: How Bronze Age Riders from the Eurasian Steppes Shaped the Modern World.* Princeton University Press, Princeton.

Anthony, D. W. 1997 Prehistoric Migration as Social Process. In *Migrations and Invasions in Archaeological Explanation*, edited by J. Chapman and H. Hamerow, pp. 21–32. British Archaeological Reports International Series 664. BAR Publishing, Oxford.

Anthony, D. W. 1990 Migration in Archaeology: The Baby and the Bathwater. *American Anthropologist* 92(4):23–42.

Anthony, D. W. 1986 The "Kurgan Culture," Indo-European Origins, and the Domestication of the Horse: A Reconsideration. *Current Anthropology* 27(4):291–313.

Anthony, D. W., and D. R. Brown 2017a Molecular Archaeology and Indo-European Linguistics: Impressions from New Data. In *Usque ad Radices: Indo-European Studies in Honour of Birgit Anette Olsen*, edited by B. S. S. Hansen, A. Hyllested, A. R. Jørgensen, G. Kroonen, J. H. Larsson, B. N. Whitehead, T. Olander, and T. M. Søborg, pp. 25–54. Museum Tusculanum, Copenhagen.

Anthony, D. W., and D. R. Brown 2017b The Dogs of War: A Bronze Age Initiation Ritual in the Russian Steppes. *Journal of Anthropological Archaeology* 38:134–148.

Anthony, D. W., D. R. Brown, P. F. Kuznetsov, O. D. Mochalov, and A. A. Khkokhlov, (editors) 2016 *A Bronze Age Landscape in the Russian Steppes: The Samara Valley Project*, Vol. 37. Monumenta Archaeologica. Cotsen Institute Press, UCLA, Los Angeles.

Bánffy, E. 2004 Neolithic Contacts: Adaptation and Exchange of Information. *Antaeus* 27:11–16.

Bellwood, P., and C. Renfrew (editors) 2002 *Examining the Farming/Language Dispersal Hypothesis.* McDonald Institute, Cambridge.

Bickle, P., and D. Hofmann 2007 Moving On: The Contribution of Isotope Studies to the Early Neolithic of Central Europe. *Antiquity* 81:1029–1041.

Bökönyi, S. 1987 Horses and Sheep in East Europe. In *Proto-Indo-European: The Archaeology of a Linguistic Problem*, edited by S. Skomal, pp. 136–144. Institute for the Study of Man, Washington, D.C.

Bramanti, B., M. G. Thomas, W. Haak, M. Unterlaender, P. Jores, K. Tambets, I. Antanaitis Jacobs, M. N. Haidle, R. Jankauskas, C.-J. Kind, F. Lueth, T. Terberger, J. Hiller, S. Matsumura, P. Forster, and J. Burger 2009 Genetic Discontinuity Between Local Hunter-Gatherers and Central Europe's First Farmers. *Science* 326:137–140.

Burmeister, S. 2017 The Archaeology of Migration: What Can and Should it Accomplish? In *Migration und Integration von der Urgeschichte bis zum Mittelalter*, edited by H. Meller, F. Daim, J. Krause, and R. Risch, pp. 57–68. Tagungen des Landesmuseums für Vorgeschichte 17, Halle.

Burmeister, S. 2000 Archaeology and Migration: Approaches to an Archaeological Proof of Migration. *Current Anthropology* 41(4):554–555.

Cavalli-Sforza, L. L., P. Menozzi, A. Piazza 1994 *The History and Geography of Human Genes*. Princeton University Press, Princeton.

Clark, J. J. 2001 *Tracking Prehistoric Migrations: Pueblo Settlers among the Tonto Basin Hohokam*. Anthropological Papers of the University of Arizona No. 65. University of Arizona Press, Tucson.

Clark, J. J., J. A. Birch, M. Hegmon, B. J. Mills, D. M. Glowacki, S. G. Ortman, J. S. Dean, R. Gauthier, P. D. Lyons, M. A. Peeples, L. Borck, and J. A. Ware 2018 Resolving the Migrant Paradox: Two Pathways to Coalescence in the Late Precontact U.S. Southwest. *Journal of Anthropological Archaeology*. DOI:10.1016/j.jaa.2018.09.004, accessed December 2018.

Clarke, D. L. 1968 *Analytical Archaeology*. Methuen, London.

Czebreszuk, J., and M. Szmyt 2011 Identities, Differentiation, and Interactions on the Central European Plain in the 3rd Millennium BC. In *Sozialarchäologische Perspektiven: Gesellschaftlicher Wandel 5000–1500 v. Chr. zwischen Atlantik und Kaukasus*, edited by S. Hansen and J. Müller, pp. 269–294. Archäologie in Eurasien 24. Philipp von Zabern, Darmstadt.

Dergachev, V. A. 2007 *O Skipetrakh, O Loshadyakh, O Voine: Etiudy v zashchitu migrationnoi konseptsii M. Gimbutas*. Nestor-Istoriya, Saint Petersburg.

Ecsedy, I. (editor) 1979 *The People of the Pit-Grave Kurgans in Eastern Hungary*. Akadémia Kiadó, Budapest.

Elster, E. S. 2015 Marija Gimbutas: Old Europe, Goddesses and Gods, and the Transformation of Culture. *Backdirt* (Cotsen Institute): 94–102.

Fernández-Götz, M. 2016 Revisiting Migrations in Archaeology: The Aisne-Marne and the Hunsrück-Eifel Cultures. In *Proceedings of the 17th Iron Age Research Student Symposium*, edited by G. J. R. Erskine, P. Jacobsson, P. Miller, and S. Stetkiewicz, pp. 1–11. Archaeopress, Oxford.

Fiedel, S., and D. W. Anthony 2003 Deerslayers, Pathfinders, and Icemen: Origins of the European Neolithic as Seen from the Frontier. In *The Colonization of Unfamiliar Landscapes*, edited by M. Rockman and J. Steele, pp. 144–168. Routledge, London.

Frînculeasa, A., B. Preda, and V. Heyd 2015 Pit-Graves, Yamnaya and Kurgans along the Lower Danube: Disentangling IVth and IIIrd Millennium BC Burial Customs, Equipment, and Chronology. *Praehistorische Zeitschrift* 90(1–2):1–69.

Furholt, M. 2018 Massive Migrations? The Impact of Recent aDNA Studies on our View of Third Millennium Europe. *European Journal of Archaeology* 21(2):159–191.

Furholt, M. 2014 Upending a "Totality": Re-evaluating Corded Ware Variability in Late Neolithic Europe. *Proceedings of the Prehistoric Society* 80:67–86.

Gerling, C., V. Heyd, A. Pike, E. Bánffy, J. Dani, K. Köhler, G. Kulcsár, E. Kaiser, and W. Schier 2012 Identifying Kurgan Graves in Eastern Hungary: A Burial Mound in the Light of Strontium and Oxygen Isotope Analysis. In *Population Dynamics in Prehistory and Early History: New Approaches Using Stable Isotopes and Genetics*, edited by E. Kaiser, J. Burger, and W. Schier, pp. 165–176. DeGruyter Open Access E-book. https://www.degruyter.com/view/product/179228

Gimbutas, M. 1963 The Indo-Europeans: Archeological Problems. *American Anthropologist* 65(4):815–836.

Gimbutas, M. 1977 The First Wave of Eurasian Steppe Pastoralists into Copper Age Europe. *Journal of Indo-European Studies* 5(4):277–338.

Gimbutas, M. 1993 The Indo-Europeanization of Europe: The Intrusion of Steppe Pastoralists from South Russia and the Transformation of Old Europe. *Word* 44:205–222.

Goldberg, A., T. Günther, N. A. Rosenberg, and M. Jakobsson 2017 Reply to Lazaridis and Reich: Robust Model-Based Inference of Male-Biased Admixture during Bronze Age Migration from the Pontic-Caspian Steppe. *Proceedings of the National Academy of Sciences* 114(20):E3875-E3877.

Haak, W., P. Forster, B. Bramanti, S. Matsumura, G. Brandt, M. Ta¨nzer, R. Villems, C. Renfrew, D. Gronenborn, K. W. Alt, and J. Burger 2005 Ancient DNA from the First European Farmers in 7500-Year-Old Neolithic Sites. *Science* 310:1016–1028.

Haak, Wolfgang, I. Lazaridis, N. Patterson, N. Rohland, S. Mallick, B. Llamas, G. Brandt, S. Nordenfelt, E. Harney, K. Stewardson, Q. Fu, A. Mittnik, E. Bánffy, C. Economou, M. Francken, S. Friederich, R. G. Pena, F. Hallgren, V. Khartanovich, A. Khokhlov, M. Kunst, P. Kuznetsov, H. Meller, O. Mochalov, V. Moiseyev, N. Nicklisch, S. L. Pichler, R. Risch, M. A. R. Guerra, C. Roth, A. Szécsényi-Nagy, J. Wahl, M. Meyer, J. Krause, D. Brown, D. Anthony, A. Cooper, K. W. Alt, and D. Reich 2015 Massive Migration from the Steppe Was a Source for Indo-European Languages in Europe. *Nature* 522(7555):207–211.

Hakenbeck, S. 2008 Migration in Archaeology: Are We Nearly There Yet? In *Archaeological Review from Cambridge* 23(2):9–26.

Halsall, G. 1995 *Early Medieval Cemeteries: An Introduction to Burial Archaeology in the Post-Roman West*. Cruithne Press, Glasgow.

Härke, H. 1998 Archaeologists and Migrations. A Problem of Attitude? *Current Anthropology* 39:19–45.

Harrison, R., and V. Heyd 2007 The Transformation of Europe in the Third Millennium BC: The Example of "Le Petit-Chasseur I + III" (Sion, Valais, Switzerland). *Praehistorische Zeitschrift* 82(2):129–214.

Haury, E. 1958 Evidence at Point of Pines for a Prehistoric Migration from Northern Arizona. In *Migrations in New World Culture History*, edited by R. H. Thompson, pp. 1–6. Social Science Bulletin No. 27. University of Arizona Press, Tucson.

Häusler, A. 2003 Nomaden, Indogermanen, Invasionen. Zur Entstehung eines Mythos. *Orientwissenschaftliche Hefte* 5.

Heather, P. 2009 *Empires and Barbarians: The Fall of Rome and the Birth of Europe*. Oxford University Press, Oxford.

Heyd, V. 2012 Yamnaya Groups and Tumuli West of the Black Sea. In *Ancestral landscapes: Burial mounds in the Copper and Bronze Ages*, edited by E. Borgna and S. M. Celka, pp. 536–555. Travaux de la Maison de l'Orient 58. MOM Editions, Lyon.

Hofmann, D. 2016 Keep on Walking: The Role of Migration in Linearbandkeramik Life. *Documenta Praehistorica* 43:235–251.

Juras, A., M. Chyleński, E. Ehler, H. Malmström, D. Żurkiewicz, P. Włodarczak, S. Wilk, J. Peška, P. Fojtík, M. Králík, J. Libera, J. Bagińska, K. Tunia, V. I. Klochko, M. Dabert, M. Jakobsson, and A. Kośko 2018 Mitochondrial Genomes Reveal an East to West Cline of Steppe Ancestry in Corded Ware Populations. *Nature Scientific Reports* 8:11603. DOI:10.1038/s41598-018-29914-5.

Kristiansen, K. 1989 Prehistoric Migrations: The Case of the Single Grave and Corded Ware Cultures. *Journal of Danish Archaeology* 8:211–225.

Machnik, J. 1999 Radiocarbon Chronology of the Corded Ware Culture on Grzęda Sokalska: A Middle Dnieper Traits Perspective. *Baltic-Pontic Studies* 7:221–250.

Mallory, J. P. 1992 Migration and Language Change. *Peregrinatio Gothica* III, Universitetets Oldsaksamlings Skrifter Ny Rekke (Oslo) 14:145–153.

Merpert, N. I. 1974 *Drevneishie Skotovody Volzhsko-Uralskogo Mezhdurechya*. Nauka, Moskva.

Meyer, C., G. Brandt, W. Haak, R. A. Ganslmeier, H. Meller, and K. W. Alt 2009 The Eulau Eulogy: Bioarchaeological Interpretation of Lethal Violence in Corded Ware Multiple Burials from Saxony-Anhalt, Germany. *Journal of Anthropological Archaeology* 28(2009):412–423.

Moch, L. P. 1992 *Moving Europeans: Migration in Western Europe Since 1650*. Indiana University Press, Bloomington.

Neustupny, E. 1982 Prehistoric Migrations by Infiltration. *Archeologicke Rozhledy* 34:278–293.

Olalde, I., S. Brace, M. E. Allentoft, I. Armit, K. Kristiansen, T. Booth, N. Rohland, S. Mallick, A. Szécsényi-Nagy, A. Mittnik, E. Altena, M. Lipson, I. Lazaridis, T. K. Harper, N. Patterson, N. Broomandkhoshbacht, Y. Diekmann, Z. Faltyskova, D. Fernandes, M. Ferry, E. Harney, P. de Knijff, M. Michel1, J. Oppenheimer, K. Stewardson, A. Barclay, K. W. Alt, C. Liesau, P. Ríos, C. Blasco, J. Vega Miguel, R. M. García, A. A. Fernández, E. Bánffy, M. Bernabò-Brea, D. Billoin, C. Bonsall, L. Bonsall, T. Allen, L. Büster, S. Carver, L. C. Navarro, O. E. Craig, G. T. Cook, B. Cunliffe, A. Denaire, K. E. Dinwiddy, N. Dodwell, M. Ernée, C. Evans, M. Kuchařík, J. F. Farré, C. Fowler, M. Gazenbeek, R. G. Pena, M. Haber-Uriarte, E. Haduch, G. Hey, N. Jowett, T. Knowles, K. Massy, S. Pfrengle, P. Lefranc, O. Lemercier, A. Lefebvre, C. H. Martínez, V. G. Olmo, A. B. Ramírez, J. L. Maurandi, T. Majó, J. I. McKinley, K. McSweeney, B.G. Mende, A. Mod, G. Kulcsár, V. Kiss, A. Czene, R. Patay, A. Endrő"di, K. Köhler, T. Hajdu, T. Szeniczey, J. Dani, Z. Bernert, M. Hoole, O. Cheronet, D. Keating, P. Velemínský, M. Dobeš, F. Candilio, F. Brown, R. F. Fernández, A. Herrero-Corral, S. Tusa, E. Carnieri, L. Lentini, A. Valenti, A. Zanini, C. Waddington, G. Delibes, E. Guerra-Doce, B. Neil, M. Brittain, M. Luke, R. Mortimer, J. Desideri, M. Besse, G. Brücken, M. Furmanek, A. Hałuszko, M. Mackiewicz, A. Rapin'ski, S. Leach, I. Soriano, K.T. Lillios, J. L. Cardoso, M. Parker Pearson, P. Włodarczak, T. D. Price, P. Prieto, P. Rey, R. Risch, M. A. R. Guerra, A. Schmitt, J. Serralongue, A. M. Silva, V. Smrčka, L. Vergnaud, J. Zilhão, D. Caramelli, T. Higham,

M. G. Thomas, D. J. Kennett, H. Fokkens, V. Heyd, A. Sheridan, K. Sjögren, P. W. Stockhammer, J. Krause, R. Pinhasi, W. Haak, I. Barnes, C. Lalueza-Fox, and D. Reich 2018 The Beaker Phenomenon and the Genomic Transformation of Northwest Europe. *Nature* 555:190–196.

Ortman, S. G. 2012 *Winds from the North: Tewa Origins and Historical Anthropology*. University of Utah Press, Salt Lake City.

Paschetta, C., S. de Azevedo, L. Castillo, N. Martínez-Abadías, M. Hernández, D. E. Lieberman, and R. González-José 2010 The Influence of Masticatory Loading on Craniofacial Morphology: A Test Case across Technological Transitions in the Ohio Valley. *American Journal of Physical Anthropology* 141:297–314.

Perles, C. 2001 *Early Neolithic Greece*. Cambridge University Press, Cambridge.

Pickrell, J. K., and D. Reich 2014 Toward a New History and Geography of Human Genes Informed by Ancient DNA. *Trends in Genetics* 30(9):377–389.

Price, T. D., R. A. Bentley, D. Gronenborn, J. Luning, and J. Wahl 2001 Human Migration in the Linearbandkeramik of Central Europe. *Antiquity* 75:593–603.

Renfrew, C. 1987 *Archaeology and Language: The Puzzle of Indo-European Origins*. Jonathon Cape, London.

Robb, J. 1993 A Social Prehistory of European Languages. *Antiquity* 67:747–760.

Roberts, B. W., and M. Vander Linden (editors) 2011 *Investigating Archaeological Cultures: Material Culture, Variability, and Transmission*. Springer, Berlin.

Schroeder, H., A. Margaryan, M. Szmyt, B. Theulot, P. Włodarczak, S. Rasmussen, S. Gopalakrishnan, A. Szczepanek, T. Konopka, T. Z. T. Jensen, B. Witkowska, S. Wilk, M. M. Przybyła, Ł. Pospieszny, K.-G. Sjögren, Z. Belka, J. Olsen, K. Kristiansen, E. Willerslev, K. M. Frei, M. Sikora, N. N. Johannsen, and M. E. Allentoft 2019 Unraveling Ancestry, Kinship, and Violence in a Late Neolithic Mass Grave. *Proceedings of the National Academy of Sciences*. https://doi.org/10.1073/pnas.1820210116.

Sjögren K.-G., T. D. Price, and K. Kristiansen 2016 Diet and Mobility in the Corded Ware of Central Europe. *PLoS ONE* 11(5):e0155083. DOI:10.1371/journal.pone.0155083.

Trigger, B. G. 1968 *Beyond History: The Methods of Prehistory*. Holt Rinehart, New York.

Van Andel, T. H., and C. N. Runnels 1995 The Earliest Farmers in Europe. *Antiquity* 69:481–500.

Von Cramon-Taubadel, N., and R. Pinhasi 2011 Craniometric Data Support a Mosaic Model of Demic and Cultural Neolithic Diffusion to Outlying Regions of Europe. *Proc. R. Soc. B* 2011. DOI:10.1098/rspb.2010.2678.

Wang, C.-C., S. Reinhold, A. Kalmykov, A. Wissgott, G. Brandt, C. Jeong, O. Cheronet, M. Ferry, E. Harney, D. Keating, S. Mallick, N. Rohland, K. Stewardson, A. R. Kantorovich, V. E. Maslov, V. G. Petrenko, V. R. Erlikh, B. C. Atabiev, R. G. Magomedov, P. L. Kohl, K. W. Alt, S. L. Pichler, C. Gerling, H. Meller, B. Vardanyan, L. Yeganyan, A. D. Rezepkin, D. Mariaschk, N. Berezina, J. Gresky, K. Fuchs, C. Knipper, S. Schiffels, E. Balanovska, O. Balanovsky, I. Mathieson, T. Higham, Y. B. Berezin, A. Buzhilova, V. Trifonov, R. Pinhasi, A. B. Belinskij, D. Reich, S. Hansen, J. Krause, and W. Haak 2018 The Genetic Prehistory of the Greater Caucasus. bioRxiv. *Nature* in review. DOI:/10.1101/32234.

Watson, P. J. 1971 *Explanation in Archaeology: An Explicit Scientific Approach*. Columbia University Press, New York.

Zilhao, J. 2001 Radiocarbon Evidence for Maritime Pioneer Colonization at the Origins of Farming in West Mediterranean Europe. *Proceedings of the National Academy of Science* 98(24):14180–14185.

Zvelebil, M., and M. Lillie 2000 Transition to Agriculture in Eastern Europe. In *Europe's First Farmers*, edited by T. D. Price, pp. 57–92. Cambridge University Press, Cambridge.

CHAPTER FOUR

The Conceptual Impacts of Genomics to the Archaeology of Movement

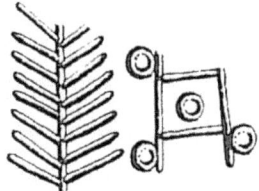

Omer Gokcumen

Abstract *We are all migrants. From our first migrations within Africa to the constant movements of present-day peoples, we have crisscrossed this earth countless times. The last ten years have witnessed an explosion of anthropological genomics studies, tracing the signatures left in our genomes by the travels of our ancestors. Charting the myriad migrations that defined our past has blurred the boundaries between ethnic and cultural groups, both past and present. Instead, we now are building maps of previously unimagined biological connections and isolations. These exciting new insights are shaping how we think about our past. Connections between the present and past peoples that had been taken for granted are now weakening, while previously unknown connections are made. The ways in which we study the social and cultural processes that shape the material culture are shifting. Wanderlust defines our species. Thus, the study of human movement takes center stage in this new era of archaeogenetics. In this short review, I will introduce the genomic tools that enabled this transformation in the field, give examples where genomic insights have transformed the way we think about our material culture, and argue that politics of migrations and nation formation remain major forces in shaping where and what kind of studies are undertaken across the world.*

The How and Why of Genomics

The human genome is an ideal subject for the study of the movements of our ancestors, given its two inherent qualities. First and foremost, the human genome is the molecule of inheritance. We each inherit half of our genome from our mother and the other half from our father. In turn, our parents inherited their genomes from their parents. All of our genomes can be traced back, generation after generation, to now-lost ancestral peoples, the stories of some we already know, and some yet to be written (Nielsen et al. 2017).

Second, DNA, the stuff of the genomes, is stable. Human genomes are simple in their helical, string-like architecture. The genome makes up for its simplicity by elongating by billions of chemical letters. Those chemical letters are constantly replicated in our bodies with amazing fidelity and protected from change by the many guardians of the genome. The sequence of our genomes, all the billions of chemical letters, remains essentially the same in each of our trillions of cells from our births to thousands of years after our deaths. The human genome is a well-protected and stable biological hard drive.

At the intersection of these properties, DNA lends itself to a new wave of investigation of our past—a new reconstruction of histories, not from the written word, but through analysis of the biological text in our genomes. Studies focusing on maternally inherited mitochondrial DNA have constructed family trees, tracing back our maternal ancestors to Africa (Cann, Stoneking, and Wilson 1987). They followed genetic breadcrumbs that our ancestors left in their migrations out of Africa (Soares et al. 2012) and into Eurasia (Macaulay et al. 2005; Richards et al. 2000), the Americas (Torroni et al. 1993), and Oceania (Duggan et al. 2014). These studies were then replicated for paternally inherited Y chromosomes (Schurr and Sherry 2004; Hammer et al. 2001). Initial anthropological genetics studies have made use of these datasets to inquire about past migrations (Hammer et al. 2001) and social structure (Pérez-Lezaun et al. 1999; Chaix et al. 2007), constructing the theoretical and methodological foundations of modern archaeogenomics. Now, with access to entire genomes inherited from both our parents, the resolution of anthropological genomics studies has dramatically increased (Veeramah and Hammer 2014).

The mode of inheritance of our *autosomal* chromosomes allows us to surpass the limited scope of the mitochondrial and Y-chromosome data to glimpse at our history at the population level (Jobling et al. 2013). Briefly, our genome is packaged into 23 pairs of chromosomes—23 from our mothers and 23 from our fathers. When we produce a gamete, a random chromosome from each pair is passed on to create the sperm or the egg. Occasionally maternal and paternal chromosomes can exchange genetic materials. This event, called recombination, results in a hybrid chromosome passed on to the gamete. Thus, the next generation's genome is comprised of both the maternal and paternal assortment of chromosomes with an occasional shuffled paternal segment on a maternal chromosome, or vice versa. Over generations, the random sorting of chromosomes and their occasional shuffling result in a quilt-tile pattern, with thousands of different segments in our genomes that can individually be traced back to different ancestors. They represent the genetic heritage from thousands of ancestors, which now is accessible to researchers thanks to genome sequencing and computational advancements.

For example, when I compare my genome to my cousin's, I can identify thousands of segments that I share with him only two generations back. These are the segments that we inherited from our grandparents. However, I also share many segments with him not because we are close relatives, but because we both have West Eurasian ancestors. Thus, we share other segments that we inherited from ancestors that were probably among the first migrants out of Africa. Going back in time, we all share genetic segments that we inherited from ancestors that roamed Africa hundreds of thousands of years ago. We even can identify segments that my cousin and I share that we inherited from a Neanderthal ancestor that lived somewhere in Eurasia some 30–40,000 years ago. Thus, just comparing my genome to my cousin's, I can find clues into my immediate family, migrations outside of Africa, the recent history of western Eurasia, and even interactions between our species and archaic humans. Overall, it is now possible to reconstruct population histories of human groups with unprecedented resolution (Nielsen et al. 2017).

A second revolution in studying ancient peoples and migrations is facilitated by the methodological advances that allow us to sequence genomes from ancient remains (Skoglund and Mathieson 2018). It gave us a candid look at ancient populations and revealed ancestral connections between present-day peoples and ancient populations. However, it is only in the last five years that ancient genomes have become relatively routine and affordable, due to two interrelated challenges with studying ancient genomes that had been prohibitive before (Handt et al. 1994). First, it is challenging to extract and sequence DNA from ancient remains due to its degradation and paucity. Second, contamination in the archaeological context complicates the analysis of the "original" DNA. The cost of genomic sequencing has dropped approximately 100,000 times in the last decade (Wetterstrand 2013). In parallel, clever new experimental methodologies were developed to better extract genomes from ancient remains (Gansauge and Meyer 2014; Kemp and Smith 2005). These allowed researchers to enrich ancient DNA in a given sample and later bioinformatically clean the resulting data to construct the genome from remains that are tens of thousands of years old (Skoglund et al. 2014; Green et al. 2006). These developments in the field make ancient genomics a relatively routine undertaking and provide us direct insight into the genomic variation of archaeological populations (Skoglund and Mathieson 2018).

The advent of these powerful genomic technologies now allows us to more realistically assess thousands of ancestors' contributions to contemporary genetic variation while providing a direct investigation of ancient populations. Instead of taking a snapshot of our genetic variation with a fixed-focus lens, as we did with initial studies of mitochondrial DNA, we can adjust our focus to answer direct questions involving specific times and specific geographies.

Culture-Historical Archaeology Is Dead; Long Live Culture-Historical Archaeogenomics

The early twentieth century, an era of colonial powers and geographical exploration, witnessed the rise of culture-historical archaeology (Trigger 1989; see Kristiansen, this volume; Daniels, this volume). Ancient material cultures were imagined to represent ethnically homogeneous peoples. Moreover, these imagined homogenous peoples, represented through archeological remains, were linked to present-day populations, often with nationalist and racist undertones (Arnold 1990). Arguably, the most striking examples of this view were presented by Gustaf Kossinna (Arvidsson 2006). He was inspired by both emerging views about Kulturkreis (the idea that cultural centers emerged and shaped human variation across geographies), and racialism (the idea that there are distinct races of peoples with different, inherent qualities). Integrating these ideas into a simplistic but politically powerful narrative, he argued for the existence of a "Germanic" material culture that was inherently linked to an imagined Nordic race. In his view, the cultures and ethnicities were monolithic entities tied to certain geographical locales.

In the broader context of the culture-historical framework, specific material culture markers are strongly tied to ethnic groups, where particular shapes, pottery practices, or symbols left in the archaeological record come to signify a particular, monolithic culture linked to a monolithic ethnic group. In Western academia, culture-historical archaeology has largely been replaced by approaches that focus on scientifically delineating cultural and demographic processes (Binford 1962).

Genomics is about biological diversity. Therefore, analyzing biological diversity in an archaeological context revives the central question asked by culture-historical archaeology: *Do genes correlate with cultures?* This is a complicated issue and has recently been scrutinized from different perspectives (Heyd 2017). At its best, archaeogenomics give unexpected and complicated answers about the relationship between genes and cultures. In some cases, they sever the accepted links between ethnicities and material cultures. In other cases, they reveal connections between peoples and cultural complexes thought to be completely isolated from each other. At its worst, archaeogenomics, almost always without intent, resurrects the white supremacist narratives in popular narratives, especially across social media (Frieman and Hofmann 2019).

Studies investigating the relationship between material culture and genomic variation of European late-Neolithic/Bronze Age peoples exemplify this conceptual leap (Allentoft et al. 2015; Jeong et al. 2018; Haak et al. 2015; Damgaard et al. 2018). Archaeologists define Early Bronze Age European material culture by two cultural components: the Corded Ware and Bell Beaker pottery cultural complexes (Price et al. 2004; Kolar 2017). Corded Ware culture was defined as early as the late nineteenth century and discussed within the context of Indo-European languages (Renfrew 1990). Genetic studies reconstructing genetic variation from graves associated with Corded Ware culture revealed that there is a genetic affinity with samples from the remains of the steppe-laden (today's Ukraine/Russia) Yamnaya burials (Haak et al. 2015). This observation later led to a new model of the peopling of present-day European populations based on genetic data where immigration of Yamnaya "peoples" into Europe plays an important part. In contrast to the rather clear link between genetic variation associated with the Yamnaya culture, genetic variation associated with Beaker Bell culture, which spread from the Western reaches of England and the Iberian peninsula into central Europe (Price et al. 2004), was remarkably diverse (Olalde et al. 2018). In other words, the genetic ancestors of peoples associated with Beaker culture had diverse origins predating the spread of specific traditions that define the Beaker culture complex itself. This observation indicates that cultural transmission, rather than the coupling of genes and material culture, explains the expansion of Beaker culture in Europe.

Geographically, a more focused look at Britain paints a different picture than what is observed in the rest of Europe. Britain, a relatively isolated geography in the European context, provides an interesting archaeological framework. In this geography, the transition from Beaker culture marks a clear transition from earlier Neolithic archaeological cultures to the Bronze Age. Moreover, the genetic variation from Neolithic and Bronze Age Britain is found to be clearly distinct (Olalde et al. 2018). This shows that people with different ancestries brought their genes *and* Beaker pottery to Britain, largely replacing the Neolithic inhabitants of the Isles.

In sum, the links between genes and culture are complicated and depend on context. For example, as a whole, Beaker culture cannot be linked to a single genetic component. It was practiced by diverse groups of people across Europe. However, it is also clear that migration of people has an impact on cultural transmission. The human movement brought new genes and Beaker culture to Britain, marking the transition to the Bronze Age in this geography, and largely replacing the genetic diversity. It is important to note here that archaeogenomics studies, perhaps because of their empirical sophistication, can sometimes be treated as definitive answers to major anthropological questions, such as the origins of Indo-European languages or the mode of cultural transitions. However, they would not give adequate answers without proper anthropological and archaeological context (see Cameron, this volume; Barnard, this volume). I argue that genetic research provides new ways to look at fundamental anthropological questions. By doing so, rather than giving definitive answers, it reveals the underappreciated complexity of human movement and its impact on material culture.

Complicating the Process

Thanks to archaeogenomics, we have now a robust view of the multiple events that shaped the Neolithic genetic variation of Anatolia. It provides a clear example of how archaeogenetics sometimes clarifies but more often complicates archaeological questions about culture change, demographic change, and migration. The transitions to sedentary, agricultural lifestyles are among the most important events in human history (Bellwood et al. 2007). They are marked by dramatic increases in population size, shifts in how humans interact with nature, massive changes in life histories, and increases in the complexity of arts and technologies (Bocquet-Appel and Bar-Yosef 2008; Ammerman and Cavalli-Sforza 2014). Collectively, they set the stage for complex societies (Hodder 2010). Anatolia, connecting the fertile crescent to the Aegean, and home to some of the oldest settlements known, is a geographical center in the study of Neolithic transition (Skourtanioti et al. 2020). Indeed, several ancient genomes published involving samples from Neolithic Anatolia have complicated three long-accepted notions, providing novel insights into the transition to agriculture in Western Asia.

First, it was found that early agriculturalists from the Levant, Zagros, and Anatolia were as genetically distinct as present-day Western Europeans and Western Asian populations are from each other (Lazaridis et al. 2016). This contrasts with the more simplistic hypothesis that agricultural lifestyle emerged from a single origin, possibly from a single Middle Eastern group in Mesopotamia, spreading rapidly to neighboring regions (Ammerman and Cavalli-Sforza 2014). Ancient genomics allowed us to ask more specific questions: *Did the transition to agriculture in these three groups happen completely independently? How were the ideas and technologies that define the Western Asian early agricultural lifestyle disseminated between these peoples? What cultural, demographic, and ecological forces prevented interactions between these groups, allowing genetic differentiation to accumulate and be maintained?*

Second, ancient genomics data demonstrated that genetic variation in earlier agricultural settlements of Anatolia (especially in Boncuklu Hoyuk) was relatively low and arguably even lower than that of contemporaneous foraging groups in Europe (Kılınç et al. 2016). This complicates a more simplistic understanding of agricultural transition in places where it happened nearly instantaneously, resulting in a major population boom (Bocquet-Appel 2011). Instead, genomic data points to more subtle and gradual transitions that lasted millennia, where foragers "experimented" with agriculture prior to establishing full-fledged agricultural societies emblematic of late Anatolian Neolithic, such as Çatalhöyük. This leads to further questions: *How long did this transition last? What were the first crops and animals to be domesticated? Especially in the light of striking discoveries at Göbekli Tepe, what was the initial driving force for more sedentary lifestyles leading to experimentation with local crops?*

Third, ancient genomics research revealed that the Western Asian Neolithic was a dynamic period. What started as relatively isolated, small forager populations experimenting with a sedentary agricultural lifestyle transformed over time to larger and genetically more diverse groups (Kılınç et al. 2016). These regional Western groups interacted with other settlements, sharing both materials and genes. This led to, for example, a significant increase in genetic variation observed in later Anatolian farmers as compared to that observed from earlier farming groups from the same settlements. The Anatolian farmers eventually migrated to Europe, bringing their genes and material culture with them, and largely replacing the hunter-gatherer inhabitants of the continent (Omrak et al. 2016; Hofmanová et al. 2016; Mathieson et al. 2018; Lazaridis et al. 2016). In a matter of a few years, our understanding of Neolithization was immensely expanded, progressing from simplistic, overarching themes to complex, multidimensional histories involving cultural innovation, demographic shifts, local social interactions, and long-range migrations. The most valuable insights come when researchers analyze genomic data within an archaeological context.

Severing the Ties from Past and Present: The Case of Anatolia

Ancient genomics was heralded as a means to find the connections between present-day peoples and ancient societies. Instead, it mostly severed the long-held beliefs about the relationships between past and present peoples, leading to public discussions of how the genetics of a people can be tied to a cultural group, a nation, or an archaeological culture (Reardon 2009). The genetic studies, both ancient and modern, of the populations residing in present-day Turkey have disrupted the national discussions of identity (Burton 2018). It is, thus, curious that archaeogenetics, which often deals with pre-Byzantian times, is celebrated by Turkish bureaucracy and the political intelligentsia. At the same time, the genetics of extant populations remain constrained due to mainly political considerations.

From the rich Neolithic cultures of its central plains to the ancient Greek cities of its coast, Anatolia has always been a central geographical home to myriad diverse peoples and cultures (Mitchell 1993; Norwich 1998; Inalcik 2013; Mellaart 1967). Historically, it is clearly documented that Anatolia has been inhabited by peoples that identify themselves distinctly from both their predecessors and contemporaries (Karpat 1985; Mango 2002). Even after the devastating events coinciding with World War I tore the peoples of Anatolia further to pieces, several Sunni and Alevi groups, Armenians, different clans of Kurds, Caucasians, Pontic, and Greek Orthodox Christians, among other smaller groups, remained in Turkey. These groups often identify with certain locales in Anatolia, have distinct cultural traditions, and often claim ancestry with specific past peoples (Gokcumen et al. 2011). This diversity contrasted (and still does) with the politics of the Turkish Republic, where "Turkishness," vaguely defined, is the bedrock of national identity (Kadioğlu 1996).

Over the last century, the academic elite of the Young Republic, especially in History, Anthropology, and Archaeology departments, promoted the notion that Anatolian populations were largely replaced by Turkic speaking nomads at the beginning of the second millennium A.D. (Toprak 2012), often symbolically marked by the Battle of Manzikert (A.D. 1071). In this scenario, the majority of Turkish citizens would trace back their ancestors to a central Asian "homeland." An interesting offshoot of this idea is the Sun-Language thesis, which put forward the idea that Turkic-speaking groups of central Asia were connected to earlier Western Asian Empires, specifically to the Hatti and Hittite peoples (Aytürk 2004). This implies that Anatolia is an original homeland for Turkic-speaking peoples and that the migration of Turkic nomads into Anatolia at the beginning of the first millennium A.D. is not an invasion, but a reclamation.

This academic narrative, coupled with ongoing political strife, makes a healthy discussion of Anatolia's present-day variation difficult. It is unsurprising that present-day genetic variation in Anatolia is virtually indistinguishable from the neighboring geographies, namely, the Middle East, Greece, Caucasus, etc. (Alkan et al. 2014). It is also unsurprising that there are likely signatures of recent population movements. These include the small, but clearly visible part of the genetic variation shared with present-day Central Asian and Turkic-speaking groups, likely a signature of the westward expansion of these groups in the last thousand years. I would argue that the careful dissection of genetic structure in Turkey would also uncover several social links, migrations, and local population movements that are currently hidden. Indeed, my own work shows patrilineal structuring of genetic variation at the village level, independent of cultural, ethnic, or religious affiliations (Gokcumen et al. 2011). Thus, the population of present-day Turkey is not a genetically homogenous entity, but a quilt that has emerged from myriad emigrations and immigrations, population collapses and expansions, cultural shifts, and regional interactions. I would argue that such genetic heterogeneity is not unique to the population of Turkey, but to the populations of virtually all nation-states. A more subtle, anthropologically contextualized understanding of human genetic variation is warranted to properly link archaeogenetics with present-day genetic variation. What is different in the case of Turkey is a stiff opposition to acknowledging the complex history of the land, stifling any major genomics project concerning the extant peoples living in Turkey.

Burton's careful historical dissection of Turkey's genetics studies (Burton 2018) provides a glimpse into the complex cultural and political dynamics that complicates genetics research in this part of the world. The potential participants in genomics research often mistrust international scientists, bureaucrats, and academics who are wary of popular and political backlash, and the general political narrative often dismisses the presence of multiple histories that shape present-day Turkey. As a result, there is a relatively small number of genetic studies in Turkey, most of which focus on medical rather than historical questions. International collaboration, otherwise promoted, is hampered when it comes to human genetics. As a result, the genetic variation in contemporary Turkey is relatively unappreciated. The lack of representation of Turkey in global maps of genomic variation (e.g., in HapMap [International HapMap Consortium 2003] and 1000 Genomes Project [1000 Genomes Project Consortium 2012]) is particularly telling.

Ancient genomics research, in contrast, thrives in Turkey. The politically problematic questions raised when studying modern-day genomes do not apply when investigating genomes dating back to thousands of years ago. Thus, Turkish archaeologists and scientists have fostered several fruitful collaborations, leading to the training of a new generation of Turkish archaeogeneticists. As a result, we know more about the population movements that shape ancient Anatolian history, from the initial migrants from Africa to demographic changes during the Neolithic, to Bronze Age movements, than we know of the population movements of the last 1,000 years of today's Turkish population.

It so happens that the early farmers of Anatolia are more genetically similar to present-day Sardinians than they are to the present-day Turkish population (Lazaridis et al. 2016; Kılınç et al. 2016). If the modern genetic variation in Turkey is neither from medieval central Asia nor from Neolithic Anatolia, it begs the question of where it did come from. Unfortunately, studying this question remains difficult in practice for several reasons. First, there is a miscommunication about how genetic variation data are understood and interpreted, given that these interpretation frameworks were designed mainly via North American and West European academic traditions (Gokcumen 2018). Due to this miscommunication and political and ideological concerns, the Turkish government and academic institutions are reluctant to commit to supporting large genetic variation studies or to participate in global consortia. The genetic databases, even those designed for solely clinical purposes, remain scattered and inaccessible. As a consequence, key questions concerning present-day genetic variation and its link to the past remain understudied. We do not know if there is genetic structuring across Anatolian geography. We can neither reliably date nor investigate the linguistic, cultural, and demographic changes that undoubtedly happened across Anatolia's recent history. We cannot test the hypothesis that at least some present-day self-identified ethnic groups might have ancestral connections to archaeological remains. However, thanks to archaeogenomics, we now know that the histories of the peoples of

Anatolia who live in modern-day Turkey are even more complicated than we thought and that they remain to be written.

Conclusion

Genomics has never been more relevant to address archaeological questions. It provides powerful empirical insights into ancestral connections between settlements and cultural complexes. In this piece, I argue that genomics complicates, rather than resolves, long-disputed questions in archaeology, opening novel avenues of research. It revives a new culture-historical perspective, challenging the processual interpretation of archaeological data, and calls the previously established links between present-day peoples with ancient remains from the same geography into question. I am hopeful that these new discussions will lead the field to move into a more sophisticated and integrative understanding of the past.

Acknowledgments

I like to thank Ozgur Taskent and Izzy Starr for their insightful suggestions.

References Cited

1000 Genomes Project Consortium 2012 An Integrated Map of Genetic Variation from 1,092 Human Genomes. *Nature* 491(7422):56–65.

Alkan, C., P. Kavak, M. Somel, O. Gokcumen, S. Ugurlu, C. Saygi, E. Dal, K. Bugra, T. Güngör, S. Cenk Sahinalp, N. Özören, and C. Bekpen 2014 Whole Genome Sequencing of Turkish Genomes Reveals Functional Private Alleles and Impact of Genetic Interactions with Europe, Asia and Africa. *BMC Genomics* 15(1):963.

Allentoft, M. E., M. Sikora, K.-G. Sjögren, S. Rasmussen, M. Rasmussen, J. Stenderup, P. B. Damgaard, H. Schroeder, T. Ahlström, L. Vinner, A.-S. Malaspinas, A. Margaryan, T. Higham, D. Chivall, N. Lynnerup, L. Harvig, J. Baron, P. Della Casa, P. Dąbrowski, P. R. Duffy, A. V. Ebel, A. Epimakhov, K. Frei, M. Furmanek, T. Gralak, A. Gromov, S. Gronkiewicz, G. Grupe, T. Hajdu, R. Jarysz, V. Khartanovich, A. Khokhlov, V. Kiss, J. Kolář, A. Kriiska, I. Lasak, C. Longhi, G. McGlynn, A. Merkevicius, I. Merkyte, M. Metspalu, R. Mkrtchyan, V. Moiseyev, L. Paja, G. Pálfi, D. Pokutta, Ł. Pospieszny, T. D. Price, L. Saag, M. Sablin, N. Shishlina, V. Smrčka, V. I. Soenov, V. Szeverényi, G. Tóth, S. V. Trifanova, L. Varul, M. Vicze, L. Yepiskoposyan, V. Zhitenev, L. Orlando, T. Sicheritz-Pontén, S. Brunak, R. Nielsen, K. Kristiansen, and E. Willerslev 2015 Population Genomics of Bronze Age Eurasia. *Nature* 522:167–172. DOI:10.1038/nature14507.

Ammerman, A. J., and L. Luca Cavalli-Sforza 2014 *The Neolithic Transition and the Genetics of Populations in Europe*. Princeton University Press, Princeton.

Arnold, B. 1990 The Past as Propaganda: Totalitarian Archaeology in Nazi Germany. *Antiquity* 64(244):464–478.

Arvidsson, S. 2006 *Aryan Idols: Indo-European Mythology as Ideology and Science*. University of Chicago Press, Chicago.

Aytürk, İ. 2004 Turkish Linguists against the West: The Origins of Linguistic Nationalism in Atatürk's Turkey. *Middle Eastern Studies* 40(6):1–25.

Bellwood, P., C. Gamble, S. A. Le Blanc, M. Pluciennik, M. Richards, and J. E. Terrell 2007 First Farmers: The Origins of Agricultural Societies, by Peter Bellwood. Malden, Mass.: Blackwell, 2005 *Cambridge Archaeological Journal* 17(01):87–109.

Binford, L. R. 1962 Archaeology as Anthropology. *American Antiquity* 28(2):217–225.

Bocquet-Appel, J.-P. 2011 When the World's Population Took off: The Springboard of the Neolithic Demographic Transition. *Science* 333(6042):560–561.

Bocquet-Appel, J.-P., and O. Bar-Yosef 2008 *The Neolithic Demographic Transition and Its Consequences*. Springer Science and Business Media, Berlin.

Burton, E. K. 2018 Narrating Ethnicity and Diversity in Middle Eastern National Genome Projects. *Social Studies of Science* 48(5):762–786.

Cann, R. L., M. Stoneking, and A. C. Wilson 1987 "Mitochondrial DNA and Human Evolution. *Nature* 325(6099):31–36.

Chaix, R., L. Quintana-Murci, T. Hegay, M. F. Hammer, Z. Mobasher, F. Austerlitz, and E. Heyer 2007 From Social to Genetic Structures in Central Asia. *Current Biology: CB* 17(1):43–48.

Damgaard, P. de Barros, N. Marchi, S. Rasmussen, M. Peyrot, G. Renaud, T. Korneliussen, J. V. Moreno-Mayar, M. W. Pedersen, A. Goldberg, E. Usmanova, N. Baimukhanov, V. Loman, L. Hedeager, A. G. Pedersen, K. Nielsen, G. Afanasiev, K. Akmatov, A. Aldashev, A. Alpaslan, G. Baimbetov, Vladimir I. Bazaliiskii, A. Beisenov, B. Boldbaatar, B. Boldgiv, C. Dorzhu, S. Ellingvag, D. Erdenebaatar, R. Dajani, E. Dmitriev, V. Evdokimov, K. M. Frei, A. Gromov, A. Goryachev, H. Hakonarson, T. Hegay, Z. Khachatryan, R. Khaskhanov, E. Kitov, A. Kolbina, T. Kubatbek, A. Kukushkin, I. Kukushkin, N. Lau, A. Margaryan, I. Merkyte, I. V. Mertz, V. K. Mertz, E. Mijiddorj, V. Moiyesev, G. Mukhtarova, B. Nurmukhanbetov, Z. Orozbekova, I. Panyushkina, K. Pieta, V. Smrčka, I. Shevnina, A. Logvin, K. G. Sjögren, T. Štolcová, K. Tashbaeva, A. Tkachev, T. Tulegenov, D. Voyakin, L. Yepiskoposyan, S. Undrakhbold, V. Varfolomeev, A. Weber, N. Kradin, M. E. Allentoft, L. Orlando, R. Nielsen, M. Sikora, E. Heyer, K. Kristiansen, and E. Willerslev 2018 137 Ancient Human Genomes from Across the Eurasian Steppes. *Nature* 557 (7705):369–374. DOI:10.1038/s41586-018-0094-2.

Duggan, A. T., B. Evans, F. R. Friedlaender, J. S. Friedlaender, G. Koki, D. A. Merriwether, M. Kayser, and M. Stoneking 2014 Maternal History of Oceania from Complete mtDNA Genomes: Contrasting Ancient Diversity with Recent Homogenization due to the Austronesian Expansion. *American Journal of Human Genetics* 94(5):721–733.

Frieman, C. J., and D. Hofmann 2019 Present Pasts in the Archaeology of Genetics, Identity, and Migration in Europe: A Critical Essay. *World Archaeology* 51(4):528–545.

Gansauge, M.-T., and M. Meyer 2014 Selective Enrichment of Damaged DNA Molecules for Ancient Genome Sequencing. *Genome Research* 24(9):1543–1549.

Gokcumen, Ö. 2018 The Year in Genetic Anthropology: New Lands, New Technologies, New Questions. *American Anthropologist* 120(2):266–277.

Gokcumen, Ö., T. Gultekin, Y. Dogan Alakoc, A. Tug, E. Gulec, and T. G. Schurr 2011 Biological Ancestries, Kinship Connections, and Projected Identities in Four Central Anatolian Settlements: Insights from Culturally Contextualized Genetic Anthropology. *American Anthropologist* 113(1):116–131.

Green, R. E., J. Krause, S. E. Ptak, A. W. Briggs, M. T. Ronan, J. F. Simons, L. Du, M. Egholm, J. M. Rothberg, M. Paunovic, and S. Pääbo 2006 Analysis of One Million Base Pairs of Neanderthal DNA. *Nature* 444(7117):330–336.

Haak, W., I. Lazaridis, N. Patterson, N. Rohland, S. Mallick, B. Llamas, G. Brandt, S. Nordenfelt, E. Harney, K Stewardson, Q. Fu, A. Mittnik, E. Bánffy, C. Economou, M. Francken, S. Friederich, R. Garrido Pena, F. Hallgren, V. Khartanovich, A. Khokhlov, M. Kunst, P. Kuznetsov, H. Meller, O. Mochalov, V. Moiseyev, N. Nicklisch, S. L. Pichler, R. Risch, M. A. Rojo Guerra, C. Roth, A. Szécsényi-Nagy, J. Wahl, M. Meyer, J. Krause, D. Brown, D. Anthony, A. Cooper, K. Werner Alt, and D. Reich 2015 Massive Migration from the Steppe Was a Source for Indo-European Languages in Europe. *Nature* 522(7555):207–211. DOI:10.1038/nature14317.

Hammer, M. F., T. M. Karafet, A. J. Redd, H. Jarjanazi, S. Santachiara-Benerecetti, H. Soodyall, and S. L. Zegura 2001 Hierarchical Patterns of Global Human Y-Chromosome Diversity. *Molecular Biology and Evolution* 18(7):1189–1203.

Handt, O., M. Höss, M. Krings, and S. Pääbo 1994 Ancient DNA: Methodological Challenges. *Experientia* 50(6):524–529.

Heyd, V. 2017 Kossinna's Smile. *Antiquity* 91(356):348–359.

Hodder, I. (editor) 2010 *Religion in the Emergence of Civilization: Çatalhöyük as a Case Study*. Cambridge University Press, Cambridge.

Hofmanová, Z., S. Kreutzer, G. Hellenthal, C. Sell, Y. Diekmann, D. Díez-Del-Molino, L. van Dorp, S. López, A. Kousathanas, V. Link, K. Kirsanow, L. M. Cassidy, R. Martiniano, M. Strobel, A. Scheu, K. Kotsakis, P. Halstead, S. Triantaphyllou, N. Kyparissi-Apostolika, D. Urem-Kotsou, C. Ziota, F. Adaktylou, S. Gopalan, D. M. Bobo, L. Winkelbach, J. Blöcher, M. Unterländer, C. Leuenberger, Ç. Çilingiroğlu, B. Horejs, F. Gerritsen, S. J. Shennan, D. G. Bradley, M. Currat, K. R. Veeramah, D. Wegmann, M. G. Thomas, C. Papageorgopoulou, and J. Burger 2016 Early Farmers from across Europe Directly Descended from Neolithic Aegeans. *Proceedings of the National Academy of Sciences of the United States of America* 113(25):6886–6891.

Inalcik, H. 2013 *The Ottoman Empire: 1300–1600*. Hachette, London.

International HapMap Consortium 2003 The International HapMap Project. *Nature* 426(6968):789–796.

Jeong, C., S. Wilkin, T. Amgalantugs, A. S. Bouwman, W. Timothy Treal Taylor, R. W. Hagan, S. Bromage, S. Tsolmon, C. Trachsel, J. Grossmann, J. Littleton, C. A. Makarewicz, J. Krigbaum, M. Burri, A. Scott, G. Davaasambuu, J. Wright, F. Irmer, E. Myagmar, N. Boivin, M. Robbeets, F. J. Rühli, J. Krause, B. Frohlich, J. Hendy, and C. Warinner 2018 Bronze Age Population Dynamics and the Rise of Dairy Pastoralism on the Eastern Eurasian Steppe. *Proceedings of the National Academy of Sciences of the United States of America*, November. DOI:10.1073/pnas.1813608115.

Jobling, M. A., M. E. Hurles, and C. Tyler-Smith 2013 *Human Evolutionary Genetics: Origins, Peoples, and Disease*. Garland Science, New York.

Kadioğlu, A. 1996 The Paradox of Turkish Nationalism and the Construction of Official Identity. *Middle Eastern Studies* 32(2):177–193.

Karpat, K. H. 1985 *Ottoman Population, 1830–1914: Demographic and Social Characteristics*. University of Wisconsin Press, Madison.

Kemp, B. M., and D. G. Smith 2005 Use of Bleach to Eliminate Contaminating DNA from the Surface of Bones and Teeth. *Forensic Science International* 154(1):53–61.

Kılınç, G. M., A. Omrak, F. Özer, T. Günther, A. Metin Büyükkarakaya, E. Bıçakçı, D. Baird, H. M. Dönertaş, A. Ghalichi, R. Yaka, D. Koptekin, S. Can Açan, P. Parvizi, M. Krzewińska, E. A. Daskalaki, E. Yüncü, N. D. Dağtaş, A. Fairbairn, J. Pearson, G. Mustafaoğlu, Y. S. Erdal, Y. G. Çakan, İ. Togan, M. Somel, J. Storå, M. Jakobsson, and A. Götherström 2016 The Demographic Development of the First Farmers in Anatolia. *Current Biology* 26(19):2659–2666.

Kolar, J. 2017 Review of Corded Ware Coastal Communities: Using Ceramic Analysis to Reconstruct Third Millennium BC Societies in the Netherlands by Sandra Mariët Beckerman. *European Journal of Archaeology* 20(4):759–763.

Lazaridis, I., D. Nadel, G. Rollefson, D. C. Merrett, N. Rohland, S. Mallick, D. Fernandes, D. Fernandes, M. Novak, B. Gamarra, K. Sirak, S. Connell, K. Stewardson, E. Harney, Q. Fu, G. Gonzalez-Fortes, E. R. Jones, S. A. Roodenberg, G. Lengyel, F. Bocquentin, B. Gasparian, J. M. Monge, M. Gregg, V. Eshed, A.-S. Mizrahi, C. Meiklejohn, F. Gerritsen, L. Bejenaru, M. Blüher, A. Campbell, G. Cavalleri, D. Comas, P. Froguel, E. Gilbert, S. M. Kerr, P. Kovacs, J. Krause, D. McGettigan, M. Merrigan, D. A. Merriwether, S. O'Reilly, M. B. Richards, O.Semino, M. Shamoon-Pour, G. Stefanescu, M. Stumvoll, A. Tönjes, A. Torroni, J. F. Wilson, L. Yengo, N. A. Hovhannisyan, N. Patterson, R. Pinhasi, and D. Reich 2016 Genomic Insights into the Origin of Farming in the Ancient Near East. *Nature* 536(7617):419–424.

Macaulay, V., C. Hill, A. Achilli, C. Rengo, D. Clarke, W. Meehan, J. Blackburn, O. Semino, R. Scozzari, F. Cruciani, A. Taha, N. K. Shaari, J. M. Raja, P. Ismail, Z. Zainuddin, W. Goodwin, D. Bulbeck, H.-J. Bandelt, S. Oppenheimer, A. Torroni, and M. Richards 2005 Single, Rapid Coastal Settlement of Asia Revealed by Analysis of Complete Mitochondrial Genomes. *Science* 308(5724):1034–1036.

Mango, C. 2002 *The Oxford History of Byzantium*. Oxford University Press, Oxford.

Mathieson, I., S. Alpaslan-Roodenberg, C. Posth, A. Szécsényi-Nagy, N. Rohland, S. Mallick, I. Olalde, N. Broomandkhoshbacht, F. Candilio, O. Cheronet, D. Fernandes, M. Ferry, B. Gamarra, G. González Fortes, W. Haak, E. Harney, E. Jones, D.Keating, B. Krause-Kyora, I. Kucukkalipci, M. Michel, A. Mittnik, K. Nägele, M. Novak, J. Oppenheimer, N. Patterson, S. Pfrengle, K. Sirak, K. Stewardson, S. Vai, S. Alexandrov, K. W. Alt, R. Andreescu, D. Antonović, A. Ash, N. Atanassova, K. Bacvarov, M. B. Gusztáv, H. Bocherens, M. Bolus, A. Boroneanţ, Y.Boyadzhiev, A. Budnik, J. Burmaz, S. Chohadzhiev, N. J. Conard, R. Cottiaux, M. Čuka, C. Cupillard, D. G. Drucker, N. Elenski, M. Francken, B. Galabova, G. Ganetsovski, B. Gély, Tamás Hajdu, V. Handzhyiska, K. Harvati, T. Higham, S. Iliev, I. Janković, I. Karavanić, D. J. Kennett, D. Komšo, A. Kozak, D. Labuda, M. Lari, C. Lazar, M. Leppek, K. Leshtakov, D. Lo Vetro, D. Los, I. Lozanov, M. Malina, F. Martini, K. McSweeney, H. Meller, M. Menđušić, P. Mirea, V. Moiseyev, V. Petrova, T. D. Price, A. Simalcsik, L. Sineo, M. Šlaus, V. Slavchev, P. Stanev, A. Starović, T. Szeniczey, S. Talamo, M. Teschler-Nicola, C. Thevenet, I. Valchev, F. Valentin, S. Vasilyev, F. Veljanovska, S. Venelinova, E. Veselovskaya, B. Viola, C. Virag, J. Zaninović, S. Zäuner, P. W. Stockhammer, G. Catalano, R. Krauß, D. Caramelli, G. Zariņa, B. Gaydarska, M. Lillie, A. G. Nikitin, I. Potekhina, A. Papathanasiou, D. Borić, C. Bonsall, J. Krause, R. Pinhasi, and

D. Reich 2018 The Genomic History of Southeastern Europe. *Nature* 555(7695):197–203. DOI:10.1038/nature25778.

Mellaart, J. 1967 *Çatal Hüyük: A Neolithic Town in Anatolia*. McGraw-Hill, New York.

Mitchell, S. 1993 *Anatolia: Land, Men, and Gods in Asia Minor*. Clarendon Press, Oxford.

Nielsen, R., J. M. Akey, M. Jakobsson, J. K. Pritchard, S. Tishkoff, and E. Willerslev 2017 Tracing the Peopling of the World through Genomics. *Nature* 541(7637):302–310.

Norwich, J. J. 1998 *A Short History of Byzantium*. Penguin, London.

Olalde, I., S. Brace, M. E. Allentoft, I. Armit, K. Kristiansen, T. Booth, N. Rohland, S. Mallick, A. Szécsényi-Nagy, A. Mittnik, E. Altena, M. Lipson, I. Lazaridis, T. K. Harper, N. Patterson, N. Broomandkhoshbacht, Y. Diekmann, Z. Faltyskova, D.Fernandes, M. Ferry, E. Harney, P. de Knijff, M. Michel, J. Oppenheimer, K. Stewardson, A. Barclay, K. W. Alt, C. Liesau, P. Ríos, C. Blasco, J. V. Miguel, R. M. García, A. A. Fernández, E. Bánffy, M. Bernabò-Brea, D. Billoin, C. Bonsall, L. Bonsall, T. Allen, L. Büster, S. Carver, L. C. Navarro, O. E. Craig, G. T. Cook, B. Cunliffe, A. Denaire, K. E. Dinwiddy, N. Dodwell, M. Ernée, C. Evans, M. Kuchařík, J. F. Farré, C. Fowler, M. Gazenbeek, R. G. Pena, M. Haber-Uriarte, E. Haduch, G. Hey, N. Jowett, T. Knowles, K. Massy, S. Pfrengle, P. Lefranc, O. Lemercier, A. Lefebvre, C. Heras Martínez, V. G. Olmo, A. B. Ramírez, J. L. Maurandi, T. Majó, J. I. McKinley, K. McSweeney, B. G. Mende, A. Modi, G. Kulcsár, V. Kiss, A. Czene, R. Patay, A. Endrődi, K. Köhler, T. Hajdu, T. Szeniczey, J. Dani, Z. Bernert, M. Hoole, O. Cheronet, D. Keating, P. Velemínský, M. Dobeš, F. Candilio, F. Brown, R. F. Fernández, A.-M. Herrero-Corral, S. Tusa, E. Carnieri, L. Lentini, A. Valenti, A. Zanini, C. Waddington, G. Delibes, E. Guerra-Doce, B. Neil, M. Brittain, M. Luke, R. Mortimer, J. Desideri, M. Besse, G. Brücken, M. Furmanek, A. Hałuszko, M. Mackiewicz, A. Rapiński, S. Leach, I. Soriano, K. T. Lillios, J. L. Cardoso, M. P. Pearson, P. Włodarczak, T. D. Price, P. Prieto, P.-J. Rey, R. Risch, M. A. Rojo Guerra, A. Schmitt, J. Serralongue, A. M. Silva, V. Smrčka, L. Vergnaud, J. Zilhão, D. Caramelli, T. Higham, M. G. Thomas, D. J. Kennett, H. Fokkens, V. Heyd, A. Sheridan, K.-G. Sjögren, P. W. Stockhammer, J. Krause, R. Pinhasi, W. Haak, I. Barnes, C. Lalueza-Fox, and D. Reich 2018 The Beaker Phenomenon and the Genomic Transformation of Northwest Europe. *Nature* 555(7695):190–196. DOI:10.1038/nature25738.

Omrak, A., Torsten G., Cristina V., E. M. Svensson, H. Malmström, H. Kiesewetter, W. Aylward, J. Storå, M. Jakobsson, and A. Götherström 2016 Genomic Evidence Establishes Anatolia as the Source of the European Neolithic Gene Pool. *Current Biology: CB* 26(2):270–275.

Pérez-Lezaun, A., F. Calafell, D. Comas, E. Mateu, E. Bosch, R. Martínez-Arias, J. Clarimón, G. Fiori, D. Luiselli, F. Facchini, D. Pettener, and J. Bertranpetit 1999 Sex-Specific Migration Patterns in Central Asian Populations, Revealed by Analysis of Y-Chromosome Short Tandem Repeats and mtDNA. *American Journal of Human Genetics* 65(1):208–219.

Price, T. D., C. Knipper, G. Grupe, and V. Smrcka. 2004 Strontium Isotopes and Prehistoric Human Migration: The Bell Beaker Period in Central Europe. *European Journal of Archaeology* 7(1):9–40.

Reardon, J. 2009 *Race to the Finish: Identity and Governance in an Age of Genomics*. Princeton University Press, Princeton.

Renfrew, C. 1990 *Archaeology and Language: The Puzzle of Indo-European Origins*. Cambridge University Press, Cambridge.

Richards, M., V. Macaulay, E. Hickey, E. Vega, B. Sykes, V. Guida, C. Rengo, D. Sellitto, F. Cruciani, T. Kivisild, R. Villems, M. Thomas, S. Rychkov, O. Rychkov, Y. Rychkov, M. Gölge, D. Dimitrov, E. Hill, D. Bradley, V. Romano, F. Cali, G. Vona, A. Demaine, S. Papiha, C. Triantaphyllidis, G. Stefanescu, J. Hatina, M. Belledi, A. Di Rienzo, A. Oppenheim, S. Nørby, N. Al-Zaheri, S. Santachiara-Benerecetti, R. Scozzari, A. Torroni, and H.-J. Bandelt 2000 Tracing European Founder Lineages in the Near Eastern mtDNA Pool. *American Journal of Human Genetics* 67(5):1251–1276.

Schurr, T. G., and S. T. Sherry 2004 Mitochondrial DNA and Y Chromosome Diversity and the Peopling of the Americas: Evolutionary and Demographic Evidence. *American Journal of Human Biology: The Official Journal of the Human Biology Council* 16(4):420–439.

Skoglund, P., and I. Mathieson 2018 Ancient Genomics of Modern Humans: The First Decade. *Annual Review of Genomics and Human Genetics* 19(August):381–404.

Skoglund, P., B. H. Northoff, M. V. Shunkov, A. P. Derevianko, S. Pääbo, J. Krause, and M. Jakobsson 2014 Separating Endogenous Ancient DNA from Modern Day Contamination in a Siberian Neandertal. *Proceedings of the National Academy of Sciences of the United States of America* 111(6):2229–2234.

Skourtanioti, E., Y. S. Erdal, M. Frangipane, F. Balossi Restelli, K. Aslıhan Yener, F. Pinnock, P. Matthiae, R. Özbal, U.-D. Schoop, F. Guliyev, T. Akhundov, B. Lyonnet, E. L. Hammer, S. E. Nugent, M. Burri, G. U. Neumann, S. Penske, T. Ingman, M. Akar, R. Shafiq, G. Palumbi, S. Eisenmann, M. D'Andrea, A. B. Rohrlach, C. Warinner, C. Jeong, P. W. Stockhammer, W. Haak, and J. Krause 2020 Genomic History of Neolithic to Bronze Age Anatolia, Northern Levant, and Southern Caucasus. *Cell* 181(5):1158–75.e28.

Soares, P., F. Alshamali, J. B. Pereira, V. Fernandes, N. M. Silva, C. Afonso, M. D. Costa, E. Musilová, V. Macaulay, M. B. Richards, V. Černý, and L. Pereira 2012 The Expansion of mtDNA Haplogroup L3 within and out of Africa. *Molecular Biology and Evolution* 29(3):915–927.

Toprak, Z. 2012 Darwinizm'den Ateizm'e Türkiye'de Tarih Eğitiminin Evrimi. *Darwin'den Dersim'e Cumhuriyet ve Antropoloji.*

Torroni, A., T. G. Schurr, M. F. Cabell, M. D. Brown, J. V. Neel, M. Larsen, D. G. Smith, C. M. Vullo, and D. C. Wallace 1993 Asian Affinities and Continental Radiation of the Four Founding Native American mtDNAs. *American Journal of Human Genetics* 53(3):563–590.

Trigger, B. G. 1989 *A History of Archaeological Thought.* Cambridge University Press, Cambridge.

Veeramah, K. R., and M. F. Hammer 2014 The Impact of Whole-Genome Sequencing on the Reconstruction of Human Population History. *Nature Reviews. Genetics* 15(3):149–162.

Wetterstrand, K. A. 2013 DNA Sequencing Costs: Data from the NHGRI Genome Sequencing Program (GSP).

PART II

Migrations, Visible and Invisible:
Toward More Inclusive Histories

CHAPTER FIVE

New Data and Old Narratives

Migrants and the Conjoining of the Cultures and Economies of the Pre-Roman Western Mediterranean

Franco De Angelis

Abstract *The study of the ancient Mediterranean and Near East has witnessed an explosion of new data and approaches over the past generation. In some cases, old historical narratives have also changed to account for these new data and approaches, but in most cases old, outdated narratives continue. A case in point concerns the conjoining of the economies and cultures of the pre-Roman western Mediterranean between the ninth and third centuries B.C. Two competing narratives currently exist. The older, and still dominant, colonialist narrative sees this region as backward before the arrival of superior immigrants, most notably Greeks and Phoenicians. From these supposedly more advanced immigrants, Etruscans, Romans, and other preexisting peoples would have been able to take the best of the immigrants' technology, innovation, and ideas and build on them by a process known as leapfrogging. The other competing postcolonial narrative is more recent and argues for greater sophistication and cultural autonomy in the western Mediterranean prior to the arrival of any immigrants. This chapter tests these narratives against the latest evidence and theory, with the intention of providing a less polarized and more nuanced working narrative for understanding these crucial centuries before the rise of the Roman Empire.*

The study of the ancient Mediterranean and Near East has witnessed an explosion of new data and approaches over the past generation. In some cases, old historical narratives have also changed to account for these new data and approaches, but in most cases old, outdated narratives continue. A case in point concerns the conjoining of the economies and cultures of the eastern and western Mediterranean in pre-Roman times, especially in Italy, which later became the historical center of the Mediterranean. This chapter focuses critically on a narrative central to this historical encounter: that it was migrants from the eastern Mediterranean who transformed the western Mediterranean through a series of earth-shattering cultural and technological transfers. The discussion is divided into two parts. In the first part, I critically evaluate the two competing narratives that currently exist to explain this fascinating and important historical encounter. In the second part, I test to what degree these narratives stand up to the latest evidence and theory. The overall intention is to formulate a less polarized and more nuanced working narrative better attuned to understanding the conjoining of the cultures and economies of the eastern and western Mediterranean in the crucial centuries before the rise of the Roman Empire.

Polarized Narratives on the Role of Immigrants

Historians of the Roman Empire have traditionally shown little interest in the first half of Rome's millennium-long history as a subject in its own right (Terrenato 2010:515). They have preferred to investigate the fully formed empire itself to its origins—always an easier task. At best they might include a chapter on this first half of Roman history in textbook accounts as a sort of rite of passage without necessarily connecting these two historical periods (e.g., Boatwright, Gargola, Lenski, and Talbert 2011), although some signs of change are starting to emerge (Terpstra 2019). This habit only reinforces the problem. As a result, Roman historians end up bypassing the formative processes that made the Roman Empire possible, and especially the raging debates found in pre-Roman historical scholarship regarding the role immigrants from the eastern Mediterranean played in that story. These debates merit attention in their own right and can be classified as currently following one of two possible narrative structures.

The older, and still dominant, colonialist narrative maintains that the western Mediterranean was backward before superior immigrants, most notably Greeks and Phoenicians, started arriving in the late ninth century B.C. Since the late nineteenth century, modern scholars have drawn upon ideas of "*Ex Oriente Lux*" ("from the East, light") as ultimately the driving force in this interpretation (Wells 1989:67). Without this external spark, no internal and independent development could otherwise occur in the western Mediterranean. From these supposedly more advanced immigrants, other preexisting cultures, such as the Etruscans and Romans, would have been able to take the best of the immigrants' technology, innovation, and ideas and build on them without having to reinvent the wheel, so to speak. The East simply laid the basis for the pre-Roman western Mediterranean and its later historical success.

For the general viewpoint, we have the following quotation from the widely read work on the Etruscans by Friedhelm Prayon (2010:47):

> Phönikern und Griechen haben die Etrusker es zu verdanken, daß sie aus prähistorischer Bedeutungslosigkeit erwacht und in kurzer Zeit zum führenden Kulturvolk Mittelitaliens aufgestiegen sind. Der Hintergrund dieses kulturhistorisch für weite Teile Westeuropas entscheidenden Vorgangs war die Kolonisation des westlichen Mittelmeerraumes.[1]

Prayon is not in doubt of the role of the Phoenicians and Greeks in the making of Italy and the entire pre-Roman western Mediterranean with it. Putting the words "Phönikern und Griechen" in the dative case at the very start of his sentence only emphasizes that point even further. The *coup de grâce* is the description of Etruscan developments as irrelevant before outside contact. Two other quotations, both from the late distinguished Italian prehistorian Luigi Bernabò Brea, add more details to this general picture. In the first quotation, Bernabò Brea (1957:136), in his important synthesis of evidence translated into English for the widely read Thames & Hudson series, *Ancient Peoples and Places*, approaches the question of the development of the western Mediterranean in the context of discussing the collapse of the Bronze Age interregional networks:

> The peaceful relations and commercial exchanges which had existed between the various Mediterranean peoples were now broken off [in the mid-thirteenth century B.C.] almost entirely. A time of war and fear began, forcing the peoples to change their whole way of life, and profoundly altering the basis of their economy. A real Dark Age set in, only to be brought to an end five centuries later with the Greek colonization of Sicily and southern Italy.

In the second quotation, Bernabò Brea picks up the discussion regarding the reopening of the Mediterranean with the arrival of the Phoenicians and Greeks in discussing the important site of Pantalica in Sicily, and he specifies iron technology as one of the features brought for the first time from the eastern Mediterranean:

> A questo vasto complesso di apporti trasmarini, abbiamo ritenuto che debba essere ascritta anche l'introduzione, in Sicilia, dei primi oggetti di ferro, in un periodo in cui la fusione di questo metallo era ancora ignota nell'isola.'

These quotations represent the tip of their iceberg, so to speak, and many other similar quotations could be cited with the same result (another example is given below in the second section). It is important to note that this line of thinking is accompanied, whether directly stated or not, by cultural and economic processes such as "The Greek Miracle," "Hellenization," "Orientalizing," "Orientalization," "Phoenicianization," and so on that were created by it to account for the spread of these innovations. These are modern coinages that derive their inspiration from numerous ancient literary sources with their tropes as civilizing narratives. This is a large topic that has been well discussed in recent years (Vogt-Spira and Rommel 1999; Braund and Gill 2003; Dench 2005; Ridgway 2010; Whitmarsh 2010). It is enough to say here, in overview, that these ancient discourses, which are full of ideology, have shaped modern discussion of East-West relations. Unfortunately, the ancient literary sources were usually taken at face value when the modern disciplines of ancient history and archaeology were being formulated. The subject requires the careful disentangling of fact from fiction with an archaeology of knowledge. For our purposes, two points must be emphasized. The first is that Greeks, before and during the Roman Empire, Hellenized the origins of peoples, products, and technologies of all kinds. The second is that the Romans themselves discussed their relationship with Greece in terms of their own civilizing narrative, the most outstanding example being the famous lines from the poet Horace (*Epistles* II.1.156): "Graecia capta ferum victorem cepit et artis intulit agresti Latio."[3]

The effects of all these civilizing processes are deemed to have been far-reaching and to have had profound influence on the preexisting populations. Put another way, migrants from the eastern Mediterranean were put on a pedestal as the prime historical actors and agents, and the regions that they settled regarded as virgin terrains passively waiting to be developed. This colonially inspired line of thinking also makes Italy and the western Mediterranean a disciplinary footnote to Classical and Near Eastern studies. That means, therefore, that this scholarly viewpoint is not necessarily restricted to scholars working in German or Italian, as in the case of the two scholars quoted earlier, but instead, as we will see further later on in this chapter, it is a general approach to pre- and post-contact Italy and the western Mediterranean.

In the last two decades, a postcolonial view has challenged this narrative. This has come about through the growth and interpretation of archaeological data in the pre-Roman western Mediterranean (Bietti Sestieri 1997; Guidi 1998, 2008; Dietler and López-Ruiz 2009; Celestino and López-Ruiz 2016; Webster 2016). It argues for greater sophistication and cultural autonomy in the western Mediterranean prior to the arrival of any immigrants. Closer and more careful analyses of the data have been taken, as recently with, for example, wall painting (Naso 2010) or ship building (Höckmann 2001), instead of automatically attributing this or that development to eastern Mediterranean origins. This reappraisal includes a revolution in absolute chronology supported by the scientific dating techniques of radiocarbon and dendrochronology (Bartoloni and Delpino 2005; Nijboer 2005; Brandherm and Trachsel 2008). The result has led to the revision of many parts of the traditional chronological system originally built up before World War II around a small number of ancient literary passages, especially from Thucydides (Book VI). These literary passages were matched up with finds of Greek Geometric and Corinthian pottery found in the sites mentioned by these ancient authors, and then extended well beyond these contexts to all points of the compass where synchronisms for relative and absolute chronology were needed. This was the routine way in which absolute chronology was constructed before archaeological science became available. Nevertheless, the traditional chronological system has become outdated in several important respects, the western Mediterranean being one of them, and revisions to it might have been regarded as normal were it not for the historical repercussions that the revisions have generated. The overall result of these recent scholarly developments, assuming them to be essentially correct, is that the western Mediterranean has emerged as more culturally developed, with some important features, such as the arrival of iron technology and state formation, now shown to be earlier than previous thought. These developments were neither dependent on immigrant stimuli for their initial development, nor did they emerge out of any sort of "Dark Age."

Let me illustrate this other, newer narrative with the following quotation from two of its leading proponents, Corinna Riva and Nicholas Vella (2006:10):

> That the Dark Age is more a historiographical construct than a historical reality of a specific time period is a given amongst prehistorians of the central Mediterranean where a continuity of activity from the end of the Bronze Age is known from the archaeological

visibility of settlements, exploitation of metal sources, and trade links between east and west Mediterranean, particularly at Cyprus. It is surprising that such evidence from the central Mediterranean has hardly been used by scholars to engage with debates on the supposed darkness of the Aegean. Even now there is certain apprehension in making explicit cross-Mediterranean links that are, by contrast, presupposed for the first millennium BC.

This quotation outlines the main features of this line of thinking. The pre-Roman western Mediterranean is viewed as more culturally and economically developed than imagined in earlier scholarship. The western Mediterranean exchanged with the eastern Mediterranean, primarily through Cyprus, but it is Greece alone, on this viewpoint, that was in a downturn (labeled in this quotation a Dark Age following traditional scholarship) and less involved with the wider world of the Early Iron Age Mediterranean. In other words, the entire Mediterranean basin was not at the whim of Greece and its regional developments. What also underlies this position are two other recent scholarly developments, besides changes in absolute chronology. The first concerns questioning inherited concepts. Riva and Vella single out the "Dark Age" as one problematic concept, but their words belong to the introductory remarks of a volume that they co-edited that critically debated the validity of the concept of Orientalization. They and some of the contributors to their edited volume are not alone in thinking about the exaggerated role that Orientalization has played in discussions of the Mediterranean as a whole. The distinguished French archaeologist Roland Étienne also feels the same way in the two chapters he has recently written (2010:372; 2017:11–13). He has gone so far as to speak of the need to "de-orientalize" the ancient Mediterranean. Even if we do not wish to go to this drastic extent (cf. Carenti and Wilkes 2006, for example), the point is that the role of the East needs to be reevaluated, to remove the excesses of previous scholarship. In any case, it remains the case that the western Mediterranean, as a historical entity in its own right, is still either not all included in historical narratives or at best treated as an appendix of the Aegean Sea basin (Schulz 2008:13; Prag and Crawley Quinn 2013).

The main reason for these polarized historical narratives is that they are based on polarized methodologies (De Angelis 2016a). The older, and still dominant, colonialist narrative is inspired by ancient and modern ideas of *"Ex Oriente Lux."* It builds on ancient literary sources with their tropes as civilizing narratives. Its archaeological practices belong to the culture history paradigm and often treat the western Mediterranean as a footnote of Classical and Near Eastern studies, which originated in the colonial and imperial discourses of the nineteenth century. The other postcolonial view that argues for more sophistication in the pre-Roman western Mediterranean has much in common with processual archaeology, in that it employs mainly archaeological data, situating them in their ecological contexts and adopting scientific techniques to enhance their interpretation. It also usually rejects altogether the ancient literary sources as a part of a wider process of decolonizing scholarship. As noted by the editor in her introduction to this volume, the result has been a methodological "standoff."

This polarization of source types and interpretative frameworks needs to be bridged with interdisciplinary methods. Extending the approach taken in my research on ancient Sicily (De Angelis 2016b), where similar narrative polarizations previously existed, I aim to establish a proper analytical framework. I adopt a rigorous methodology involving the critical combination of ancient literary and material sources, awareness of the ancient and modern historiographies shaping them, and informed with comparative and theoretical perspectives. My methodology also establishes objective criteria to test both opposing viewpoints with our available evidence. This allows me to steer a careful course between over- and understating the roles of the eastern and western Mediterranean. This kind of methodology is essential to study the pre-Roman western Mediterranean between the ninth and third centuries B.C. For one of the cultural items transmitted from the eastern to western Mediterranean was alphabetic writing (see the various essays throughout Étienne and Esposito 2010). Although the uses of writing and literacy remained confined to narrow elite circles, we hear the voices of some cultures, most notably the Greeks, versus the silences of others, for which archaeology and etic commentaries form the core of our knowledge. Put another way, the study of the pre-Roman western Mediterranean has been affected, like so many other similar periods of history worldwide, by traditional disciplinary divisions between prehistoric, protohistoric, and historic studies and by their objects of study cast as essentialized cultures, often in opposition to one another. Bridging these divides with cross-cultural, interdisciplinary methods better captures the nature of this period and our evidence for it (De Angelis 2016a). Applying an anthropological perspective that seeks to be as neutral as possible in this highly debated encounter between ancient East and West is also required, because previous scholarship has tended, whether or not it acknowledges the fact, to self-identity with particular peoples and their source types.

Even with the application of all of the foregoing methodological and theoretical advances, Classical Mediterranean studies must be infused with further anthropology. These studies ought to be brought more in line with the groundbreaking work by anthropological archaeologists working on mobility and migrations (for starters, one can refer to the chapters by Kristian Kristiansen and David Anthony contained in this volume). Genetic and stable isotopic research has been scarcely developed for the pre-Roman western Mediterranean between the ninth and third centuries B.C., centuries which we well know were characterized by one of the most important episodes of mobility and migration in human history (the few studies that exist only whet the appetite for more: Matisoo-Smith et al. 2016, 2018; Tanasi et al. 2017). Considerably more data and analyses are needed before definitive answers to more sophisticated questions can be provided. We can be certain that these new data will impact current historical narratives just as they have for the study of prehistoric Europe. For the time being, we have to work with the data and arsenal of methods and theory available to us. My research moves the field in this new direction by taking the next logical step in reformulating current historical narratives that are in dire need of modification. I put these principles into practice in the next part of this chapter.

Testing the Backwardness Narrative and Proposing an Alternative

The obvious place to begin is by testing the longstanding backwardness narrative, which is still exerting its influence on most historical reconstructions. Thereafter, I put forward a less polarized and more nuanced working narrative better attuned to understanding the conjoining of the cultures and economies of the eastern and western Mediterranean between the ninth and third centuries B.C.

The civilizing narratives of the ancient and modern discourses, as already discussed, have provided the appropriate context for thinking about the pre-Roman western Mediterranean as backward before the arrival of Greek and other supposedly superior immigrants from the eastern Mediterranean. What made such ancient thinking about the pre-Roman western Mediterranean seem applicable in modern eyes was, arguably, the advent of the Industrial Revolution in the late eighteenth and nineteenth centuries, and the discussion that ensued from it of why some European regions industrialized and others fell behind economically. Peter Musgrave (1999: back cover) has succinctly summed up the problem in his thought-provoking book *The Early Modern European Economy*: "Until recently, study of the early modern economy in Europe has tended to have heroes and villains: the former being the progressive and 'modern' economies of the Netherlands and England, and the latter being doomed, backward and Catholic Italy and Spain." Therefore, at the same time that scholarship on the ancient western Mediterranean was developing, Italy and Spain were regarded as economically backward when compared to the Netherlands and England (for full discussion of this North-South European divide, see Dainotto 2007). This modern backwardness was directly applied without acknowledgment or much thought to pre-Roman Italy and the western Mediterranean as a feature of their economic history. This was not the first and only instance of this modern to ancient back-projection happening in ancient history (for another example, see De Angelis 2006). Italy's timelessness was interrupted only by two periods of "modernity" in the eyes of Europeans: the Roman Empire and the Renaissance. That Italy could not capitalize on the latter efflorescence in particular in an enduring way to produce its own Industrial Revolution invited intense internal, and especially, external scrutiny.

These negative framings predate the important research by Russian American economic historian Alexander Gerschenkron (1962) before and after World War II. There is a positive side to backwardness that Gerschenkron revealed in his discussions of the Industrial Revolution. He argued that late industrializers, such as Germany, Russia, and Italy, diverged in their development from early industrializers, like Britain. The so-called backward countries could skip several stages, which the former had to go through by adopting and adapting their advanced technology, to catch up with their predecessors, without necessarily having to reinvent the wheel or make the kind of investments that the early industrializers had had to. There were not just disadvantages to backwardness, as we might normally think, but also advantages in coming late to the game that could be transformed into rapid development, where latecomers could overtake the preceding leaders to become the new leaders through a process usually referred to as leapfrogging or, less commonly, the retarding lead (Burke 2005:147–148). To the best of my knowledge, only a small handful of scholars working on antiquity has ever picked up on this potentially powerful argument to explain the development of the Mediterranean (Morris 2010:34–36; Broodbank 2013:399–400, 467). Certainly, the concept has not been systematically applied and tested for the pre-Roman western Mediterranean between the ninth and third centuries B.C.

In order to test whether backwardness existed and led to leapfrogging, we must start with what Gerschenkron and others have singled out as the defining features of backwardness. It must be remembered that these discussions have generally occurred in the context of the Industrial Revolution, and that some of the features either did not exist at all in antiquity or to the same degree as later. The model suggests that the more backward the economy, the more likely it is that the following things will occur (Gerschenkron 1962:353–354):

- Special institutions, including banks or the state, will be necessary to properly channel physical and human capital to industries.

- There will be an emphasis on the production of producer goods rather than consumer goods.

- There will be an emphasis on capital-intensive production rather than labor-intensive production.

- There will be a great scale of production and enterprise.

- There will be a reliance on borrowed rather than local technologies.

- The role of the agricultural sector, as a market for new industries, will be small.

- There will be a reliance on productivity growth.

Our evidence, derived mainly from archaeology, does in fact allow us to say whether, for instance, there was greater reliance on borrowed rather than local technologies, whether there was greater emphasis on the production of producer versus consumer goods, and whether the role of the agricultural sector was smaller as a market for new industries.

Let us test the backwardness criteria against metallurgy, which is one of the features constantly singled out in both of the current historical narratives. For scholars who view the western Mediterranean as essentially backward before the arrival of Phoenician and Greek immigrants, metallurgy of every kind is usually thought to have been brought wholesale from the eastern to the western Mediterranean in the ninth century B.C. (besides one of the quotations from Bernabò Brea above, similar statements are made more recently by the distinguished Italian American Etruscologist Larissa Bonfante [2002:43]). Of the traditions of pre-Roman western Mediterranean metallurgy, that of Etruscan bronzes is a highly visible and well-investigated sphere of activity. So the question may be posed: Is it true that the Phoenicians and Greeks ultimately taught the Etruscans to make their famed crested helmet or so-called antenna swords, the two most common and widely distributed artefact types?

The views of the so-called Backwardness School contrast drastically with those of Anne Lehoërff (2007) in her book on central Italian bronze metallurgy from 1200 to 750 B.C. Lehoërff addresses a variety of issues in her big and important book, though the bulk of it is dedicated to an in-depth treatment of the technology of Etruscan metallurgy over these centuries. Her methodology involves a microscopic scientific analysis of a large set of bronze objects conducted in a laboratory setting, accompanied by close visual examination of these objects and close attention to their chronology and archaeological and historical contexts. In her conclusions, she begins by making the important point that temperate Europe was not tributary only to the Mediterranean for its history. Central and northern Europe were more advanced than usually imagined by Classical and Near Eastern scholars, and Italy and the western Mediterranean as a whole fit into a twofold picture as representing a kind of fulcrum throughout history for cultural contacts and relations between points East and West. It is difficult, Lehoërff continues, to accept the classic axis of directionality from the southeastern Mediterranean to northwestern Europe. In the crucial tenth to eighth centuries, close analysis of the evidence indicates that no innovation occurred, and that all the techniques needed for producing eighth-century objects, the century when East and West had become conjoined in a permanent way, were already previously known. This Etruscan expertise included a wide range of skilled specialists, such as mold and hammer workers; the internal division of labor was already quite articulated in all the necessary ways to produce that fine workmanship for which the Etruscans were known.

The arguments against Etruscan backwardness can also be extended to other sectors of the economy, in which the export of many agricultural and craft products may be documented or postulated, along with the import of high-quality consumer goods in large quantities (De Angelis forthcoming). The argument can be extended even further to the entire pre-Roman western Mediterranean (the focus of a book project under contract with Oxford University Press), where my working hypothesis is that the "From Backwardness to Leapfrogging" framework cannot explain the entire history of the pre-Roman western Mediterranean, simply because there is too much contrasting evidence and arguments for it to be entirely applicable. It may apply in some cases, such as Sicily (as I argue in De Angelis 2016b), but it cannot apply to the whole, as becomes visible when informed by the microregionalism that underlies the quotation from Riva and Vella discussed earlier (see more fully Horden and Purcell 2000). The concept of microregionalism applies well to the pre-Roman western Mediterranean. As we have seen, Etruria and Sardinia emerged as important microregions at the beginning of history for their sociopolitical complexity and interregional connections. Etruria and Sardinia were already highly developed when Greeks and Phoenicians encountered them; they were "prehistoric powerhouses," which stood out when compared to other parts of the western Mediterranean. About this, there can no longer be any doubt. The main problem, as discussed earlier, lies in the disciplinary divisions across the pre-Roman western Mediterranean that have hindered the necessary dialogue, along with their respective colonialist and postcolonialist viewpoints. Pre-Roman specialists have long sought to establish a dialogue with Classical and Near Eastern scholars, if only because their field is heavily overwritten by Classical and Near Eastern written sources. It is Classical and Near Eastern scholarship in general that still seems blissfully unaware of the direct relevance of pre-Roman studies, although that is gradually changing. Nowhere is this more evident and more glaring than in the practices of Roman historians discussed at the beginning of the first part of this chapter. Introspection is needed for the disciplines of Classical and Near Eastern scholarship. One of the ways that this could be done, for purposes most germane to this chapter, is for practitioners to stop viewing their disciplines and subject matter as idealized monolithic blocks. It is wrong to state that Greece and the Near East were uniformly developed and more advanced; they too had microregions (however defined) that were and were not as dynamic and complex as parts of the contemporary western Mediterranean (Liverani 2017). As we increasingly define the Mediterranean as microregional, it only follows that movement and interaction in the Mediterranean occurred not only in the traditional East to West manner, but also in a West to East manner and a North to South manner. It also follows that we should keep pace with viewing the ancient world as decentered and, consequently, polycentric. My research situates itself within *The Corrupting Sea* (Horden and Purcell 2000) scholarly paradigm emphasizing historical ecology, microregionalism, and connectivity, but it also updates the paradigm in light of the second-wave criticisms made of it (see introduction, this volume).

The Etruscans and Sardinians can no longer be contained within central Italy; there is simply too much evidence for them all over the ancient world for which their agency in distributing their material culture can also no longer be denied (Camporeale 2004; Webster 2016:221). Any arguments to the contrary must be grounded in tangible evidence; otherwise, we are reverting to the privileged special pleadings of earlier generations of scholarship. One can sense a very slow and, so far, small turning of the tide. Other scholars, besides Riva and Vella quoted earlier, have been bold enough to state as much outright; they include both Italian prehistorians, as is only to be expected, and Greek historians/archaeologists (for example, Bietti Sestieri, Cazzella, and Schnapp 2002:425–426; Osborne 2009:121). My comparative and theoretical reading suggests that we should be seeing human interactions not under the microscope, but as a system of overlapping regional trajectories that could be linked together by heightened levels of mobility and connectivity. This is the basic idea of the late Janet Abu-Lughod's (1989) classic book *Before European Hegemony: The World System A.D. 1250–1350*. She depicts the global, Old World situation in the century before the arrival of the so-called Black Death in Europe as a series of eight overlapping regional systems of various shapes and sizes that stretch from southeastern Asia to southern England in a kind of Venn Diagram framework (Abu-Lughod 1989:34 Figure 1). This cartographic rendering of the world system that Abu-Lughod has delineated provides us with food for thought. It allows us to imagine how regional systems developed and existed on their own in the ancient pre-Roman western Mediterranean in the first instance. Later, through the settlement of migrants from the eastern Mediterranean, this world could become polycentric and linked together to form a more integrated larger global whole. This is also the basic idea behind Horden and Purcell's (2000) groundbreaking work *The Corrupting Sea* with its emphasis on historical ecology, microregionalism, and connectivity. Our case study involving the pre-Roman western Mediterranean can help revise and refine their scholarly paradigm.

The Corrupting Sea has spurred on further research by others on applying theories of globalization to the ancient world. This includes the creation of two new coinages for its ancient equivalent: "Mediterraneanization" by Ian Morris (2003), speaking of Archaic Sicily, and "oikoumenisation" by Eivind Heldaas Seland (2008), speaking in the context of the Indian Ocean and its relations with the Roman Empire. Morris was among the first to spearhead the second-wave criticisms of *The Corrupting Sea*'s intellectual paradigm with which I am in full agreement. Morris underlines the human costs of connectedness and talks about winners and losers in terms not necessarily defined by ethnicity, illustrating his argument with a case study from Archaic Sicily. His ideas can certainly be extended to the entire western Mediterranean before the rise of the Roman Empire. We can begin by solving the problem of our polarized historical narratives involving the pre-Roman western Mediterranean outlined above by adopting cross-cultural interdisciplinary methods that do not self-identify with one side or the other and that think in terms of networks. We can also think more deeply about the pace of connectivity, which does not necessarily need to be "constant," as often currently imagined, and does not necessarily only belong to some chosen peoples (like the Phoenicians and Greeks) to the detriment of others (like the Etruscans and Sardinians). All sides, both local and immigrant groups (themselves no longer immigrant after a couple of generations and now also to be considered local, or perhaps "glocal" because they were diasporic cultures that joined their places of origin with the new settlements they established) played a role in the development of the pre-Roman western Mediterranean. No group, however, was particularly favored because it was local or because it had emigrated from the eastern Mediterranean. Instead, this appears to be another instance from history of how once-dominant cultures and economies, when conjoined with others in conditions of coexistence, collaboration, and competition, fall behind for various reasons and are replaced by hungrier, more focused and better institutionally organized ones, sometimes accompanied no doubt by serendipity. Who produced, sustained, and altered these long-term trajectories in the pre-Roman western Mediterranean changed over the course of time. No one, not even Rome, was predestined to come out on top.

Conclusions

It is important to get right the history of the pre-Roman western Mediterranean between the ninth and third centuries B.C., for two reasons. First, the Roman Empire was forged in this period, and so was Western civilization by extension. Second, the historical processes that occurred in these centuries supply more evidence and case studies that are relevant to understanding similar moments throughout time, including the present. Outlining what is potentially at stake should embolden us to take the cross-cultural and interdisciplinary risks needed to get right the history of these centuries. Here, I can only reiterate the pleas of Michel Gras (2000) for such work made more than two decades ago.

In this chapter, I have made a first attempt at doing so by looking closely at the two competing historical narratives and how far they match up with our available evidence. The pre-Roman western Mediterranean cannot any more be characterized with blanket descriptions of backwardness, nor can we swing the pendulum in the opposite direction and claim no role for Greeks, Phoenicians, and the eastern Mediterranean during these centuries. Instead, we need to argue and nuance our narratives with evidence and be prepared to see shifting historical agents and complexities. However, we have only touched the tip of the iceberg. The groundbreaking work by anthropological archaeologists working on mobility and migrations, some of it contained in this volume, has hardly made a dent on our subject. Genetic and stable isotopic research remains largely absent from what we well know was one of the most important episodes of mobility and migration in human history. The dynamic centuries of history addressed in this chapter await new research horizons.

Acknowledgments

I am grateful to Megan Daniels for the invitation to take part in the conference on which this volume is based and for her editorial comments on the original oral version of the text and its final written version. Megan is to be commended for organizing a most stimulating conference, during which I received considerable helpful feedback on my paper from various participants whom I also acknowledge here. I also would like to thank the three anonymous reviewers of my chapter who provided useful comments, which I have taken on board.

Notes

1. Translation of the German original: "It is the Phoenicians and Greeks that the Etruscans are to thank for awakening them out of their prehistoric irrelevance and for raising them to the leading people of central Italy. The reason for this decisive event, for large parts of Western Europe, was the colonization of the western Mediterranean."
2. Translation of the Italian original: "To this vast complex of overseas transferences, we have maintained that the introduction of the first iron objects in Sicily must be assigned, in a period in which the fusion of this metal was still unknown in the island."
3. Translation of the Latin original: "Captive Greece took her savage victor captive and brought the arts into rustic Latium."

References Cited

Abu-Lughod, J. 1989 *Before European Hegemony: The World System A.D. 1250–1350*. Oxford University Press, New York.

Bartoloni, G., and F. Delpino (editors) 2005 *Oriente e Occidente: metodi e discipline a confronto. Riflessioni sulla cronologia dell'età del ferro in Italia. Atti dell'incontro di studi, Roma, 30–31 ottobre 2003*. Fabrizio Serra, Pisa.

Bernabò Brea, L. 1957 *Sicily before the Greeks*. Thames and Hudson, London.

Bernabò Brea, L. 1990 *Pantalica: ricerche intorno all'anáktoron*. Centre Jean Bérard, Naples.

Bietti Sestieri, A. M. 1997 Italy in Europe in the Early Iron Age. *Proceedings of the Prehistoric Society* 63:371–402.

Bietti Sestieri, A. M., A. Cazzella, and A. Schnapp. 2002 The Mediterranean. In *Archeology: The Widening Debate*, edited by B. Cunliffe, W. Davies and C. Renfrew, 411–438. Oxford University Press, Oxford.

Boatwright, M. T., D. J. Gargola, N. Lenski, and R. J. A. Talbert. 2011 *The Romans: From Village to Empire*. 2nd Ed. Oxford University Press, New York.

Bonfante, L. 2002 The Greeks in Etruria. In *The Greeks beyond the Aegean: From Marseilles to Bactria. Papers Presented at an International Symposium Held at the Onassis Cultural Center, New York, 12th October, 2002*, edited by V. Karageorghis, pp. 43–58. Alexander S. Onassis Foundation, New York.

Brandherm, D., and M. Trachsel (editors) 2008 *A New Dawn for the Dark Age? Shifting Paradigms in Mediterranean Iron Age Chronology*. Archaeopress, Oxford.

Braund, D., and C. Gill (editors) 2003 *Myth, History, and Culture in Republican Rome. Studies in Honour of T. P. Wiseman*. University of Exeter Press, Exeter.

Burke, P. 2005 *History and Social Theory*. 2nd Ed. Cornell University Press, Ithaca, New York.

Broodbank, C. 2013 *The Making of the Middle Sea: A History of the Mediterranean from the Emergence of the Classical World*. Oxford University Press, Oxford.

Camporeale, G. (editor) 2004 *The Etruscans outside Etruria*. Translated by T. M. Hartmann. J. Paul Getty Museum, Los Angeles.

Carenti, G., and B. Wilkes 2006 La colonizzazione fenicia e punica e il suo influsso sulla fauna sarda. *Sardinia, Corsica et Baleares Antiquae* 4:173–186.

Celestino, S., and C. López-Ruiz 2016 *Tartessos and the Phoenicians in Iberia*. Oxford University Press, Oxford.

Dainotto, R. M. 2007 *Europe (In Theory)*. Duke University Press, Durham.

De Angelis, F. 2006 Going Against the Grain in Sicilian Greek Economics. *Greece and Rome* 53(1):29–47.

De Angelis, F. 2016a *E pluribus unum*: The Multiplicity of Models. In *Conceptualising Early Colonisation*, edited by L. Donnellan, V. Nizzo, and G.-J. Burgers, pp. 97–104. Brepols, Turnhout.

De Angelis, F. 2016b *Archaic and Classical Greek Sicily: A Social and Economic History*. Oxford University Press, Oxford.

De Angelis, F. forthcoming Exchange Networks with the West. In *The Oxford Handbook of Pre-Roman Italy*, edited by M. Maiuro. Oxford University Press, New York.

Dench, E. 2005 *Romulus' Asylum: Roman Identities from the Age of Alexander to the Age of Hadrian*. Oxford University Press, Oxford.

Dietler, M., and C. López-Ruiz (editors) 2009 *Colonial Encounters in Ancient Iberia: Phoenician, Greek, and Indigenous Relations*. University of Chicago Press, Chicago.

Étienne, R. 2010 Conclusion: Réalités du VIIe s. In *La Méditerranée au VIIe siècle av. J.-C. (Essais d'analyses archéologique)*, edited by R. Étienne and A. Esposito, pp. 369–372. De Boccard, Paris.

Étienne, R. 2017 Introduction: Can One Speak of the Seventh Century BC? In *Interpreting the Seventh Century BC: Tradition and Innovation*, edited by X. Charalambidou and C. Morgan, pp. 9–14. Archaeopress, Oxford.

Étienne, R., and A. Esposito (editors) 2010 *La Méditerranée au VIIe siècle av. J.-C. (Essais d'analyses archéologique)*. De Boccard, Paris.

Gerschenkron, A. 1962 *Economic Backwardness in Historical Perspective: A Book of Essays*. Belknap Press, Cambridge, Mass.

Gras, M. 2000 Fra storia greca e storia dei Greci. *Quaderni di Storia* 51:227–231.

Guidi, A. 1998 The Emergence of the State in Central and Northern Italy. *Acta Archaeologica* 69:139–161.

Guidi, A. 2008 Archeologia dell'*Early State*: il caso di studio italiano. *Ocnus* 16:175–192.

Höckmann, O. 2001 Etruskische Schiffahrt. *Jahrbuch des Römisch-Germanischen Zentralmuseums*,

Mainz 48:227–308.

Horden, P., and N. Purcell 2000 *The Corrupting Sea: A Study of Mediterranean History*. Blackwell, Oxford.

Lehoërff, A. 2007 *L'artisanat du bronze en Italie centrale (1200–750 avant notre ère): le métal des dépôts volontaires*. École Française de Rome, Rome.

Liverani, M. 2017 Conservative versus Innovative Cultural Areas in the Near East ca. 800–400 BC. In *Eurasia at the Dawn of History: Urbanization and Social Change*, edited by M. Fernández-Götz and D. Krausse, pp. 198–210. Cambridge University Press, Cambridge.

Matisoo-Smith E. A, A. L. Gosling, J. Boocock, O. Kardailsky, Y. Kurumilian, S. Roudesli-Chebbi, L. Badre, J.-P. Morel, L. Ladjimi Sebaï, and P. A. Zalloua 2016 A European Mitochondrial Haplotype identified in Ancient Phoenician Remains from Carthage, North Africa. *PLoS ONE* 11(5):e0155046. DOI:10.1371/journal.pone.0155046.

Matisoo-Smith E., A. L. Gosling, D. Platt, O. Kardailsky, S. Prost, S. Cameron-Christie, C. J. Collins, J. Boocock, Y. Kurumilian, M. Guirguis, R. Pla Orquín, W. Khalil, H. Genz, G. Abou Diwan, J. Nassar, and P. Zalloua 2018 Ancient Mitogenomes of Phoenicians from Sardinia and Lebanon: A Story of Settlement, Integration, and Female Mobility. *PLoS ONE* 13(1):e0190169. DOI:10.1371/journal.pone.0190169.

Morris, I. 2003 Mediterraneanization. *Mediterranean Historical Review* 18(2):30–55 (reprinted in 2005, with the same pagination, as I. Malkin [editor], *Mediterranean Paradigms and Classical Antiquity*. Routlege, London).

Morris, I. 2010 *Why the West rules—for now: The Patterns of History, and What They reveal about the Future*. Farrar, Straus and Giroux, New York.

Musgrave, P. 1999 *The Early Modern European Economy*. Palgrave, London.

Naso, A. 2010 The Origin of Tomb Painting in Etruria. *Ancient West and East* 9:63–86.

Nijboer, Albert J. 2005 The Iron Age in the Mediterranean: A Chronological Mess or "Trade before the Flag," Part II. *Ancient West and East* 4:255–277.

Osborne, R. 2009 *Greece in the Making, 1200–479 BC*. 2nd Ed. Routledge, London.

Prag, J. R. W., and J. Crawley Quinn (editors) 2013 *The Hellenistic West: Rethinking the Ancient Mediterranean*. Cambridge University Press, Cambridge.

Prayon, F. 2010 *Die Etrusker: Geschichte—Religion—Kunst*. 5th Ed. Beck, Munich.

Ridgway, D. 2010 Greece, Etruria and Rome: Relationships and Receptions. *Ancient West and East* 9:43–61.

Riva, C., and N. C. Vella 2006 Introduction. In *Debating Orientalization: Multidisciplinary Approaches to Change in the Ancient Mediterranean*, edited by C. Riva and N. C. Vella, pp. 1–20. Equinox, London.

Schulz, R. 2008 *Kleine Geschichte des antiken Griechenland*. Reclam, Stuttgart.

Seland, E. H. 2008 The Indian Ocean and the Globalisation of the Ancient World. *Ancient West and East* 7:67–79.

Tanasi, D., R. H. Tykot, A. Vianello, and S. Hassam 2017 Stable Isotope Analysis of the Dietary Habits of a Greek Community in Archaic Syracuse (Sicily): A Pilot Study. *STAR: Science & Technology of Archaeological Research* 3.2:466–477. DOI:10.1080/20548923.2018.1441695.

Terpstra, T. 2019 *Trade in the Ancient Mediterranean: Private Order and Public Institutions*. Princeton University Press, Princeton.

Terrenato, N. 2010 Early Rome. In *The Oxford Handbook of Roman Studies*, edited by A. Barchiesi and W. Scheidel, pp. 507–518. Oxford University Press, Oxford.

Vogt-Spira, G., and B. Rommel (editors) 1999 *Rezeption und Identität. Die kulturelle Auseinandersetzung Roms mit Griechenland als europäisches Paradigma*. Franz Steiner, Sttutgart.

Webster, G. 2016 *The Archaeology of Nuragic Sardinia*. Monographs in Mediterranean Archaeology vol. 14. Equinox Publishing, London.

Wells, P. S. 1989 Cross-cultural Interaction and Change in Recent Old World Research. *American Antiquity* 54:66–83.

Whitmarsh, T. 2010 Hellenism. In *The Oxford Handbook of Roman Studies*, edited by A. Barchiesi and W. Scheidel, pp. 728–747. Oxford University Press, Oxford.

CHAPTER SIX

Captives

The Invisible Migrant

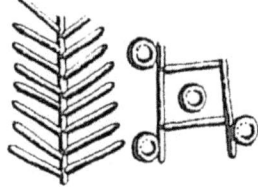

Catherine M. Cameron

Abstract *Forced migration has been largely neglected by archaeologists, but ethnohistoric, ethnographic, and archaeological data suggest that warfare and captive taking were common practices in the small-scale societies of the past. Captives tended to be women and children. They could be moved significant distances, and they often made up a significant proportion of the societies they joined. The forced movement of captives formed a constant background to the more formal migration archaeologists typically study. Recognizing captives as common and constant migrants compels us to rethink the ways in which we view the boundaries we draw around archaeological cultures and to acknowledge their permeability. This chapter develops a new model of migration that focuses on captives, allowing us to explore their role in shaping social boundaries and in cultural transmission. aDNA and isotopic studies are transforming how we see population movement, allowing us to distinguish the movement of individuals in the past. Modeling captive behavior should be an important tool for interpreting the results of these new scientific studies, ultimately refining our understanding of how people moved in and among ancient societies. Bringing captives out of the shadows, we should recognize the contributions they made to the societies they joined.*

A paradigm shift is taking place in archaeology. Megan Daniels (this volume) declares that archaeology and other disciplines that study the past are increasingly developing a migration-centered worldview of human history, "a view that sees mobility and migration as fundamental, constant features of human development and adaptation over the long term." Simultaneously, emerging data from isotope analysis and aDNA are transforming our understanding of ancient movements in many parts of the world, a scientific revolution in archaeology akin to the one that accompanied the discovery of radiocarbon dating (Kristiansen 2014 and this volume; also Anthony this volume; Gokcumen this volume). I hope to contribute to these developments by revealing the existence of a type of forced migrant that, while extremely common in societies of all types and time periods, has been largely overlooked by archaeologists: captives. The forced movement of captives formed a constant background to the sorts of movement archaeologists typically study. Isotope and aDNA data open new doors for the study of captive migration because they can track the movement of individuals. Remarkably, we can learn the age and sex of prehistoric migrants, as well as their treatment during life and after death, and sometimes their relationship to other members of the community in which they died. In order to make full use of these data, however, we need to develop new interpretative models that will help us understand migration at the level of the individual. This chapter aims to provide one framework for such a model.

I use ethnohistoric, ethnographic, and archaeological data to document the presence of captives in small-scale (pre-state) societies. Warfare and captive taking in small-scale societies caused the movement of many individuals in the past, especially women and children. These forced migrants spread both genetic material and cultural practices as they were dragged from their homes and driven across ancient landscapes. Recognition of the forced movement of captives challenges assumptions derived from modern migration studies that migrants make carefully considered decisions about when, how, and where to migrate. It disrupts our view of typical migrants as young men or families and it adds important nuance to our models of the effects of migrants on the communities they join.

The chapter begins with an overview of the archaeological study of migration that sees population movement as an intentional and carefully considered process generally linked to economic concerns. Such concepts are challenged in the remainder of the chapter. The next section presents early ethnohistoric and ethnographic accounts from around the globe to document the origin of captives in raiding and warfare, the significant distances they could be taken, the large numbers of captives involved, and the preference of captors for women and children. The following section explores the effect of these people on the social boundaries they crossed and then suggests that captives might have played important roles in cultural transmission, even when they appeared to blend in with the culture of their captors.

In the final sections of the paper I address the questions around which this volume is organized. I argue that recognition of the forced migration of captives casts doubt on the lingering assumptions that our archaeological cultures represented bounded social or ethnic groups in the past. Exploring the forced migration of captives allows us develop better models with which to interpret new aDNA and isotope data (other chapters in this volume also emphasize the importance of placing genomic data in anthropological and archaeological context. See especially Gokcumen this volume; also Anthony this volume; Barnard this volume; Kristiansen this volume). However, challenges to identifying captives in the archaeological record remain.

Migration, Forced Migrants, and Archaeology

Migration has been a fundamental concept in archaeology since the inception of the field. With changing theoretical perspectives during the twentieth century, our understanding of migration and its importance as an explanation for patterns in the archaeological record also changed (see Cabana 2011 for an overview). Vast population dislocations throughout the world today have provided additional impetus to archaeologists to explore human movement in the past. The study of migration has expanded dramatically in the past few decades (Anthony 1990, 2007; Cabana and Clark 2011; Cameron 2013; Ortman and Cameron 2011; Clark 2001; Daniels this volume; Fix 1999; Fowles 2011; Mills 2011; Peregrine et al. 2009; van Dommelen 2014). Archaeologists, especially in the American Southwest where I work, have made significant advances in understanding migration as a multilayered process (contra van Dommelen 2014), exploring the size and structure of groups that moved (Bernardini 2005; Ortman and Cameron 2011), the duration of the relocation (Cabana and Clark 2011:5–6; Cameron 1995, Clark 2001:2), the social consequences of the entry of migrants into host communities (Herr and Clark 1997; Mills 1998; Neuzil 2005; Stone 2003), and much more.

As it is commonly used today in public discourse, *migration* refers to the movement of small groups of people across political boundaries, generally for economic reasons, and their reestablishment in a new community where, at least for a time, they maintain an identity related to (but not necessarily identical to) that of their homeland (UNESCO 2019; Ortman and Cameron 2011; see also Isayev, this volume, for historical perspective on political boundaries and migrants). The news today is awash in images of people fleeing warfare, ethnic cleansing, social disorder, or other sorts of violence, but these unfortunate people are generally called *refugees,* not migrants (but see the United Nations definition of refugees: https://refugeesmigrants.un.org/definitions). Forced migration has been a distinct topic in modern migration studies since at least the 1980s, but most theories of migration seek to explain only voluntary migration (Chatty 2013; see also Koser 2007). Scholars feel that forced migration is too unpredictable for empirical study and the difference between voluntary and forced migration has been constructed mainly on descriptive characteristics. Political scientists see recent forced migration as a political tool used by states who expel minority groups from their borders or otherwise move people around (Weiner 1995, cited in Chatty 2013:5). Even those scholars who do attempt systematic studies of forced migration imagine the refugee as having choices, however restricted, about when and where to move (Chatty 2013:3).

In archaeology, there has been little study of the types of migrants that today might be called refugees (but see Camano, this volume; also Chapman 1997). Instead, most archaeologists see migration as carefully planned and in line with voluntary migration undertaken by modern migrants (Anthony 1990, 1997, 2007; Clark 2001:2–3; Cabana and Clark 2011; Cordell 1995; Cordell et al. 2007; Duff and Wilshusen 2000). Where historical accounts are available, archaeologists are aware of invasions and the forced movement of peoples in the past (see Camano this volume), but such accounts are limited largely to

Eurasia (primarily Europe) and have not generally been applied to prehistoric migration in other parts of the world. Anthony's (1990) now iconic "baby and the bathwater" article brought the study of migration back to life, arguing that method and theory developed in modern migration studies might be applied to the past and would allow archaeologists to study ancient migration as structured behavior. The sorts of voluntary migration on which Anthony focuses almost certainly explain a great deal of population movement in the past, as is clear from his contribution to this volume. But there are other common types of movement that require the development of different models.

This chapter focuses on movement that was not voluntary and cannot be explained by "push-pull" models that characterize voluntary migration. I hope to begin the process of developing models that will explain other sorts of migration. Until recently, archaeologists relied primarily on material culture distributions to define social groups and to identify migration across the landscape and across social group boundaries. New scientific methods, especially aDNA and isotope analysis, have the potential to transform our understanding of past movements by adding an unprecedented level of precision concerning who was moving, as well as when and where they moved (see especially Gokcumen, this volume). However, in an insightful recent article Stefan Burmeister (2016) reasons, "Scientific results alone provide no historical knowledge, but have to be interpreted within the context of cultural studies" (see also Bernard this volume; Gokcumen this volume). The remainder of this chapter provides a model that can help us link the scientific results emerging from aDNA and isotopic analysis with human behavior in the past.

A Global Look at Captives as Forced Migrants

In this section, I describe the characteristics of captives in small-scale societies, drawing on my research over the past decade (Cameron 2008, 2011, 2013, 2015, 2016). I have gathered dozens of ethnohistoric, ethnographic, and early historic accounts of warfare and captive taking from small-scale societies around the world, as well as archaeological data where it is available. Accounts come from North and South America, Africa, Europe, and Southeast Asia. Because of the scale of the study, I often use secondary sources. I have tried to avoid accounts from state-level societies because so much has been written about warfare, war captives, and slavery in states. Still, I have been influenced by the innumerable studies of Greek and Roman slavery and the even more abundant research on the African diaspora and post-Columbian New World slavery. Many captives became slaves and I have made considerable use of the slavery literature, which is far more extensive than the literature on captives. Because enslavement was part of the continuum of statuses a captive might experience, in the following discussion at times I use the terms *captive* and *slave* interchangeably.

The ethnohistoric and other accounts used in the study come from historic time periods and many of these societies were being deeply impacted by European colonization at the time the accounts were made. Because colonization intensified warfare and captive taking, the earliest accounts in each region, when the impacts of colonization were just beginning, are especially useful. On the first day he first landed in the Caribbean, Columbus wrote in his diary that islanders told him of enemies who had tried to capture them (Santos-Granero 2009:1). Such early accounts establish that warfare and captive taking predate European intrusion. I have found that warfare and captive taking were ancient and common practices in small-scale societies worldwide and that they had predictable demographic patterns and cultural impacts (Cameron 2016).

Warfare and Male Prestige

For many small-scale societies, especially horticultural societies, warfare was frequent and was often the best or even the only way for males to achieve status in their social group (Chacoan and Mendoza 2007; Dye 2004; Junker 2008; Keeley 1996; Santos-Granero 2009; Thornton 1999). The ideal male was a successful warrior who returned with captives and loot. These ideals were constantly reinforced by group ideology and oral history. For example, along the North Pacific Rim (from the lower Alaska Peninsula to the end of the Aleutian Islands) and Northwest Coast of North America, male status was linked to warfare and captive taking, especially of women (Donald 1997; Maschner and Reedy-Maschner 1998) (Figure 6.1). Male status and revenge were also causes for warfare among Iroquoian and other groups in the Northeast (Richter 1983:530; Rushforth 2012; Trigger 1976).

FIGURE 6.1. A Northwest Coast Village. Men are returning from a raid, with bound captives and trophy heads. By François Girard, courtesy Canadian Museum of History, 1-a-42, s95-23505.

In the Southeast, captives embodied a warrior's success in war, and returning from a raid with a captive was the highest achievement a warrior could attain (Snyder 2010:91–93). The same was true of the Kalinago of the Lesser Antilles who made extensive raids on other islands and the mainland of South America (Santos-Granero 2009:49–55). For Kalinago men, success in war and evidence of great courage were essential to allow them to marry or for any sort of social advancement. Raids were aimed at capturing as many women, children, and adult males as possible. For the Conibo of the western Amazon, success in warfare was integral to the ideals of manhood and courage in battle was essential if a young man wanted a Conibo wife (DeBoer 1986:237; Santos-Granero 2009:55). Other South American groups including Tupinamba (Bowser 2008:269–272), and the Quimbaya of the Cauca Valley (Carneiro 1991:177–178) based male status on performance in warfare and especially the taking of captives. In Southeast Asia, ethnohistoric accounts of coastal chiefdoms in the Philippines describe slave raiding as a fundamental part of local ideologies of male prestige (Junker 2008; Warren 1985). Myths and epic tales tell of a warrior elite who gained great status through successful raids. Raiders were successful if they took many captives; bringing back loot was secondary.

The Geography and Demography of Captive Taking

The effect of captives on large-scale genetic and cultural patterns was heightened because they could be moved long distances. Raiding and warfare were common between neighbors, but raiders could go much farther afield. Moreover captives were often traded, sold, or given as gifts to more distant groups. This was in part so they could not escape or be rescued. Archaeologist Warren DeBoer's (2008) extensive ethnohistoric study of captive taking in North and South America found that captives were generally taken from beyond the regions where men normally looked for wives. Distances usually were greater than 50 km, but could exceed 1000 km.

Where raiders had access to rivers or ocean margins, they made much longer distance raids to take captives. For example, the Kalinago of the Caribbean conducted long distance maritime raids against Arawak-speaking people of the Greater Antilles and Guiana coast (Santos-Granero 2009:49–55). Sometimes they covered distances of more than 800 km. The Conibo of the Amazonian part of Peru made raids of up to 600 km along the extensive river systems there, destroying villages and taking women and children captive as they traveled (DeBoer 1986; Santos-Granero 2009:55–63). In Africa, captives were moved as far as possible from their homelands to lessen the possibility that they would escape (Robertshaw and Duncan 2008:65). For example, captives were moved up and down the lengthy Congo River, mixing populations throughout the river basin. In Island Southeast Asia, female slaves were taken from throughout the Philippine archipelago and integrated into chiefly villages along the coast (Junker 2008:114–119).

Raiding moved people around, but for societies in which captives became slaves they also became highly valuable items of trade. This often removed them even farther from their homeland. Ancient trade routes on the Northwest Coast have been identified along which slaves and other goods likely moved (Ames 2008:144–146). In the late seventeenth century, the early French explorer Robert de La Salle received an Indian boy as a gift from the Michigamea tribe of the Upper Mississippi River. The boy "had been captured by the Panimahas, next taken by the Osages, then conveyed to the Emissourites (Missouris), who had sold him to the Michigamea tribe" (Ekberg 2007:12). The boy's experience was part of a widespread trade in slaves across much the central part of North America.

The first Spanish explorers to enter the Southwest found slaves held by Pueblo people who had been captured from Plains tribes (Brooks 2002). During the colonial era, the Pawnee tribes sold Apache captives to the French along the Mississippi and the Apache sold Pawnee to Pueblo villages, linking the Southwest into a widespread, almost continental-scale slave trade. In the Northeast, seventeenth-century Iroquois ranged widely to attack other groups and take captives. They raided the Algonquians far to the north and the peoples of the Upper Mississippi area far to the south, as well as areas between (Richter 1983:541).

The earliest accounts of slave trading in Island Southeast Asia offer evidence that captive slaves were traded across vast expanses of ocean by these maritime societies, beginning by at least the twelfth century A.D. (Junker 2008:110). Reid (1983:31–32) describes patterns in the Southeast Asian slave trade from the early fifteenth to the late seventeenth century as the sources of slaves and major slave importers changed through time. The trade tended to take slaves from small, divided states in the east and deliver them to wealthier ones farther west. Muslims groups took slaves from non-Muslims. Junker (2008:110) found that female captives from the Philippines might be traded as far away as Vietnam, Thailand, and Sumatra.

In Europe the "Germanic tribes" north of the Roman Empire also raided for, kept, and traded slaves (Lenski 2008). Germanic groups attacked and captured Romans, but captives were also taken during battles between different Germanic groups. Evidence of an active trade of slaves among Germanic tribes is found in Roman texts that mention slaves and slave traders; shackles have been found in Germanic sites (Lenski 2008:90–92). After the fifth century and the end of the Roman Empire, widespread raiding, captive taking, enslavement, and an extensive trade in slaves continued during the medieval period in the Mediterranean world (Bonnassie 1991:32; Pelteret 1981, 1995). Slaves were typically taken from foreign populations that were ethnically different from their captors and practiced different religions (Karras 1988). Slave trade routes "ran from Bohemia through Bavaria and Alemannia to Venice or across Carolingian Francia, from the Elbe to Koblenz and the Moselle to Verdun, then to Lyon, Arles, and Spain." (Karras 1988:14) Wars in Britain resulted in slaves sold to slave markets in Gaul (Bonnassie 1991:33).

Viking warriors raided extensively throughout the North Atlantic and into the Mediterranean, moving captives great distances (Walvin 2006:7). Genetic studies of contemporary Icelandic people suggest that Iceland's founding population was comprised of males from Scandinavia and females originating in the British Isles, a result that accords with historic records of widespread Viking raids on Ireland (Raffield 2017:316). Vikings raided much farther than the North Atlantic: "Ibn Hawqal, an Arab geographer, described a Viking slave trade in 977 CE that extended across the Mediterranean from Spain to Egypt. Others recorded that slaves from northern Europe were funneled from Scandinavia through Russia to Byzantium and Baghdad" (Lawler 2015).

Who Was Taken?

Although men were certainly taken captive in many parts of the world, the overwhelming pattern in small-scale societies was the capture of women and children (Figure 6.2). In fact, raids and warfare were often instigated with the goal of obtaining women to serve as wives, concubines, agricultural labor in horticultural societies, or as producers of other sorts of goods. Women and children were easier than men to subdue and transport. With men there was the added danger that they would try to escape or overpower their captors. Where evidence is available, it is apparent that reproductive-age women were most highly valued. As women reproduce the next generation, their prominence in the practice of captive taking has significant implications for patterns of genetic distribution. Child captives were valued because they could be easily enculturated, readily forgetting their origin. For most

FIGURE 6.2 Guaraní women and children captured by slave hunters. Image by French artist Jean-Baptiste Debret, who lived in Brazil during the early decades of the nineteenth century. From *Voyage pittoresque et historique au Brésil* [A picturesque and historic voyage to Brazil], Imprimerie Nationale Éditions (Arles: Actes Sud, 2014) (Public Domain).

small-scale societies power was in numbers (rather than control of territory) and captive taking increased population.

A recent study of the causes of Viking raiding is exemplary of the factors that were often behind the capture of women. Raffield and his colleagues (2017) use archaeological, textual, and ethnographic data to argue that elite males in Scandinavia began to monopolize marriageable women through practices of polygyny and concubinage. These men (perhaps younger sons) were motivated to increase their wealth and reputation by organizing distant raids. At the same time, low status, unmarried men were willing to engage in raiding in order to achieve the status and wealth they needed to gain a wife. Texts report that Vikings captured many women in the British Isles, as well as areas as distant as Spain, Morocco, Azerbaijan, and beyond who might have become wives or concubines for Viking raiders (Raffield et al. 2017:316, 320–321).

Similar causes of raiding have been found among the Conibo of the Amazon. Marriageable Conibo women were monopolized by older men, leaving younger men without wives (DeBoer 1986:237–238). Men wanted many wives, in part for their labor. Male status was based on the production of beer to be consumed at large fiestas, and women were the primary horticulturalists and beer producers. Many wives produced more beer, resulting in higher status for their husbands. Captive children usually became domestic servants and most Conibo men owned at least one of these children (Santos-Granero 2009:132). In the Caribbean, the Kalinago seem to have captured everyone they could, but men and boys were eventually killed and eaten, while women and girls became concubines and domestic servants (Santos-Granero 2009:54).

On the North Pacific Rim, archaeological and ethnohistoric accounts provide evidence of raids and warfare, even prior to European contact, and ethnographic accounts suggest that raids were fueled by the desire for revenge, women, and slaves (Maschner and Reedy-Maschner 1998). Farther south along the Northwest Coast, for those groups where a preference could be determined, women and children were preferred as slaves. In the Northeast, captives of the Iroquois were subject to a selection process, with some, especially men, suffering horrendous torture and death. Women and children were more frequently spared to become wives and replenish declining Iroquois populations (Rushforth 2012:46). This was especially true when village mortality was high and women and children could help replenish population. The same pattern of sparing women and children from torture and death was practiced in the Southeast among the Cherokees (Perdue 1979:6).

African males were preferred for the Atlantic slave trade because they were sought as laborers, but the internal African slave trade favored females. Women functioned as field laborers in the horticultural systems that dominated Africa, as domestic slaves, and, perhaps most importantly, as concubines or wives for their masters, producing children for the master's lineage (Robertshaw and Duncan 2008:61; for a discussion see Klein 1983:72–76). A nineteenth-century Nigerian price list for slaves shows that regardless of age, women were always more highly valued than men, but that the prices for girls and young women were far higher than any other age/sex category (Goody 1980:39).

Numbers

Captives were not an occasional feature of small-scale societies. Although determining the numbers of captives or slaves in any past society is problematic, the ethnohistoric and ethnographic data compiled for my study suggest that captives would have formed a substantial subset of people in many, perhaps most, small-scale societies. The implications of these data for the spread of genetic and cultural material across prehistoric landscapes are enormous and require that we rethink some fundamental archaeological concepts, as discussed below.

On the Northwest Coast, slave numbers varied by community (Donald 1997:185–193 provides detailed ethnohistoric data on slave numbers). When slaves were enumerated in the Stikine Tlingit subcommunities in 1845, their proportions ranged from 5 to 25% (Donald 1997:189). Among the groups along the Greater Lower Columbia River, slaves might have comprised 20–24% of village populations (Ames 2008:150). Farther inland among the Tutchone bands, slaves composed about 10% of the population, although some of these were described as debt slaves (Legros 1985:50). On the Great Plains, foreign-born women made up 8% of Southern Cheyenne women as reported in the 1892 allotment census (Moore 1994:936–937). In the Northeast, "mourning wars" in the seventeenth century had caused significant population loss for the Iroquois and they replaced dead family members with captives (Richter 1983:541). As these wars became more violent and extensive, the numbers of adopted captives grew significantly. By the 1660s, missionaries estimated that many Iroquois villages were two-thirds adopted captives and only one-third native-born Iroquois people. In Tropical America, Santos-Granero (2009) used information from ethnohistoric accounts to estimate numbers of slaves in six slaveholding societies. He found proportions ranging from 5 to 19% of the population of these groups. Among the Yanamamö (an Amazonian group, but not one of Santos-Granero's six slaveholding groups) Chagnon found that between 12 and 17% of wives were captives who had been taken in raids (1992:106–107).

Raiding and captive taking was prevalent among the tribes and small polities that emerged in Europe after the fall of the Roman Empire. Lenski's (2008) examination of the Germanic Law Codes found slaves and semi-slaves mentioned in between one-quarter to one-third of chapters, suggesting that slaves were a significant element of Germanic society after the mid-fifth century. In Britain, "Slaves were an integral and numerically important part of English society throughout the Anglo-Saxon period" (fifth to eleventh centuries; Pelteret 1981:99). The Domesday Book census of 1086 A.D. reports a slave population of 5 to 25%, depending on the region (McDonald and Snooks 1986:16–17). Early law in Norway suggest that a typical farm had three slaves, although other lines of evidence suggest that they might not have been quite that common (Karras 1988:78–80).

In a set of studies of African societies, slave numbers ranged from 1 to 50% of the population depending on the level of complexity of the group and access to trade routes (Kopytoff and Miers 1977:60–61). Slaves were a majority of the population in several Southeast Asian groups during the seventeenth and eighteenth centuries (Reid 1983:29–31). The nineteenth-century Sulu sultanate (also Southeast Asia) used slave labor for as much as 50% of their work force in agricultural fields and craft workshops (Junker 2008:118).

Captives, Material Culture, and Social Boundaries

Acknowledging captives as a common type of migrant forces us to contemplate commonly assumed links between human mobility and material culture. Archaeological cultures are constructed by mapping boundaries of material culture distributions and although few would argue that archaeological cultures represent exactly prehistoric ethnic or cultural groups, we often use them as if they do. (Note that Gokcumen [this volume] emphasizes that the new genetic data complicates, rather than resolves old questions about prehistoric ethnic groups derived from material culture; we need to beware of substituting genes for material culture in defining prehistoric groups.) Most archaeologists recognize that ethnicity is the result of a myriad of historical and social processes, that identity is constantly negotiated, and that there are multiple layers of identity upon which any individual can draw. Still, archaeologists find this understanding difficult to operationalize in the study of migration (Burmeister 2016; Jones 1997; Ortman and Cameron 2011; see also De Angelis this volume, for another example of old concepts that persist in spite of new data).[1] Conceding that captives moved in substantial numbers across the boundaries of archaeological cultures merging with the societies of their captors forces us to question the implicit assumption that circumscribed ethnic groups can be traced across time and space. It requires us to explore how captives impacted the societies they joined, including their effects on material culture and other cultural elements.

If the composition of people who made up the ancient societies we study changes, we might imagine ethnic boundaries dissolving or growing in size as members of different groups were incorporated. But captives are distinctive sorts of migrants. Ethnographic and ethnohistoric data suggest that even when large numbers of captives had been incorporated social boundaries evident at an archaeological level might remain the same. In other words, while the genetics of a group might change significantly as captive women and children were introduced, these new group members may not be immediately apparent in the material culture that archaeologists study.

Rather than dissolving social boundaries, captives help maintain them in several ways. They enter their captors' society at the lowest end of the social spectrum. This was especially true when they were incorporated as slaves rather than wives or adoptees. In small-scale societies kinship was generally a more important structuring principle than ethnicity (Albers 1993) and the defining characteristic of a captive was that she lacked kin in her captor's society. Unless she was incorporated as a wife or was adopted, she was an abject outsider, usually considered less than human (Cameron 2016). Since social boundaries are defined almost as much on negative criteria as on positive—we define ourselves in *contrast* to others—a lowly strata of captives makes a perfect foil for highlighting the superior characteristics of the captors. The Fulani of West Africa considered their slaves naive, irresponsible, uncultivated, and shameless (Riesman 1977:117), in contrast to the Fulani themselves who were, of course, none of these things. In other words, simply by their presence and low status, captives in many small-scale societies strengthened their captors' ethnic boundaries (for other examples see Karras 1988:63; Perdue 1979:17; Santos-Granero 2009).

While captives do not seem to have dissolved social boundaries, in many cases they instead created links between social groups, especially those that were alternately engaged in raiding and trading. We might think that stolen women disappear into the society of their captors, and this certainly happened in some cases. But at times families continued to have contact with their abducted daughters. Because captives often became multilingual, they could serve as intermediaries or social brokers between their family and their captors (Albers 1993; Brooks 2002; Chernela 2011). They functioned as social channels or nodes that linked different groups together—in essence, bypassing social boundaries. Especially in areas where groups engaged in both trading and raiding, multilingual women captives could play important roles as intermediaries, facilitating negotiations between groups who were sometimes friendly and sometimes hostile. The social interactions that captives promoted almost certainly resulted in additional population movement, although the scale of such movement is hard to determine.

For example, in the Great Plains we tend to view tribes as distinct and bounded ethnic groups—the Arapaho, the Cheyenne, the Kiowa, the Arikara, the Hidatsa, the Mandan, and so on. But anthropologist Patricia Albers (1993) has argued that historically known Plains tribes had overlapping regions and social formations (see also Moore 1994:936–937).[2] However, relations among these groups were often hostile with frequent raiding and captive taking. Captive women and children might be items of trade, they might be incorporated into the group to increase group size, and they might be used for their labor. Perhaps most importantly, captives served as channels for developing peaceful relationships among enemy groups. In ethnohistoric accounts, captives were visited by their birth families and those visits started cycles of gift giving and trade. In other words, captives provided an opportunity for interactions of a variety of types among groups who might otherwise be at war. They opened avenues for cooperation that might end up being advantageous to both groups. Albers describes the role of captives: "[T]he capture of women and children was both a quintessential element of war, and a fundamental opportunity for peace. It maintained, yet rearranged, the social nexus through which tribes were able to rework their relationships" (Albers 1993:128). Of course, eighteenth- and nineteenth-century Plains tribes were heavily involved in European trade networks. But small-scale societies elsewhere in the world show a similar pattern (for example, Chernela 2011). Captives can create important social and economic connections between groups that might appear to have strong ethnic group boundaries and sometimes have very hostile relations. They served as conduits for the movement of people, things, and ideas.

While the boundaries of captor groups did not dissolve or expand as captives moved in, these forced migrants did not simply disappear. Most archaeologists do not insist on a site-unit intrusion to signal the movement of a large group (Cordell 1995:207); similarly, we should not imagine that bedraggled captives, no matter their number, would continue to express their natal identity materially in ways archaeologists can easily see. But I believe captives were important elements in the transmission of cultural practices, introducing new ways of doing to the groups they joined.

Elsewhere, I have argued that archaeologists have not yet developed detailed understandings of how cultural practices were transmitted between groups (but see Kristiansen and Larson 2005) and have urged archaeologists to explore captives as a source of cultural transmission (Cameron 2016). I found that captors in small-scale societies might probe their captives to extract useful information about new technologies, ideologies, curing practices, or foodways. Archaeological and other data show that such transfers did occur. Plainware pottery discovered on the southern High Plains during the protohistoric period (1500–1700 A.D.) was apparently introduced by women captured from Pueblo groups in adjacent parts of Southwest (Habicht-Mauche 2008). In Southeast Asia, archaeological and ethnohistoric data suggest that captive women who became potters in the chiefly societies of the Philippines introduced design styles from their original homes (Junker 2008). Sometimes captives with particular skills were specifically targeted for capture. Metal objects made in a Mediterranean style have been found in archaeological sites in Denmark dating to the fifth century A.D. These objects suggest the capture and transport of skilled Roman metalsmiths (Lenski 2008:90–91). These are just a few examples of technological methods and stylistic elements captives introduced. They also affected the social organization and ideological practices of many of the societies they joined (Cameron 2011, 2013, 2016). Archaeologists exploring the process of cultural transmission should consider the role of forced migrants—captives—in this process.

Broadening Our View of Migration

Archaeology deals in broad patterns that cover great sweeps of time. Our strength lies in seeing change through time, although our reconstruction of the events of the past is unavoidably coarse. In fact, we rarely see events, but instead patterns in the past. David Anthony (1990) convinced us that migration was a process, not an event, and at the most common level of archaeological resolution he is, of course, right (see Anthony this volume). However, aDNA and strontium isotope studies do allow us to track the movements of individuals, and recognizing captives as a distinct sort of migrant should help us bring patterns of movement in the past into clearer focus. Suddenly we can transcend the limitations of archaeological cultures and their material correlates and create new understandings of the process of migration and especially of those who migrated. We have been given the opportunity to move beyond the "faceless blobs" (Tringham 1991) that populate archaeological accounts of the past and see the women, children, and men who created the patterns we find in the archaeological record.

Seeing captives in the past will not be easy, but there are a suite of methods that are currently being developed and these methods, in conjunction with aDNA and isotope studies, should permit the identification and characterization of captives (see Isayev this volume, for difficulty seeing migrants in the past). Here is a partial list of these developing methods. Given the close association between warfare and captive taking, evidence of warfare (defensive sites, weapons of war, "no-man's land," trauma to human remains) should lead us to suspect the presence of captives (see Keeley 1996; LeBlanc and Register 2003). Where captives are marginalized or enslaved, their bodies may show evidence of violence and abuse including cranial fractures, lower arm fractures (an effort to deflect a blow), and evidence of repeated beatings (Harrod 2012; Martin 2008; Martin et al. 2010; Martin et al. 2012). Skewed sex ratios in burial populations might suggest the capture of women; more females may indicate populations that took women captive, while more men might indicate a source for female captives (Cybulski 1990; Keeley 1996:68; Kohler and Turner 2006). Other lines of evidence include iconography showing what appear to be captives (Dye 2004), female-linked intrusive traits at a site and a lack of male-linked intrusive traits (Lowell 2007), regional-scale distributions of gender-linked artifact types that suggest captive taking (DeBoer 2011; Trigger 1976:159–161), and words for captives or slaves in indigenous languages where the words do not appear to be loanwords (demonstrating the antiquity of captive taking; Averkieva 1966; Rushforth 2012; Starna and Watkins 1991).

As Burmeister (2016) pointed out in the quote cited above, archaeologists cannot simply take new scientific results and apply them to the past. We must use knowledge developed from anthropology, archaeology, and historical studies to interpret them. This is not a new challenge for archaeology. We are an interdisciplinary field accustomed to borrowing theory and method from other disciplines and applying them to the past. But we must work closely with the scholars undertaking genetic and isotopes studies to ensure we understand the data they are providing and that they understand what sorts of information we need to understand the past.

What do we gain by combining a recognition of captives as a common element in most small-scale societies with the new data emerging from aDNA and isotopic laboratories? Here is one example. Knipper and colleagues (2017) described a large population of human remains from the Lech valley of southern Bavaria of the Late Neolithic Bell Beaker Complex and the Early Bronze Age that dated over an 800-year period. mtDNA analyses showed considerable diversity in the maternal lineages represented in this group of burials, with increasing diversity during the later Early Bronze Age. Strontium isotope data showed that, while the males and subadults in this population were local, 60% of the women were nonlocal, as well as a few males and subadults. Most of the nonlocal women had arrived at an age older than 16 years, although one seems to have arrived in childhood. One male seems to have begun life in the Lech Valley, moved elsewhere during childhood, and returned to the Lech Valley as an adult. Interestingly, none of the subadults were related to the nonlocal women; their offspring, if any, were not present in the burial population. Knipper et al. (2017) note that the nonlocal women were interred using the same burial positions as local females. Some even wore the particular elaborate headdress commonly worn by local women. No differences in grave goods were noted between local and nonlocal women.

Knipper et al. (2017) interpret the isotopic patterns they uncovered as the result of patrilocal residence rules and female exogamy and note that a diversity of maternal lineages in human remains has been linked by others to the same residence and marriage rules.

But the evidence is also consistent with captive taking as described above, especially the high proportion of nonlocal reproductive-aged women and the occasional nonlocal child or male. How might we distinguish these two interpretations? The fact that these women had no children in the local population might be the result of the sample size, but it could suggest that the nonlocal women were marginalized and not incorporated as wives or adoptees. If they were captives, we might look for other evidence that they were treated differently than local women. This could include evidence that they were subject to frequent trauma (beatings or other abuse; Martin et al. 2012), that they were overworked, or given insufficient nutrition. But lack of evidence for poor treatment does not ensure that the nonlocal women described by Knipper et al. (2017) were not captives. Captives often become wives or adoptees and might wear the same clothing and ornaments and be buried using the same practices as local women.

Additional lines of evidence that might be considered to distinguish these two interpretations includes the distance nonlocal women were taken—the farther they traveled, the less likely they were part of regular marriage exchange patterns. The prevalence of warfare during the time periods under consideration should also be examined. If warfare was common, captive taking was almost certainly practiced. Other lines of evidence, described above, should also be considered. Finally, the human remains described by Knipper and her colleagues represented a period of more than 800 years and over time women might have entered the Lech Valley in a variety of ways and statuses. Recognizing captives as a common type of forced migrant in small-scale societies significantly broadens our understanding of how people moved in ancient Europe (see Anthony this volume; Kristiansen this volume). Knipper et al. note, "It appears that part of what archaeologists understand as migration is the result of large-scale institutionalized and possibly sex- and age-related individual mobility" (2017:10083). I could not agree more, but I urge scholars to consider not only marriage patterns but captive taking as one possible explanation for individual movement.

Conclusions

In this chapter, I highlight one aspect of the continuum of population movement, the forced movement of captives. Coordinated movements of large numbers of people in the past are well documented but the sorts of migrations we most commonly envision took place against a background of persistent forced movement and trade of captives, especially women and children. These migrants had a significant effect on ancient genetic and material culture (and likely language) distributions and should be explored worldwide. I argue that recognizing the prevalence of captive taking in prehistory provides a model that can help explain some of the patterns that the new isotope analyses and ancient DNA data have revealed.

Ethnohistoric and ethnographic data presented above provides strong cross-cultural evidence that raiding, warfare, and captive taking were widely practiced in small-scale societies, that captives could be moved significant distances either by their original captors or through trade, and that captives made up a significant proportion of many small-scale societies. Acknowledging the presence of captives moving across cultural boundaries forces us to question the nature of the archaeological cultures we create and recognize the permeability of their borders. We have known for some time that social identities are constantly in the process of construction, that individuals identify themselves with an increasingly inclusive set of social groups, and that material culture plays an active role in the creation of social identities (Ortman and Cameron 2011; Stark 1998; Wiessner 1983; Wobst 1977).

Still, we have struggled to bring this understanding into our exploration of migration. Recognition that captives moved across the boundaries of the archaeological cultures we study should force us, once and for all, to drop the idea that cultures are like biological species that move as unitary entities through time and space. It gives us a new view of small-scale societies as fluid, hybrid entities. Perhaps most importantly, we must recognize the contributions of captives to processes of cultural transmission. They might well have existed in the lowest stratum of the societies they joined, but their impact on material culture and other aspects of prehistoric societies could be significant.

A view of migration that includes captives and other forced migrants helps to bring into focus the "blurry" migrants of the past and their effects on the cultures they joined. An important obstacle is the difficulty of seeing captives in the archaeological record, especially those that were not enslaved but blended into captor culture as wives or adoptees. Ancient DNA and isotope studies are in the process of transforming what we know about the past, but the data produced by these new scientific methods must be informed by our knowledge of human behavior. This chapter argues that a better understanding of captives and their place in the small-scale societies they joined provides one model that should be used in conjunction with the new scientific methods to reconstruct the past.

Acknowledgments

Thanks to Dr. Megan Daniels for inviting me to the *Homo Migrans* conference and to Drs. Peter Biehl and Stephen Dyson of the IEMA for hosting the conference. Megan did a magnificent job of developing and framing an extremely important topic and the conference was an exceptionally stimulating and broadening experience. I thank other conference participants for inspiring papers and conversations. My several conversations with Dr. Elena Isayev at the conference and since have been particularly valuable. Special thanks to Dr. David Anthony whose work on migration has been an inspiration to me for several decades and to Dr. Kristian Kristiansen whose scholarship has similarly inspired my interest in cultural transmission. As always, my thanks go to Jim Skibo and Jeff Grathwohl who first gave me the opportunity to develop my interest in captives, and to my childhood "aunt" Tien Fuh Wu whose experience of slavery shaped my understanding of the world.

Notes

1. Not all social scientists would agree. Some take a "primordalist" approach to ethnicity and argue that ethnic identity "is fixed once it is constructed" (Bayar 2009). The rapidity with

which a young captive can lose her previous ethnicity (including language) and take on that of her captors is strong evidence of the folly of the primordialist stance.
2. Others have pointed out that small-scale societies tend to be hybrid instead of the sorts of bounded entities we tend to imagine. Using demographic work on historic Plains tribes as well as accounts of small-scale societies in other parts of the world, Moore (1994) shows that bands and tribes frequently blend, becoming culturally and linguistically hybrid. He likens the process to a river where channels separate and recombine (Moore 1994:930). Unfortunately, calls by Moore and others for a more accurate understanding of how ethnicity is expressed and what this means for our understanding of prehistoric migration have not triggered much change in archaeological methods.

References Cited

Albers, P. 1993 Symbiosis, Merger, and War: Contrasting Forms of Intertribal Relationship among Historic Plains Indians. In *The Political Economy of North American Indians*, edited by J. H. Moore, pp. 94–132. University of Oklahoma Press, Norman.

Ames, K. M. 2008 Slavery, Household Production, and Demography on the Southern Northwest Coast: Cables, Tacking, and Ropewalks. In *Invisible Citizens: Captives and Their Consequences*, edited by C. M. Cameron, pp. 138–158. The University of Utah Press, Salt Lake City.

Anthony, D. W. 1990 Migration in Archaeology. *American Anthropologist* 92(4):895–914.

Anthony, D. W. 1997 Prehistoric Migration as Social Process. In *Migrations and Invasions in Archaeological Explanation*, edited by J. Chapman and H. Hamerow, pp. 21–32. British Archaeological Reports, Archaeopress.

Anthony, D. W. 2007 *The Horse, the Wheel, and Language*. Princeton: Princeton University Press.

Averkieva, J. 1966 [1941] *Slavery Among the Indians of North America*. Translated by G. R. Elliot. Victoria College, Victoria, B.C.

Bayar, M. 2009 Reconsidering Primordialism: An Alternative Approach to the Study of Ethnicity. *Ethnic and Racial Studies* 32(9):1639–1657.

Bernardini, W. 2005 *Hopi Oral Tradition and the Archaeology of Identity*. University of Arizona Press, Tucson.

Bonnassie, P. 1991 *From Slavery to Feudalism in Southwestern Europe*. Cambridge University Press, Cambridge.

Bowser, B. J. 2008 Captives in Amazonia: Becoming Kin in a Predatory Landscape. In *Invisible Citizens: Captives and Their Consequences*, edited by C. M. Cameron, pp. 262–282. University of Utah Press, Salt Lake City.

Brooks, J. F. 2002 *Captives and Cousins: Slavery, Kinship, and Community in the Southwest Borderlands*. University of North Carolina Press, Chapel Hill.

Burmeister, S. 2016 Archaeological Research on Migration as a Multidisciplinary Challenge. *Medieval Worlds* 4:42–64.

Cabana, G. S., and J. J. Clark, (editors) 2011 *Rethinking Anthropological Perspectives on Migration*. University Press of Florida, Gainesville.

Cameron, C. M. 1995 Migration and the Movement of Southwestern Peoples. *Journal of Anthropological Archaeology* 14(2):104–124.

Cameron, C. M. 2008 *Invisible Citizens: Captives and Their Consequences*. University of Utah Press, Salt Lake City.

Cameron, C. M. 2011 Captives and Culture Change: Implications for Archaeologists. *Current Anthropology* 52(2):169–209.

Cameron, C. M. 2013 How People Moved Among Ancient Societies: Broadening the View. *American Anthropologist* 115(2): 218–231.

Cameron, C. M. 2015 Commodities or Gifts: Captives and Slaves in Non-State Societies. In *The Archaeology of Slavery: A Comparative Approach to Captivity and Coercion*, edited by L. W. Marshall, pp. 24–40. Center for Archaeological Investigations, Southern Illinois University, Carbondale.

Cameron, C. M. 2016 *Captives: How Stolen People Changed the World*. University of Nebraska Press, Lincoln

Carneiro, R. L. 1991 The Nature of the Chiefdom as Revealed by Evidence from the Cauca Valley of Colombia. In *Profiles in Cultural Evolution: Papers from a Conference in Honor of Elman R. Service,* edited by A. T. Rambo and K. Gillogly, pp. 167–190. Anthropological Papers, Museum of Anthropology, University of Michigan. Ann Arbor.

Chacoan, R. J., and R.G. Mendoza, (editors) 2007 *North American Indigenous Warfare and Ritual Violence*. The University of Arizona Press, Tucson.

Chagnon, N. 1992 *Yanomano: The Last Days of Eden*. Harcourt Brace Jovanovich, San Diego.

Chapman, J. 1997 The Impact of Modern Invasions and Migrations on Archaeological Explanation. In *Migrations and Invasions in Archaeological Explanation,* edited by J. Chapman and H. Hamerow, pp. 11–20. British Archaeological Reports, Archaeopress, Oxford.

Chatty, D. 2013 Forced Migration. In *The Encyclopedia of Global Human Migration*, pp. 1–5. Wiley On-Line Library.

Chernela, J. M. 2011 Comment on: Captives and Culture Change: Implications for Archaeologists. *Current Anthropology* 52(2):196.

Clark, J. J. 2001 *Tracking Prehistoric Migrations: Pueblo Settlers among the Tonto Basin Hohokam*. Anthropological Papers of the University of Arizona, Number 65. University of Arizona Press, Tucson.

Cordell, L. 1995. Tracing Migration Pathways from the Receiving End. *Journal of Anthropological Archaeology* 14(2):203–211.

Cordell, L. S., C. R. Van West, J. S. Dean, and D. A. Muenchrath 2007 Mesa Verde Settlement History and Relocation: Climate Change, Social Networks, and Ancestral Pueblo Migration. *Kiva* 72(4):379–406.

Cybulski, J. S. 1990 Human Biology. In *Northwest Coast,* edited by Wayne Suttles, pp. 52–59. *Handbook of North American Indians*, Vol. 7, W. C. Sturtevant, general editor, Smithsonian Institution Press, Washington, D.C.

DeBoer, W. 1986. Pillage and Production in the Amazon: A View through the Conibo of the Ucayali Basin, Eastern Peru. *World Archaeology* 18(2):231–246.

DeBoer, W. 2008 Wrenched Bodies. In *Invisible Citizens: Captives and Their Consequences,* edited by Catherine M. Cameron, pp. 233–261. University of Utah Press, Salt Lake City

DeBoer, W. 2011 Deep Time, Big Space: An Archaeologist Skirts the Topic at Hand. In *Ethnicity in Ancient Amazonia*, edited by A. Hornborg and J. D. Hill, pp. 75–98. University Press of Colorado, Boulder.

Donald, L. 1997 *Aboriginal Slavery on the Northwest Coast of North America*. University of California Press, Berkeley.

Duff, Andrew I., and Richard H. Wilshusen 2000 *Prehistoric Population Dynamics in the Northern San Juan Region, A.D. 950–1300*. Kiva 66(1):167–190.

Dye, D. H. 2004 Art, Ritual, and Chiefly Warfare in the Mississippian World. In *Hero, Hawk, and Open Hand: American Indian Art of the Ancient Midwest and South*, edited by R. V. Sharp, pp. 190–205. The Art Institute of Chicago and Yale University Press, New Haven.

Ekberg, C. J. 2007 *Stealing Indian Women: Native Slavery in the Illinois Country*. University of Illinois Press, Urbana.

Fix, A. G. 1999 *Migration and Colonization in Human Microevolution*. Cambridge University Press, Cambridge.

Fowles, S. 2011 Movement and the Unsettling of the Pueblos. In *Rethinking Anthropological Perspectives on Migration*, edited by G. Cabana and J. Clark, pp. 45–67. University of Florida Press, Gainesville.

Goody, J. 1980 Slavery in Space and Time. In *Asian and African Systems of Slavery*, by J. L. Watson. pp. 16–42. University of California, Berkeley.

Habicht-Mauche, J. 2008 Captive Wives? The Role and Status of Non-Local Women on the Protohistoric Southern High Plains. In *Invisible Citizens: Captives and Their Consequences*, edited by C. M. Cameron, pp. 181–204. University of Utah Press, Salt Lake City.

Harrod, R. P. 2012 Centers of Control: Revealing Elites Among the Ancestral Pueblo During the "Chaco Phenomenon." *International Journal of Paleopathology* 2(2–3):123–135.

Herr, S., and J. J. Clark 1997 Patterns in the Pathways: Early Historic Migrations in the Rio Grande Pueblos. *Kiva* 62:365–389.

Jones, S. 1997 *The Archaeology of Ethnicity: Constructing Identities in the Past and Present*. Routledge Press, London.

Junker, L. 2008 The Impact of Captured Women on Cultural Transmission in Contact Period Philippine Slave-Raiding Chiefdoms. In *Invisible Citizens: Captives and their Consequences*, edited by C. M. Cameron, pp. 110–138. University of Utah Press, Salt Lake City.

Karras, R. M. 1988 *Slavery and Society in Medieval Scandinavia*. Yale University Press, New Haven.

Keeley, L. H. 1996 *War before Civilization: The Myth of the Peaceful Savage*. Oxford University Press, Oxford.

Klein, M. A. 1983 Women in Slavery in the Western Sudan. In *Women and Slavery in Africa*, edited by C. C. Robertson and M. A. Klein, pp. 67–88. The University of Wisconsin Press, Madison.

Knipper, C., A. Mittnik, K. Massy, C. Kociumaka, I. Kucukkalipci, M. Maus, F. Wittenborn, S. E. Metz, A. Staskiewicz, J. Krause, and P. W. Stockhammer 2017 Female Exogamy and Gene Pool Diversification at the Transition from the Final Neolithic to the Early Bronze Age in Central Europe. *Proceedings of the National Academy of Science* 114(38):10083–10088.

Kohler, T. A., and K. K. Turner 2006 Raiding for Women in the Pre-Hispanic Northern Pueblo Southwest? *Current Anthropology* 47(6):1035–1045.

Kopytoff, I., and S. Miers 1977 Introduction: African "Slavery" as an Institution of Marginality. In *Slavery in Africa: Historical and Anthropological Perspectives*, edited by S. Miers and I. Kopytoff, pp. 3–81. University of Wisconsin Press, Madison.

Koser, K. 2007 *International Migration: A Very Short Introduction*. Oxford University Press, Oxford.

Kristiansen, K., and T. B. Larsson 2005 *The Rise of Bronze Age Society: Travels, Transmissions, and Transformations*. Cambridge University Press, Cambridge.

Lawler, A. 2015 Kinder, Gentler Vikings? Not According to Their Slaves. *National Geographic*. Electronic document, https://news.nationalgeographic.com/2015/12/151228-vikings-slaves-thralls-norse-scandinavia-archaeology/, accessed August 3, 2018.

LeBlanc, S., and K. E. Register 2003 *Constant Battles: Why We Fight*. St. Martin's Press, New York.

Legros, D. 1985 Wealth, Poverty, and Slavery among 19th century Tutchone Athapaskans. *Research in Economic Anthropology* 7: 37–64.

Lenski, N. 2008 Captivity, Slavery, and Cultural Exchange between Rome and the Germans from the First to the Seventh Century CE. In *Invisible Citizens: Captives and their Consequences*, edited by C. M. Cameron, pp. 80–109. University of Utah Press, Salt Lake City.

Lowell, J. C. 2007 Women and Men in Warfare and Migration: Implications of Gender Imbalance in the Grasshopper Region of Arizona. *American Antiquity* 72(1):95–124.

Martin, D. L. 2008 Ripped Flesh and Torn Souls: Skeletal Evidence for Captivity and Slavery from the La Plata Valley, New Mexico (AD 1100–1300). In *Invisible Citizens: Captives and Their Consequences*, edited by C. M. Cameron, pp. 159–180. University of Utah Press, Salt Lake City.

Martin D. L, R. P. Harrod, and M. Fields 2010 Beaten Down and Worked to the Bone: Bio-archaeological Investigations of Women and Violence in the Ancient Southwest. *Landscapes of Violence* 1(1): 1–19.

Martin, D. L., R. P. Harrod, and V. R. Pérez 2012 *The Bioarchaeology of Violence*. University Press of Florida, Gainesville.

Maschner, H. D. G., and K. L. Reedy-Maschner 1998 Raid, Retreat, Defend (Repeat): The Archaeology and Ethnohistory of Warfare on the North Pacific Rim. *Journal of Anthropological Archaeology* 17(1): 19–51.

McDonald, J., and G. D. Snooks 1986 *Domesday Economy: A New Approach to Anglo-Norman History*. Oxford University Press, New York.

Mills, B. J. 1998 Migration and Pueblo IV Community Reorganization in the Silver Creek Area, East-Central Arizona. In *Migration and Reorganization: The Pueblo IV Period in the American Southwest*, edited by K. A. Spielmann, pp. 65–80. Anthropological Research Papers No. 51. Tempe, Arizona State University.

Mills, B. J. 2011 Themes and Models for Understanding Migration in the Southwest. In *Movement, Connectivity, and Landscape Change in the Ancient Southwest*, edited by M. C. Nelson and C. Strawhacker, pp. 345–362. Boulder: University Press of Colorado.

Moore, J. H. 1994 Putting Anthropology Back Together Again: The Ethnogenetic Critique of Cladistic Theory. *American Anthropologist* 96(4):925–948.

Neuzil, A. 2005 Corrugated Ceramics and Migration in the Pueblo III to Pueblo IV Transition, Silver Creek, Arizona. *Kiva* 71(1):101–124.

Ortman, S. G., and C. M. Cameron 2011 A Framework for Controlled Comparisons of Ancient Southwestern Movement. In *Movement, Connectivity, and Landscape Change in the Ancient Southwest*, edited by M. Nelson and C. Strawhacker, pp. 233–252. University Press of Colorado, Boulder.

Pelteret, D. 1981 Slave Raiding and Slave Trading in Early England. In *Anglo Saxon England*, edited by P. Clemoes, pp. 99–114. Cambridge University Press, Cambridge.

Pelteret, D. 1995 *Slavery in Early Mediaeval England: From the Reign of Alfred until the Twelfth Century*. The Boydell Press, Woodbridge, UK.

Perdue, T. 1979 *Slavery and the Evolution of Cherokee Society, 1540–1866*. The University of Tennessee Press, Knoxville.

Peregrine, P. N., I. Peiros, and M. Feldman (editors) 2009 *Ancient Human Migrations: A Multidisciplinary Approach.* University of Utah Press, Salt Lake City.

Raffield, B., N. Price, and M. Collard 2017 Male-biased Operational Sex Ratios and the Viking Phenomenon: An Evolutionary Anthropological Perspective on Late Iron Age Scandinavian Raiding. *Evolution and Human Behavior* 38:315–324.

Reid, A. 1983 Introduction: Slavery and Bondage in Southwest Asian History. In *Slavery, Bondage, and Dependency in Southeast Asia*, edited by Anthony Reid and J. Brewster, pp. 1–43. St. Martin's Press, New York.

Richter, D. K. 1983 War and Culture: The Iroquois Experience. *The William and Mary Quarterly* 40(4):528–559.

Riesman, P. 1977 *Freedom in Fulani Social Life: An Introspective Ethnography.* University of Chicago Press, Chicago.

Robertshaw, P., and W. L. Duncan 2008 African Slavery: Archaeology and Decentralized Societies. In *Invisible Citizens: Captives and Their Consequences*, edited by C. M. Cameron, pp. 57–79. University of Utah Press, Salt Lake City.

Rushforth, B. 2012 *Bonds of Alliance: Indigenous and Atlantic Slaveries in New France.* University of North Carolina Press, Chapel Hill.

Santos-Granero, F. 2009 *Vital Enemies: Slavery, Predation, and the Amerindian Political Economy of Life.* University of Texas Press, Austin.

Snyder, C. 2010 *Slavery in Indian Country. The Changing Face of Captivity in Early America.* Harvard University Press, Cambridge.

Stark, M. T. 1998 *The Archaeology of Social Boundaries.* Smithsonian Institution Press, Washington D.C.

Starna, W. A., and R. Watkins 1991 Northern Iroquoian Slavery. *Ethnohistory* 38(1):34–57.

Stone, T. T. 2003 Social Identity and Ethnic Interaction in the Western Pueblos of the American Southwest. *Journal of Archaeological Method and Theory* 10.31–67.

Thornton, J. K. 1999 *Warfare in Atlantic Africa 1500–1800.* Routledge, London.

Trigger, B. G. 1976 *The Children of Aataentsic I: A History of the Huron People to 1660.* McGill-Queen's University Press, Montreal.

Tringham, R. 1991 Households with Faces: the Challenge of Gender in Prehistoric Architectural Remains. In *Engendering Archaeology: Woman and Prehistory*, edited by J. M. Gero and M. W. Conkey. Blackwell, Oxford.

UNESCO 2019 "Migration and Inclusive Societies." Electronic document, https://wayback.archive-it.org/10611/20171126022441/http://www.unesco.org/new/en/social-and-human-sciences/themes/international-migration/glossary/migrant/, accessed October 2020.

van Dommelen, P. 2014 Moving On: Archaeological Perspectives on Mobility and Migration. *World Archaeology* 46(4): 477–483.

Walvin, J. 2006 *Atlas of Slavery.* Pearson, Harlow, England.

Warren, J. F. 1985 *The Sulu Zone 1768–1898.* New Day Publishers, Quezon City.

Weiner, M. 1995 The Global Migration Crisis: Challenge to States and to Human Rights. *Harper Collins Series in Comparative Politics.* Longman, New York.

Wiessner, P. 1983 Style and Social Information in Kalahari San Projectile Points. *American Antiquity.* 48(2):253–276.

Wobst, H. M. 1977 Stylistic Behavior and Information Exchange. In *For the Director: Research Essays in Honor of James B. Griffin*, edited by C.E. Cleland, pp. 317–342. University of Michigan, Museum of Anthropology, Ann Arbor.

CHAPTER SEVEN

The In/Visibility of Migration

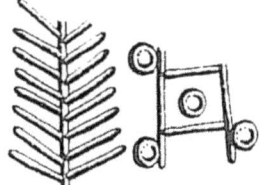

Elena Isayev

Abstract *The material record provides a complex source for identifying individuals who may have been perceived as outsiders in the ancient world. What is it that makes one's presence as an outsider in/visible? Or what would be the characteristics that would identify someone as not being a member of those who are deemed to be the native inhabitants? One of the issues is the different conceptions through time as to who is considered an outsider. Hence, in approaching the in/visibility of migration, the following paper first addresses the term migration and the roots of its contemporary English usage. It then draws on three Mediterranean case studies from the last two centuries B.C., to explore the contexts in which individuals and groups become visible as newcomers, and the challenges of recognizing them as such.*

What is it that makes one's presence as an outsider in/visible? Of the traces that a person might leave in the fabric of a place—or the traces that a birthplace might leave on them—which of these would indicate that the individual was not born on that soil? Or expressed differently: What would identify someone as not being a member of the group that saw itself as the native inhabitants of a site? The questions here do not directly address the movement of the body through space or communities, but rather the moments of stasis that intercept and bracket it. It is such moments that are anticipated and encompassed within the process of migration—not a neutral concept, but one historically and culturally contingent. Hence, in approaching the in/visibility of migration, the following paper will first consider the term *migration* and the roots of its contemporary English usage. Then three case studies, situated in the Mediterranean setting of the last two centuries B.C., will be used to explore the contexts in which individuals and groups become visible as newcomers to a place, and the challenges of recognizing them as such.

Migrant Terminologies

News reports of these early twenty-first-century decades are filled with the threat of border controls or conversely the threat of the "migrant." Whether the reader supports the views within them or finds them abhorrent s/he has no trouble understanding the references, nor imagining the scenarios described—they are easily materialized in the mind, even if never having been experienced firsthand. However, we cannot assume that people in the ancient Mediterranean would have had a similar understanding, despite the seemingly recognizable familiarity of certain situations, especially of displacement during periods of conflict. How appropriate is our terminology to a time some 2,000 years ago when two key elements of mobility appear to be missing, namely: (1) a national border, whether offshored or not; and (2) the fear of migration, as distinct from that of armed conquest or colonization? The ancient world was one of city-states, empires, areas of hegemony and regional powers, but not of countries that we might recognize in the guise of the modern nation-state. Nor were there any regional maps to scale on which the borders of such entities could be drawn. Depictions of the known world, such as the fourth-century A.D. Peutinger map, reveal an interest, not in the landmass nor any abstract Euclidian space, but the dynamism of the journey, connectivities, and place-moments. They do not provide a spatial framework—such as the gridded maps of today—with empty spaces onto which new locations can be plotted onto delineated territory.[1]

The ancient boundaries that were difficult to cross were not physical but of status; managing immigration would have made little sense in this period. This should not surprise us, as passports and border controls were mostly unknown even 200 years ago, and, as we will see below, were initially perceived as a burden during states of emergency, even as they became the norm. The use of "migration" and its derivatives as a description is not an objective statement of fact, but an interpretation, which differs from its ancient Latin form *migrare* that was much more fluid. Latin Republican usage did not differentiate between moving away from one's own state or community to a foreign one, nor was the motion it encompassed seen as a single event in one direction. The various derivatives of *migrare* seem largely interchangeable, as we first encounter them in the earliest Latin texts of the third century B.C. The Latin comic playwright Plautus equally used them to describe a move next door, a colony, or a journey overseas. The most frequently used form is *commigrare*—a move to a different residence with one's family and belongings (Plautus *Poenulus* 94; *Cistellaria* 177; *Trinummus* 1084–1085). But the same kind of move could equally be expressed by *emigrare* or *migrare* (Plautus *Mostellaria*, 470–472; *Epidicus*, 342). These were not used to articulate distance, duration, or border crossing. The characters of the Plautine comedies dart around a seemingly borderless world for trade, love, adventure, tourism, or due to poverty, war, brigandage, and slavery. In just three of his plays, *Curculio*, *Persa*, and *Poenulus*, the characters' journeys take them from North Africa, to India and onto the reaches of the Black Sea. For Plautus and his audience, it was not only that mobility was part of the everyday—rather than outside the norm—but that movement was not a subject of interest in itself.

Ancient writings, at least those produced before the Late Roman Imperial period, give no indication that migration as such was a problem, nor was it articulated as a single coherent phenomenon that could be the object of study, policy, or control, in and of itself. Today's demographers get frustrated due to the lack of good statistical data for ancient mobility, and the wide range of possibilities when calculating figures: as, for example, the persisting question of whether the total number of movements through Italy in the last 200 years B.C. was 5 or 40 million (the latter being highly plausible).[2] The preoccupation with measuring and limiting human flows is a modern phenomenon. As Betts and Collier write in their, not uncontroversial, recent book *Refuge*: the current crisis is not one of numbers but of politics (Betts and Collier 2017:2). In the context of ancient states, mobility was anticipated by authorities whose trouble was not keeping foreigners out but how to keep one's own citizens in one place long enough to count them, tax them, and recruit them into the army. This does not mean that ancient society was necessarily more inclusive, but rather that there were different modes of understanding inclusivity, and the way that geo-political space related to it.

Our own current usage of "migrate" and its derivatives, meaning to move across an international border in a "permanent" way with the purpose of "residence," is very recent. Its roots lie in the context of eighteenth-century North America. The novelty of its use was noted at the time by the philologist John Pickering, who included the terms—to *immigrate, immigration,* and *immigrant*—as neologisms in his 1816 work on vocabulary that was peculiar to the United States of America (Pickering 1816:108; Shumsky 2008:132; Thompson 2003:195). By 1828, the new meaning appeared in *Webster's Dictionary* (Webster 1828). It made "space, time, and purpose, fundamental characteristics of migration" (Shumsky 2008:131). As such, it cemented the relationship between territory, citizenship, and belonging. This new social construction of migration encouraged a fear of displacement and overcrowding by a seeming swarm of new arrivals (Shumsky 2008:134). It fueled a particular view of the foreigner and a protectionist migration policy by autonomous states. It brought in the modern passport, which became a mechanism for criminalizing unauthorized movement (Torpey 2000). The exceptionality of its normalization may be summed up in the views outlined by Reuben Fink in his 1921 article for the *Nation,* entitled: *Visas, Immigration and Official Anti-Semitism.*

> The passport and visa system is one of the evil heritages of the Great War. It emerged as a natural corollary of war logic. In this country it had its birth on May 22, 1918 through the adoption by Congress of the so-called Passport Control Act. It provided that no one should leave the United States without a passport or a permit from the Department of State, or enter this country without a passport properly visaed by the American consul or other accredited representatives abroad. The term of this act was to expire with the declaration of peace. [Fink 2014 (1921):29]

Even only a century ago, the outlook was significantly different, and hardly a given that such controls should exist, "[I]n other words, we've had nations before without any conception of a passport, or a visa system. . . . It is not just that the nation can be imagined differently, it has been practiced differently" (Magee et al. 2019:299). So writes Paul Magee, in our co-created piece with Aref Hussaini entitled *The Sky Is Hidden: On the Opening up of Language and National Borders*. Today's conception of migration, as already encompassed in Webster's early-nineteenth-century dictionary entry, arising out of a specific historical context, has gained in strength and has been projected into history, wrongly, as the norm. Such a definition would not have been possible in a world prior to the 1648 treaty, or Peace of Westphalia, which created sovereign states with territorial integrity, and hence the notion of an international border, which could, or could no longer, be easily crossed.

The difference in the conceptualization of migration across time, especially in relation to our current twenty-first-century context, becomes more apparent when trying to find a direct ancient equivalent for the seemingly generic, if highly loaded term—*migrant*—at least in Latin before the Late Imperial period. There were terms for the friendly outsider—*hospes,* and for the enemy—*hostis*. *Peregrinus* was the most common term used to mean a person from elsewhere, and *alienus* or *ignotus*[3] identified someone as being unknown.[4] The closest Latin term to *migrant* is *transitor*—literally meaning he who goes over or is a passer-by, but it only appears in the early Middle Ages when concepts of immobility were beginning to be associated with virtue (Ammianus 15.2.4). The categorization of someone as *transitor,* in the same way as *migrant* today, implies a negative state, which was then associated with vagrancy. Its appearance in this period reflects shifting attitudes to mobility, the status of individuals, and methods of control. Yet, even in Late Antiquity, the interest for authorities was not the policing of borders, but a reification of different levels of freedom, in part expressed through mobility and obligations, especially for those who were in a state of dependency. People had to be able to show that they had a reason to be where they were, whether that was as part of a particular household of an agricultural estate, a city, or region.

Being Visible

In light of the conceptual differences, it is not migration or the migrant, as understood today, that can be made visible in the ancient context. What is most prominently traceable in our material and written record are mass mobility events, which at times we know are state-initiated, as in the form of colonies, or relocations of enemies, soldiers, slaves, and veterans. Where these result in creation or dissolution of settlements, processes that are particularly prominent in our material record, but beyond the scope of this short paper,[5] we may consider as to why people chose to come together or move apart. But there are other forms of mobility—many evident in the studies within this volume—through individual and small group movements that are of equal if not of greater magnitude. It is the visibility of these non-state-initiated mobilities that will be the focus in this second part of the chapter. The key concerns here are: How is the fact of people being from elsewhere visible on the ground? And more specifically, which people, and at what point do they become visible as being from elsewhere? What makes their "fromness," whether geographically or culturally, a distinction to be exhibited?

The most visible traces are those left by the environment in the fabric of the body—in the bones and teeth. Bio-archaeological data, especially stable isotope analysis with its potential to provide an individual's geographic position at birth and at death, can reveal one part of this mobility history. The isotopic studies carried out in Italy, for example at the Roman cemeteries of Isola Sacra, at Casal Bertone and Castellaccio Europarco,[6] suggest that about one-third of the buried individuals were not of local origin. The visibility of outsiders through isotopic evidence is necessarily different from their visibility through self-representation, whether on inscriptions, which include foreign names and indications of origin, or through material evidence that points to the presence of external cultural elements. In terms of proportion; interestingly, where other data are available, the nonlocal origin of one-third of buried individuals seems to be a common trend, at least in some Italian urban contexts.[7] At the cemeteries belonging to Etruscan Volsinii (modern Crocifisso del Tufo, Orvieto), some one-third of the hundreds of names recorded for the Archaic period are of nonlocal origin.[8] At Caere and Rome, the onomastic data, although notoriously difficult to use for determining geographic origins, suggests that outsiders would have formed a significant proportion of the population (Bourdin 2012:532–551, Annex 2.12, 532–534). As the number of case studies increases, it will be interesting to see how robust this proportion of one-third is across the ancient world, whether it changes over time, and whether it is solely an urban feature. But just because someone was nonlocal does not necessarily mean that they would have been perceived as foreign. Self-representation is affected by factors of confidence, status, exclusivity, ideology, the extent of integration, and the nature of the site.

ITALIANS IN THE EASTERN MEDITERRANEAN DURING THE REPUBLIC—THE LAST THREE CENTURIES B.C.

The following three case studies from the Italian context will be used to consider the challenges of recognizing, materially, people of Italian origin in the Eastern Mediterranean who, according to textual sources, were there in the tens of thousands during the Roman Republican period.[9] Plenty of archaeological and other evidence indicates that communities in Italy had ties with sites around the Mediterranean from early on in their history, and we can detect a significant increase in contacts and exchange from the eighth century B.C. onward.[10] In terms of how the material culture of interaction, especially that found in domestic spaces and assemblages, relates to self-perception or belonging, an investigation in dialogue with Deleuzian notions of becoming is articulated by Marín-Aguilera (2018), focusing partly on the settlements in the Bay of Naples. One of the sites with which these communities on the coast had interactions was Pithekoussai. This settlement, located on the island of Ischia, just off the Campanian coast, was home to a successful socioeconomic enterprise that grew substantially in the eighth century B.C. Many of its incomers may have come from the Eastern Mediterranean, and especially Euboea, judging by the dominance of Euboean material in the funerary evidence, but they were not the only ones.[11] The variety of cultural trends represented in the archaeological record indicates that diverse communities participated in the creation of the site, including those "indigenous" to the island, along with Phoenicians, Greeks, and others from Italy. One example is an inscription dating to the seventh to sixth centuries B.C. on a locally made amphora in tomb 285 at S. Montano (Jeffery 1990:453, C). It carries the name Dazimos in the Greek alphabet, which is believed to be a Hellenized version of the Messapic name Dazminas. As for mobility flows in the opposite direction—Italians living in the East only become visible in the late third century B.C. While we might expect that, with the spread of Roman power at that time, more Italians would be moving to these regions of the Mediterranean, it is likely that they would have ventured East prior to this period.[12] The Plautine comedies, at least, suggest there was a good familiarity with this part of the world by the late third century B.C. Outside of the plays, the Italians who moved abroad in the period of the third to second centuries B.C. are most visible in the epigraphic record (Hatzfeld 1919; Ferrary 2002; Hasenohr 2007). While this is also sparse, at least it is direct evidence of presence, which is difficult to identify through other material remains.

Individuals who arrived from Italy or had roots in the peninsula have been recognized as such on inscriptions, either by the nature of their name, or because they are cited as *Rhômaioi* or *Italikoi* in Greek inscriptions and *Italici* in Latin ones.[13] Our inability to identify earlier evidence of their presence may be due to a lack of interest in displaying Italian cultural traits materially prior to the spread of Roman power. But the lack of an earlier record of Italians on inscriptions is also the result of the epigraphic habit on the peninsula itself. In Italy, the substantial growth of inscribed names came in the third to second centuries B.C., especially with the diffusion of elite funerary inscriptions and epitaphs.[14] For the whole of Italy, the total number of Latin inscriptions known from the third century B.C. is in the range of 600, of which only about 146 are from Rome (Gordon and Reynolds 2003:219–220). In the following two centuries, the figure from Italy rises to over 3,000, and most of these date to the final 160 years (Gordon and Reynolds 2003:220, note 37, 227–228; Crawford 1998:38; Panciera 1997; Pobjoy 2000), precisely the point at which Italians overseas become more visible. However, even then, the number of Italians listed on inscriptions in the East does not give a sense of the significant Italian population that would have made their new home in this part of the Mediterranean.

Massacre in Asia Minor

The extent of the discrepancy may be captured in a particular episode of the early first century: the massacre in 88 B.C. of Romans and Italians living in Asia Minor, by order of Mithridates VI king of Pontus. The total number killed, according to some authors, was 80,000.[15] It is probably an exaggeration, but even if reduced to 8,000 it is still significant, especially if we consider that the population of Italy at the time, on some estimates, was about 8 million.[16] Without the references to this event we would have no sense that so many Italians lived in this area of the Mediterranean, as there is only a handful of inscriptions from the region that record Italian origin dating to this period.[17] Our earliest inscriptions, which include names that are distinctly recognizable as Italian, are from Pergamum (von Prott and Kolbe 1902:44–151) and precede, by a few years, the direct Roman administration and formation of the province of Asia Minor, overseen by M. Aquillius from 129–126 B.C. (Strabo 13.4.2 [C624]; Appian *BC*, 1.111; Livy *Periochae*, 58, 59: Gruen 1984:592–610). What is of particular interest in this episode is that these people were not in Asia Minor as a result of any collective movement or an event such as colonization, at least none that we know about. They lived across numerous cities of the region, having arrived as individuals for a variety of reasons and especially commercial opportunities.

This form of independent and private mobility is the hardest to quantify. The extent of this group of Romans and Italians in Asia Minor may not be visible epigraphically, but we know that they were visible as Italians on the street, since they had to be recognized as such to be killed (Alcock 2007). The toga would have likely been a giveaway sign of their origin or affiliation (Amiotti 1980:134; Wilson 1966:154–155). Cicero tells of how the exiled Publius Rutilius Rufus, who was living in Mytilene, had to exchange his toga for a Greek cloak—*pallium*—in an attempt to escape the executioners.[18] The choice to hold on to, or reintroduce, one's distinctive external cultural signifiers, such as dress, language, or name, is a sign of privilege and confidence. The privilege and confidence afforded by being a Roman, and to some extent also Italian citizen, may have meant a disinterest in integrating into the local culture. Such a shift in one's self-perception is another reason why individuals from this newly emerging Romano-Italian empire become more visible in our written sources and material evidence from this time on.

Visibility and the Case of Delos

My final case is that of the Italians operating from the free port of Delos (Polybius 30.31), one of the major trading hubs of the Mediterranean. Hasenohr's detailed studies of the monuments and inscriptions show that the presence of Italians at Delos can be traced back at least to the third century B.C. (Hasenohr 2007). The Italians are discernible not only as individuals, but also as a defined group that was responsible for collective action. This is most visible in the creation of the Delian college of *Competaliastai* which oversaw the Italian cult of the *Lares Compitales* from the early second century B.C. (Hasenohr 2001; Hasenohr 2002; Hasenohr 2003; Ferrary 2002). Delos was also home to other *consortia* that exercised collective action. There was a Delian association of Alexandrians, and the Phoenicians had a cult organization corresponding to a *marzeah* (Baslez 2007:228–230; Hasenohr 2007). We can also trace the movements of some of the merchant families operating there, such as the Castricii, believed to be of Campanian origin, but, by then, of multiple homes (Müller and Hasenohr 2002:18–20). Their *gens* name first appears not in Italy but in Delos and Boeotia. They only (re?)-appear in Italy several generations later once the port at Puteoli superseded the one in Delos in the first century B.C.[19]

While there is evidence of collective action at Delos, it seems to be lacking in Athens, where Roman and Italian names also appear in this period. Follet's findings show that here they do not stand out as a group, either in collective dedications, or as members of professional or cultural associations (Follet 2002). It is also apparent that some of those with Romano-Italian names may have come from different regions of the Mediterranean and not directly from Rome or Italy (Follet 2002:85). Perhaps Delos is special in this period in its role as a self-contained central trade hub,[20] with a fluid populace, and no dominant majority. It was more akin to an ancient stock exchange, which created an environment conducive to cultural enclaves and the prioritization of external links, rather than integration or intermixing. It may also be the case that we are witnessing a shift, which appears most visibly at Delos. These Italians and Romans—in particular—were becoming conspicuous in a way they had not been prior to the spread of Roman power in the second century B.C. Their visibility demonstrates an interest in being recognized as part of a group with rising influence and privilege, fueled by a desire to be associated with an imperial power.

Furthermore, some of the collective activities might not be recognizable as Italian. For example, Rizakis showed that Romano-Italian communities were keen worshippers of Eastern deities. Serapis was particularly favored, as revealed in the dedications by Italian *negotiatores* at the Serapeion of Thessalonike. The financial success of these traders helped to fund renovations in the temple.[21] These Italians were important benefactors of these cults, and contributed to their dissemination. Communal acts such as the organization of colleges, or the creation of religious and cultural spaces, required wealth, influence, and power to sustain them, as well as the permission to build them on foreign soil in the first place, as the Romano-Carthaginian early treaties outline. They are endeavors that reflect a heightened state of confidence, which these Italic individuals carried with them to their homes abroad from the second century onward, supported by their newly acquired imperial origins.

Conclusions

Despite the low levels of material visibility of civilian outsiders in the contexts described above, multiple forms of evidence make it beyond doubt that ancient communities were highly mobile and often mixed. The studies presented in this volume support this trend, and demonstrate that those individuals who can be identified as being away from their place of birth are only the tip of the iceberg of those on the move or living abroad. At what point does one's presence as an outsider become visible? As I have tried to show, status plays a key role in this visibility. As bio-archaeological methods of analysis improve, and it becomes more feasible to look at larger samples of buried individuals, we should gain more robust data for the proportion of outsiders in a community, their provenance, the comparative mobility of men and women, between different age groups and diverse social sectors. It will allow insight as to whether those who were not local were treated differently at burial, across different sites. It will also highlight integrative practices, which can make nonlocals invisible.

One sector of those largely invisible in the material record are the people who have been forcefully displaced, especially if they are moving as individuals or small groups. Forced displacement is most apparent in our record when it occurs en masse.[22] Some of its characteristic signs are the rapid abandonment and destruction of certain sites, and the appearance and hurried creation of new settlements, often on marginal land with structures made of poor materials. Distinctive material culture, in terms of moveable objects and small finds in any quantity are rare in such contexts, since people who are fleeing do not tend to take many belongings with them. It is unusual to find even today the kind of collection that exists, for example, at Trieste, a city that sat precariously on opposite sides of the border between Italy and what was then Yugoslavia, during the first half of the twentieth century. Trieste still houses, in Magazzino 18—one of its vast harbour warehouses—an incredible collection of chairs, cupboards, tables, beds and other remnants of households that were transported in the tens of thousands following World War II. These were the material remains of the consequences of the 1947 Treaty of Paris—which redrew the boundaries between Italy, Austria, and the Socialist Federal Republic of Yugoslavia, with Italy losing control over Istria. It triggered the forced displacement (or repatriation) of the majority of those Italians who were living in what became Yugoslav territory overnight—a total of some 300,000 people (Gori and Ravello-Lami 2018). Interestingly, this move of some magnitude, over this contested border, would have remained largely invisible to bio-archaeological investigations. For, unlike the deep divisions forced by a line on the map, the environment is the same on both sides of the border, and would have left few traces in the body.

Acknowledgments

I am grateful to Megan Daniels and her team at the University of Buffalo, and especially the students, for creating such a dynamic meeting to exchange ideas. This paper draws on these exchanges, especially with Catherine Cameron, and the research published in Isayev 2017. The final shaping and nuances of this piece are thanks to nourishing discussions with Staffan Müller-Wille.

Notes

1. For discussion on ancient mapping see Isayev 2017, ch. 10, esp. 377ff.
2. The 5 million figure is based on the calculations made by Scheidel 2004, 2005. Forty million is the theoretical figure projected by Erdkamp (2008:419), in his critique of Osborne's 1991 calculations for Greece, which used Laslett's 1977 studies of seventeenth-century populations in the villages of Clayworth and Cogenhoe. For discussion on demographic approaches to ancient migration, their opportunities and limitations see Isayev 2017, ch. 2.
3. Cicero in his *de Officiis*, 1.37 notes that the term *hostis,* meaning enemy by the later Republican period, in Archaic times had the same meaning as *peregrinus*—stranger. He provides examples of its use from the Twelve Tables. Varro also notes this same change in the use of the word *hostis:* Varro *Lingua Latina,* 5.3. For commentary, and the texts of the Twelve Tables, 2.2 and 6.4 see: *Roman Statutes* Law 40: Tab. 2.2e; Tab. 6.4 (Vol. II, 622–624, 660–661).
4. *Alienus* is used in *Captivi,* 145; *Rudens,* 115; *Stichus,* 480; and *Truculentus,* 178, which also uses *ignotus* in the same phrase, implying there is some distinction between them or for emphasis; *pro ignoto alienoque*. The term *ignotus* is also used in *Curculio,* 280; *Menaechmi,* 335, 373, 495. A similar term meaning someone who is unknown—*non novit*: *Asinaria,* 495–496.

5. For an in-depth study of this subject relating to ancient Italy of the sixth to the third centuries B.C., see Isayev 2017, ch. 3–4.
6. Prowse et al. 2019, with reference to the studies by Killgrove (2010a, 2010b).
7. As also observed by Hin 2013:219, 234–237.
8. For the most recent analysis of this epigraphic collection, the site, and the extent to which it can tell us about the origins of those in the buried community: Bourdin 2012:532–534, Annex 2.12; van Heems 2009.
9. See Isayev 2017, ch. 2.
10. See ibid., ch. 3–5 for overview and references.
11. Ancient authors writing hundreds of years after the events recount the different peoples that settled the island over time, Strabo 5.4.9, starting from the Chalcidians and Eretrians in the eighth century B.C.; Livy 8.22.5.–6, states that those who came to found Cumae from Chalcis in Euboea, first landed on Pithekoussai as well as other nearby islands. Questioning whether Pithekoussai should be seen as a colony rather than an emporion: Osborne 1998:257–259; Cuozzo 2007:246; Coldstream 1994; Riva 2010:53; Izzet 2007:216. The funerary practice and material remains from the burials at the site show strong links with Euboea: Buchner and Ridgway 1993.
12. For the visibility of Etruscans and other Italians abroad from the Archaic period: Isayev 2017, ch. 3 and 4.
13. The term *Italici*, continued to be used even after the Social War—despite the fact that all were Roman citizens: Ferrary 2002:135.
14. Berrendonner 2009:192. Non-aristocratic ones proliferating from about 200 B.C.
15. For the details of the events: Appian *The Mithridatic Wars* 22–24. For the figure of 80,000: Valerius Maximus 9.2.3 (ext); Memnon of Heraclea Pontica 31.9 (= FGH III B, p352, ll 16–21).
16. For discussion of the population figures, and debates over high and low counts, see: Hin 2013; De Ligt 2012; Bowman and Wilson 2011.
17. For Italians in Asia Minor: Frank 1975 [1938]:543–545; Fränkel 1890–1895:249, lines 14ff; with Wilson 1966:125; Ferrary 2001.
18. Cicero, *For Rabirius Postumus* 10.27. For details of Rufus's life: Kelly 2006:89–91, 181 (note 25).
19. For the importance of Puteoli as a draw for international traders see: Cébeillac-Gervasoni 2002.
20. Italians were well embedded in the thriving community on Delos by the time that the island was given free port status in 166 B.C., when it was assigned to Athens by Rome (Polybius 30.31.10). For context see Wilson 1966:99–120.
21. Some of the earliest *gens* names linked with Nilotic cults are Salarii, Herennii, Avii, Papii (Rizakis 2002:122).
22. For the challenges of identifying forced displacement materially see Driessen 2018.

References Cited

Alcock, S. 2007 Making Sure You Know Whom to Kill: Spatial Strategies and Strategic Boundaries in the Eastern Roman Empire. *Millennium—Jahrbuch* 4:13–23.

Amiotti, G. 1980 I Greci ed il massacro degli Italici nell 88 a.C. *Aevum* 54:132–139.
Baslez, M.-F. 2007 La question des étrangers dans les cités grecques (Ve–1er siècles). Immigration et partenariat économique. *Pallas* 74:213–236.
Berrendonner, C. 2009 L'Invention des épitaphes dans la Rome médio-républicaine. In *Ecritures, cultures, sociétés dans les nécropoles d'Italie ancienne: table ronde des 14–15 décembre 2007. Mouvements et trajectoires dans les nécropoles d'Italie d'époque pré-républicaine et républicaine*, edited by M. L. Haack, pp. 181–201. ENS Paris, Paris.
Betts, A., and P. Collier 2017 *Refuge: Transforming a Broken Refugee System*. Penguin Random House, Milton Keynes.
Bourdin, S. 2012 *Les peuples de l'Italie préromaine: identités, territoires et relations inter-ethniques en Italie centrale et septentrionale (VIIIe–Ier s. av. J.-C.)*. École française de Rome, Rome.
Bowman, A., and A. Wilson (editors) 2011 *Settlement, Urbanization, and Population: Oxford Studies on the Roman Economy 2*. Oxford University Press, Oxford and New York.
Bradley, G., E. Isayev, and C. Riva (editors) 2007 *Ancient Italy, Regions Without Boundaries*. University of Exeter Press, Exeter.
Buchner, G., and D. Ridgway 1993 *Pithekoussai. Vol. 1: La necropoli: tombe 1-723 scavate dal 1952 al 1961*. Accademia nazionale dei Lincei, Rome.
Cébeillac Gervasoni, M. 2002 Note relative aux élites du Latium et de la Campanie et à leurs rapports avec la Méditerranée orientale. In *Les italiens dans le monde grec : IIe siècle av. J.-C.–Ier siècle ap. J.-C.: circulation, activités, intégration: actes de la table ronde, École normale supérieure, Paris, 14–16 mai 1998*, edited by C. Müllerand and C. Hasenohr, pp. 21–28. De Boccard, Paris.
Coldstream, N. 1994 Prospectors and Pioneers: Pithekoussai, Kyme and Central Italy. In *The Archaeology of Greek Colonisation: Essays Dedicated to Sir John Boardman*, edited by G. Tsetskhladze and F. De Angelis, pp. 47 59. Oxford University School of Archaeology, Oxford.
Crawford, M. H. 1998 How to Create a *Municipium*: Rome and Italy after the Social War. In *Modus Operandi: Essays in Honour of Professor G. E. Rickman*, edited by M. Austin, J. Harries, and C. Smith, pp. 31–46. Institute of Classical Studies, London.
Crawford, M. H. 1996 *Roman Statutes*. Institute of Classical Studies, School of Advanced Study, University of London, London.
Cuozzo, M. 2007 Ancient Campania: Cultural Interaction, Political Borders, and Geographical Boundaries. In *Ancient Italy, Regions without Boundaries*, edited by G. Bradley, E. Isayev, and C. Riva, pp. 224–267. University of Exeter Press, Exeter.
De Ligt, L. 2012 *Peasants, Citizens, and Soldiers: Studies in the Demographic History of Roman Italy 225 BC–AD 100*. Cambridge University Press, Cambridge.
Driessen, J. (editor) 2018 *An Archaeology of Forced Migration. Crisis-Induced Mobility and the Collapse of the 13th c BCE Eastern Mediterranean. AEGIS*, edited by J. Driessen. UCL, Louvain.
Erdkamp, P. 2008 Mobility and Migration in Italy in the Second Century BC. In *People, Land, and Politics: Demographic Developments and the Transformation of Roman Italy 300 BC–AD 14*, edited by L. De Ligt and S J. Northwood, pp. 417–450. Brill, Leiden and Boston.
Ferrary, J.-L. 2001 Rome et les cités grecques d'Asie Mineure au IIe siécle. In *Les cités d'Asie mineure occidentale au IIe siècle a.C.*, edited by A. Bresson and R. Descat, pp. 93–106. Ausonius, Bordeaux.
Ferrary, J.-L. 2002 La création de la province d'Asie et la présence italienne en Asie Mineure. In *Les italiens dans le monde grec : IIe siècle av. J.-C.–Ier siècle ap. J.-C. : circulation, activités,*

intégration: actes de la table ronde, Ecole normale supérieur, Paris, 14–16 mai 1998, edited by C. Müller and C. Hasenohr, pp. 133–146. École française d'Athènes, Paris.

FGH (1923–) *Fragmente der griechischen Historiker*. Leiden.

Fink, R. 2014[1921] Visas, Immigration, and Official Anti-Semitism. In *This Immigrant Nation: Perspectives on an American Dilemma, Articles from The Nation 1868—The Present*, edited by R. Lingeman, pp. 29. Special volume of *The Nation*.

Follet, S. 2002 Les Italiens à Athènes (IIe siècle av. J.-C.–Ier siècle ap. J.-C). In *Les italiens dans le monde grec : IIe siècle av. J.-C.–Ier siècle ap. J.-C. : circulation, activités, intégration : actes de la table ronde, Ecole normale supérieur, Paris, 14–16 mai 1998*, edited by C. Müller and C. Hasenohr, pp. 79–88. De Boccard, Paris.

Frank, T. (editor) 1975 *An Economic Survey of Ancient Rome*, Vol. IV, 2nd ed. Octagon Books, New York.

Fränkel, M. 1890 *Die Inschriften von Pergamon—Bd. 1. Bis zum Ende der Königszeit*. Spemann, Berlin.

Gordon, R., and J. Reynolds 2003 Roman Inscriptions 1995–2000. *Journal of Roman Studies* 93:212–294.

Gori, M., and M. Revello Lami 2018 From Lampedusa to Trieste: An Archaeological Approach to Present Forced Migrations and Identity Patterns. In *An Archaeology of Forced Migration. Crisis Induced Mobility and the Collapse of the 13th c BCE Eastern Mediterranean. AEGIS*, edited by J. Driessen, pp. 31–54. UCL, Louvain.

Gruen, E. S. 1984 *The Hellenistic World and the Coming of Rome*. University of California Press, Berkeley.

Hasenohr, C. 2001 Les monuments des collèges italiens sur l'agora des Compétaliastes à Délos. In *Constructions publiques et programmes édilitaires en Grèce entre le IIe siècle av. J.-C. et le Ier siècle ap. J.-C. : actes du colloque organisé par l'École française d'Athènes et le CNRS, Athènes, 14–17 mai 1995* (BCH Supplément 39), édité by J.-Y. Marc and J.-C. Moretti, pp. 329–348. École française d'Athènes, Athens.

Hasenohr, C. 2002 Les collèges de magistri et la communauté italienne de Délos. In *Les italiens dans le monde grec : IIe siècle av. J.-C.–Ier siècle ap. J.-C. : circulation, activités, intégration : actes de la table ronde, École normale supérieur, Paris, 14–16 mai 1998*, édité by C. Müller and C. Hasenohr, pp. 67–76. École française d'Athènes, Paris.

Hasenohr, C. 2003 Les *Compitalia* à Délos. *Bulletin de Correspondence Hellénique* 127:167–249.

Hasenohr, C. 2007 Les Italiens à Délos: entre romanité et hellénisme. *Pallas* 73:221–232.

Hatzfeld, J. 1919 *Les trafiquants italiens dans l'Orient hellénique*. Bibliothèque des Écoles françaises d'Athènes et de Rome 115. De Boccard, Paris.

Hin, S. 2013 *The Demography of Roman Italy: Population Dynamics in an Ancient Conquest Society (201 BCE–14 CE)*. Cambridge University Press, Cambridge.

Hussaini, A., E. Isayev, and P. Magee 2019 "The Sky is Hidden": On the Opening up of Language and National Borders. *GeoHumanities*: 295–311.

Isayev, E. 2017 *Migration, Mobility, and Place in Ancient Italy*. Cambridge University Press, Cambridge.

Izzet, V. 2007 *The Archaeology of Etruscan Society*, Cambridge University Press, Cambridge.

Jeffery, L. H. 1990 *The Local Scripts of Archaic Greece. A Study of the Origin of the Greek Alphabet and its Development from the Eighth to the Fifth Centuries B.C.* (rev. ed.). Oxford University Press, Oxford.

Kelly, G. P. 2006 *A History of Exile in the Roman Republic.* Cambridge University Press, Cambridge.

Killgrove, K. 2010a Migration and Mobility in Imperial Rome. PhD dissertation, University of North Carolina at Chapel Hill.

Killgrove, K. 2010b Identifying Immigrants to Imperial Rome Using Strontium Isotope Analysis. In *Roman Diasporas: Archaeological Approaches to Mobility and Diversity in the Roman Empire* (Journal of Roman Archaeology Supplementary Series 78), edited by H. Eckardt, pp. 157–174. Journal of Roman Archaeology, Portsmouth, RI.

Laslett, P. 1977 *Family Life and Illicit Love in Earlier Generations: Essays in Historical Sociology.* Cambridge University Press, Cambridge.

Marín-Aguilera, B. 2018 Inhabiting Domestic Space: Becoming Different in the Early Iron Age Western Mediterranean. *Journal of Mediterranean Archaeology* 31(1):77–100.

Müller, C., and C. Hasenohr 2002 Gentilices et circulation des Italiens : quelques réflexions méthodologiques. In *Les italiens dans le monde grec : IIe siècle av. J.-C.–Ier siècle ap. J.-C. : circulation, activités, intégration : actes de la table ronde, Ecole normale supérieur, Paris, 14–16 mai 1998*, edited by C. Müller and C. Hasenohr, pp. 11–20. De Boccard, Paris.

Osborne, R. 1991 The Potential Mobility of Human Populations. *Oxford Journal of Archaeology* 10(2):231–252.

Osborne, R. 1998 Early Greek Colonization? The Nature of Greek Settlements in the West. In *Archaic Greece. New Approaches and New Evidence,* edited by N. Fisher and H. van Wees, pp. 251–270. Duckworth, London.

Panciera, S. 1997 L'evergetismo civico nelle iscrizioni latine d'età repubblicana. In *Actes du Xe Congrès International d'Épigraphie Grecque et Latine, Nîmes, 4–9 octobre 1992*, edited by M. Christol and O. Masson, pp. 249–290. Publications de la Sorbonne, Paris.

Pickering, J. 1816 [1974] *A Vocabulary or Collection of Words and Phrases Which Have Been Supposed to be Peculiar to the United States of America.* Burt Franklin, New York.

Pobjoy, M. P. 2000 Building Inscriptions in Republican Italy: Euergetism, Responsibility, and Civic Virtue. In *The Epigraphic Landscape of Roman Italy* (BICS Supplement 73), edited by A. E. Cooley, pp. 77–92. Institute of Classical Studies, London.

Prowse, T., R. Stark, and M. Emery 2019 Stable Isotope Analysis and Human Migration in the Ancient Mediterranean and Near East. In *Migration and Migrant Identities in the Near East from Antiquity to the Middle Ages*, edited by A. Zerbini and J. Yoo. Routledge, London.

Riva, C. 2010 *The Urbanisation of Etruria. Funerary Practices and Social Change, 700–600 BC.* Cambridge University Press, Cambridge.

Rizakis, A. 2002 L'émigration romaine en Macédoine et la communauté marchande de Thessalonique : perspectives économiques et sociales. In *Les italiens dans le monde grec : IIe siècle av. J.-C. Ier siècle ap. J.-C. : circulation, activités, intégration : actes de la table ronde, École normale supérieure, Paris, 14–16 mai 1998*, edited by C. Müller and C. Hasenohr, pp. 109–132. De Boccard, Paris.

Scheidel, W. 2004 Human Mobility in Roman Italy, I: The Free Population. *Journal of Roman Studies* 94:1–26.

Scheidel, W. 2005 Human Mobility in Roman Italy, II: The Slave Population. *Journal of Roman Studies* 95:64–79.

Shumsky, N. L. 2008 Noah Webster and the Invention of Immigration. *The New England Quarterly* 81(1):126–135.

Thompson, P. 2003 "Judicious Neology" The Imperative of Paternalism in Thomas Jefferson's Linguistic Studies. *Early American Studies: An Interdisciplinary Journal*, 1(2):187–224.

Torpey, J. 2000 *The Invention of the Passport: Surveillance, Citizenship and the State*. Cambridge University Press, Cambridge.

Van Heems, G. 2009 La naissance des traditions épigraphiques funéraries dans l'Étrurie archaïque ; le cas de Cocifisso del Tufo. In *Écritures, cultures, sociétés dans les nécropoles d'Italie ancienne : table ronde des 14–15 décembre 2007 'Mouvements et trajectoires dans les nécropoles d'Italie d'époque pré-républicaine et républicaine,' ENS Paris*, edited by M. L. Haack, pp. 15–44. De Boccard, Paris.

Von Prott, H., and W. Kolbe 1902 Die Arbeiten zu Pergamon: Inschriften. *Mitteilungen des Deutschen Archäologischen Instituts, Athenische Abteilung* 27:44–151.

Webster, N. 1828 *An American Dictionary of the English Language*. S. Converse, New York.

Wilson, A. J. N. 1966 *Emigration from Italy in the Republican Age of Rome*. Manchester University Press, Manchester.

CHAPTER EIGHT

A Harbor Scene

Reassessing Mobility in the Bronze Age
Eastern Mediterranean Following the
Archaeological Science Revolution

Assaf Yasur-Landau

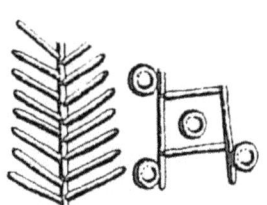

Abstract *The archaeology of the Levant is currently going through a fully fledged scientific revolution, with the results of new analytical methods being heavily integrated in the effort to reconstruct ancient societies and to understand the social processes of the last decade. The main challenge for current users of these methods will be to create a mechanism of feedback between analytical and interpretative tools in the same or similar pace as that of scientific developments in analytical methods.*

This Mediterranean reality in which a multiplicity of interactions involving mobility occur simultaneously (from trade to migration etc.) does not enable discussing each form of mobility separately—not even the very wide range of migration. Rather, a unified model of interaction is required that allows the identification of each event of mobility within the significantly wider interaction continuum. This article suggests some possible directions for more inclusive modeling of human mobility in complex societies, with the use of data procured from aDNA and stable isotope analyses in tandem with historical and archaeological data. A point of departure for this discussion are the complex interactions depicted in a unique harbor scene from the Tomb of Kenamun (TT162), dating to the days of Amenhotep III.

THE NEED FOR NEW AND IMPROVED THEORETICAL MODELS FOR MOBILITY IN ARCHAEOLOGY

Why do we now need new and improved theoretical models for mobility in archaeology? As we shall see below, the new analytical methods in archaeology, such as aDNA studies and stable isotope analysis, pose considerable challenges for archaeological theory as an interpretative tool, as they advance at a much faster pace than does current migration and mobility theory in archaeology. Ion (2019) has recently defined the expectation for a research design for the study of environmental data in the era of new scientific methods in archaeology:

> Interdisciplinary archaeology projects require us to follow a two-step process: (1) more refined methodologies, with more data points, and complex interpretive frameworks instead of "one-shot" explanations, and (2) a shift in points of view, by bringing environmental data into anthropological frameworks. [Ion 2019:12]

To my mind, similar expectations should be directed at the study of ancient mobility; that is, the need to create a mechanism of feedback between the development of earth and life sciences analytical tools and the development of interpretative frameworks that rely on the social sciences. The aim of this article is therefore to explore—through the use of examples from the second-millennium B.C. eastern Mediterranean—some of the considerations needed in order to modify the theoretical frameworks in the archaeology of mobility.

The complicated relationship between archaeogenetics, language, and material culture is at the heart of the current debate on the use of the newly available genetic sequencing and clustering. The heavy shadow of the past with its semidark heritage of cultural history seems to still loom (mainly) over European archaeology, in cases such as the problematic history of the Beaker phenomenon and the challenges for present archaeogenetic research (see also Callaway 2018; see Daniels this volume; Gokcumen this volume). This is, in some ways, an almost startling iteration of the taxonomic challenge faced by the founders of processual archaeology when explaining the multifaceted aspects of culture. Thus, for example, Clarke (1978:372–374) explored Bantu identity through the partially overlapping ovals of culture group, technocomplex, language group, and "subrace," creating in their intersection the Bantu ethnopolitical group, while arguing that the same sets can be used for archaeological elements (Clarke 1978:Figure 76). Yet in order to avoid the pitfalls of cultural history with its (sometimes) racial overtones, efforts to establish due caution in the question of the naming of genetic clusters and to differentiate them from material culture clustering are, of course, justified, as "genetic clusters are as flexible and dynamic as archaeological groupings. Both are theoretical constructions and result from our epistemological need to create space-time-entities as aids for further understanding" (Eisenmann et al. 2018:10).

In a way, the extensive use of natural and earth sciences in archaeology as integrated parts of the discipline's research, combined with global concerns for current climate change, have ushered in, perhaps unintentionally, an era characterized by elements of positivist, neo-processual archaeology (Kristiansen 2014:25). This is evident by a new emphasis on climate change as a cause, not only for collapse, as in the case of the Bronze Age (e.g., Langgut et al. 2013; Kaniewski et al. 2013; Finne et al. 2017), but also for culture change as an effort to adapt to these changes (e.g., Flohr et al. 2016; Roffet-Salque 2018; Biehl and Nieuwehuyse 2016). In terms of the current stance of archaeology in the track of the theory pendulum, it may well be that it is in the midst of the shift seen already in social sciences and elsewhere from "postmodernity to a revised modernity" (Kristiansen 2014:23). The quantum leap in ancient DNA (aDNA) research is indeed bringing to the front of the stage the vigorous return to the study of mobility and migration, themes that were almost unthinkable in the era of post-processual archaeology (Burmeister 2000; Hakenbeck 2008). This is indeed an era of experimentations and rapid changes following the demise of post-processualism (Kristiansen 2014:13).

The archaeology of the Levant is currently going through a fully fledged scientific revolution, with the results of new analytical methods being heavily integrated in the effort to reconstruct ancient societies and to understand the social processes of the last decade (Yasur-Landau et al. 2019). The work on aDNA is just now beginning to reach the eastern Mediterranean and is expected to provide considerable breakthroughs regarding patterns of mobility. Thus, research on the aDNA of early farming communities has exposed the significant complexity of large-scale and prolonged movement of people in the Levant in the Neolithic period (Lazaridis et al. 2016), perhaps connected also with the striking genetic variability in the Peqi'in Cave during the Chalcolithic period (Harney et al. 2018). With current, and doubtless future, research in the Levant dealing with finds from the Bronze and Iron Ages—periods from which a rich written historical record exists—aDNA studies and other scientific methods such as stable isotope analysis will surely be used for looking beyond large-scale population movements, into the intricate, co-occurring mobility-related events and phenomena, such as trade, smaller-scale human migration (whether voluntary or forced), and even animal mobility.

The Mediterranean Sea with the short-distance sailing routes between its surrounding lands was a convenient medium for connectivity in antiquity, as it is today. Here, various ranges of interaction co-occurred in the same regions, sometimes at the same location as migration, trade, maritime colonization, the movement of refugees, and piracy (e.g., Horden and Purcell 2000:293–291; Knapp and van Dommelen 2014:109). This Mediterranean reality in which a multiplicity of interactions involving mobility occur simultaneously (from trade to migration, etc.) does not enable discussing each form of mobility separately—not even the very wide range of migration. Rather, a unified model of interaction is required that allows the identification of each event of mobility within the significantly wider interaction continuum (Figure 8.1) (Yasur-Landau 2010:10–12, Figure 1.1).

A previous suggestion for such a model combines parameters suggested by studies of acculturation (e.g., Berry 1997; Kuo and Roysircar 2004) with insights from the study of migration and trade in archaeology and history. It includes six parameters for which values may be entered, describing any form of interaction, such as trade, migration, and conquest, among others (Figure 1.2, Yasur-Landau 2010:10–13; 2017):

1. The number of people involved in the interaction

2. The duration of the interaction

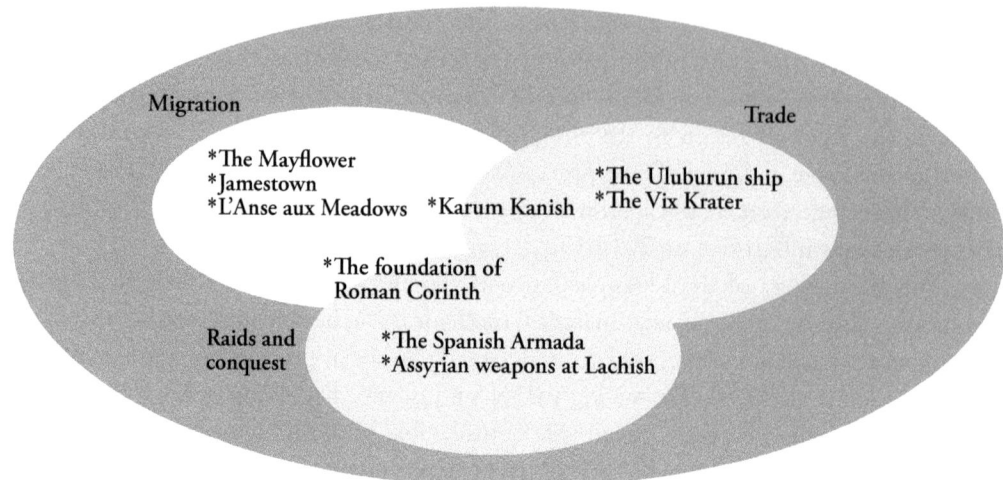

FIGURE 8.1. Overlapping interaction ranges; after Yasur-Landau 2010, Figure 1.1.

3. The cultural distance between the cultures involved in the interaction

4. The segment of population involved in the interaction

5. The balance of power between the cultures involved in the interaction

6. The level of pluralism and tolerance within the interacting societies

A criterion of *deep change* in material culture connected with activities that are mainly domestic was used to differentiate between migration and other forms of interaction (Yasur-Landau 2010:13–26). While the new potent tools of aDNA and stable isotope analyses do not influence the description of the modes of human mobility in the variables above, they do provide new data for the identification of such events and phenomena. Such an endeavor for more inclusive modeling of human mobility in complex societies is indeed on its way, and I wish to suggest some possible directions for the use of data procured from the new analytical tools of the current scientific revolution in archaeology including aDNA and stable isotope analyses in tandem with historical and archaeological data.

A Snapshot of Co-Occurring Mobility in the Harbor Scene in the Tomb of Kenamun

The complex Levantine societies in the second millennium B.C. grew accustomed to a reality in which maritime interregional interaction developed into a remarkable variety of co-occurring activities, fit for the growing social and economic needs of the local elites. Just how complex these interactions were can be seen in a unique harbor scene from the Tomb of Kenamun (or Qenamun, TT162), dating to the days of Amenhotep III (Figure 8.2). While complex, these interactions, as we shall see in the following sections of this article, can be at least partially reconstructed using new scientific methods. The tomb's owner had been the mayor of Thebes and overseer of the granary—his career spanning the reigns of Thutmose IV and Amenhotep III (Davies and Faulkner 1947, Plate 8; Shirley 2005:258; Wachsmann 1998, Figure 14.6; Yasur-Landau 2019:553–555) [Figure 8.2 herein]. Although the depiction is not accompanied by an inscription, it is likely that as part of his role as mayor Kenamun inspected the arrival of Levantine ("Syrian") ships to the major port of Thebes (Shirley 2007:388). The arrival of Levantine ships at the Egyptian port is followed by several scenes demonstrating different types of interaction, on various scales, involving different participants:

1. Small-scale trade: Upon disembarking, Levantine sailors dressed in short skirts and merchants dressed in heavier robes, depicted in the lower register, are seen approaching a series of small shops in which Egyptian men and women are selling textiles and sandals.

2. Foreign families and human mobility: In the top register, two women and a child in Levantine dress face an Egyptian official. A Levantine man wearing a heavy robe is seated to the official's left, raising his hands toward another Egyptian official.

FIGURE 8.2. Interactions in a harbor scene, tomb of Kenamun (after Davies and Faulkner 1947: pl. 8, additions by Yasur-Landau) (Public Domain).

3. Tribute: The middle register shows a presentation scene in which Levantine men clad with heavy robes, some bowing down, stand among Egyptian officials; the former are depicted carrying metal vessels and other finished products.

4. Large-scale bulk trade, including animal mobility: The lower register also shows the import of Canaanite amphorae, bowls, and some finished products, such as a metal statue of a bull and two very prominent, huge humped-back or zebu bulls.

How can we disentangle, using archaeological tools, such a baffling array of mobility types that occur simultaneously following the arrival of several boats at a harbor? It may be expected that each interaction type left a different imprint on the archaeological record, as each has a different value in the interaction parameters suggested above. Table 8.1 suggests

TABLE 8.1.
THE USE OF INTERACTION PARAMETERS TO ANALYZE
THE VARIOUS INTERACTIONS IN THE KENAMUN HARBOR SCENE

	1. Number of Levantine people involved	2. Duration of interaction	3. Cultural distance between people interacting	4. Segment of population involved	5, 6. Balance of power and level of tolerance
Arrival of foreign families	Few–up to 10	Years-long stay in Egypt	Different culture; different language group	Elite men and women interacting with Egyptian administrators	Egyptian culture considered superior by Egyptian elite
Sailors conducting trade at the port	Crews of 4–5 ships, ca. 20 people	Days to months	Same as above	Non-elite men interacting with non-elite Egyptian women and men shopkeepers	Same as above
Tribute	Few–up to 10	Days to months	Same as above	High-status men interacting with high Egyptian officials (including Kenamun?)	Same as above

hypothetical values for three of the interactions seen in the Kenamun harbor scene. It may be possible to differentiate between migration and other forms of interactions by the high values that the former has in the criterion of time; that is to say that longer presence of foreigners will result in a stronger impact on the material culture of the target country. This, however, depends on additional criteria, such as the cultural distance between the societies. Mobility of complete families or kinship groups will also create a more visible impact on the material culture of the target country (Yasur-Landau 2010:16).

While the Kenamun tomb imagery shows events presumably framed within a short period of time, the archaeological reality of multiperiod tells in the Levant is a bewildering palimpsest even within a single archaeological period, or "stratum." The remainder of this paper will be dedicated to exploring aspects of two of the interactions seen in the harbor scene in the tomb of Kenamun—the arrival of foreign families, and the mobility of cattle—and assessing the impact of the new methods of aDNA and stable isotope analyses on current and future methods of understanding mobility in the Bronze Age eastern Mediterranean.

Multicultural Families in Coastal and Harbor Sites

The complex situation of multicultural coastal cities can be seen in a census of Alashian (Cypriot) households in Ugarit, RS 11.857, found in the Royal Palace of Ugarit (KTU 4.108; Schloen 2001:324; McGeough and Smith 2011:38–40). It records 27 Alashian households, each named after its head, and mentions 93 individuals: 30 wives, 4 sons, 4 daughters, 9 youths, 12 maidens, and 7 retainers. The designation as Alashian may, however, mask more complex relations between geographic origin, cultural attribution, and even language, as at least two heads of households have distinctively Semitic names, not necessarily connected with Cyprus (obverse line 13 $^{tptb^cl}$ and reverse line 23 $^{sdqš[lm]}$). Different purposes have been suggested for the recording of foreign families, from keeping track of foreign slaves through lists of people eligible for service, to temple household laborers (McGeough and Smith 2011:40). Astour (1970:123) suggested that these people were part of a foreign community established in or around the port of Ma'hadu, the main port of Ugarit. It is possible that one of the reasons for the registration of foreigners was connected with the occasional allocations they received from the palace because of their status. For example, the wine allocation list RS 15.039 (KTU 4.149; McGeough and Smith 2011:111–112; Astour 1970:121) included one *kd* measure for the "Hittite at Mahadu" (reverse line 5) and two *kd* measures were allocated "as a present to the Alashian" (reverse lines 7–8).

The new tool of aDNA analysis may well provide additional information that can be compared to the literary and archaeological evidence to reconstruct the complex processes of interaction occurring in Bronze Age coastal cities. The work of Haber et al. (2017) on aDNA from the Middle Bronze Age cemetery at Sidon exposed genetic similarity between five people interred in the tombs (two males and three females) and the Neolithic and Early Bronze Age populations in Jordan, as well as similarity to the current population of Lebanon, with an emphasis put on genetic continuity. This is an exciting result, which should be reexamined with a larger dataset containing more samples. The coastal town of Sidon was a hub of maritime activity in the Middle Bronze Age and later, with connections to Cyprus and to the Aegean area, as seen in examples of ceramic imports (Doumet-Serhal 2003). An aDNA analysis skeleton of a woman found interred at the bottom of a well from the sixteenth century B.C. in Alalakh was interpreted as an indication for a migration of an individual from a location in Eastern Iran or Central Asia. Several healed skeletal traumata in addition to the irregular interment further hint to a personal story of individual suffering (Skourtanioti et al. 2020). It should be noted that aDNA and the relationship between the individuals interred in tombs, as well as their relations to other populations, both ancient and modern, can shed light on but one part of mobility—that of ancestry. At the same time, a stable isotope analysis of these burials may provide important data on the personal history of the people interred in such tombs. While they belong to a genetically similar group, they might have traveled extensively during their lifetime before being interred in their home town.

A study by Schrenk et al. (2016) demonstrates the significant value of stable isotope analysis for identifying migrants as well as for reconstructing their individual life histories. In four cases of people interred within a Bronze Age tomb (ca. 2100–2000/1950 B.C.) at Tell Abraq in the United Arab Emirates, a study of strontium, oxygen, and carbon isotopes has discovered that the individuals migrated to the site. One of them was a young (18–20-year-old) female who migrated after the age of fifteen. Upon moving to the more densely populated settlement of Tell Abraq, the conditions in the new county had left her more vulnerable to contracting and developing paralytic poliomyelitis in her late teens. A recent genetic study of 73 individuals from five archaeological sites across, mostly from the Bronze Age Southern Levant, modeled populations associated with "Canaanite" material culture as descending from both earlier local Neolithic populations and populations related to the Chalcolithic Zagros or the Bronze Age Caucasus. Some were rather recent (yet not first generation) migrants, as two individuals in a Middle Bronze Age Megiddo tomb were siblings and with a large genetic component of the Zagros or Caucasus area. A strontium isotope analysis has demonstrated that both siblings were raised locally (Agranat Tamir et al. 2020).

The significant potential for understanding Mediterranean mobility and the creation of intercultural families is explored by Matisoo-Smith et al. (2018), who suggest that women's mobility played an important role in the Iron Age maritime migrations connected with Phoenician settlements. The study implied movement of women from sites in the Near East or North Africa to Sardinia, and also a possible movement of women from Europe to Phoenician sites in Lebanon. While it is easy to see how the new available tools of aDNA and stable isotope analyses can contribute to the study of aspects of gender in migration and other forms of mobility, it can only be done within a combined methodological framework in which the new evidence is assessed with the existing historical and archaeological data (Yasur-Landau 2010:26–28; see other papers in this volume).

Multicultural families can potentially be identified in the archaeological record, using lessons learned from historical archaeology case studies (Yasur-Landau 2011, 2012). The depiction of women from different cultural origins among the Sea People migrants in the Medinet Habu reliefs opened the possibility for the existence of a similar situation in the Philistine migration to the southern Levant in the twelfth century B.C. (Sweeney and Yasur-Landau 1999). Following this possibility, a close examination of twelfth-century assemblages in houses at Tel Miqne/Ekron, Ashdod, and Ashkelon has yielded two coexisting sets of domestic behavior in almost every house: food was cooked in both Aegean-style cooking jugs and open Canaanite cooking pots using both Aegean-style hearths and local round *tannur*s (bread ovens). The food and drinks were served in Aegean-style LH IIIC bowls, kraters, and jugs, as well as in local, Canaanite-style bowls, kraters, and jugs. This binary set of domestic behavioral patterns was interpreted as resulting from the intercultural household created by Aegean immigrants and members of the local, Canaanite population (Yasur-Landau 2011, 2012, 2016). A recent aDNA study from Ashkelon included a comparison between the genome of individuals from three periods: an MB-LB cemetery, four burials of infants found under twelfth-century-B.C. houses, and an Iron IIA cemetery. The four infants were genetically distinct from the tested individuals of the MB-LB and the Iron IIA, exhibiting what was termed as "a European-related admixture": 25 to 70% of their DNA was inherited from southern European ancestors, linked to the migration of the Philistines (Feldman et al. 2019). The formal burial of these infants beneath the houses indicates an inclusion in the community, and to my mind may well be to some extent a reflection of the ancestry of the families that reside within these houses. While ancestry is by no means equal to culture, and genetic makeup cannot be compared directly to the behavioral patterns and cultural traditions (cf. Ion 2017), it does not mean that a methodology for the study of ancient mobility should not develop the ability to include both sets of data. Indeed, the Ashkelon case shows the great potential for more sharpened methodological tools for analyzing events of mobility reflected in aDNA and their possible connection to archaeological evidence of material culture change connected with intercultural families.

Interpreting Mobility of Cattle and Other Domestic Animals

Pioneer studies of animal mobility conducted by Meiri et al. (2017) and by Pereira Verdugo et al. (2019) found evidence for crossbreeding between taurine and zebu cattle observed in the Late Bronze Age, Iron I and Iron IIA in the southern Levant. Meiri et al. (2017) have cautiously suggested, based on historical considerations, that this is an indication of the introduction of zebu, or hump-backed cattle, from Egypt to Canaan during the New Kingdom as an adaptation to the conditions of increasing aridity at the end of the Late Bronze Age. While this remains a plausible explanation, it might be worthwhile to suggest that pictorial evidence from Egyptian tombs of the New Kingdom suggests a much more complex image of the mobility of hump-back bulls between Egypt and Canaan. The large humps of these bulls, very plausibly identified as zebu cattle, are present in a clear context of Levantine ("Syrian") tribute in the tomb of Kenamun. This is by no means the sole representation of such cattle in the early to mid-Eighteenth Dynasty. Another tomb that shows a possibly Syrian boat is the tomb of Nebamun (TT17), who was a royal scribe and a physician to the king during the mid-Eighteenth Dynasty, before or at the beginning of the reign of Amenhotep II. The tomb contains a depiction of the owner, Nebamun, receiving offerings from his brother Sheni while gift-bearing Levantine people are depicted behind him, arranged in two registers. The upper of the two includes a seated Levantine noble and his wife. The bottom register depicts a ship and more Levantine people leading hump-backed bulls pulling two wagons (Shirley 2007:382–383; Mark 2017:Figure 1). In Shirley's opinion (2007:386–389), this scene occurs in a Syrian port, where tribute is carried into a ship destined for Egypt, reflecting the role of the owner of the tomb as a scribe present in foreign lands. To Mark's mind, on the other hand, the boat is Egyptian and the scene shows a noble "Syrian" patient departing from Egypt (Mark 2017:68–69). Whether this scene takes place in Syria with the bulls used as carriers of the tribute, or in Egypt with Levantine people conducting zebu bulls toward a ship, it nevertheless shows the intricate nature of mobility of animals at an age of vastly developed maritime trade.

Zebu bulls, are included among scenes of tribute and gift giving in two or three additional Theban tombs of the mid-Eighteenth Dynasty (TT42, TT119, and TT367) (Shirley 2007:389). Mark (2017:80–81) suggests that such depictions are an indication that these bulls were a prized import. At the same time, they also appear in contemporary Egyptian breeding herds in TT86, and were therefore likely imported to Thebes in the days of Thutmose III and owned by the local elite during the days of Nebamun.

The mobility of bulls as a luxury items from the Levant to Egypt began even before the New Kingdom. The tribute of Asiatic princes to Amenemhat II (nineteenth century B.C.) in the Mit Rahina inscription includes cattle and small domestic animals brought by "the children of the princes of Asia," and there is another reference to Asiatic cattle brought to Egypt, dated either to the reign of Amenemhet II or to that of Amenemhet III (Marcus 2007:139, 172). Another text from the Middle Bronze Age suggests the mobility of cattle was by no means unidirectional from Canaan to Egypt. A cuneiform text from Mari refers to the shipment of 84 head of cattle to Hazor, perhaps accompanied by six mules or onagers. This is direct evidence for the mobility of cattle from Mesopotamia to Canaan during the early part of the MB II (ARMT [Archives Royales de Mari] 23:505; Malamat 1998:42).

The great potential of stable isotope analysis for the reconstruction of animal mobility in the Levant is exemplified by the work of Arnold et al. (2016), who demonstrate that the remains of a donkey and a goat found at Tell es-Safi/Gath originated in the Nile valley. The combined use of carbon, oxygen, and strontium isotopes allows the recreation of the life history of the donkey that was found: its early tooth development took place while it was in the Nile valley; it later migrated, very likely within a trade caravan, to Tell es-Safi/Gath where the formation of its third molar was completed, before the donkey was ceremoniously sacrificed.

Returning to the question of zebu mobility, zebu remains have been found in Late Bronze Age contexts in inland Levantine sites: Tell Jemmeh in the Negev, Kamid el-Loz in the Beqaa valley, and Tell Deir 'Alla in the Jordan valley (Chahoud and Vila 2011:268). One may expect that in this case too, stable isotope analysis will be most useful in recreating mobility patterns within cattle, determining whether these were introduced from Egypt, from other places in the Levant, or from both, as well as the circumstances of this introduction: from the acquisition of impressive and rare animals to the adaptation to changing climate conditions.

Conclusions

After a long period of theoretical quasi-stagnations in the theoretically informed archaeological study of migration and mobility, the advent of scientific methods in archaeology is bringing new and exciting analytical tools. The promise of the scientific revolution is that of the return of the *great ideas* (Kristiansen 2014). It is my hope, however, that as the pendulum swings away from post-processualism and toward an era of scientific discovery, the resulting interpretative models will indeed reflect lessons learned from both processual and post-processual pasts. The application of network modeling as well as agent-based models in archaeology does suggest that multivariate models may indeed create a stronger theoretical framework that can keep in pace with the advances in scientific methods and will provide us with a better grasp of the complex realities of the past (Kristiansen 2014:17–18; 2019). This will have to be done, however, with the awareness and indeed the moral responsibility that this is a human story, in many cases a story of human suffering, and the literary, material, or other evidence is directly related to the aspirations, fears, and hopes of a great number of real people who went through intense experiences of conflict, travel, and settlement (Yasur-Landau 2010:345).

References Cited

Agranat-Tamir, L., S. Waldman, M. A. S. Martin, D. Gokhman, N. Mishol, T. Eshel, O. Cheronet, N. Rohland, S. Mallick, N. Adamski, A. M. Lawson, M. Mah, M. Michel, J. Oppenheimer, K. Stewardson, F. Candilio, D. Keating, B. Gamarra, S. Tzur, M. Novak, R. Kalisher, S. Bechar, V. Eshed, D. J. Kennett, M. Faerman, N. Yahalom-Mack, J. M. Monge, Y. Govrin, Y. Erel, B. Yakir, R. Pinhasi, S. Carmi, I. Finkelstein, L. Carmel, and D. Reich 2020 The Genomic History of the Bronze Age Southern Levant. *Cell* 181, 1146–1157. DOI:10.1016/j.cell.2020.04.024.

Arnold E. R., G. Hartman, H. J. Greenfield, I. Shai, L. E. Babcock, and A. M. Maeir 2016 Isotopic Evidence for Early Trade in Animals between Old Kingdom Egypt and Canaan. *PLOS ONE* 11(6):e0157650. DOI:10.1371/journal.pone.0157650.

Astour, M. C. 1970 Maʾḫadu, the Harbor of Ugarit. *Journal of the Economic and Social History of the Orient* 13(2):113–127.

Berry, J. W. 1997 Immigration, Acculturation, and Adaptation. *Applied Psychology: An International Review* 46(1):5–34.

Biehl, P. F., and O. P. Nieuwenhuyse (editors) 2016 *Climate and Cultural Change in Prehistoric Europe and the Near East*. The Institute for European and Mediterranean Archaeology Distinguished Monograph Series 6. State University Press of New York, Albany.

Burmeister, S. 2000 Archaeology and Migration: Approaches to an Archaeological Proof of Migration. *Current Anthropology* 41(4):539–567.

Chahoud, J., and E. Vila 2011 The Role of Animals in Ancient Sidon: An Overview of Ongoing Zooarchaeological Studies. *Archaeology and History in Lebanon* 34–35:259–284.

Callaway, E. 2018 The Battle for Common Ground. *Nature* 555:573–576.

Clarke, D. L. 1978 *Analytical Archaeology*. 2nd ed. Methuen, London.

Davies, N. de G., and R. O. Faulkner 1947 A Syrian Trading Venture to Egypt. *The Journal of Egyptian Archaeology* 33:40–46.

Doumet-Serhal C. 2003 Excavating Sidon, 1998–2003. *Archaeology and History in Lebanon* 18:2–19.

Eisenmann, S., E. Bánffy, P. van Dommelen, K. P. Hofmann, J. Maran, I. Lazaridis, A. Mittnik, M. McCormick, J. Krause1, D. Reich, and P. W. Stockhammer 2018 Reconciling Material Cultures in Archaeology with Genetic Data: The Nomenclature of Clusters Emerging from Archaeogenomic Analysis. *Scientific Reports* 8:13003. DOI:10.1038/s41598-018-31123-z.

Feldman, M., D. M. Master, R. A. Bianco, M. Burri, P. W. Stockhammer, A. Mittnik, A. J. Aja, C. Jeong, and J. Krause 2019 Ancient DNA Sheds Light on the Genetic Origins of Early Iron Age Philistines. *Science Advances* 5(7):eaax0061. DOI:10.1126/sciadv.aax0061, accessed July 3, 2019.

Finne, M., K. Holmgren, C.-C. Shen, H.-M. Hu, M. Boyd, and S. Stocker 2017 Late Bronze Age Climate Change and the Destruction of the Mycenaean Palace of Nestor at Pylos. *PLoS ONE* 12(12):e0189447. DOI:10.1371/journal.pone.0189447.

Flohr, P., D. Fleitmann, R. Matthews, W. Matthews, and S. Black 2016 Evidence of Resilience to Past Climate Change in Southwest Asia: Early Farming Communities and the 9.2 and 8.2 ka Events. *Quaternary Science Reviews* 136:23–39.

Haber, M., C. Doumet-Serhal, C. Scheib, Y. Xue, P. Danecek, M. Mezzavilla, S. Youhanna, R. Martiniano, J. Prado-Martinez, M. Szpak, E. Matisoo-Smith, H. Schutkowski, R. Mikulski, P. Zalloua, T. Kivisild, and C. Tyler-Smith 2017 Continuity and Admixture in the Last Five Millennia of Levantine History from Ancient Canaanite and Present-Day Lebanese Genome Sequences. *The American Journal of Human Genetics* 101:274–282.

Hakenbeck, S. 2008 Migration in Archaeology: Are We Nearly There Yet? *Archaeological Review from Cambridge* 23(2):9–26.

Harney, É., H. May, D. Shalem, N. Rohland, S. Mallick, I. Lazaridis, R. Sarig, K. Stewardson, S. Nordenfelt, N. Patterson, I. Hershkovitz, and D. Reich 2018 Ancient DNA from Chalcolithic Israel Reveals the Role of Population Mixture in Cultural Transformation. *Nature Communications* 9:3336. DOI:10.1038/s41467-018-05649-9.

Horden, P., and N. Purcell 2000 *The Corrupting Sea: A Study of Mediterranean History*. Oxford University Press, Oxford.

Ion, A. 2017 How Interdisciplinary Is Interdisciplinary? Revisiting the Impact of aDNA Research for the Archaeology of Human Remains. *Current Swedish Archaeology* 25:177–198.

Ion, A. 2019 Beyond Determinism. A Case for Complex Explanations and Human Scale in Framing Archaeological Causal Explanations. *Archaeological Dialogues* 26:10–12. DOI:10.1017/S1380203819000084.

Kaniewski D., E. Van Campo, J. Guiot, S. Le Burel, and T. Otto 2013 Environmental Roots of the Late Bronze Age Crisis. *PLOS ONE* 8(8):e71004. DOI:10.1371/journal.pone.0071004.

Knapp A. B., and P. van Dommelen (editors) 2014 *The Cambridge Prehistory of the Bronze and Iron Age Mediterranean*. Cambridge University Press, New York.

Kristiansen, K. 2014 Towards a New Paradigm? The Third Science Revolution and Its Possible Consequences in Archaeology. *Current Swedish Archaeology* 22:11–34.

Kristiansen, K. 2019 Who Is Deterministic? On the Nature of Interdisciplinary Research in Archaeology. *Archaeological Dialogues* 26:12–14. DOI:10.1017/S1380203819000060

Kuo B. C. H., and G. Roysircar 2004 Predictors of Acculturation for Chinese Adolescents in Canada: Age of Arrival, Length of Stay, Social Class, and English Reading Ability. *Journal of Multicultural Counselling and Development* 32:143–154.

Langgut, D., I. Finkelstein, and T. Litt 2013 Climate and the Late Bronze Collapse: New Evidence from the Southern Levant. *Tel Aviv* 40:149–175.

Lazaridis, I., D. Nadel, G. Rollefson, D. C. Merrett, N. Rohland, S. Mallick, D. Fernandes, M. Novak, B. Gamarra, K. Sirak, S. Connell, K. Stewardson, E. Harney, Q. Fu, G. Gonzalez-Fortes, E. R. Jones, S. A. Roodenberg, G. Lengyel, F. Bocquentin, B. Gasparian, J. M. Monge, M. Gregg, V. Eshed, A.-S. Mizrahi, C. Meiklejohn, F. Gerritsen, L. Bejenaru, M. Blüher, A. Campbell, G. Cavalleri, D. Comas, P. Froguel, E. Gilbert, S. M. Kerr, P. Kovacs, J. Krause, D. McGettigan, M. Merrigan, D. A. Merriwether, S. O'Reilly, M. B. Richards, O. Semino, M. Shamoon-Pour, G. Stefanescu, M. Stumvoll, A. Tönjes, A. Torroni, J. F. Wilson, L. Yengo, N. A. Hovhannisyan, N. Patterson, R. Pinhasi and D. Reich 2016 Genomic Insights into the Origin of Farming in the Ancient Near East. *Nature* 536:419–424.

Malamat, A. 1998 *Mari and the Bible*. Studies in the History and Culture of the Ancient Near East 12. 2nd edition. Brill, Leiden.

Marcus, E. S. 2007 Amenemhet II and the Sea: Maritime Aspects of the Mit Rahina (Memphis) Inscription. *Egypt and the Levant* 17:137–190.

Mark, S. 2017 The Ship Depiction in the Tomb of Nebamun: The Earliest Egyptian Ship without a Hogging Truss. *Journal of Ancient Egyptian Interconnections* 16:68–86.

Matisoo-Smith, E., A. L. Gosling, D. Platt, O. Kardailsky, S. Prost, S. Cameron-Christie, C. J. Collins, J. Boocock, Y. Kurumilian, M. Guirguis, R. Pla Orquôin, W. Khalil, H. Genz, G. Abou Diwan, J. Nassar and P. Zalloua 2018 Ancient Mitogenomes of Phoenicians from Sardinia and Lebanon: A Story of Settlement, Integration, and Female Mobility. *PLoS ONE* 13(1):e0190169. DOI:10.1371/journal.pone.0190169.

McGeough, K., and M. S. Smith_2011 *Ugaritic Economic Tablets: Text, Translation and Notes*. Ancient Near Eastern Studies Supplement Series 32. Peeters, Leuven.

Meiri M., P. W. Stockhammer, N. Marom, G. Bar-Oz, L. Sapir-Hen, P. Morgenstern, S. Macheridis, B. Rosen, D. Huchon, J. Maran, and I. Finkelstein 2017 Eastern Mediterranean Mobility in the Bronze and Early Iron Ages: Inferences from Ancient DNA of Pigs and Cattle. *Scientific Reports* 7:701. DOI:10.1038/s41598-017-00701-y.

Pereira Verdugo, M., V. E. Mullin, A. Scheu, V. Mattiangeli, K. G. Daly, P. Maisano Delser, A. J. Hare, J. Burger, M. J. Collins, R. Kehati, P. Hesse, D. Fulton, E. W. Sauer, F. A. Mohaseb, H. Davoudi, R. Khazaeli, J. Lhuillier, C. Rapin, S. Ebrahimi, M. Khasanov, S. M. F. Vahidi, D. F. MacHugh, O. Ertuğrul, C. Koukouli-Chrysanthaki, A. Sampson, G. Kazantzis, I. Kontopoulos, J. Bulatovic, I. Stojanović, A. Mikdad, N. Benecke, J. Linstädter, M. Sablin, R. Bendrey, L. Gourichon, B. S. Arbuckle, M. Marjan, D. Orton, L. Kolska Horwitz, M. D. Teasdale, and D. J. Bradley 2019 Ancient Cattle Genomics, Origins, and Rapid Turnover in the Fertile Crescent *Science* 365:173–176. DOI:10.1126/science.aav1002.

Roffet-Salque, M., A. Marciniak, P. J. Valdes, K. Pawłowska, J. Pyzel, L. Czerniak, M. Krüger, C. N. Roberts, S. Pitter, and R. P. Evershed 2018 Evidence for the Impact of the 8.2-kyBP Climate Event on Near Eastern Early Farmers. *PNAS* 115(35):8702–8709. DOI:10.1073/pnas.1803607115.

Schloen, J. D. 2001 *The House of the Father as Fact and Symbol: Patrimonialism in Ugarit and the Ancient Near East*. Eisenbrauns, Winona Lake, Indiana.

Schrenk, A., L. A. Gregoricka, D. L. Martina, and D. T. Potts 2016 Differential Diagnosis of a Progressive Neuromuscular Disorder Using Bioarchaeological and Biogeochemical Evidence from a Bronze Age Skeleton in the UAE. *International Journal of Paleopathology* 13:1–10.

Shirley, J. J. 2005 *The Culture of Officialdom: An Examination of the Acquisition of Offices during the Mid-18th Dynasty*. PhD Dissertation, Johns Hopkins University, Baltimore.

Shirley, J. J. 2007 The Life and Career of Nebamun, the Physician of the King in Thebes. In *The Archaeology and Art of Ancient Egypt: Essays in Honor of David B. O'Connor*, edited by Z. Hawas and J. Richards, pp. 381–401. Annales du Service des Antiquités de l'Égypte cahier 36, vol. II. Publications du Conseil Suprême des Antiquités de l'Égypte, Cairo.

Skourtanioti, E., Y. S Erdal, M. Frangipane, K. Balossi Restelli, A. Yener, F. Pinnock, P. Matthiae, R. Özbal, U.-D. Schoop, F. Guliyev, T. Akhundov, B. Lyonnet, E. L. Hammer, S. E. Nugent, M. Burri, G. U. Neumann, S. Penske, T. Ingman, M. Akar, R. Shafiq, G. Palumbi, S. Eisenmann, M. D'Andrea, A. B. Rohrlach, C. Warinner, C. Jeong, P. W. Stockhammer, W. Haak, and J. Krause 2020 Genomic History of Neolithic to Bronze Age Anatolia, Northern Levant, and Southern Caucasus. *Cell* 181:1158–1175. DOI:10.1016/j.cell.2020.04.044.

Sweeney, D., and A. Yasur-Landau 1999 Following the Path of the Sea Persons: The Women in the Medinet Habu Reliefs. *Tel Aviv* 26:116–145.

Wachsmann, S. 1998 *Seagoing Ships and Seamanship in the Bronze Age Levant*. Texas A&M University Press, College Station, Texas, and London.

Yasur-Landau, A. 2010 *The Philistines and Aegean Migration in the Late Bronze Age*. Cambridge University Press, Cambridge and New York.

Yasur-Landau, A. 2011 *Deep Change* in Domestic Behavioural Patterns and Theoretical Aspects of Interregional Interactions in the 12th-Century Levant. In *On Cooking Pots, Drinking Cups, Loom Weights, and Ethnicity in Bronze Age Cyprus and Neighbouring Regions: Proceedings of an International Archaeological Symposium, Nicosia, 6th–7th November 2010*, edited by V. Karageorghis and O. Kouka, pp. 239–249. A. G. Leventis Foundation, Nicosia.

Yasur-Landau, A. 2012 The Role of the Canaanite Population in the Aegean Migration to the Southern Levant in the Late 2nd Millennium BC. In *Materiality and Social Practice: Transformative Capacities of Intercultural Encounters*, edited by J. Maran and P. W. Stockhammer, pp. 190–197. Oxbow, Oxford.

Yasur-Landau, A. 2016 Women in Philistia: The Archaeological Record of the Iron Age. In *Women in Antiquity: Real Woman across the Ancient World*, edited by S. Budin and J. M. Turfa, pp. 501–510. Routledge, New York.

Yasur-Landau, A. 2017 Some Notes on Philistines, Migration and Mediterranean Connectivity. In *"Sea Peoples" Up-to-Date: New Research on Transformations in the Eastern Mediterranean in the 13th–11th Centuries BCE*, edited by P. M. Fischer and T. Bürge, pp. 141–148. Austrian Academy of Sciences Press, Vienna.

Yasur-Landau, A. 2018 Towards an Archaeology of Forced Movement of the Deep Past. In: *An Archaeology of Forced Migration. Crisis-induced Mobility and the Collapse of the 13th c. BCE Eastern Mediterranean* (AEGIS 15), edited by J. Driessen, pp. 177–185. Louvain University Press, Louvain.

Yasur-Landau, A. 2019 The Archaeology of Maritime Adaptation. In *The Social Archaeology of the Levant: From Prehistory to the Present*, edited by A. Yasur-Landau, Y. M. Rowan, and E. H. Cline, pp. 551–569. Cambridge University Press, Cambridge and New York.

Yasur-Landau, A., Y. M. Rowan, and E. H. Cline 2019 Epilogue. In *The Social Archaeology of the Levant: From Prehistory to the Present*, edited by A. Yasur-Landau, Y. M. Rowan, and E. H. Cline, pp. 633–637. Cambridge University Press, Cambridge and New York.

PART III

Computational Models of Migration

Chapter Nine

Surfing with the Alien

Simulating and Testing the Spread of Early Farming across the Adriatic Basin

Marc Vander Linden, Cornelis Drost,
Jane Gaastra, Ivana Jovanović,
Sébastien Manem, Anne de Vareilles

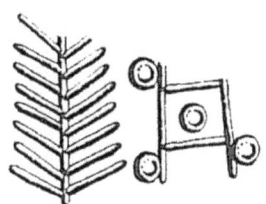

Abstract *The spread of animal and plant domesticates across Europe offers a good laboratory of the many fortunes of migration and mobility in archaeology. From all mighty deus ex machina during the culture-historical days, to conceptual monstrosity throughout the late twentieth century A.D., human mobility has experienced a recent revival under the impetus of new scientific techniques, especially stable isotopes (Sr, O), and ancient DNA. In this sense, if the—partial—link between the new domesticates and migrants is warranted in several instances, the scale and cultural impact (i.e., how much does this help us to understand the period) of early Neolithic human mobility remains extensively debated.*

After a brief review of the existing aDNA evidence and of the ^{14}C record, considered as an alternative population proxy, this paper assesses the temporal variation of the Early and Late Neolithic of the Adriatic basin. We first devise an agent-based model (ABM) simulating the spread of a population and concomitant changes in its cultural diversity. The results of this ABM provide as many hypotheses, which are then tested against the archaeological record, with a focus on zooarchaeological remains.

One of the most enduring debates in Later European prehistory has concerned the potential role of human mobility, and especially migration, in the introduction and dispersal of early farming practices across Europe. Although there is no doubt that the majority of plant and animal domesticates were introduced from the Near East, for decades archaeologists have fought an entrenched battle opposing, on the one hand, externalists supporting the role of migrants and, on the other hand, localists stressing the importance of local late foraging communities in this process of dispersal. Countless arguments have been evoked by both camps, especially perceived (dis-)continuities in the material record, and patterning in the ^{14}C chronology (for a review, see Vander Linden 2011).

Over the past few years, the inception on the archaeological stage of a new technology, ancient DNA (hereafter aDNA) seems to have settled the controversy. Several studies published in high-profile journals have indeed demonstrated that, across all regions of Europe, the introduction of early farming is paralleled by the migration of a new population, characterized by a specific genomic signature and whose origins must eventually be sought in the Near East (e.g., Lazaridis et al. 2016; Mathieson et al. 2018). Although there are both temporal and spatial divergences in the admixture proportion of local and new genomic components, it is now impossible to deny the potent role of migrants in the diffusion of early farming across Europe.

Does the undeniable success of aDNA however mean that the controversy is to be cast away in the drawers of the historiographic past of our discipline? Arguably not, and for several reasons. Firstly, and as has been obvious since the 1960s (e.g., Binford 1962; Clark 1966), one should not confuse the positive identification of a past migration with an explanation of the past. Yes, migration is a major historical force, but its positive identification, however significant, only raises further questions regarding the nature of the underlying responsible principles (Anthony 1990). Secondly, the early Neolithic archaeological record cannot be reduced solely to the introduction of domesticated plants and animals across the European peninsula. Local early Neolithic archaeological assemblages exhibit a staggering variation, which does not merely reflect the corresponding genetic diversity. This should not come as a surprise since biological relatedness, investigated by geneticists, does not passively reproduce social relationships, whether for the early European Neolithic or for any period, for that matter (Johannsen et al. 2017).

What is left remaining is that we, as archaeologists, still have a fairly poor understanding of how human migrations, especially large-scale ones, impact material culture and eventually shape the archaeological record. David Anthony (1990) made clear nearly thirty years ago that the archaeologists' role is to explain the reasons for past human mobility. Current biomolecular tools such as isotopic measures and aDNA are undoubtedly pivotal techniques for such undertaking, and must be accompanied by concerted theoretical and methodological efforts to reinterrogate the archaeological record as a source of documentation in itself about the evolutionary and historical role of human mobility (see also Racimo et al. 2020).

To this effect, this paper outlines one particular methodology, articulated in two distinct, successive steps. The first one consists of the creation of a computational model. In this case, an agent-based model (e.g., Cegielski and Rogers 2016) aims at replicating under a narrow but strict set of rules the effects of a migrating population upon its cultural diversity. The resulting simulations indicate a strong link between migration, here triggered by demographic expansion, and fluctuating levels of cultural diversity. The second methodological step is to then test some of the predictions derived from the preceding simulations through a renewed analysis of archaeological data. Here, the testing procedure focuses on the zooarchaeological record of the western Balkans and the Adriatic basin, though theoretically this could be extended to any facet of the archaeological record and/or any other region. Two main reasons justify the selection of this case study. Firstly, this area lies at the gateway of Europe and is home to the formation of archaeological complexes linked to the introduction of early farming across much of the western Mediterranean (Impresso complex) and central Europe (Linearbandkeramik complex). Secondly, despite its key geographical location, the archaeological record of this area remains comparatively understudied. As part of an ongoing research project, we aim at filling this documentary gap through a combination of literature review (e.g., Orton et al. 2016; Pilaar Birch and Vander Linden 2017; Gaastra and Vander Linden 2018), targeted fieldwork (e.g., Pandžić and Vander Linden 2014; Vander Linden et al. 2014), and reexamination of existing collections (Gaastra et al. 2018).

The structure of this chapter reproduces the suggested methodology, starting with a presentation of the computational model and of the resulting simulations, which in turn allow us to formulate a series of formal hypotheses, tested against zooarchaeological data. The implications of this work for both the European early Neolithic and the archaeology of human mobility are then briefly explored.

Simulating a Demographically Driven Migration

The first methodological step corresponds to the creation and implementation of a computational model. As pointed out by an extensive body of literature, computational models articulate together a series of assumptions so that, in this sense, they do not present any conceptual difference from more "narrative-led" models favored by other theoretical flavors (Steele and Shennan 2009). But, as computational models ultimately lead to simulations, they require a strict formal architecture so that assumptions and rules might be converted into mathematical equations and computing codes. For the present purpose, our aim is not to set a model that explains migration, but rather a model that simulates a migration and its potential effects upon cultural diversity.

In this perspective, rather than designing an entirely new model, we decided to work within the framework of a well-established agent-based model, namely, the Cultural Dissemination Model (hereafter CDM) devised by the political scientist R. Axelrod in the late 1990s (Axelrod 1997). The original CDM aims at evaluating the role and impact of homophily, that is, the tendency of similar people to interact more closely, upon the formation of cultural boundaries. The resulting model consists of a population of agents organized on a regular—traditionally quadrangular, here hexagonal—lattice. Each agent is characterized by a series of features, each one possessing a unique trait taken from a given range of possible variants. The number of features and traits is set at the beginning of the simulation and does not change during its course (see Drost and Vander Linden 2018 for variants). During each run, an agent (or "source") is randomly chosen across the entire grid, and one of its neighbors ("target") is then selected for interaction. With a probability equal to their cultural similarity, calculated on the basis of the number of existing shared traits, the source copies a previously diverging trait from the target, thus leading to increased similarity between them. At the beginning of the simulation, each agent is randomly given a selection of traits, so that the overall cultural diversity across the grid is very high. Under these conditions, the probability of neighboring agents sharing identical traits is low and their ability to interact therefore relatively limited. As the simulation proceeds, agents increasingly exchange traits and the overall level of cultural diversity therefore drops. This process is accompanied by the gradual formation of so-called regions, blocks of neighboring agents sharing all traits. These agents most often can still share traits with agents belonging to other regions, unless total diversity is reached. The number of individual regions gradually decreases through time until the simulation reaches an equilibrium stage whereby the grid is filled by several regions whose respective agents are entirely different and thus unable to interact anymore.

Axelrod's original CDM thus demonstrates how the same interaction process, homophily, leads to both local convergence, as uniform regions are created, and global disparity, as overall homogeneity is never achieved. It also shows that the eventual number of regions depends upon several parameters, including the grid size, the number of agents, as well as the number of features and traits used for the simulation (Axelrod 1997; see Castellano et al. 2009). For instance, a higher number of features leads to fewer, larger regions as it increases the probability of interactions between agents, while a higher number of traits has the reverse effect as the larger repertoire minimizes the probability of successful interaction between agents.

As part of a series of modifications made to the CDM (Drost and Vander Linden 2018), we use this modeling framework to simulate the effect of an expanding population upon its cultural package and diversity. This is achieved by adding two changes to the simulation process. Firstly, at the beginning of the simulation, only a contiguous fraction of the grid is populated with agents while the rest is left empty, corresponding to the area to be colonized. Secondly, in order to simulate a population expansion, we slightly modify the original interaction process. Interaction between agents follows the same rules as in the standard CDM. But, if either the randomly chosen source or the target is empty, no interaction occurs. This additional rule is, however, relaxed at a fixed rate of D times per interaction step: then, if the source chooses an empty target, it propagates itself through cloning, that is, the grid of populated agents expands by one, with identical features to its source of origins.

Figure 9.1 compares, to the left, a normal CDM with, to the right, a CDM with expansion rate D set at 1/5. The right panel clearly shows the gradual expansion of the original population as the simulation proceeds. Most importantly, this dispersal is associated with the creation, behind the expansion front, of large regions. These eventually break down during a second phase characterized by increased cultural diversity, and thus smaller regions. In order to measure these fluctuations in cultural diversity, we use Shannon's diversity index, a measure of diversity derived from information theory and routinely used for instance in numerical ecology (e.g., Borcard et al. 2011). Here, the Shannon index is calculated for eight segments of identical size, allowing us to track the progress of the expanding population across time and space. As shown in Figure 9.2, as the original population expands

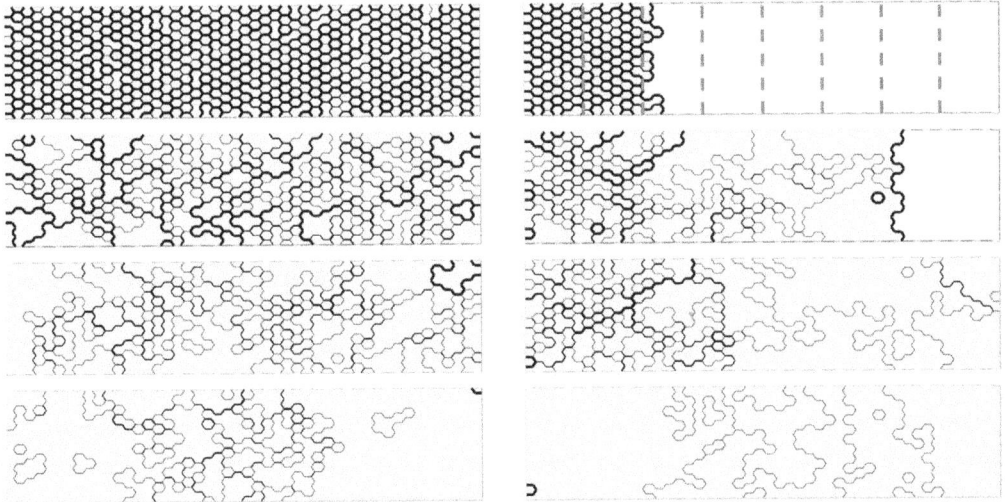

FIGURE 9.1. Top left: behavior of the unmodified CDM model at steps 5 k, 100 k, 500 k, and 1.500 k. Top right: Behavior of the wave toy model for corresponding steps. The red dotted lines indicate the eight vertical slices used to calculate Shannon's diversity index values (after Drost and Vander Linden 2018:Figure 5).

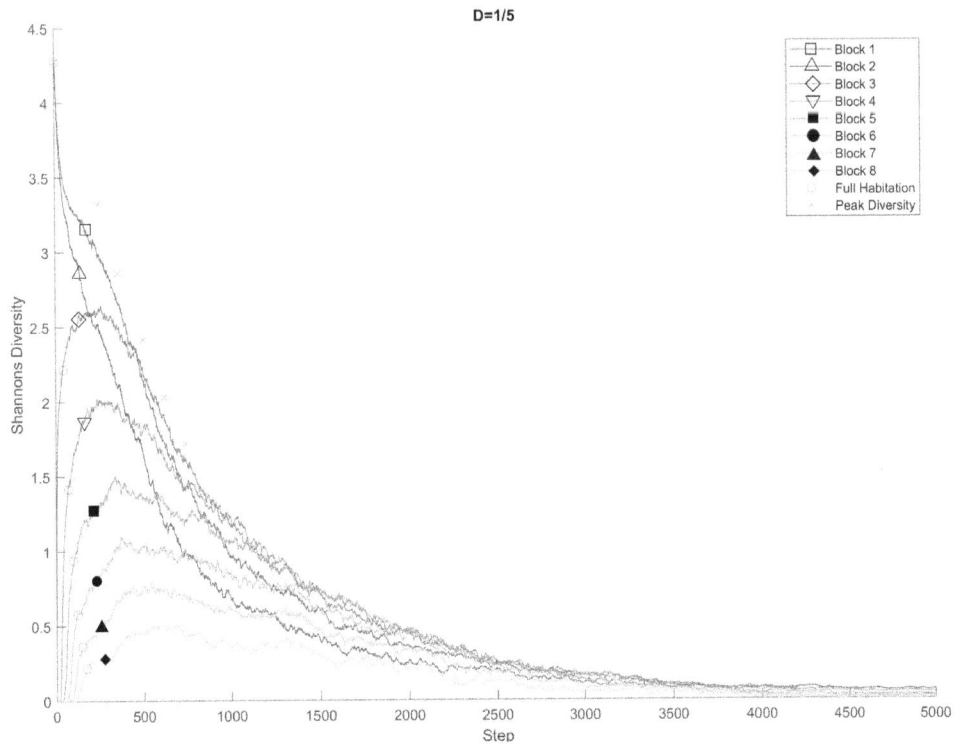

FIGURE 9.2. Plot of Shannon's diversity values for all vertical blocks (after Drost and Vander Linden 2018:Figure 5).

across the grid, there is a gradual loss of diversity indicated by a recurrent drop in the Shannon index values for the first total inhabitation of the corresponding slice. With the exception of the first two slices, where the population was initially set, the Shannon index values then rise for a relatively short period of time, corresponding to the rise in local diversity associated with the breaking down of the original large expanding regions. Afterward, the modified CDM follows the same trajectory as the original version, with a gradual decay of diversity until eventual equilibrium is reached.

The modeling literature hosts an extensive debate regarding the level of complexity associated with agent-based models (e.g., Vander Linden and Saqalli 2019). Here, we adopt an explicit simple stance, by limiting the number of parameters to a bare minimum. Although other factors might theoretically be considered (see below), previous work indicates that the addition of many parameters to the CDM quickly leads to a complex, non-predictable behavior (e.g., Drost and Vander Linden 2018). By contrast, the present version allows for the formulation of a number of predictions, which constitute as many formal hypotheses to be tested against the archaeological record:

- Firstly, a population under condition of demographic growth and corresponding spatial dispersal will experience a drop in its cultural diversity. This process results from the cloning of agents at the front, and is analogous to a founder effect in population genetics (see Currat et al. 2010);

- Secondly, there is a narrow repertoire of traits at the expansion front. The apparent success of these traits, suggested by their overrepresentation, is not related to any higher adaptive power, but to the mere outcome of their random selection and subsequent multiplication through cloning;

- Thirdly, this initial episode of cultural homogeneity is followed by a second phase characterized by a comparatively higher cultural diversity. This is explained by the fact that, under the normal rules of the CDM, agents never stop to interact together, and thus the cultural diversity present in the original populated zone gradually encroaches upon the homogeneous regions of the expanding front, leading to their eventual demise.

The next two sections examine the implementation and implications of this modified CDM for the dispersal of early farming across the western Balkans, and especially the Adriatic basin. After verifying that the assumptions behind the computational model are warranted by archaeological data, we then test the three aforementioned predictions briefly against the extensive and high-resolution zooarchaeological record.

Testing Assumptions

The demographic variant of the CDM presented here rests upon three main assumptions: (1) the importance of homophily as an evolutionary force; (2) the existence of a demographically driven wave of expansion during the period under consideration; (3) an empty—or at least comparatively lowly populated—landscape within which the wave advances.

The first assumption rests upon a purely theoretical point regarding the general relevance of homophily for human evolutionary history, as it governs the interaction and exchange of traits between agents within the framework of the CDM. While archaeological computational approaches to cultural transmission, especially under the influence of evolutionary thought, have devoted much energy to identifying and quantifying biased transmission (see review in Lake 2014), comparatively limited attention has been paid to specific forms of biased transmission such as homophily (e.g., Shennan et al. 2014; Madsen and Lipo 2015). This theoretical gap is, however, damageable as an extensive sociological and evolutionary literature demonstrates the key role of homophily in structuring social networks (see reviews in McPherson et al. 2001; Haun and Over 2013).

The second assumption rests upon the existence of a demic wave of expansion in the chosen research area in the corresponding period. Testing this assumption requires the ability to directly identify a process of expansion and to link it to a regime shift in the demography of the corresponding human populations. In both cases, the ^{14}C record provides the necessary data. Although, at a local scale, the history of research in the area prevents systematic in-depth analysis, the dataset meets all minimum quantitative criteria for exploratory data analysis at a macro scale (see Williams 2012). Figure 9.3 provides an interpolation of the oldest ^{14}C dates associated with the local introduction of plant and animal domesticates. The chosen geostatistical technique is an ordinary kriging, undertaken in the R statistical environment (R core team 2018) using the gstat (for spatial statistics: Gräler et al. 2016) and tmap (for thematic mapping; Tennekes 2018) packages. This figure shows a

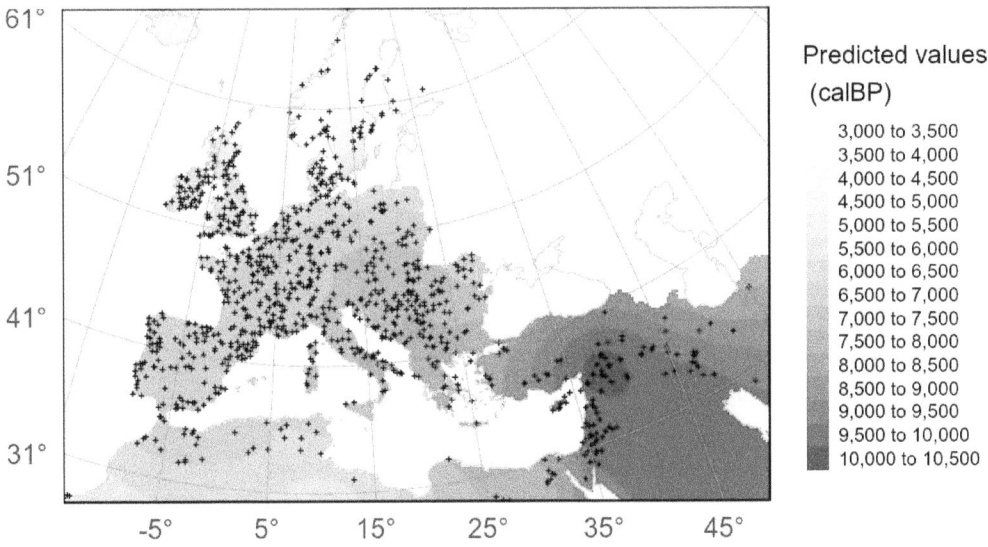

FIGURE 9.3. Interpolated dates for the dispersal of early farming across Europe.

clear SE-NW gradient—i.e., aligned with the main axis of the Adriatic Sea—in the dispersal of domesticates, as well as a relative pause between a major expansion at the turn of the ninth and eighth millennia cal B.P. then resuming toward 7600–7500 cal B.P. to encompass the entire northern part of the Adriatic basin (see also Silva and Vander Linden 2017). The radiocarbon record can also be used to evaluate if this dispersal is associated with a change of demographic regime. Figure 9.4 shows temporal variations of the demographic growth rate, calculated using the function spd2rc in the R package rcarbon (Bevan and Crema 2018), for the period between 9000 and 7000 cal B.P. in the Adriatic basin, expressed on the left as an annual growth rate and, on the right, in relative percentage. The expansion phase centered upon 8000 cal B.P. clearly corresponds to a peak of the annual growth rate, with values slightly superior to 0.004, suggesting that, in the corresponding interval, the population size more than doubled. As such figures can be neither achieved nor sustained by any preindustrial society (Bocquet-Appel 2008), the only possibility is to assume the existence of an incoming population. Although aDNA samples are lacking for the Neolithic period in the Adriatic basin, evidence from all neighboring regions and the rest of the European subcontinent confirms this interpretation (Mathieson et al. 2018).

The third assumption depends on the absence, or low population density, of the local foraging communities. This is not the place to review the local archaeological record of the late foraging populations (see Pilaar Birch and Vander Linden 2017). Keeping this in mind, several arguments point to a relatively thin overall Mesolithic population density, privileging specific ecological niches characterized by high availability of various types of

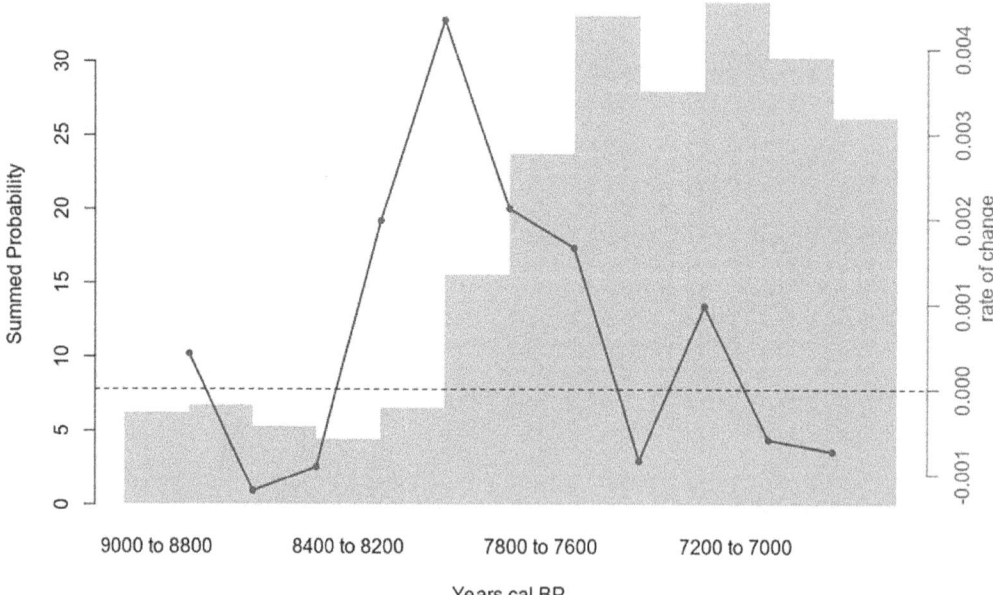

Figure 9.4. Plot of absolute population growth rate for the Adriatic Neolithic, as inferred from the analysis of the ^{14}C record.

prey, including the Danube gorges (Bonsall and Boroneanț 2018), the shores of the Skadar Lake (Vander Linden et al. 2015), the Montenegrin karst (Borić et al. 2019), or the Italian Alpine piedmonts (Franco 2011). In a similar vein, Gurova and Bonsall also pointed out the dearth of Mesolithic sites in areas with otherwise rich evidence of Late Pleistocene human occupation, suggesting an extensive reorganization of the settlement pattern and behavior of the corresponding foraging groups (Gurova and Bonsall 2014; see also Runnels 1995). Lastly, despite long-lasting systematic sampling, the early Holocene sequence of the Croatian Adriatic coast presents a noticeable gap centered upon the late Mesolithic/Early Neolithic transition (Forenbaher et al. 2013). This being said, if all available evidence points to a low population density of the last local foragers, especially when compared to the incoming farming groups (see above), interaction did happen between both populations, as inferred from both material culture (Borić et al. 2019) and, at least in neighboring areas, aDNA data (Mathieson et al. 2018).

Testing the Model: The Zooarchaeological Record

Before actually testing our agent-based model against archaeological data, it must be stressed that the original CDM, or the present version for that matter, does not take into consideration properties of the features and traits. As traits are neutral (i.e., they do not increase the fitness of the agent, nor is their dispersal favored or hampered by any property of the landscape, for instance), the predictions of the model can thus theoretically be tested against any facet of the archaeological record, or possibly several. For the purpose of the present paper, this test focuses on zooarchaeological record for the Adriatic basin, following several publications of our research group (Orton et al. 2016; Gaastra and Vander Linden 2018; Gaastra et al. 2019).

Zooarchaeological data are chosen here for a series of reasons. Firstly, there is a relative abundance of data for the Adriatic Neolithic, as bones have been routinely kept and recorded during excavations in the research area. Secondly, although recovery and analytical standards vary enormously, taxonomic abundance by a number of identified specimens (NISP) are consistently reported in the literature, thus allowing for systematic analysis. Thirdly, there is a growing literature on the meta-analysis of zooarchaeological remains, and the present contribution outlines some of the key results outlined in greater detail in previous publications (e.g., Gaastra and Vander Linden 2018; see also Orton et al. 2016). Lastly, as far as domesticated animals are concerned, these constitute without any ambiguity a series of species previously absent in the Adriatic basin. Set in terms of our modified CDM, this implies that we are here dealing with traits intricately associated with the expansion process, and thus potentially robust markers of the corresponding changes.

Although the details are available elsewhere, a few words are required regarding the nature of the data in order to consider potential biases resulting from the uneven history of local archaeological research. In total, the dataset holds records for 111 500-year phases spread over 93 sites, accounting for 85,955 specimens. In the vast majority of cases, the phasing is enabled by directly associated ^{14}C dating, although in 20 cases, the sites were assigned on the basis of their associated chronological group. A minimum NISP cutoff of 100 was applied and, given the large range of assemblage size (min. = 100, max. = 5,696), we first tested for possible correlation between number of taxa and assemblage size, showing a weak correlation between both variables (see details in Gaastra and Vander Linden 2018). In addition to various statistical techniques, we extensively resorted to correspondence analysis to explore variation in the dataset. This multivariate technique, increasingly used in zooarchaeological meta-analysis (e.g., VanDerwarker 2014), illustrates the relationship between sets of categorical variables by a series of measures explaining a decreasing percentage of the total variance of the studied population. Here, plots found in Figure 9.5 account for nearly 70% of the total variance (see Gaastra and Vander Linden 2018 for full discussion).

These methodological precautions having been taken, it is time to turn our attention to testing the three predictions listed above. The first prediction concerns the fact that, during

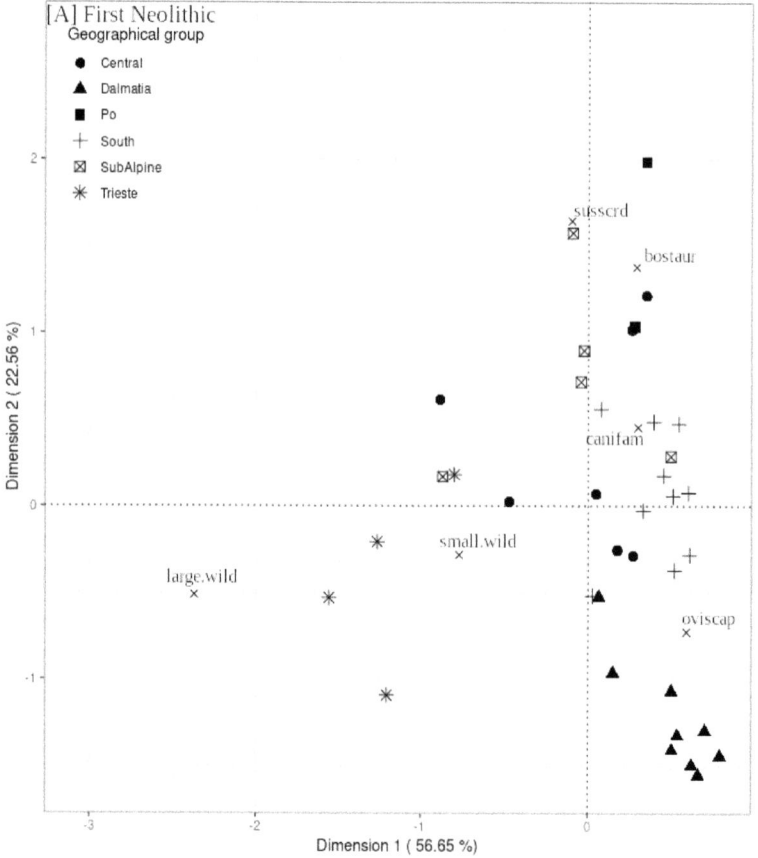

Figure 9.5. Taxonomic representation of sites by region for initial and secondary phases of Neolithic settlement expressed via correspondence analysis (after Gaastra and Vander Linden 2018:Figure 8).

an episode of demographically fueled spatial expansion, a population will experience a drop in its cultural diversity. Translated into archaeological terms, we therefore expect the earliest zooarchaeological assemblages to be characterized by a low variation. To this purpose, and given the time span of the dispersal of early farming across the Adriatic, we grouped zooarchaeological data and corresponding phases in two main classes. Class 1 ("First Neolithic") encompasses all archaeological sites dated within the first 500 years following the date of local introduction of domesticates; class 2 ("Second Neolithic") includes all archaeological sites dated 500 to 1,000 years after the local introduction of early farming. These classes are thus based on the relative chronology of the spread of early farming, since in our model the effects of the wave are systemic and thus reproduced through time and space as long as the expansion front progresses. As seen on Figure 9.5, zooarchaeological assemblages belonging to Class 1 cluster largely in the right half of the biplot, pointing to a limited amount of variation, although regional differences do occur, and are explored in the following section.

The second prediction, as a logical correlate of this reduced diversity, implies the presence of a narrow repertoire of traits at the expansion front. As already stated, it is essential to recognize that, in our modified CDM, the success of these traits, indicated by their overrepresentation in the corresponding assemblages, is not the reflection of any higher adaptive power. As all traits are neutral, this pattern is linked to the internal dynamics of the modified CDM, rather than any external factor such as environmental pressure. While a similar process is well described for crop and pulse packages in both the Adriatic basin and other European regions (e.g., limited presence of peas in the Adriatic: Gaastra et al. 2019; absence of lentils in the Linearbandkeramik of central Europe: Colledge et al. 2005; see also Coward et al. 2008), the situation is more difficult to assess for domesticated animals given their restricted repertoire (i.e., four species: *Bos taurus, Ovis aries, Capra hircus, Sus domesticus*). It is however noticeable that the overall reduced variation in Class 1 sites is even more marked when considering individual regions, each occupying different parts of the CA biplot. This being said, contrary to the premises of our CDM, this interregional variation can partly be explained by environmental factors. Dalmatian and, to some extent, southern Italian sites indeed present a higher proportion of ovicaprids, while the relative weight of more water-demanding species such as pigs and cattle gradually increases northward, reflecting the general north-south gradient across the Adriatic in precipitation. To some extent, this situation echoes other regional trends in the Danube basin, characterized by staggered temporal and geographical adaptation to local ecological conditions, although Pannonian sites retained for a few centuries an emphasis on sheep and goats despite the damp conditions theoretically more favorable for pigs and/or cattle (Orton et al. 2016). So, while indeed the narrow repertoire predicted by our model finds some empirical grounding, the archaeological reality proves—without much surprise, it must be said—more complex, given the role of environmental factors not considered in our computational model.

The third prediction states that the initial episode of relative cultural homogeneity gives way to a second phase of higher cultural diversity, linked to continuous interactions between agents located in both the original populated zone and the former expansion front. This larger variation is easily visible through visual inspection of the correspondence analysis for Class 2 sites, which occupy a much larger space on the biplot than Class 1 sites. The nature of this difference is easier to grasp when directly comparing the eigenvalues of Dimension 1, which marks the distinction between wild (to the left of the CA biplot, with low values) and nonwild species (to the right, with high values), and of Dimension 2, with, on the one hand, sheep and goats (with low values) and, on other hand, cattle and pigs (with higher values). Figures 9.6 and 9.7 provide a visual representation of these differences in the form of violin plots of the eigenvalues for Dimensions 1 and 2 respectively. As evident by comparing both figures, there are no significant differences in terms of Dimension 1, as confirmed by a further t-test (as both distributions are parametric; p.value = 0.5841). On the contrary, the boxplots illustrate a clear difference for Dimension 2 values, which prove statistically significant (as both distributions are non-parametric, a Mann-Whitney u-test was used; p.value = 0.012). This analysis demonstrates the existence of differences between both phases, and that these are largely related to regional differences in the proportions of domesticated animals. It is equally important to note that this increased diversity is not the mere outcome of increased adaptation to the local conditions and/or specialization. Although regional trends are still present, each regional group actually exhibits less focused strategies than before. The Dalmatian and southern Italian sequences provide good examples, as both experience a growing importance of cattle to the detriment of ovicaprids, a trend that carries on during the seventh millennium cal B.P. despite increasingly arid conditions, a priori more favorable for sheep and goats on the basis of the local ecological

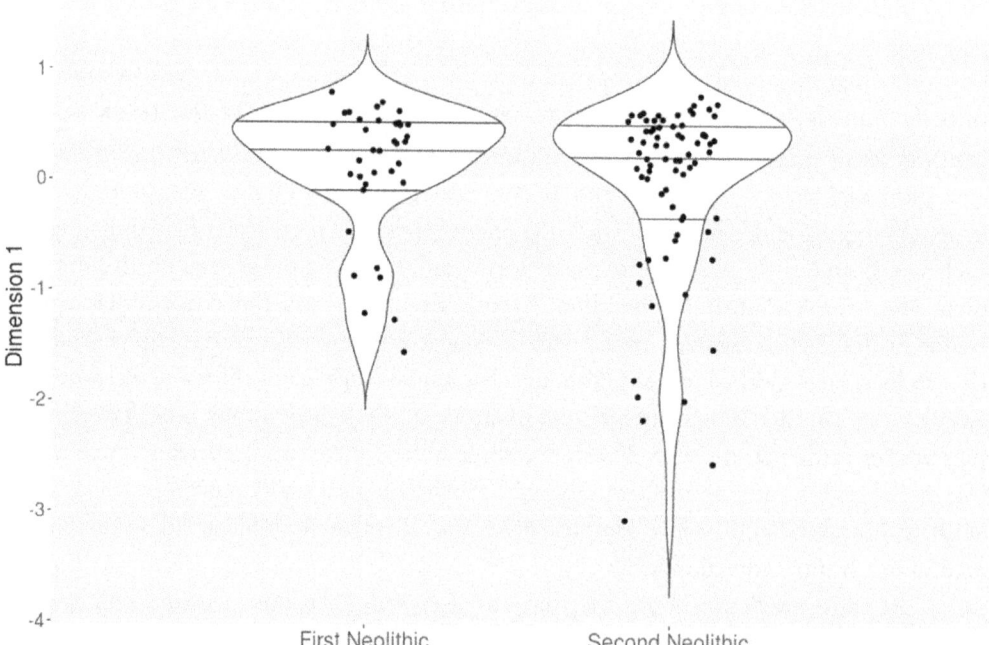

FIGURE 9.6. Violin plots of eigenvalues for Dimension 1 for first and second Adriatic Neolithic zooarchaeological assemblages.

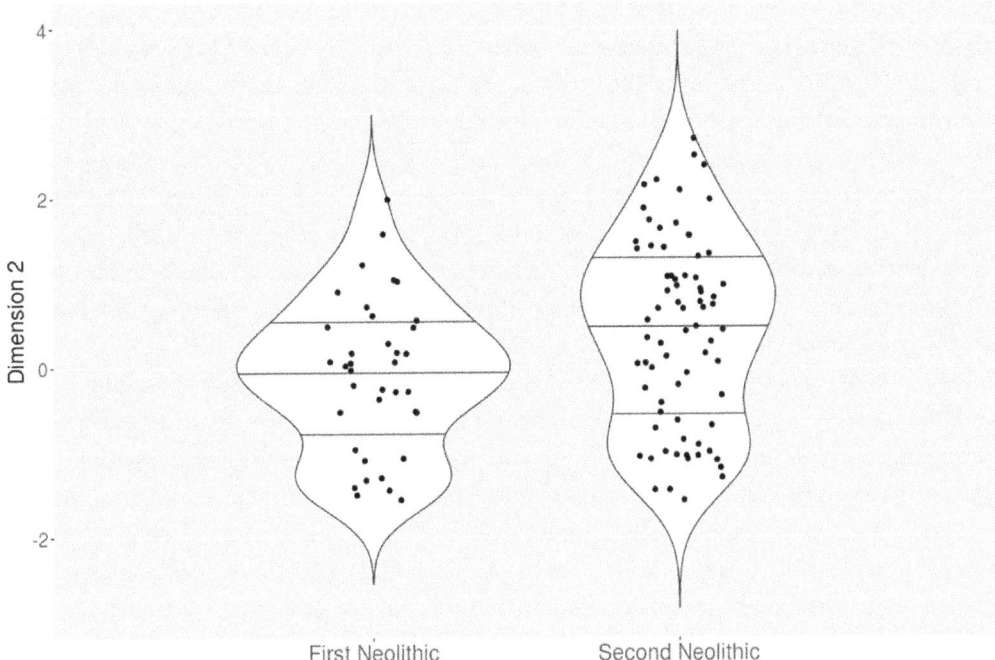

FIGURE 9.7. Violin plots of eigenvalues for Dimension 2 for both first and second Adriatic Neolithic zooarchaeological assemblages.

conditions. The same applies to hunting. Cave sites in southern and central Italy present a greater proportion of wild animals, suggesting differential usages of the landscape away from open-air settlements, while, by contrast, hunting levels remain low along the western Adriatic and with considerable diversity, including between cave and open-air sites (Gaastra and Vander Linden 2018).

Conclusion

The simple model proposed here allowed us to examine, admittedly under a narrow range of parameters, what happens to the culture of a population experiencing a phase of expansion. While possibly limiting, such a parsimonious approach has the advantage of providing general, widely applicable hypotheses, readily testable against the archaeological record (Drost and Vander Linden 2018). Indeed, our modified CDM suggests that, during a demographically induced dispersal, a population will undergo an initial phase of reduced cultural diversity, followed by a second stage of increased variation. We tested these predictions against the zooarchaeological record of the early Neolithic in the Adriatic basin. After classifying corresponding assemblages from a chronological relative—rather than a more classical absolute—point of view, we showed that, as predicted by our model, sites chronologically associated with or close to the local introduction of plant and animal domesticates were characterized by a low diversity, clearly identified for instance through correspondence analysis of zooarchaeological data. It is noteworthy that this pattern has been recognized and discussed previously, with competing interpretations stressing either the role of random drift (Pérez-Losada and Fort 2011) or of biased cultural transmission (Conolly et al. 2008). In comparison, our model, wherein cultural transmission is regulated by a combination of homophily and cloning, concurs with the importance of biased transmission in explaining this early horizon of reduced cultural variation. But, different from earlier work, our model is the first to identify and explain the existence of a second phase, characterized by a rise in cultural diversity. This hypothesized phase also appears in the zooarchaeological record for the Adriatic Neolithic.

Although two of the predictions of the model were met, this does not imply that the model provides a perfect fit for the available archaeological data. As discussed above, environmental factors, not considered in our computational approach, have shaped to some extent variation in Neolithic zooarchaeological assemblages. This effect seems more obvious during the early stages of the Adriatic sequence, as the preference for certain types of domesticates broadly corresponds to certain characteristics of the landscape. Comparatively, environmental variables do not seem to explain the higher diversity of the second phase, with no obvious trajectory toward increased local adaptation and/or specialization. All in all, the role of environment—or other variables for that matter—thus requires further testing, which can to some extent be done with the conceptual and methodological framework of our model, but also requires alternative techniques. It is, however, necessary to recognize that, while the model would gain in complexity and "reality," this is likely to come at the cost of losing some of the predictive power of the approach (as too many parameters drive the model in chaotic directions), as well as its general applicability (as the model becomes increasingly rigged toward one particular situation and set of parameters).

To conclude, partly under the impetus of new scientific techniques, archaeology has recently rediscovered the central role of migration in human history. Given this new technical arsenal, there have been calls for archaeologists to put less emphasis on recognizing migrations, as the task can seemingly be left to the hard sciences, and rather to focus on questions of understanding how they arise. These are assuredly essential goals, but they cannot come at the expense of any basic understanding of what a migration looks like in the material archaeological record, as, after all, scientific techniques are not always a possibility through a combination of conservation biases (i.e., suitable samples may not have entered the archaeological record), ethics (i.e., unwillingness of certain stakeholders to undertake destructive analysis), and practicalities (i.e., lack of funding). In this sense, it is equally paramount to come back to the basic task of how migrations and their underlying factors shape the archaeological record.

Acknowledgments

This paper is an output from the European Research Council project EUROFARM, funded under the European Union's Seventh Framework Programme (FP/20072013; ERC Grant

Agreement. no. 313716), led by MVL. The authors acknowledge the use of the UCL Legion High Performance Computing Facility (Legion@UCL) and associated support services in the completion of this work. Lastly, many thanks are due to all participants of the Buffalo 2018 conference for their comments, and especially to Megan Daniels for her outstanding editorial work and patience.

References Cited

Anthony, D. 1990 Migration in Archaeology: The Baby and the Bathwater. *American Anthropologist* 92(4):895–914.

Axelrod, R. 1997 The Dissemination of Culture: A Model with Local Convergence and Global Polarization. *Journal of Conflict Resolution* 41(2):203–226.

Bevan, A., and E. R. Crema 2018 *rcarbon v1.2.0: Methods for Calibrating and Analysing Radiocarbon Dates*. Electronic document, https://CRAN.R-project.org/package=rcarbon.

Binford, L. 1962 Archaeology as Anthropology. *American Antiquity* 28(2):217–225.

Bocquet-Appel, J.-P. 2008 *La paléodémographie. 99,99 % de l'histoire démographique des hommes ou la démographie de la Préhistoire*. Errance, Paris.

Bonsall, C., and A. Boroneanţ 2018 The Iron Gates Mesolithic—A Brief Review of Recent Developments. *L'anthropologie* 122(2):264–280.

Borcard, D., F. Gillet, and P. Legendre 2011 *Numerical Ecology with R*. Springer, New York.

Borić, D., N. Borovinić, L. Đurič, J. Bulatović, K. Gerometta, D. Filipović, E. Allué, Z. Vušović-Lučić, and E. Cristiani 2019 Spearheading into the Neolithic: Last Foragers and First Farmers in the Dinaric Alps of Montenegro. *European Journal of Archaeology*. DOI:10.1017/eaa.2019.14.

Castellano, C., S. Fortunato, and V. Loreto 2009 Statistical Physics of Social Dynamics. *Review of Modern Physics* 81(2):591–646.

Cegielski, W. H., and J. D. Rogers 2016 Rethinking the Role of Agent-Based Modeling in Archaeology. *Journal of Anthropological Archaeology* 41:283–298.

Clarke, G. 1966 The Invasion Hypothesis in British Archeology. *Antiquity* 40:172–189.

Colledge, S., J. Conolly, and S. Shennan 2005 The Evolution of Early Neolithic Farming from SW Asian Origins to NW European Limits. *European Journal of Archaeology* 8(2):137–156.

Conolly, J., S. Colledge, and S. Shennan 2008 Founder Effect, Drift, and Adaptive Change in Domestic Crop Use in Early Neolithic Europe. *Journal of Archaeological Science* 35(10):2797–2804.

Coward, F., S. Shennan, S. Colledge, J. Conolly, and M. Collard 2008 The Spread of Neolithic Plant Economies from the Near East to Northwest Europe: A Phylogenetic Analysis. *Journal of Archaeological Science* 35:42–56.

Drost, C. J., and M. Vander Linden 2018 Toy Story: Homophily, Transmission, and the Use of Simple Models in Assessing Variability in the Archaeological Record. *Journal of Archaeological Method and Theory* 25(4):1087–1108.

Forenbaher, S., T. Kaiser, and P. T. Miracle 2013 Dating the East Adriatic Neolithic. *European Journal of Archaeology* 16:589–609.

Franco, C. 2011 *La fine del Mesolitico in Italia. Identità culturale e distribuzione territoriale degli ultimi cacciatori-raccoglitori*. Società per la preistoria e protoistoria della regione Friuli-Venezia Giulia, Trieste.

François, O., M. Currat, N. Ray, E. Han, L. Excoffier, and J. Novembre 2010 Principal Component Analysis under Population Genetic Models of Range Expansion and Admixture. *Molecular Biology and Evolution* 27(6):1257–1268.

Gaastra, J., and M. Vander Linden 2018 Farming Data: Testing Climatic and Palaeo-Environmental Effect on Neolithic Adriatic Stockbreeding and Hunting through Zooarchaeological Meta-Analysis. *The Holocene*. DOI:10.1177/0959683618761543.

Gaastra, J., H. Greenfield, and M. Vander Linden 2018 Gaining Traction on Cattle Exploitation: Zooarchaeological Evidence from the Western Balkan Neolithic (6000–4500 cal BC). *Antiquity* 92:1462–1477.

Gaastra, J., A. de Vareilles, and M. Vander Linden 2019 Bones and Seeds: An Integrated Approach to Understanding the Spread of Farming Across the Western Balkans. *Environmental archaeology: the journal of human palaeoecology*. DOI:10.1080/14614103.2019.1578016.

Gräler, B., E. Pebesma, and G. Heuvelink 2016 Spatio-Temporal Interpolation Using gstat. *The R Journal* 8(1):204–218.

Gurova, M., and C. Bonsall 2014 "Pre-Neolithic" in Southeast Europe: a Bulgarian Perspective. *Documenta Praehistorica* 15:95–109.

Haun, D. B. M., and H. Over 2013 Like Me: a Homophily-Based Account of Human Culture. In *Cultural Evolution: Society, Technology, Language, and Religion*, edited by P. J. Richerson and M. Christiansen, pp. 75–85. MIT Press, Cambridge.

Johannsen, N. N., G. Larson, D. J. Meltzer, and M. Vander Linden 2017 A Composite Window into Human History. Better Integration of Ancient DNA Studies with Archaeology Promises Deeper Insights. *Science* 356:1118–1120.

Lake, M. 2014 Trends in Archaeological Simulation. *Journal of Archaeological Method and Theory* 21(2):258–287.

Lazaridis, I., D. Nadel, G. Rollefson, D. C. Merrett, N. Rohland, S. Mallick, D. Fernandes, M. Novak, B. Gamarra, K. Sirak, S. Connell, K. Stewardson, E. Harney, Q. Fu, G. Gonzalez-Fortes, E. R. Jones, S. A. Roodenberg, G. Lengyel, F. Bocquentin, B. Gasparian, J. M. Monge, M. Gregg, V. Eshed, A.-S. Mizrahi, C. Meiklejohn, F. Gerritsen, L. Bejenaru, M. Blüher, A. Campbell, G. Cavalleri, D. Comas, P. Froguel, E. Gilbert, S. M. Kerr, P. Kovacs, J. Krause, D. McGettigan, M. Merrigan, D. A. Merriwether, S. O'Reilly, M. B. Richards, O. Semino, M. Shamoon-Pour, G. Stefanescu, M. Stumvoll, A. Tönjes, A. Torroni, J. F. Wilson, L. Yengo, N. A. Hovhannisyan, N. Patterson, R. Pinhasi, and D. Reich 2016 Genomic Insights into the Origins of Farming in the Ancient Near East. *Nature* 536:419–424.

Madsen, M. E., and C. P. Lipo 2015 Behavioral Modernity and Cultural Transmission of Structured Information: The Semantic Axelrod model. In *Learning Strategies and Cultural Evolution during the Palaeolithic*, edited by A. Mesoudi and K. Aoki, pp. 67–83. Springer, New York.

Mathieson, I., S. Alpaslan-Roodenberg, C. Posth, A. Szécsényi-Nagy, N. Rohland, S. Mallick, I. Olalde, N. Broomandkhoshbacht, F. Candilio, O. Cheronet, D. Fernandes, M. Ferry, B. Gamarra, G. González Fortes, W. Haak, E. Harney, E. Jones, D. Keating, B. Krause-Kyora, I. Kucukkalipci, M. Michel, A. Mittnik, K. Nägele, M. Novak, J. Oppenheimer, N. Patterson, S. Pfrengle, K. Sirak, K. Stewardson, S. Vai, S. Alexandrov, K. W. Alt, R. Andreescu, R. Antonović, A. Ash, N. Atanassova, K. Bacvarov, M. Balázs Gusztáv, H. Bocherens, M. Bolus, A. Boroneanţ, Y. Boyadzhiev, A. Budnik, J. Burmaz, S. Chohadzhiev, N. J. Conard, R. Cottiaux, M. Čuka, C. Cupillard, D. G. Drucker, N. Elenski, M. Francken, B. Galabova,

G. Ganetsovski, B. Gély, T. Hajdu, V. Handzhyiska, K. Harvati, K., T. Higham, S. Iliev, I. Janković, I. Karavanić, D. J. Kennett, D. Komšo, A. Kozak, D. Labuda, M. Lari, C. Lazar, M. Leppek, K. Leshtakov, D. Lo Vetro, D. Los, I. Lozanov, M. Malina, F. Martini, K. McSweeney, H. Meller, M. Menđušić, P. Mirea, V. Moiseyev, V. Petrova, T.D. Price, A. Simalcsik, L. Sineo, M. Šlaus, V. Slavchev, P. Stanev, A. Starović, T. Szeniczey, S. Talamo, M. Teschler-Nicola, C. Thevenet, I. Valchev, F. Valentin, S. Vasilyev, F. Veljanovska, S. Venelinova, E. Veselovskaya, B. Viola, C. Virag, J. Zaninović, S. Zäuner, P. Stockhammer, G. Catalano, R. Krauß, D. Caramelli, G. Zariņa, B. Gaydarska, M. Lillie, A.G. Nikitin, I. Potekhina, A. Papathanasiou, D. Borić, C. Bonsall, J. Krause, R. Pinhasi, and D. Reich 2018 The Genomic History of Southeastern Europe 555:197–203.

McPherson, M., L. Smit-Lovin, and J. M. Cook 2001 Birds of a Feather: Homophily in Social Networks. *Annual Review of Sociology* 27:425–444.

Orton, D., J. Gaastra, and M. Vander Linden 2016 Between the Danube and the Deep Blue Sea: Zooarcheological Meta-Analysis Reveals Variability in the Spread and Development of Neolithic Farming across the Western Balkans. *Open Quaternary* 2. DOI:10.5334/oq.28.

Pandžić, I., and M. Vander Linden (editors) 2014 *The Neolithic site of Kočićevo in the lower Vrbas Valley, Republika Srpska, Bosnia and Herzegovina: Results of the 2009–2014 Investigations*. Muzej Republike Srpske, Banja Luka (with Serbian translation).

Pérez-Losada, J., and J. Fort 2011 Spatial Dimensions Increase the Effect of Cultural Drift. *Journal of Archaeological Science* 38(6):1294–1299.

Pilaar Birch, S., and M. Vander Linden 2017 A Long Hard Road: Reviewing the Evidence for Environmental Change and Population History in the Eastern Adriatic and Western Balkans during the Late Pleistocene and Early Holocene. *Quaternary International* 465B:177–191.

R Core Team 2018 *R: A Language and Environment for Statistical Computing. R Foundation for Statistical Computing*. Vienna, Austria. Electronic document, https://www.R-project.org/.

Racimo F., M. Sikora, M. Vander Linden, H. Schroeder, and C. Lalueza-Fox 2020 Beyond Broad Strokes: Sociocultural Insights from the Study of Ancient Genomes. *Nature Reviews Genetics* 21:355–366. DOI:10.1038/s41576-020-0218-z.

Runnels, C. 1995 Review of Aegean Prehistory IV: The Stone Age of Greece from the Paleolithic to the Advent of the Neolithic. *American Journal of Archaeology* 99:699–728.

Shennan, S. J., E. R. Crema, and T. Kerig 2014 Isolation-by-Distance, Homophily, and Cultural Evolution Models in Neolithic Europe. *Evolution and Human Behaviour* 36:103–109.

Silva, F., and M. Vander Linden 2017 Amplitude of Travelling Front as Inferred from ^{14}C predicts Levels of Genetic Admixture among European Early Farmers. *Nature Scientific Reports* 7:11985.

Steele, J., and S. Shennan 2009 Introduction: Demography and Macrocultural Evolution. *Human biology* 81(2–3):105–119.

Tennekes M. 2018 tmap: Thematic Maps in R. *Journal of Statistical Software* 84(6):1–39. DOI:10.18637/jss.v084.i06.

VanDerwarker, A. M. 2014 Correspondence Analysis and Principal Components Analysis as Methods for Integrating Archaeological Plant and Animal Remains. In *Integrating Zooarchaeology and Paleoethnobotany. A Consideration of Issues, Methods, and Cases*, edited by A. M. VanDerwarker and T. M. Peres, pp. 75–95. Springer, New York.

Vander Linden M. 2011 In Constant Motion? Recent Advances in Mathematical Modelling and Radiocarbon Chronology of the Neolithisation of Europe. In *Dynamics of Neolithisation:*

Studies in Honour of Andrew Sherratt, edited by A. Hadjikoumis, E. Robinson and S. Viner, pp. 41–61. Oxbow, Oxford.

Vander Linden, M., G. Marriner, D. Orton, A. de Vareilles, D. Gazivoda, and D. Mihailović 2015 Seocka Pećina: An Early Mesolithic Site in South-Eastern Montenegro. *Mesolithic Miscellany* 23(2):49–54.

Vander Linden, M., and M. Saqalli 2019 Introducing Qualitative and Social Science Factors in Archaeological Modelling: Necessity and Relevance. In *Integrating Qualitatve and Social Science Factors in Archaeological Modelling*, edited by M. Saqalli and M. Vander Linden, pp. 1–14. Springer, New York.

Williams A. N. 2012 The Use of Summed Radiocarbon Probability Distributions in Archaeology: A Review of Methods. *Journal of Archaeological Science* 39:578–589. DOI:10.1016/j.jas.2011.07.014.

CHAPTER TEN

The Settlement Record, Paleodemography, and Evidence for Migrations in Eneolithic Ukraine

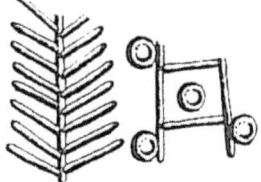

Thomas K. Harper

Abstract *Neo-Eneolithic settlement systems throughout Europe were highly mobile from one generation to the next, engaging in serial relocation of sites and gradually colonizing new regions. The typochronology of the Cucuteni-Tripolye cultural complex (ca. 5050–2950 B.C.) suggests an added feature: large-scale, spatially targeted migrations in the forest-steppe region of Moldova and Ukraine, which attained their peak during the first half of the fourth millennium B.C. Recent examination of diachronic trends in the distribution and size of settlements in this area enables the reconstruction of quantitative demographic histories by region. However, it remains difficult to discern which population changes result from endogenous growth and which are the result of migrations. In order to highlight those instances in which population growth is potentially migratory in nature, it is necessary to combine settlement archaeology with an understanding of the vital statistics of an ancient society (paleodemography). By calculating the potential natural increase (PNI), researchers might come to an understanding of the probable limits of endogenous growth. In turn, this allows us to highlight those situations in which archaeologically observed population growth exceeds PNI and therefore likely has a migratory component. The presented case study explores PNI from the perspectives of both paleodemographic meta-analysis and a generalized model of preindustrial sex-age structure. Comparisons between the two have the added effect of revealing potential biases within regional paleodemographic data sets. Results support the idea that some regional examples of population agglomeration, as well as the sudden emergence of certain archaeological horizons, are manifestations of migratory behavior.*

Identifying incidences of migration within regional population trends is a complicated proposition, often dependent on archaeometric means such as stable isotope analyses of human remains (e.g., $\delta^{13}C$, $\delta^{15}N$, $^{87}Sr/^{86}Sr$). Given a large and representative skeletal sample, as well as a comprehensive understanding of regional trophic behaviors and environmental background values, these methods can be used to distinguish between local and nonlocal populations and, ideally, even determine the approximate source location of migrants. Meanwhile, large-scale studies in population genomics are increasingly explicating population movements on relatively broad space-time scales (see Anthony, this volume). However, these methods are contingent on actively sampling skeletal populations representative of an array of local contexts, which may vary wildly in terms of their archaeological preservation due to differences in taphonomy and mortuary practice. This paper explores an alternative multipart approach for understanding migratory behavior on the regional level, using settlement-based population reconstruction and available data from past paleodemographic studies.

Here, I examine a case study from Eastern Europe during the Neo-Eneolithic period (ca. 6300–2950 B.C.), specifically in the modern countries of Romania, Moldova, and Ukraine west of the Dnieper River. For this area and time period there exists an extensive amount of archaeological settlement data and a finely tuned pottery typochronology that, while not perfect, is synchronized at various positions by cross-dating of exchange goods and a small corpus of radiocarbon data (Diachenko and Harper 2016; Harper 2016). Meanwhile, human remains are conspicuously absent in many contexts; where present, they represent a biased record in a region divided between competing practices of cremation and inhumation burials. Both settlement-based population reconstructions and pottery typology and seriation suggest that large-scale, medium-distance population movements occurred at specific times within subregions of this study area. The most notable examples occurred during the first half of the fourth millennium B.C., when the largest settlements of prehistoric Europe (the giant-settlements of the middle-to-late Tripolye culture) appeared in the territory between the Southern Bug and Dnieper rivers in Central Ukraine. When taken in unison, the available data make a reasonable case for migrations, especially given that Neolithic settlement practices were largely predicated on continual, short-distance movement of habitational sites to begin with (Milisauskas and Kruk 1989). However, it is important to note that (1) pots are not people; and (2) there is a substantial difference between moving 10 km and 300 km. As admittedly unlikely as it would be for a geographically discrete population to suddenly adopt the material culture of another group simply on the basis of exchange or some other vague "influence," it is important to find some means of corroborating regional-level migrations beyond qualitative examination of the dispersion of diagnostic archaeological materials.

I employ a method of empirically identifying migrations in the archaeological record through the combined use of two forms of analysis. The first step, a settlement archaeology approach, calculates the population of a given analytical region over a desired series of time references. The second step—which relies on inferences from paleodemographic data—estimates the potential natural increase (PNI) of a given population, enabling the assessment of whether episodes of observed population growth outstrip the population's reproductive capacity. Both analyses are outgrowths of well-established components of processual archaeology, particularly spatial and demographic approaches codified in the 1970s and '80s (Ammerman et al. 1976; Hassan 1981; Zubrow 1975, 1976). Even if the theoretical agenda of that time might be considered by some to be ambivalent to the topic of migration (Cabana and Clark 2011), many fundamental methods in archaeological demography remain essentially unchanged. Current revisions and reapplications of these methods (in a similar vein to Zubrow et al., this volume) might be considered novel due to the addition of modern computing. This allows for greater operational complexity while also simplifying the construction and analysis of very large space-time data sets. Few researchers are currently approaching population estimation from the perspective of large-scale observational analysis, generally preferring the use of meta-analysis (extrapolating superregional populations from compilations of disparate regional analyses; e.g., Müller 2015) or proxy records derived from environmental or archaeometric data sources (especially ^{14}C summed probability distributions; e.g., Shennan and Edinborough 2007). Such approaches often have poor theoretical foundations and, at least within the geographic and temporal frame I examine, little to no correlation with archaeological settlement data (Harper forthcoming).

Since the operation of my method for obtaining population estimates from settlement data sets is explored elsewhere, in whole or in part (Harper 2016; Harper et al. 2019; Harper forthcoming), emphasis here will mostly be placed on the calculation of PNI and its role in identifying migratory episodes. I will assess two scenarios for performing this calculation: one involving the use of available Neo-Eneolithic paleodemographic data, and the other involving a generalized model of preindustrial sex-age structure. First, I will address the regional archaeological record and what may be inferred regarding population development over time.

The Settlement Record and Population Development

The Cucuteni-Tripolye Complex

Many of the archaeological materials from Ukraine, Moldova and Romania during the Eneolithic (ca. 5050–2950 B.C.) can be ascribed to the Cucuteni-Tripolye cultural complex, a diverse group of regional assemblages descended from a common initial developmental period (Precucuteni) centered in northeastern Romania. At its greatest territorial extent, the complex extended from the Dnieper to the Carpathians, and from Volyn to the Black Sea littoral (Figure 10.1). While there is considerable space-time variability in pottery styles throughout the complex, development is often casually denoted in three main ("early-middle-late") periods: Precucuteni/Tripolye A (ca. 5050–4500 B.C.); Cucuteni A and A-B/Tripolye B (ca. 4500–3900 B.C.); and Cucuteni B and Horodoștea-Foltești/Tripolye C (ca. 3900–2950 B.C.).

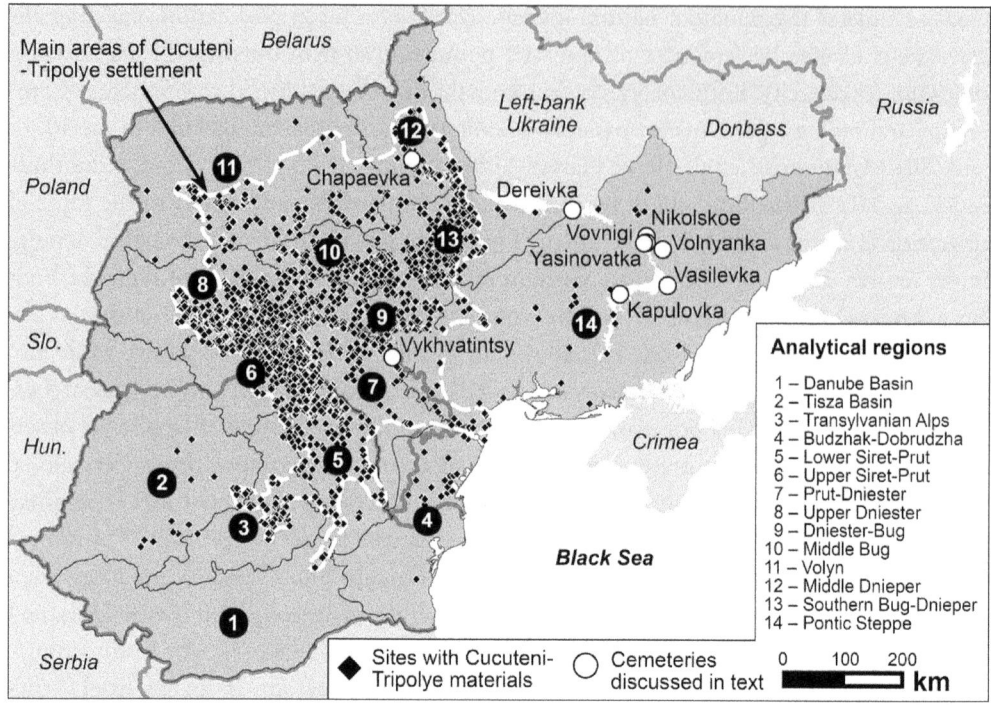

FIGURE 10.1. The study area, overlaid with the distribution of Cucuteni-Tripolye sites and the positions of cemeteries discussed in the text.

Cucuteni-Tripolye sites are particularly numerous; within the study area, sites belonging to this complex may account for up to 50% of all sites during the entire Neo-Eneolithic period. However, there are a variety of other neighboring and overlapping material assemblages that must be taken into account when generating population estimates (Harper 2016). Other major archaeological groups that contribute substantially to regional population estimates include the Bug-Dniester, Starčevo-Körös-Criş and Linear Pottery cultures of the Early and Middle Neolithic, the Boian and Hamangia cultures of the Late Neolithic, the Gumelniţa and Tiszapolgár complexes of the Eneolithic, and a variety of groups during the Terminal Eneolithic and Early Bronze Age (EBA) transition (notably including the Baden and Coţofeni cultures). Due to the interrelatedness and geographical overlap of archaeological cultures in the region, it makes far more sense to use all available data instead of adopting a freestanding "culture area" approach.

Population History

The role of medium-range migrations in establishing the Tripolye giant-settlements in the forest-steppe region of Ukraine was first suggested by material specialists (notably Sergei Ryzhov), who noted the close relationship of ceramic assemblages and settlement architecture between Moldova and Central Ukraine during the periods of Tripolye B2 and C1

(Ryzhov 1999). This time period (ca. 4000–3600 B.C.) is roughly contemporaneous with the onset of the 5.9 ka climate change event, a period of prevailingly cooler and wetter conditions lasting nearly a millennium that left a perceptible signature in regional pollen records (Harper 2019). Substantial changes in settlement patterns can be observed in a variety of contexts throughout the study area and have been discussed in the context of climate by several studies (Anthony 2007; Diachenko 2010; Dolukhanov et al. 2009; Manzura 2005; Weninger and Harper 2015). Against a backdrop of increased climatic variability, Late Eneolithic societies in this region gradually adopted a more dispersed and mobile way of life over the course of the fourth millennium, at least partially prefiguring the vast socioeconomic changes that characterize the transition to the EBA several centuries later (Harper et al. 2019). Based on available radiocarbon data and stratigraphic sequences in Ukraine west of the Dnieper River, it is highly probable that the first century of the third millennium (ca. 3000/2900 B.C.) marks the emergence of the EBA Yamnaya horizon (and, in turn, the *terminus ante quem* for the Neo-Eneolithic period). The sudden nature of this change in material culture (by the standards of archaeological time) has long been thought by some researchers to be due to large-scale migrations from the Eurasian steppe (Anthony, this volume), a viewpoint that has been corroborated by recent studies of European population genomics (e.g., Mathieson et al. 2018).

Recent investigations indicate that *Yersinia pestis* was present in Eastern Europe by the fourth millennium B.C., and the suggestion is made that there may be a link between its emergence and the collapse of densely populated settlements such as the Tripolye giant-settlements (Rascovan et al. 2019). While it cannot be excluded that the spread of plague may have influenced the events of the Late Eneolithic and EBA transition, an understanding of the time depth and cultural variability of this ~600-year period tends to temper sensationalistic notions of sudden calamitous collapse or mass-mortality events, which are almost universally archaeologically uncorroborated. Additionally, discussion of PNI will reveal that—plague or no plague—we should consider distressingly high mortality rates to be the prevailing norm in ancient and traditional societies.

Population histories were reconstructed for fourteen subregions across Romania, Moldova, and Ukraine during the Neo-Eneolithic period through the use of a mathematical model derived from the *SARP* model (Harper 2016; Harper forthcoming). *SARP* is a basic model in concept, simply consisting of multiplying the number of synchronous settlements (S) by their area (A), number of rooms (R), and persons per room (P) to achieve a population estimate for a given time reference (Ammerman et al. 1976). However, the relative simplicity of this approach's calculations belies a labor-intensive process of chronology building and data collection. For the present study area, I compiled a comprehensive archaeological site database (n = 8,164) called the Eastern European Neo-Eneolithic Sites Repository (EENSR; Harper et al. 2019), which enabled the calculation of population time series along a 48-phase chronology. The general trends in the spatial distribution of the population revealed by this model are summarized in Figure 10.2.

SARP provides the best available population reconstruction for this region and time period, allowing interregional comparison of population values and calculation of growth rates. Over the course of evaluating results from this model, growth rates from one

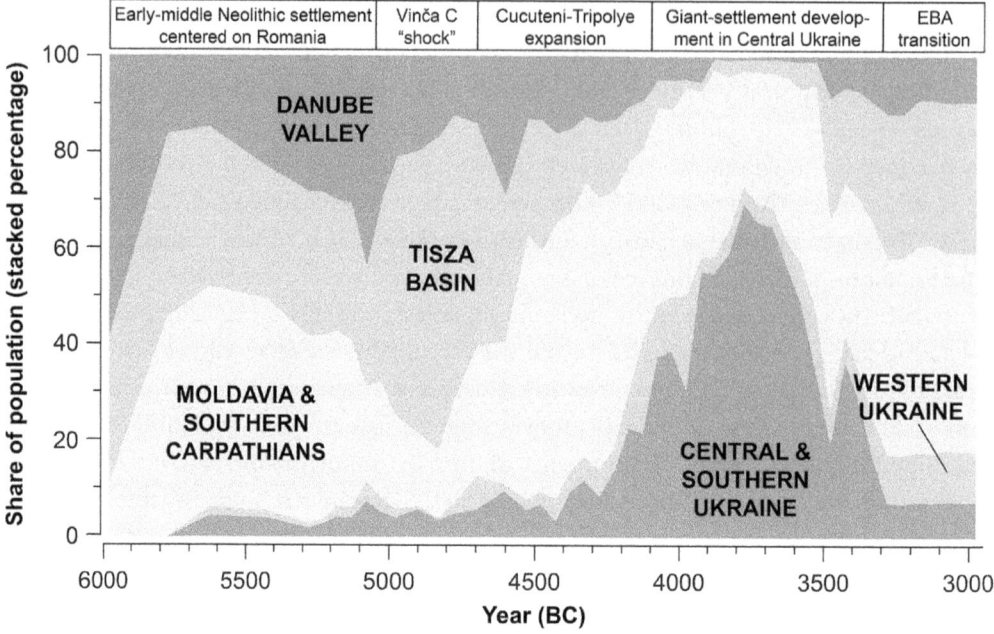

FIGURE 10.2. Population expansion and movement over the course of the Neo-Eneolithic period in Romania, Moldova, and Ukraine, expressed as a stacked percentage (simplified to five regions for clarity).

chronological phase to the next stood out as the most promising quantitative indicator of migrations. They, however, lack any inherent attribute that indicates whether this growth is endogenous or exogenous. The addition of PNI allows us to consider a threshold beyond which the endogenous growth of a population is improbable.

METHODS AND ANALYSIS

NEO-NEOLITHIC PALEODEMOGRAPHY

In order to calculate the PNI of a prehistoric population we must address human remains themselves, with the most important data being the sex-age structure of burials within a given archaeological population. By establishing the age and sex of deceased individuals, we can then derive life expectancies for a given age cohort, mortality profiles (most importantly, childhood mortality), and the adult survivorship and reproductive potential of a given population.

While human remains within the Cucuteni-Tripolye complex are sparse, two Late Tripolye inhumation cemeteries stand out: the Tripolye C1 cemetery at Chapaevka in the Kiev region, Ukraine (29 burials; Kruts 1977), and the Tripolye C2 cemetery at Vykhvatintsy in Transnistria, Moldova (56 burials; Dergachev 1978). Additional cemeteries belonging to the neighboring Dnieper-Donets culture allow the expansion of the Ukrainian Neo-Eneolithic skeletal sample to 561 individuals. These cemeteries—Dereivka 1, Kapulovka, Nikolskoe, Vasilevka 2 and 5, Volnyanka, Vovnigi 1 and 2, and Yasinovatka (Potekhina 1981, 1988, 1999)—are mostly dated to phase 2 of the Dnieper-Donets culture, which for the most part can be roughly synchronized with the early and middle periods of the Cucuteni-Tripolye complex (Telegin 1987). They are situated within a 100 km radius of each other in the Lower Dnieper region, with half concentrated along the historical Dnieper Rapids between the modern cities of Zaphorozhye and Dnipropetrovsk. While these "Steppe Neolithic" areas are outside of the main area of Cucuteni-Tripolye settlement, Tripolye ceramics are present at cemeteries and kurgans throughout the Pontic Steppe, and it may be characterized as an extensive and porous interaction zone.

The actual remains associated with these studies are scattered across numerous collections throughout the former USSR and their availability for morphometric reanalysis is dubious. A quick means of data verification is to examine the approximate adult age-at-death observed in other studies of Neo-Eneolithic paleodemography (Table 10.1). Compared to a more recent study of roughly contemporaneous remains in Hungary (Ubelaker and Pap 2009) the Soviet and Ukrainian studies tend to observe a higher adult age-at-death. This amounts to one year for females (33.9 versus 32.9) and three and one-half years for males (37.0 versus 33.4). In a premodern setting, this is a substantial difference, and can probably

TABLE 10.1.
MEAN ADULT AGE-AT-DEATH FROM SELECTED STUDIES THROUGHOUT THE NEAR EAST AND SOUTHEASTERN EUROPE

Site/Area	n	All	Female	Male	Data source(s)
HaYonim Cave, Israel (Epipaleolithic)	17	28.9	—	—	Bar-Yosef and Goren 1973
Çatalhüyük, Turkey (Early Neolithic)	216	32.0	29.8	34.3	Angel 1971
Alepotrypa Cave, Greece (Early Neolithic)	81	28.8	—	—	Papathanasiou 2005
Cucuteni-Tripolye and Dnieper-Donets cemeteries (Neo-Eneolithic)	438	35.9	33.9	37.0	See text
Northeastern Hungary (Eneolithic)	155	—	32.9	33.4	Ubelaker and Pap 2009
Scythian burials in Ukraine (Iron Age)	813	38.6	35.1	41.8	Potekhina and Kislyj 1994

be ascribed to the use of different reference populations (as discussed by Bocquet-Appel and Masset [1982], and many others since).

In the absence of modern reanalysis, it cannot be known whether these differences are wholly due to methodological factors or whether they include some genuine regional variability in vital statistics. However, the elevated values seen in both the Neo-Eneolithic and Scythian (Potekhina and Kislyj 1994) samples suggest a systematic bias in method or the reference population used in Soviet and post-Soviet studies, particularly concerning males. Studies from other contexts showcase a slight upward increase in age-at-death over the course of the Holocene, but in general it is appropriate to generalize a fairly consistent preindustrial mortality profile characterized by high childhood mortality and low life expectancy (Hassan 1981).

Modern developments in paleodemographic methods tend to eschew life tables in favor of probabilistic age models (Hoppa and Vaupel 2002; Wood et al. 2002). However, the more old-fashioned life table–based approach is still used in some contexts (particularly where detailed morphometric data are unreported) and I retain it here due to the data available for input and the desire to produce at least some regionally sourced estimates for adult life expectancy. Age data from Ukrainian sources were resampled to adhere to commonly used age classes and assigned to life tables (Tables 10.2–4). The variables listed in each life table are: x, the age cohort; D_x, the number of deaths observed between age x and $x+1$; d_x, the proportion of total deaths occurring between age x and $x+1$; l_x, the number of survivors of age x; q_x, the probability of death between age x and $x+1$; L_x, the number of years lived by survivors between age x and $x+1$; T_x, the total years lived beyond age x; and E_x, the life expectancy at age x. Due to the majority of children and a minority of adults lacking sex identifications, unclassified individuals were assigned categories based on the observed distribution of the overall sample. This is the reason for non-integer values for D_x.

Aside from probable reference biases, the overall sex-age distribution shows a marked bias against childhood mortality that is unexpected in preindustrial society, with an l_{15} of 75.09 (meaning that 75% of the population can be expected to survive to age 15). This is even more exaggerated in the available data from Hungary, where l_{15} = 84.70 (Ubelaker and Pap 2009). Taphonomic bias surely plays a role at many sites, though we cannot neglect the possibility that burial practices also differed depending on sex and age; in Ukraine, males outnumber females by nearly two to one in mortuary populations, while the number of child burials fluctuates widely from zero to 62.5%. When compared against a model life table assembled from ethnographic observations (Weiss 1973), values of q_x (the probability of death for an individual in age cohort x) are substantially lower than are to be expected for the lowest age categories (Figure 10.3). In general, mortality trends should adhere to what is called the "bathtub curve" (Wood et al. 2002), where the force of mortality is most keenly observed among the very young and very old. This is evident in Weiss's model life table while the biases of the Ukrainian sample render the left side of our "bathtub" missing.

An expected and reassuring aspect of the available skeletal sample lies in the way that it showcases differential mortality between males and females (Figure 10.4). This is represented most keenly by the prominent spike in observed deaths in the 25–29 age bracket, the

Table 10.2.
Life Table for Neo-Eneolithic Inhabitants of Ukraine and Moldova (Both Sexes; n = 562)

x	D_x	d_x	l_x	q_x	L_x	T_x	E_x
0–4	34.79	6.19	100.00	0.06	484.52	3070.80	30.71
5–9	59.21	10.54	93.81	0.11	442.71	2586.28	27.57
10–14	46.00	8.19	83.27	0.10	395.91	2143.57	25.74
15–19	33.78	6.01	75.09	0.08	360.42	1747.66	23.27
20–24	35.49	6.31	69.08	0.09	329.61	1387.24	20.08
25–29	54.58	9.71	62.76	0.15	289.54	1057.64	16.85
30–34	48.55	8.64	53.05	0.16	243.66	768.10	14.48
35–39	62.92	11.20	44.41	0.25	194.08	524.43	11.81
40–44	69.54	12.37	33.22	0.37	135.16	330.35	9.95
45–49	32.25	5.74	20.84	0.28	89.88	195.20	9.36
50–54	31.54	5.61	15.11	0.37	61.50	105.32	6.97
55–59	37.00	6.58	9.49	0.69	31.01	43.82	4.62
60–64	10.13	1.80	2.91	0.62	10.04	12.81	4.40
65–69	6.22	1.11	1.11	1.00	2.77	2.77	2.50

Table 10.3.
Life Table for Neo-Eneolithic Inhabitants of Ukraine and Moldova (Females; n = 135, Plus ~56 Assigned Children and Indeterminates)

x	D_x	d_x	l_x	q_x	L_x	T_x	E_x
0–4	11.79	6.17	100.00	0.06	484.58	2863.05	28.63
5–9	21.91	11.46	93.83	0.12	440.51	2378.47	25.35
10–14	15.99	8.36	82.37	0.10	390.96	1937.95	23.53
15–19	13.40	7.01	74.01	0.09	352.53	1546.99	20.90
20–24	18.50	9.68	67.00	0.14	310.82	1194.46	17.83
25–29	25.02	13.09	57.33	0.23	253.91	883.63	15.41
30–34	17.21	9.00	44.24	0.20	198.68	629.72	14.23
35–39	15.47	8.09	35.23	0.23	155.94	431.04	12.23
40–44	19.58	10.24	27.14	0.38	110.11	275.10	10.14
45–49	8.00	4.18	16.90	0.25	74.05	164.99	9.76
50–54	8.58	4.49	12.72	0.35	52.37	90.94	7.15
55–59	11.15	5.83	8.23	0.71	26.57	38.57	4.69
60–64	2.29	1.20	2.40	0.50	9.00	11.99	5.00
65–69	2.29	1.20	1.20	1.00	3.00	3.00	2.50

Table 10.4.
Life Table for Neo-Eneolithic Inhabitants of Ukraine and Moldova (Males; n = 258, Plus ~113 Assigned Children and Indeterminates)

x	D_x	d_x	l_x	q_x	L_x	T_x	E_x
0–4	23.00	6.20	100.00	0.06	484.49	3177.92	31.78
5–9	37.30	10.06	93.80	0.11	443.84	2693.43	28.72
10–14	30.01	8.09	83.74	0.10	398.46	2249.59	26.86
15–19	20.38	5.50	75.64	0.07	364.48	1851.13	24.47
20–24	16.99	4.58	70.15	0.07	339.29	1486.65	21.19
25–29	29.56	7.97	65.57	0.12	307.91	1147.36	17.50
30–34	31.33	8.45	57.60	0.15	266.86	839.45	14.57
35–39	47.45	12.80	49.15	0.26	213.74	572.59	11.65
40–44	49.96	13.47	36.35	0.37	148.07	358.85	9.87
45–49	24.25	6.54	22.88	0.29	98.04	210.77	9.21
50–54	22.96	6.19	16.34	0.38	66.21	112.74	6.90
55–59	25.85	6.97	10.15	0.69	33.30	46.53	4.59
60–64	7.84	2.11	3.17	0.67	10.58	13.23	4.17
65–69	3.93	1.06	1.06	1.00	2.65	2.65	2.50

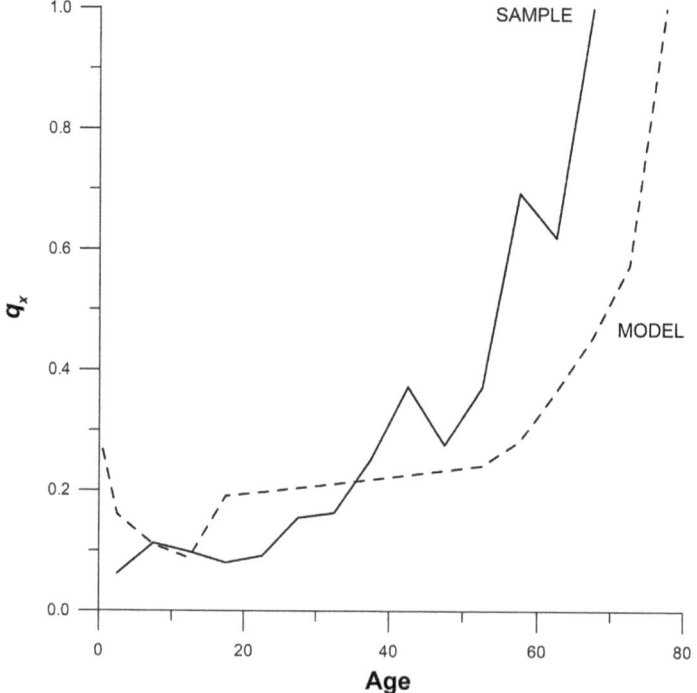

Figure 10.3. Comparison of observed values of qx (probability of death for a given age cohort) with a generalized model life table drawn from global ethnographic observations of traditional societies (data from Weiss 1973).

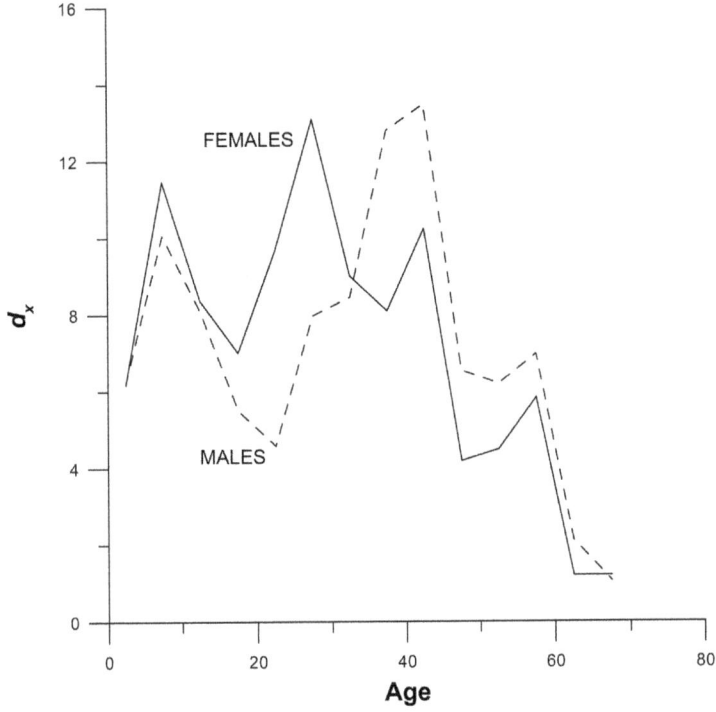

FIGURE 10.4. Percentage distribution of deaths for a given age cohort x (dx).

cohort in which the greatest number of female individuals died (reflecting the dangers and health complications inherent to childbirth). Conversely, most male deaths occur in the age ranges of 35–39 and 40–44. As a result, certain indices derived from the sex-age structure of the population can be presumed to be broadly accurate, even assuming a slight bias to the data. For example, among well-represented cohorts such as young and mature adults, determinations of life expectancy (E_x) should be more or less accurate, at least in a sense relative to the accuracy of the initial age determinations. In our case, the most important single metric is the E_{15} of the female portion of the population (20.9 years), because this gives an estimate of their adult life expectancy and attendant reproductive lifespan. This result corresponds well, albeit at the top of the expected range, with Weiss's assumption that the value of E_{15} for preindustrial societies can be generalized to 15–20 years.

CALCULATING POTENTIAL NATURAL INCREASE

For the calculation of PNI, I consider both the observational Neo-Eneolithic data as well as Weiss's model, particularly in order to illustrate the effect of differences in perceived mortality rates. The calculations themselves are derived from the methodology of Fekri Hassan, who presented a model for assessing prehistoric fertility and population growth (Hassan 1981). This model requires several assumptions, which must be informed by historical and modern data. Based on analogy to ethnographic examples, Hassan places the mean generational time span for prehistoric societies at approximately 20 years, the spacing of live births at 40 months, a constant ratio of female-male offspring at 0.488, and the female attainment of reproductive age at around 18 years.

By plugging in the adult female life expectancy of 35.9, derived from the Ukrainian and Moldovan skeletal sample, we can deduce a reproductive period of 17.9 years. Based on a 40-month spacing of live births, the potential total fertility (the maximum number of children per woman) is 5.37. However, we can then exclude male children, since they are mostly inconsequential to the reproductive capacity of the subsequent generation. Given the sex ratio of 0.488, the actual gross reproduction rate, which describes the number of female offspring replacing each mother, is 2.62. In order to receive the net reproduction rate (R_0), this total is then modified by the rate of childhood mortality. It is here that the model must be broken into different scenarios, due to the divergence of mortality rates between the observed data and Weiss's model. Assuming that the results from the calculated life tables are accurate and that female childhood mortality is roughly 26% (a dubious proposition), the net reproduction rate is 1.94. If childhood mortality is instead estimated along the lines of Weiss's model life tables (50%), R_0 is equal to 1.31.

From these results, the maximum rate of endogenous population growth can be determined using the equation

$$r = \ln R_0 / 20$$

where r is the rate of population growth, R_0 is the net reproduction rate, and 20 is equal to the time span of an average reproductive generation. For the different scenarios of childhood mortality (26% versus 50%), the resultant rates of potential natural increase are 3.31% and 1.35%. For a value of R_0 of 1.31 (assuming Weiss's observations of an adult life expectancy of 35 and childhood mortality of 50%), $r = 1.09\%$.

Discussion

If we assume that 50% is an appropriate approximation of childhood mortality, the close agreement of PNI between both the observational data and Weiss's model (1.35% and 1.09%) indicate that the adult skeletal sample in Moldova and Ukraine is not substantially different from what one may expect for a "typical" preindustrial population. Population growth rates for much of the modern period have been anomalously high, influenced by continually increasing life expectancies and decreasing mortality rates. Among preindustrial populations, maximum rates of growth can be expected to be substantially lower than we are accustomed to today; from 0.52% for Paleolithic hunter-gatherers (Hassan 1981) to 2.71% for ethnographically observed traditional agriculturalists (Van Arsdale 1978). These values take into account the substantially higher rates of disease prevalence and mortality (especially among children) that are, unfortunately, endemic to societies lacking modern medicine. The childhood mortality rate of 26% observed in the sample, and its attendant

PNI of 3.31%, outstrips even Van Arsdale's observations of historically attested populations and can be considered to be beyond credulity.

By applying the estimates of PNI to the *SARP*-based population model, we can now categorize episodes of regional population growth (Figure 10.5), at least in a qualitative sense, by their likelihood of being migratory in nature. Four categories are delineated: (1) population loss, or growth under 1% per annum, is taken as a baseline; (2) the range of 1–2% is considered to be possibly indicative of a migratory component; (3) at 2–3%, migration is highly probable; and (4) the few cases of population growth exceeding 3% are taken to definitely be indicative of migration, even by the standard of the improbably low observed childhood mortality values. Instances of growth outstripping 3% are overwhelmingly situated in places and times where sudden "events" in material culture are perceived. Nearly half can be associated with the period of forest-steppe expansion of the early-middle Tripolye culture, while most of the rest seem to reflect the advent of the Late Eneolithic horizons (Cernavodă 3-Baden-Boleráz) in Romania.

Overall, regions in Ukraine and Moldova experienced a 70% greater incidence of periods of population growth over 1% than Romanian regions, supporting the notion that

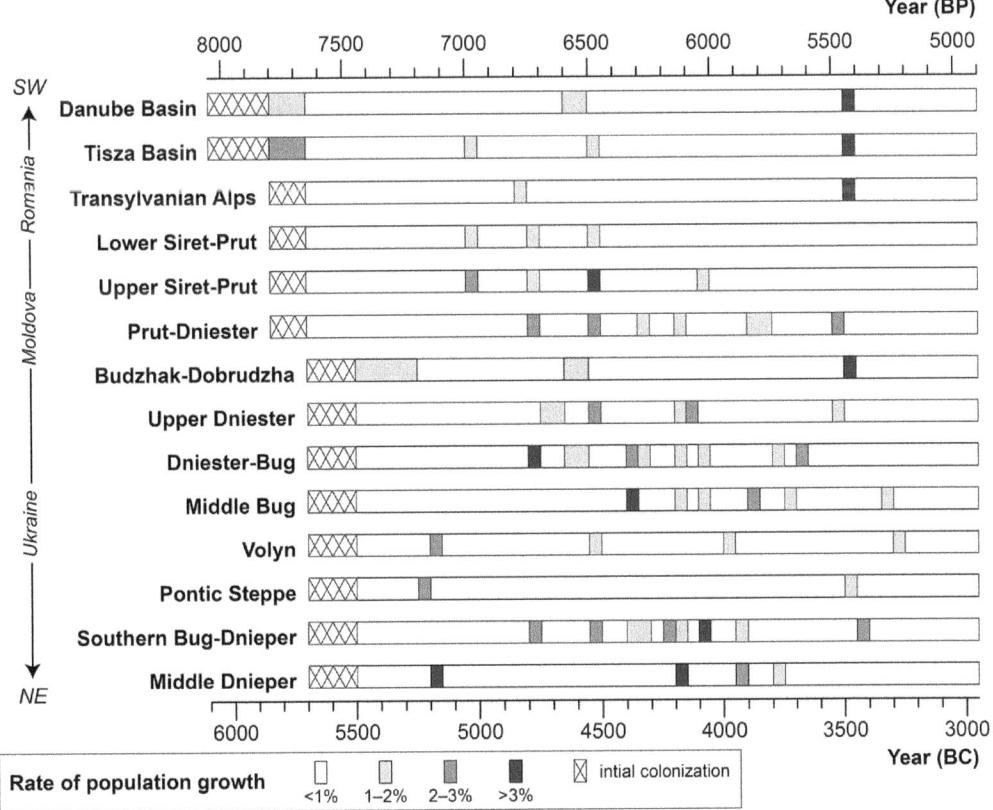

FIGURE 10.5. The spatio-temporal distribution of population growth episodes probably outstripping PNI.

most population movements were targeted toward peripheral regions and away from the Cucuteni-Tripolye "core" area in northeastern Romania. Population growth events in the range of 1–3% can generally be related to the emergence of specific settlement and material complexes. While I cannot explore each individual instance here, we may examine the sequence of one forest-steppe region—the Southern Bug-Dnieper—for which there is an extensive preexisting body of settlement research (cf. Diachenko and Menotti 2012).

In this region there are seven periods in which population growth outstrips 1%. Two of these occur during the interval of 4800–4500 B.C., when the first Cucuteni-Tripolye communities (Tripolye A2/1 to A3/3) were established in the region. Two periods during the interval of 4400–4150 B.C. correspond with the Cucuteni A/Tripolye B1 expansion; during the latter, a large number of Tripolye B1 sites proliferated, which may be cross-dated by ceramics with the Cucuteni A3 site of Hăbășești-Holm (Palaguta 2007). The most outstanding example of population growth rates in the Southern Bug-Dnieper region occurs ca. 4100–4050 B.C., and may almost entirely be associated with the Eastern Tripolye settlement of Veselyj Kut, first of the giant-settlements. Further giant-settlement development attributed to migrating components of the Western Tripolye culture can be identified ca. 3950–3900 B.C. (associated with the giant-settlement of Nebelevka) and ca. 3450–3400 B.C. (associated with the giant-settlement of Kosenovka). In each case, material culture from these settlement phases has a typological lineage pointing to the Prut-Dniester region.

The key limitation of the PNI-based approach, at least as it is implemented here on fairly broad regional scales, is that it does not identify all situations in which migration played a role; only those in which migration likely (or, in the case of our upper limits of population growth, *had to have*) played a role. Notably, in the case of the Southern Bug-Dnieper region above, it failed to identify one period of intensive growth associated with the arrival of the Tomashovskaya local group during Tripolye C1, identified in the more fine-scaled population study of Diachenko and Zubrow (2015). In this case, concurrent growth and decline in different microregions serves to conceal the migratory component on the broader regional level. At any rate, it shows promise for informing meso-scale hypotheses of mobility and migration, bridging the gap between microscale investigation of individual settlements and movements of artifact classes and continental-scale archaeogenomic studies focusing on large-scale population turnover.

Conclusion

Population growth almost never exists in a stable and isolated state, but is nearly always influenced by endogenous growth potential as well as in- and outmigration. The use of PNI as a determinant for identifying migrations can serve as a systematic framework for corroborating observations from settlement data sets, while complimenting other forms and scales of analysis in the areas of conventional material culture studies, archaeometry and population genomics. The case study explored here examined two methods for dealing with PNI, one based on regional particularism and the other based on model life tables of general ethno-historical observations. The regional method highlights several deficiencies that can be introduced by meta-analysis of extant paleodemographic data, which might or might not be systematically biased due to: (1) the use of old, less-reliable reference data sets; and (2) a very incomplete picture of childhood mortality and adult survivorship due to biases introduced by taphonomic conditions and cultural practices. Assessment of both observational and model-derived data can provide a range of probable growth values. However, for most preindustrial applications, and especially in areas where existing paleodemographic data is biased or deficient, the use of generalized data based on model life tables would seem most appropriate. This does not, however, exclude the possibility of refining the approach in specific contexts in conjunction with modern specialists in paleodemography and paleopathology.

Acknowledgments

This research was partially enabled by grant BCS-1725067 from the National Science Foundation ("Long Term Population Response to Environmental Fluctuation," D. J. Kennett and T. K. Harper). I give my sincere thanks to Megan Daniels for inviting me and the board of IEMA for supporting research in archaeological demography.

References Cited

Ammerman, A. J., L. L. Cavalli-Sforza, and D. K. Wagener 1976 Toward the Estimation of Population Growth in Old World Prehistory. In *Demographic Anthropology: Quantitative Approaches*, edited by E. B. W. Zubrow, pp. 27–62. University of New Mexico Press, Albuquerque.

Angel, J. L. 1971 Early Neolithic Skeletons from Çatal Hüyük: Demography and Pathology. *Anatolian Studies* 21:77–98.

Anthony, D. W. 2007 *The Horse, the Wheel, and Language: How Bronze-Age Riders from the Eurasian Steppes Shaped the Modern World*. Princeton University Press, Princeton.

Bar-Yosef, O., and N. Goren 1973 Natufian Remains in Hayonim Cave. *Paléorient* 1(1):49–68.

Bocquet-Appel, J.-P., and C. Masset 1982 Farewell to Paleodemography. *Journal of Human Evolution* 11:321–333.

Cabana, G. S., and J. J. Clark (editors) 2011 *Rethinking Anthropological Perspectives on Migration*. University Press of Florida, Gainesville.

Dergachev, V. A. 1978 (in Russian) Выхватинский могильник (Vykhvatintsy cemetery). Shtiintsa, Kishinev.

Diachenko, A. V. 2010 (in Russian) Эвстатические колебания уровня Черного моря и динамика развития населения кукутень-трипольской общности [Eustatic Fluctuations of the Black Sea Level and the Dynamics of the Development of the Cucuteni-Tripolye Population]. Stratum Plus 2010(2):37–48.

Diachenko, A., and T. K. Harper 2016 The Absolute Chronology of Late Tripolye Sites: A Regional Approach. *Sprawozdania Archeologiczne* 68:81–105.

Diachenko, A., and F. Menotti 2012 The Gravity Model: Monitoring the Formation and Development of the Tripolye Culture Giant-Settlements in Ukraine. *Journal of Archaeological Science* 39(4):2810–2817. DOI:10.1016/j.jas.2012.04.025.

Diachenko, A., and E. B. W. Zubrow 2015 Stabilization Points in Carrying Capacity: Population Growth and Migrations. *Journal of Neolithic Archaeology.* DOI:10.12766/jna.2015.1.

Dolukhanov, P. M., A. Shukurov, K. Davison, G. Sarson, N. P. Gerasimenko, G. A. Pashkevich, A. A. Vybornov, N. N. Kovalyukh, V. V. Skripkin, G. I. Zaitseva, and T. V. Sapelko 2009 The Spread of Neolithic in the South East European Plain: Radiocarbon Chronology, Subsistence, and Environment. *Radiocarbon* 51(2):783–793.

Harper, T. K. 2016 *Climate, Migration, and False Cities on The Old European Periphery: A Spatial-Demographic Approach to Understanding the Tripolye Giant-Settlements.* PhD dissertation, Department of Anthropology, SUNY at Buffalo. Proquest, Ann Arbor.

Harper, T. K. 2019 Demography and Climate in Late Eneolithic Ukraine, Moldova, and Romania: Multiproxy Evidence and Pollen-Based Regional Corroboration. *Journal of Archaeological Science: Reports* 23:973–982. DOI:10.1016/j.jasrep.2017.06.010.

Harper, T. K. (forthcoming) SARP Revisited: Reconstructing Population Trends in Neo-Eneolithic Eastern Europe Through Large-Scale Analysis of Archaeological Settlement Data. In *Quantifying Stone Age Mobility: Scales and Parameters*, edited by I. Sobkowiak-Tabaka, A. Diachenko, and A. Wiśniewski. Springer, New York.

Harper, T. K., A. Diachenko, Yu. Ya. Rassamakin, and D. J. Kennett 2019 Ecological Dimensions of Population Dynamics and Subsistence in Neo-Eneolithic Eastern Europe. *Journal of Anthropological Archaeology* 53:92–101. DOI:10.1016/j.jaa.2018.11.006.

Hassan, F. A. 1981 *Demographic Archaeology.* Academic Press, New York.

Hoppa, R. D., and J. W. Vaupel 2002 The Rostock Manifesto for Paleodemography: The Way from Stage to Age. In *Paleodemography: Age Distributions from Skeletal Samples*, edited by R. D. Hoppa and J. W. Vaupel, pp. 1–8. Cambridge University Press, New York.

Kruts, V. A. 1977 (in Russian) *Позднетрипольские памятники Среднего Поднепровья* [Late Tripolye Monuments in the Middle Dnieper Region]. Naukova Dumka, Kiev.

Manzura, I. 2005 Steps to the Steppe: or, How the North Pontic Region was Colonised. *Oxford Journal of Archaeology* 24(4):313–338. DOI:10.1111/j.1468-0092.2005.00239.x.

Mathieson, I., S. Alpaslan-Roodenberg, C. Posth, A. Szécsényi-Nagy, N. Rohland, S. Mallick, I. Olalde, N. Broomandkhoshbacht, F. Candilio, O. Cheronet, D. Fernandes, M. Ferry, B. Gamarra, G. González Fortes, W. Haak, E. Harney, E. Jones, D. Keating, B. Krause-Kyora, I. Kucukkalipci, M. Michel, A. Mittnik, K. Nägele, M. Novak, J. Oppenheimer, N. Patterson, S. Pfrengle, K. Sirak, K. Stewardson, S. Vai, S. Alexandrov, K.W. Alt, R. Andreescu, D. Antonović, A. Ash, N. Atanassova, K. Bacvarov, M.B. Gusztáv, H. Bocherens, M. Bolus, A. Boroneanţ, Y. Boyadzhiev, A. Budnik, J. Burmaz, S. Chohadzhiev, N. J. Conard, R. Cottiaux, M. Čuka, C. Cupillard, D. G. Drucker, N. Elenski, M. Francken, B. Galabova, G. Ganetsovski, B. Gély, T. Hajdu, V. Handzhyiska, K. Harvati, T. Higham, S. Iliev, I. Janković, I. Karavanić, D.J. Kennett, D. Komšo, A. Kozak, D. Labuda, M. Lari, C. Lazar, M. Leppek, K. Leshtakov, D. Lo Vetro, D. Los, I. Lozanov, M. Malina, F. Martini, K. McSweeney, H. Meller, M. Menđušić, P. Mirea, V. Moiseyev, V. Petrova, T. D. Price, A. Simalcsik, L. Sineo, M. Šlaus, V. Slavchev, P. Stanev, A. Starović, T. Szeniczey, S. Talamo, M. Teschler-Nicola, C. Thevenet, I. Valchev, F. Valentin, S. Vasilyev, F. Veljanovska, S. Venelinova, E. Veselovskaya, B. Viola, C. Virag, J. Zaninović, S. Zäuner, P. W. Stockhammer, G. Catalano, R. Krauß, D. Caramelli, G. Zariņa, B. Gaydarska, M. Lillie, A. G. Nikitin, I. Potekhina, A. Papathanasiou, D. Borić, C. Bonsall, J. Krause, R. Pinhasi, and D. Reich 2018 The Genomic History of Southeastern Europe. *Nature* 555:197–203.

Milisauskas, S., and J. Kruk 1989 Neolithic Economy in Central Europe. *Journal of World Prehistory* 3(4),403–446.

Müller, J. 2015 Eight Million Neolithic Europeans: Social Demography and Social Archaeology on the Scope of Change—from the Near East to Scandinavia. In *Paradigm Found: Archaeological Theory—Present, Past and Future. Essays in Honour of Evžen Neustupny*, edited by K. Kristiansen, L. Šmejda, and J. Turek, pp. 200–214. Oxbow Books, Oxford.

Palaguta, I. 2007 *Tripolye Culture during the Beginning of the Middle Period (BI): The Relative Chronology and Local Grouping of Sites*. BAR International Series 1666. Hadrian Books, Oxford.

Papathanasiou, A. 2005 Health Status of the Neolithic Population of Alepotrypa Cave, Greece. *American Journal of Physical Anthropology* 126:377–390. DOI:10.1002/ajpa.20140.

Potekhina, I. D. 1981 (in Russian) К вопросу о продолжительности жизни человека каменного века на Украине [On the Question of Life Expectancy of Stone Age Man in Ukraine]. In *Древности среднего Поднепровья: сборник научных трудов*, edited by I. I. Artemenko. pp. 21–30. Naukova Dumka, Kiev.

Potekhina, I. D. 1988 (in Russian) Краниологические материалы из неолитического могильника Ясиноватка на Днепре [Anthropological Materials from the Neolithic cemetery Yasinovatka on the Dnieper]. *Sovetskaya Arkheologia* 1988(4):18–25.

Potekhina, I. D. 1999 (in Russian) *Население Украины в эпохи неолита и раннего энеолита по антропологическим данным* [Population of Ukraine in the Neolithic and Early Neolithic According to Anthropological Data]. Institut Arkheologii NAN Ukrainy, Kiev.

Potekhina, I. D., and A. E. Kislyj 1994 (in Russian) Реконструкция демиграфической структура скифов лесостепной и степной зон Украины [Demographic Reconstruction of Scythians in the Forest-Steppe and Steppe Zones of Ukraine]. In *Палеодемография скифского населения Северного Причерноморья*, edited by N. A. Gavrilyuk, pp. 12–39. Institut Arkheologii NAN Ukrainy, Kiev.

Rascovan, N., K.-G. Sjögren, K. Kristiansen, R. Nielsen, E. Willerslev, C. Desnues, and S. Rasmussen 2019 Emergence and Spread of Basal Lineages of *Yersina pestis* during the Neolithic Decline. *Cell* 176(1–2):295–305. DOI:10.1016/j.cell.2018.11.005.

Ryzhov, S. M. 1999 (in Ukrainain) *Кераміка поселень трипільської культури Буго-Дніпровського межиріччя як історичне джерело* [Ceramics from the Tripolye settlements of the Bug-Dnieper interfluve as a historical source]. Institut Arkheologii NAN Ukrainy, Kiev.

Shennan, S., and K. Edinborough 2007 Prehistoric Population History: From the Late Glacial to the Late Neolithic in Central and Northern Europe. *Journal of Archaeological Science* 34:1339–1345. DOI:10.1016/j.jas.2006.10.031.

Telegin, D. J. 1987 Neolithic Culture of the Ukraine and Adjacent Areas and Their Chronology. *Journal of World Prehistory* 1(3):307–331.

Ubelaker, D. H., and I. Pap 2009 Skeletal Evidence for Morbidity and Mortality in Copper Age Samples from Northeastern Hungary. *International Journal of Osteoarchaeology* 19:23–35. DOI:10.1002/oa.969.

Van Arsdale, P. W. 1978 Population Dynamics among Asmat Hunter-Gatherers of New Guinea: Data, Methods, Comparisons. *Human Ecology* 6, 435–467.

Weninger, B., and T. Harper 2015 The Geographic Corridor for Rapid Climate Change in Southeast Europe and Ukraine. In *Neolithic and Copper Age Between the Carpathians and the Aegean Sea: Chronologies and Technologies From the 6th to the 4th Millennium BCE,* edited by S. Hansen, P. Raczky, A. Anders, and A. Reingruber, pp. 475–505. Archäologie in Eurasien 31. Deutsches Archäologisches Institut, Berlin.

Weiss, K. M. 1973 Demographic Models for Anthropology. *American Antiquity* 38(2), Part 2, Memoir 27.

Wood, J. W., D. J. Holman, K. A. O'Connor, and R. J. Ferrell 2002 Mortality Models for Paleodemography. In *Paleodemography: Age Distributions from Skeletal Samples*, edited by R. D. Hoppa and J. W. Vaupel, pp. 129–168. Cambridge University Press, New York.

Zubrow, E. B. W. 1975 *Prehistoric Carrying Capacity: A Model*. Cummings Archaeology Series. Cummings Publishing Company, Menlo Park.

Zubrow, E. B. W. (editor) 1976 *Demographic Anthropology: Quantitative Approaches*. University of New Mexico Press, Albuquerque.

CHAPTER ELEVEN

N Site Continuous Model for Migration

Parameter and Prehistoric Tests

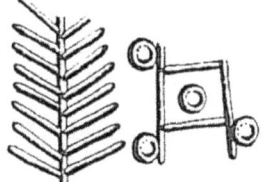

Ezra B. W. Zubrow,
Aleksandr Diachenko, Jay Leavitt

Abstract *The problem of migration is one of the most important demographic issues today. It underlies many development crises as well as the politics of inclusion and exclusion. Today terrorism, warfare, and refugee catastrophes are both determinants and consequences. Yet migration has always been a component of the human condition. As one of the most successful adaptive radiations of all time, our hominid ancestors moved out of Africa and around the entire globe. Every human individual is either a migrant or a descendant of one.*

This paper is the first of a series of papers by the authors. It creates a new theory and model for migration among any number of locations—hence the term "N sites" in its title. It revises and expands upon a Malthusian determinant theory that was proposed in the 1960s and '70s by Zubrow. This fundamental theory was temporally discontinuous. Not only is time in this new theory continuous, but population growth and migration are calculated by continuous functions. The previously static resources in Zubrow's (1975) model are made dynamic. Moreover, in- and out-migration are calculated in a far more sophisticated and realistic manner. They are calculated not only on the basis of the real resources at the loci of out-migration and in-migration as well as those controlled by the migrants, but by the perceived resources at the loci of out-migration and in-migration by the local populations and the perceived resources by the migrant population.

The new theory is operationalized using a simulation model written in Visual Basic and the impact of changing the parameters is explored. Finally, a successful demonstration of the theory and the simulation model uses a case study provided by analyzing the movements among three Cucuteni-Tripolye settlements in modern Ukraine where migration is evident from paleodemographic and material cultural studies.

Introduction

Migration has been, is, and will be a critical issue for human societies. One only needs to look to the present "refugee crisis" to place it in the continuum of major policy issues and substantive responses (e.g., Del Pinto et al. 2018; Fekete 2018; Ohanian 2018). There is no reason to doubt its importance in the near and long-term past (e.g., Alexander and Steidl 2012; Codding and Jones 2013; Engbersen 2013; Gibbons 2015; Groote and Tassenaar 2000; McColl et al. 2018). In fact, the entire history of hominid evolution is a long history of the continuous process of migration. This process was not only expansive and unidirectional, but, as is increasingly being shown by new research, migration is not simply mass movements of people from one point to another. It is a multidirectional process continuously operating at multiple scales (Garcea 2016; Anthony this volume; Yasur-Landau, this volume). This process began more than two million years ago and accelerated with *Homo erectus*. As a genus and as a species we have had considerable practice migrating.

As Megan Daniels notes in the introductory chapter to this volume, it is increasingly common to call the modern period "the age of migration." If one is not migrating, one is thinking about migration either as a migrant or as a member of the communities from which and to which migration takes place. Therefore, it is extremely relevant for this book to have a chapter that integrates the process of migrating with the process of thinking about migration. Migration studies are taking place across the entire world. Table 11.1 shows a sample of scholars in a sample of countries studying this topic.

This paper provides a new theory for migration among and between N site locations. It is built upon a long tradition of "determinant" models but "undeterminizes" them. It begins from an assumption base that Zubrow (1971, 1974, 1975) used in his original "carrying capacity" models, but extends it by making knowledge at the N sites not only critical but also probabilistic and dynamic. Furthermore, it is cognitive in that it not only encompasses the knowledge of what the migrant believes about the point of origin and the point of the destination but also what they believe about both places after they migrate. In short, in- and out-migration are partially dependent upon perceived resources as well as real resources at both the origin and the destination. Migrants are able to change their mind and return to the place of origin. The model uses group agency (Lindstrøm 2015), whereby groups make decisions based on perceived risks.

By adding perception and relaxing many assumptions that are made about migration, this new model not only mingles processual, post-processual and cognitive archaeology, but allows scholars to analyze migratory problems in far greater geographic and temporal domains. In addition, it is easily accessible and may be widely used by students and scholars because the programs are written in Visual Basic.

Our case study concerns the population movement between three Cucuteni-Tripolye settlements located in modern Ukraine, where migration is evident from paleodemographic estimations and material culture studies. The Cucuteni-Tripolye cultural complex (hereafter, CTCC) was formed at the northeastern periphery of the Neolithic and Eneolithic cul-

Table 11.1.
Migration Researchers by Country

Australia	Peter Bellwood, Stephen Castles, James Forrest, Fei Guo, Lesleyanne Hawthorne, Graeme Hugo, Robyn Iredale, Siew-Ean Khoo, Peter McDonald, Paul W. Miller
Austria	Michael Jandl
Belgium	Marco Martiniello, Karen Phalet
Canada	Eric Fong, Shiva S. Halli, Feng Hou, Patricia Landolt, Bruce Newbold, Ravi Pendakur
Denmark	Kristian Kristiansen
Fiji	Carmen Voigt-Graf
Germany	Claudia Diehl, Thomas Faist, Bram Lancee, Stephen Vertovec
Greece	Nicholas P. Glytsos, Theodore P. Lianos
Israel	Anastasia Gorodzeisky, Yitchak Haberfeld, Rebeca Raijman, Larissa Remennick, Moshe Semyonov, Assaf Yasur-Landau
Italy	Anna Triandafyllidou
Kuwait	Nasra M. Shah
Netherlands	Maurice Crul, Kees Groenendijk, Arjen Leerkes, Valentina Mazzucato, Clara H. Mulder, Marlou Schrover, Maarten van Ham, Frank van Tubergen, Maykel Verkuyten
New Zealand	Richard Bedford
Norway	Jørgen Carling, Marta Bivand Erdal
Portugal	João Peixoto
Singapore	Md Mizanur Rahman, Brenda S.A. Yeoh, Min Zhou
South Korea	In-Jin Yoon
Sweden	Pieter Bevelander, Marita Eastmond
Switzerland	Khalid Koser
Taiwan	Hong-zen Wang
Turkey	Ahmet İçduygu
United Kingdom	Claire Alexander, Richard Black, Alice Bloch, Katharine Charsley, Michael Collyer, Hein de Haas, Franck Düvell, Alan M.Findlay, Ralph Grillo, Ron Johnston, Russell King, Eleonore Kofman, Ewa Morawska, Nicola Piper, Parvati Raghuram, Louise Ryan, Nina Glick Schiller, Ludi Simpson, Ronald Skeldon, Miri Song, Aileen Stockdale, Kevin J.A. Thomas, Nicholas Van Hear
United States	David W. Anthony, Victor Agadjanian, Ilana R. Akresh, Richard Alba, Rogers Brubaker, Barry R. Chiswick, Jeffrey H. Cohen, Philip Connor, Megan Daniels, Katharine M. Donato, Mark Ellis, Patricia Fernandez-Kelly, Nancy Foner, Lingxin Hao, José Itzigsohn, Philip Kasinitz, Loren B. Landau, Peggy Levitt, Zai Liang, Ivan Light, John R. Logan, Lindsay Lowell, Philip Martin, Susan Martin, Douglas S. Massey, Cecilia Menjívar, Pyong Gap Min, Alejandro Portes, Marta Tienda, Roger Waldinger, Andreas Wimmer, Richard Wright

tural complexes of the Balkans and Danube region. At the complex's maximum expansion, its westernmost border was located in the Carpathian Mountains, while the eastern bank of the River Dnieper marked its easternmost border. The CTCC includes several cultures. Its Tripolye part was divided into two cultures. One is the Western Tripolye Culture (WTC), whose settlements are characterized by painted ceramics (Ryzhov 2007, 2012). The other is the Eastern Tripolye Culture (ETC), which Tsvek (2006) noted had ceramics mostly characterized by incised ornamentation in their settlements.

The WTC is known by its mega-sites, with the largest settlements in Neolithic Europe located in the southern part of forest-steppe zone in the Southern Bug and Dnieper interfluve (territory of modern Ukraine), ca. 4100–3400 B.C. The size of five largest sites—Nebelevka, Dobrovody, Chichirkozovka, Talianki, and Maidanetske—reached a size of 150–340 ha. Most dwellings at these settlements were two-storied. They were arranged into elliptic patterns recognized from aerial photos and geophysical plans (Chapman et al. 2014; Kruts 1989; Menotti and Korvin-Piotrovskij 2012; Müller et al. 2016). Relatively large WTC settlements, reaching a size of 30–60 ha, are also notable for the Middle Dniester region, Southern Bug and Dniester interfluve, and Middle Bug region (Diachenko 2012; Rassmann et al. 2016).

Theory

The Fundamental Theory

Our theory is generalized and generalizable. By this, we mean that it applies to a broad range of domains, varied conditions, and different contexts. The phrase "general theory" is not common, but it normally means a theory meant to apply widely across various contexts, rather than a theory that is focused on specific material. The term is usually reserved for the kinds of broad, overarching theories that lie at the hearts of scientific disciplines.[1] The model incorporates population growth and stabilization points. More precisely, the growth function is based on a continuous probabilistic logistic implementation. At the most fundamental level, it is a dynamic equilibrium system where there are two interacting processes: fertility and mortality. The fundamental interaction principle is "die or migrate." People will migrate when they believe or the reality is that at the point of origin there are not enough resources to support themselves or their family. Resources may be broadly defined to include not only subsistence resources but also such factors as safety. Our model is a variation on the zero-sum game but it is a dynamic zero-sum game allowing for both resources and population to grow and decline as well as be redistributed.

In short, it completely revolutionizes Zubrow's old study. In the old study, development of populations in marginal resource zones was shown to be a function of optimal zone exploitation. In addition, a deviation-amplifying model originally developed by MacArthur and Connell (1966) was presented as an alternative to the model's diminishing resource curves as a possible explanation of diminishing population and potential total abandonment of an area. The effects of population excess disequilibriums as defined by the model were examined in relationship to the settlement pattern variables of population aggregation, spatial aggregation, and residential area (Zubrow 1975).

Underlying this paper, we once again assume the validity of a "neo-Malthusian approach." Malthus's (1958) major argument that first appeared in the "Essay on Population" has been encapsulated by an anonymous writer in the following doggerel:

> *To get land's fruit in quantity,*
> *Takes jolts of labor ever more*
> *Hence, food will grow like one, two, three,*
> *While numbers grow like one, two, four.* [Samuelson 1961:16]

Since its original publication in 1798, there have been many criticisms of the Essay.[2] First and most trivial, Malthus's ratios have been shown to be in error. Second, he hypothesized that each advance in technology is absorbed by a subsequent increase in population, which prevents any increase in the standard of living. This hypothesis was disproved by the Industrial Revolution. As an empirical generalization, it was valid for most of the preindustrial world prior to 1760. However, as a general law, it fell due to the fallacious assumption that increases in production could never exceed increases in population. The neo-Malthusians such as Boulding (1959) and Peacock (1952) feel that the general Malthusian model applies where the Industrial Revolution has not changed the potential for production by several quantum leaps. In these labor-intensive economies, population is a major factor in determining the production function and the law of diminishing returns eventually limits production. Although Malthus's stability of the standard of living is rejected, the conclusion that population growth is a correlate of technological change is viable. Thus, in our neo-Malthusian model the ratios are replaced by population pressure in a series of organized, spatially differentiated ecosystems, each with its own level of consumption expectations based on food chains with internal and external ecological connections. Our second assumption is that it is possible to measure prehistoric populations and resources through indirect indices of archaeological data resulting from excavations and surveys.

In the next few paragraphs, we will build the new theory and model.

We assume a population will grow until it reaches a resource limit. This can be a real limit, a perceived limit, or an actual carrying capacity. There is a nomenclature issue of which we are aware. We use the terms *limit* and *carrying capacity* interchangeably to mean the same thing, namely a finite number of people that a region can support. The assumption is that at this limit there is no degradation of the environment. In a future paper we consider the frequent case of degrading environment and a decreasing carrying capacity. This is a general theory and clearly for hunters and gatherers natural carrying capacity will set the limit, while for more technically sophisticated societies the resource limits will be based on more culturally processed resources such as agricultural and energy production. In short, we are focusing on the limit. Of course, it is complicated to estimate the exact resource limit or carrying capacity based on standard ecological techniques or such models as site catchment analysis. There are numerous concerns that include a variety of cultural factors such as religious and social preferences. Alternatively, Diachenko and Zubrow (2015) introduced a way of estimating carrying capacity out of demographic trends. The population may grow at slower or faster rates. The difference is that at a slower rate it still will reach the limit. Figure

11.1 shows a population growing toward that limit at a faster or slower rate. In the following graphs, essentially theoretical simplifications, the values on the x axis and the y axis are broad estimates of what the actual dates and population sizes are for the sites.

Figure 11.1 assumes that although the resources are limited they do not decline with consumption because they are immediately replaceable. If one relaxes this replacement assumption, the graph is portrayed in Figure 11.2a. As population increases, the amount of resources will decrease until an equilibrium point is reached. The reader will recognize this figure as the standard graphical formulation of a dynamic equilibrium system. Of course, with a dynamic system there may be considerable movement around the equilibrium point prior to the equilibrium being reached, as illustrated in Figure 11.2b.

Figure 11.3 shows a growing population that reaches the resource level, with the resource level then increasing. Let the reader imagine four areas; none of them are occupied. For the sake of theoretical expediency, one should imagine that they are arranged sequentially in decreasing order by the amount of resources or carrying capacity. One suggests that an initial population will grow in the area with the highest resource level. When the initial population surpasses the resources, the surplus population, given a choice between starving, dying, or migration, will choose to migrate. This population will migrate to area 2, where they will begin to grow. Once the secondary population surpasses the resource level they will move to area 3, where the process repeats itself, and then repeats again into area 4 *ad infinitum*. Figure 11.4 illustrates this process.

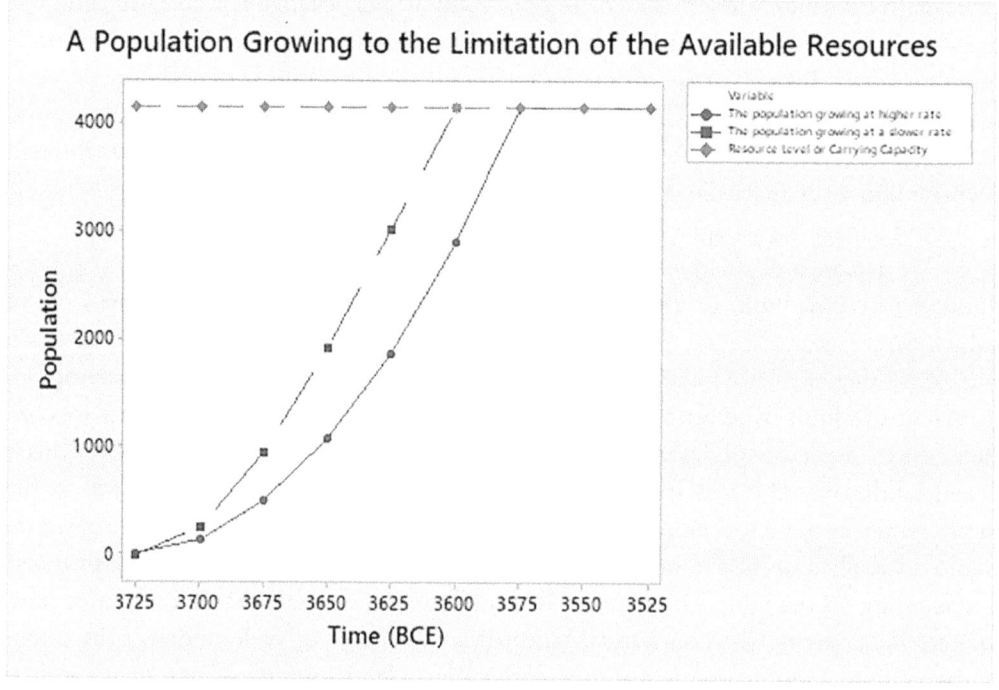

FIGURE 11.1. A comparison between a population growing at a faster and slower rate to an available resource limit (expressed in population).

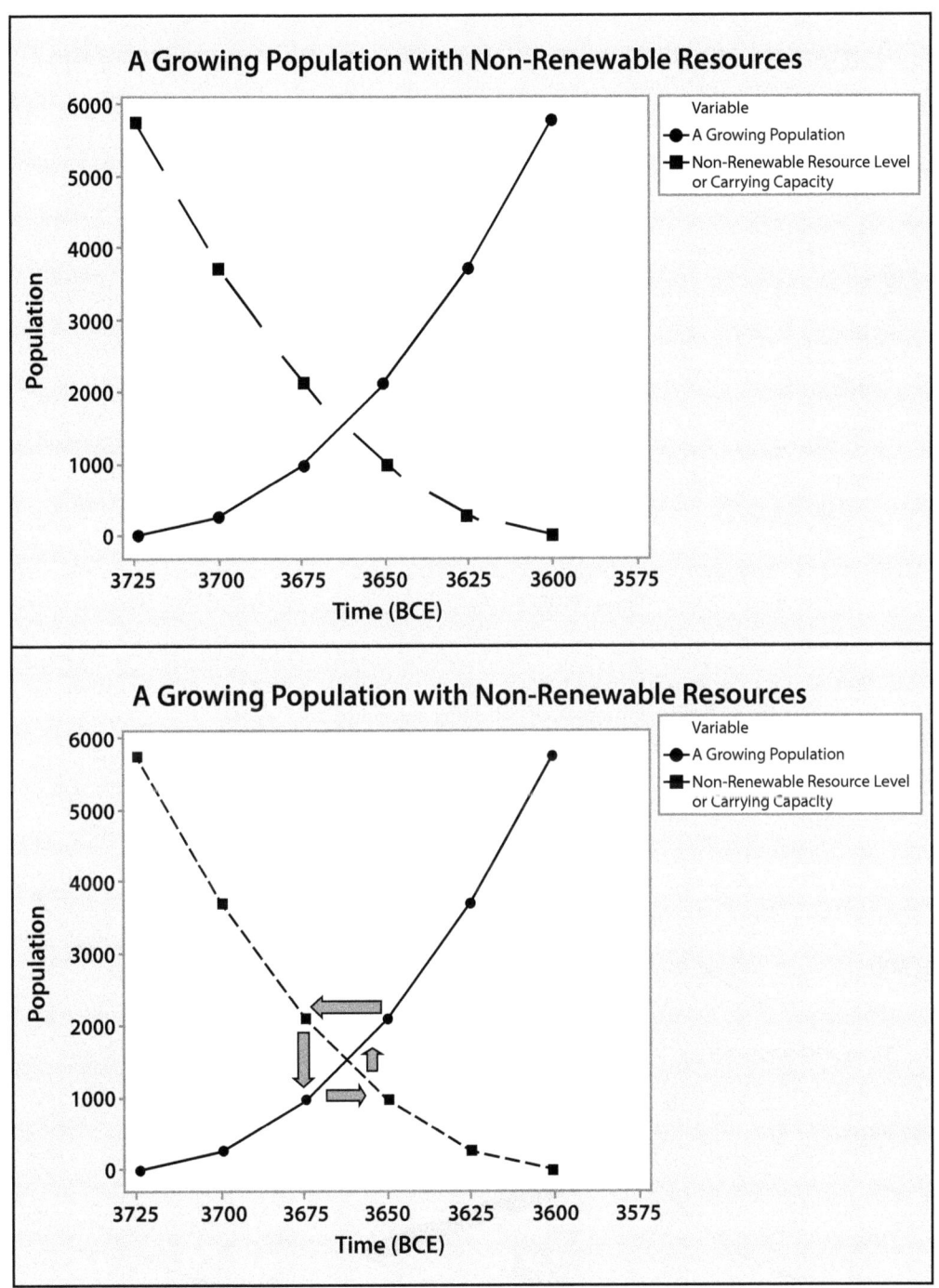

FIGURE 11.2. A growing population with nonrenewable resources: 2a—as population increases, resources decrease to an equilibrium point; 2b—the dynamic process of reaching equilibrium.

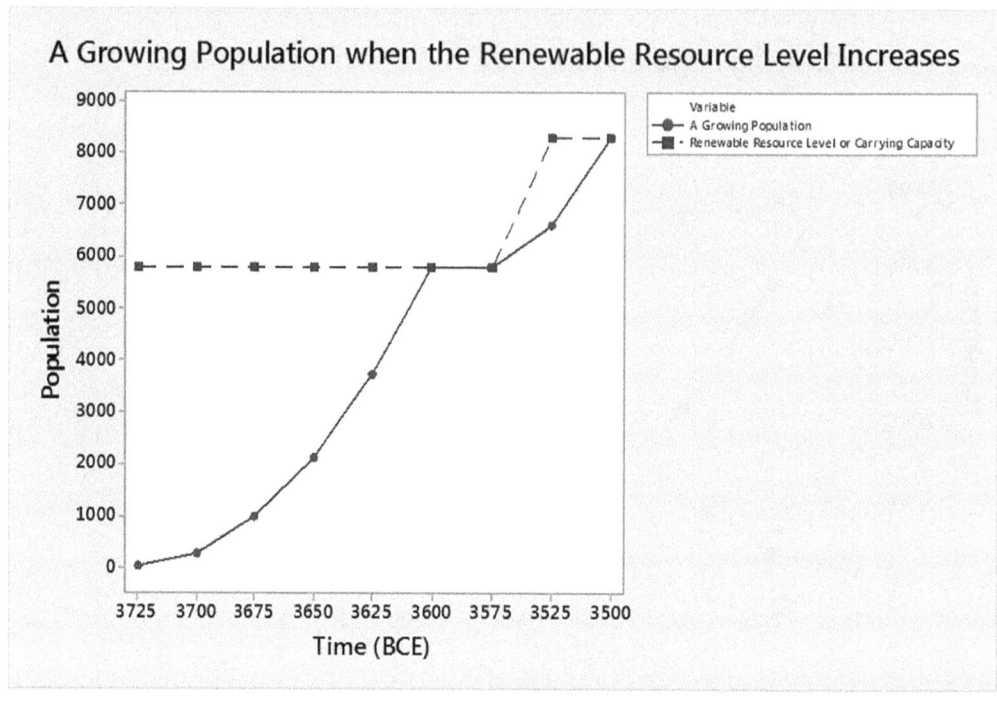

FIGURE 11.3. A growing population with nonrenewable resources—as population grows, resources decline appropriately reflecting consumption.

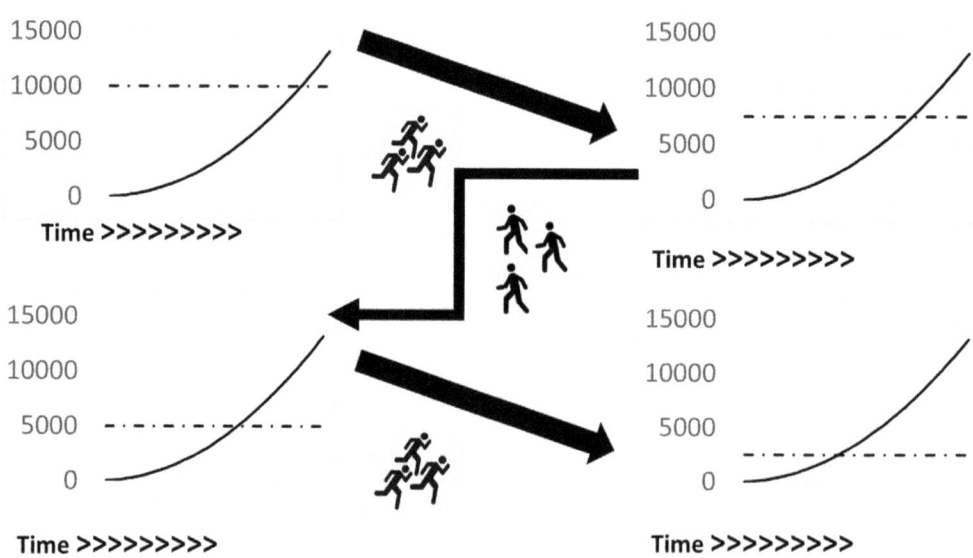

FIGURE 11.4. Surplus population migrating sequentially from areas of higher resources to areas of lower resources.

The Extended Theory

The following section presents the mathematical background of our model. Reading the following section carefully will not require putting too much effort for nonmathematical readers for there is considerable ancillary text explaining in nonmathematical terms most of the concepts. Our work has focused on the ratio of population to resource levels or carrying capacity. We recognize that they are not the same but shall use them interchangeably. Carrying capacity is defined as the maximum size of a population that can be maintained indefinitely within an area (Zubrow 1975). Our rationale is that the significant factor is the "limiting threshold." The "limiting threshold" might be the "carrying capacity" or another "limiting threshold" such as amount of water or salt or "cattle for protein." For our purposes, it makes no difference as long as the "limiting threshold" limits population growth.

We will examine all of the N sites both substantively and analytically contemporaneously as an integrated network and system. However, although integrated we do not use the aggregate values of the system as a whole but examine each location as a unit. Each site has its own carrying capacity. In our theory, not only can the carrying capacity for each site grow or fall but it also might or might not have an interactive relationship with the carrying capacity of the other sites.

Other researchers have previously performed simulations based on discrete periods. A large number of these earlier simulations used a gravity model as their underlying theoretical and operational structure (e.g., Abrams 1943; Marches 1953; Haggett 1979; see Nakoinz and Knitter 2016 for the most recent overview). The gravity model is expressed as follows:

$$p = \frac{P_I P_J}{D_{IJ}^a} \quad \text{(Equation 1)},$$

where p is the probability for migration from location I to location J, P_I and P_J and are the population size at these locations, and D_{IJ}^a is the distance between them raised to a power of a.

The outcomes of these previous simulations may be summarized by stating that sometimes the gravity model works and sometimes it does not. Perhaps, more accurately, one might state that the application of the gravity model in different cases produces both precise and weak predictions when compared to empirical evidence. There are a variety of reasons for its failure. One is its determinant nature, which does not allow for random variation. Another is going and coming distances are not the same. In addition, no consideration is taken of the following: differential knowledge, growth in the threshold level by the discovery of new resources, changes in technology or even labor practices, etc. Moreover, the precision of the model results decreases with the decrease of the population size. In short, the product of population size divided by distance between them is a rough approximation for migration because some important parameter(s) for the locations are taken for constants.

In order to reduce failures and weak predictions we introduce two new factors into the model at this point (others will be added later in the chapter). They are, first, the carrying capacity, C, and, second, the changing of the system from deterministic to probabilistic. We assume that the probability for migration from the original location increases with the increase in population and the consequent decline in carrying capacity prior to out-migration. In the end, migration is a two-sided sword. With increased stress comes increased probability to leave. On the other hand, looking from the perspective of the receiving population, the degree of their welcome will be determined by the perceived available resources. The C at one site might be based on food supply while at another water limitations are the "limiting factor." The model is probabilistic because many of the drivers are implemented using probabilistic variables, which means that they are completely described using a statistical distribution rather than a value.

The next factors one adds to the model are perceptual. It is with these factors that we move from a determinant processual model to an integrated processual/post-processual model. We recognize that the information held by the locals or the migrants need not be complete, nor does it need to be equally known by both locals and migrants.[3] Therefore, we add perceptions into the model in the following sections.

If the actual carrying capacity directly affects demographic properties of a population, such as the growth rate, fertility, and mortality, then migratory behavior depends not only on these properties but also on how migrants perceive them. For example, how do potential migrants perceive the available resources or carrying capacity not only at their present locations but also at the places to which they are considering migrating? Moreover, the local population that is not planning to migrate also perceives their own local situation regarding their limiting factors and their carrying capacity. Based on these perceptions as well as the basis of the reality they may accept the migrants or refuse them. Therefore, our model includes variables to stipulate these perceptions. We differentiate the actual carrying capacity (P_{max}) and two parameters describing the carrying capacity as presumed by migrants and local population (respectively C_e and C_{loc}).

To summarize, we may express the probability that an individual will migrate between two locations as:

$$p = k \frac{P_e C_{i(mig)}}{C_e P_{i(mig)} D_{oi}^a} \quad \text{(Equation 2)},$$

where P_e is the site of out-migration, which has the carrying capacity C_e. $P_{i(mig)}$ and $P_{i(loc)}$ is the population size at the site of in-migration as presumed by migrants and local population respectively, which has the carrying capacity $C_{i(mig)}$ and $C_{i(loc)}$ as presumed by migrants and local population respectively. Coefficient k represents the relationship between the perceptions of the locals at the place of in-migration and the perception of the migrants as follows:

$$\text{If } \frac{C_{i(loc)}}{P_{i(loc)}} \geq \frac{C_{i(mig)}}{P_{i(mig)}}, k = 1 \quad \text{(Equation 3)},$$

If $\dfrac{C_{i(loc)}}{P_{i(loc)}} < \dfrac{C_{i(mig)}}{P_{i(mig)}}$, $k = \left(\dfrac{C_{i(loc)} P_{i(mig)}}{P_{i(loc)} C_{i(mig)}}\right)$ (Equation 4),

To understand these formulas, one needs to keep in mind various perceptual possibilities as seen from the view of different populations—namely the locals and the migrants. What is *k*? It is a variable that expresses the relationship between the perceptions of migrants and local population. Therefore, for migrants who are estimating their own locality, it is *P/C*. For example, migrants in Lybia and Tunisia, thinking about their locations, estimate the population to carrying capacity ratio as 96% and the area seems to be saturated. From the perspective of the same migrants looking to travel to Malta, Italy, or Germany, the perceived value is *C/P*. The carrying capacity is 130% of the population and thus it is an ideal target area. The migrants are thus concerned with *C/P*. For them, they want to make sure that there is always a surplus and that they as in-migrants will not destroy the livelihood and will want *C/P* to be well over 100%. For the local population looking at what is happening at the location from which the migrants come, the short but brutish answer is that they essentially do not care. If the local population estimate that the demographic and economic parameters of the place where they live is higher or equal to the migrants' perception, then they will be receptive to migrants. If the local population holds the opposite perception—namely, that resources in their area are lower than the migrants perceive—they will be more restrictive on the influx of people allowed into their territory. With the above scenarios in mind, we now turn to the local and migrant populations. The above is summarized in Table 11.2.

We assume that most of the time the population size will reach *C*/2. The stabilization of population growth below the carrying capacity is caused by the experience of generations in resource management (Ostrom 1990; Feinman 2016). The traditional explanation of the logistic curve of population growth describes an initial population that increases at an increasing rapid rate and then decreases at a decreasing rapid rate. This situation frames the state of constant risks to exceed carrying capacity resulting in death for the part of population. Instead, self-regulation in population size and density, which is also described by an S-shaped curve, suggests that a certain number of people are removed from the location by migration as soon

TABLE 11.2.
THE DECISION TABLE FOR MIGRANTS AND LOCAL POPULATIONS

	Migrant	Local
Looking at own place	*P/C*	*C/P*
Looking at other place	*C/P*	Don't care what has happened elsewhere, only care what happened in my own place.

as the population size exceeds a certain proportion of the carrying capacity. Simulations show that populations tend to stabilize at nearly one-half of the carrying capacity, $C/2$ (Strogatz 1994). These stable platforms we call stabilization points. Surprisingly, stabilization sometimes occurs at an even lower degree than half the carrying capacity. For instance, recent simulations have shown the stabilization of the WTC populations in the Southern Bug and Dnieper interfluve area at nearly 40 % of the carrying capacity (Diachenko and Zubrow 2015). If P exceeds C and continues its pattern of continuous growth during a single cycle/sub-cycle,[4] it is replaced by a massive migration of a size of $\frac{C^2}{P}$. The reason is that once the population is above the carrying capacity, the population will begin to reduce (all other things being equal) according to an inverse logistic curve. The analytical solution to the inverse logistic is $\frac{C^2}{P}$. If we are calculating the migration that takes place before the population reaches the carrying capacity but over the stabilization point, then the migration is estimated at $\frac{C^2}{P}$. (In either case, a massive migration will begin to release the stress.)

We use probability continuous functions. By a probability function, we mean that function will return a single point when given some input, but this point is chosen randomly according to a particular random distribution. By a continuous function, we mean a function for which one can make infinitely small changes in the input that results in changes in the output.[5] In order to develop a continuous model based on N sites, it is necessary to represent the probability of migration as instantaneous in time for a single person. The number of migrants is calculated as the integral of the probability over the duration of the period. Initial work demonstrates this to be a zero-sum game in terms of migrants. What this means is that the number of emigrants who leave a location equals the number of immigrants who reach the new location. In other words, emigrants do not die along route or change location midway as they travel the route. However it does not mean that the number of emigrants from village m to another village, village n, needs to equal the number of emigrants from village n to village m.

In order to change from discrete time to continuous time one needs to replace the population size in equation 2 with the logistic equation. Therefore, the next 15 equations are mathematical derivations and expansions of equation 2.

Assume the population at the location of the out-migration is less than one-half the carrying capacity at the site of out-migration and the population at the site of possible in-migration is less than one-half of the in-migration site's carrying capacity, namely, $P_e < C_e/2$ and $P_{i(mig)} < C_{i(mig)}/2$ (the first scenario).

Symbolically, P_e is the population at the site of out-migration, which has the carrying capacity C_e. $P_{i(mig)}$ is the population at the site of in-migration as perceived by migrants going from location e to a destination i before they migrate. If these conditions are met, then the probability for an individual to migrate will be the growing population at the site of out-migration P_e multiplied by the sum of the carrying capacity and growing population for the site of possible in-migration as viewed by the migrants. These growing populations are the "logistic replacement" and are of the form $P_e e^{gel}$. This is divided by the growing population at the site of possible in-migration as viewed by migrants times the distance between the sites raised to a power times the sum of the carrying capacity and growing population at the site of out-migration. This probability may or may not be reduced depending on the perception of the local population at i, the place of in-migration, as well as the perception of the migrants themselves before they migrate. We assume that g_e is the natural growth rate as presumed by migrants and locals respectively, and l is the duration of the cycle/sub-cycle.

$$p = k \frac{P_e e^{g_e l}(C_{i(mig)} + P_{i(mig)}(e^{g_i l}-1))}{P_{i(mig)} e^{g_i l}(C_e + P_e(e^{g_e l}-1))} * D_{ei}^{-a} \quad \text{(Equation 5)}.$$

The next two equations reflect the scenario of one population less than one-half of the carrying capacity and another one exceeding one-half of the carrying capacity. The difference between the two is that the former refers to the "under" half carrying capacity of the out-migrant population. The latter is when the "under" half carrying capacity applies to the in-migrant population.

If $C_e/2 < P_e < C_e$ and $P_{i(mig)} < C_{i(mig)}/2$,

$$p = k \frac{C_e^2(C_{i(mig)} + P_{i(mig)}(e^{g_i l}-1))}{2 P_e P_{i(mig)} e^{g_i l}} * D_{ei}^{-a} \quad \text{(Equation 6)}$$

If $P_e < C_e/2$ and $C_{i(mig)}/2 < P_{i(mig)} < C_{i(mig)}$,

$$p = k \frac{2 P_{i(mig)} P_{i(mig)} P_e e^{g_e l}}{C_{i(mig)}^2 (C_e + P_e(e^{g_e l}-1))} * D_{ei}^{-a} \quad \text{(Equation 7)}$$

The next four equations correspond to the scenario of one population exceeding the carrying capacity and another one staying below one-half of the carrying capacity (equations 8 and 9), or exceeding one-half of the carrying capacity (equations 10 and 11):

If $P_e > C_e$ and $P_{i(mig)} < C_{i(mig)}/2$,

$$p = k \frac{C_e^2(C_{i(mig)} + P_{i(mig)}(e^{g_i l}-1))}{P_e P_{i(mig)} e^{g_i l}} * D_{ei}^{-a} \quad \text{(Equation 8)}$$

If $P_e < C_e/2$ and $P_{i(mig)} > C_{i(mig)}$,

$$p = k \frac{P_{i(mig)} P_e e^{g_e l}}{C_{i(mig)}^2 (C_e + P_e(e^{g_e l}-1))} * D_{ei}^{-a} \quad \text{(Equation 9)}$$

If $P_e > C_e$ and $C_{i(mig)}/2 < P_{i(mig)} < C_{i(mig)}$,

$$p = k \frac{2C_e^2 P_{i(mig)}}{P_e C_{i(mig)}^2} * D_{ei}^{-a} \quad \text{(Equation 10)}$$

If $C_e/2 < P_e < C_e$ and $P_{i(mig)} > C_{i(mig)}$,

$$p = k \frac{C_e^2 P_{i(mig)}}{2P_e C_{i(mig)}^2} * D_{ei}^{-a} \quad \text{(Equation 11)}$$

The following equation represents the scenarios of both populations exceeding one-half of the carrying capacity or exceeding the carrying capacity:

If $C_e/2 < P_e < C_e$ and $C_{i(mig)}/2 < P_{i(mig)} < C_{i(mig)}$, or $P_e > C_e$ and $P_{i(mig)} > C_{i(mig)}$,

$$p = k \frac{C_e^2 P_{i(mig)}}{P_e C_{i(mig)}^2} * D_{ei}^{-a} \quad \text{(Equation 12)}$$

The following set of seven equations represents the scenario of one of two populations reaching the carrying capacity:

If $P_e < C_e/2$ and $P_{i(mig)} = C_{i(mig)}$,

$$p = k \frac{P_e e^{g_e l}}{C_{i(mig)} C_e + C_{i(mig)} P_e(e^{g_e l} - 1))} * D_{ei}^{-a} \quad \text{(Equation 13)}$$

If $C_e/2 < P_e < C_e$ and $P_{i(mig)} = C_{i(mig)}$,

$$p = k \frac{C_e^2}{2P_e C_{i(mig)}} * D_{ei}^{-a} \quad \text{(Equation 14)}$$

If $P_e > C_e$ and $P_{i(mig)} = C_{i(mig)}$,

$$p = k \frac{C_e^2}{P_e C_{i(mig)}} * D_{ei}^{-a} \quad \text{(Equation 15)}$$

If $P_e = C_e$ and $P_{i(mig)} < C_{i(mig)}/2$,

$$p = k \frac{C_e C_i + C_e P_{i(mig)}(e^{g_i l} - 1)}{P_{i(mig)} e^{g_i l}} * D_{ei}^{-a} \quad \text{(Equation 16)}$$

If $P_e = C_e$ and $C_{i(mig)}/2 < P_{i(mig)} < C_{i(mig)}$,

$$p = k \frac{2C_e P_{i(mig)}}{C_{i(mig)}^2} * D_{ei}^{-a} \quad \text{(Equation 17)}$$

If $P_e = C_e$ and $P_{i(mig)} > C_{i(mig)}$,

$$p = k \frac{C_e P_{i(mig)}}{C_{i(mig)}^2} * D_{ei}^{-a} \quad \text{(Equation 18)}$$

If $P_e = C_e$ and $P_{i(mig)} = C_{i(mig)}$,

$$p = k \frac{C_e}{C_i} * D_{ei}^{-a} \quad \text{(Equation 19)}$$

Changes in population size at the locations are a combined result of the processes of emigration, immigration and natural growth (sub-cycle). The last follows Verhulst's (1838, 1845) logistic model:

$$P_{t+1} = \frac{(P_t + G - L)e^{g_e l}}{1 + \frac{P_t + G - L}{P_{max}}(e^{g_e l} - 1)} \quad \text{(Equation 20),}$$

where P_t is the population in the beginning of a sub-cycle, and P_{t+1} is the population in the end of a sub-cycle.

Population does not grow when it reaches the carrying capacity for there are insufficient resources. It does not, however, immediately decrease after exceeding carrying capacity:

If $P_t = P_{max}$, $P_{t+1} = P_t$ (Equation 21);

if $P_t > P_{max}$, $P_{t+1} = \frac{P_{max}^2}{P_t}$ (Equation 22).

For the purposes of this paper, the authors make an important simplifying assumption—namely, that all the perceived carrying capacities (carrying capacity at the location from which the migrants emigrate, C_e, and the location to which the migrants immigrate, C_i) equal the objective carrying capacity P_{max}. This is the null hypothesis. It is the only hypothesis that this paper will test. However, the mechanisms within the model allow for the potential for none of these to be equal to each other. If the null hypothesis is shown to be true, one might argue that in this particular case one does not need to test the alternatives.

Nevertheless, the authors recognize that there might be combination of inequalities that together would produce a similar result; however, it was decided that a full exploration of the potential behavior of the inequalities needs a study of its own.

The Simulation Model

Having developed a robust extended theory, one needs to develop a robust simulation model in order to test the reality of the theory. There are all types of simulations ranging from "instant coffee" through agency-based simulations, which follow individuals through each action and each decision. This simulation model is a testing platform. It allows one to change the initial parameters such as population size, growth rates, resource levels, time, number of cycles, etc. It then calculates the outcome values of such variables as the number of migrants, the distances they cover, the size of the villages to which they migrate before and after migration, and the perception of available resources by the migrants and the local populations before and after migration. These can then be compared to the archaeological and/or demographic realities.

The authors wanted to make the simulation model accessible to the largest number of archaeologists possible. In no way do we wish to denigrate the technical ability of most archaeologists, but we decided to forgo broad high-level simulation programming languages and generalized simulation programs that tend to be written in advanced languages.[6] The front end of this model is an Excel spreadsheet where users can change various parameters such as number of sites, population, carrying capacity, distance, number of cycles, and sub-cycles. Cells that are user-controlled have a black background. When the model is run, it displays the gain and loss of each site's migration for each sub-cycle in columns R through W. The sum of the growth of the population plus the net migration (immigration minus emigration) in both directions are shown in columns M and N. These values also are shown graphically. The right column, X, contains the totals of the populations including the amounts from population growth (Figure 11.5).

The back end of the model is written in Visual Basic for Applications (VBA) in terms of discreet modules consisting of groups of macros. This setup results in great flexibility. Migration between sites is handled pairwise with the order being irrelevant. Thus, it is not difficult to add additional sites.[7] Distance between two sites may be asymmetric for a variety of noneconomic reasons such as geography or politics. The integration is approximated using Simpson's eight-point rule (Cartwright 2016). Its error is $\frac{1}{h^5}$, where h is the duration. The total integration is from zero to one. Thus the duration is $\frac{1}{cycles} \times sub-cycles^5$. This means the error in this presentation's calculation is of order $1/8^5$ or 1 in 35000.

If the population exceeds the resource level or carrying capacity then we impose the dictator's rule. The probability of immigration in the receiving village is set to zero by our imaginary dictator. If the population of the sending village drops to zero we impose the zombie rule. The zombie rule states that if the number of migrants is zero or below they are no longer counted in the population. Without this rule, they are at least metaphorically the "walking dead" and produce bizarre results. The probability of emigration from the site is set to zero.

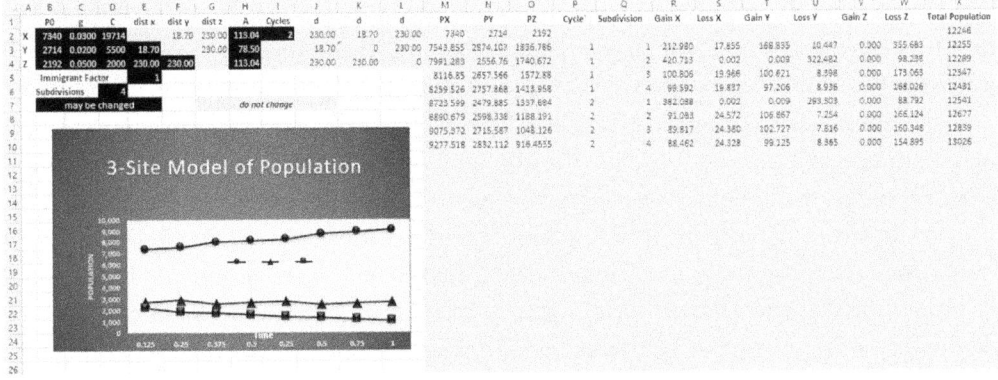

FIGURE 11.5. User interface for the N Site Migration Model.

Figure 11.6 examines the Excel and VBA model in its simplest form. Each of the rectangles in the flowchart might seem like a *Charlie and the Chocolate Factory* machine, but the spreadsheet initiates the process of running through all the cycles and sub-cycles. Each round trip is an idealization of a single cycle and starts with the "White Rectangle."

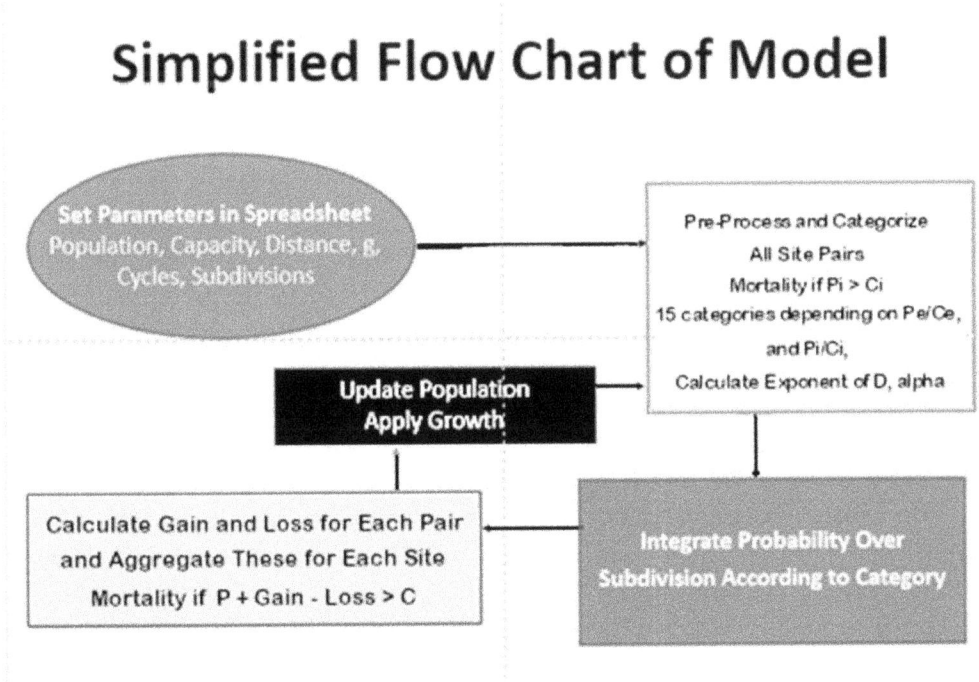

FIGURE 11.6. Flowchart for the N Site Migration Model.

The "White Rectangle" processes six pairs taking three sites, two at a time. Immediately the dictator's rule may be imposed on the immigrating site. Then mortality is ascribed to death along the way if the rule is imposed.

Next, each pair is assigned a category depending on the emigration site's ratio of population to carrying capacity as well as the immigrating site's similar ratio. If the population amounts to less than one-half of the carrying capacity then the exponent of the distance is squared for the emigrating site. If it is greater than the carrying capacity for the sites located in the same microregion (X and Y in our case study), then it is set to four. Site Z is already far from the other sites. Imposing an exponent of four would result in the calculation of a denominator in the order of 10^{16}. Therefore, its exponent is left at two.

Depending on the category derived from the "White Rectangle," the "Darker Gray Rectangle" represents the integration of a pair over the length of the duration. The "Light Gray Rectangle," more or less, represents the completion of the migration for a single cycle. The probability is multiplied by the population of the emigrating site. Then the population gains and losses are calculated. For example, if we are looking at migration from X to Y the loss in X is equal to the gain in Y. The gains and losses for each site need to be accumulated so that we finally have the gain and the loss across time for each of the sites and for the system as a whole. Some of these may result in the dictator rule being imposed, resulting in additional mortality (simply saying, the dictator's rule does not allow negative values for population size). The "Darker Gray Rectangle" is the completion of the subdivision. The populations are updated with their gains and losses and finalized with the integration of the growth in the "Black Rectangle."

Data Input

This case study involves the WTC (Western Tripolye Culture) settlement of Chechelnitskaya group Stena I, IV, in the interfluve of the Dniester and the Southern Bug, and the Tomashovskaya group sites of the WTC Maidanetske and Romanovka in the Southern Bug and Dnieper interfluve, (3700–3650 B.C.) (Figure 11.7: 1, 6, 7). The average duration of settlements caused by their periodical abandonment and population movement to the new places is estimated to ca. 50 years (Kruts 1989; Markevich 1981). However, the duration of large settlements, or the so-called mega-sites, with the size exceeding 100 ha, reached durations of approximately 100 years (Diachenko 2012; Diachenko and Zubrow submitted; cf. Chapman and Gaydarska 2016; Müller et al. 2016; Nebbia et al. 2018).

The number of synchronous dwellings at the settlement Maidanetske increases to 2,327 comparing to 1,631 synchronous dwellings at Maidanetske's predecessor, the settlement of Talianki (Figure 11.7: 5; Diachenko 2016). At the same time, the number of dwellings at the settlement Stena I, IV decreases to 129 comparing to ca. 488 synchronous dwellings in Stena's predecessor, the settlement of Belyj Kamen (Figure 11.7: 3; Tarapata 2015; for the corrections to estimated number of dwellings see Ohlrau 2015; Diachenko 2016). Decrease in population from Belyj Kamen to Stena I, IV corresponding to the increase in population

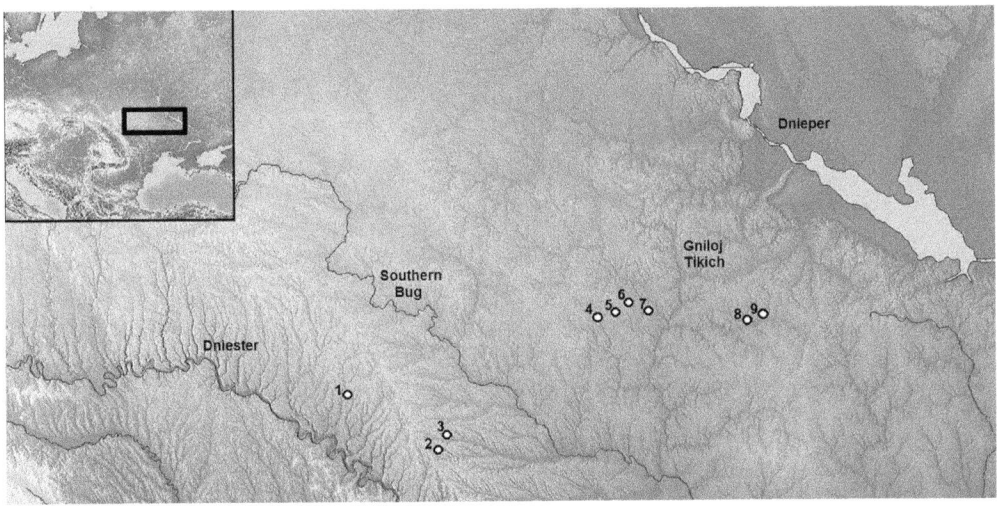

FIGURE 11.7. Location of sites concerned in this study: 1—Stena I, IV, 2—Chechelnik, 3—Belyj Kamen, 4—Dobrovody, 5—Talianki, 6—Romanovka, 7—Maidanetske, 8—Chichirkozovka, 9—Vasilkov.

from Talianki to Maidanetske suggests a direct migration. This assumption is supported by the numerous Chechelnitskaya group imports and imitations in ceramic assemblage of Maidanetske (Shmaglij and Videiko 2003; Tkachuk 2005; Ryzhov 2007).

Let us consider the variables from the model. The average number of people per dwelling reached 4–5 persons (Diachenko 2016). Taking the value of 4.5 persons per dwelling, we assume 7,340 inhabitants of Maidanetske, 2,714 persons at Romanovka, and 2,192 people at Stena I, IV in the beginning of the analyzed period. The distance between Maidanetske and Romanovka is estimated at 18.7 km and the distance between each of these sites and Stena I, IV is estimated at 230 km. Recent simulations have shown that the carrying capacity of the largest WTC settlement in the Southern Bug and Dnieper interfluve among the smaller sites reached a population of 4,381 dwellings (Diachenko and Zubrow 2015). Considering 4.5 persons per one house, the carrying capacity of Maidanetske is estimated at 19,714 people. The carrying capacity of Romanovka is postulated to be a doubled population of this settlement as shown by simulations (Strogatz 1994). We assume the local population perceives the carrying capacity of Stena I, IV, as 2,000 people.

Results

Figure 11.8 presents the results of simulations. Initially, Maidanetske had a population approximately one-third of the carrying capacity. Romanovka's was just below one-half of the carrying capacity. Stena I, IV, on the other hand, exceeded the carrying capacity.

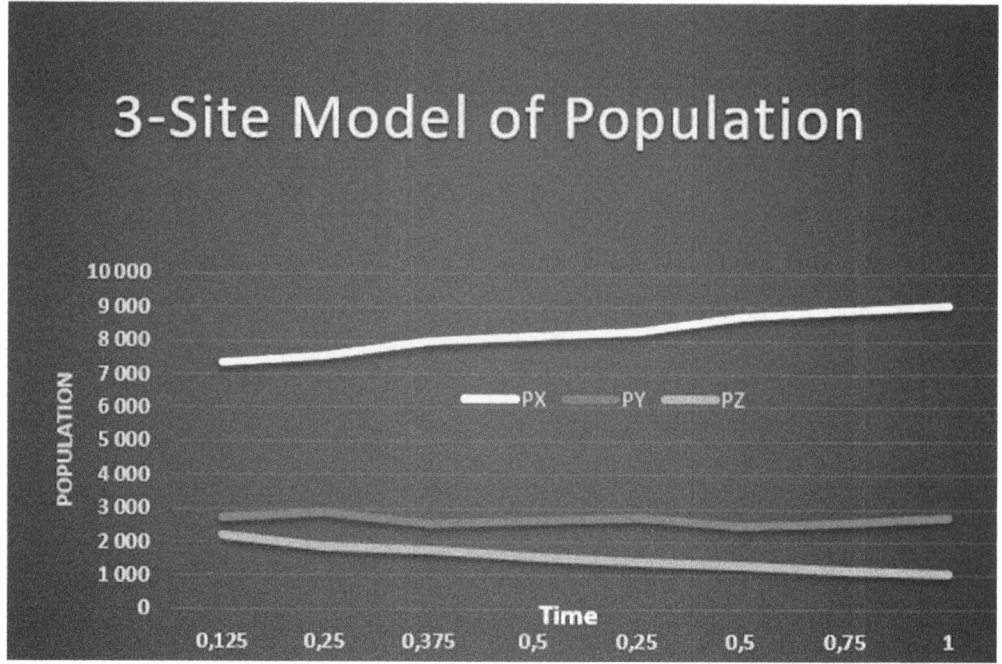

FIGURE 11.8. Model of Migration combined with growth.

The model behaved as expected. Stena I, IV never showed any gain in population. Maidanetske generally had a greater gain than Romanovka, especially at cycle 2, sub-cycle 1. Therefore, most of Maidanetske's gains came from Romanovka's losses. Romanovka exceeded 2,750, its critical point, at the end of cycle 2. Total population gradually increased over time from 12,246 to 12,765.

The combination of losses with growth for Stena I, IV is a linearly decreasing curve. The graph of Maidanetske consistently increases. Its periods of maximum growth come at the expense of Romanovka. Romanovka's maximum growth periods coincide with Stena's maximum losses. All of these combined migration and growth curves are shown in the graph of the 3-Site Model of Population (Figure 11.8).

Our simulations allow three important conclusions considering the demographic development at the analyzed sites. These could be extended to more general issues of paleodemography. The modeled population size of Maidanetske is less than its population size estimated from empirical evidence. This divergence may be explained by another migration, probably, related to the Tomashovskaya group mega-site of Vasilkov (Figure 11.7: 9). The latter site was built by former inhabitants of Chichirkozovka, which is synchronous to Dobrovody (Figure 11.7: 4, 8; Diachenko and Menotti 2012). Hence, the decline of Vasilkov may correspond to the difference between modeled and empirical values for Maidanetske. This issue will be solved with further application of the model to the whole range of known settlements.

The model has shown significant issues in the estimation of the population size based on empirical evidence. Population exchange between Maidanetske and Romanovka may be reflected in the related dynamics in the ratio of inhabited and abandoned dwellings at both sites. At the same time, population exchanges within the WTC settlement system confirm the hypothesis by Diachenko and Zubrow (submitted). They argue that the formation of spatio-demographic structure of such systems are the result of self-regulation caused by density-dependence.

Finally, the tested null hypothesis on equal and presumed carrying capacity has shown that both are important to consider in simulations. There is no empirical evidence to support the decrease in actual carrying capacity in the Dniester and Southern Bug interfluve, where Stena I, IV is located. Thus, the migration to Maidanetske rather represents the change in perception of carrying capacity.

Conclusion

The N site model of migration is a multifaceted project. This chapter is the simplified first stage of the project. What we have done is create, from a theory, an expanded and more generalized theory. Fundamentally, we took a variant of the Hobbesian/Malthusian worldview rooted deeply in history and added evidence-based cognitive psychology (Lindstrøm 2015). We then created the generalized operational model by which to test this theory. However, having once created the generalized theory and generalized operational model for this paper, we have returned to simplicity and first principles by testing the simplest "null hypothesis." The theory is simplified because although the generalized theoretical and operational structures are there, the following conditions are included solely to simplify. The simplifications are as follows:

- Simplification 1. We use only three sites (e.g., three body problem).
- Simplification 2. The carrying capacity for each site is a constant.
- Simplification 3. Each of the three sites has different actual carrying capacities, but those values are the same whether they are perceived by the immigrants, the emigrants, or the members of each village.

The new null hypothesis is that given these restrictions the theory will not predict the migratory behavior of three sites in the Tripolye area. As one can tell from the results section, the predictions do work and thus the null hypothesis needs to be rejected.

We believe the theory and model deserve more effort because, if valid, the model has political, public policy, demographic, anthropological, and archaeological implications. It politically speaks to the issues of hard and soft borders, Brexit, human rights, political as well as economic migrants, free labor movement, and government policy toward detention camps, to name only a few issues. With better prediction tools, it would not be necessary to compensate ex-post facto for too many or too few economic or political immigration policies.

Demographically it is inclusive. It allows for all types of migration from stable or unstable, stationary or unstationary populations. It can be either a population push or population pull model, or both. It can be either a network or a wave model. Unlike many weaker models, it is a population model that is not solely determined by economic values. Anthropologically, it is highly relevant to the "what we count rather than what counts" debate. When one is considering the role of the power of measurement and the limitations of numerical values, it has a strong ethnographic component and incorporates the bottom-up as well as the more common top-down control of population movement.

Archaeologically it fits right on the transition line between processual and post-processual archaeology. Not only does it incorporate the traditional values of the "new archaeology," namely, studying the population rather than the individual, and population behavior rather than individual introspection, yet it simultaneously incorporates perception, cultural bias, and the decision making emphasized by post-processual archaeology. Nevertheless, because it is population-based and evidence-based, it might be more similar to the new world "symmetric" archaeology, Kristian Kristiansen's (2013) evidence-based archaeology, as well as Renfrew and Zubrow's (1994) cognitive archaeology.

Given that the N site model works with these restrictions, the initial stage of the research demonstrates that more work is worth putting into the model. For example, one may relax the carrying capacity simplification and allow it to change dynamically. A very preliminary examination shows that increasing the carrying capacity by 5% or 10% creates a strong oscillation in the migrants. Similarly, a decrease of as little as 5% or 10% results in demographic stabilization. The stabilization points likely change over time. We believe we should relax the carry capacity assumption, increase the number of sites, examine the asymmetric aspects of the distance relationships, increase the diversity of original populations, and allow the cognitive and perceptual differences to increase. However, these steps await the next study, which we plan to publish in the near future.

Notes

1. Standard examples are the general theory of evolution, the general theory of gravitation, and the general theory of relativity, among others. Generalized theories are frequently tested on more specific cases such as the famous three-body problem that held out without a solution for generations (Marchal 1990).
2. Some critiques emerged as soon as the ideas were published, including those of Booth and Malthus (1823). A letter to the Rev. T. R. Malthus, M.A. F.R.S. being an answer to the criticism, on Mr. Godwin's work on population, which was inserted in the LXXth number of the Edinburgh review: To which is added an examination of the censuses of Great Britain and Ireland. London: [Printed for Longman, Hurst, Rees, Orme, and Brown].
3. Kenneth J. Arrow showed mathematically that there were better and worse strategies for reaching an equilibrium with complete and incomplete knowledge. In a theorem of stunning generality, Professor Arrow proved that no system of action worked satisfactorily

(in a formal sense). Furthermore, his book *Social Choice and Individual Values* (1951) was far more sweeping. Not only do sequential action systems prove unsatisfactory but nonsequential ones do as well when one does not know the equilibrium parameters. For example this is the case for whether to emigrate or not. This theorem became known as Arrow's "impossibility theorem." Later, he defined the price equations that bring everything including migrating labor into a voluntary equilibrium. Most importantly for our purposes, he brought forth the "learning by doing" notion. Namely, the more a company produces, the smarter it gets. This concept evolves into the sophisticated theories of "endogenous growth," depending on internal policies. This concept applies to out-migrants. The more frequently one migrates, the more one knows how to do it and the easier it becomes. Those individuals or families that migrate several times are called "hyper migrants." There are numerous studies of hypermigration (e.g., Bauböck 2011; Ho 2016).

4. Subcycles are analytical time periods that are used in the model and in the simulation. They are combined in a variety of ways, depending upon the simulation run, into larger time periods that are labeled "cycles."

5. One might look at time in a variety of manners. Consider, for instance, time to be a rectangular cuboid loaf of bread. In a discontinuous framework one examines time as a cuboid loaf with time slices, one after another. Einstein's contribution was essentially to discover that the slices should be cut on an angle so that time becomes relative. In a continuous framework, however, one no longer has vertical or angular slices; rather, one has cores drilled continuously between the two ends of the loaf (Lightman1994).

6. Since Gordon's famous 1969 book, numerous generalized as well as field-specialized simulation packages have been developed. Some are open source and some are proprietary. Here are a few of the nonproprietary generalized packages: *ASCEND*, an open-source equation-based modeling environment; *Elmer*, an open-source multiphysical simulation software for Windows/Mac/Linux; *Facsimile*, a free, open-source discrete-event simulation library; *Freemat*, a free environment for using the same language as MATLAB and GNU Octave; *Galatea*, a multi-agent, multiprogramming language, simulation platform; *Open-Modelica*, an open-source modeling environment based on *Modelica* (the open standard for modeling software); *NetLogo*, an open-source multi-agent simulation software; *ns-3*, an open-source network simulator; *OpenEaagles*, a multiplatform simulation framework to prototype and build simulation applications; *Tortuga*, an open-source software framework for discrete-event simulation in Java; and *UrbanSim*, an open-source software to simulate land use, transportation, and environmental planning.

7. VBA (Visual Basic for Applications) is the programming language of Excel and other Office programs (Mansfield 2016).

References Cited

Abrams, R. H. 1943 Residential Propinquity as a Factor in Marriage Selection: Fifty Year Trends in Philadelphia. *American Sociological Review* 3(3):288–294.

Alexander, J. T., and A. Steidl 2012 Gender and the "Laws of Migration": A Reconsideration of Nineteenth-Century Patterns. *Social Science History* 36(2):223–241.

Arrow, K. J. 1951 *Social Choice and Individual Values*. Yale University Press, New Haven.

Bauböck, R. 2011 Temporary Migrants, Partial Citizenship, and Hypermigration. *Critical Review of International Social and Political Philosophy* 14(5):665–693.

Booth, D., and T. R. Malthus 1823 *A Letter to the Reviewer. T.R. Malthus, M.A., F.R.S. Being an Answer to the Criticism, on Mr. Godwin's Work on Population, which was Inserted in the LXXth Number of the Edinburgh Review: To which is Added an Examination of the Censuses of Great Britain and Ireland*. Printed for Longman, Hurst, Rees, Orme, and Brown, London.

Boulding, K. E. 1959 (1964 printing) Thomas Robert Malthus, 1766–1834. In T. R. Malthus *Population: The First Essay (with a foreword by Kenneth E. Boulding)*. University of Michigan Press, Ann Arbor.

Cartwright, K. V. 2016 Simpson's Rule Integration with MS Excel and Irregularly-Spaced Data. *Journal of Mathematical Science and Mathematics Education* 11(2):34–42.

Chapman, J., and B. Gaydarska 2016 Low-Density Agrarian-Based Cities: A Principle of the Past and Present. In *Trypillia Mega-Sites and European Prehistory, 4100–3400 BCE*, edited by J. Müller, K. Rassmann, and M. Videiko, pp. 289–300. Routledge, London.

Chapman, J., M. Videiko, D. Hale, B. Gaydarska, N. Burdo, K. Rassmann, C. Mischka, J. Müller, A. Korvin-Piotrovskiy, and V. Kruts 2014 The Second Phase of the Trypillia Mega-Site Methodological Revolution: A New Research Agenda. *European Journal of Archaeology* 17(3):369–406.

Codding, B., and T. Jones 2013 Environmental Productivity Predicts Migration, Demographic, and Linguistic Patterns in Prehistoric California. *Proceedings of the National Academy of Sciences of the USA* 110(36):14569–14573.

Del Pinto, R., D. Pietropaoli, U. Russomando, P. Evangelista, and C. Ferri 2018 Health Status of Afro-Asian Refugees in an Italian Urban Area: A Cross-Sectional Monocentric Study. *Public Health* 158:176–182.

Diachenko, A. 2012 Settlement System of West Tripolye Culture in the Southern Bug and Dnieper Interfluve: Formation Problems. In *The Tripolye Culture Giant-Settlements in Ukraine: Formation, Development and Decline*, edited by F. Menotti and A. G. Korvin-Piotrovskiy, pp. 116–138. Oxbow Books, Oxford.

Diachenko, A. 2016 Demography Reloaded. In *Trypillia Mega-Sites and European Prehistory, 4100–3400 BCE*, edited by J. Müller, K. Rassmann, and M. Videiko, pp. 181–194. Routledge, London.

Diachenko, A., and F. Menotti 2012 The Gravity Model: Monitoring the Formation and Development of the Tripolye Culture Giant-Settlements in Ukraine. *Journal of Archaeological Science* 39(4):2810–2817.

Diachenko, A., and E. B. W. Zubrow 2015 Stabilization Points in Carrying Capacity: Population Growth and Migrations. *Journal of Neolithic Archaeology* 17:1–15.

Diachenko, A., and E. B. W. Zubrow (submitted) Spatio-Demographic Structure and Social Organization: A Linear Trajectory or Overlapping Trends? In *What if We Build This Here? Spatial Patterns, Community Organization, and Identity at Nucleated Settlements*, edited by A. Gyucha and R. Salisbury. State University of New York Press, Buffalo.

Engbersen, G. 2013 Labour Migration from Central and Eastern Europe and the Implications for Integration Policy. In *Making Migration Work: The Future of Labour Migration in the European Union*, edited by J. W. Holtslag, M. Kremer and E. Schrijvers, pp. 105–122. Amsterdam University Press, Amsterdam.

Feinman, G. M. 2016 Reframing Ancient Economies: New Models, New Questions. In *Eurasia at the Dawn of History: Urbanization and Social Change*, edited by M. Fernández-Götz and D. Krausse, pp. 139–152. Cambridge University Press, Cambridge.

Fekete, L. 2018 Migrants, Borders and the Criminalization of Solidarity in the EU. *Race & Class* 59(4):65–83.

Garcea, E. A. A. 2016 Dispersals Out of Africa and Back to Africa: Modern Origins in North Africa. *Quaternary International* 408(15):79–89.

Gibbons, A. 2015 Human Evolution: Prehistoric Eurasians Streamed into Africa, Genome Shows. *Science* 350(6257):149.

Gordon, G. 1969 *System Simulation (Prentice-Hall Series in Automatic Computation)*. Prentice-Hall, Englewood Cliffs, New Jersey.

Groote, P., and V. Tassenaar 2000 Hunger and Migration in a Rural-Traditional Area in the Nineteenth Century. *Journal of Population Economics* 13(3):465–483.

Haggett, P. 1979 *Geography. A Modern Synthesis*. Harper and Row, New York, Hagerstown, Philadelphia, San Francisco, London.

Ho, E. 2016 Incongruent Migration Categorisations and Competing Citizenship Claims: "Return" and Hypermigration in Transnational Migration Circuits. *Journal of Ethnic and Migration Studies* 42(14):2379–2394.

Kristiansen, K. 2014 Towards a New Paradigm? The Third Science Revolution and its Possible Consequences in Archaeology. *Current Swedish Archaeology* 22:11–71.

Kruts, V. A. 1989 K Istorii Naseleniya Tripolskoj Kultury v Mezhdurechye Yuzhnogo Buga i Dnepra. In *Pervobytnaya Arkheologiya: Materialy i Issledovaniya*, edited by S. S. Berezanskaya, pp. 117–132. Naukova Dumka, Kiev.

Lightman, A. 1994 *Einstein's Dreams*. Sceptre, London.

Lindstrøm, T. 2015 Agency "in Itself." A Discussion of Inanimate, Animal, and Human Agency. *Archaeological Dialogues* 22(2):207–238.

MacArthur, R., and J. Connell 1966 *Biology of Populations*. John Wiley and Sons, New York.

Malthus, T. R. 1958 (1967 reprint) *An Essay on the Principle of Population*. Everyman's Library, London and Dent.

Mansfield, R. 2016 *Mastering VBA for Microsoft Office 2016*. 3rd. Ed. John Wiley and Sons, Indianapolis.

Marchal, C. (editor) 1990 *The Three-Body Problem. Studies in Astronautics* 4. Elsevier, Amsterdam and Oxford.

Marches, J. R. 1953 The Effect of Residential Propinquity on Marriage Selection. *The American Journal of Sociology* 58(6):592–595.

Markevich, V. I. 1981 *Pozdnetripolskie Plemena Severnoj Moldavii*. Shtiintsa, Kishinev.

McColl, H. et al. 2018 The Prehistoric Peopling of Southeast Asia. *Science* 361(6397):88–92.

Menotti, F., and A. G. Korvin-Piotrovskiy (editors) 2012 *The Tripolye Culture Giant-Settlements in Ukraine: Formation, Development and Decline*. Oxbow Books, Oxford.

Müller, J., R. Hofmann, L. Brandtstätter, R. Ohlrau, and M. Videiko 2016 Chronology and Demography: How Many People Lived in a Mega-Site? In *Trypillia Mega-Sites and European Prehistory, 4100–3400 BCE*, edited by J. Müller, K. Rassmann, and M. Videiko, pp. 133–170. Routledge, London.

Müller, J., K. Rassmann, and M. Videiko (editors) 2016 *Trypillia Mega-Sites and European Prehistory, 4100–3400 BCE*. Routledge, London.

Nakoinz, O., and D. Knitter 2016 *Modelling Human Behavior in Landscapes: Basic Concepts and Modelling Elements*. Springer, New York.

Nebbia, M., B. Gaydarska, A. Millard, and J. Chapman 2018 The Making of Chalcolithic Assembly Places: Trypillia Megasites as Materialized Consensus among Equal Strangers. *World Archaeology*. DOI:10.1080/00438243.2018.1474133.

Ohanian, D. 2018 The Migration of Child and Women Survivors of the Armenian Genocide from the Eastern Mediterranean to Canada, 1923–1930. *Genocide Studies International Volume* 11(2):197–215.

Ostrom, E. 1990 *Governing the Commons: The Evolution of Institutions for Collective Action*. Cambridge University Press, Cambridge.

Peacock, A. 1952 Theory of Population and Modern Economic Analysis. *Population Studies* 6:114–122.

Rassmann, K., A. Korvin-Piotrovskiy, M. Videiko, and J. Müller 2016 The New Challenge for Site Plans and Geophysics: Revealing the Settlement Structure of Giant Settlements by Means of Geomagnetic Survey. In *Trypillia Mega-Sites and European Prehistory, 4100–3400 BCE*, edited by J. Müller, K. Rassmann, and M. Videiko, pp. 29–54. Routledge, London.

Renfrew, C., and E. B. W. Zubrow (editors) 1994 *The Ancient Mind: Elements of Cognitive Archaeology*. Cambridge University Press, Cambridge.

Ryzhov, S. M. 2007 Suchasnyj Stan Vyvchennia Kulturno-Istorychnoi Spilnosti Cucuteni-Trypillya. In *O. Olzhych. Archeologiya*, edited by Yu. Ya. Rassamakin and S. M. Ryzhov, pp. 437–477. Vydavnytstvo im. Oleny Teligy, Kiev.

Ryzhov, S. 2012 Relative Chronology of the Giant-Settlement Period BII–CI. In *The Tripolye Culture Giant-Settlements in Ukraine: Formation, Development, and Decline*, edited by F. Menotti and A. G. Korvin-Piotrovskiy, pp. 79–115. Oxbow Books, Oxford.

Samuelson, P. A. 1961 *Economics. An Introductory Analysis*. McGraw-Hill, New York.

Shmaglij, N. M., and M. Yu. Videiko 2003 Maidanetskoe-Tripolskij Protogorod. *Stratum Plus* 2:44–140.

Strogatz, S. H. 1994 *Nonlinear Dynamics and Chaos with Applications to Physics, Biology, Chemistry, and Engineering*. Westview Press, Cambridge, Massachusetts.

Tkachuk, T. M. 2005 *Znakovi Systemy Trypilsko-Cucutenskoi Kulturno-Istorychnoi Spilnosti (Maliovanyj Posud), Ch. 2: Semiotychnyj Analiz Trypilsko-Kukutenskyh Znakovyh System (Maliovanyj Posud)*. Nova Knyha, Vinnytsia.

Tsvek, E. V. 2006 *Posellenia Skhidnotrypilskoi Kultury: Korotkyj Narys*. Institute of Archaeology of the NAS of Ukraine, Kyiv.

Verhulst, P. F. 1838 Notice sur la loi que la population poursuit dans son accroissement. *Correspondance mathématique et physique* 10:113–121.

Verhulst, P. F. 1845 Recherches mathématiques sur la loi d'accroissement de la population. *Nouveaux Mémoires de l'Académie Royale des Sciences et Belles-Lettres de Bruxelles* 18, Art. 1:1–45.

Zubrow, E. B. W. 1971 Carrying Capacity and Dynamic Equilibrium in the Prehistoric Southwest. *American Antiquity* 36(2):127–138.

Zubrow, E. B. W. 1974 Population, Climate, and Contact in the New Mexican Pueblos. *University of Arizona Anthropological Papers* 24. University of Arizona Press, Tucson.

Zubrow, E. B. W. 1975 *Prehistoric Carrying Capacity: A Model*. Cummings Press, Menlo Park.

PART IV

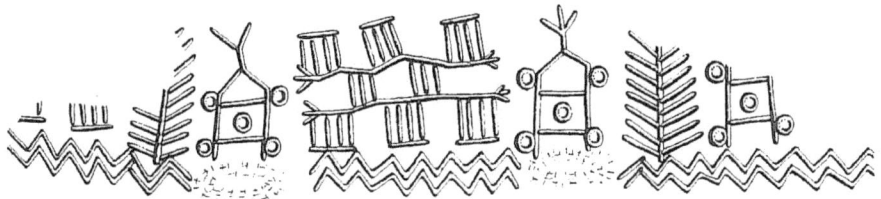

Sociohistorical Models of Migration

CHAPTER TWELVE

Toward a Social Archaeology of Forced Migration

Rebuilding Landscapes of Memory in Medieval Armenian Cilicia

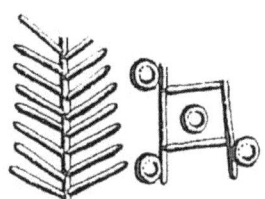

Aurora E. Camaño

Abstract *Despite a recent surge in scholarship on the resettlement of refugees across many social disciplines in response to current global events, the study of forced migration within archaeology has lagged. There exists a widening lacuna in our understanding of the experiential, affective, and mnemonic engagements of migrant groups due to our field's continued preference for research that focuses on identifying migration events and mobility patterns. This chapter analyzes the historiographic factors leading to the neglect of migrant experience within archaeology and advocates for a social archaeology of forced migration that invites research on the restoration of migrant identity and place. Drawing from contemporary anthropological studies of forced migration and landscape archaeology, it is proposed that comparative analysis between built landscapes of origin and resettlement provides an opportunity to address the question of how memory is manipulated and monumentalized through the medium of resettlement. Using the resettlement of the Armenians in the eleventh and early twelfth century in Cilicia as a case study, this chapter offers a look into how the structural and architectural landscape can be used to reconstruct narratives of identity and belonging, as well as understand the role of myth following the trauma of forced relocation.*

Displacement, by means of both state-enforced population transfer and impelled migration due to threat of violence, was a consistent element of life in the eastern medieval world (Charanis 1961:141; Ahrweiler and Laiou 1998; Stouraitis 2016:11; Göçek 1995:2). Byzantine rulers regularly used mass deportation and the relocation of ethnic and religious minority groups as political strategy for the repopulation and Christianization of new and reclaimed territories throughout their empire (Charanis 1961:145, 150–151; Stouraitis 2016:9–11). Despite the frequency of such events in the medieval east, as well as those across regional and chronological boundaries, the topic of forced migration, until recently, has been left behind within archaeological scholarship. While contemporary social anthropology boasts a lengthy history of research on forced migration, having undergone decades of theoretical and methodological development to navigate the experiences and perceptions of resettled refugees (cf. Chatty 2014), the subject of migrant experience and memory within archaeological contexts has comparatively seen neglect.

The present-day global refugee crisis has propelled forced migration studies to the forefront across many social disciplines. However, research arising out of this renewed interest within the field of archaeology has largely concentrated building methodologies for the geographic and material identification of migration events (e.g., Burke 2011, 2018a; Driessen 2018) and tracing movement patterns of affected populations (e.g., Martin 2018). This emphasis on identification remains critical, particularly for periods and regions of study that lack accompanying historical documentation. Nonetheless, for medieval archaeological contexts in which primary source materials have long illuminated such details, this narrowed focus of study has resulted in a significant void in our collective knowledge of the social, experiential, and mnemonic responses to trauma and the social disarticulation caused by involuntary relocation.

This chapter advocates the need for archaeological research beyond the identification of events and sites associated with forced movement, and calls for a social archaeology of forced migration which ultimately seeks to reconstruct past migrant narratives and the often-overlooked societal impacts of mass displacement and resettlement. A shift toward social anthropological explorations of forced migration within archaeology will allow archaeologists to reconstruct how forcibly resettled populations in the past responded to the disruption of place-based identity and the loss of social legitimacy as a result of mass displacement. More specifically, such an approach provides archaeologists an opportunity to explore the changing role that historical memory and myth played in the reformation of cultural identities, political legitimacy, and place-belonging through the multigenerational process of permanent resettlement.

Beyond calling attention to the need for further social enquiry into the minds and lives of forcibly resettled groups within archaeology, this chapter offers new theoretical and methodological directions for this work using the medieval resettlement of the Armenians in Cilicia as a preliminary case study. Drawing from approaches used in contemporary anthropological scholarship and archaeological landscape studies, this study aims to expose how mnemonic responses to the trauma of forced resettlement can present within the material record.

Defining Forced Migration

The term *forced migration* has been assigned a host of definitions, depending on the disciplinary and sociohistorical context it is framed within. The complexities of forced migration, as Catherine Cameron notes (this volume), does not always fit easily within the "push-pull" paradigm borrowed by archaeologists to explain voluntary migrations (Anthony 1990:898). Instead, to encompass the many channels and structures of displacement in both present-day contexts and the archaeological past, this chapter defers to the definition set forth by *The International Association for the Study of Forced Migration*, which broadly classifies forced migration as "the movements of refugees and internally displaced people" (Hansen, Mission of the IASFM), including individuals and groups displaced by conflict as well as development, resource crises, or environmental disasters. Impelled migration has also been included under the umbrella of forced migration. This term denotes groups that, while not forcibly removed from their homeland by an activating agent, such as an invading body or state authority, leave en masse due to perceived unsuitable living environments, increasing threat to social freedoms, or danger to human life.

During the relocation of the Armenians to Cilicia in the eleventh century there are clear occurrences of both forced and impelled conflict-induced displacement. A state-activated population transfer occurred under the orders of Constantine IX Monomachos, who, prior to his annexation of the Bagratid capital of Ani in 1045, enforced a mass relocation of Armenian nobility and related parties living within Greater Armenia to allotted lands in Cappadocia, Sivas, Northern Syria, and Cilicia (Charanis 1963:51; Boase 1978:2). Seljuk interactions in the following decades, particularly the Seljuk capture of Ani in 1064 and the aftermath of the Battle of Manzikert in 1071, sparked a secondary exodus of Armenians who sought domicile in Cilicia (Weyl Carr 1993:xi; Der Nersessian 1962:630). These migration events, which lead to the establishment of a new Armenian Kingdom in the twelfth century, remain severely under-studied from both archaeological and historical perspectives.

Researching Forced Migrants in Archaeology and Anthropology

The small number of archaeological studies centered on forced migration cannot be blamed on a lack of historical examples. In the Near East, documentary sources mentioning forced exiles or the movement of minority populations appear as early as the second millennium B.C. (Burke 2018b:2). Instead, the lack of scholarship on forced migration within archaeology mirrors the avoidance and overcautiousness which befell archaeological migration and mobility studies more generally in the late 1960s. Barbara Bender once called it the "one domain in which archaeological theorizing has been slow to keep pace with anthropology" (Bender 2001:76). Several other archaeologists have noted this pause in the academic literature, explaining it as a response to problematic migrationist and diffusionist theories and their role as drivers of nationalist culture-historical narratives (Anthony 1990:895–897; Hackenbeck 2008:13–15; van Dommelen 2014:477–478).

One regretful consequence of this temporal break is that the study of human mobility within archaeology largely missed out on the post-processualist lens of the 1980s and early 1990s. In particular, the archaeological study of migration seemingly skipped over the postmodernist shift toward investigations of power and agency, the embodied subject, and place making. Cabana and van Dommelen have both noted that studies arising from the recent return to migration and mobility in archaeology have predominantly reverted to processualist modes of framing and inquiry, with a primary focus on proving the existence and scales of mass human movements over time and space (Cabana 2011:24; van Dommelen 2014:479). Speaking on migration studies more widely, van Dommelen notes that "there has been very little consideration of the implications of migration" (van Dommelen 2014:479). This reality has had a particularly detrimental cost for the archaeological study of conflict-induced forced migration. Overlooking the implications and aftermaths of forced relocations has aided in further silencing the voices of marginalized pasts—where the archaeological impacts of migration events cannot be separated from the layers of social trauma carried by those subjected to forced dislocation.

In contrast, the study of forced migration within social and cultural anthropology received continued attention and has progressed significantly throughout the past 70 years. The earliest systematic studies of displaced peoples from an anthropological perspective date to the mid-1940s (e.g., Colson 1943). However, much like the pitfalls of early archaeological explorations of migration, many of these initial studies painted refugees as agency-less survivalists by prioritizing notions of territorialization and social disintegration (Malkki 1995; Chatty 2014:77, 81). Rather than throwing the baby out with the bathwater, as David Anthony (1990) suggests occurred within archaeology, social anthropologists in the late 1960s and 1970s responded by activating a move past the structuralist studies of forced movement and resettlement, which had defined the field (Chatty 2014:80). Alongside Elizabeth Colson's later work on memory and resettlement (Colson 2003), research conducted by Peter Loizos (1981), Anthony Oliver-Smith (1982), Akhil Gupta and James Ferguson (1992), Liisa Malkki (1992, 1995), Renee Hirschon (1998), and Dawn Chatty (2010) contributed to the adoption of postmodernist and social constructivist frameworks within anthropological forced migration studies (Chatty 2014:80–83).

The advent of the postmodernist turn in social anthropology during the 1960s and 1970s created space for new and deeper considerations of refugee and migrant agency, lived experiences, perceptions, and social memories on both individual and collective scales. These themes continue to form the core of forced migration research in anthropology today (Chatty 2014:75,77). Dawn Chatty, who has written on the history of forced migration studies within anthropology, summarizes the current motivations of the discipline by stating:

> The primacy of the vision of anthropology has been the perspective and voice of the forced migrant, the phenomenological encounter that permits the uprooted, the displaced, and the refugee to break out from the category of "object of study" and to bring to life the individual experience of dispossession. [Chatty 2014:83]

Recent anthropological studies on refugee and migrant populations have showcased a growing program of research which explores multigenerational notions of identity, belonging, and mnemonic engagements with place and past as expressed through resettlement and the act of place making. It is precisely these modes of inquiry and analysis that are presently lacking within archaeological scholarship on forced migration. It is, therefore, increasingly necessary that archaeologists studying past groups affected by traumatic forced relocation turn to this corpus of literature to confront the ways in which the trauma of displacement manifests during and through the course of resettlement.

In his influential work *Migration in Archaeology: The Baby and the Bathwater*, David Anthony re-poses the controversial question of whether modern migration studies are irrelevant to the study of human mobility in the archaeological past (Anthony 1990:898). Anthony himself advocates the necessity of using present-day social science research within archaeological studies of human movement (Anthony 1990:898). Although his question is posed within the framework of understanding prehistoric migration patterns, his statement is equally pertinent to archaeological investigations of forced resettlement within the historic past, as this chapter explores. Modern social anthropological studies offer significant contributions both methodologically and theoretically to the archaeology of forced migration. Perhaps most importantly, they can provide a basis for understanding and identifying affective, behavioral, and mnemonic responses to the traumatic social conditions of forced displacement.

Nevertheless, as highlighted by Aaron Burke (2018a:230), it is necessary that archaeologists acknowledge the different conditions faced by many in present-day examples of conflict-induced resettlement and those which appear within historical records, and use caution when attempting to draw direct parallels. Although affective responses to the trauma of being forcibly removed from a perceived homeland appear universal, such as feelings of loss of belonging or place attachment and nostalgia, the scale and medium of their expression is dictated by both cultural and state dynamics. Today, refugees are typically first relocated to temporary places of asylum before dispersal to host countries, thus undergoing long governmental immigration processes resulting in widespread diaspora. The act of resettlement under such circumstances is heavily controlled and requires newcomers to integrate into preexisting built environments and communities. In the eastern medieval world, the spectrum of autonomy among forcibly uprooted groups varied. Byzantine-led deportations and population relocations of minority groups, such as the Armenians, often afforded arriving migrants greater levels of control over their newly resettled landscape: an experience that differs drastically to that of many contemporary migrants and refugees.

In medieval Armenian Cilicia, arriving migrants were, comparatively, presented with a near-blank canvas upon which to rebuild their home. Asa Eger has suggested, despite the Byzantine reconquest of 965, that there is little archaeological evidence to suggest a significant Byzantine reoccupation in Rough Cilicia after the steep population decline experienced in the seventh century until the arrival of the Armenians (Eger 2015:170). Although Byzantine military strongholds remained at the sites of Sis, Pardzerpert, Anavarsa, and Adana until the reign of Prince T'oros in the early twelfth century, the Armenians quickly became an ethnic majority in Cilicia. Furthermore, Cilicia's geographic position was within the political reaches of Philaretos Brachamios, an Armenian-born Byzantine general who controlled the territory between Antioch and Melitene. An Armenian himself, Philaretos was sympathetic to the plight of the arriving migrants and saw strategic benefit in their arrival—making more noteworthy arrivals such as Ruben I, the originator of the Rubenid line, his vassal. The combination of these geopolitical factors allowed the incoming

Armenians a level of self-determination over their new landscape that would be uncommon for groups undergoing forced resettlement today. It is imperative that these complex social dynamics are considered fully when archaeologists draw from anthropological research concerning recent and present-day contexts.

Subject focus and theoretical frameworks within the anthropological study of forced migration have changed considerably over recent decades. However, knowledge acquisition remains deeply rooted in the traditional methodologies of the discipline; namely, participant-based and material-based approaches—with the former being most widely applied. According to Dawn Chatty, social anthropology involves "two interrelated, fundamental research strategies and tools, participant observation and the ethnographic method" (Chatty 2014:83). Participant-based observation, ethnological comparative analysis, and the collection of ethnographic narratives and materials remain the foundation of nearly all major anthropological contributions to the study of refugees and displaced peoples (e.g., Loizos 1981; Malkki 1995; Hirschon 1998; Colson 1999; Davies 2010; Rishbeth and Powell 2013; Philipp and Ho 2010). The value of this ethnographic and participant-centered research when attempting to reconstruct refugee narratives cannot be disputed. Chatty refers to these practices as giving "voice and agency" to forced migrants (Chatty 2014:74). However, without access to living informants to drive research, this objective becomes more difficult to achieve.

As archaeology primarily deals with the nonliving and ancient past, one of the challenges archaeologists face is the acquisition of suitable material substitutes to replace the ethnographic narrative sources central to contemporary anthropology, while retaining the humanistic elements of social anthropological inquiry that archaeological scholarship on forced migration frequently lacks. This challenge is further emphasized by the perceived invisibility of portable material culture associated with contexts of involuntary movement. In addition to the previously deterred interest in human mobility due to past problematic applications, concerns of material visibility in the archaeological record, due to the transient and ephemeral nature of forced migration (as noted by Pistrick and Bachmeier 2016:210; Gori and Revello Lami 2018:32; Legendre 2018:71; Martin 2018:114), have also contributed to the dearth of social archaeological investigations on the topic of forced migration.

Recent work out of contemporary archaeology, bridging anthropological research of modern peoples and archaeological materials-based methodologies, has addressed several of these issues. Anthropologist Jason De León has used materials-based methods to illuminate contemporary experiences and narratives of individuals crossing the borders between Latin America and the United States of America through the *Undocumented Migration Project* (De León 2013, 2015). Building on such approaches explored by De León, the *Journal of Contemporary Archaeology* released a special issue on archaeologies of undocumented migration in 2016 that was later expanded into an edited volume in 2018. Edited by Yannis Hamilakis, the volume showcases Hamilakis's own fieldwork at the refugee camps of Lesvos, Greece, where he applies archaeological methods to study the abandonment of portable material culture in present-day contexts of conflict-induced displacement. (Hamilakis 2016, 2018). In this work, Hamilakis questions how refugees maintain a sense of connection to their lost homeland through material means, and he highlights the great need for sensorial and affective considerations that can shed light on how both migrant experience and materiality transform landscapes of relocation (Hamilakis 2016:128)—or, as Helen Armstrong asks: "How is the turbulence of migration inscribed in the landscape?" (Armstrong 2004:241). Although considerable work has been undertaken to address such questions within contemporary studies, much less has been written from this perspective regarding the ancient world. Assaf Yasur-Landau has critically reminded archaeologists studying migratory groups of the "deep past" to remember and embrace the humanity of their subjects (Yasur-Landau 2018:177). Although the activating factors and governmental systems involved in current migration crises can differ greatly from those of the ancient and medieval past, the lines of social enquiry exhibited in recent contemporary archaeological studies remain essential to the exploration of forced migration within traditional archaeological contexts seeking to understand peoples and events from the distant past. The necessary question therefore becomes: *How* is this best achieved in the absence of the portable material culture and ethnographic narratives with which both Hamilakis and De León engage?

A Comparative Landscape Approach

Without access to living informants or assemblages of portable material culture to consult, the most accessible datasets for archaeologists studying forcibly relocated groups are their physical landscapes of origin and resettlement. The study of human interactions with their landscape has long been acknowledged as a rich archaeological resource. Landscape archaeology approaches both altered and unaltered landscapes as cultural products, which are assigned meaning and physically transformed through human activity and experience (Branton 2009:51, 55; Rubertone 1989:50; Darvill 1998:107). The perceptions, myths, and meanings that become attached to a landscape by a group are entrenched in their shared history, social memories, and experiences with and within that place. The reciprocal relationship between people and their environment (Turner 2006:387), therefore, becomes entwined with the construction of collective identities and historical narratives (Branton 2009:54; Stobbelaar and Bas 2011:323). In turn, this contributes to building a sense of *place attachment,* that is, the "emotional, symbolic, and affective dimensions of people's thinking and feeling for places" (Rishbeth and Powell 2013:161).

Cultural landscapes, thus, provide an ideal platform from which to study cognitive relationships with place and the ways that the collective social memories of migrant groups take shape and manifest architecturally and structurally through resettlement. Identifying the physical expressions of shared memories, perceptions, motivations, and imagined histories within the built landscape affords insight into the evolving narratives of migrant identity and legitimacy reclamation. Furthermore, comparative analysis of migrant landscapes illuminates how enduring memories and perceptions of the pre-migration past were reframed through the experience of dislocation and social disarticulation caused by the loss of their ancestral home and way of life. The acclaimed anthropologist Elizabeth Colson, who worked for several decades with the formerly displaced Gwembe Tonga in Zambia and Zimbabwe, merited the use of ethnological comparison of collected narratives. She referred to ethnology as a tool that provides a "deeper understanding of the human condition" in times of trauma and social upheaval (Colson 2003:3). For archaeological contexts of displacement, this chapter submits that performing a comparative analysis of the cultural landscapes associated with a forced migration event is likewise essential for tapping into the repository of migrant memory held by these lived spaces. Migrants carry ideals, perceptions, motivations, and memories rooted in the experiences of their ancestral lands onto the new territories to which they are transplanted. Therefore, using a direct historical approach (Abramiuk 2012:66), it is possible to conduct a systematic cross-comparison between a (perceived) landscape of origin and the landscape of resettlement, including comparison of site placement, social and structural organization, and architectural traditions.

Depending on site access and the archaeological resolution of the study group, comparative landscape analysis can take shape in many ways. Evidence from traditional archaeological and architectural survey, GIS-based approaches using available satellite imaging, as well as archival resources such as historic maps, photographs, and early travel literature and ephemera from the regions in question can all aid in forming a foundation for landscape and architectural comparison between places of origin and resettlement. Such an approach can highlight scales of cultural retention and transformation and be used to explore how memory and perception of the pre-migration past were constructed and monumentalized through the medium of resettlement.

Migrant Memory, Place Making, and Myth in Armenian Cilicia

The Armenians who settled in Cilicia in the eleventh and early twelfth century originated predominately from the Bagratid Kingdoms in Western Armenia, a region that straddles the Akhurian River, which today delineates the borders of Turkey and the modern Republic of Armenia. Although a significant number of Armenians later relocated to Cilicia from the Anatolian plateau following their initial transfer to lands in and around Cappadocia and Sivas, the landscape of Western Greater Armenia was considered their ancestral home. Upon initial assessment, it is easily observed that the natural landscapes of Rough Cilicia and Western Armenia share numerous visual and sensory environmental parallels, including a rugged and cave-speckled mountainous terrain, cliff-framed river valleys and gorges, and expansive agrarian plains. The topographic resemblance of the natural landscape of origin and resettlement offered the arriving Armenian migrants a familiar foundation upon which to rebuild their lost home.

This environmental familiarity makes the medieval forced movement of the Armenians to Cilicia an ideal model for trialing a comparative study of the built landscapes of origin and relocation. From comparative landscape studies we can observe and extract physical expressions of historical memory, identity management, and identity negotiation among migrant groups and their descendants as shaped by their experiences of forced resettlement. Furthermore, the swift reacquisition of political autonomy in Cilicia from the clutches of Byzantium by the relocated Armenians, allows us to consider the subsequently built landscape of Cilicia as a true physical expression of Armenian ideals and values regarding place and identity at the time of their rebuilding. By 1080 Cilicia had been declared to be an independent Armenian principality, one that was self-governing with minimal interference from Byzantium (Ghazarian 2000:45). This independence provided the resettled population in Cilicia with the capacity to self-manage their new social environment to a degree that many forcibly relocated groups throughout history could not. Their internal authority over the expanding principality continued to grow, leading to the crowning of the first Rubenid King, Levon the Magnificent, in 1198. This event inaugurated the official, and fully sovereign, Armenian Kingdom of Cilicia (Ghazarian 2000:55). The combination of environmental similarity and growing self-determinacy over their region of relocation invites the opportunity to trace how the Armenians physically and affectively manipulated their new home to reconstruct sentiments of familiarity, place attachment, belonging, and historical legitimacy within Cilicia.

Building Familiarity and Place Attachment

In a participant-based study of first-generation migrants in the United Kingdom and their interactions with and perceptions of new social spaces, conducted by Claire Rishbeth and Mark Powell, the authors found that visual familiarity and the performance of familiar activities in a space acted as mnemonic aides. They noted that these aids played a critical role in developing new feelings of belonging, place attachment, and continuity with the past (Rishbeth and Powell 2013:168, 174). Their research suggests that individuals who have undergone displacement place high value on building visual and sensory familiarity within new spaces they occupy. This is further supported by the work of Helen Armstrong, who through focus groups and coded textual analysis, studied place value, belonging, and the symbolic ways in which different migrant groups made the unfamiliar feel familiar following their arrival in Australia (Armstrong 2004:245, 257). Following relocation, familiar spaces not only provide comfort to those undergoing social upheaval, but also facilitate continuity of daily routines and activities central to identity maintenance.

Stefan Burmeister (2000) also engages with the concept of maintaining familiarity following migration. Burmeister proposes that, through resettlement, "external" material culture (i.e., public facing objects, namely, architecture) is more frequently subject to acclimatization and change, whereas "private" material culture (i.e., portable material culture, residence interiors, and furnishings) is likely to reflect cultural traditions from the place of origin (Burmeister 2000:542). However, this hypothesis assumes that the circumstances of moved groups are limited to integration into preexisting social fabrics and does not account for the broad spectrum of autonomy involved in many historic population transfers. For relocated groups such as the Armenians of medieval Cilicia, where self-control over the landscape was increasingly gained in the decades following resettlement, it should be anticipated that external material culture, particularly examples of monumental architecture, would similarly mirror the level of cultural retention Burmeister noted within the private and portable materials in his study. The strong topographic similarities between the natural landscapes of Rough Cilicia and Western Armenia means we can evaluate whether this familiarity was further emphasized by the resettled through structural modifications to the built landscape. An initial literature survey of the monuments and settlements of medieval Armenian Cilicia documented by Robert W. Edwards in the 1980s and 1990s shows evidence of structural continuity carried from the pre-migration past in Greater Armenia. Through preliminary comparative study, consisting of previous archaeological and architectural surveys alongside relevant archival literature and images, emerging patterns in site selection, settlement formation, as well as architectural design suggest that memory of the Greater Armenian homeland continued to inform and influence locational and structural preferences across multiple generations of Cilician Armenians.

Settlement Structure. Architectural impact is only one component of the built landscape. While monumental constructions are perhaps the most obvious markers of memory within a landscape, acting as both internal and external projections of identity and legacy, site selection and the overall structural organization of a settlement can also be manipulated to evoke familiarity and connection to the past. In reference to settlement formation and planning, Edwards's survey of Armenian Cilicia notes (with some confusion) that from the eleventh to the thirteenth century Armenian Cilicia appears to have lacked, according to classical tradition, the density and grandeur that would be expected of a rising principality-turned-kingdom (Edwards 1993:180–182). Edwards maintained that the results of his architectural survey supported that Armenian settlements in Cilicia were not structured in a way that would be recognized as traditionally urban, noting that Armenian society in Cilicia appeared "very different" to the models followed in either Roman-Byzantine or Islamic traditions (Edwards 1993:183). Rather than comparing the medieval Armenian settlements of Cilicia to the earlier Roman and Byzantine cities in the region, it is instead more effective to look to the ancestral lands the resettled population identified with and drew inspiration from.

Scholars of medieval Armenia have often painted the city as an "alien element" (see Franklin et al. 2017:121). Nina Garsoïan, in studying perceptions of classical cities within early medieval Armenian text, noted that cities were only rarely mentioned in such contexts and that their position in the early medieval Armenian tradition could be viewed as both "peripheral" and "exceptional" (Garsoïan 1984:68). She concluded, as others have suggested, that large urbanized centers or cities in the classical sense were not a central part of the settlement vernacular within Late Antique and early medieval Armenia. Like Edwards's characterization of Armenian Cilicia, Garsoïan, Robert W. Thomson, and Anne Elizabeth Redgate have each branded the broader social landscape of medieval Greater Armenia as largely nonurban (Garsoïan 1984:75; Thomson 1982:148), even at the economic height of the Bagratid dynasty (Redgate 1998:209). Instead, the archetypal settlement unit in medieval Armenia was fortified and agriculturally based villages with strong intergenerational familial ties, in the form of princely houses (*nakharars*) that were linked to the quasi-feudal social undercurrents of medieval Armenian society. Franklin et al.'s examination of the late medieval Armenian village challenges earlier perceptions of the rural village as contracted or remote landscapes; rather, their work underscores that the medieval village of the South Caucasus served as interconnected loci of vibrant social, political, and economic activity (Franklin et al. 2017). Christina Maranci has similarly characterized the built environment of Armenian Cilicia as "a landscape not of cities but of strongholds" (Maranci 2018:93). Acknowledging the centrality and social vibrancy of the village unit in the Western medieval

Armenian tradition, it should be no surprise that—despite the physical remnants of Byzantium's early presence in the region—the traditional highland settlement networks comprised of rural villages and family estates associated with fortified strongholds and agricultural pursuits prevailed and was preserved for generations by the resettled Armenians of Cilicia.

Settlement Location. To date, limited field research has been conducted on the medieval Armenian settlements of Cilicia, leaving a great need for deeper analysis. However, a survey conducted by Edwards at nine Armenian settlements associated with major fortifications in Cilicia (cf. Edwards 1993) reveals that not only was Armenian Cilicia emulating medieval Greater Armenia in settlement organization and structure, but locational preference for these villages also appears to follow a historical model that traces back to their pre-migratory past. Cilicia was a center of considerable commercial activity from antiquity until its decline in the seventh century (Eger 2015:170; Blanton 2000). However, Edwards notes that during the period of Armenian occupation, former classical cities, such as Seleucia, Adana, and Tarsus, appear in sources only as geographic markers or military posts, rather than as sites of significant residential or commercial activity. Edwards remarks that there is an absence of archaeological evidence to support large-scale occupation during the period of Armenian rule at these sites. However, it must be noted that few excavations have taken place in the region that have included later medieval materials (Edwards 1993:183). Instead of inhabiting what most would consider to be the "prime real estate" of Cilicia, at present it appears that the Armenians built the foundations of their new kingdom in more secluded, elevated locations within the interior of Level Cilicia and amid the difficult karst highland terrain of Rough Cilicia (Edwards 1993:183; Pringle 1995:177). Consequently, these preferred locales evoke the rugged orogenic topography of Western Armenia to which they were accustomed. Furthermore, eight of the nine Cilician settlements studied by Edwards overlook a major river (Edwards 1993:185), producing familiar viewsheds to the former Bagratid capitals of Bagaran, Shirakavan, Kars, and Ani which lined the Akhurian and Kars Rivers.

Settlement Formation. The abundance of fortresses, castles, and defensive walls in Armenian Cilicia, and their placement in securable highland areas (Edwards 1993:185), is often explained as merely a response to the regional turbulence of the Crusades and subsequent invasions (Pringle 1995:177). However, settlements formed in connection to strategic fortifications are in no way exceptional within the Western medieval Armenian tradition, whose existence was frequently plagued by threats from powerful neighbors. As such, larger settlement centers in early medieval Armenia were most often positioned at the base of an earlier fortress or acropolis (Garsoïan 1986:72). This practice carried through to the Bagratid period, with all of the former Bagratid capitals following a similar structural evolution. Bagaran, often described as a royal fortress, became the first Bagratid capital in 885 (Sinclair 1989:18, 440). In 890, the capital was moved to nearby Shirakavan which is seated at the foot of the Tignis fortress. In 929 the capital was relocated briefly to Kars, which is more commonly described as a key fortified stronghold and treasury than a residential or economic center (Garsoïan 1986:77; Sinclair 1989:440). Finally, in 961, Ani was appointed as the capital. Considered the most prolific of the Bagratid capitals due to its role as a major trading point, Ani also grew out from a citadel and garrison that had been built due to its strategic position overlooking the Akhurian River (Sinclair 1989:18; Garsoïan 1986:78–79). When comparing the positioning and evolution of these Bagratid settlements to the formation of two key Rubenid royal centers and former capitals in Cilicia, Sis, and Anavarsa, a similar course of development is revealed. Both Sis and Anavarsa were initially occupied for their use as critical fortified defensive points that later produced nearby settlements (Edwards 1993). Similarly, all nine of the settlements chronicled in the Edwards survey were discovered due to their being within one kilometer of a major fortification (Edwards 1993:185, 188).

Constructing the social landscape in a way that retains both visual and structural familiarity functions as a mnemonic aid for the lost homeland and reinforces social memories of the past, building a sense of belonging and place attachment to the new landscape. Elizabeth Colson noted that forced migration not only disrupts geographic familiarity but also upsets migrants' social constructions, internal hierarchical patterns, and the distributions of power that have culturally defined them. Displaced groups must, therefore, adapt and compensate internally for the loss of role structure and sense of identity—which can take generations to restore—through the process of their resettlement (Colson 2003:8–10). The physical likeness between the two above landscapes, both natural and constructed, facilitated the performance of traditional lifeways and the reinstatement of internal societal structures central to their sense of cultural identity, including a reinvention of the traditional *nakharar* system with the addition of new titles influenced by Western nobility.

Imagined Histories and the Role of Myth

Place attachment is an integral part of human identity. The term *place attachment* characterizes the reciprocal relationship humans develop with their natural environment through social interaction with and within a specific place over time (Altman and Low 1992; Seamon 2013:19; Lewicka 2011:676; Cooper Marcus 1992:87–88). Removal from a perceived homeland, however, does not remove the deeply ingrained sense of attachment to that place, and shared memories play a critical role in sustaining a sense of place attachment and longing for generations (Lewicka 2013:51). Anthropological studies show that emotional connection to a landscape, and the place-based identity that stems from this attachment, can be intergenerational even in instances where a group is no longer able to interact with that place (Colson 2003). For instance, Colson notes that the Gwembe Tonga still identified themselves as "people of the river," despite their dislocation from this spatial milieu 40 years previous, leading her to ultimately conclude that "resettlement does not wipe out memory, but rather provides a medium through which it is reworked" (Colson 2003:9).

Imagined histories are one of the inventive and selective ways in which a group collectively remembers their past. These imagined pasts often manifest as ancestry or origin myths, reimaginings of historic events, or as romanticized versions of life in a former place or time. The invention of these alternative pasts performs as an explanatory coping mechanism (Pistrick 2015:157) and can assist migrant groups with maintaining a sense of continuity with their former lives through the social disruption of displacement (Dudley 2010:159). These reworkings of historical memory become engrained within a group's new shared history and serve to build a sense of social and cultural legitimacy following the social disarticulation of forced relocation. The formation of imagined pasts is not unique to refugee communities; numerous historical examples of adopting fictionalized genealogies and ancestral legends exist across spatial and temporal bounds. Often these myths assert relationships to the divine or heroic as means of earning social currency. Anthropological studies have shown that the reinvention of ancestry or origin myths and historic events within communities that have been forcibly resettled is exceptionally commonplace (Malkki 1995; Colson 2003:9). Colson dubbed this phenomenon the "role of myth as validation," and—in regard to the creation of new shared histories and founding myths—stated that resettled communities are "seed beds most conducive to the growth of memory and the pursuit of myth" (Colson 2003:9).

Although Colson worked with contemporary refugee groups, we can extrapolate that the trauma of forced movement would elicit similar social responses within the archaeological past. Idealized histories provide a window into how cultural identity and historical legitimacy were resiliently refashioned following the distress of dislocation. These newly introduced ancestral myths and expressions of restorative nostalgia are difficult to reconstruct from the archaeological record alone. However, evidence of selectively romanticizing the past through the revival of old architectural forms and motifs can, when studied in conjunction with historical texts in cases where imagined histories have been chronicled, be used to infer how such stories and myths were manipulated to drive narratives of historical/social legitimacy and demonstrate continuity with the past. An example of this can be found within chronicles detailing the Rubenid dynasty's ascent to power in Cilicia. By the early thirteenth century, the Chronicler Vahram of Edessa introduces the Rubenids' assertion that they were blood heirs of the beloved former rulers in Greater Armenia, the Bagratids (Vahram d'Édesse, Chronique:497, ll. 161–68). Historians today agree this is an unlikely story (Adontz 1970:431; Garsoïan 1998:123). Instead, this declaration has long been considered an ancestry myth used to acquire political status and trust as figures of authority. Nonetheless, this declaration quickly became engrained into the collective memory of Armenian Cilicia, as featured within both literary models and artistic traditions from the period (Der Nersessian 1993:29; Bozoyan 2008:72).

Further archaeological survey of Armenian Cilicia is still necessary in order to initiate a holistic comparative study of the monumental architecture of Rubenid Armenia and Bagratid Armenia—only then will it be possible to fully see the imprint that this imagined history left on the built environment of Cilicia. Still, both Edwards and Maranci have noted that the Rubenids appropriated earlier models of construction and design aesthetics, such as the inclusion of exterior niches, from the Greater Armenian tradition at the royally commissioned church of T'oros at Anavarsa (Figure 12.1) (Edwards 1993:185; Edwards 1982:161; Maranci 2018:96). It is my expectation that a comprehensive comparison between the two built landscapes will demonstrate further architectural examples of the Rubenids adopting a romanticized version of the Bagratid past, linking the grand legacy and security of what was considered the "golden days of medieval Armenia" with their new and uncertain future in Cilicia. Monumental architecture must be viewed as vessels of identity and ideological expression. The visual and tangible relationship to the historic past being built within the mountains and plains of Rough Cilicia would have strengthened the Rubenid Armenian's sense of identity, validity, and authority as the heirs to a new Armenian Kingdom constructed out of the dramatic loss inflicted by their displacement.

Figure 12.1. Church of T'oros at Anavarza, taken c. 1905 (Gertrude Bell Archive, Newcastle University, Image: C-198).

Conclusions

The trauma of mass displacement ruptures a group's sense of belonging, legitimacy, and identity, forever altering how they view themselves and their history (Smith et al. 2008:18, 23). The built landscape serves as a medium of identity and ideological expression; thereby, changes made to the landscape are reflective of both the way in which its modifiers perceive themselves and how they wish to be perceived by others. How displaced groups rebuild their sense of legitimacy and identity through the physical processes of resettlement can aid archaeologists in reconstructing migrant memories, experiences, and the affective narratives of trauma and resilience that often go untold in our interpretations of the past. This chapter followed the relocation of the Armenians from the former Bagratid Kingdom to Cilicia as they sought to reestablish their social positions, identities, and sense of place. The example of medieval Armenian Cilicia showcases how landscapes of resettlement are repositories for the myths and shared memories that are integral to identity management and rebuilding senses of belonging and place attachment. A comprehensive comparison of the architectural landscapes of origin and subsequent resettlement remains to be done. However, it is the hope of the author that furthering this study will assist in reviving some of the multigenerational narratives of displacement and resettlement of the Armenians in medieval Cilicia that have been overlooked. Nevertheless, by conducting a broad evaluation of the structural and locational preferences of the resettled Armenians, framed within the historical context of their ancestral home and shared experience of dislocation, this chapter has aimed to demonstrate why social anthropological inquiry is critical to archaeology's understanding of the social and environmental impacts of forced resettlement.

The archaeology of conflict-induced migration did not undergo the postmodernist transition of the 1970s that led the field of social anthropology to expand into phenomenological and affective inquiries of the mind, memory, and experience of resettled refugees. Instead, with few exceptions from contemporary archaeology, archaeological explorations of forced migration have remained relatively processual in their approach, frequently focusing efforts on tracking and identifying examples of forced movement in the material record. Contemporary anthropological participant and ethnographically based studies have provided needed insight into human responses toward the loss of cultural identity, social legitimacy, and place attachment. The importance of anthropology's contributions to refugee studies needs recognition within archaeological scholarship and must inspire a shift toward a social archaeology of forced migration that aims to give voice to the motivations of displaced populations within our historic past as they rebuilt the material world around them.

Acknowledgments

I wish to acknowledge the time given and the valuable conversations had with Mark Jackson, Sam Turner, Ross Jamieson, Sabrina Higgins, Christina Maranci, Dimitris Krallis, and Anne Elizabeth Redgate concerning this research in its various forms, the Gertrude Bell Archive at Newcastle University, as well as the Stavros Niarchos Foundation Centre for Hellenic Studies at Simon Fraser University for their support. I also wish to extend my appreciation to IEMA, particularly Megan Daniels, for the invitation to contribute to this collection and for her thoughtful comments on this chapter.

References Cited

Abramiuk, M. A. 2012 *The Foundations of Cognitive Archaeology*. The MIT Press, Cambridge.
Adontz, N. 1970 *Armenia in the Period of Justinian: The Political Conditions Based on the Naxarar System*. Peeters, Leuven.
Altman, I., and S. Low (editors) 1992 *Place Attachment*. Plenum, New York.
Anthony, D. 1990 Migration in Archaeology: The Baby and the Bathwater. *American Anthropologist* 92(4):895–914.
Armstrong, H. 2004 Making the Unfamiliar Familiar: Research Journeys Towards Understanding Migration and Place. *Landscape Research* 29(3):237–260.
Ahrweiler, H., and A. Laiou (editors) 1998 *Studies on the Internal Diaspora of the Byzantine Empire*. Harvard University Press, Cambridge.
Bender, B. 2001 Landscapes on-the-Move. *Journal of Social Archaeology* 1(1):75–89.
Blanton, R. 2000 *Hellenistic, Roman, and Byzantine Settlement Patterns of the Coast Lands of Western Rough Cilicia*. Archeopress, Oxford.

Branton, N. 2009 Landscape Approaches in Historical Archaeology: The Archaeology of Places. In *International Handbook of Historical Archaeology*, edited by T. Majewski and D. Gaimster, pp. 51–65. Springer, New York.

Boase, T. S. R. 1978 *The Cilician Kingdom of Armenia*. Scottish Academic Press, Edinburgh.

Bozoyan, A. A. 2008 Armenian Political Revival in Cilicia. In *Armenian Cilicia*, edited by R. G. Hovannisian and S. Payaslian. Mazda, California.

Burke, A. A. 2011 An Anthropological Model for the Investigation of the Archaeology of Refugees in Iron Age Juda and its Environs. In *Interpreting Exile: Displacement and Deportation in Biblical and Modern Contexts*, edited by B. E. Kelle, F. R. Ames, and J. L. Wright, pp. 41–56. Society of Biblical Literature, Houston.

Burke, A. A. 2018a The Decline of Egyptian Empire, Refugees, and Social Change in the Southern Levant, ca. 1200–1000 BCE 229. In *An Archaeology of Forced Migration Crisis-induced Mobility and the Collapse of the 13th c. BCE Eastern Mediterranean*, edited by J. Driessen, pp. 229–261 AEGIS Presses Universitaires de Louvain, Louvain-la-Neuve.

Burke, A. A. 2018b Refugees in the Near East and Mediterranean, Archaeology of. In *Encyclopedia of Global Archaeology*, edited by C. Smith, pp. 1–6. Springer, New York

Burmeister, S. 2000 Archaeology and Migration. *Current Anthropology* 41(4):539–567.

Cabana, G. 2011 The Problematic Relationship Between Migration and Culture Change. In *Rethinking Anthropological Perspectives on Migration*, edited by G. Cabana and J. Clark, pp. 16–27. University Press of Florida, Gainesville.

Charanis, P. 1961 The Transfer of Population as Policy in the Byzantine Empire. *Comparative Studies in Society and History* 3(2):140–154.

Charanis, P. 1963 *Armenians in the Byzantine Empire*. Fundação Calouste Gulbenkian, Lisbon.

Chatty, D. 2010 *Dispossession and Displacement in the Modern Middle East*. Cambridge University Press, Cambridge.

Chatty, D. 2014 Anthropology and Forced Migration. In *The Oxford Handbook of Refugee and Forced Migration Studies*, edited by E. Fiddian-Qasmiyeh, G. Loescher, K. Long, and N. Sigona, pp. 74–84. Oxford University Press, Oxford.

Colson, E. 1999 Gendering Those Uprooted by "Development." In *Engendering Forced Migration: Theory and Practice*, edited by D. M. Indra, pp. 23–39. Berghahn, Oxford.

Colson, E. 1943 Assessing Public Opinion in a Dislocated Community. *Public Opinion Quarterly* 7(4):652–668.

Colson, E. 2003 Forced Migration and the Anthropological Response. *Journal of Refugee Studies* 16(1):1–18.

Cooper Marcus, C. 1992 Environmental Memories. In *Place Attachment*, edited by I. Altman and S. M. Low, pp. 87–112. Plenum, New York.

Darvill, T. 1998 The Historic Environment, Historic Landscapes and Space-Time-Action Models in Landscape Archaeology. In *Archaeology and Anthropology of Landscape: Shaping Your Landscape*, edited by R. Layton and P. Ucko, pp. 106–120. Routledge, London.

Davies, R. 2010 *Palestinian Village Histories: Geographies of the Displaced*. Stanford University Press, Stanford.

De León, J. 2013 Undocumented Migration, Use Wear, and Materiality of Habitual Suffering in the Sonoran Desert. *Journal of Material Culture* 18:321–345.

De León, J. *The Land of Open Graves: Living and Dying on the Migrant Trail*. University of California Press, Berkeley.

Der Nersessian, S. 1962 The Kingdom of Cilician Armenia. In *A History of the Crusades*, Vol. II, edited by K. M. Setton, pp. 630–660. University of Pennsylvania Press, Philadelphia.

Der Nersessian, S., and S. Agémian 1993 *Miniature Painting in the Armenian Kingdom of Cilicia from the Twelfth to the Fourteenth Century*, Vol. 1. Dumbarton Oaks, Washington.

Driessen, J. 2018 An Archaeology of Forced Migration—Introduction. In *An Archaeology of Forced Migration Crisis-induced Mobility and the Collapse of the 13th c. BCE Eastern Mediterranean*, edited by J. Driessen, pp. 19–25, AEGIS Presses Universitaires de Louvain, Louvain-la-Neuve.

Dudley, S. H. 2010 *Materialising Exile: Material Culture and Embodied Experience among Karenni Refugees in Thailand*. Berghahn Books, New York.

Edwards, R. W. 1982 Ecclesiastical Architecture in the Fortifications of Armenian Cilicia. *Dumbarton Oaks Papers* 36:155–176.

Edwards, R. W. 1993 Settlement and Toponymy in Armenian Cilicia. *REarm* 24:181–249.

Eger, A. 2015 *The Islamic-Byzantine Frontier: Interaction and Exchange among Muslim and Christian Communities*. IB Tauris, London.

Franklin, K., T. Vorderstrasse, and F. Babayan 2017 Examining the Late Medieval Village from the Case at Ambroyi, Armenia. *Journal of Near Eastern Studies* 76(1):113–138.

Garsoïan, N. 1984 The Early Medieval City: An Alien Element? *Journal of the Ancient Near Eastern Society* 16(1):67–83.

Garsoïan, N. 1998 The Problem of Armenian Integration into the Byzantine Empire. In *Studies on the Internal Diaspora of the Byzantine Empire*, edited by H. Ahrweiler, and A. Laiou. Harvard University Press, Cambridge.

Ghazarian, J. G. 2000 *The Armenian Kingdom in Cilicia During the Crusades: The Integration of Cilician Armenians with the Latins 1080–1393*. Curzon Press, Richmond.

Göçek, F. M. 1995 Population Transfers in Mediterranean History: The Ottoman Empire in the Fourteenth–Seventeenth Centuries, http://www-personal.umich.edu/~gocek/Work/ja/Gocek.Muge.ja.population.transfers.pdf, accessed November 2020.

Gori, M., and M. Ravello Lami 2018 From Lampedusa to Trieste: An Archaeological Approach to Contemporary Forced Migrations and Identity Patterns. In *An Archaeology of Forced Migration Crisis-induced Mobility and the Collapse of the 13th c. BCE Eastern Mediterranean*, edited by J. Driessen, pp. 31–55, AEGIS Presses Universitaires de Louvain, Louvain-la-Neuve.

Gupta, A., and J. Ferguson. 1992 Beyond "Culture": Space, Identity, and the Politics of Difference. *Cultural Anthropology* 7:6–23.

Hackenbeck, S. 2008 Migration in Archaeology: Are We Nearly There Yet? *Archaeological Review from Cambridge* 23(2):9–26.

Hansen, A. *Mission of the IASFM*. International Association for the Study of Forced Migration. Electronic document, http://www.efms.uni-bamberg.de/iasfm/mission.htm, accessed July 20, 2019.

Hirschon, R. 1998 *Heirs of the Greek Catastrophe: The Social Life of Asia Minor Refugees in Piraeus*. Berghahn, Oxford.

Hamilakis, Y. 2016 Archaeologies of Forced and Undocumented Migration. *Journal of Contemporary Archaeology* 3(2):121–139.

Hamilakis, Y. (editor) 2018 *The New Nomadic Age: Archaeologies of Forced and Undocumented Migration*. Equinox Publishing, Sheffield.

Legendre, J. 2018 Vestiges of the Spanish Republican Exodus to France: An Archaeological Study of the Retirada. In *An Archaeology of Forced Migration Crisis-induced Mobility and the Collapse of the 13th c. BCE Eastern Mediterranean, edited by J. Driessen, pp. 55–75, AEGIS Presses Universitaires de Louvain, Louvain-la-Neuve.

Lewicka, M. 2011 On the Varieties of People's Relationships with Places: Hummon's Typology Revisited. *Environment and Behaviour* 43(5):676–709.

Lewicka, M. 2013 In Search of Roots: Memory as Enabler of Place Attachment. In *Place Attachment: Advances in Theory, Methods, and Applications*, edited by L. Manzo, and P. Devine-Wright. Routledge, New York.

Loizios, P. 1981 *The Heart Grown Bitter: A Chronicle of Cypriot War Refugees*. Cambridge University Press, Cambridge.

Malkki, L. H. 1992 National Geographic: The Rooting of Peoples and the Territorialization of National Identity among Scholars and Refugees. *Cultural Anthropology* 7(1):24–44.

Malkki, L. H. 1995 *Purity and Exile: Violence, Memory, and National Cosmology among Hutu Refugees in Tanzania*. University of Chicago Press, Chicago.

Maranci, C. 2018 *The Art of Armenia: An Introduction*. Oxford: Oxford University Press.

Martin, S. 2018 Forced Migration after Natural Disasters, The Late Bronze Age Eruption of Thera. In *An Archaeology of Forced Migration Crisis-induced Mobility and the Collapse of the 13th c. BCE Eastern Mediterranean*, edited by J. Driessen, pp. 107–177. AEGIS Presses Universitaires de Louvain, Louvain-la-Neuve.

Oliver-Smith, A., and A. Hansen 1982 *Involuntary Migration and Resettlement: The Problems and Responses of Dislocated People*. Westview Special Studies, Boulder.

Pistrick, E. 2015 *Performing Nostalgia: Migration Culture and Creativity in South Albania*. Routledge, New York.

Pistrick, E., and F. Bachmeier 2016 Empty Migrant Rooms: An Anthropology of Absence through the Camera Lens. *Journal of Contemporary Archaeology* 3(2):205–215.

Philipp, A., and E. Ho 2010 Migration, Home, and Belonging: South African Migrant Women in Hamilton, New Zealand. *New Zealand Population Review* 36:81–101.

Pringle, D. 1995 Architecture in the Latin East 1098–1571. In *The Oxford Illustrated History of the Crusades*, edited by J. Simon and C. Riley-Smith. Oxford University Press, Oxford.

Redgate, A. E. 1998 *The Armenians*. Wiley-Blackwell, Oxford.

Rishbeth C., and M. Powell 2013 Place Attachment and Memory: Landscapes of Belonging as Experienced Post-Migration. *Landscape Research* 38(2):160–178.

Rubertone, P. E. 1989 Landscape as Artifact: Comments on the Archaeological Use of Landscape Treatment in Social, Economic, and Ideological Analysis. *Society for Historical Archaeology* 23(1):50–54.

Seamon, D. 2013 Place Attachment and Phenomenology: The Synergistic Dynamism of Place. In *Place Attachment: Advances in Theory, Methods, and Applications*, edited by L. Manzo, and P. Devine-Wright, pp. 11–22. Routledge, New York.

Sinclair, T. A. 1987 *Eastern Turkey: An Architectural and Archaeological Survey*, Vol. I. Pindar Press, London.

Stobbelaar, D. J., and P. Bas 2011 Perspectives on Landscape Identity: A Conceptual Challenge. *Landscape Research* 36(3):321–339.

Stouraitis, Y. 2016 Byzantium and Migration: An Introduction. Keynote address Presented at Mobility and Migration in Byzantium: Sources and Concepts, Vienna Austria. Electronic document, https://www.academia.edu/28964265/_Byzantium_and_Migration_an_introduction_keynote_speech_at_the_International_Conference_Mobility_and_Migration_in_Byzantium_Sources_and_Concepts_Vienna_June_17_2016, accessed July 24 2018.

Thomson, R. W. 1982 The Formation of the Armenian Literary Tradition. In *East of Byzantium: Syria and Armenia in the Formative Period*, edited by N. Garsoïan, T. Mathews, and R. W. Thomson. Dumbarton Oaks, Washington, District of Columbia.

Turner, S. 2006 Historic Landscape Characterisation: Landscape Archaeology for Research, Management, and Planning. *Landscape Research* 31:385–398.

Vahram d'Édesse 1869 Chronique rimée des rois de Petite Arménie, Recueil des historiens des Croisades. *Documents arméniens*, Vol. I, pp. 491–537. Paris, imprimerie impériale.

van Dommelen, P. 2014 Moving On: Archaeological Perspectives on Mobility and Migration. *World Archaeology* 46(4):477–483.

Weyl Carr, A. 1993 Introduction. In *Miniature Painting in the Armenian Kingdom of Cilicia from the Twelfth to the Fourteenth Century*, Vol. I, edited by S. Der Nersessian. Dumbarton Oaks, Washington, District of Columbia.

Yasur-Landau, A. 2018 Towards an Archaeology of Forced Movement of the Deep Past. In *An Archaeology of Forced Migration Crisis-induced Mobility and the Collapse of the 13th c. BCE Eastern Mediterranean*, edited by J. Driessen, pp. 177–187. AEGIS Presses Universitaires de Louvain, Louvain-la-Neuve.

Chapter Thirteen

Macro- and Micro-Mobilities and the Creation of Identity in the Ancient Near East

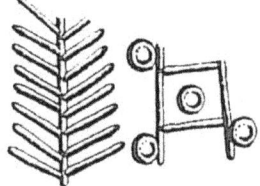

Anne Porter

Abstract *Macro- and micro-mobilities have always been a feature of existence in the Near East. A survey of archaeological and historical evidence of such mobilities shows that it is not movement itself, nor biological ancestry that is the critical factor in shaping history and culture, but the creation of, and ascription to, identities to which the dynamic intersection of diverse populations gives rise.*

Although deeply entrenched in Western cultural knowledge as the place where sedentism and its civilizational consequences such as labor specialization, class, writing, urbanism, and the state were first established, mobility was a continuous dynamic in shaping culture, society, politics, and especially the course of history in the ancient Near East. Whether in pursuit of pasture, as victims of conflict, fleeing ecological disaster, or in the service of private or palatial trade, there is no time period in this region in which humans, individually, or as groups of varying sizes, have not moved beyond the confines of their original locale to engage with the world beyond. Macro- and micro-mobilities have been as much a critical dynamic in the transformations that emerged from this region as its environmental affordances.

The terms "macro" and "micro" migrations may be understood in a variety of ways. They may refer to length of movement, frequency of movement, intensity of movement, or scale of the groups that move. In this paper, I denote scale by these terms, contrasting the outcomes of movements of individuals with those of larger population groups, albeit of varying and unspecified size. The usefulness of these labels lies primarily in the contrasts they denote, serving especially to draw our attention to the historical as well as personal significance of isolated migrations that are only now becoming identifiable in the archaeological record. But although isotopic maps are available for several parts of the world, they are not yet possible for much of Mesopotamia.

These terms also allow us to consider potential commonalities in the social and political outcomes of migration of all kinds. Categorizations based on length or frequency of movement highlight distinctions in ways of life and economic concerns rather than confront an issue central to migrants of any category: identity construction. The scope of this paper does not allow for the detailed survey of macro- and micro-mobilities that the rich archaeological and textual documentation to be found in the Near East warrants. But I propose that if such a survey were to be undertaken, among the salient features that would emerge is the critical role of identity. For mobility is not in and of itself a determinative. That is, there can be no expected outcome to a certain kind of movement—no one model of how refugees or mobile pastoralists behave. The factors involved in the choices people make, and the material manifestations of those choices, on relocation to a new place, temporarily, repetitively, or permanently, are, if not infinitely variable, certainly close to it. A comparison of even a few examples, as follows, shows that mobile groups in similar circumstances might manifest very differently in terms of material culture, whereas groups in different circumstances might manifest similarly. On the other hand, certain commonalities do seem to emerge in terms of the creation of, and ascription to, identity that arises from the volatile intersection of different social, political, and not only ethnic, entities. Such identities may, or may not, be based in biological ancestry.

Micro-Mobilities

Macro-mobilities are a well-known, if not well understood, component of the archaeological and historical record. Large-scale nomadic movements, invasions and conquests, forced migrations, and diasporas have all been given some degree of theoretical and empirical attention. But the significance of micro-mobilities should not be overlooked. While on the one hand micro-mobilities might be understood simply as small-scale or short-term movements rather than long distance ones, there are, in addition to examples of "wholesale" movements, the migrations of individuals or small groups that constitute a constant ebb and flow of people across the Near East. While many such movements are occasioned by professions requiring mobility, such as state representatives and messengers, many other micro-mobilities are recognizable largely because of claims and attributions of identity that arise when strangers appear, or conflict arises. No doubt the further development of isotope analyses for the Near East will remedy this in the future, but at the moment our awareness of such micro-movements comes primarily from textual and linguistic evidence. Therefore, we know more about such movements in Mesopotamia than in other parts of the Near East. Mesopotamians were often careful to note someone's place of origin, accurately or not, and certainly did not hesitate to use ethnicity in their various battles for political supremacy. One of the most common identifiers of difference in this regard is the Sumerian term MARDU, Akkadian *Amurru*, English Amorrite. Exactly what MARDU means—whether it is an ethnicity or profession, a direction, a polity, or place, or all of the above—is as yet unresolved (Kamp and Yoffee 1980; Whiting 1995; Buccellati 2008; Michalowski 2011; Porter 2012; Burke 2017). It is attributed to an entire population, and to individuals performing tasks within the Mesopotamian administrative system long before there is evidence of any such definable population. It accompanies people registered as coming from outside Mesopotamia in some way, including those whose names indicate ethnic origins distinct from their Amorriteness. At a certain point in history it is claimed by some. And perhaps denied by others.

The very notion of a population to be identified as MARDU was largely a creation of the Third Dynasty of Ur in the late third millennium, who often used the label in creation of an "other" whose defining attribute was some kind of mobility. Calling its political rivals "monkeys" and "an abomination" as in *The Marriage of Martu* (ECTSL c.1.7.1: 126–141) did little in the end, though, to exclude MARDU from the centers of power. One of those MARDU who may have contributed to, but certainly benefited from, the downfall of the Third Dynasty of Ur, was a man named Naplanum, the head of the Emutbal mobile pastoralist group (Figure 13.1). From lists of the chancellery's expenditures we can

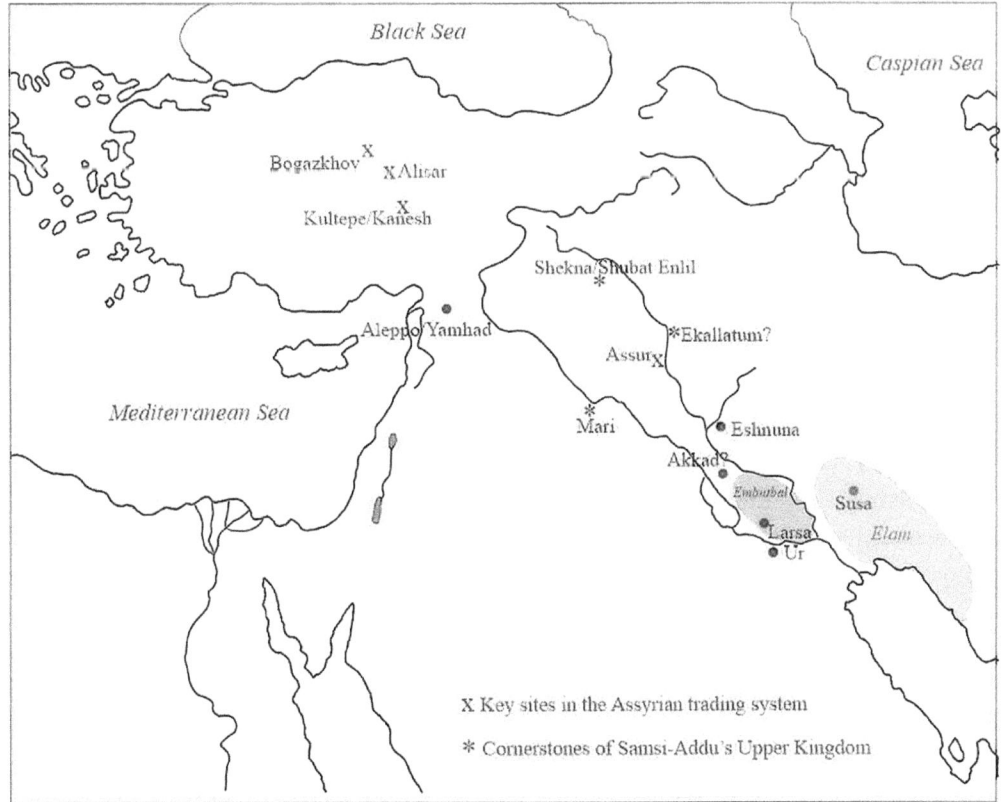

FIGURE 13.1. Map of the Near East showing key sites of the Upper Kingdom of Samsi-Addu and the Assyrian trading system, with the location of Elam and Emutbal territories.

trace Naplanum's close connections to the Third Dynasty of Ur and his movements from various pasturages to his residence in the town of Kisig (Steinkeller 2004). The implications of this data are that as his identity—nomad or not, inside the system or not—is difficult for modern scholars to reconcile, so it was irreducible to a single dimension in the past. Indeed, it was his very social as well as physical mobility that allowed him to traverse the different sectors of the society he came to control, and integrated its various components into the power base that allowed him to found the dynasty at Larsa, thus heralding the beginning of the political supremacy of Amorrites.

We have no documents that tell us what Naplanum called himself, but a couple of generations later, kings of Larsa started using the term MARDU of themselves (Porter 2012:315). Warad-Sin referred to his father, Kudur-mabuk (who was never in fact king of Larsa but rather leader of the Emutbal), as "father of the Amorrites" (Seri 2005:67) and yet not only is Kudur-mabuk's name Elamite in origin, he calls himself the son of the Elamite Simti-shilhak (Frayne 1990). Elam is the kingdom in the Zagros Mountains adjacent to Mesopotamia, and characters such as Kudur-mabuk, as well as multiple cultural influences, show that there was fairly constant contact across these regions for millennia.

But this duality too has long been a problem for modern scholarship—was Kudur-mabuk an Amorrite or was he an Elamite? Does an Elamite name mean that MARDU does not designate an ethnicity? Yet it need not be a matter of either/or. Such labels do not require a biological reality, for socially constructed membership of a group is well attested in the ancient Near East (and see Gokcumen, this volume, for a detailed discussion of this and related issues). Laying claim to multiple identities was also an established way of facilitating political legitimacy—something the Third Dynasty of Ur were themselves masters of with the creation of false historical relationships to the fictional character of Gilgamesh (Porter 2012:251–277). At the same time, that dual identity is very informative. It tells us of the physical, as well as sociopolitical, mobility of this figure and of the way ancestral groups could include people of diverse origins, as well as affirming an eastern presence for the Amorrite groups against whom the Third Dynasty of Ur railed.

Another case where the manipulation of a dual identity in the name of political aspiration has confused modern scholarship is that of Samsi-Addu. Samsi-Addu, in the Amorrite spelling of his name, or Shamshi-Addad in the Akkadian, invokes multiple mobilities. He was a member of a mobile pastoralist ancestral group, the Numha (Heimpel 2003:18), with whom he maintained close political ties. While not known to have spent time as a pastoralist, he certainly extolled the virtues of a rugged mobile life, at least to his indolent and pampered son, Yasmah-Addu. He was born and raised in the city of Ekallatum (Figure 13.1), which his father ruled, it seems (Charpin 2004:148; cf. Durand 1998:107), and he had vast imperialist ambitions. In the furtherance of these ambitions he moved around the region that was to become his domain. He transferred his seat from Ekallatum on the Tigris to the city of Shekna, in the Upper Habur, renaming it Shubat Enlil. One son was appointed in his place over Ekallatum, and the other was given the city of Mari, which Samsi-Addu had taken from a rival Amorrite family. Thus was born the Upper Kingdom, which, with the conquest of the city of Assur, was ultimately to become the Old Assyrian empire that gained much of its wealth from the trading enterprise that saw a regular traverse of the distance between Assur and Anatolia (Highcock 2018:Figure 1). And yet despite the many letters that raise Samsi-Addu's relationship to his Amorrite brethren, many scholars believe that this figure is really Akkadian in descent (Durand 1998:108) and therefore civilized, in contrast to the mobile Amorrites. But being sedentary does not negate an Amorrite ancestry, biological or otherwise.[1] And yet, an Akkadian identity *was* created, perpetuated by events such as a trip to Akkad (Charpin 2004) that has been interpreted as a kind of ancestral pilgrimage, and by the manipulation of practices of descent. For found in the throne room of the palace of Mari was a text of Samsi-Addu's commemorative mortuary ritual known as *kispu,* which presumably Samsi-Addu's son Yasmah-Addu performed for his father.[2] This ritual invokes the two great kings of Akkad, Sargon and Naram-Sin. Since the *kispu* is, among other things, an affirmation of descent,[3] their inclusion would seem to be a statement of a biological heritage. At the same time, both the genealogy of Samsi-Addu and that other great Amorrite king, Hammurabi, lay claim to a rootedness in mobility and association with various ancestral groups (Gelb 1954; Finkelstein 1966). In fact, the assertion of descent through mortuary ritual and the iteration of ancestors is a critical part of identity construction for Amorrites. But it is not just a hallmark of this period, nor of micro-mobilities. Nor is it only a matter of political expediency. The dead seem to be deployed as time-space distanciation—the stretching of social relations across time and space, as Anthony Giddens delineates (1981)—in multiple examples of macro-mobility.

Macro-Mobilities

The Uruk and Kura-Araxes Expansions

If micro-mobilities are registered through language one way or another, macro-mobilities are very often recognized by the distribution of distinctive kinds of material culture to which modern scholarship, if not ancient users, attribute a specific identity, often an ethnic one. Well known, albeit still mysterious, are the Uruk expansion of the fourth millennium B.C. (Figure 13.2), and the partially contemporaneous, but longer-lived, Kura-Araxes phenomenon (Figure 13.3).[4] The first is marked by the widespread distribution of a distinctive material cultural complex that included everything from architecture to imagery, but especially pots. It has long been understood as an essentially one-way movement of people and/or goods originating in the urban world of southern Mesopotamia. Traditional explanations have generally understood this movement as an economic, and fundamentally exploitative, enterprise (Algaze 1989).

The second is a far more extensive, but rather more amorphous, situation, based largely on the determination that a very particular kind of pottery, Kura-Araxes, or Red Black Burnished, Ware, originated in the southern Caucasus, subsequently to be found unevenly distributed across Syro-Anatolia, eventually to reach as far as the Southern Levant (Batiuk 2013). Despite the fact that various maps show the distribution of this phenomenon (such as Simonyan and Rothman 2015) as a unified field, in fact it is not. The chrono-

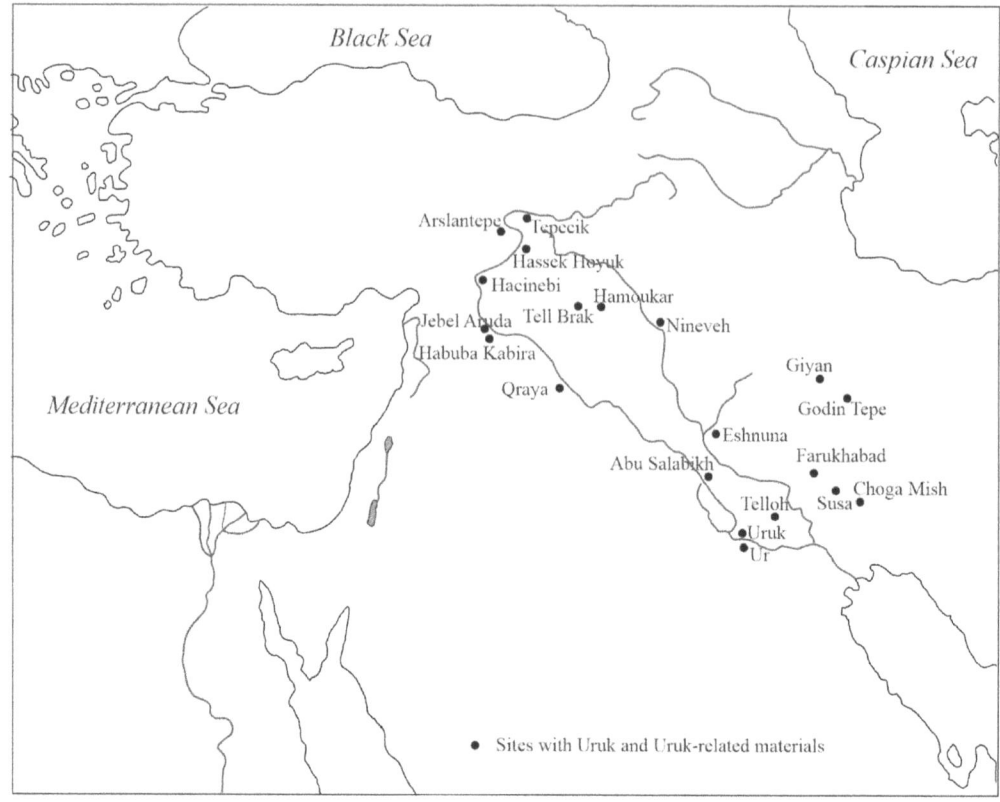

Figure 13.2. Map of the Near East showing core distribution of sites with Uruk and Uruk-related materials.

logical lag between its appearance in these different regions is thought by some to reflect the slow filtering of a population outward, perhaps emerging from the homeland in successive waves (Batiuk and Rothman 2007). Somehow, over this vast temporal and spatial distribution, this population maintained the integrity of its cultural, if not biological, identity. In contrast to the general understanding of the Uruk phenomenon (but see Porter 2012), the Kura-Araxes culture is not only nonurban, but closely associated with mobile pastoralism as its basic form of subsistence. Although the relationship is little explicated, the pastoralist regime also includes small settlements throughout the homelands and beyond (Sagona 2018:213–215).

In both these examples there are serious underlying theoretical as well as empirical problems. They are treated as if one explanation fits every situation, when it is far more likely multiple processes are occurring in different arenas, all at the same time, even if we cannot identify them. But understanding what simultaneous events and processes are shaping the distribution of Mesopotamian and Transcaucasian material cultures is first and foremost a question of chronology, and it should be noted that for the Kura-Araxes in particular this is highly problematic. Each discussion of the topic seems to use its own chronological

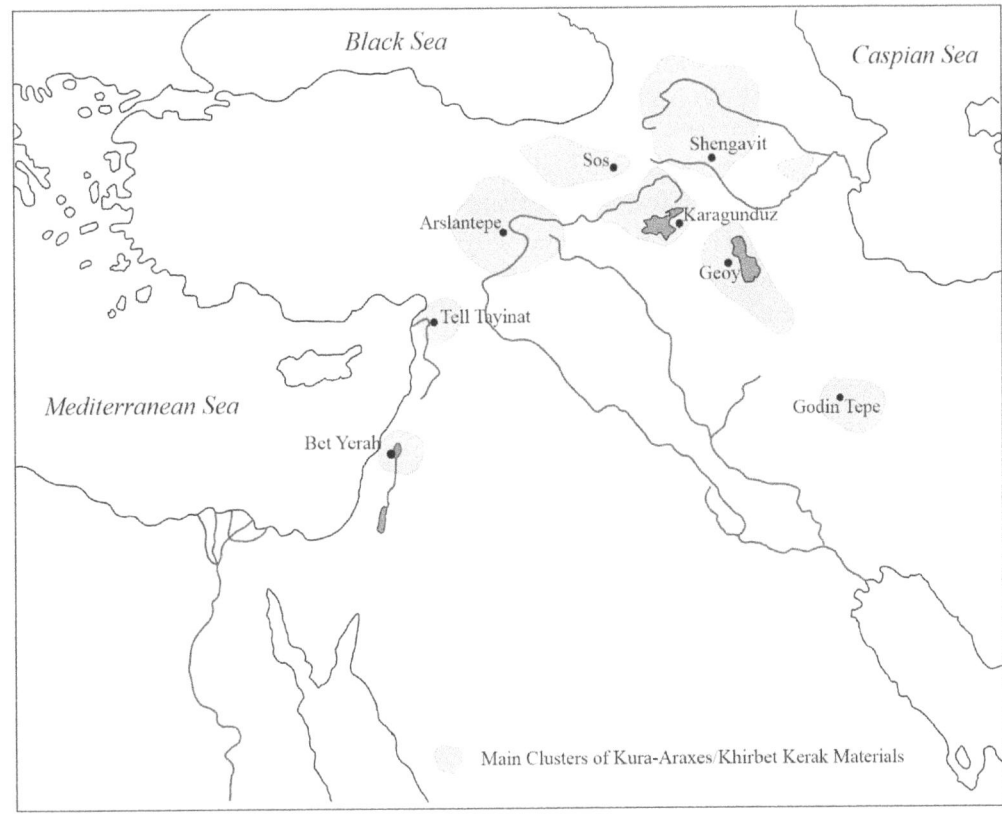

FIGURE 13.3. Map of the Near East showing main clusters of settlements with Kura-Araxes/Khirbet Kerak materials.

scheme.[5] Much interpretation of the processes of expansion is also based on assumption rather than careful interrogation of a mass of seemingly conflicting evidence. And both are often treated as if they are "pure" cultures with a single point of origin.

Given the extensive interaction already in the fifth millennium between north and south, south and east, that which we identify as "Uruk culture" is doubtless already a result of interculturality. Moreover, specific elements of the ceramic repertoire included within this assemblage are northern in origin. The degree to which the movement of Uruk material culture is tied to the movement of people is debatable. Because of course, not all movement is undertaken by humans. Raw materials and the objects created from them have been shown to travel vast distances, and it is also often the case that it is the idea of the object that moves rather than the object itself. While through neutron activation analysis of 385 clay and pottery samples Emberling and Minc (2016) undermine any suggestion that the broad distribution of southern-style materials is merely the result of long-distance trade, whether these archaeological patterns were the remains of wholesale or specialized intrusive populations, that is, colonists, refugees, or traders, or local elites who sought to share the prestige of the south through emulation (Stein 1999), is still contentious. Moreover, the conclusion that southern potters participated in the foundation of so-called colony sites begs as many questions as it answers. Why did some communities keep replicating the material attributes of another society hundreds of years after the initial emigration/emulation?

Because some remarkable archaeological facts still remain. A body of material culture is distributed across a vast expanse and remains remarkably unchanged over an extremely long period of time—some 500–700 years (Porter 2012). One of the reasons the duration of this period was difficult to detect before Wright and Rupley's (2001) reexamination of Late Chalcolithic radiocarbon dates was the fact that there was so little evidence of stylistic change in ceramic materials.

But rather than a simultaneous expansion across the four quarters of the Near East, there is a directional pattern to the temporal framework of this distribution that is reflective of changing geopolitical relationships between different regions, and that should, at least in theory, result in regionally distinct material interculturalities and third spaces. Both time and space provide ample opportunities for gradual but substantial dilution of the southern style. Compared to the much shorter lifespan of cultural assemblages in the adjacent fifth and third millennia, this persistent maintenance of a cultural tradition is itself instructive. It takes effort, especially since it has been demonstrated that northern and eastern settlements at this time were manifesting their own signs of an indigenous complexity (Frangipane 2018; Oates and Oates 2006). If emerging polities in their own right, with multiple interregional contacts in place that surely exert their own "push and pull" on material culture, why does southern style material culture look exactly the same, wherever and whenever we encounter it beyond the Mesopotamian realm, especially when the south itself shows material changes during this period?

One clue lies in the spatial distribution of these materials, as has always been acknowledged. Found primarily in new sites established in previously unoccupied areas (e.g., Habuba Kabira and Jebel Aruda), that is, those termed colony sites, or in defined spaces within established towns (enclaves) either contemporaneously with local occupation or after abandonment (e.g., Haçinebi and Hassek Höyük), the precise nature of the materials is also informative. On a very general level, there are two components: living spaces with associated tools and vessels; and specialized spaces and specialized vessels that speak to the performance of rituals through which identity is created and reproduced. Living spaces are arranged around specialized spaces in both the so-called colony and enclave sites, and in those cases where this has been studied, the large-scale manufacturing and processing of goods destined for consumption in those specialized spaces, such as bread and beer, is attested in the living spaces (van Driel 2002).

These specialized spaces themselves constitute two basic kinds of structure. There are those that stand apart and are highly elaborated, and those that replicate the domestic structures among which they are embedded. This last kind is only distinguishable from living spaces by the fixtures within them and the materials distributed around those fixtures. The distinction between the two kinds of specialized space may be characterized as housing town-based and kin-based religious practices. The first, as evidenced in Southern Mesopotamian materials, embodies the identity of the settlement, for each city belongs to a particular god. Participation in public religious structures transcends the social cleavages (in both senses of the word) of kin and class. The second embodies the quotidian identity of the family groups that constitute these communities and that are the fundamental reason for their existence. If the motivation for the Uruk expansion is economic, whatever the commodities at stake, then some means of maintaining the intrinsic connection between the home communities and their expatriates is essential for the long-term survival of the endeavor.

In my interpretation of the evidence (explicated in full in Porter 2012), the Uruk expansion represents the intersection of two kinds of movement: that of mobile pastoralists who provided wool for the burgeoning textile industry, with economic migrants, the latter moving to facilitate both the economic success of the former and their continued connection to the home community. At the heart of the settlements established by the economic migrants are ritual practices that create and maintain identity. These practices of identity construction have a dual outcome—an outcome I would argue is intended—that maintains both internal social cohesion and external difference and separation from the local communities in which immigrants find themselves. Archaeologically it is clear that those who used the material assemblage, defined as southern outside the south, kept themselves apart, either in whole fortified settlements, in walled enclaves within local settlements or by moving into abandoned local settlements. This is not to say that there was no interaction with local populations. On the contrary, there are plenty of both empirical data and theoretical constructs to demonstrate there was. For example, the presence of tools in local styles indicates some dependence on local agriculture, or at the very least, adoption of local methods of production. But it is in that very interaction that the potential threat to the system lies. If affective ties within communities might dissolve after only a couple of generations of separation (Lees and Bates 1974:191), if daily interactions and intermarriage with others dilute natal identities and give rise to third spaces, simply barricading oneself behind a wall will not prevent this.

We do not yet have any real understanding of the social effects of the Uruk expansion on the communities of origin, although the economic outcomes seem obvious. Most students of the Uruk expansion assume that it contributed vastly to the wealth and power of the south, even if we do not know exactly how. The general assumption is that there was a feedback relationship between the administrative ability of the state to organize, and probably to control, the expansion, which fed back exotic goods that allowed young institutions to visibly display and enhance their status, simultaneously providing the wealth to further expand their administrative capacity. That is, it is thought that some level of state formation must have been in place to generate the expansion, but that the expansion also furthered, if not caused, state formation. What most of this work does not address, however, is how that feedback relationship was maintained over space, and over time, be it 150 years or 700. It is certain that there was no coercive power, and little practical way southern entities could keep their far-flung members in check. It was the practices of identity, based in complex networks of social linkages, that sustained the connection between communities of origin and the communities of expansion. And as the domestic shrines suggest, it is likely that households and kin groups also participated—and benefited—as independent entities. The situational effect of mobility, then, on those who were mobile was to reify a social identity (expressed materially) that was itself changing at home. By "situational" I mean that it is not mobility per se that has this effect, but the purposes behind mobility, the way it was practiced, and the processes by which social cohesion was maintained.

Kura-Araxes culture was also the outcome of "multi-cultural contact" (Marro et al. 2015:157; Rothman 2015:9192). Although the subsistence practices of the home region of this culture were closely associated with pastoralism of some kind (Sagona and Zimansky 2009:190), the ultimate movement of interest here is largely argued to be emigration. While not all scholars concede that emigration, or emigration alone, is appropriate to explain the distribution of Kura-Araxes materials,[6] the consensus is that in some way, at some point, people from this region moved beyond their homeland. And when they did, just as in the Uruk phenomenon, they maintained a distinct material identity over a very long time—some thousand years and more (Batiuk and Rothman 2007:8).

An overemphasis on the urban versus rural origins, the agricultural versus pastoralist subsistence practices, and the hierarchical versus egalitarian social structure of the Uruk and Kura-Araxes phenomena respectively have obscured the fact that there are many informative parallels in their extended presences. We recognize both by a long-lived and highly distinct ceramic repertoire. Indeed, as with the Uruk, where in "the extreme longevity of Uruk forms ... what we see ... is not so much the absence of change, as it is concerted efforts *not* to change" (Porter 2012:121), the even greater longevity of Kura-Araxes material culture can be characterized as a "tenacious adherence to certain fundamental elements ... [in] a conscious attempt to preserve a common social identity" (Sagona 2018:215; see also Batiuk 2013:452).

As Algaze (1989) did for the Uruk, Batiuk (2013) has defined three patterns of distribution for the Kura-Araxes materials in external contexts: where the Kura-Araxes constitutes all, or definitively outnumbers, local materials; where there are more or less equal quantities of intrusive and local materials; and where there are only a few Kura-Araxes materials intermingled with the local assemblage. Both cultures are located in their diaspora in very different geographic situations to their homelands. The southern presence is now found in often empty areas not particularly productive for agriculture. Whether along the riverbanks or in the mountains, the one feature all sites with Uruk materials have in common is that they are in, or adjacent to, landscapes most conducive to pastoralism. The Kura-Araxes appears in good agricultural areas, which would suggest an abandonment of native practices of mobile pastoralism. As with Uruk settlements, whether on the outskirts of, or within, local settlements, the populations associated with Kura-Araxes materials seem to have kept themselves spatially, if not necessarily socially, separate from local communities (Batiuk 2013:452; Greenberg et al. 2014). And both deploy their own, very specific kinds of fireplace and ceramic vessels in what seem to be ritual contexts. The rather strict maintenance of associations between items; the presence of cups in one lobe of the hearth; and shared imagery on cooking pots and andirons, all elevate mundane items into a symbolic system of meaning.

And yet, unlike the Uruk, the Kura-Araxes expansion does result in regionally distinct material interculturalities and third spaces. It is this factor that has confounded attempts to explain the expansion as a single emigration. But Sagona and Sagona (2009), Simonyan and Rothman (2015), and Adam T. Smith (2015) all argue from varying perspectives that there is a religio-ritual artifact complex that defines, and unites, the communities that fit within the Kura-Araxes material culture in the northern arc of expansion at least. The most sophisticated of these arguments is Smith's, who understands the fixedness of the artifactual repertoire across time and space as the process of building a "civilization," a concept not too far from my own focus on practices of identity as time-space distanciation (Porter 2009, 2012). "Civilization" here is understood as "a machine that reproduces the terms of inclusion and exclusion" (Smith 2015:9–99), where "machine" is the material culture—specifically, objects—that creates the identity of the group, thereby making manifest boundaries between groups (Smith 2015:22). For Smith (2015:120), the distribution of animal figurines around the distinctive Kura-Araxes hearth unites the subsistence practices of the mobile members of the community with a core concept of the social unit as based in the immovable house, reproduced through domestic ritual. As I do for the Uruk expansion, Smith views this civilizing process within the Kura-Araxes as an outcome of social fragmentation initially wrought by pastoral mobility (Porter 2009).

This takes us to a very different place than that accepted by the majority of scholars of the Kura-Araxes, because it is not based on emigration, nor on the movement of a single ethnicity, but indeed, on the maintenance of a way of life, specifically in contrast—resistance for Smith—to the hierarchical and exploitative system emerging in southern Mesopotamia (Smith 2015). Thus, assemblage diversity is readily accommodated—not as a product of hybridity, but because different social entities, whether based in ethnicity, ancestral group, or some other definition, were all incorporated within this civilization because they shared a similar social structure and way of life.

Not surprisingly, I find Smith's arguments very convincing, for the northern rather than southern distribution of Kura-Araxes at least. But it does not quite explain what is happening in those places where, as in the Uruk, there are segregated enclaves of Kura-Araxes material adjacent to or within a local community (Batiuk's second type, as above). And I am not so sure it is applicable, without incorporating emigration, to the most far flung of the phenomenon's extension—the Southern Levant (Greenberg et al. 2014), where the Kura-Araxes material is known as Khirbet Kerak Ware.

The fact that the southernmost version of Kura-Araxes culture appears (virtually) simultaneously at a number of sites, either in spatially discrete locations within local settlements, or replacing previous occupations (Greenberg and Palumbi 2015:127) suggests immigration, rather than the spread of a new cultural repertoire taken on by specific sectors of the community. Rightly or wrongly, we usually understand such adoption to be an elite process in furtherance of its own position, a process that involves some public display of difference. Such would not seem to be the case here. Khirbet Kerak habitation areas are hardly elite, and the materials and practices of Khirbet Kerak culture are housebound and internalized (Greenberg and Palumbi 2015:130). This is demonstrated by the detailed work at Bet Yerah, which best explicates the Kura-Araxes presence in the Southern Levant. This group seems to have moved into an abandoned sector of the community, maintaining its distinctness for several phases of occupation. The material labeled Khirbet Kerak at Bet

Yerah does not just look like the Kura-Araxes material culture, it is a spatially distinct body of practices that has been specifically linked to the Kura-Araxes homeland through common manufacturing techniques (Greenberg et al. 2014; Iserlis et al. 2010). Those who are using Khirbet Kerak material culture are using it to live in the same ways as in the Kura-Araxes, reproducing the domicile. As in the north, the key element is the hearth, with decorated andirons, pots, and animal figurines materializing the symbolic sphere.

There are certain elements of this religio-ritual assemblage, wherever it is found, that suggest a very similar means of identity construction to that of the Uruk: the invocation of ancestors as the practice of descent structures through specialized preparation and consumption of food and drink (Wilkinson 2014). The focus on the hearth; the anthropomorphic and even stylized imagery that nevertheless suggests the face or body found on the very items of food preparation, andirons, and pots (see for example Smith 2015:Figure 22; Sagona 2018:Figures 5.7, 5.11–12); the role of drink, the locus in the home rather than some external place, all suggest eating with and feeding the dead. As with the much later *kispu* ritual, the bodily presence of the dead, such as in subfloor graves, is not required, for ancestors are ontologically distinct from their physical remains even when a conception of connection between them is maintained.

This question of emigration is important, for it potentially points to a fundamental difference between the Uruk expansion and the Kura-Araxes one in terms of the first point of this paper: there can be no expected outcome to a certain kind of movement—no one model of how refugees or mobile pastoralists behave. Consensus views of both the Uruk (Algaze 1989; Stein 1999) and Kura-Araxes (Batiuk 2013; Wilkinson 2014; Rothman 2015) result in two very different kinds and processes of mobility, two very different kinds of settlement establishment in the extension, yet two highly similar material outcomes. If the reproduction of southern identity in the Uruk expansion was to ensure the economic and perhaps social well-being of the homeland, there has been no suggestion that such a relationship existed for the Kura-Araxes, especially not in the Southern Levant. And yet the outcome, materially, is the same: an exclusionary identity maintained by the things of everyday life, deployed in the cultural practices of another place. The expansion of Kura-Araxes material culture seems to be confronting, at its core, exactly the same issue as the Uruk: how to maintain the integrity of the social unit, however it is defined, when part of it is not present.

Yet there is a quandary here. Because, according to my interpretation of the evidence for the Uruk expansion, indeed for the nature of southern Mesopotamian economy and society from the fourth millennium and beyond (Porter 2012), and Smith's (2015) understanding of the patterns in material culture of the Kura-Araxes expansion, the root causes, and the relationship between material culture and social construction in these two examples, seem to be exactly the same. Through a close adherence to a specific material repertoire that is used in both ritual and quotidian practices, and is itself the practice of identity, the populations associated with the Uruk and the Kura-Araxes expansions, whatever their biological identity, are reproducing the social bonds that link sedentary and mobile sectors of the community. In both situations, mobile pastoralism is a potential source of fracture and disintegration and in both situations the household is where those social bonds are located. In the one, though, the Uruk, whole communities are established to prevent fracture, so that a one-way migration follows the shifting patterns of mobile pastoralism over the long term. In the other, those communities are already established, but the practices of social integration and the objects that perform them migrate.

In fact, the Kura-Araxes is not "an absolutely original social and cultural model that was radically different to the Mesopotamian and North Caucasian models," as Palumbi (2016:4) and others have asserted. This is a reductionist view not only of the settlements of the Mesopotamian expansion, but of the homeland too, where mobility and kinship did not just coexist with sedentary, class-based households, but were integral parts of urban social and political fabric. The fundamental difference is that the Kura-Araxes seems to lack the institutional sector that is the real location of social differentiation in greater Mesopotamia at this time, allowing us to see more clearly the functioning of "ordinary" households in the north than in the south.

If, as Smith states (2015:98), "a necessary corollary to the manufacture of an imagined community is the simultaneous material inscription of exclusion that sets a collectivity off from its neighbors"—resulting in the very distinctiveness of the assemblage that has so engaged scholars for generations—what are we to make of a situation parallel in most respects to the Uruk expansion that shows *no* material exclusion? A similarly economic mobility, from a similarly based sociopolitical system marked by strong institutions, the presence of Old Assyrian traders from northern Mesopotamia in Anatolia in the second millennium B.C., reveals very different material outcomes. Yet here too, the need to maintain social, political, and especially economic linkages with the homelands was vital to the enterprise. And here too, there are indications that ancestor traditions defined the expatriate community.

THE ASSYRIAN TRADERS

The "Old Assyrian Colony Period," dated to the first centuries of the second millennium B.C., is characterized by an extensive network of installations designed to facilitate trade that crisscrossed the landscape from the Tigris River to central Anatolia and beyond (Barjamovic 2008, 2011). The texts relating to this period tell us just how endemic movement was—an extensive network of roads, bridges and inns served not just merchant caravans, but fast messengers and ordinary travelers as well (Barajmovic 2011).

Distinguished by the Assyrians themselves as *karum* and *wabartum,* usually translated as colonies[7] (without any necessary imperialist implications) and stations, the system revolved around a core network of trader settlements attached to key "consumer cities" (Barjamovic 2008:91) such as Boğazköy, Alişar, and Kultepe in central Anatolia. Traders in those settlements were members of merchant families from the northern Mesopotamian city of Assur. Assyrians also distinguished between kinds of traders: " 'travellers on the road to the City' (*āliku ša harrān ālim*) and the 'residents' (*wašbūtum*)" (Highcock 2018:40), where residents were those permanently living abroad, and the travelers were those who moved the goods, and who maintained practical links between branches of the trading families across distance. Shorter-lived than the previous examples (although comparable to earlier assessments of the length of the Uruk expansion), "residents" were established in these settlements for generations, maintaining over that time an Assyrian identity and citizenship.

We know far more about the organization of this system than we ever will for the Uruk because some 23,000 tablets documenting it have been recovered from Kultepe (ancient Kanesh). Nevertheless, parallels are evident. The mobility of both the Uruk and Old Assyrian expansions may be characterized as a patchwork of one-directional migratory, but ultimately sedentary, components in conjunction with periodically mobile, bi-, or multidirectional components. Both groups, as best we know, are pursuing the economic goals of their places of origin. Both groups are present in their host locations for multiple generations. The first group, the Uruk, seems to have preserved its natal culture in fine detail and for several centuries (Porter 2012); the second, the Assyrian, shows little obvious material evidence of its original identity. Indeed, if it were not for the discovery of the archives of the Assyrian trading families at Kultepe, we would not even have thought to look for a foreign presence there (Larsen and Lissen 2014). It has taken several decades of research before any material indications of a foreign identity have been recognized (Highcock 2018), and they remain slight, consisting primarily of tools of the trade.[8]

By one estimate, some 900 Assyrians lived at Kultepe (Barjamovic 2014:60) outside the main mound, as a *karum*, or quay. The traditional location of trading enterprises in Mesopotamian cities, in the expansion *karum* seems to designate not so much a physical space as an administrative and juridical body (Highcock 2018:301). For this lower town was not an exclusively Assyrian enclave. Assyrians lived among local Anatolians (Barjamovic 2011:56), in houses of Anatolian design, and used pots of Anatolian manufacture. Assyrian men—and women (Veenhof 2008; Larsen and Lassen 2014:178)—married Anatolians, although some also had wives and children left in Assur (Larsen 2015).

The transitory nature of a merchant's presence abroad might explain the lack of Assyrian material features, as has been argued, but these were not in the end temporary existences at Kanesh. Moreover, initially at least, personal items such as pins, jewelry, and even weapons such as knives and daggers would be carried by merchants on their trips abroad. Historically, travelers also frequently carry their personal utensils such as a cup and plate, and metal ones would be lighter and more durable than ceramics. If anticipating at the outset a longer stay, a broader range of household and personal goods might be packed for the voyage. It is often stated that merchants would *not* carry Assyrian-made pots and pans with them (Larsen 2015:244), and yet of course, since the very essence of the Assyrian enterprise was the shipment of tin and textiles, among other goods, via caravans ranging in size from 2 to 300 donkeys (Larsen 2015:171ff.), it is not impossible that they might have packed a pannier with a few things from home. Nor is there any reason, if material items of home were so desired, that potters themselves could not have accompanied caravans, as they seem to have in the Uruk expansion. Certainly, Assyrian metalsmiths took up residence in Anatolia (Larsen and Lassen 2014:173).

The point is this: *not* taking and reproducing Assyrian personal and household goods in migration is a choice of complex dimensions. Pragmatism and short-term intentions are only small parts of that complexity. On the surface, the fact that the Assyrians are living in fully urban contexts seems to differentiate conditions from the Uruk. In the fourth-millennium example, new settlements such as Habuba Kabira and Jebel Aruda were established in sparsely occupied regions. But it must be remembered that at Arslantepe and Tell Brak, sites of Late Chalcolithic indigenous complexity that would equally be able to provide pots and pans, Southern-style materials are highly recognizable.

There is one fundamental material difference, though, between the Assyrian expatriate world and that of the Uruk, and that is the existence of writing. Assyrians maintained a juridical and political identity *as* Assyrians, established by written treaties with local polities (Larsen and Lassen 2014; Highcock 2018). They were in certain matters answerable to Assur, and tablets dealing with trade, family matters, and legal issues "flew" back and forth between the periphery and the center. It was this constant communication, unavailable to the emigrants of Uruk and Kura-Araxes, that obviated any particular need, sentimental or political, for objects of the homeland.

Yet as in the Uruk expansion, social fragmentation threatened both institutional and household relationships. This is abundantly clear in letters from wives left behind to manage on their own (Michel 2001) and from official correspondence as well as communications with Anatolian powers, especially once Samsi-Addu assumed control of the city of Assur (Highcock 2018:125ff). One contentious issue under Samsi-Addu was his interference in matters of religion, for Assyrian expatriates also maintained a religious identity tied to the city god Assur. This is evident primarily in seal imagery and texts (Lassen 2017) in the absence of any archaeological evidence for temples or religious objects. And as with both the Uruk and Kura Araxes, there is evidence to suggest domestically based ritual practices centered on ancestor traditions at Kanesh.

As in the Uruk period sites of Habuba Kabira and Jebel Aruda (see above), certain buildings contained features that distinguished them from others around them, thus rendering them specialized spaces. Four houses in the *karum* contained undecorated stelae[9] that, while not obviously anthropomorphic, nevertheless echoed the general shape of a human. The rooms in which the stelae were found also contained installations such as a basin situated in front of the stele, horseshoe hearths, distinctive and specialized vessels, and sub-floor burials, in varying combinations in each house. The sum total of this material indicates that libation rituals were performed in association with the house, iterating the identity of the house—most likely, given textual evidence for Assyrian mortuary behavior, the Assyrian house (Heffron 2016). Not every house has these features, suggesting that those that do may provide the core of a clustering of houses, possibly defined by kin group (Porter 2012; also Heffron 2016:38–39), possibly, by community founders—the first generation traders at Kanesh.

Conclusion

Culture, material and otherwise, is always in the process of being made. So too is identity. But how culture and identity are made is highly variable. Adherence to a specific identity over generations, not to mention many hundreds of miles, and in the midst of others, involves more than rules. It involves a certain knowledge of who one is. Descent systems do just that. They establish one's place in time and space, the nature of relations to others, and while certainly malleable, they establish boundaries when desired. All that knowledge travels with the person and the group no matter where they might be. Commemorative mortuary practices enact descent systems, just as written genealogies do.

There is a mutually enhancing relationship between such systems, practices, and artifacts, particularly in the context of macro-mobilities. Descent practices in all their potential variety bulwark the meaning of artifacts and facilitate continuity of form and fabrication, just as making and using the same artifacts over generations keeps the system intact. Identity takes a very different turn in consideration of micro-mobilities. Since the cases considered here concern the identity of leaders, it may be argued that there is a political pragmatism involved in the presentation of an individual's identity. In ruling multiple constituencies, the reification of identity is disadvantageous. But the multiple identifiers demonstrated in the examples discussed here are also a product of the mobility and fluidity of individual lives—lives that take different directions over time, ending up in different places.

Notes

1. See Porter 2009 and 2012 for detailed discussions.
2. Although knowing the degree to which Samsi-Addu attempted to control Yasmah-Addu because of his perception of his son's incompetence, I would not be surprised if he had prepared this document himself in the eventuality of his death.
3. See Jacquet 2012 for details of the *kispu* ritual.
4. The precise chronology of the Kura-Araxes culture in the homeland and its subsequent distribution beyond, is contentious. ^{14}C dates however shows an initial presence of varieties of Red-Black burnished ware in the Late Chalcolithic in both Anatolia and the Southern Caucasus (Smith 2015:102).
5. See Simonyan and Rothman 2015 and Sagona 2018 for an overview of the chronological issues.
6. Smith 2015:107–108, for example, points out that a corresponding depopulation of the Kura-Araxes homelands is not in evidence.
7. Although, see Highcock 2018:32ff for a thorough discussion of the problems with this term.
8. Highcock provides a comprehensive and detailed analysis of this material in her 2018 dissertation.
9. Other stelae were found out of context.

References Cited

Algaze, G. 1989 The Uruk Expansion: Cross-Cultural Exchange in Early Mesopotamian Civilization. *Current Anthropology* 30:571–608.

Barjamovic, G. 2008 The Geography of Trade. Assyrian Colonies in Anatolia c. 1975–1725 BC and the Study of Early Interregional Networks of Exchange. In *Anatolia and the Jazira During the Old Assyrian Period* edited by J. Dercksen, pp. 87–100. NIINO, Leiden.

Barjamovic, G. 2011 *A Historical Geography of Anatolia in the Old Assyrian Colony Period*. The Carsten Niebuhr Institute of Ancient Near Eastern Studies, Museum Tusculanum Press, Copenhagen.

Barjamovic, G. 2014 The Size of Kanesh and the Demography of Early Middle Bronze Age Anatolia. In *Current Research at Kültepe-Kanesh: An Interdisciplinary and Integrative Approach to Trade Networks, Internationalism, and Identity*, edited by L. Atici, F. Kulakoğlu, G. Barjamovic, and A. Fairbairn, pp. 55–68. Journal of Cuneiform Studies Supplemental Studies 4. Lockwood Press, Atlanta.

Batiuk, S. 2013 The Fruits of Migration: Understanding the "Longue Durée" and the Socio-Economic Relations of the Early Transcaucasian Culture. *Journal of Anthropological Archaeology* 32:449–447.

Batuik, S., and M. Rothman 2007 Early Transcaucasian Cultures and Their Neighbors: Unraveling Migration, Trade, and Assimilation. *Expedition: The Magazine of the University of Pennsylvania*, 49(1):7–17.

Buccellati, G. 1966 *The Amorites of the Ur III Period*. Pubblicazioni del Seminario di Semitistica 1. Istituto Orientale di Napoli, Naples.

Buccellati, G. 2008 The Origin of the Tribe and of "Industrial" Agropastoralism in Syro-Mesopotamia. In *The Archaeology of Mobility: Old World and New World Nomadism*, edited by H. Barnard and W. Wendrich, pp. 141–159. Cotsen Advanced Seminars 4. Cotsen Institute of Archaeology Press, Los Angeles.

Burke, A. 2017 Amorites, Climate Change, and the Negotiation of Identity at the End of the Third Millennium B.C. In *The Late Third Millennium in the Ancient Near East: Chronology C, 14, and Climate Change*, edited by F. Höflmayer, pp. 261–307. Oriental Institute Publications, Chicago.

Charpin, D. 2004 Histoire politique du Proche-Orient Amorrite (2002–1595). In *Mesopotamien: Die altbabylonische Zeit*, edited by P. Attinger, W. Sallaberger, and M. Wäfler, pp. 23–480. Orbis Biblicus et Orientalis 160/4. Academic Press, Fribourg.

van Driel, G. 2002 Jebel Aruda: Variations on a Late Uruk Domestic Theme. In *Artefacts of Complexity: Tracking the Uruk in the Near East*, edited by J. N. Postgate, pp. 191–205. Iraq Archaeological Reports 5. British School of Archaeology in Iraq, Cambridge.

Durand, J.-M. 1998 *Documents épistolaires du palais de Mari. Tome II. Littératures anciennes du Proche-Orient*. Les Éditions du Cerf, Paris.

Emberling, G., and L. Minc 2016 Ceramics and Long-Distance Trade in Early Mesopotamian States. *Journal of Archaeological Science: Reports* 7:819–834.

Finkelstein, J. 1966 The Genealogy of the Hammurapi Dynasty. *Journal of Cuneiform Studies* 20:95–118.

Frangipane, M. 2018 Different Trajectories in State Formation in Greater Mesopotamia: A View from Arslantepe (Turkey). *Journal of Archaeological Research* 26(1):3–63.

Frayne, D. 1990 *Old Babylonian Period (2003–1595)*. The Royal Inscriptions of Mesopotamia, Vol. 4. University of Toronto Press, Toronto.

Gelb, I. 1954 Two Assyrian King Lists. *Journal of Near Eastern Studies* 13:209–230.

Giddens, A. 1981 *A Contemporary Critique of Historical Materialism*. Vol. 1: Power, Property and the State. University of California Press, Berkeley.

Greenberg, R., M. Iserlis, and R. Shimelmitz 2014 New Evidence for the Anatolian Origins of "Khirbet Kerak Ware People" at Tel Bet Yerah (Israel), ca 2800 BC. *Paléorient* 40(2):183–201.

Greenberg, R., and G. Palumbi 2014 Corridors and Colonies: Comparing Fourth-Third Millennia BC Interactions in Southeast Anatolia and the Levant. In *The Cambridge Prehistory of the Bronze and Iron Age Mediterranean*, edited by A. B. Knapp and P. van Dommelen, pp. 111–138. Cambridge University Press, Cambridge.

Heffron, Y. 2016 Stone Stelae and Religious Space at Kültepe-Kaneš. *Anatolian Studies* 66:23–42.

Heimpel, W. 2003 *Letters to the King of Mari: A New Translation, with Historical Introduction, Notes, and Commentary*. Eisenbrauns. Winona Lake, Indiana.

Highcock, N. 2018 *Community across Distance: The Forging of Identity between Aššur and Anatolia*. PhD dissertation. New York University, New York.

Iserlis M., R. Greenberg, R. Badalyan, and Y. Goren 2010 Beth Yerah, Aparan III, and Karnut I: Preliminary Comments on Kura-Araxes Homeland and Diaspora Ceramic Technology. *TÜBA-AR* 13:245–262.

Jacquet, A. 2012 Funerary Rituals and Cult of the Ancestors during the Amorite Period: The Evidence of the Royal Archives of Mari. In *(Re-)Constructing Funerary Rituals in the Ancient Near East*, edited by P. Pfälzner, H. Niehr, E. Pernicka, and A. Wissing, pp. 123–136. Qatna Studien Supplementa 1, Wiesbaden.

Kamp, K., and N. Yoffee 1980 Ethnicity in Ancient Western Asia During the Early Second Millennium BC. *Bulletin of the American Schools of Oriental Research* 237:85–103.

Lees, S. H., and D. G. Bates 1974 The Origins of Specialized Nomadic Populations: A Systemic Model. *American Antiquity* 39(2.1):187–193.

Larsen, M. T. 2015 *Ancient Kanesh: A Merchant Colony in Bronze Age Anatolia*. Cambridge University Press, New York.

Larsen, M. T., and A. Lassen 2014 Cultural Exchange at Kültepe. In *Extraction and Control: Studies in Honor of Matthew W. Stolper*, edited by M. Kozuh, pp. 171–188. Studies in Ancient Oriental Civilization 68. Oriental Institute Publications, Chicago.

Lassen. A. 2017 The Bull-Altar in Old Assyrian Glyptic: A Representation of the God Assur? In *Movement, Resources, Interaction: Proceedings of the 2nd Kültepe International Meeting, Kültepe, 26–30 July 2015: Studies Dedicated to Klass Veenhof*, edited by F. Kulakoğlu and G. Barjamovic, pp. 177–194. Subartu XXXIX/ KIM 2. Brepols, Turnhout.

The Marriage of Martu. Electronic document. Corpus of Sumerian Literature, c.1.7.1. http://etcsl.orinst.ox.ac.uk/cgi-bin/etcsl.cgi?text=t.1.7.1&charenc=j#. Accessed on October 13, 2019.

Marro, C., R. Berthon, and V. Bakhshaliyev 2015 A reply to G. Palumbi and C. Chataigner. *Paléorient*, 41(2):157–162.

Michalowski, P. 2011 *The Correspondence of the Kings of Ur: An Epistolary History of an Ancient Mesopotamian Kingdom*. Eisenbrauns, Winona Lake.

Michel, C. 2001 *Correspondance des marchands de Kaniš au début du IIe millenaire av. J.-C.* Littératures du Proche-Orient ancien 19. CERF, Paris.

Oates, D., and J. Oates 2006 Tripartite Buildings and Early Urban Tell Brak. In *Les espaces Syro-Mésopotamiens. Dimensions de l'expérience humaine au Proche-Orient ancient. Volume d'hommage offert à Jean-Claude Margueron*, edited by P. Butterlin, M. Lebeau, J.-Y. Monchambert, J. Montero Fenollós, and B. Muller, pp. 33–40. Subartu XVII. Brepols, Turnhout.

Palumbi, G. 2016 The Early Bronze Age of the Southern Caucasus. Oxford Handbooks Online, Oxford University Press, Oxford.

Porter, A. 2009 Beyond Dimorphism: Ideologies and Materialities of Kinship as Time-Space Distanciation. In *Nomads, Tribes, and the State in the Ancient Near East: Cross-Disciplinary Perspectives*, edited by J. Szuchman, pp. 201–225. Oriental Institute Publications, Chicago.

Porter, A. 2012 *Mobile Pastoralism and the Formation of Near Eastern Civilizations: Weaving Together Society.* Cambridge University Press, New York.

Rothman, M. 2015 Early Bronze Age Migrants and Ethnicity in the Middle Eastern Mountain Zone. *Proceedings of the National Academy of Sciences* 112(30):9190–9195.

Sagona, A. 2018 *The Archaeology of the Caucasus: From Earliest Settlements to the Iron Age.* Cambridge University Press, Cambridge.

Sagona, C., and A. Sagona 2009 Encounters with the Divine in the Late Prehistoric Period of Eastern Anatolia and Southern Caucasus. In *Studies in Honour of Altan Cilingiroglu. A Life Dedicated to Urartu, on the Shores of the Upper Sea*, edited by H. Saglamtimur, E. Abay, Z. Derin, A. Ü. Erdem, A. Batmaz, F. Dedeoğlu, M. Erdalkiran, M. B. Baştürk, and E. Konakcı, pp. 537–563. Arkeoloji ve Sanat, Istanbul.

Sagona, A., and P. Zimansky 2009 *Ancient Turkey.* Routledge, New York.

Seri, A. 2005 *Local Power in Old Babylonian Mesopotamia.* Equinox, London.

Simonyan, H., and M. Rothman 2015 Regarding Ritual Behaviour at Shengavit, Armenia. *Ancient Near Eastern Studies* 52:1–45.

Smith, A. T. 2015 *The Political Machine: Assembling Sovereignty in the Bronze Age Caucasus.* Princeton University Press, Princeton.

Stein, G. 1999b *Rethinking World Systems: Diasporas, Colonies and Interaction in Uruk Mesopotamia.* University of Arizona, Tucson.

Steinkeller, P. 2004 A History of Mashkan-shapir and Its Role in the Kingdom of Larsa. In *The Anatomy of a Mesopotamian City: Survey and Soundings at Mashkan-shapir*, edited by E. Stone and P. Zimansky, pp. 26–42. Eisenbrauns, Winona Lake.

Veenhof, K. 2008 The Death and Burial of Ishtar-Lamassi in kārum Kanish. In *Studies in Ancient Near Eastern World View and Society—presented to Martin Stol on Occasion of his 65th Birthday*, edited by R. J. van der Spek, pp. 97–119. CDL Press, Bethesda.

Whiting, R. 1995 Amorite Tribes and Nations of Second-Millennium Western Asia. In *Civilizations of the Ancient Near East*, vols. 1–2, edited by J. M. Sasson, pp. 1231–1242. Charles Scribner's Sons, New York.

Wilkinson, T. C. 2014 The Early Transcaucasian Phenomenon in Structural-Systemic Perspective: Cuisine, Craft and Economy. *Paléorient* 40(2):203–229.

Wright, H., and E. Rupley 2001 Calibrated Radiocarbon Age Determination of Uruk-Related Assemblages. In *Uruk Mesopotamia and its Neighbors. Cross-Cultural Interactions in the Era of State Formation*, edited by M. Rothman, pp. 85–122. School of American Research Advanced Seminar Series. School of American Research Press, Santa Fe.

CHAPTER FOURTEEN

Wandering Ports on the Datça Peninsula

Exploring Regional Mobility in a Maritime Landscape

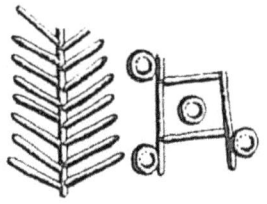

Elizabeth S. Greene and Justin Leidwanger

Abstract *The site of Burgaz in southwest Turkey's Datça Peninsula flourished from the Archaic period through Late Antiquity, spanning its transformation from civic center to workshop and industrial hub around the fourth century B.C. This shift was concurrent with the expansion of Knidos at Tekir to the west as the center of religious and cultural life and interaction on the peninsula even as Burgaz remained an important engine behind regional economic prosperity. As dozens of sites emerged throughout the peninsula, these two urban centers represented major poles for mobility. In this paper we address the regular short-distance mobilities that might have developed in this regional context, particularly those linking urban centers, agricultural production communities, and the ports that tied them into the world beyond. In modeling these micro-mobilities at the scale of a single peninsula, we aim to consider diachronic changes in the nature and frequency of interactions, and to track the ebb and flow of central places in the landscape concurrent with regional sociopolitical, economic, and technological development, expanding maritime networks, as well as catastrophic and gradual local environmental pressure.*

The papers in this volume are largely concerned with human migration and mobility across large scales, where evidence for movement and change is written into the biological and archaeological records. Also significant but far more prevalent in populations ancient and modern are smaller movements within and around spaces that are geographically, intellectually, and socially closer to home, generally corresponding to a regional cultural scale (Anthony 1990:901). Such small-scale movement can intersect with and in turn influence larger-scale shifts within and beyond a particular region. The Mediterranean has long been defined by intensive connectivity among its many parts (Braudel 1972; Horden and Purcell 2000). Delving deeper into ideas of generalized interaction, Woolf (2016:451) imagines the Mediterranean as a "mosaic of locally caged societies" in which movement within those small worlds was very frequent. The "inside-out geography" (Horden and Purcell 2000:133) of the Mediterranean means that many of these movements are structured at least in part by the ubiquitous presence of the sea and the often mountainous topography that privileges certain vectors and generally orients communities toward the coasts.

Earlier in this volume, Anne Porter identifies micro-mobilities as the regular ebb and flow of peoples across the Near East, movements that are more easily seen in textual and linguistic than archaeological evidence. Similarly, movements from port to port, inland center to port, and among such communities are less archaeologically detectable on an individual level—as such close connections led nearby peoples to share material cultures and practices, and DNA—but formed a regular feature of interconnected Mediterranean worlds. Conceptualizing how to account for these and other patterns of ancient mobility, Woolf (2016:442) challenges scholars to consider explicitly a series of parameters: the kinds of mobility, the demographics and numbers of those moving, and the variability in these patterns over time. In this paper, we address regular short-distance mobility across the Datça Peninsula in southwest Turkey between urban centers, rural spaces of agricultural production, and the connecting nodes of ports and adjacent islet settlement (Figure 14.1). We define micro-mobilities as journeys of economic, religious, political, or social activity, which could be completed over land or sea within a few hours, ensuring a routine that facilitated return in a single day. Using network visualizations, we explore how to conceptualize these micro-mobilities at the scale of a single peninsula, and how to utilize this modeling to understand larger shifts of peoples and places, including diachronic change in the nature and frequency of human interactions, and the ebb and flow of central places in this regional landscape.

Forming the basis for economic, social, and political interaction and integration, these regular patterns of small-scale movement are also wrapped up with larger population shifts prompted by intensive changes in settlement occupation and agricultural exploitation as well as both slow environmental change and sudden catastrophe. Examples of such community migrations, including whole relocations and mergers of cities, in the Greek world have been detailed by Demand (1990), who reviews literary and historical data for urban relocation (*metoikesis*) and amalgamation (*synoikesis*), generally as a result of political or military pressures. Addressing urban abandonment and the strategic relocation of communities as a response to environmental and economic pressures, Mackil (2004:494–97) considers the example of Myous in the Maeander River basin. Ongoing siltation of its port eventually reduced to negligible the settlement's once-significant harbor. Pausanias (7.2.11; see also Strabo 14.10.1) describes newly inland marshes swarming with mosquitoes such that the Myesians abandoned their city, likely in the third century B.C.: "They departed for Miletus, taking with them the images of the gods and their other movables, and on my visit I found nothing in Myous except a white marble temple of Dionysus." In this case, the Myesians

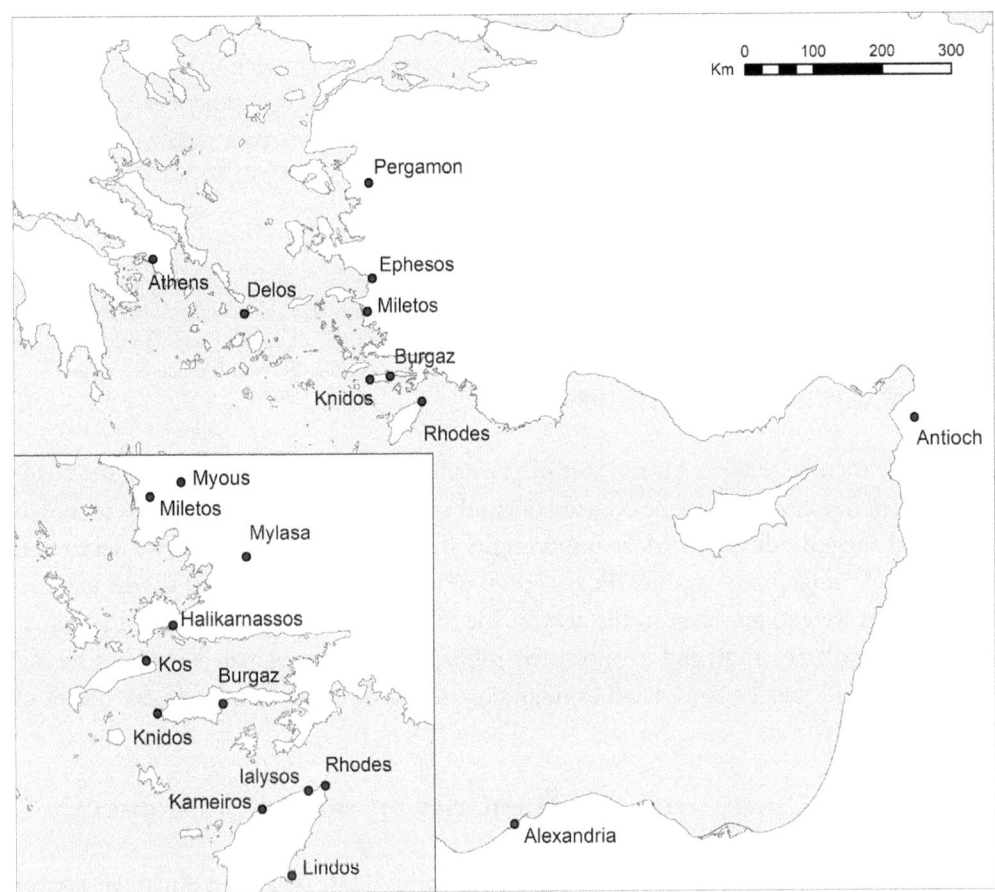

FIGURE 14.1. Map of the eastern Mediterranean and Aegean, with detail of the southeast Aegean, showing locations of major sites of interest (J. Leidwanger).

make a choice to join forces with the Milesians in a new locale, leaving their city behind. A marble block inscribed with a decree of Myous, used in the second-century theatre of Miletus, for Mackil (2004:495) stands as a *pierre errante*, wandering along with the city and its residents. While this relocation receives a dramatic portrayal, it is made possible through the regular economic interactions and sociopolitical bonds between the two nearby cities.

Less extreme examples of *synoikism* or *sympoliteia*—the political union of cities that converge on a single location—are frequent in the eastern Mediterranean; for island and coastal cities, these relocations often have their basis in the degree to which the local harbor was able to meet community needs. In the late fifth century B.C., the citizens of Ialysos, Lindos, and Kameiros are said to have banded together to establish the city of Rhodes (Diodorus 13.75; Gabrielsen 2000). The new urban center was arranged around a large deep port astride an important channel between the island and the adjacent Anatolian mainland that saw considerable movement between the Aegean and eastern Mediterranean littoral. Demand (1990:92) suggests that the topography of the new site allowed for the construction of multiple harbors, a new necessity in an era of growing military threats and commercial opportunities. A few decades later, Diodorus (15.76.2) describes residents of Astypalaia moving northeast to Kos, where they quickly constructed a noteworthy harbor that facilitated access to broader Hellenistic networks (Demand 1990:127–131; Höghammar 2016). But as Boehm explains:

> The archaeological evidence for the synoikisms of the early Hellenistic period and their effects on patterns of settlement, though incomplete, shows no signs of systematic destruction on the scale that the sources suggest. . . . The "destruction" of a city, then, should be understood primarily as the eclipse of an autonomous unit and the transference of some or all of its population to a new site. [2018:19]

Should we then be looking for the sort of permanent movements that demand the abandonment of one city to allow the creation of another, when contemporary models of mobility would suggest otherwise? More importantly, with what parameters can we detect and analyze such "migrations" against the backdrop of routine movements and shared material cultures that were so prevalent in the ancient Mediterranean? How do monumental migrations relate to, arise from, and in turn exert influence on these regular patterns of mobility? And should they be considered as migrations at all, or rather large-scale extensions of micro-mobilities?

Shifting Centralities and Mobilities on the Datça Peninsula

To address such questions we turn to the Datça Peninsula in southwest Anatolia. Jutting out from the Carian mainland and home to the Knidians, the narrow stretch of land offers a dramatic mountainous terrain that strongly influenced its socioeconomic development. A prominent ridge runs across the north and outcrops cleave the south into small valleys, making for uneven settlement and agriculture as well as challenging communication. By contrast, the low-lying strip across the middle of the peninsula offers the best agricultural land and comparatively easy overland transit. While the peninsula was dominated variously by two major urban centers throughout antiquity—Burgaz (or "Old Knidos") and Knidos (or "New Knidos") at Tekir some 30 km to the west—a string of other religious sites, ports, towns, and farmsteads appeared and faded across the landscape between the Archaic and late Roman eras (Figures 14.2 and 14.3).

The site of Burgaz, situated midway along the southern shore of the peninsula, was identified by Bean and Cook (1952:202–204) as "Old Knidos," or the early settlement of the Knidians before the intensive growth of the city at Tekir at the western tip of the peninsula. The late Classical "removal" (Bean and Cook 1952:202, 210) of the Knidians from Burgaz to Tekir has been generally adopted by scholars (e.g., Bresson 1999; 2013; Berges 2006; Tuna et al. 2009, but cf. Demand 1989), though neither literary nor archaeological evidence offers definitive proof of anything like a sudden or complete uprooting of people,

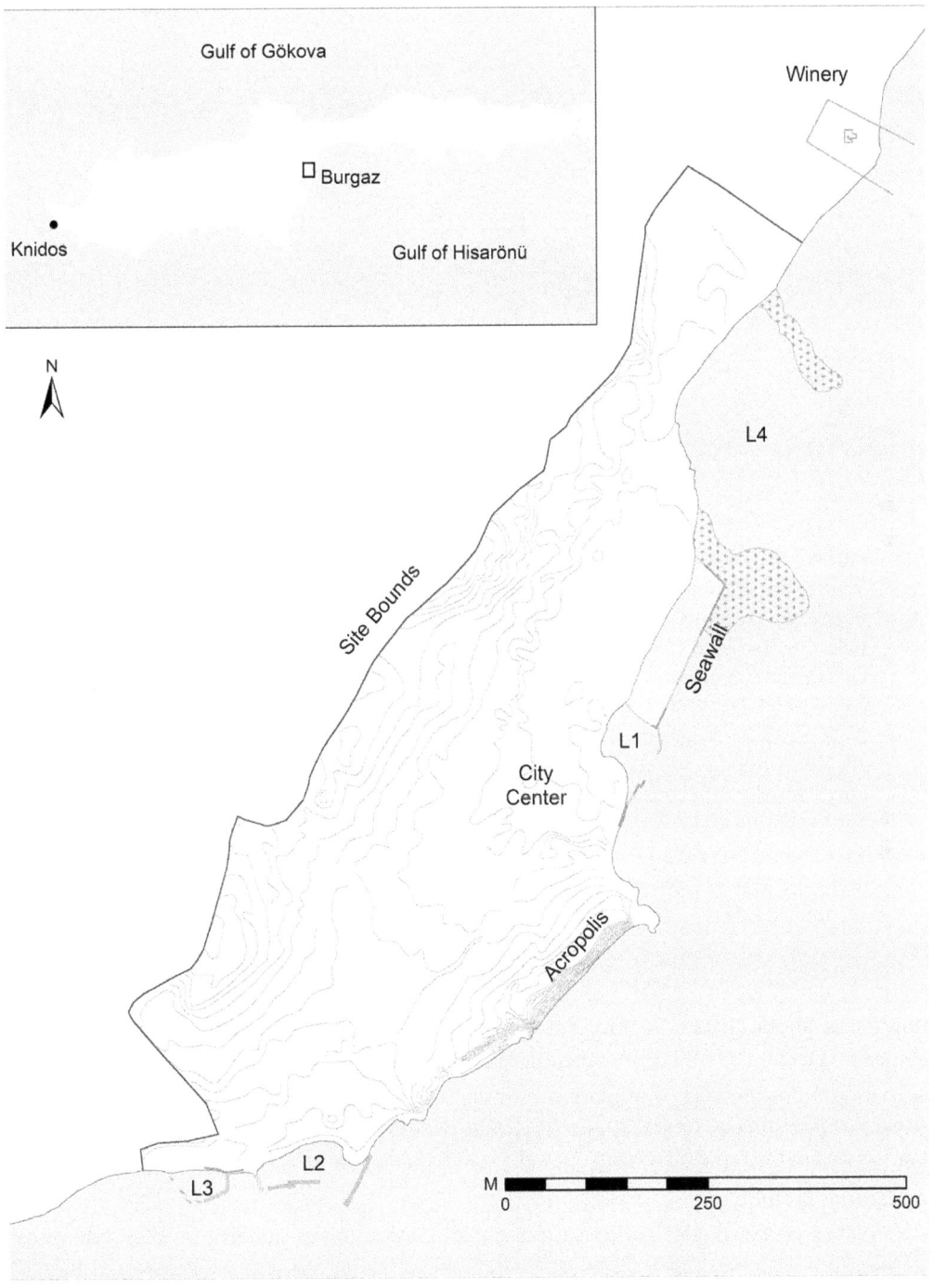

FIGURE 14.2. General plan of Burgaz showing locations of the settlement, harbors, and other features (J. Leidwanger and N. Riddick).

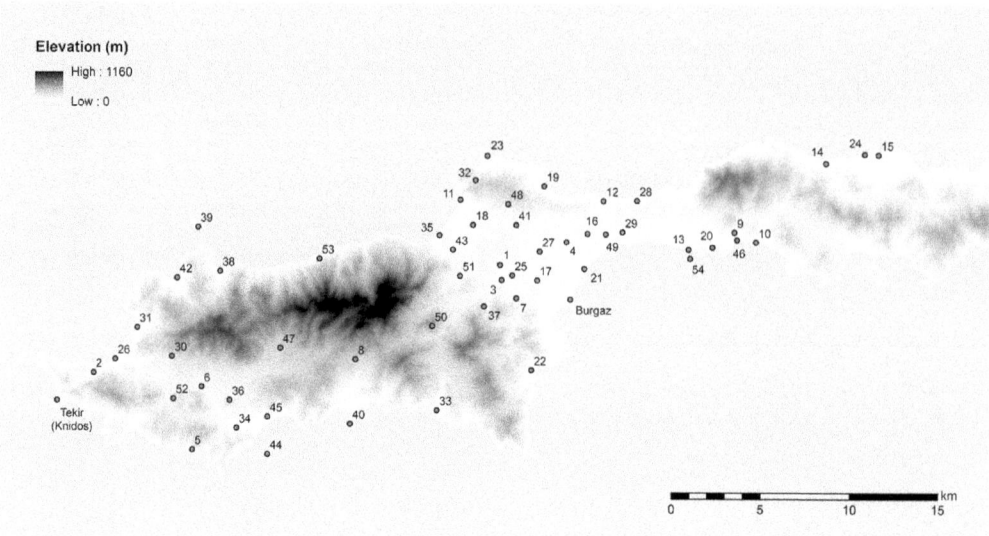

FIGURE 14.3. Map of 56 sites on the Datça peninsula recorded by Tuna (1983) and Sevimli (2016) ranging in date from the Archaic through the Late Roman period: 1. Bağharımı; 2. Barkaz; 3. Batıraltı; 4. Billiktepe; 5. Bükceğiz; 6. Çeşmeköy; 7. Datça Kalesi; 8. Döşeme Kalesi; 9. Emecik; 10. Gavurdere; 11. Gerenci; 12. Germe; 13. Gökçedere/Kabakkoyu; 14. Göktaş; 15. Gölyeri; 16. Göztepe/Yanıkharman; 17. Gümüş-Ülüklü; 18. Güznetepe; 19. Harıplık; 20. Karaincir; 21. Karfitepe; 22. Kargı; 23. Katıyalı; 24. Kepçemel Burnu; 25. Kiliseyanı; 26. Killik; 27. Killiktepe/Karakuştepe; 28. Kislebükü; 29. Kisletepe; 30. Kisleyanı; 31. Kızılağaç; 32. Kızılağaç kezi; 33. Kızılbükü; 34. Kızılkilise/Karıncalı; 35. Körmen; 36. Kumyer; 37. Maltepe; 38. Mersincik; 39. Mersincik Adası; 40. Mesudiye; 41. Muhaltepe; 42. Murdala; 43. Olgun Boğazı; 44. Palamutbükü Adası; 45. Sakızyakası; 46. Sarılimanı; 47. Sındı/Asartepe; 48. Tekirlikyolu; 49. Yağtaşı-Devtaşı; 50. Yarıkdağ; 51. Yassıdağaltı; 52. Yazıköy Kalesi; 53. Yelimli; 54. Yollucu Adası.

objects, or public spaces. For this reason, based on a review of the literary and epigraphic evidence, Demand (1989:237) concludes that Knidos did not really move. In this paper we shift away from the idea of migration of individuals or cities in favor of a broader regional approach that situates such trajectories within the context of routine movement within the landscape of the entire peninsula and the functional shift of centralities tied to changing patterns of mobility.

While archaeological evidence points to early religious activity at Tekir, the most important Archaic and early Classical civic center of the Knidians was seemingly at Burgaz, which capitalized on its close proximity to the only extensive arable land on the peninsula (Figure 14.2). On either side of a low plateau that served as the acropolis, coastal features include four built harbors with three distinct phases (Greene and Leidwanger 2019; Greene et al. 2019). From its foundation through much of the mid-fifth century B.C., the city relied on a natural harbor (Harbor 1) immediately adjacent to the city center and protected from the prevailing northwest winds. Considerable sedimentation has reduced the depth and total area of this inlet today, which probably extended into the low-lying fields during its early phases. This single harbor served as a multifunctional space to meet varied commercial, civic, communication, and military needs. The next phase saw built moles, probably mid-Classical in date, enhance the harbor's protection (and significantly increase its rate of siltation). This same brief period also saw expansion and fortification of the city, with side-by-side basins (Harbors 2 and 3) constructed on the other side of the acropolis to the southwest around 400 B.C. Today the lower courses of two long walls of Harbor 2 are the most conspicuous features, each integrating a square tower of roughly 8 to 9 m on a side. At this stage, port functions at Burgaz may have been divided between military in this new space and more general communication and commerce in the older Harbor 1. The archaeological record suggests early-fourth-century activity followed by a relatively rapid disuse into the early Hellenistic era, after which the harbor saw only limited use.

From the mid-fourth century, Burgaz underwent a transformation that marks its third major phase (Greene and Leidwanger 2019; Greene et al. 2019). Domestic and civic spaces were converted into workshops for industrial and agricultural activities (Tuna et al. 2009). All three ports were left to silt, while larger-scale workshops and warehouses were constructed just to the northeast, where its largest Harbor 4 was built. This deeper but less sheltered facility features simple curving breakwaters made from massive rubble mounds enclosing more than 3 ha. A series of Hellenistic wine workshops line the shore, complete with built storage basins and possible docking facilities (Tuna et al. 2010; Koparal et al. 2014). A long seawall extends toward the silting Harbor 1, setting off a low-lying rectangular area of open space likely given over to such routine activities as the assembly and transshipment of cargos as well as perhaps ship maintenance and repair.

This fundamental shift in infrastructure, economic activity, and urbanism at Burgaz was concurrent with the rapid expansion and reorganization of Tekir on the western tip of the peninsula. Since at least the seventh century B.C., the site at Tekir held important religious centrality, drawing celebrants from around the region for cultural, and perhaps also economic exchange (Love 1974; Bruns-Özgan 2013; Doksanaltı et al. 2015); Tozluca and Doksanaltı (2019) record a scattering of Protogeometric and Geometric ceramics in the eastern harbor area and bull-shaped figurines from both the Geometric and Archaic periods. A newly organized and expanded urban core, however, appears during the mid- to late fourth century, with the construction of extensive civic buildings, theatres, and temples. Blackman (1982:193) and Büyüközer (2012:40) both suggest that the double harbor basins for which the city was famous were built up in this period. Strabo (14.2.15) notes a naval station for twenty ships, likely the smaller basin protected by towers to the north. The massive commercial harbor to the south was augmented with 100- to 150-m long walls that rise from more than 25 m of depth (Büyüközer 2012:42). This new monumentality projected Knidos's preeminent status on the peninsula, and the city found itself well situated to host the growing interregional maritime traffic between the Aegean and eastern Mediterranean over the late Classical and Hellenistic period, a role it played throughout the rest of antiquity.

This is where the Knidian maritime story typically ends, with the ebb and flow of facilities and traffic at two major ports. But understanding the internal dynamics of this peninsular system requires a finer-grained view of small-scale networks and evolving patterns of mobility across the peninsula. Surface survey by Tuna in the 1980s revealed a wide range of sites that may form the basis for a study of regional mobility and interaction (Tuna 1983, 2012:31–40; Sevimli 2016). Identified primarily through surface ceramics as well as limited architecture, these 56 sites range from Archaic through late Roman in date (Figure 14.3).[1] One basic observation should be noted immediately regarding the numbers and distribution of sites, particularly with regard to ports. Port locales are more numerous than inland agricultural sites from the Archaic/early Classical period, only surpassed by noncoastal settlement, production, or agricultural sites from the fourth century. But this late Classical through early Roman expansion throughout the peninsula's inland areas was short-lived, and in its wake, ports seem more resilient moving into the mid-/late Roman world than the small agricultural settlements that dotted the earlier landscape. Connected by the sea, these maritime outposts provided an additional opportunity for mobility within and beyond the peninsula, particularly useful when such movements involved the bulk agricultural produce that was the Knidians' economic backbone. Some of the new Hellenistic sites were inland farmsteads that capitalized on small but fertile valleys and extensive terracing to expand the agricultural base; others are ports of various sizes, from the more obvious protected inlets to the least conspicuous but evidently sufficient sandy beaches.

Given the peninsula's distinctive geography, these ports provide a crucial facet of local structures of movement and interaction. Among the many such examples, a few will suffice to signal the diverse roles in which these simple sites supported movements of goods and people, becoming focal points for mobility across the peninsula and beyond.

Backed by high mountains, the small valley around Mersincik (Figure 14.3: No. 38) on the north shore is challenging to access except by sea. While hardly an ideal port location, it offers some shelter from prevailing winds behind the headland to the west, where still today small vessels anchor. Other craft are simply pulled up onto the sandy and cobbly beach. No traces of harbor infrastructure are visible, but Tuna (1983:385–386, 1989:148; Sevimli 2016:29) records the remains of a pottery kiln eroding into the sea, with associated debris (mostly transport amphoras), walls, and a freshwater source. The scale of production seems larger than necessary for the few farmsteads that could have thrived here, suggesting that empty amphoras were likely shipped up and down the coast for the packaging of produce by neighboring communities (Leidwanger 2019).

The opposite, southern shore of the peninsula is more naturally protected from the prevailing northerly winds. Roughly halfway along this undulating coastline between Tekir and Burgaz, Mesudiye (Figure 14.3: No. 40) sits at the outlet of a narrow but fertile valley winding from the mountainous interior. Its well-sheltered cove at Ovabükü shows no traces of built harbor, but its depth and sandy/pebbly beach would have allowed anchoring and pulling small vessels ashore. Tuna (1983:363–365; see also Love 1978:1119–1120) describes the eroded remains of another workshop for amphoras and other ceramics, with wine- or oil-processing installations strung along most of the shore here, including built stone dolia in several groups with associated structures.

As a third example, Bean and Cook (1952:178, 188–189) record the presence of an early Archaic architectural piece, later inscribed "horos limenos," that seems itself to have moved (Figure 14.4). The stone was subsequently reused in the construction of a mosque located about 2 km from the modern ferry port on the north of the peninsula at Körmen (Figure 14.3: No. 35), and likely once marked the ancient port's boundary. Tuna (1983:365–366) and Sevimli (2016:38, 55) record a Hellenistic pottery workshop here producing amphoras as well as common wares, and the scattered ceramics might indicate a functional port as early as the Geometric period. Bean and Cook argue that this port and its workshops served boats coming to and from Burgaz across the Gulf of Keramos from centers to the north in order to avoid the difficult and longer journey around the cape at Tekir, but the agricultural productivity of the landscape in the vicinity here too might have been a significant draw that should not be overlooked.

These are just three of many small ports strung along the coastlines of the Datça Peninsula. No two sites are identical, but the various appearance of storage and processing structures as well as amphora workshops underscores the extent to which agricultural production was diffused along the coast and dependent on short-haul movements to and over

FIGURE 14.4. Boundary stone, perhaps of the harbor at Körmen, inscribed *horos limenos*, in its contemporary context, built sideways into a mosque at Karaköy, about 2 km inland (E.S. Greene).

the sea: grapes or olives for pressing, empty amphoras for packaging, finished products for warehousing, and assembled cargos for export. Simple jetties or breakwaters could transform basic coves into effective harbors, but even those lacking maritime infrastructure could service the types of occasional traffic and small vessels that were sufficient to handle such movements and likely embedded within such small maritime communities where sailors were well aware of local winds and other conditions. While Tuna (2012:35–36) follows Bean and Cook (1952:179) in suggesting a vital road running the length of the peninsula (largely corresponding to the modern road), economic connections seem also to have utilized both overland communication as well as this archipelagic-like chain of settlements along the coast linked by the sea.

Network Modeling of Routine Regional Mobilities

Formal modeling of micro-mobilities between these sorts of ports and other sites allows us to hypothesize how diachronic shifts in the locations of settlement and activity may have both reflected and helped to generate changing patterns of movement and centrality across the peninsula. Using the relational structure of Social Network Analysis (SNA) we can consider connections between sites (or nodes) as a series of social relationships (or edges). The immediate problem for creating such networks using the archaeological evidence is how to systematically map relationships in the absence of a differentiated material record in which objects specific to particular locations can serve as proxies linking geographic areas (Leidwanger 2017; Greene 2018), or where concentrations of objects can allow for the spatial modeling of varying contours of interaction (Blake 2014). In light of the shared material culture visible across the Datça Peninsula and with an eye toward establishing a replicable system for generating links between communities, we utilize a combination of fixed-radius modeling and proximal point analysis (PPA) (Broodbank 2000; Rivers et al. 2013).

This approach assumes that sites interact most frequently with their nearest neighbors, and have regular interactions up to certain thresholds of distance, beyond which connections become markedly less frequent. These egalitarian factors lend both strengths and weaknesses to the analytical utility of the models. They allow consideration of all sites without preexisting assumptions about their relative importance in a broader network (Broodbank 2000:181; Collar 2014:102–103), but do not take into account known archaeological or historic evidence regarding the size or significance of a site in a particular period. As Rivers et al. (2013:109) have noted, such null models that assume fixed parameters of interaction reflect a necessarily simplified approach to the realities of interaction. Nonetheless, in light of the ongoing controversy over the relative importance of different sites on the peninsula at different periods, we have consciously sought a method that allows for the modeling of mobility in a less directed manner. The inherent unevenness of survey data resolution on site size, importance, connectedness, and the like makes this baseline geographical approach preferable. Our goal is to analyze change in network connections, and by association likely frequencies of mobility, using the same parameters but shifting distributions of sites across four broad periods: the Archaic/early Classical period, the late Classical/early Hellenistic period, the late Hellenistic/early Roman period, and the Roman/late Roman period. These periods reflect the major divisions that can be read reliably through archaeological survey across the peninsula, wherein each period exhibits a sufficient number of sites to generate analytically robust network structures.

Since our focus is on the development of human mobility, we have created our network to reflect the relative costs of basic movement within this particular landscape. While most spatial network models are built from linear ("as the crow flies") distances (e.g., Blake 2014; Broodbank 2000), we opted here to calculate distance in terms of temporal cost that can vary widely across the topography of the peninsula, as well as between movement by land and by sea. In practical terms, this entailed running least cost path analyses (in ArcGIS 10.4.1, using Tobler's hiking function with a digital elevation model of the peninsula) to derive approximate overland travel times in hours from each site to each other site on the peninsula (Gorenflo and Gale 1990; Tobler 1993; Herzog 2014). To account for the impact of the only securely identified road, the one running through the middle of the peninsula from Tekir to Burgaz and beyond toward the mainland, we reduced speed by 40% when traveling off this path on rough terrain (Tobler 1993; Irmischer and Clarke 2018). Where travel by sea was possible—among ports and the several small islets just off the coast—we also calculated times at "best average" sailing speeds of merchant vessels based on relative wind speed (i.e., the speed a mariner might reasonably hope to make in generally positive conditions). This approach grows out of a previously published method that incorporates not only wind speed but direction (Leidwanger 2013), but we justify the simplification here on the basis of several factors: first, mariners along the Datça Peninsula could simply wait out unhelpful winds when setting out to cover the short distances of interest; and second, the prevailing wind direction throughout the entire extended major sailing season is consistently from the north, allowing ships to make generally similar progress on a beam reach in either of the two major directions (westward and eastward) along these coasts (Heikell and Heikell 2013:187). From these calculations, sets of times were extracted in a tabular format that allowed us to find those sites that could be most quickly reached from each location, and to threshold these distances at meaningful values.

As a framework for connecting sites across the peninsula during each of our four periods, we determined two basic thresholds of two and four hours in each direction for journeys by land and sea, and a maximum of six connections originating from each site. Both the two- and four-hour trips would leave a certain amount of time to conduct necessary economic, political, religious, or social business at the destination before returning, effectively capturing a day's activity. Two hours represents a more manageable distance on a routine basis between agricultural villages; farmers often travel up to an hour or so to their own fields daily (Halstead and Jones 1989; Halstead 2014:110; cf. Marchetti 1994), and market centers in preindustrial contexts show a similar catchment of two to three hours in travel time (Bintliff 2002:245; McHugh 2019:229). Such distances suggest that the closest ties of less than a couple of hours should be weighted more strongly than those links produced over a distance representing as much as four hours' journey. But trips of up to four hours in duration, particularly those imagined during the longer days of summer, still allowed for establishing regular and productive connections across the peninsula. This approach to creating hypothetical connections must also balance the practical demands of modeling, where sufficient links are necessary to create effective network structure; test networks built solely from journeys of the shorter duration did not provide sufficient connectivity across the peninsula, particularly in earlier periods. Certain sites in certain periods had fewer than six connections within this four-hour threshold; in this case, we included only those sites reachable within four hours. Other sites had more than six connections within the threshold, in which case we included only the six sites most quickly reached. While the methodology did not privilege relationships between ports, islets, or inland sites, we found that virtually every site in every period was within a four-hour journey to some port site, highlighting the powerful connective role of maritime activity across the peninsula. The data generated by these connections based on proximity thresholds were visualized with the network-graphing program Gephi 0.9.2. The resulting visualizations explore how ease of mobility might have helped to generate different networks of communication among sites within a landscape marked by varying settlement densities, coastal access, and the distinctive challenges and opportunities of both overland and seaborne movement.

Connections between the limited number of port (n = 5), islet (n = 1), and other (n = 5: farmstead, settlement, artifact concentration) sites known from the Archaic and early Classical period can be visualized in a network graph based on the relational scheme described previously (Figure 14.5). The graph defines connections between sites using those parameters: namely, a maximum of six sites and a four-hour threshold. The resultant network is depicted in a ForceAtlas 2 layout. This layout spatializes the network by simulating a physical system in which nodes repulse each other like charged particles, while edges attract their nodes like springs (Jacomy et al. 2014:2). As a result, better-connected nodes are

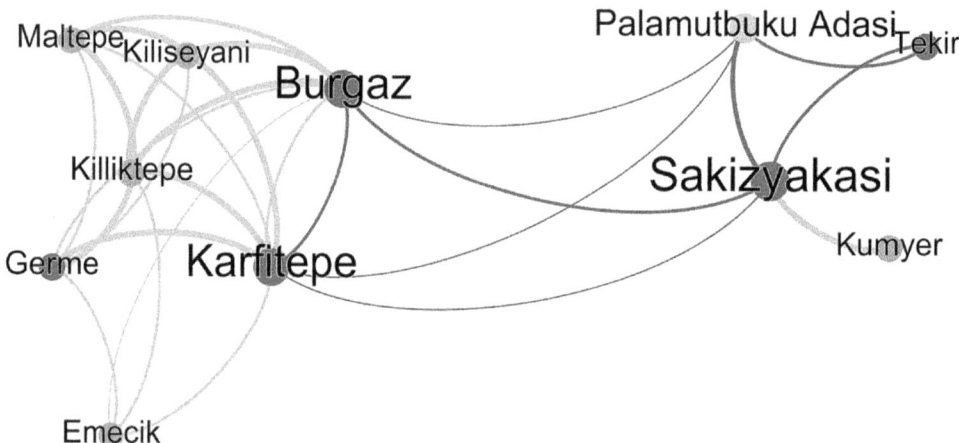

FIGURE 14.5. Network visualization (ForceAtlas2 layout) of connections across the Datça Peninsula during the Archaic/early Classical period.

drawn toward the center of the graph, while more distant nodes are located on the graph's periphery. Such a layout is based on network centrality, rather than geographic coordinates (for the location of each site, see Figure 14.3). Nodes are distinguished by shades according to their category: ports in darker grey, islets in medium gray, and all others in lighter gray. Their sizes reflect their betweenness centrality, or their role as connecting paths between other node pairs.[2] Edges are colored to differentiate between types of voyage: land in light gray and sea in dark gray. In instances where the same site was located within the four-hour threshold from another site by both land and sea, the shorter journey was prioritized. The thicknesses of the edges that connect sites are weighted according to proximity: journeys shorter than two hours are considered to have twice the strength or weight of those that take between two and four hours. The thickness of each resulting line on the graph indicates the relative strength of the link between sites, often comprising the cumulative strength of individual ties in either direction (i.e., from site A to site B and from site B to site A). The strengths of these connections can reflect the relative frequency of such journeys in our null model, in which civic, religious, infrastructural, and other parameters are not considered but could of course overlay and affect this network topology. In prior models, we variously dictated that each inland site connects to its closest port, that all sites link to religious or civic centers and the like, but here we have opted to explore the most neutral modeling.

Evolving Networks on the Datça Peninsula

The graph for the Archaic/early Classical period reflects a strongly connected center of the peninsula, with dense and robust links between interior agricultural sites (Kiliseyani, Maltepe, Killiktepe) and ports (Burgaz, Karfitepe, Germe) from which goods could be shipped. Because of its strong connections to multiple sites in this part of the peninsula, as well as its connection to port sites farther to the west (Sakızyakası, Palamutbükü), Burgaz takes on a highly central and structurally important role in the network. The sea links that connect Burgaz and Karfitepe in the center to Sakızyakası and Palamutbükü Adası in the west, though weaker, are fundamental to keeping the full network intact. The centrality of Palamutbükü Adası is perhaps overrepresented by the graph; as an islet, it can reach other sites only by sea, which in practice might have been a more limiting geographical reality. The religious sites at Emecik and Tekir stand at the periphery of these topographically focused networks, though their likely status (even in the early period) as important religious centers for the entire regional community may in fact have increased their centrality on certain occasions, creating another form of link. Without these weak links we would see two separate and disconnected networks at either end of the peninsula. As Rivers et al. (2013:120–121) explain for their archaeological networks following Granovetter's (1973, 1983) influential modeling, these weaker links facilitate movement across a network and promote stability, but may be costly to maintain. How then, does this network view of mobility develop over the periods that follow?

While the number of sites nearly doubles (n = 21: 7 ports, 1 islet, 13 other) in the late Classical/early Hellenistic period (Figure 14.6), the primary network connections across the

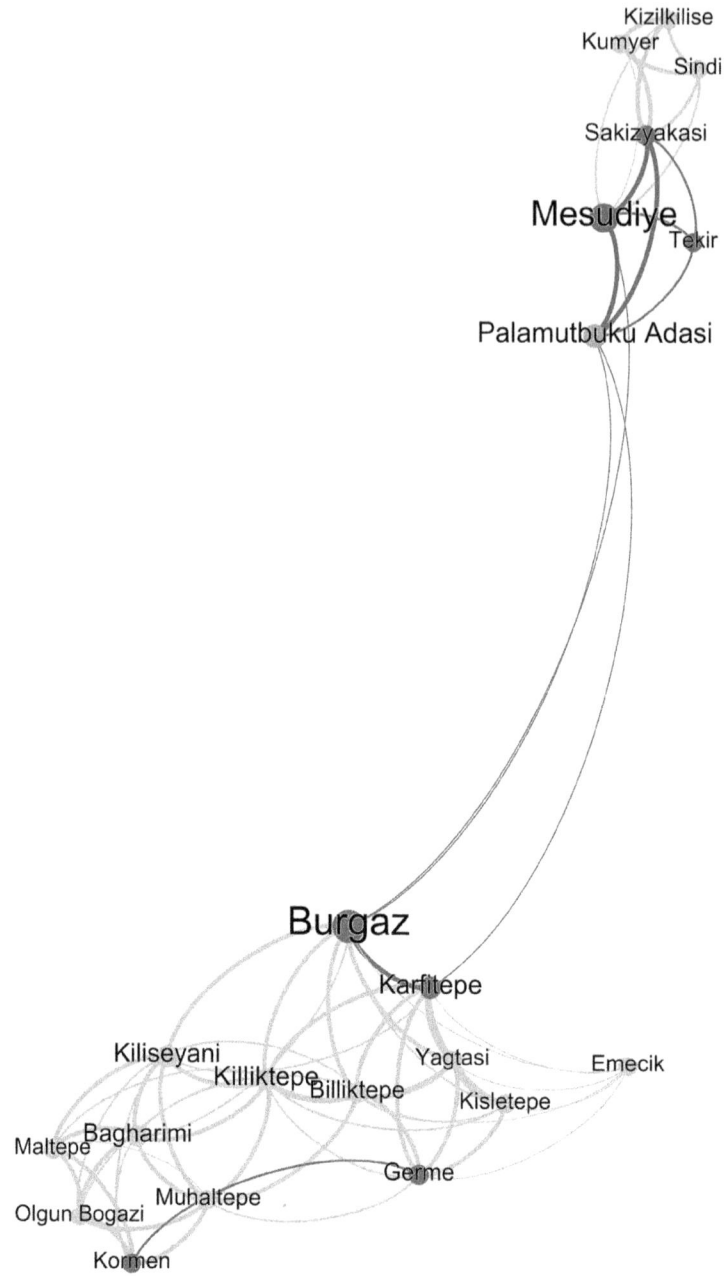

FIGURE 14.6. Network visualization (ForceAtlas2 layout) of connections across the Datça Peninsula during the late Classical/early Hellenistic period.

peninsula change little, suggesting generally consistent patterns of basic mobility despite the archaeological evidence for the growth of Tekir as a cultural center in the mid- to late fourth century. In this phase we see even stronger links between the closely connected agricultural sites and nearby ports in the center of the peninsula. Burgaz, and the nearby Karfitepe on the southern shore are highly central both to the local inland production sites and through weak seaborne ties to the ports and islets along the western peninsula, including Palamutbükü Adası and now Mesudiye, located to the east of Sakızyakası. As in the graphs for the Archaic/early Classical period, Emecik and Tekir are peripheral to the peninsula-wide network, even in a period when we know that the Tekir was developing as a thriving civic and commercial center. By their nature, proximity networks will favor sites that are geographically central, but the peripheral nature of Emecik and Tekir cannot be explained only by this phenomenon. As in the earlier era, these religious centers might have drawn visitors on festivals and public occasions, but such numerous weak links are invisible in a graph based on mobility routines in the landscape. Neither site seems particularly well-connected to its agricultural hinterlands, and this may not be surprising if they were not initially transshipment hubs. In the case of Tekir, however, stronger ties to farther-flung centers beyond the region may have been more important than weak links within the peninsula, suggesting this city developed, at least in its initial stages, as part of a wider maritime network phenomenon than just the Datça Peninsula.

But the situation changes rather dramatically in the late Hellenistic/early Roman period (Figure 14.7), as the number of sites jumps yet again, this time more than doubling (n = 47: 24 ports, 2 islets, 21 other). The peninsular network now looks entirely transformed, suggesting very different patterns of routine mobility. Despite its notional decline discussed above, Burgaz remains well connected to the agricultural hinterland and a series of ports on the southern coast. New ports on the northern coast now form an alternate path for the central valley sites, which can just as easily move their produce across new sea routes. Strong connections now link the two ends of the peninsula, with Körmen, Katıyalı, and Germe standing out on the north, while Burgaz, Kargı, and Karfitepe are similarly central to movement on the south. No longer does a single port demonstrate key centrality or a unique and fundamental structural role without which the network would fragment. On the western end of the peninsula, Tekir moves into a central position, concentrating mobility in its direction with increased connections to ports and agricultural sites on both the north and south of the peninsula. Slowly, the networks of the peninsula have developed connections to supply the population and export markets at Tekir, and the weak links that joined east to west have strengthened. In the east, mobility to Emecik is also now more facilitated, better reflecting its religious role in Knidian life. The process speaks for gradual expansion of paths and mobilities rather than a single movement that offers new priority to the west.

While this extension of small-scale mobility to encompass the complete peninsula marks the late Hellenistic/early Roman period, the situation changes yet again in the Roman/late Roman world (Figure 14.8), when the number of identified sites drops sharply to 27 (13 ports, 2 islets, 12 other). At this stage, both the number of sites and the general connectivity around the peninsula more closely resemble the late Classical/early Hellenistic period, with a few important exceptions. On the eastern end of the peninsula, Burgaz reassumes its position of centrality, a situation that aligns with the renewed activity focused on its large Harbor 4 (Leidwanger et al. 2015). But the ports at Germe, Gerenci, and Körmen highlight an ongoing mobility of goods from the interior as well as the maintenance of

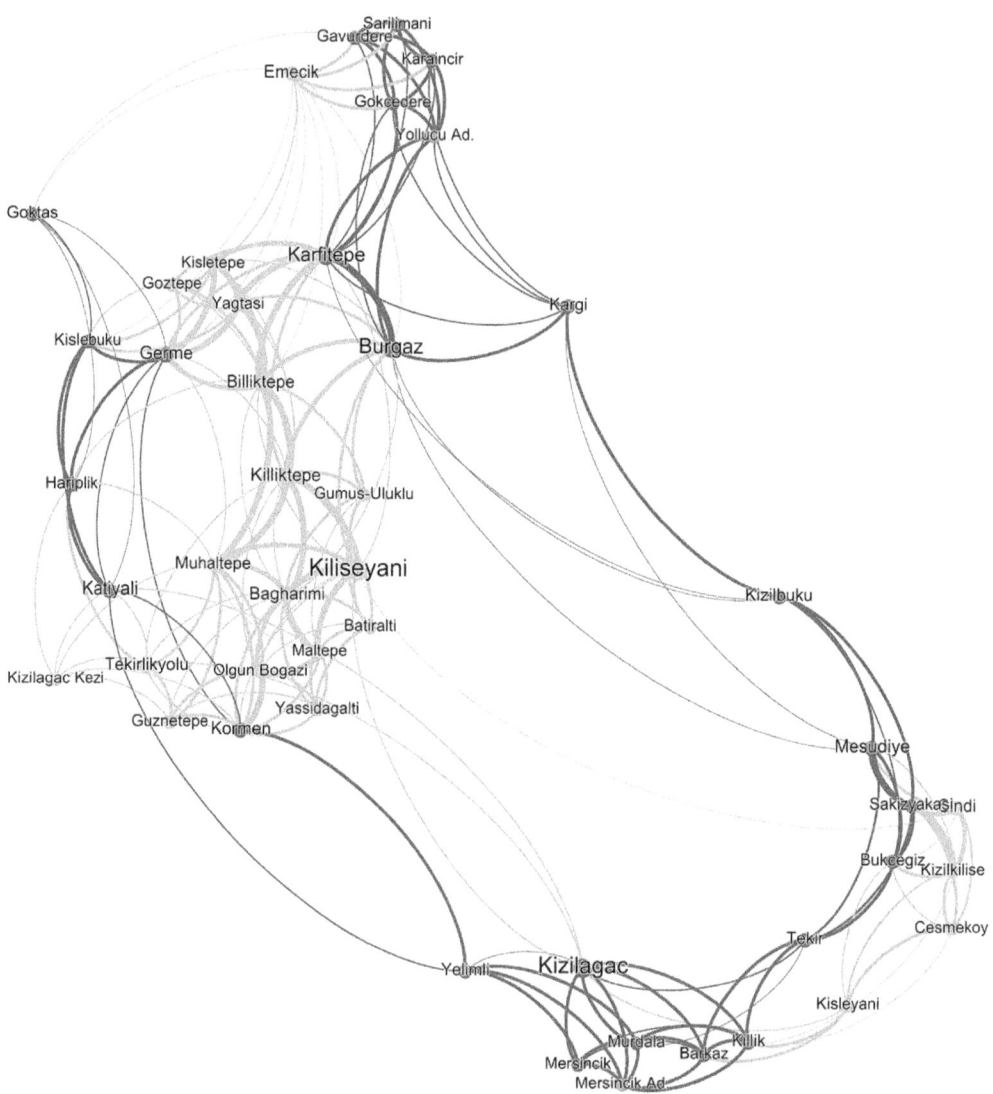

FIGURE 14.7. Network visualization (ForceAtlas2 layout) of connections across the Datça Peninsula during the late Hellenistic/early Roman period.

strong ties between east and west; weak ties by land also serve to integrate the overall peninsula. Tekir remains at the center of activity in the west, with its more crucial links surely also expanding outward from the peninsula toward farther-flung areas not considered in these graphs. In general network terms, ports prove to be somewhat more resilient than inland sites, perhaps because of their ability to interact through maritime connections over longer distances despite a general decline of population and agricultural exploitation that left fewer interior sites to connect. In each period, betweenness centrality figures calculated by Gephi (see Brandes 2001 for the algorithm) tend to be higher for ports and islets than inland sites.

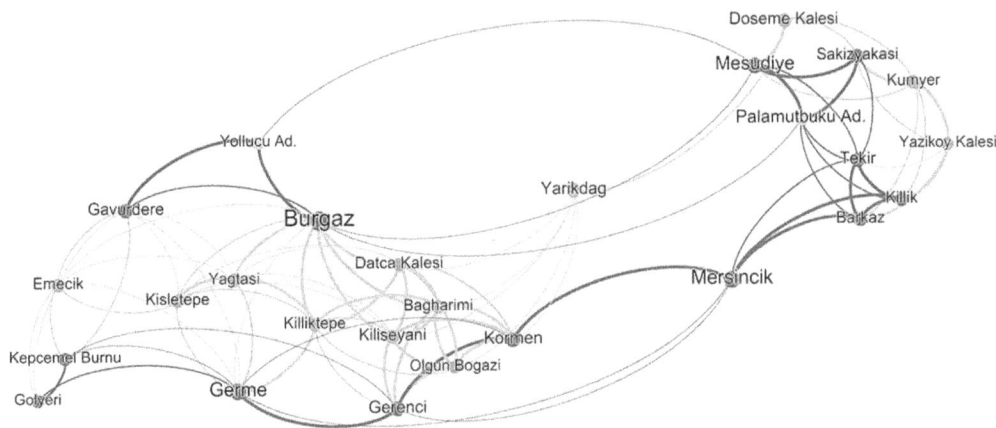

FIGURE 14.8. Network visualization (ForceAtlas2 layout) of connections across the Datça Peninsula during the mid-/late Roman period.

Nodes with high betweenness centrality lie on the shortest paths between multiple node pairs and are crucial to communication in the network; removal of these nodes would lead to large disruptions in the network structure.

Conclusions: Network Mobilities on the Datça Peninsula and Beyond

Population mobilities, and the associated shifts in centrality that accompany them, are not uncommon in regional contexts in the ancient Mediterranean world. Historical sources record movement by other communities in the Dorian hexapolis toward more advantageous locations, in most cases strategic coastal locations that afforded increased maritime centrality. In addition to the examples of Myous and Rhodes discussed above, a shift from inland Mylasa allowed coastal Halikarnassos to become the Carian capital. As along the Datça Peninsula, each of these cases seems to reflect a growing awareness of the critical role of networks that connect local communities through larger maritime mobilities; cities with good harbors that sit astride growing seaborne routes become increasingly central to dynamics of mobility within and beyond their regional contexts. But unlike the movement of Myous, Rhodes, and Halikarnassos, historical sources are silent about the population "removal" from Burgaz to Tekir, which Bean and Cook proposed for the Datça Peninsula. Bresson (1999:101) suggests that the shift was not worthy of mention, and it seems that the two sites had long been playing different and complementary roles within a common regional civic identity. All were Knidians regardless of whether they remained at Burgaz, migrated to Tekir, or moved elsewhere throughout the peninsula. In the literary record (see Porter in this volume for other examples of how ancient literary sources inform us on micro-mobilities), Herodotus himself uses the collective regional identifier "Knidia" interchangeably with the more specific geographic label of Knidos for a unique city, and the boundary stone found near Körmen seems to mark the borders of one of the many ports that helped people move around the region.

We should of course not be surprised that mobility within such contexts tends to be difficult to track archaeologically, given not only the shared material culture noted previously, but also the ongoing web of regional networks in which such larger-scale movements were embedded. The shift toward Tekir is one manifestation of its increasing centrality as part of the evolving socioeconomic situation on the peninsula as a whole. The uptick in agricultural communities markedly shifted regional centrality. It set the stage for Knidos at Tekir to eclipse Burgaz through its maritime connections to both shores. Yet it takes two more centuries of this settlement growth before significant new ports are established, suggesting that Tekir and Burgaz continued to dominate regional maritime activity. When more ports do appear, the largest growth is in the peninsula's northwest, probably taking advantage of the centrality of Knidos at Tekir. Of course, the network graphs reflect activity only on the peninsula. They do not account for Knidos's growing international connections, nor do they reveal, for example, potential links of minor ports north to Kos and Halikarnassos. Nonetheless, they highlight patterns in the bulk data that can help us propose hypotheses for how regional dynamics unfolded amid the growing mobility and interaction on the Datça Peninsula.

The emerging importance of not only Knidos at Tekir but other ports throughout the area, seen through this lens of network mobility, reflects the variability, vulnerability, resilience, and adaptation of coastal communities navigating the changing broader geopolitical and local socioeconomic conditions of an increasingly mobile and connected Mediterranean. Focusing on small-scale mobility and routine interaction throughout the peninsula offers one path forward in interrogating how the cadences of socioeconomic life can help generate larger network structures that result in population migrations normally ascribed to environmental catastrophe or polis-wide decisions. This one regional case study may hold clues also to larger questions about the movement of populations toward or between cities, the mobilization of goods and people in globalizing societies, and the impact of such shifts across spatial and temporal scales.

Acknowledgments

We are grateful to Megan Daniels for the invitation to participate in the IEMA conference and for the comments and insights offered by its participants and the anonymous reviewers of this volume. Thanks are due to the Turkish Ministry of Culture and Tourism for permission to conduct research at Burgaz, to Numan Tuna for his long-term collaboration on the harbor research, and to the organizations that provided financial and logistical support for this work: the Social Sciences and Humanities Research Council of Canada, Loeb Classical Library Foundation, Honor Frost Foundation, Canada Foundation for Innovation, Stanford University's Department of Classics, Brock University, Middle East Technical University, and the Institute of Nautical Archaeology (INA). Particular thanks are owed to INA's

Bodrum Research Center, especially Tuba Ekmekçi Littlefield and Esra Altınanıt Biçer for their ongoing support, and to James Gross for help compiling the site data used here for network modeling.

NOTES

1. Tuna (1983) and Sevimli (2016) record sites on the peninsula dating from the Geometric period; due to the paucity of sites in this early phase, our study takes the Archaic/early Classical period as its starting point.
2. As Collar et al. (2015:17–18) explain, "A node's betweenness centrality is defined as the fraction of the number of geodesics passing through this node over the number of geodesics between all pairs of nodes in the network. Nodes with a high betweenness centrality are often considered to be important intermediaries for controlling the flow of resources between other nodes, because they are located on paths between many other node pairs."

REFERENCES CITED

Anthony, D. 1990 Migration in Archeology: The Baby and the Bathwater. *American Anthropologist* 92(4):895–914.
Bean, G. E., and J. M. Cook 1952 The Cnidia. *Annual of the British School at Athens* 47:171–212.
Berges, D. 2006 *Knidos: Beiträge zur Geschichte der archaischen Stadt*. Philipp von Zabern Verlag, Mainz.
Bintliff, J. 2002 Going to Market in Antiquity. In *Stuttgarter Kolloquium zur historischen Geographie des Altertums 7, 1999: zu Wasser und zu Land*, edited by E. Olshausen and H. Sonnabend, pp. 209–250. Franz Steiner Verlag, Stuttgart.
Blackman, D. J. 1982 Ancient Harbours in the Mediterranean. Part 2. *International Journal of Nautical Archaeology* 11(3):185–211.
Blake, E. 2014 *Social Networks and Regional Identity in Bronze Age Italy*. Cambridge University Press, Cambridge.
Boehm, R. 2018 *City and Empire in the Age of the Successors: Urbanization and Social Response in the Making of the Hellenistic Kingdoms*. University of California Press, Berkeley.
Brandes, U. 2001 A Faster Algorithm for Betweenness Centrality. *Journal of Mathematical Sociology* 25(2):163–177.
Braudel, F. 1972 *The Mediterranean and the Mediterranean World in the Age of Philip II*. Translated by S. Reynolds. Harper Colophon Books, New York.
Bresson, A. 1999 Cnide à l'époque classique : la cité et ses villes. *Revue des études anciennes* 101:83–114.
Bresson, A. 2013 Knidos. In *The Encyclopedia of Ancient History*, edited by R. S. Bagnall, K. Brodersen, C. B. Champion, A. Erskine, and S. R. Huebner, pp. 3793–3794. 1st Ed. Blackwell, London.
Broodbank, C. 2000 *An Island Archaeology of the Early Cyclades*. Cambridge University Press, Cambridge.
Bruns-Özgan, C. 2013 *Knidos: Ergebnisse der Ausgrabungen von 1996–2006*. Ege Yayınları, Istanbul.
Büyüközer, A. 2012 *Knidos limanları*. PhD thesis, Selçuk University, Konya.

Collar, A. C. F. 2014 Networks and Ethnogenesis. In *A Companion to Ethnicity in the Ancient World*, edited by J. McInerney, pp. 97–111. Blackwell, London.

Collar, A., F. Coward, T. Brughmans, and B. J. Mills 2015 Networks in Archaeology: Phenomena, Abstraction, Representation. *Journal of Archaeological Method and Theory* 22:1–32.

Demand, N. 1989 Did Knidos Really Move? The Literary and Epigraphical Evidence. *Classical Antiquity* 8(2):224–237.

Demand, N. 1990 *Urban Relocation in Archaic and Classical Greece: Flight and Consolidation*. University of Oklahoma Press, Norman.

Doksanaltı, E. M., S. Sevmen, İ. Karaoğlan, L. U. Erdoğan, and C. Özgan 2015 Knidos Kazı ve Araştırmaları: 2012–2013. *Kazı Sonuçları Toplantısı* 36(2):517–546.

Gabrielsen, V. 2000 The Synoikized Polis of Rhodes. In *Polis and Politics: Studies in Ancient Greek History. Presented to Mogens Herman Hansen on his Sixtieth Birthday, August 20, 2000*, edited by T. Flensted-Jensen, H. Nielsen, and L. Rubinstein, pp. 177–205. Museum Tusculanum Press, Copenhagen.

Granovetter, M. 1973 The Strength of Weak Ties. *American Journal of Sociology* 78(6):1360–1380.

Granovetter, M. 1983 The Strength of Weak Ties: A Network Theory Revisited. *Sociological Theory* 1:201–233.

Gorenflo, L. J., and N. Gale 1990 Mapping Regional Settlement in Information Space. *Journal of Anthropological Archaeology* 9:240–274.

Greene, E. S. 2018 Shipwrecks as Indices of Archaic Mediterranean Trade Networks. In *Maritime Networks in the Ancient Mediterranean World*, edited by J. Leidwanger and C. Knappett, pp. 132–162. Cambridge University Press, Cambridge.

Greene, E. S., and J. Leidwanger 2019 Knidian "Anyports": A Model of Coastal Adaptation and Socioeconomic Connectivity from Southwest Turkey. *Mediterranean Historical Review* 34(1):9–25.

Greene, E. S., J. Leidwanger, and N. Tuna 2019 Archaeological Investigations in the Harbors of Burgaz, Turkey: 2011–2015 Field Seasons. *International Journal of Nautical Archaeology* 48(1):103–122.

Halstead, P. 2014 *Two Oxen Ahead: Pre-Mechanized Farming in the Mediterranean*. Wiley Blackwell, Malden.

Halstead, P., and G. Jones 1989 Agrarian Ecology in the Greek Islands: Time Stress, Scale and Risk. *Journal of Hellenic Studies* 109:41–55.

Heikell, R., and L. Heikell 2013 *Turkish Waters and Cyprus Pilot*. 9th Ed. Imray, Laurie, Norie and Wilson, St Ives.

Herzog, I. 2014 A Review of Case Studies in Archaeological Least-Cost Analysis. *Archeologia e calcolatori* 25:223–239.

Höghammar, K. 2016 International Networks of an Island Port—the Case of Kos. In *Ancient Ports: The Geography of Connections. Proceedings of an International Conference at the Department of Archaeology and Ancient History, Uppsala University, 23–25 September 2010*, edited by K. Höghammar, B. Alroth, and A. Lindhagen, pp. 95–165. Boreas—Uppsala Studies in Ancient Mediterranean and Near Eastern Civilizations 34. Uppsala Universitet, Uppsala.

Horden, P., and N. Purcell 2000 *The Corrupting Sea: A Study of Mediterranean History*. Blackwell, Oxford.

Irmischer, I., and K. C. Clarke 2018 Measuring and Modeling the Speed of Human Navigation. *Cartography and Geographic Information Science* 45(2):177–186.

Jacomy, M., T. Venturini, S. Heymann, and M. Bastian 2014 ForceAtlas2, A Continuous Graph Layout Algorithm for Handy Network Visualization Designed for the Gephi Software. *PLoS ONE* 9(6):e98679. DOI:10.1371/journal.pone.0098679.

Koparal, E., N. Tuna, and A. E. İplikçi 2014 Hellenistic Wine Press in Burgaz/Old Knidos. *METU Journal of the Faculty of Architecture* 31(2):93–107.

Leidwanger, J. 2013 Modeling Distance with Time in Ancient Mediterranean Seafaring: A GIS Application for the Interpretation of Maritime Connectivity. *Journal of Archaeological Science* 40:3302–3308.

Leidwanger, J. 2017 From Time Capsules to Networks: New Light on Roman Shipwrecks in the Maritime Economy. *American Journal of Archaeology* 121(4):595–619.

Leidwanger, J. 2019 The *Knidia* and Its Amphoras: Taking Stock of a Regional Agricultural Economy. *HEROM: Journal on Hellenistic and Roman Material Culture* 8:237–255.

Leidwanger, J., E. S. Greene, and N. Tuna 2015 A Late Antique Ceramic assemblage at Burgaz, Datça Peninsula, South-west Turkey, and the "Normality of the Mixed Cargo" in the Ancient Mediterranean. *International Journal of Nautical Archaeology* 44(2):300–311.

Love, I. C. 1974 Excavations at Knidos, 1971. *Türk Arkeoloji Dergisi Sayı* 20(2):97–142.

Love, I. C. 1978 A Brief Summary of Excavations at Knidos 1967–1973. In *The Proceedings of the Xth International Congress of Classical Archaeology*, edited by E. Akurgal, pp. 1110–1133. Türk Tarih Kurumu, Ankara.

Mackil, E. 2004 Wandering Cities: Alternatives to Catastrophe in the Greek Polis. *American Journal of Archaeology* 108(4):493–516.

Marchetti, C. 1994 Anthropological Invariants in Travel Behavior. *Technological Forecasting and Social Change* 47:75–88.

McHugh, M. 2019 Going the Extra Mile: Travel, Time, and Distance in Classical Attica. *The Annual of the British School at Athens* 114:207–240.

Rivers, R., C. Knappett, and T. E. Evans 2013 Network Models and Archaeological Spaces. In *Computational Approaches to Archaeological Spaces*, edited by A. Bevan and M. Lake, pp. 99–126. Left Coast Press, Walnut Creek.

Sevimli, E. 2016 *Development of Burgaz (Palaia Knidos) and Its Hinterland in Context of Settlement Pattern Analysis*. MA thesis, Middle East Technical University, Ankara.

Tobler, W. 1993 *Non-Isotropic Geographic Modeling*. Technical Report No. 93-1. National Center for Geographic Information and Analysis, Santa Barbara.

Tozluca, D. O., and E. M. Doksanaltı 2019 A Group of Protogeometric and Geometric Pottery Found in Knidos. *Anodos: Studies of the Ancient World* 14:217–225.

Tuna, N. 1983 *Batı Anadolu Kent-Devletlerinde Mekan Organizasyonu: Knidos Örneği*. PhD thesis, Dokuz Eylül University, Izmir.

Tuna, N. 1989 Datça Yarımadası Arkeolojik Yüzey Araştırmaları, 1987. *Araştırma Sonuçları Toplantısı* 6:141–158.

Tuna, N. 2012 *Knidos Teritoryumu'nda Arkeolojik Araştırmalar (Archaeological Investigations at the Knidian Territorium)*. ODTÜ Tarihsel Çevre Araştırma ve Değerlendirme Merkezi (TAÇDAM), Ankara.

Tuna, N., N. Atıcı, İ. Sarkaya, and E. Koparal 2009 The Preliminary Results of Burgaz Excavations within the Context of Locating Old Knidos. In *Die Karer und die Anderen: internationales Kolloqium an der Freien Universität Berlin*, edited by F. Rumscheid, pp. 517–532. Rudolf Habelt Verlag, Bonn.

Tuna, N., N. Atıcı, and İ. Sakarya 2010 Burgaz Yerleşimindeki M.Ö. 4.-3. Yüzyıl Zeytinyağı ve Şarap Atölyeleri Üzerine Değerlendirmeler. In *Olive Oil and Wine Production in Anatolia during Antiquity, International Symposium Proceedings (06–08 November 2008 Mersin)*, edited by Ü. Aydınoğlu, and A. K. Şenol, pp. 199–212. Kilikia Arkeolojisini Araştırma Merkezi, Istanbul.

Woolf, G. 2016 Movers and Stayers. In *Migration and Mobility in the Early Roman Empire*, edited by L. de Ligt, and L. E. Tacoma, pp. 438–461. *Studies in Global Social History* 23. Brill, Leiden.

PART V

Migration and Complexity

CHAPTER FIFTEEN

Assessing the Possibility of Trans-Maritime Mobility in Archaic Hominins

Does Afro-Eurasian Coastal Paleogeography Support Sweepstakes Dispersal in *Homo*?

Thomas P. Leppard

Abstract *Did archaic species of our genus cross oceans and arrive at insular landmasses during the Pleistocene? The data—from Island Southeast Asia, but perhaps also from the Mediterranean—increasingly appear to suggest that, rarely, they may have done so. Does this mean we should abandon our overall model of oceans and seas as, in general, inhibitors rather than facilitators of hominin mobility? In this chapter I explore this question. In particular, I emphasize that deliberate, strategic dispersal is not the only mode of dispersal which accounts for island colonization; molecular phylogenies also point to the existence of "sweepstakes" or long-distance dispersal. I evaluate the paleogeographies of the glacial and interglacial Mediterranean and Island Southeast Asia, suggesting that, during glacials, they were likely conducive to enabling sweepstakes dispersal events. This means we need not necessarily assume that limited evidence for over-water dispersal in more archaic members of* Homo *is evidence for hitherto unsuspected technological, cognitive, and social sophistication.*

This chapter considers human mobility and migration in their longitudinal dimension, extending the analysis offered elsewhere in this volume back into deep time. In particular, I consider the extent to which biogeographic barriers did or did not impose mobility constraints on our own, and on more archaic, hominin species. I do this in the wider context of what might appropriately be called the "Paleolithic seafaring debate"—the ongoing contention regarding whether hominins beside our own species were capable of deliberately crossing large water gaps to colonize new habitats (Leppard and Runnels 2017).

It is becoming increasingly clear that archaic taxa, including perhaps Neanderthals and *Homo erectus,* did indeed traverse maritime boundaries during the Lower and Middle

Paleolithic. Some scholars have accordingly assumed that the qualitative aspects of this mobility (motivation, means, cognitive and technological process) precisely paralleled the qualitative aspects of mobility in our own species—that is, that dispersal of this sort was intentional, involving goal-directed thought and action and reliant on technological adaptations to long-distance maritime travel, comparable to the other examples of mobility discussed in the preceding and succeeding chapters. If they are correct, and oceans have always been facilitators of mobility in *Homo* rather than inhibitors of it, this would have major, revisionist implications for how we understand human evolution and the archaeology of the Paleolithic; not only for understanding how and when modern strategies of mobility and migration developed in our genus, but also for broader models of the emergence of the package of neurosocial traits that we collectively characterize as "modern behavior." For example, if *H. erectus* were engaging in behaviors of this sort in Southeast Asia a million years ago, our overall conception of the behavioral suites and capacities (including capacity for language) of that species would necessarily have to be reevaluated.

It is not clear, however, that this assumption—that the cognitive, social, and ecological patterns driving over-water movement in all species of *Homo* are identical—is warranted (see now Gaffney 2021). Choosing between oceans as inhibitors of mobility versus facilitators of it, is then of enormous importance; but assessing whether or not the assumptions of the deliberate transmaritime mobility model are warranted is rendered intractable by the nature of the problem. In particular, evaluating the motivation driving intrinsically unrecoverable and extremely rare behavior, deep in the Pleistocene and with little or no material correlates, is prodigiously challenging.

I have argued elsewhere, from a number of perspectives, that the forces driving and circumstances surrounding transmaritime dispersal by archaic hominin taxa should not be understood as homologous to intentional over-water migration in our own species (e.g., Leppard 2014, 2015a, 2015b; cf. Dennell et al. 2014; Gaffney 2021). Here, I build on and develop a previous argument (Leppard 2015b), approaching the problem via spatial analysis of the data for maritime dispersal in *Homo*. First, I briefly review (1) the data that are held to be indicative of transmaritime mobility by hominins and (2) modes of dispersal for mammals in general, highlighting the difference between deliberate and "sweepstakes" dispersal. I then evaluate these data within their paleogeographic, paleohydrological, and paleoenvironmental contexts, attempting to identify patterns that might be indicative of this mobility representing either deliberate or sweepstakes dispersal. I suggest that key differences between the environmental and geographic contexts of archaic hominin and modern human dispersal events indicate that it is unlikely that they were comparable in terms of motivation and mechanism. I conclude by highlighting the implications of this observation.

The Ocean as Barrier to—or Facilitator of—Movement?

The majority of scholarship regarding the distribution of various hominin species during the Pleistocene has explicitly or implicitly understood large water barriers to have been impediments to movement (e.g., Boivin et al. 2017; Dennell 2009; Gamble 2003). These impediments—along with those offered by mountains, deserts, and the higher latitudes—are held to explain the directionality and restriction of out-of-Africa dispersal, with archaic hominins confined to Eurasia below about fifty degrees north (depending on the glacial-interglacial cycle). Only with the advent of our own species were these last, substantive eco-geographic barriers—salt water and extreme cold—overcome with the colonization of the Americas and Australia, along with high-altitude and high-latitude adaptations. This general model is now subject to critique (Bednarik 2003, 2014; Runnels 2014; Runnels et al. 2014a; Simmons 2012, 2014), with this critique fueled by apparent evidence for maritime dispersal prior to the appearance of our own species (now at perhaps 400,000 to 300,000 years ago; Hublin et al. 2017) and, in particular, prior to the appearance of anatomically modern members of that species.

Before reviewing this evidence, it is important to briefly emphasize the role that paleo-geographic reconstruction plays in this debate (and will play in this chapter). Over the course of the Quaternary, the planet has oscillated between glacial and interglacial periods. Because of the capture of liquid water in polar icecaps during glacials, sea levels during glacial periods were much lower than during interglacials (Lambeck and Chappell 2001). Many of the fringing islands of the Afro-Eurasian megacontinent are on continental rather than oceanic crust; accordingly, many were united by falling sea levels with the mega-continental landmass during glacials, facilitating biotic exchange. However, a number of factors further complicate this, including: (1) that not all glacials witnessed comparable levels of eustatic drawdown, glacials being of differing severity; and (2) that isostatic crustal rebound from ice-sheet loss, and the highly dynamic geotectonic nature of various parts of the Afro-Eurasian fringe (i.e., Island Southeast Asia, the Aegean), combine to render locally specific calculations of insularity frustratingly inexact. Suffice it to say that hominin skeletal or artifactual material from what is currently an insular landmass does not necessarily imply over-water dispersal. Attention to local paleogeographic specifics is vital when considering what does, and what does not, constitute evidence for maritime (as opposed to cyclically terrestrial) dispersal.

NORTHWEST EURASIA: GIBRALTAR, BAB-EL-MANDEB, AND THE BALKANS

Understanding the likelihood of transmaritime dispersal in Northwest Eurasia is complicated by the geography of the African plate's interactions with tectonic units to the north and northeast. For the duration of the existence of the genus *Homo,* the only terrestrial route out of (or indeed back into) Africa has been via the Sinai (Figure 15.1); but the proximity of Africa to Eurasia at both the Straits of Gibraltar and Bab-el-Mandeb ("Gate of Tears") between the Horn of Africa and Yemen has meant that these straits have featured substantially in discussion of hominin exit routes from Africa. The complicating factor is, of course, that archaeologically visible presence of hominins in—for example—Iberia or Arabia (both in fact home to early extra-African hominin populations) could as equally well be explained by dry-shod, if roundabout, dispersal via Sinai. Bab-el-Mandeb is often mentioned in passing as a potential dispersal route (e.g., Abbate and Sagri 2012:4–5; Dennell

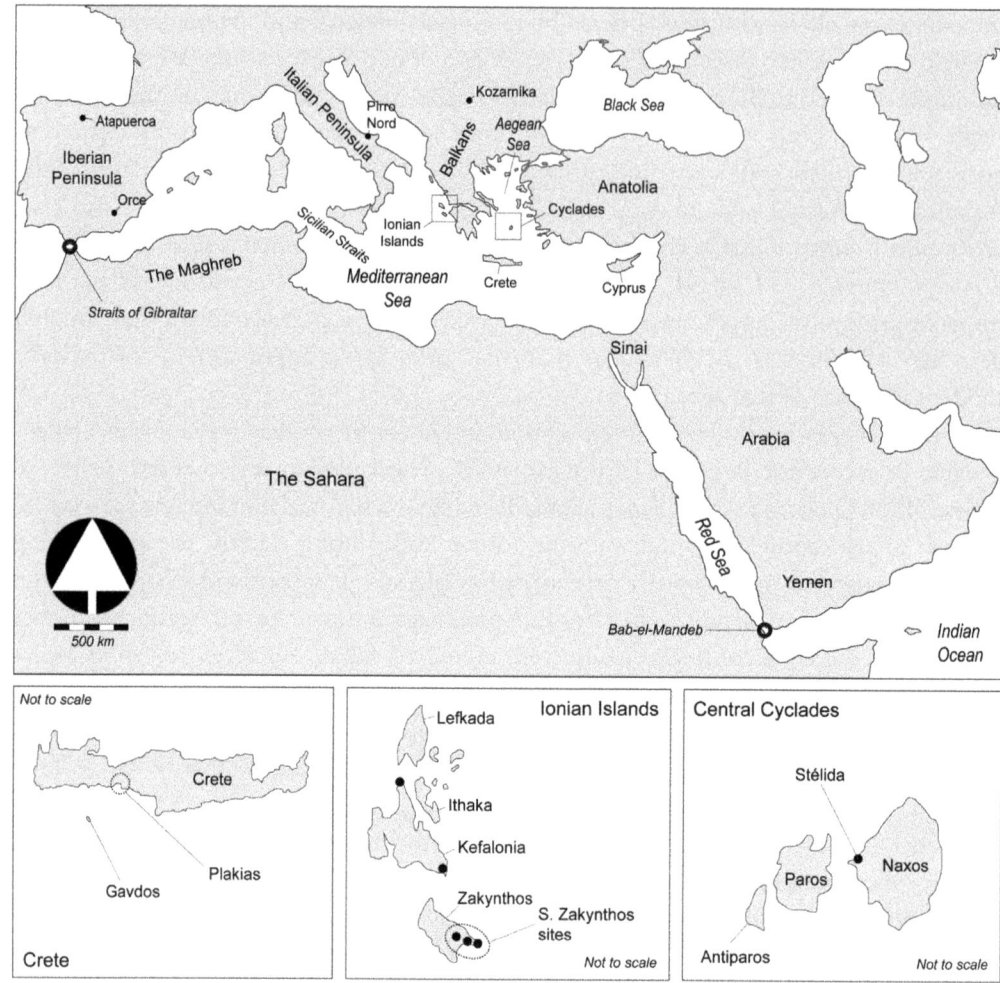

FIGURE 15.1. Contexts of possible over-water hominin dispersal in Northwest Eurasia, with sites and locations mentioned in the text and modern sea level depicted. Note that, because Lefkada/Leukas has definitely been connected to the mainland during glacials, Middle Paleolithic sites on it are not depicted. Sites on the other Ionian Islands after Ferentinos et al. 2012.

2003:435; Mithen and Reed 2002; Tchernov 1992:116–117; but Petraglia 2003:169–170 for a sensible and critical commentary), although this discussion may in part be premised on the assumption that the terrestrial connection at the foot of the Red Sea lasted until the Plio-Pleistocene, which is not correct (Fernandes et al. 2006; cf. Bailey 2009). The well-attested and early hominin presence in Iberia (Carbonell et al. 2008; Toro-Moyano et al. 2013) has similarly suggested to some the possibility of trans-Gibraltar maritime dispersal (for a review, see O'Regan 2008), although when it comes to the Atapuerca hominins themselves scholarship is laudably circumspect on assigning a maritime route.

With regard to evidence for maritime dispersal elsewhere in the Mediterranean, the archaeology is arguably clearer, but the paleogeography less so, and here the Balkan Peninsula and the islands between it and Anatolia loom large (Figure 15.1). Claims for an archaic hominin presence on islands that almost certainly remained separated from the Afro-Eurasian mainland since 5.33 million years ago were made by Chelidonio (2001) and Kopaka and Mantzanas (2009), for Melos and Gavdos respectively. It was, however, a high-profile project on Crete, an island similarly resolutely insular over the Plio-Pleistocene, which made more substantial claims for colonization of the insular Aegean by premodern hominins. Strasser and colleagues (2010, 2011) reported a series of surface assemblages from the Plakias region of the island that contained chipped stone artifacts that might reasonably be interpreted as belonging to an Acheulean (i.e., a Lower Paleolithic) industry. Subsequent to this, comparable finds have been reported from elsewhere on Crete (Runnels et al. 2014b) and Cyprus (Strasser et al. 2016; Moutsiou 2021), as well as Rodafnidia on Lesvos (Galanidou et al. 2016a). In addition to material assigned to the Acheulean on morphotypological grounds, chipped stone artifacts in a Mousterian Middle Paleolithic tradition—and usually associated with *H. neanderthalensis* or *heidelbergensis*—are reported from Naxos (Carter et al. 2014; supported now by infrared stimulated luminescence dates; Carter et al. 2019), in the central Aegean, as well as from the Ionian Islands, on the western side of the Balkan Peninsula (Ferentinos et al. 2012; Galanidou et al. 2016b). Here, the majority are reported from Lefkada/Leukas, which has often been conjoined with the mainland, but surface finds are also reported from Kefalonia and Zakynthos.

How do we begin to parse this complex situation? I return to the topic below, but a good starting point for now is close attention to the paleogeography. Rodafnidia provides excellent evidence for an Acheulean tradition with associated absolute dates: but Lesvos has been cyclically connected to the Anatolian seaboard during glacials, so this is inadmissible as evidence for maritime dispersal. Naxos, too, in several paleogeographic reconstructions of the Aegean during severe glacials (i.e., Lykousis 2009) is joined to the continental landmass. The presence of Mousterian technology at Stélida may, then, be more parsimoniously explained as an outcome of terrestrial dispersal during a severe Middle Pleistocene glacial (e.g., Marine Isotope Stage, or MIS, 12). Crete (and also Gavdos) appears to have been truly insular since the in-filling of the Mediterranean basin after the Messenian Salinity Crisis at the end of the Miocene, and the Ionian Islands may have been tenuously connected to or slightly separated from the Balkan mainland (Lykousis 2009; Zavitsanou et al. 2015; Lefkada/Leukas certainly was connected). That notwithstanding, much of the central Aegean could have been reached terrestrially.

The temporal resolution of the data is also a concern. With Naxos and Lesvos removed, all the remaining artifacts are surface finds, dated by morphotypological characteristics. This is clearly problematic in that the technological choices that determine morphology are not always intrinsically chronologically diagnostic (or, indeed, diagnostic to species, and recent claims for very early *Homo sapiens* presence in the Aegean further muddy the waters in terms of hominins responsible for Middle Paleolithic assemblages [Harvati et al. 2019]). Strasser et al. (2011) purported to date the artifacts by their association with uplifted (and dated) geological deposits, suggesting that they should be considered at least 110,000 years old, but Sakellariou and Galanidou are not convinced by the method (2016) and, in any case, a date of this sort could support a Middle Paleolithic just as well as a Lower Paleolithic attribution. Regardless, the dates on this material should be considered open to revision, especially as Sakellariou and Galanidou (2016) would rather interpret the Plakias material—simply on morphological and technological criteria—as Middle Paleolithic, and similarly Papoulia (2017) sees the majority of the data fitting more comfortably within a Middle Paleolithic tradition. With the suspect evidence pared away, then, we are left with a body of data that is nonetheless suggestive of a Middle Paleolithic, and potentially late Lower Paleolithic, presence on potentially two insular landmasses: Crete, and the paleo-Ionian islands.

SOUTHEAST ASIA: ACROSS THE WALLACE-HUXLEY LINE

Data suggesting transmaritime dispersal in tropical Southeast Asia (referred to as Island Southeast Asia, or ISEA) are more persuasive. The paleogeographic context (which I consider in more detail in the latter part of this chapter) has varied substantially over the Quaternary (Bird et al. 2005; Hall 2009, 2013; Hanebuth et al. 2011; Robles et al. 2015). During interglacials, as in our current one, the landmasses between the Malay Peninsula and Australia were decidedly insular in their organization, with the large islands of Borneo, Java, and Sumatra separated from New Guinea and Australia by a sea of small islands of various geotectonic pedigrees, from the subduction-derived Lesser Sundas in the south to the Philippines in the north (Figure 15.2). These islands substantially differ in their biotic composition from the large islands to the west: accordingly, and reflecting that this observation was first made by Wallace, they are referred to as "Wallacea" (with Wallace's line, modified by Huxley, the biogeographic boundary separating the Wallacean from continental faunas). During glacials, however, this picture changes dramatically. Borneo, Sumatra, and Java were highlands united into a large extension of the paleo-Malay peninsula, known as Sundaland (of which the Lesser Sunda islands, crucially, were not part) and drained by a now-drowned river system. The Makassar Strait between Borneo and Sulawesi, and the Lombok Strait between Bali and Lombok, were substantially narrower, and Sundaland reached toward the paleo-Philippines—either united with Palawan (during severe draw-down) or minutely separated from it by the Balabac Strait (although the Mindoro Strait, between Palawan and Mindoro, probably remained open). Australia, New Guinea, and associated islands were united in the paleo-landmass of Sahul.

Archaeological and fossil data from east of the Wallace-Huxley line, while not plentiful, are more reliably indicative of transmaritime dispersal than in Northwest Eurasia (Figure 15.2). The best evidence comes from Flores, a small island in the Lesser Sundas. Here, from sites in the So'a Basin, hominin activity—in the form of an expedient chipped stone technology—can be dated to just over a million years ago (at Wolo Sege), while the nearby site at Mata Menge yielded comparable artifacts alongside isolated hominin teeth and a mandible fragment dated to 700,000 years ago (Brumm et al. 2010, 2016; van den Bergh

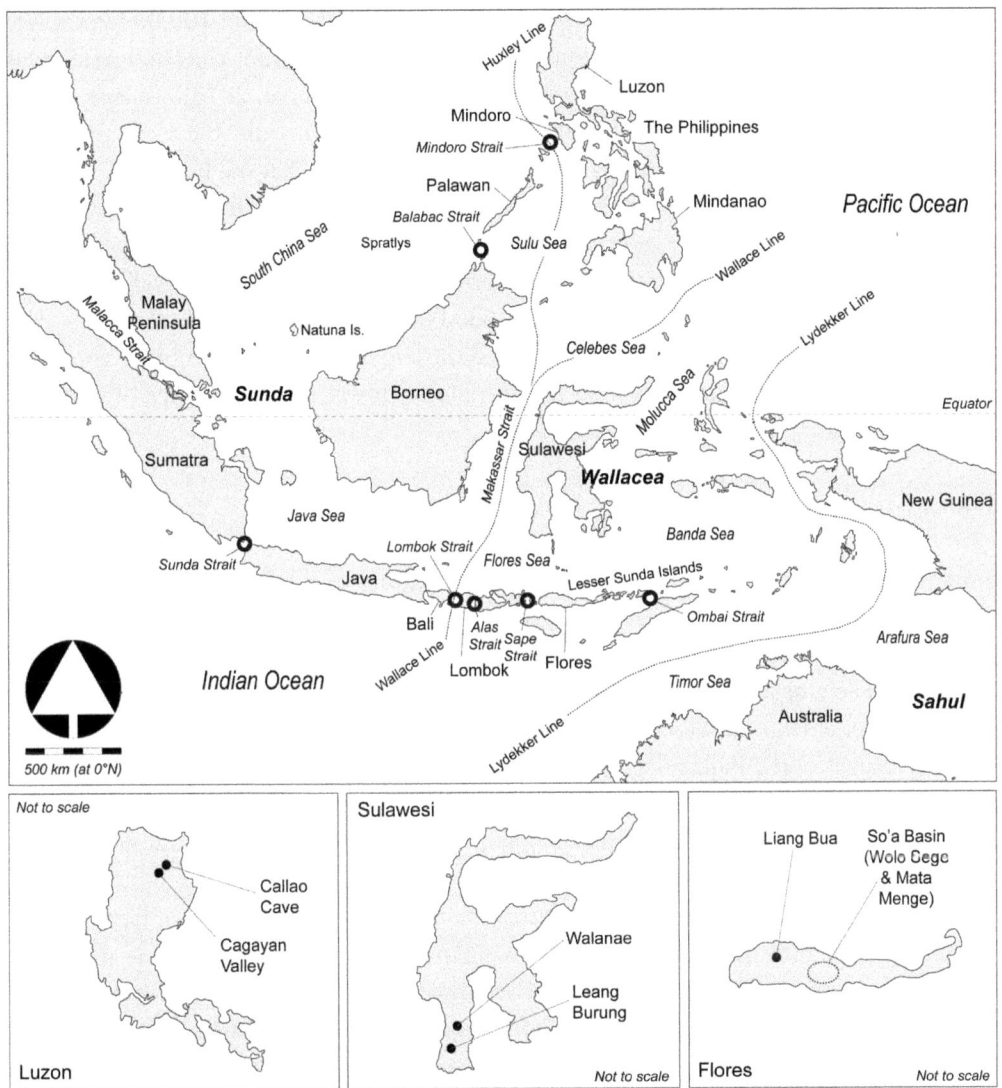

FIGURE 15.2. Contexts of possible over-water hominin dispersal in ISEA, with sites and locations mentioned in the text and modern sea level depicted. Biogeographic regions (Sahul etc.) in italic boldface, and biogeographic boundaries as dashed lines.

et al. 2016a). These fossils have been assigned, on a morphological basis, to the hominin taxon otherwise known uniquely from the Liang Bua cave on Flores, *Homo floresiensis*. The most complete fossil of this taxon, LB1, is now dated to between 100,000 and 60,000 years ago (Sutikna et al. 2016),[1] and *floresiensis* remains (excepting *H. luzonensis*) the only skeletal evidence for over-water dispersal in premodern *Homo*.

Since the discovery of the Early-Middle Pleistocene presence of hominins in southern Wallacea, there have been additional finds in central and northern Wallacea. Van den Bergh et al. (2016b) report the presence of chipped stone artifacts from the Talepu site in the Walanea basin of southern Sulawesi dated to between 200,000 and 100,000 years ago, and a comparably expedient hard-hammer technology is noted from the basal stratum at Leang Burung 2 in the mountains behind Makassar (Brumm et al. 2018). To this we can now add new data from the insular Philippines. A metatarsal from the Callao Cave in northern Luzon, dated to 67,000 years ago, has a morphology that might hint at affinities to *floresiensis,* although no associated stone tools were recovered (Mijares et al. 2010), and is recognized as the novel taxon *Homo luzonensis* (Détroit et al. 2019). More recently, evidence of a butchered endemic rhinoceros, *Rhinoceros philippinensis,* in the Cagayan Valley pushes a hominin presence in Luzon back to 780,000–630,000 years ago (Ingicco et al. 2018). Further work in the Callao Cave itself has increased the size of the fossil assemblage associated with *H. luzonensis,* demonstrating that this diminutive taxon exhibits a range of primitive and derived features (Détroit et al. 2019).

TAKING STOCK OF THE DATA

From both the northwestern and southeastern extremities of the Afro-Eurasian landmass, archaeological data (albeit of variable quality) suggest limited over-water dispersal by archaic hominins. These data are clearly more convincing when surface assemblages or assemblages comprised solely of archaeological material can be related to excavated assemblages and/or fossil material (e.g., on Flores). Nonetheless, from across the Wallace-Huxley Line, and from the fringes of the Balkan Peninsula, there is evidence for transmaritime movement in premodern hominins after approximately one million years ago (i.e., from the late Early Pleistocene onward), with this evidence apparently becoming richer after about 700,000 years ago.

Some scholars have suggested that these data support a revised model of hominin dispersal during the Pleistocene. Rather than proving to be a biogeographic barrier to the movement of our genus, it is suggested that the evidence from the eastern Mediterranean and from Wallacea rather indicates that premodern hominins were well accustomed to intentional over-water voyaging; and that, consequently, we must not only reevaluate our general model of the spread of *Homo* around the planet,[2] but also of the cognitive/behavioral parameters of more archaic members of our genus (see, most recently, discussion in Barras 2018; Leppard and Runnels 2017; also Bednarik 2003, 2014; Runnels 2014; Runnels et al. 2014a; Simmons 2012, 2014).[3] This represents a profound challenge to the more established understanding of global hominin dispersal, in which bodies of water have been considered to be a constraint on mobility, not a facilitator of it. We are left with two choices: either we must substantially revise our understanding of hominin mobility during the Pleistocene; or we must nuance the standard dispersal model in a manner that can account for these outlying data.

A key element often overlooked in this discussion relates to qualitative difference in types of mobility in hominins. Proponents of the facilitationist model tend to make the uniformitarian assumption that over-water mobility in archaic *Homo* must have been driven by the same factors that drives over-water dispersal in our own species: that as our own species makes complex, strategic, technologically advanced plans for maritime mobility, so must more archaic humans. It is not clear if this was necessarily the case, however. If we could demonstrate that a type of occasional transmaritime mobility was prevalent in archaic hominins that did not necessarily imply the series of interrelated cognitive and social tasks we closely associate with behavioral modernity, we need not abandon our overall model of (1) islands as biogeographically restrictive and (2) modern humans as uniquely evolutionarily equipped to overcome such restrictions. What forms would such mobility take? And which paleogeographic contexts would facilitate or militate against it?

The Paleogeographic Contexts of Overwater Dispersal in *Homo*

Modes of Dispersal in Terrestrial Mammals

Not unreasonably, we are used to understanding our actions, and those of our ancestors, as informed by thought, reflection, data gathering, consultation, and planning. If we (or they) cross a water barrier—or travel any long distance—it is because we or they intended to do so; presumably, because some good would thereby accrue to us, or some negative effect be mitigated. This highly anthropocentric view, however, only captures one possible dimension of mobility. I have reviewed the range of dispersal modes in terrestrial mammalian taxa at length elsewhere (Leppard 2015b), and here will only summarize briefly, before moving on to assess whether the paleogeographic contexts of maritime dispersal in archaic *Homo* support or do not support a model of intentional, strategic dispersal. Suffice it to say that such deliberate action is not the only means by which mammals (indeed, organisms more generally) cross biogeographic barriers. Far more common over evolutionary time, and with profound evolutionary effects, is sweepstakes dispersal.

Sweepstakes dispersal (Simpson 1940; also now Long Distance Dispersal, or LDD; Nathan 2005, 2006; also "waif" dispersal) involves an organism crossing a biogeographic barrier in a stochastic fashion. In normal circumstances, the organism would be unlikely to cross the barrier, or to survive a crossing: but, given enough time and situational possibility, intrinsically rare, chance crossings occur. Nathan and Nathan (2014:153) refer to "very low probabilities and innumerable trials," and this eloquently captures the ultimate inevitability of unlikely events over huge timescales. Unlikely LDD events vary across taxa: they might include improbably long-distance seed dispersal; a migrating bird with fertilized eggs blown far off course; fish transported between usually unconnected river systems during flood; or a terrestrial vertebrate surviving being washed out to sea. Part of the problem in ascribing evolutionary agency to outlier dispersal phenomena such as this lies in observer bias: it is clearly difficult to observe intrinsically highly rare events, and this can drive skepticism regarding their existence at all. Nonetheless, molecular phylogenies make it clear that these events do occur, that their evolutionary impact (as engines of allopatry) is prodigious, and that they happen to primates, as well as mammals more generally (Ali and Huber 2010; Kay et al. 1997; Loss-Oliviera et al. 2012; Schüle 1993).

In the absence of flight and brine-tolerance, and with high energetic demands, modes of sweepstakes dispersal open to other taxa are largely unavailable to large primates, which are quite poor candidates for LDD. One possibility, however, is rafting. Various processes on the earth's surface can lead to the oceanic deposition of floating material. Inadvertent transport on such material is a major driver of LDD (for review, see Thiel and Gutow 2005a, 2005b; Thiel and Haye 2006; references in Fraser et al. 2011; Gillespie et al. 2012); rafting is, for example, the assumed mode of dispersal for the New World monkeys (Loss-Oliviera et al. 2012). There is no genetic data to support raft dispersal in the Hominidae (the great apes), but this itself hints at the difficulties in observing LDD events: molecular reconstruction of phylogenies clearly relies upon extant genetic material, which in turn requires that dispersing populations survive over evolutionary time to allow for genome sequencing. However, the rarity of such events, multiplied by (1) the rarity of a K-selected organism surviving such an event and (2) the rarity of successful establishment of a population surviving to the present makes LDD intrinsically difficult to observe. In short, sweepstakes events in large primates should theoretically be possible (and proportionally more so over longer periods of time), but extremely rare and almost impossible to detect (Dennell et al. 2014; Leppard 2015b; Leppard and Runnels 2017).

With that said, there are certain environmental configurations that should militate for and against such dispersal (cf. Thiel and Gutow 2005a). Coastal geographies that increase rather than decrease the chance of terrestrial stranding favor LDD, such that densely spaced archipelagos and peninsulas are better contextual candidates, whereas unintended coastline which opens onto open ocean is much less favorable. Hydrological dynamics also have a role to play, both riverine and oceanic: riverine, to transport vegetation mass downstream to coasts; and oceanic currents that flow toward, rather than away from, neighboring landmasses. Oceanic and riverine flooding may also be advantageous, as may be the presence of cyclones (to dislodge and move vegetative mats). Warm seas are conducive, to prevent or prolong the onset of hypothermia in the organism (cf. Anderson 2018), as is the presence of vegetation, especially trees rather than grasses. Finally, large and established source populations of would-be dispersing organisms also increase the chances of LDD: clearly, other factors being equal, the more members of a species there are roaming a given patch over a greater period of time, the more opportunity for rare stochastic events to occur.

SPATIAL PATTERNING IN PLEISTOCENE DATA

The best evidence of transmaritime dispersal in archaic *Homo* (the caveats noted above notwithstanding) come from Wallacea and the circum-Balkans, although the Straits of Gibraltar and Bab-el-Mandeb are also sometimes invoked as possible dispersal avenues. I now address the following questions: To what degree do the paleogeographic, paleohydrological, and paleoenvironmental contexts of these dispersal events parallel or diverge from one another? And what might this indicate about the nature of that dispersal?

1. These contexts are all either on continental shelves (e.g., the Balkans to the Ionian Islands; Borneo to Palawan), or across narrow submarine troughs to neighboring continental shelves (e.g., Palawan to Mindoro; Borneo to Sulawesi). There are no instances of possible dispersal from the continental shelf to truly oceanic islands (i.e., islands that form

on oceanic crust via convection in the upper mantle driving hotspot formation); for example, from western Africa to the Cape Verde Islands, or from eastern Africa to the Seychelles.

2. These contexts are constrained between approximately 10 degrees south and 40 degrees north; in terms of climatic zones, the tropics and subtropics. As Anderson notes (2018), this has a series of implications, one of which is that seas maintain relatively high year-round temperatures. Indeed, under interglacial conditions, the seas of ISEA are the warmest on the planet, maintaining mean annual sea surface temperatures of 28–30 degrees Celsius (Anderson 2018:227–228), although during glacial maxima this would fall to perhaps 25–29 degrees Celsius. The Mediterranean would be cooler, especially during glacials—but still substantially warmer than unenclosed seas at comparable latitudes.

3. Again, as Anderson emphasizes, this latitudinal constriction has implications in terms of vegetative cover, and in particular the presence of forests in both contexts. Glacial Sundaland seems to have been home to large expanses of tropical forest interspersed with tropical savannah (Bird et al. 2005), and home to a range of bamboo taxa (Anderson 2018). Wang et al. (2009), for example, report an LGM (Last Glacial Maximum) predominance of bamboo and fern pollen from a core near the mouth of the North Sunda River (see below). The glacial Mediterranean (interpolating from pollen cores that reflect vegetative cover at the LGM and MIS 6, but which arguably provide decent proxies for earlier glaciations) seems to have witnessed range expansion of *Pinus* at the expense of deciduous *Quercus* (Roucoux et al. 2011; Pickarski et al. 2015), although to what extent this expansion prevailed in now-submerged (thus: low-elevation) environments is less clear.

4. These contexts are associated with embayments and highly interdigitated coastlines. This is illustrated in Figures 15.3 and 15.4. The Aegean relies on the reconstruction of Lykousis (2009); because it is so tectonically dynamic; the reconstruction of Wallacea derives from LGM models (which essentially involve relying on the current 120 m isobath; Voris 2000), but we might suppose more severe glacials to have exacerbated the trends observed. In Wallacea (Figure 15.3), the straits of (from north to south) Mindoro, Balabac, Makassar, and Lombok would all be reduced to gaps of around or less than 20 km (including emerged mid-strait islands in the Strait of Mindoro). The Sulu Sea would be almost entirely enclosed, as would the Celebes Sea, with its southern extension into the Makassar Strait almost enclosed at its southern end. The Flores Sea would also be substantially enclosed, and with Flores itself probably united with the islands to the east. During severe glacials, the Sape and Alas straits may also have been closed (although not the Lombok Strait).

In the Mediterranean and Red Sea (Figure 15.4), the Straits at Gibraltar and Bab-el-Mandeb would be narrowed, possibly with intervening islands in Bab-el-Mandeb. More interesting is the circum-Balkan situation, where models differ substantially. Interpretations range from Zakynthos, Kefalonia, and Ithaka being united in a larger barrier island minutely separated from Lefkada/Leukas, which forms an extension of the mainland (e.g., Ferentinos et al. 2012:Figure 7; and Zavitsanou et al. 2015:Figure 4), to a tenuous connection from this barrier island to the mainland (e.g., Sakellariou and Galanidou 2016:Figure 22.7), to the entire archipelago completely incorporated into the Balkan landmass (e.g., Lykousis 2009:Figure 5; this is the maximalist reconstruction adopted in Figure 15.4).

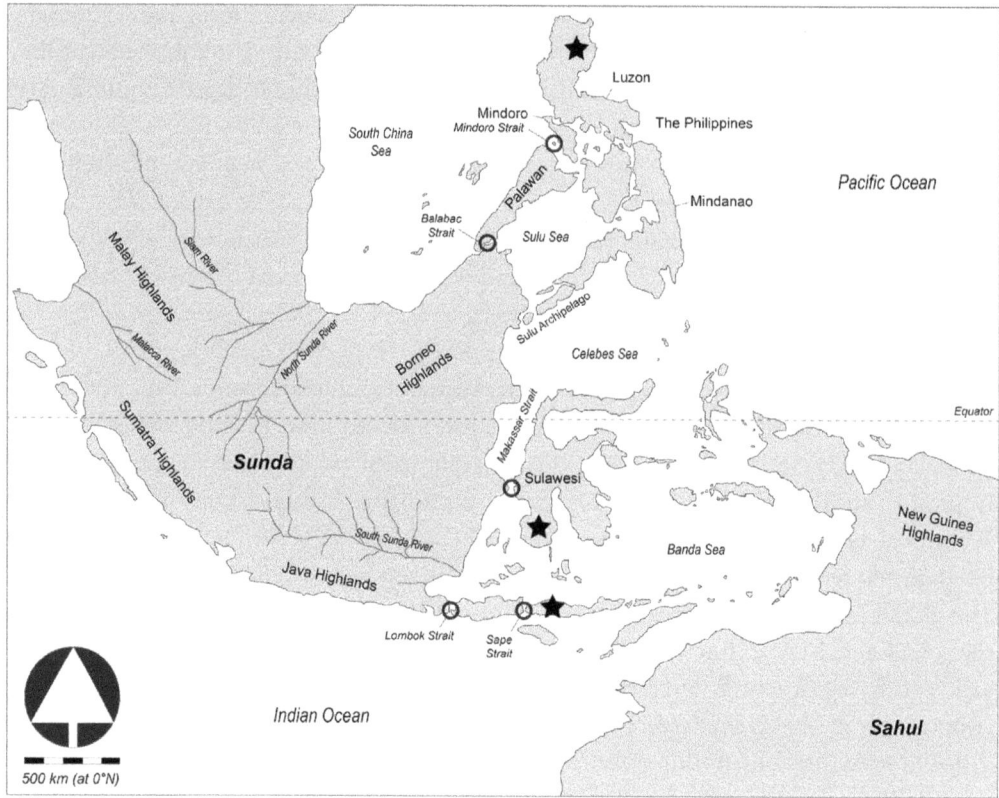

FIGURE 15.3. Reconstruction of the paleogeography of ISEA during a moderate glacial. After Voris 2000 and Hall 2011. Stars indicate Lower and Middle Paleolithic sites noted in Figure 15.2.

Whichever model is correct (and this depends in large part upon the relevant MIS), either the Ionians would be connected to the continent via Lefkada or they would form a barrier island to a highly enclosed Gulf of Patras; in both cases we are dealing with a highly enclosed embayment. In the Aegean, Crete remains insular—but forming a huge barrier landmass to a massively reduced Aegean, almost enclosed at its western extremity by the unification of Kythera and Antikythera into a peninsula (with the Antikythera Strait less than 10 km) and by paleo-Karpathos at its eastern extremity.

5. This altered glacial paleogeography would have reconfigured in comparable manners the hydrological systems in both ISEA (especially Sundaland) and in the eastern Mediterranean, especially in the Aegean. In ISEA, the existence of paleorivers on the Sunda shelf during eustatic drawdown has been known since Molengraaff (e.g., 1921; now Voris 2000). The largest of these rivers would have been the North Sunda, or Molengraaff River, draining parts of Sumatra and western Borneo and emptying northward into the South China Sea somewhere beyond Natuna Island and south of the Spratly archipelago. A second major river system would have flowed from west to east under what is now the Java Sea, draining

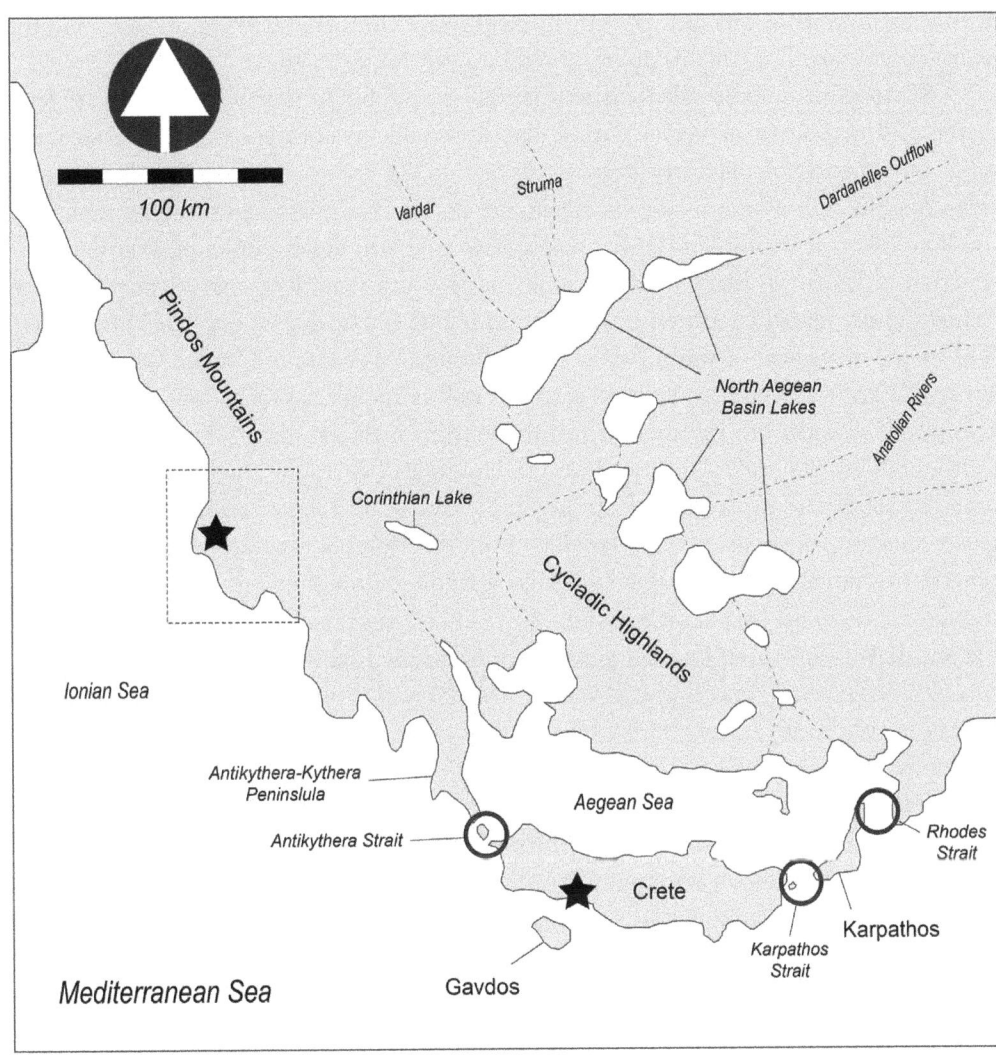

FIGURE 15.4. Reconstruction of the paleogeography of the Balkan and Aegean during a severe glacial (e.g., MIS 12). After Lykousis 2009. Note that reconstructed rivers (dashed lines) are fully hypothetical. Dashed box indicates the Ionian Islands, whose insularity during severe glacials is debated. Stars indicate possible Lower and Middle Paleolithic sites noted in Figure 15.1.

Sumatra, Java, and Borneo and debouching into the Flores Sea. Both of these would have been substantial drainages, transporting large amounts of sediment and vegetative detritus from their watersheds into the South China and Flores Seas. In the Aegean the situation is less clear, but modeling of severe glacial drawdown suggests the presence of large lakes in what is now the northern and central Aegean. The major westward-flowing Anatolian rivers (the Cayster/Küçük Menderes, Meander/Büyük Menderes, and Hermos/Gediz) and the major rivers of the north Aegean (the Strymon/Struma and Axios/Vardar) would have debouched into these, but then potentially might have continued flowing south toward the paleo-Aegean coastline, by this point united into very large drainages.

6. Modeling oceanic paleo-currents is challenging, but withdrawal of global sea level to the 120 m isobath or below during glacials would, in both contexts, have reconfigured some aspects of planetary oceanic circulation. In the enclosed basin of the glacial paleo-Aegean, influx from major Anatolian and Balkan rivers, lessened surface evaporation (under cooler conditions), and eddies would have governed the dynamics of waterflow. The situation in ISEA was likely more dynamic, and we can tentatively better grasp probable changes under glacial conditions. The reason for this is that the Indonesian Throughflow (ITF)—the movement of warm Pacific water through ISEA into the Indian Ocean (Sprintall et al. 2009)—operates under both glacial as well as interglacial conditions. Considerable volumes of seawater are transported in this manner, with the main flow being from the Celebes Sea via the Makassar Strait into the Flores Sea (where the shallow Dewakang Sill prohibits southward progression of deeper, colder water) and then through the gaps in the Lesser Sundas; there is also a secondary flow from the Molucca Sea into the Banda Sea. The general directionality of ocean flow in Wallacea is, then, from north to south, with current strength in the straits (Makassar, Lombok, and Ombai) exacerbated by constriction. During eustatic drawdown—even if under glacial conditions the Pacific/Indian temperature gradients were less severe—flows in the Makassar Strait (as well as the inter-Lesser Sundas) would have been even stronger, drawing vast amounts of water from the Celebes Sea and southern Philippines into the Flores Sea.

7. Finally, both these contexts of potential dispersal are on the fringes of ranges with long-established hominin populations. The presence of Javan *erectus* in Sunda now dates to perhaps 1.6 to 1.2 million years ago (Broadfield et al. 2001; Kaifu 2017; Matsu'ura et al. 2020), although data from Shangchen (Zhu et al. 2018) might now push an "early *Homo*" (*sensu* Scardia et al. 2020) East Asian presence back to at least 2 million years ago. In the Mediterranean, the earliest fossil dates remain those from Iberia: at Atapuerca, also around 1.2 or 1.1 million years old (Carbonell et al. 2008), but with contemporaneous or possibly older dates reported from Orce in southern Iberia (Toro-Moyano et al. 2013) and now from southern France (Michel et al. 2017). Closer to the Balkans, however, chipped stone assemblages without accompanying hominin fossils have been dated comparably, from around 1.6 to 1.4 million years ago (at Pirro Nord in Italy and Kozarnika in Bulgaria; Arzarello et al. 2015; Sirakov et al. 2010). Accordingly—and here deliberately avoiding debates about species attribution, refugia, and/or colonization and localized extinction cycles—we are secure in positing an archaic hominin population in the northern Mediterranean littoral at about 1.5 million years ago. Accordingly, there is quite a substantial time lag between initial arrival of hominin populations and instances of dispersal in both contexts. Where we have radiometric dates (ISEA), this time lag is upward of perhaps 200,000 to 400,000 years or more, if there is a pre-Javan *erectus* presence that is invisible in the record; in the Mediterranean, where we do not have radiometric dates, but arbitrarily assigning a late Lower or Middle Paleolithic date, upward of perhaps 500,000 years.

Paleogeography and Sweepstakes Dispersal in *Homo*

Based on what we know about the likely geographic and environmental contexts of over-water mobility in archaic *Homo*, and knowing what ecogeographic contexts facilitate or inhibit sweepstakes dispersal, how likely or unlikely is it that the Wallacean and circum-Balkan data are indicative of sweepstakes (as opposed to deliberate) dispersal? In the absence of a full review of all available paleoenvironmental data (beyond the scope of this chapter, but an important future project), any answer must necessarily be impressionistic and tentative. Nonetheless, in general there is a good correlation between the contexts of over-water dispersal in premodern hominins and environments that would promote sweepstakes events. Glacial Wallacea and Sundaland were separated at several points by only very small gaps, with these gaps interspersed by large, warm embayments (the Sulu, Celebes, and Flores Seas). Into these constrained waterways large rivers flowed, bringing terrestrial sediment but also floating vegetation, all derived from a landscape with an established population of Asian *H. erectus*, and possibly earlier hominins. This is, in general terms, an environment which would be expected to enable over-water LDD/waif dispersal in *K*-selected taxa.

It is further interesting to note that the most likely axis of entry across the Wallace-Huxley line lies in the north, being the Borneo-Palawan-Mindoro route (crossing the narrow straits at Balabac and Mindoro), where there is now evidence for an early Middle Pleistocene hominin presence in Luzon (Ingicco et al. 2018). Sulawesi and Flores (admitting that the dates on Flores are about 300,000 years earlier: but the Cagayan Valley is unlikely to represent the earliest hominin infiltration to Luzon) lie downcurrent from the Philippines on the Indonesian Throughflow. Are we perhaps grasping the faintest wisps of sweepstakes dispersal into the Philippines, followed by subsequent waif dispersal southward along the Indonesian Throughflow? At this point it is impossible to say, but downcurrent drift from the north is a more likely means of arriving on Flores, as opposed to unintentional embarkation from the Bali coast (most likely to end up in the middle of the Indian Ocean), and there is support for waif dispersal dynamics in non-hominin vertebrate taxa (e.g., stegodons, varanids, and murids) in a north to south direction in Wallacea (Turvey et al. 2017).

The situation in the Mediterranean is comparable, if on a smaller scale and in cooler conditions. As demonstrated in the review of the data, the best evidence for archaic hominin transmaritime dispersal in the Mediterranean comes from the Ionian Islands and Crete. Both of these would have formed barrier islands to constrained embayed seas (the Gulf of Patras and the Aegean respectively), embayed seas into which large rivers flowed from watersheds containing pine forest. This situation is further complicated by the fact that here the morphotypological pedigree of the artifacts in question might be more readily associated with *H. heidelbergensis* or *neanderthalensis* than more archaic taxa. Neanderthals in particular have a cranial architecture that more closely approximates that of our own species than, for example, *H. erectus*, and are often thought to have been capable of behaviors that we understand to parallel our own "modern" behavior (e.g., Hoffman et al. 2018; but Aubert et al. 2018). Might this combination of factors have promoted more active mobility than in ISEA? That is, could we modify the waif dispersal model (which seems a good fit for ISEA and a more archaic hominin taxon) into one in which Neanderthals were capable of short-distance hops to visible, large landmasses under optimal conditions for such behavior, taking advantage of their more substantial capacity to model long-term risk and reward? The short answer is that this is currently unclear; here, it is for now only necessary to note that, in the Mediterranean under moderate to severe glacial conditions, a sweepstakes dispersal event would be more likely in the Aegean than in the remainder of the basin.

That sweepstakes dispersal was the mechanism driving hominin dispersal into Wallacea is supported by the fossil evidence, which might indicate the operation of specifically insular evolutionary processes. While *H. floresiensis* remains contentious, it increasingly finds support as a valid taxon (Baab et al. 2016; Argue et al. 2017), and in this context the recovery of further Pleistocene hominin fossils from the So'a Basin and *H. luzonensis* from the Callao Cave might be considered suggestive of a wider Wallacean distribution of one or more small hominin species (van den Bergh et al. 2016a; Mijares et al. 2010). This is potentially illuminating in that LDD events are, more generally, drivers of allopatric speciation, with gene flow between colonizer and source population reduced to essentially zero. For a variety of reasons, islands exercise peculiar evolutionary pressures on colonizing taxa, and one frequent outcome in large-bodied vertebrates is overall reduction in body size once gene flow with source population ceases; morphological studies of LB1 suggest that *H. floresiensis* underwent such an island dwarfing process (Bromham and Cardillo 2007; Diniz-Filho and Raia 2017). If dwarfed archaic hominins characterize the Pleistocene Wallacean fauna, this evolutionary process could only have occurred in a situation with no gene flow across the Wallace-Huxley line.[4] In the Mediterranean, absence of fossils or excavated contexts precludes any comparable speculation; although it should be highlighted that, even in our own species, the Mediterranean appears to have been a barrier to gene flow in the immediate aftermath of the LGM (e.g., van de Loosdrecht et al. 2018).

Conclusions: Variability in Hominin Maritime Dispersal

In explaining the presence of archaic hominins in Wallacea, and their possible presence on Crete and the Ionian Islands, we can either overturn established and powerful explanatory systems or we can nuance them by recognizing that hominin mobility can take a range of forms. From the principle of parsimony, the second option is more attractive. It becomes increasingly so when we consider from where and when good evidence for over-water dispersal in *Homo* is derived—that is, from paleogeographic contexts that should be amenable to sweepstakes, LDD, or waif dispersal. The likelihood of such dispersal in hominins, as in other large mammalian taxa, remains extraordinarily rare: but, given the right concatenation of circumstances, a big enough source population, and enough time, we would expect sweepstakes dispersal to occur in *Homo*. The fact that our best evidence for transmaritime movement in our genus comes from two such ideal contexts might well be considered uncoincidental (as Dennell et al. 2014 conclude).

By contrast, maritime dispersal in our own species provides a stark (and, in terms of process, illuminating) contrast. Since the arrival of modern humans in Sahul, there is evidence for modern human maritime dispersal, which is global, latitudinally broad, coastal, transpelagic, rapid, multidirectional, and almost ubiquitous. This is substantially and qualitatively different from limited transmaritime mobility in more archaic taxa. "Maritime dispersal" then, becomes a hugely variable and taxon-specific phenomenon, in that qualitatively distinct types of maritime dispersal seem to correlate with species. In our own species, such mobility is most often deliberate, involving a cluster of intertwined cognitive, social, and technological processes closely tied with emergence of other aspects of behavioral modernity. Reviewing the paleogeographic contexts of maritime dispersal in more archaic hominins suggests that, over the evolutionary history of our genus, other types of transmaritime mobility have had a more prominent role to play.

ACKNOWLEDGMENTS

I should like to thank the editor, Megan Daniels, both for her invitation to the conference from which this chapter derives and for her tenacity in wrestling the resulting volume together. Ezra Zubrow, Marc Vander Linden, David Anthony, Willeke Wendrich, Anne Porter, and Hans Barnard all offered kind feedback on the initial version of this paper, and John Cherry and Elizabeth Murphy read and commented upon the resulting text with their usual perspicacity. The graduate students in SUNY Buffalo's Department of Anthropology were incisive interlocutors, especially Sarah Hoffman and Christopher Troskosky. Thanks are also due to IEMA and SUNY Buffalo for their hospitality. This research was completed while I held a Renfrew Fellowship in the McDonald Institute for Archaeological Research in the University of Cambridge, for which support I am very thankful.

NOTES

1. I ignore here the controversy surrounding the attribution of LB1 and comparable fossils to this taxon. See Argue et al. (2017) for a recent review.
2. Recent attempts to argue for an American Lower Paleolithic have been met with justifiably substantial skepticism (Braje et al. 2017), and I gloss the issue here.
3. It should be emphasized that much of this discussion revolves around Mediterranean scholarship: ISEA scholarship has approached the dispersal issue in a more nuanced and agnostic fashion; e.g., Dennell et al. 2014.
4. In general, while the Wallacean fauna clearly diverges from the Asian, the evolutionary assembly of this fauna is imperfectly understood, as is the role of sweepstakes dispersal in this assembly over the Quaternary. A review of non-hominin LDD events in the Quaternary of the Mediterranean and ISEA would represent a useful means of further evaluating the likelihood of such dispersal in *Homo*.

REFERENCES CITED

Abbate, E., and M. Saggri 2012 Early to Middle Pleistocene *Homo* Dispersals from Africa to Eurasia: Geological, Climatic and Environmental Constraints. *Quaternary International* 267:3–19.

Ali, J. R., and M. Huber 2010 Mammalian Biodiversity on Madagascar Controlled by Ocean Currents. *Nature* 463:653–657.

Anderson, A. 2018 Ecological Contingency Accounts for Earliest Seagoing in the Western Pacific Ocean. *Journal of Island and Coastal Archaeology* 13(2):224–234.

Argue, D., C. P. Groves, M. S. Y. Lee, and W. L. Jungers 2017 The Affinities of *Homo floresiensis* Based on Phylogenetic Analyses of Cranial, Dental, and Postcranial Characters. *Journal of Human Evolution* 107:107–133.

Arzarello, M., C. Peretto, and M-H. Moncel 2015 The Pirro Nord site (Apricena, Fg, Southern Italy) in the Context of the First European Peopling: Convergences and Divergences. *Quaternary International* 389:255–263.

Aubert, M., A. Brumm, and J. Huntley 2018 Early Dates for "Neanderthal Cave Art" May Be Wrong. *Journal of Human Evolution.* DOI:10.1016/j.jhevol.2018.08.004.

Baab, K. L., P. Brown, D. Falk, J. T. Richtsmeier, C. F. Hildebolt, K. Smith, and W. Jungers 2016 A Critical Evaluation of the Down Syndrome Diagnosis for LB1, Type Specimen of *Homo floresiensis*. *PLOS ONE* 11(6): e0155731.

Bailey, G. 2009 The Red Sea, Coastal Landscapes, and Hominin Dispersals. In *The Evolution of Human Populations in Arabia*, edited by M. D. Petraglia and J. I. Rose, pp 15–37. Springer, Dordrecht.

Barras, C. 2018 Have Humans Been Sailors for a Million Years? *New Scientist* 3180:36–43.

Bednarik, R. G. 2003 Seafaring in the Pleistocene. *Cambridge Archaeological Journal* 13:41–66.

Bednarik, R. G. 2014 The Beginnings of Maritime Travel. *Advances in Anthropology* 4:209–221.

Bird, M. I., D. Taylor, and C. Hunt 2005 Palaeoenvironments of Insular Southeast Asia during the Last Glacial Period: a Savanna Corridor in Sundaland? *Quaternary Science Reviews* 24:2228–2242.

Boivin, N., R. Crassard, and M. Petraglia (editors) 2017 *Human Dispersal and Species Movement: From Prehistory to the Present*. Cambridge University Press.

Braje, T. J., T. D. Dillehay, J. M. Erlandson, S. M. Fitzpatrick, D. K. Grayson, V. T. Holliday, R. L. Kelly, R. G. Klein, D. J. Meltzer, and T. C. Rick 2017 Were Hominins in California ~130,000 Years Ago? *PaleoAmerica* 3(3):200–202.

Broadfield, D. C., R. J. Holloway, K. Mowbray, A. Silvers, M. S. Yuan, and S. Márquez 2001 Endocast of Sambungmacan 3 (Sm 3): A New *Homo erectus* from Indonesia. *Anatomical Record* 262(4):369–379.

Bromham, L., and M. Cardillo 2007 Primates Follow the "Island Rule": Implications for Interpreting *Homo floresiensis*. *Biology Letters* 3:398–400.

Brumm, A., G. M. Jensen, G. D. van den Bergh, M. J. Morwood, I. Kurniawan, F. Aziz, and M. Storey 2010 Hominins on Flores, Indonesia, by One Million Years Ago. *Nature* 464:748–752.

Brumm, A., G. D. van den Bergh, M. Storey, I. Kurniawan, B. V. Alloway, R. Setiwan, E. Setiyabudi, R. Grün, M. W. Moore, D. Yurnaldi, M. R. Puspaningrum, U. P. Wibowo, H. Insani, I. Sutisna, J. A. Westgate, N. J. G. Pearce, M. Duval, H. J. M. Meijer, F. Aziz, T. Sutikna, S. van der Kars, F. Flude, and M. J. Morwood 2016 Age and Context of the Oldest Known Hominin Fossils from Flores. *Nature* 534:249–253.

Brumm, A., B. Hakim, M. Ramli, M. Aubert1, G. D. van den Bergh, B. Li, B. Burhan, A. M. Saiful, L. Siagian, R. Sardi, A. Jusdi, Abdullah, A. P. Mubarak, M. W. Moore, R. G. Roberts, J-X. Zhao, D. McGahan, B. G. Jones, Y. Perston, K. Szabó, M. I. Mahmud, K. Westaway, Jatmiko, E. W. Saptomo, S. van der Kaars, R. Grün, R. Wood, J. Dodson, and

M. J. Morwood 2018 A Reassessment of the Early Archaeological Record at Leang Burung 2, a Late Pleistocene Rock-Shelter Site on the Indonesian Island of Sulawesi. *PLOS ONE* 13(4): e0193025.

Carbonell E., J. M. Bermúdez de Castro, J. M. Parés, A. Pérez-González, G. Cuenca-Bescós, A. Ollé, M. Mosquera, R. Huguet, J. van der Made, A. Rosas, R. Sala, J. Vallverdú, N. García, D. E. Granger, M. Martinón-Torres, X. P. Rodríguez, G. M. Stock, J. M. Vergès, E. Allué, F. Burjachs, I. Cáceres, A. Canals, A. Benito, C. Díez, M. Lozano, A. Mateos, M. Navazo, J. Rodríguez, J. Rosell, and J. L. Arsuaga 2008 The First Hominin of Europe. *Nature* 452:465–469.

Carter, T., D. Contreras, S. Doyle, D. D. Mihailović, T. Moutsiou, and N. Skarpelis 2014 The Stelída Naxos Archaeological Project: New Data on the Middle Palaeolithic and Mesolithic Cyclades. *Antiquity* 341: Project Gallery.

Carter, T., D. A. Contreras, J. Holcomb, D. D. Mihailović, P. Karkanas, G. Guérin, N. Taffin, D. Athanasoulis, and C. Lahaye 2019 Earliest Occupation of the Central Aegean (Naxos), Greece: Implications for Hominin and Homo Sapiens' Behavior and Dispersals. *Science Advances* 5:eaax0997.

Chelidonio, G. 2001 Manufatti litici su ciottolo da Milos (Isole Cicladi). Nota preliminare. *Pegaso* 1:117–144.

Dennell, R. 2003 Dispersal and Colonisation, Long and Short Chronologies: How Continuous is the Early Pleistocene Record for Hominids outside East Africa? *Journal of Human Evolution* 45:421–440.

Dennell, R. 2009 *The Palaeolithic Settlement of Asia*. Cambridge University Press, Cambridge.

Dennell, R., J. Louys, H. J. O'Regan, and D. M. Wilkinson 2014 The Origins and Persistence of *Homo floresiensis* on Flores: Biogeographic and Ecological Perspectives. *Quaternary Science Reviews* 96:98–107.

Détroit, F., A. S. Mijares, J. Corny, G. Daver, C. Zanolli, E. Dizon, R. Grün, and P. J. Piper 2019 A New Species of *Homo* from the Late Pleistocene of the Philippines. *Nature* 568:181–186.

Diniz-Filho, J. A. F., and P. Raia 2017 Island Rule, Quantitative Genetics and Brain–Body Size Evolution in *Homo floresiensis*. *Proceedings of the Royal Society B*. DOI:10.1098/rspb.2017.1065.

Ferentinos, G., M. Gkioni, M. Geraga, and G. Papatheodorou 2012 Early Seafaring Activity in the Southern Ionian Islands, Mediterranean Sea. *Journal of Archaeological Science* 39:2167–2176.

Fernandes, C. A., E. J. Rohling, and M. Siddall 2006 Absence of Post-Miocene Red Sea Land Bridges: Biogeographic Implications. *Journal of Biogeography* 33:961–966.

Fraser, C. I., R. Nikula, and J. M. Waters 2011 Oceanic Rafting by a Coastal Community. *Proceedings of the Royal Society B* 278:649–655.

Gaffney, D. 2021 Pleistocene Water Crossings and Adaptive Flexibility within the *Homo* Genus. *Journal of Archaeological Research* 29:255–326.

Galanidou, N., C. Athanassas, J. Cole, G. Iliopoulos, A. Katerinopoulos, A. Magganas, and J. McNabb 2016a The Acheulian Site at Rodafnidia, Lisvori, on Lesbos, Greece: 2010–2012. In *Paleoanthropology of the Balkans and Anatolia: Human Evolution and Its Context*, edited by K. Harvati and M. Roksandic, pp. 119–138. Springer, Dordrecht.

Galanidou, N., G. Iliopoulos, and C. Papoulia 2016b The Palaeolithic Settlement of Lefkas: Archaeological Evidence in a Palaeogeographic Context. *Journal of Greek Archaeology* 1:1–32.

Gillespie, R. G., B. G. Baldwin, J. M. Waters, C. I. Fraser, R. Nikula, and G. K. Roderick 2012 Long-distance Dispersal: A Framework for Hypothesis Testing. *Trends in Ecology and Evolution* 21:47–56.

Hall, R. 2009 Southeast Asia's Changing Palaeogeography. *Blumea* 54:148–161.

Hall, R. 2011 The Palaeogeography of Sundaland and Wallacea Since the Late Jurassic. *Journal of Limnology* 72:1–17.

Hanebuth, T. J. J., H. K. Voris, Y. Yokoyama, Y. Saito, and J. Okuno 2011 Formation and Fate of Sedimentary Depocentres on Southeast Asia's Sunda Shelf Over the Past Sea-Level Cycle and Biogeographic Implications. *Earth-Science Reviews* 104:92–110.

Harvati, K., C. Röding, A. M. Bosman, F. O. Karakostis, R. Grün, C. Stringer, P. Karkanas, N. C. Thompson, V. Koutoulidis, L. A. Moulopoulos, V. G. Gorgoulis, and M. Koulouk-oussa. 2019 Apidima Cave Fossils Provide Earliest Evidence of *Homo sapiens* in Eurasia. *Nature* 571:500–504.

Hoffmann, D. L., C. D. Standish, M. García-Diez, P. B. Pettitt, J. A. Milton, J. Zilhao, J. J. Alcolea-González, P. Cantalejo-Duarte, H. Collado, R. de Balbín, M. Lorblanchet, J. Ramos-Munoz, J., G-Ch. Weniger, and A. W. G. Pike 2018 U-Th Dating of Carbonate Crusts Reveals Neandertal Origin of Iberian Cave Art. *Science* 359:912–915.

Hublin, J.-J., A. Ben-Ncer, S. E. Bailey, S. E. Freidline, S. Neubauer, M. M. Skinner, I. Bergmann, A. Le Cabec, S. Benazzi, K. Harvati, and P. Gunz 2017 New Fossils from Jebel Irhoud, Morocco, and the Pan-African Origin of *Homo Sapiens*. *Nature* 546:289–292.

Ingicco, T. G. D. van den Bergh, C. Jago-on, J-J. Bahain, M. G. Chacón, N. Amano, H. Forestier, C. King, K. Manalo, S. Nomade, A. Pereira, M. C. Reyes, A-M. Sémah, Q. Shao, P. Voinchet, C. Falguères, P. C. H. Albers, M. Lising, G. Lyras, D. Yurnaldi, P. Rochette, A. Bautista, and J. de Vos 2018 Earliest Known Hominin Activity in the Philippines by 709 Thousand Years Ago. *Nature* 557:233–237.

Kaifu, Y. 2017 Archaic Hominin Populations in Asia before the Arrival of Modern Humans. *Current Anthropology* 58(S17):S418-S433.

Kay, R. F., C. Ross, and A. B. Williams 1997 Anthropoid Origins. *Science* 275(5301):797–804.

Kopaka, K., and C. Mantzanas 2009 Palaeolithic Industries from the Island of Gavdos, Near Neighbour to Crete in Greece. *Antiquity* 321:Project Gallery.

Lambeck, K., and J. Chappell 2001 Sea Level Change through the Last Glacial Cycle. *Science* 292:679–686.

Leppard, T. P. 2014 Modeling the Impacts of Mediterranean Island Colonization by Archaic Hominins: The Likelihood of an Insular Lower Palaeolithic. *Journal of Mediterranean Archaeology* 27(2):231–253.

Leppard, T. P. 2015a The Evolution of Modern Behaviour and Its Implications for Maritime Dispersal During the Palaeolithic. *Cambridge Archaeological Journal* 25(4):829–846.

Leppard, T. P. 2015b Passive Dispersal Versus Strategic Dispersal in Island Colonization by Hominins. *Current Anthropology* 56(4):590–595.

Leppard, T. P., and C. Runnels 2017 Maritime Hominin Dispersals in the Pleistocene: Advancing the Debate. *Antiquity* 356:510–519.

Loss-Oliveira, L., B. O. Aguiar, and C. G. Schrago 2012 Testing Synchrony in Historical Biogeography: The Case of New World Primates and Hystricognathi Rodents. *Evolutionary Bioinformatics* 8:127–137.

Lykousis, V. 2009 Sea-Level Changes and Shelf Break Prograding Sequences During the Last 400 ka in the Aegean Margins: Subsidence Rates and Palaeogeographic Implications. *Continental Shelf Research* 29:2037–2044.

Matsu'ura, S., M. Kondo, T. Danhara, . . . M. Sudo, Y. Danhara, and F. Aziz 2020 Age Control of the First Appearance Datum for Javanese *Homo erectus* in the Sangiran Area. *Science* 367:210–214.

Michel, V., C-C. Shen, J. Woodhead, H-M. Hu, C-C. Wu, P-É. Moullé, S. Khatib, D. Cauche, M-H. Moncel, P. Valensi, Y-M. Chou, S. Gallet, A. Echassoux, F. Orange, and H. de Lumley 2017 New Dating Evidence of the Early Presence of Hominins in Southern Europe. *Scientific Reports* 7:10074.

Mijares, A. S., F. Détroit, P. Piper, R. Grün, P. Bellwood, M. Aubert, G. Champion, N. Cuevas, A. De Leon, and E. Dizon. 2010 New Evidence for a 67,000-Year-Old Human Presence at Callao Cave, Luzon, Philippines. *Journal of Human Evolution* 59(1):123–132.

Mithen, S., and M. Reed 2002 Stepping Out: A Computer Simulation of Hominid Dispersal from Africa. *Journal of Human Evolution* 43(4):433–462.

Molengraaff, G. A. F. 1921 Modern Deep-Sea Research in the East Indian Archipelago. *Geographical Journal* 57:95–121.

Moutsiou, T. 2021 Climate, Environment, and Cognition in the Colonisation of the Eastern Mediterranean Islands during the Pleistocene. *Quaternary International* 577:1–14.

Nathan, R. 2005 Long-Distance Dispersal Research: Building a Network of Yellow Brick Roads. *Diversity and Distributions* 11:125–130.

Nathan, R. 2006 Long-Distance Dispersal of Plants. *Science* 313:786–788.

Nathan, R., and O. Nathan 2014 Unlikely Yet Pivotal Long Dispersals. *Science* 344:153–154.

O'Regan, H. J. 2008 The Iberian Peninsula—Corridor or Cul-de-sac? Mammalian Faunal Change and Possible Routes of Dispersal in the Last 2 Million Years. *Quaternary Science Reviews* 27:2136–2144.

Papoulia, C. 2017 Seaward Dispersals to the NE Mediterranean Islands in the Pleistocene. The Lithic Evidence in Retrospect. *Quaternary International* 431:64–87.

Petraglia, M. D. 2003 The Lower Paleolithic of the Arabian Peninsula: Occupations, Adaptations, and Dispersals. *Journal of World Prehistory* 17(2):141–179.

Pickarski, N., O. Kwiecien, D. Langgut, and T. Litt 2015 Abrupt Climate and Vegetation Variability of Eastern Anatolia during the Last Glacial. *Climate of the Past* 11:1491–1505.

Robles, E., P. Piper, J. Ochoa, H. Lewis, V. Paz, and W. Ronquillo 2015 Late Quaternary Sea-Level Changes and the Palaeohistory of Palawan Islands, Philippines. *Journal of Island and Coastal Archaeology* 10:76–96.

Roucoux, K. H., P. C. Tzedakis, I. T. Lawson, and V. Margari 2011 Vegetation History of the Penultimate Glacial Period (Marine Isotope Stage 6) at Ioannina, North-West Greece. *Journal of Quaternary Science* 26(6):616–626.

Runnels, C. 2014 Early Palaeolithic on the Greek Islands? *Journal of Mediterranean Archaeology* 27:211–230.

Runnels, C., C. DiGregorio, K. W. Wegman, S. F. Gallen, E. Panagopoulou, and T. F. Strasser 2014a Lower Palaeolithic Artifacts from Plakias, Crete: Implications for Hominin Dispersals. *Eurasian Prehistory* 11(1–2):129–152.

Runnels, C., F. McCoy, R. Bauslaugh, and P. M. Murray 2014b Palaeolithic Research at Mochlos, Crete: New Evidence for Pleistocene Maritime Activity in the Aegean. *Antiquity* 342:Project Gallery.

Sakellariou, D., and N. Galanidou 2016 Pleistocene Submerged Landscapes and Palaeolithic Archaeology in the Tectonically Active Aegean Region. In *Geology and Archaeology: Submerged Landscapes of the Continental Shelf*, edited by J. Harff, G. Bailey, and F. Lüth, pp. 145–178. Geological Society, London.

Scardia, G., W.A. Neves, I. Tattersall, and L. Blumrich 2020 What Kind of Hominin First Left Africa? *Evolutionary Anthropology* doi: 10.1002/evan.21863.

Schüle, W. 1993 Mammals, Vegetation, and the Initial Human Settlement of the Mediterranean Islands: A Palaeoecological Approach. *Journal of Biogeography* 20(4):399–411.

Simmons, A. H. 2012 Mediterranean Island Voyages. *Science* 338:895–897.

Simmons, A. H. 2014 *Stone Age Sailors: Paleolithic Seafaring in the Mediterranean*. Left Coast Press, Walnut Creek.

Simpson, G. G. 1940 Mammals and Land Bridges. *Journal of the Washington Academy of Sciences* 30:137–163.

Sirakov, N., J-L. Guadelli, S. Ivanova, S. Sirakova, M. Boudadi-Maligne, I. Dimitrova, F. P. C. Ferrier, A. Guadelli, D. Iordanova, N. Iordanova, M. Kovatcheva, I. Krumova, J-C. Leblanc, V. Miteva, V. Popov, R. Spassov, S. Taneva, and T. Tsanova 2010 An Ancient Continuous Human Presence in the Balkans and the Beginnings of Human Settlement in Western Eurasia: A Lower Pleistocene Example of the Lower Palaeolithic Levels in Kozarnika Cave (North-Western Bulgaria). *Quaternary International* 233–224:94–106.

Sprintall, J., S. E. Wijffels, R. Molcard, and I. Jaya 2009 Direct Estimates of the Indonesian Throughflow Entering the Indian Ocean: 2004–2006. *Journal of Geophysical Research* 114. DOI:10.1029/2008JC005257.

Strasser, T. F., E. Panagopoulou, C. Runnels, P. M. Murray, N. Thompson, P. Karkanas, F. W. McCoy, and K. W. Wegmann 2010 Stone Age Seafaring in the Mediterranean: Evidence from the Plakias Region for Lower Palaeolithic and Mesolithic Habitation of Crete. *Hesperia* 79:145–190.

Strasser, T. F., C. Runnels, K. W. Wegmann, E. Panagopoulou, F. W. McCoy, C. DiGregorio, P. Karkanas, and N. Thompson 2011 Dating Palaeolithic Sites in Southwestern Crete, Greece. *Journal of Quaternary Science* 26:553–560.

Strasser, T. F., C. Runnels, and C. Vita-Finzi 2016 A Possible Palaeolithic Handaxe from Cyprus. *Antiquity* 350:Project Gallery.

Sutikna, T., M. W. Tocheri, M. J. Morwood, E.nW. Saptomo, Jatmiko, R. Due Awe, S. Wasisto, K. E. Westaway, M. Aubert, B. Li, J-X. Zhao, M. Storey, B. V. Alloway, M. W. Morley, H. J. M. Meijer, G. D. van den Bergh, R. Grün, A. Dosseto, A. Brumm, W. L. Jungers, and R. G. Roberts 2016 Revised Stratigraphy and Chronology for *Homo floresiensis* at Liang Bua in Indonesia. *Nature* 532:366–369.

Tchernov, E. 1992 Eurasian-African Biotic Exchanges through the Levantine Corridor during the Neogene and Quaternary. In *Mammalian Migration and Dispersal Events in the European Quaternary*, edited by W. von Königswald and L. Werdelin, pp. 103–123. Courier Forschunginstitute Senckenberg, Frankfurt.

Thiel, M., and L. Gutow 2005a The Ecology of Rafting in the Marine Environment. I. The Floating Substrata. *Oceanography and Marine Biology: An Annual Review*. 42:181–263.

Thiel, M., and L. Gutow 2005b The Ecology of Rafting in the Marine Environment. II. The Rafting Organisms and Community. *Oceanography and Marine Biology: An Annual Review* 43:279–418.

Thiel, M., and P. A. Haye 2006 The Ecology of Rafting in the Marine Environment. III. Biogeographical and Evolutionary Consequences. *Oceanography and Marine Biology: An Annual Review* 44:323–429.

Toro-Moyano, I., B. Martínez-Navarro, J. Agustí, C. Souday, J.M. Bermúdez de Castro, M. Martinón-Torres, B. Fajardo, M. Duval, C. Falguères, O. Oms, J.M. Parés, P. Anadón, R. Julià, J. M. García-Aguilar, A-M. Moigne, M. P. Espigares, S. Ros-Montoya, and P. Palmqvist 2013 The Oldest Human Fossil in Europe, from Orce (Spain). *Journal of Human Evolution* 65(1):1–9.

Turvey, S. T., J. J. Crees, J. Hansford, T. E. Jeffree, N. Crumpton, I. Kurniawan, E. Setiyabudi, T. Guillerme, U. Paranggarimu, A. Dosseto, and G. van den Bergh 2017 Quaternary Vertebrate Faunas from Sumba, Indonesia: Implications for Wallacean Biogeography and Evolution. *Proceedings of the Royal Society B*. DOI:10.1098/rspb.2017.1278

Van de Loosdrecht, M., A. Bouzouggar, L. Humphrey, C. Posth, N. Barton, A. Aximu-Petri, B. Nickel, S. Nagel, E. H. Talbi, M. A. E. Hajraoui, S. Amzazi, J-J. Hublin, S. Pääbo, S. Schiffels, M. Meyer, W. Haak, C. Jeong1, and J. Krause 2018 Pleistocene North African Genomes Link Near Eastern and Sub-Saharan African Human Populations. *Science*. DOI:10.1126/science.aar8380.

Van den Bergh, G. D., Y. Kaifu, I. Kurniawan, R. T. Kono, A. Brumm, E. Setiyabudi, F. Aziz, and M. J. Morwood 2016a *Homo floresiensis*-like Fossils from the Early Middle Pleistocene of Flores. *Nature* 534:245–248.

Van den Bergh, G. D., B. Li, A. Brumm, R. Grün, D. Yurnaldi, M. W. Moore, I. Kurniawan, R. Setiawan, F. Aziz, R. G. Roberts, Suyono, M. Storey, E. Setiyabudi, and M. J. Morwood 2016b Earliest Hominin Occupation of Sulawesi, Indonesia. *Nature* 529:208–211.

Voris, H. 2000 Maps of Pleistocene Sea Levels in Southeast Asia: Shorelines, River Systems, and Time Durations. *Journal of Biogeography* 27:1153–1167.

Wang, X., X. Sun, P. Wang, and K. Stattegger 2009 Vegetation on the Sunda Shelf, South China Sea, during the Last Glacial Maximum. *Palaeogeography, Palaeoclimatology, Palaeoecology* 278:88–97.

Zavitsanou, A., D. Sakelleriou, G. Rousakis, P. Georgiou, and N. Galanidou 2015 Paleogeographic Reconstruction of the Inner Ionian Sea during Late Pleistocene Low Sea-Level Stands: Preliminary Results. *Proceedings of the 11th Panhellenic Symposium on Oceanography and Fisheries*: 997–1000.

Zhu, Z., R. Dennell, W. Huang, . . . J. Xie, J. Han, and T. Ouyang 2018 Hominin Occupation of the Chinese Loess Plateau since about 2.1 Million Years Ago. *Nature* 559:608–612.

CHAPTER SIXTEEN

Homo mobilis

Interactions, Consciousness, and the Anthropocene

Hans Barnard

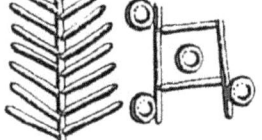

Abstract *Our ability to control our movements seems intricately connected with our sentience, which creates a sense of unity and continuity, both in time and in space, as well as a sense of urgency to keep the individual functional, whole, and safe. These phenomena are often approached as exclusive functions of the brain; a problematic hypothesis, as a brain is as ineffective without a body and its senses as a body is without a brain. The relevant output of the brain, irrespective of what may or may not go on inside it, is control over our movements. The body of living animals, including humans, maintains a central platform identified as sentience, which integrates the often complex input and decides on a course of action. Movements connect individuals in the creation of signs and symbols, but also at a physiological level as illustrated by contagious laughter and yawning, mirror neurons and the related motor theory of speech perception. At a larger scale this may translate into a group of social animals developing a common sense of cohesion by moving across the landscape, most clearly when dancing, marching, or on a pilgrimage.*

When asked to participate in the conference at the basis of this volume, I initially responded that my scholarly interest had shifted from the movement of people in the past (Barnard and Duistermaat 2012; Barnard and Wendrich 2008), to what I think is the vital importance of our ability to move in a controlled fashion for our being in the world. Reflected in a single sentence, and explained in some detail below, I argue that in bilateral symmetric living beings sentience, and ultimately consciousness, evolved as a platform integrating sensory input and establishing motor responses. Prudently invoking the theory of recapitulation—summarized as *"ontogeny recapitulates phylogeny"* (Foster 1994;

Medicus 1992)—it can be proposed that the movement of individuals or groups of people across the landscape likewise creates physical phenomena and mental abilities that may otherwise not arise. Such movement similarly has significant, long-term consequences for our social and physical environment (Leppard, this volume).

This chapter is not meant to be an interpretative conclusion to the volume in hand, but rather aims to widen the subjects of motility, movement, and mobility beyond a narrow archaeological or anthropological focus. Archaeology is fundamentally a multidisciplinary field of research in which archaeological and anthropological research methods are habitually combined with analytical techniques adapted from the natural sciences. This makes the discipline the most scientific branch of the humanities and the most humanistic branch of the sciences. Too often, however, its investigations remain confined to ancient peoples and cultures, and focused on temples, tombs, and treasure. It is becoming increasingly clear that archaeology as a discipline should spend more time and effort on public engagement (Altschul et al. 2017), not only by involving local stakeholders and the interested general public (Effros and Lai 2018; Jameson and Musteață 2019; Schmidt and Pikirayids 2016), but also by demonstrating that archaeological methods and theories can and should be applied to address contemporary issues (Arnold et al. 2012; Farrier 2020; Graves-Brown et al. 2013; Harrison and Schofield 2010).

Spontaneous movement and the ability of living organisms to control their movements are fundamental to our being in the world. Aristotle states that "it is impossible to say that their motion [of things that move spontaneously] is derived from themselves: this is a characteristic of life and peculiar to living things" *(Physics, Book 8, Part 4,* around 300 B.C., translated by Barnes 1991:136)—an intuitive notion elegantly demonstrated by Fritz Heider and Marianne Simmel (1944).[1] In the more than two millennia since Aristotle it has been shown that our ability to control our movements and our mobility across the landscape are closely associated with human culture, religion, intelligence, evolution, and consciousness. It is thus much more than the phenomenon that is the subject of this volume. In this chapter, I aim to unify motility (at the cellular level), movement (at the individual level), and mobility (at the group level) by highlighting a few aspects of the primary phenomenon as meant by Aristotle, including its significance for cultural *versus* genetic evolution, (human) consciousness, and (artificial) intelligence—using the game of chess as paradigm—and the sway of *Homo mobilis*.

DNA Analysis in Archaeological Research

DNA analysis seems sometimes advocated as a panacea able to provide solutions to all archaeological and anthropological research questions. Similar hopes were in the recent past expressed toward radiocarbon dating and the analysis of inorganic and organic compounds in ancient materials using methods such as X-ray fluorescence and immunological or mass spectrometric techniques (Briuer 1976; Eerkens 2005; Evershed 2008; Gurfinkel and Franklin 1988; Hyland et al. 1990; Libby et al. 1949; Loy 1983, 1993; Malainey et al. 1999; Mottram et al. 1999; Newman and Julig 1989; Oudemans and Boon 1991; Rainey and Ralph 1966; Sears 1973; Shanks et al. 1999; Solazzo et al. 2008). Obviously, all these methods and techniques can provide valuable data, but because of practical and fundamental problems their results can only be meaningfully interpreted within a larger archaeological or anthropological theoretical framework (Clark 2010; Diamond 2000; Downs and Lowenstein 1996; Fiedel 1996; Nigra et al. 2015; Killick and Goldberg 2009; Kooyman et al. 1992; Lambert et al. 2000; Lyman and VanPool 2009; Pollard and Bray 2007; Shackley 2010; Shott 2010; Smith and Wilson 1992).

The human species occupies a special niche in the ecology of the world from more than one perspective. Worldwide we are around 7.5 billion individuals, all belonging to the same species (*Homo sapiens*). This is remarkable compared to around 250,000 individuals (<0.005%) of the three next most numerous primate species—the Bornean gibbon *(Hylobates muelleri)*, chimpanzee *(Pan troglodytes)*, and gelada *(Theropithecus gelada)*—and certainly given the fact that most of the 200–400 primate species are listed as vulnerable to endangered by the *International Union for Conservation of Nature*. The striking difference can be explained by the unique human response to entering new environments after migrating across the landscape: cultural adaptation rather than speciation by genetic evolution (Boyd and Richerson 2009a; Henrich 2016; Henrich and McElreath 2003; Wade 2009). "Cultural evolution can solve many of the same adaptive problems as genetic evolution, only faster and without speciation" (Henrich 2016:239). A comparison, for instance, between the diversity of bats (another mammal with a worldwide distribution)—which can be a proxy for speciation (there are more than 1,400 bat species)—with the variety of human languages (there are between 5,000 and 7,000 living languages)—which can be a proxy for cultural evolution—reveals strikingly similar taxonomies.

Between 1990 and 2003 the *Human Genome Project* determined the sequence of around three billion base pairs and identified 20–25,000 genes in human DNA. Included in this large international project were the mapping of the genomes of the most frequently used laboratory organisms: *Caenorhabditis elegans* (a nonparasitic nematode), *Drosophila melanogaster* (fruit fly), *Escherichia coli* (a coliform bacterium), and *Saccharomyces cerevisiae* (baker's or brewer's yeast). The success of this enterprise and the greatly improved techniques that it generated led to an abundance of research into the genome of other organisms, but also revealed the fact that individual human beings are not defined by their genetic makeup. Although such comparisons are ultimately not very meaningful, the human genome appeared to be about 96–98% the same as that of bonobos *(Pan paniscus)* and chimpanzees *(Pan troglodytes)*—the species most closely related to humans—70–80% the same as in nonprimate mammals, and 40–50% the same as in birds and insects (Bovine Genome Sequencing and Analysis Consortium et al. 2009; Pertea and Salzberg 2010; Varki et al. 2008). On the one hand this should not be surprising, as all life on Earth is biochemically analogous, with all organisms encountering similar evolutionary challenges, but on the other hand it leaves unexplained the fundamental differences between humans and other organisms, including primates, as well as between human individuals.

Evidently, the expression of genes, the conversion of genotype into phenotype, is greatly influenced by factors outside the genome, some of which may be otherwise biological and inherited—such as the level of testosterone—while others may originate elsewhere. Very few human traits appear to be determined by a single gene (one example being the color of the iris), while the great majority, including skin color and physical appearance, is polygenetic or determined by a combination of genetic and other factors (Richerson and Boyd 2005; Schmitz et al. 2017; Varki et al. 2008). This is reminiscent of the old nature-versus-nurture debate, in which time and again our psychosocial, cultural, and physical environment appears to be of crucial importance to our being in the world (Baines 1985; Boroditsky et al. 2011; Carrigan et al. 2015; Ehrlich and Feldman 2003; Flegr 2007; Frank et al. 2008; Guerra-Doce, 2015; Held et al. 2011; Hockings 2015; Hoffman et al. 2015; Leach 2003; Oppezzo and Schwartz 2014; Regier and Kay 2009; Roberson et al. 2005; Wnuk and Majid 2014), as well as our well-being (Gros 2014; Ingold 2011; Kok and Fredrickson 2010; Kozorovitskiy et al. 2005; Lafferty 2006; Link et al. 2013; Lövheim 2012; Morris et al. 1953a, 1953b; Shusterman 2012; Tuk et al. 2011). It is also becoming increasingly clear that our well-being and being in the world are not solely based on human genes, securely stored in human DNA, but partly also on genes of microbiological origin (Bosch and McFall-Ngai 2011; Cho and Blaser 2012; Turnbaugh et al. 2007). Ethnicity, culture, and identity are not at all properties wholly or partly embedded in our DNA (Boyd and Richerson 2009b; Derricourt 2005; Ehrlich and Feldman 2003; Leach 2003; Richerson and Boyd 2005; Varki et al. 2009), as are eye color or physical appearance, but rather like clothes that are worn, tailored, and selected to fit the occasion. Indeed, in most human societies clothing forms a more important part of psychosocial identities than physical traits (Boytner 2004; Gilling 2007; Gordon 2011; Lemire and Riello 2008; McCorriston 1997). "To argue that social identity can be identified from DNA takes away people's ability to alter who and what they are" (Mirza and Dungworth 1995:352). Instead, "cultural differences are biological differences but not genetic differences. . . . Cultural evolution is a type of biological evolution; it's just not a type of genetic evolution" (Henrich 2016:263).

What can be securely determined by comparing DNA of two or more living or deceased individuals is the closeness in which they are related, as discussed in detail in other chapters in this volume. As such, it is comparable to radiocarbon dating, which can provide a relatively secure age for organic materials, but it likewise shares the necessity for interpretation of the results within a theoretical archaeological or anthropological framework. Archaeology is the study of humanity based upon their material remains, mostly the objects that they used and produced, but also their physical remains. All of these materials produce secondary data, the most important being the context in which recovered objects were deposited, preserved, and ultimately found, and occasionally extending to their dimensions, form and shape, origin, production technique, material composition, radiocarbon age, selected stable isotope ratio, DNA profile, among many more. Objects can locally appear homogeneous or greatly variable; an explanation for this is not in the data per se, but in our interpretation of these. DNA analysis cannot readily provide answers to archaeological or anthropological research questions, but only adds further elements to already complex and multifaceted datasets (Chaubey et al. 2017; Chen et al. 2009; Weinstein 2007; Wen et al. 2004; Zhao et al. 2015; Gokcumen, this volume). Variability can often be explained by the movement of ideas (styles that are more or less successfully imitated or emulated), the movement of the objects (direct trade or a side effect of trade), or the movement of people (mobility or migration).

Analogous to DNA analysis and radiocarbon dating, no single analytical technique can replace archaeological and anthropological reasoning in the study of mobility and migration. Stable isotopes ratios, for instance, can provide valuable information, but it should be kept in mind that food and water can be transported over substantial distances, for practical, prestigious, or religious reasons. Examples include cereals, wine, olive oil, and *garum* (fermented fish sauce) in the Greco-Roman World during the first century A.D. (Bowman and Wilson 2009, 2013) and the sustenance of the Wari overlords living on near-inaccessible Andean mountaintops (Moseley et al. 2005). Using only stable isotope ratios, most humans in the modern, wealthy Western World would likely be identified as originating somewhere in Illinois, Iowa, Minnesota, or Nebraska where most of the corn (maize, *Zea mays*) that is present in nearly all our food is grown. Given the subject matter of the discipline, archaeology should claim the field of human mobility, much as it should not leave the study of the Anthropocene exclusively the domain of geologists (Barnes et al. 2013; Braje et al. 2014; Erlandson and Braje 2013; Krauss 2015; Lane 2015; Palsson et al. 2013; Pétursdóttir 2017). Such claims should be firmly based in all data available and combine, confront, and integrate as many lines of evidence as possible, including archaeological information, (art) history, material analysis (including DNA analysis), as well as statistical, explanatory, and predictive models. Models and theories, however, will not emerge from data, but only from our human interpretation of the facts. Scholarly research necessarily starts in facts, but equally necessarily needs to explain and understand these as they present themselves to us today.

Movement and Consciousness

The complexity of our humanity can likewise not be explained as the function of a single organ, but seems deeply rooted in our ability to move in a controlled fashion, both at an individual level as well as in groups across the landscape. It is often suggested that our brain has an all-important function in creating our consciousness and intelligence. Around 400 B.C., Hippocrates stated that "men ought to know that from nothing else but [from the brain] come joys, delights, laughter and sports, and sorrows, griefs, despondency, and lamentations. . . . And by the same organ we become mad and delirious, and fears and terrors assail us . . . and ignorance of present circumstances, desuetude, and unskillfulness" (Adams 1886:344). A notion repeated until modern times: "[Y]ou, your joys and your sorrows, your memories and your ambitions, your sense of personal identity and free will, are in fact no more than the behavior of a vast assembly of nerve cells and their associated molecules" (Crick 1994:3). Francis Crick later nuanced his statement, but others remain convinced of its accuracy: "There is no such thing as 'mind.' It ultimately reduces down to neurons firing and neurochemical transmitter substances flowing across synaptic gaps between neurons, combining in complex patterns to produce something we call mind but is actually just brain" (Shermer 2011:22–23).

Only cursory macroscopic inspection, however, can sustain the impression that the human brain is a single entity separate from the rest of the body. It is instead a complex organ comprising two hemispheres—connected by the corpus callosum—the diencephalon (thalamus and hypothalamus), two olfactory bulbs, the cerebellum, pons, and medulla oblongata, as well as the pineal and pituitary glands. To consider this a single large organ or an interconnected array of smaller organs is a matter of scholarly priorities. Blood vessels penetrate all parts of the brain while nerve cells, including those combined into twelve pairs of cranial nerves, extend uninterrupted into many organs. Next to these indispensable, interconnected anatomical elements, the brain can likewise not function without sensory input (Held et al. 2011; Kozorovitskiy et al. 2005; Sasakura et al. 2012). Even closer inspection reveals that the interface between the body and the world is equally ambiguous. Every day we exchange 5–10% of our body mass with gasses, liquids, and solids from the environment. Even a conservative 1% implies that our current material self has a half-life of only 70 days. Meanwhile we mark the world with our fingerprints and footprints (Ingold 2011:115–125), which sometimes survive in the archaeological record (Leary 2014). Moreover, of the cells we understand to compose our self only about 30–60% are human, containing a mere 0.1–0.01% of the total number of genes present, the majority being of microbiological origin (Bosch and McFall-Ngai 2011; Cho and Blaser 2012; Turnbaugh et al. 2007). We are truly indivisibly part of an *Umwelt* (Uexküll 1992), or a weather-world (Ingold 2011:120), and our ability to monitor and control our movements determines our interactions with it (Figure 16.1).

There is thus no single part of our body responsible for our consciousness; it is a function of the living whole and a vital part of the systems that integrate sensory input and decide on our motor actions. A crude analogy would be to identify the part of an airplane that makes it fly. A plane will not fly without its wings, but it cannot be maintained that the wings make it fly as it also needs one or more engines. It is not, however, the engines that make a plane fly as it also needs a pilot, as well as the air that not only carries the plane, but also keeps the engines running and the pilot alive. All these elements are indispensable for the plane to get and remain airborne. "Brain processes cannot be understood by looking at the brain alone: in order to understand the function of the brain, we must consider embodiment; we must deal with the coupling between brain, body, and environment" (Pfeifer and Bongard 2007:20).

Reversely, it must be recognized that the human mind can extend into inanimate objects (Bruner and Lozano 2014; Clark and Chalmers 1998). "Consider a blind man with a stick. Where does the blind man's self begin? At the tip of the stick? At the handle of the stick? Or at some point halfway up the stick?" (Bateson 2000:318). By itself the blind man's stick is just a stick, but it can be imbued with agency by communicating with a living body, including its brain and sensory organs (Figure 16.2). "The boundaries between bodies, tools, and the environment are fluid and dependent upon relationships more than materials" (Woolford and Dunn 2014:125). Archaeological research into mobility and otherwise is greatly facilitated by the resulting fact that in all objects created and used by humans func-

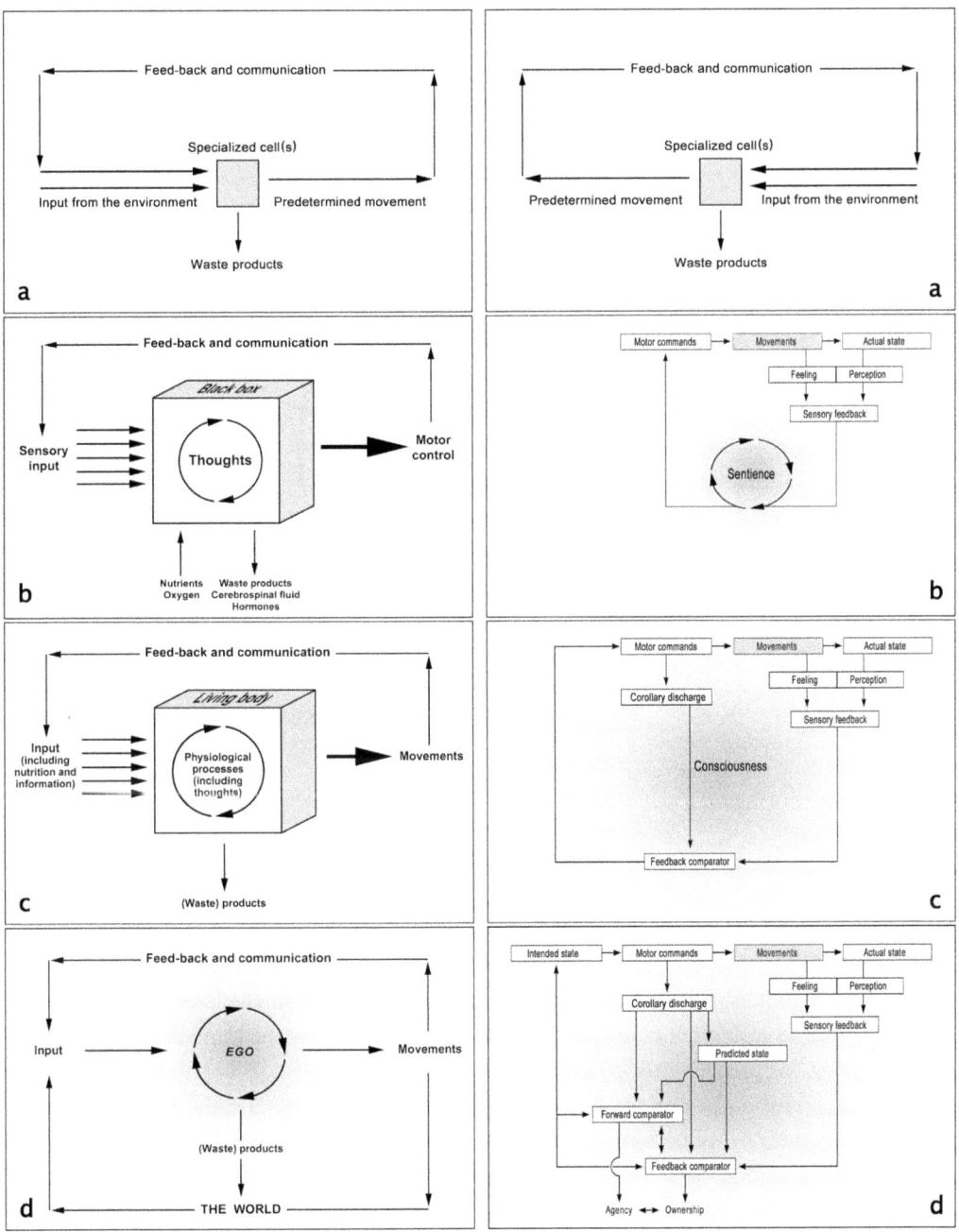

FIGURE 16.1. Left column (a–d): The deconstruction of the boundaries we experience between brain, body, and the world around us. Right column (a–d): The emergence of sentience, consciousness, agency, and ownership out of our systems for motor control.

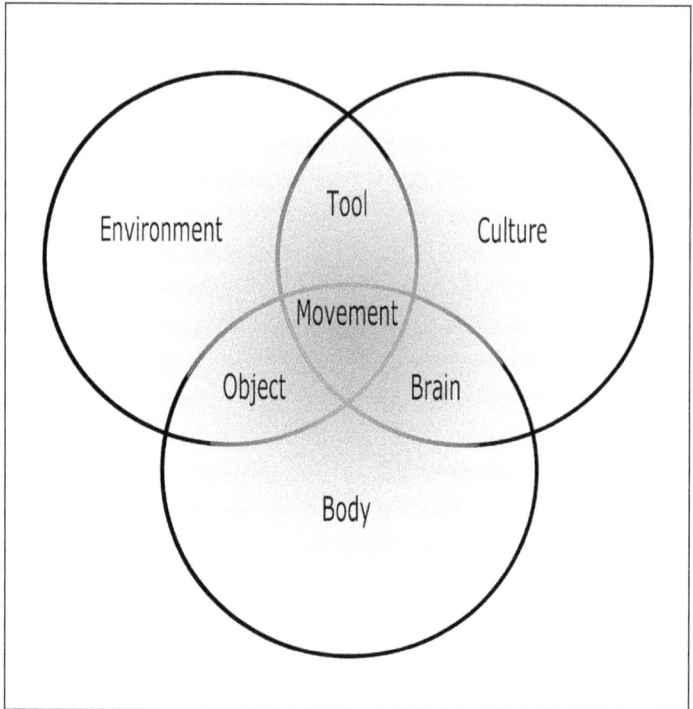

FIGURE 16.2. The interconnections between our body, environment, and culture. The grey background symbolizes our sentience or consciousness that arises from the interactions within this system as a whole.

tionality is intricately complimented with meaning (Bennett 2010; Hodder 2012; Ingold 2013; Malafouris 2013). "The extraordinary stability of tools such as hand-axes over time (1.5 million years) and over space (Europe, Africa, Asia) could not have been an accident, nor due solely to inertia. . . . When manufacturing tools, the toolmaker would be making a sign as well as an instrument, and he would want his sign to say the same things as had the tools made by his predecessors" (Tallis 2003:234).

The relevant output of the brain, irrespective of what may or may not go on inside it, is control over our movements, and our ability to move in a controlled fashion is at the basis of our knowledge and our being in the world. "Bodily movement and brain activity are functionally interdependent" (Wilson 1999:10) because "movement is the only way we have of interacting with the world. . . . All sensory and cognitive processes may be viewed as inputs that determine future motor outputs" (Wolpert et al. 2001:487). "Whether accompanied by consciousness or not, all brain excitation has ultimately but one end, to aid in the regulation of motor coordination" (Sperry 1952:298–299). These processes do give rise to sentience and ultimately consciousness. "The function of consciousness is coordinated movement" (Sheets-Johnstone 2011:377), and "the relations between moving and thinking are in fact quite straightforward . . . intelligence cannot be understood if we do not understand basic movement" (Pfeifer and Bongard 2007:25). "In the beginning, after all, we do not try to move, think about movement possibilities, or put ourselves to the task of moving. We come straightaway moving into the world; we are precisely not stillborn. . . . In effect, our first cognitive steps are taken by way of our movement" (Sheets-Johnstone 2011:117–118). Although the evocative term *stillborn* may only be used in English, "it may even be possible to say that bodily movement, transformed onto the level of action, is the very thing that constitutes the self" (Gallagher 2005:9).

All this is not to take away from the importance of the brain, but rather to demonstrate that a brain is as ineffectual without a body as a body is without a brain. Since the studies of Pierre Paul Broca and Carl Wernicke at the end of the nineteenth century, much research of the brain has been based on the effects of the loss of brain tissue after trauma or a failing blood supply. The damaged part was inferred to have controlled the function that was lost. There are obvious epistemological problems with this approach: a frog does not hear with its legs, even though it no longer jumps when startled by a sound after its legs have been removed. This issue is widely recognized, but the success of the method nevertheless allowed it to become a major source of information. "Neurology's favorite term is / Deficit / . . . / A word for every specific / Neural and mental function / Of which patients may find themselves deprived / Deficit / Loss / Everything that patients aren't / And nothing that they are" (from the beginning of the 1986 opera *The Man Who Mistook His Wife for a Hat,* by Michael Nyman and Christopher Rawlence after a book with the same title by Oliver Sacks). At the end of the twentieth century Paul Lauterbur and Seiji Ogawa developed functional magnetic resonance imaging (fMRI) into an important research technique allowing the visualization of blood-oxygen-level-dependent (BOLD) contrast in an active brain. An increase in oxygen consumption is interpreted as indicative of increased activity directly related to the task performed. This is exactly the reverse of the earlier method and suffers the same epistemological issues. As it shows areas of increased activity in an already universally active brain, the question remains what exactly the contribution is of the newly active region (Libet 1985; Passingham et al. 2013; Raichle 2006). Furthermore, it has been shown that the necessary manipulation of raw data can result in the detection of activity in the brain of a dead Atlantic salmon (Gewin 2012).

Seen from a methodological distance, sentience or consciousness appear little more than a platform that evolved to integrate sensory input and decide on motor actions. This is highly unlikely to be limited to humans, primates, or even mammals (Griffin and Speck 2004; Pompilio et al. 2006; Rowe and Healy 2014). "You have to deeply deny the evidence to conclude that humans alone are conscious, feeling beings who can enjoy living and desire to continue doing so" (Sapina 2015:288); "[T]he question is not, can [animals] reason? nor, can they talk? but, can they suffer?" (Bentham 1907:309). This notion seems intuitively accepted by psychopaths, many of which started their criminal career torturing animals (Cawthorne 2007; Hensley et al. 2009). "At the beginning of his reign [Emperor Domitian] used to spend hours in seclusion every day, doing nothing but catch flies and stab them with a keenly-sharpened stylus" (Rolfe 1914:345). If we accept that animals other than humans possess some degree of consciousness and intelligence, the question arises what the minimum requirements would be. Charles Darwin wrote in *On the Origin of Species* (1859, chapter 7): "I could show that none of these characters of instinct are universal. A little dose, as Pierre Huber expresses it [when reporting on his research of caterpillars], of judgment or reason, often comes into play," and in his last book *The Formation of Vegetable Mould Through the Action of Worms* (1881, chapter 7): "[Earthworms] do not act in the same unvarying manner in all cases, as do most of the lower animals; for instance, they do not drag in leaves by their footstalks, unless the basal part of the blade is as narrow as the apex, or narrower than it" (Reed 1982).

Not many creatures are generally considered "lower animals" than earthworms and sentience, consciousness, and intelligence without doubt evolved relatively early; I propose around the transition between the Proterozoic and Cambrian Periods (Figure 16.3). The

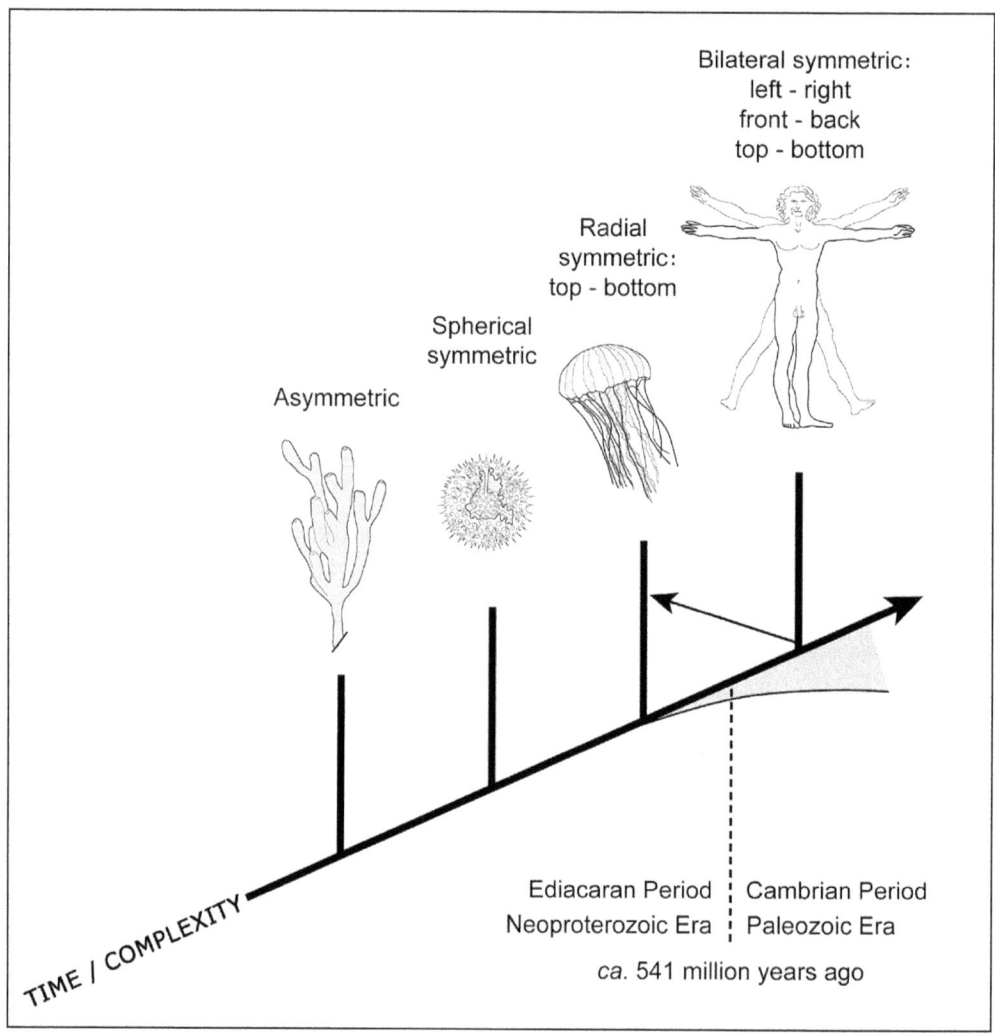

FIGURE 16.3. The development of bilateral symmetric organisms and sentience (in grey) from the transition between the Neoproterozoic and the Cambrian Periods, around 541 million years ago, onward.

so-called Cambrian explosion took place around 541 million years ago and is characterized by the occurrence of bilateral symmetric organisms that have a different top and bottom, front and back, and left and right. This arrangement appeared to be evolutionarily highly advantageous as different areas could specialize to perform specific tasks and the majority of species alive today share this basic ground plan (Smith and Harper 2013). One major consequence of bilateral symmetry was that the direction of motion became fixed and both specialized sensory and propulsion organs could evolve to control motility. Intricately interwoven with this appears to have been the evolution of a system replacing some of the simple feedback loops between input and output with a platform integrating sensory input to decide on motor actions (Figure 16.1) "[Basic cognitive embodiment,] a fundamental cognitive/perceptual toolkit for tracking certain spatial properties and relations ... is required for effective control of a complex active animal body" (Trestman 2013:89).

Certain animals bridge the transition between radial and bilateral symmetry. They revert back from the latter to the former as they mature, suggesting that bilateral symmetry in higher animals is an example of neoteny: the retention of juvenile features, including the flexibility to develop and learn. The eggs of most sea squirts *(Ascidiacea)* develop into nonfeeding tadpoles that swim around to find a place to settle. There they attach themselves irreversibly and turn into sessile, feeding, and sexually mature adults. In the process they lose not only their tail, but also the rudimentary brain that innervated it, as well as their eyes and equilibrium organs (Sasakura et al. 2012). We must assume that at the same time they also lose what little sentience they possessed. Starfish *(Asteroidea)* very similarly metamorphosize from bilateral symmetric larvae into pentaradially symmetric mobile adults, often passing through a short sessile stage. Comb jellies *(Ctenophora)* are radial symmetric, yet have rudimentary sensory organs and a nerve net—all biochemically quite different from the nervous systems of other animals—which might be remnants of an intermediate evolutionary stage or developed independently (Moroz 2015). These examples serve to show how sensory, motor, and nervous systems are evolutionarily closely connected and deeply rooted in control over movements; "[T]hinking and moving are not separate happenings but are aspects of a *kinetic bodily logos*" (Sheets-Johnstone 2011:xxxi–xxxii). The latter is most likely not just valid at an individual level, but equally for groups of animals or humans.

Human Grasp and the Game of Chess

What sets humans apart from the rest of the animal kingdom resulted from the rapid coevolution of our hands and brain that took place during the final two million years of human evolution (Bruner and Lozano 2014; Bruner et al. 2016; Coolidge et al. 2015; Tallis 2003; Wilson 1999), developments that are illustrated here with the uniquely human activity of playing chess (Brooks 1990). Chess has served as model for the world since medieval times (Ferm 2005; O'Sullivan 2012), and became the holy grail of computer engineering during the Cold War (Ensmenger 2012). Much has been written about the victory in May 1997 of IBM's hard- and software array *Deep Blue*, developed in the United States, over the Russian former world chess champion Garry Kasparov (Brooks 2001; Campbell et al. 2002; Newborn 2000). After these events, the game of go *(wéiqí)* replaced chess as the *"drosophila of artificial intelligence"* (Ensmenger 2012; Müller 2002; Silver et al. 2016), until the victory of Google's algorithm *AlphaGo* over South Korean professional go player Lee Sedol, at the time the second strongest player in the word, in March 2016 (Gibney 2016; Silver et al. 2016).

If chess is to serve as model for human intelligence, however, all aspects of the game should be taken into consideration. For a human player, chess requires considerable intellectual efforts, even after significant time is spent to become proficient in the game. Physically moving the pieces seems almost effortless (Figure 16.4), but reflects skills deeply rooted in our evolutionary makeup. Because the same is true for most human behavior we are convinced that thinking is challenging and moving trivial. "Classical artificial intelligence . . . has been successful at those tasks that humans normally consider difficult—playing chess, applying rules of logic, proving mathematical theorems, or solving abstract problems—whereas actions that we experience as very natural and effortless, such as . . . walking, drinking from a glass, assembling a car from a Lego kit . . . have proved notoriously hard" (Pfeifer and Bongard 2007:34). This biased perspective, enhanced by the robots that surround us and the movies that we watch, explains why almost all attention is on the intellectual aspects of chess and so little on its motor components.

Figure 16.4. The hand of the author moves a piece of an alternative chess set. Our ability to initiate and control such movements (grasp in the most literal sense) may be more relevant to our being in the world than our ability to appreciate and compute where to place the piece (grasp in a more figurative sense).

Although computers now seem able to beat humans at chess and go, León and others (2014:1) remark that "although many researchers have partially studied various aspects of the human hand from the neuro-physiological and biomechanical viewpoints, to date there has been no comprehensive characterization of the human hand function for grasping and manipulating of everyday life objects, mainly because of the lack of a sufficiently detailed and accurate tool for its simulation." This observation was confirmed by Suárez-Ruiz et al. in their report on developing a robot able to assemble an IKEA chair:

> Robots can autonomously achieve a highly complex manipulation task . . . working in an unstructured environment. . . . There is still an important limitation: Although all the steps were automatically planned and controlled, their sequence was hard-coded through a considerable engineering effort. One can envision such a sequence being automatically determined. . . . Combining the capabilities and the framework developed here with the recent advances in [artificial intelligence] could lead, in the near future, to such fully autonomous assembly. [2018:2]

Although it is doubtlessly possible for robots to achieve fully autonomous grasping and manipulating movement capabilities, such as moving chess pieces or assembling an IKEA chair, while sentience or consciousness may not be indispensable for such activities, it remains unclear when this "near future" will arrive (Al-Saedi et al. 2015; Becker-Asano et al. 2015; Dreyfus 1972; Matuszek et al. 2011; Randell 1982).

Our partiality toward mental as opposed to physical agility becomes evident when considering whether somebody with both the intelligence and the physical limitations of, for instance, the late theoretical physicist Stephen Hawking, would be able to play chess. Many are tempted to respond in the affirmative. Reversely, almost all reject the notion that he would be able to play tennis, even though this is also a game between two players that, governed by strict rules, requires both strategic insight and choreographed movements. To identify a chess algorithm, or the hardware that enables it, as the intelligence that controls the movements of the chess pieces is an oversimplification of a fundamentally more complex reality. Even if all the necessary anatomical and physiological components are introduced or restored, as could be envisioned for Hawking, this might not inevitably lead to the desired result. This may be illustrated by the anecdote about a patient with a broken wrist who asks his doctor whether it would be possible for him to play the piano after his injuries have healed. Upon a positive response he remarks how wonderful that would be as he was never able to do so before his accident. Another, less whimsical analogy is the Molyneux problem (Held et al. 2011; Nagel 1974; Patrick 1899; Tunstall 2011), named after its formulation by John Locke in his *An Essay Concerning Human Understanding*:

> Suppose a man born blind . . . and taught by his touch to distinguish between a cube and a sphere. . . . Suppose then the cube and sphere placed on a table, and the blind man be made to see: quaere, whether by his sight, before he touched them, he could now distinguish and tell which is the globe, which the cube. [1690, Book 2, chapter 9]

Chess and go are old, but not quite old enough to be evolutionarily embedded. Aptitude in these games is the result of exaptation—the application of traits and skills for entirely different purposes than for the specific challenges in response to which they evolved—combined with sufficient deliberate practice ensuing from a *"rage to master"* (Hambrick et al. 2014; Vandervert 2009; Winner 1996). The material substrates of the unique human development include increasingly complex tools (Ambrose 2001; Hodder 2012; Malafouris 2013), as well as increasingly meaningful artifacts (Ingold 2011; Zilhão 2007). Only about 130,000 years after the last Acheulean hand-axe the first Boeing 747 airliner was built and within 30,000 years the Périgord rock-art and the Venus of Dolní Věstonice developed into the works of Pablo Picasso, Henry Moore, and all modern literary and scientific publications. Playing chess combines these avenues and requires strategic insight, the chess-specific parts of which have to be actively learned, as well as fine motor control, which is almost entirely evolutionarily embedded. As with every human endeavor the two are inseparably intertwined.

In his critical review of the optimism of his colleagues at the Massachusetts Institute of Technology (MIT) in achieving artificial intelligence, Hubert Dreyfus used chess as paradigm for intelligence, but focused entirely on the strategic aspects of the game. "In the context of a game of chess, the weight of the pieces is irrelevant" (Dreyfus 1972:169). This ignores the various levels of movement involved in an actual game of chess and denied Dreyfus the opportunity to question the intelligence of machines when he was beaten by chess algorithm *MacHack VI* (MIT 1967). In a volume printed at the same institution, Lambros Malafouris (2013:28) acknowledges that "in implementing computational theory in the laboratories of artificial intelligence, it soon became manifest that, although simulations based on computational logic proved extremely effective in performing complex analytical tasks (such as running a program capable of winning a chess game), they were extremely ineffective in performing tasks as simple as instructing a robot to find its way out of a room without running into walls." Robots, computers, and algorithms are obviously still far from playing chess the way humans do. They are certainly better in the strategic aspects of the game, but hopeless at its motor aspects. They are even farther from enjoying the game or becoming frustrated as they lose. The human experience is maybe best expressed by Vladimir Nabokov when he describes the fictional chess grandmaster Aleksandr Luzhin contemplating his next move in an adjourned game:

> Luzhin narrowed his eyes and almost in a whisper, pursing his lips as for a careful kiss, emitted not words, not the mere designation of a move, but something most tender and infinitely fragile. The same expression was on his face—the expression of a person blowing a tiny feather from the face of an infant—when the following day he embodied this move on the board. [Nabokov 1990 (1930):122, translated by V. Nabokov and M. Scammell]

Still more aspects of chess need to be taken into account when employing it as a model for the world. It is, for instance, not the position of the pieces that is important, but rather their individual potential. After a piece is moved, the significance of all remaining potential moves has changed and it is this continuously changing web of potential moves that defines a game. These moves do not exist without the pieces and neither do the pieces exist without their moves. "Take a knight, for instance. By itself is it an element in the game? Certainly not, for by its material make-up—outside its square and the other conditions of the game—it means nothing to the player; it becomes a real, concrete element only when endowed with value and wedded to it" (de Saussure 1959:110). Furthermore, a game of chess can only exist between two players. While playing, they reach out—literally as well as figuratively—and together create a game that could not otherwise exist. No game exists without the players, nor are they players without the game. Similarly, humans and human groups can only exist within a landscape where their movements bring them into contact with different environments as well as other humans, resulting in continuous psychosocial and cultural development.

Movement as Catalyst of History

The complex mechanisms that over long time periods resulted in specific properties at the individual level, such as controlled movement generating sentience as argued above, will have similar effects on groups of individuals encountering comparable challenges, especially in social beings such as humans (Boyd and Richerson 2009a; Foster 1994; Gallese 2009; Henrich 2016; Iacoboni 2009; Leach 2003; Medicus 1992). No human individual or human group is entirely settled or continuously mobile; we are all somewhere within the continuum between these two scholarly constructs. Mobile groups do not move across the landscape simply because they are nomads, but will stay in one place until their inertia is overcome by push and pull factors that make them move. Modern settled humans are born in one place and are educated in several others. After graduating they start a career in yet another place, more often than not far from both their childhood home and their place of professional education. They may subsequently move several times before retiring in a place with much sun and little taxes. Also on a daily and seasonal scale most modern people move significantly: they travel considerable distances from home to work and back, and a multitude when on their yearly vacation. Although the scale of this mobility may have increased over time it is not a modern phenomenon, but has been attested from the dawn of humanity onward. The difference between settled and mobile people, or between various mobile groups, is thus not as clear as it might appear upon cursory inspection (Sheller and Urry 2006; Wendrich and Barnard 2008).

The last two million years of human evolution are characterized by the swift coevolution of our hands and brain, resulting in the current separation of the human species from all other animals. Although the exact details remain elusive, partially because of a paucity of data, the events seem to be initiated by adaptive behavior and microevolution in response to climatic change (Antón et al. 2014; Hughes et al. 2007; Naya et al. 2016). Among the first steps in the process was the fostering of bipedal movement (Bramble and Lieberman 2004; Crompton et al. 2010; Thorpe et al. 2014), which sparked a virtuous cycle of increased agility of our hands (Forrester et al. 2013; Tallis 2003; Uomini 2009; Wilson 1999), now liberated from their previous tasks (Bruner and Lozano 2014; Coolidge et al. 2015; Schmitz et al. 2017), and a dramatic increase in both the volume of our brain and our intelligence (Antón et al. 2014; Koyabu et al. 2014; Lefebvre 2012; Rightmire 2004; Roth and Dicke 2012), necessary to control the multitude of newly developed movements. Among the properties emerging from this cycle, and at the same time driving it, are changes in the human diet (Babbitt et al. 2010), increasingly complex tools (Ambrose 2001; Diogo et al. 2012; Key and Dunmore 2015), and the development of pyrotechnology (Archibald et al. 2012; Wrangham and Carmody 2010), as well as language (Ocklenburg et al. 2014; Wilson 1999).

Human cultural evolution is intricately intertwined with human movement and social interaction. As humanity moved out of its heartland in eastern Africa, individuals and groups of individuals arrived in new and unfamiliar landscapes and environments with not previously encountered climatic properties, food sources, raw materials, prey and predator animals, and many other novelties (Leppard this volume). Although these sometimes must have proven detrimental, human culture was often able to create opportunities out of these challenges. This became especially relevant when anatomically modern humans successfully and permanently moved "out of Africa," around 90,000–70,000 years ago, after migrating either across the Red Sea at Bab-el-Mandeb, much narrower at the time due to continental drift and a lower average ocean level, or along the Red Sea coast and across the Sinai Peninsula (Armitage et al. 2011; Beyin 2006; Derricourt 2005; Oppenheimer 2009; Petraglia 2003; Vermeersch 2001). Next to a multitude of adjustments (Kuper and Kröpelin 2006; Zhang et al. 2007), two events similarly combined, on a global scale, the movement of people with rapid and fundamental developments in human material and immaterial culture, their mental and physical abilities, as well as the world around them. The first was the so-called Neolithic wave of advance (Diamond and Bellwood 2003; Pinhasi et al. 2005; Sjödin and François 2011), starting around 12,000–8,000 years ago, and discussed in other chapters in this volume. The second resulted in the "Columbian exchange" around 500–300 years ago (Boivin et al. 2012; Mann 2011; Nunn and Qian 2010), which refers to the anthropogenic introduction of many Old World species of plants and animals in the Americas, and vice versa, almost completely reversing their previous separation by continental drift about 150 million years earlier.

A series of interconnected phenomena that resulted from these developments are of interest here. First is that anatomically modern humans needed personal protection from the environment and achieved this in the form of clothing. Their garments quickly became imbued with abundant psychosocial meaning (Boytner 2004; Gilling 2007; Gordon 2011; Lemire and Riello 2008; McCorriston 1997), as they remain today. The production chain that resulted in wearable garments over time developed into the most complex and valuable human enterprise, possibly only surpassed by the aerospace industry in the second half of the twentieth century. Given the large role of women in this process, it is remarkable that "female mobility is rarely or never used as an explanation for the spread of material culture or technology transfer between communities in prehistory" (Brown 2014:170). The Industrial Revolution, which between 1760 and 1840 resulted in our modern society, was largely driven by the textile industry (Temin 1997; Knick Harley and Crafts 2000; Lemire and Riello 2008), while organic chemistry developed out of the need to understand and improve textile dyes and soaps. Textiles and clothing, as well as the technological, economic, and social changes of the Industrial Revolution greatly facilitated all aspects of human mobility.

Recently, it became poignantly clear that because of the interconnections between humans and the world around them, our activities result in irreversible changes in the environment. The continuous movement of humans into new territories combined with the expanding movement of humans on a daily basis appears to have launched a new geological period, identified as the Anthropocene (Barnes et al. 2013; Erlandson and Braje 2013; Farrier 2020; Lane 2015; Palsson et al. 2013; Pétursdóttir 2017). Comparable geological phenomena ensuing from biological activity include the free oxygen in the air, as well as the fossil fuels and limestone under our feet, primarily generated around 2–1 billion years ago (the Great Oxygenation Event), 323–299 million years ago (the Upper Carboniferous or Pennsylvanian Period), and 100–66 million years ago (the Upper Cretaceous Period), respectively. Irrespective of whether we define the beginning of the Anthropocene to coincide with the first human use and control of fire, the gradual shift to settled agriculture (about 10,000 years ago), the Industrial Revolution (around 1800), or the development of nuclear energy (1945), the movements of humans are leading to a loss of biodiversity, pollution, ocean acidification, ozone depletion, the alteration of global climate systems, and changes in the global carbon, nitrogen, and phosphorus cycles.

Mobility of people can likewise have significant social, political, and historical impacts. Next to the large-scale, long-term events discussed above, more recent examples include the Atlantic slave trade and the expulsion of Jews out of Spain and Portugal at the end of the fifteenth century, and subsequently out of Europe in the first half of the twentieth century. Apart from unfathomable grief, these events also created new cultural expressions and mental abilities that would otherwise not have arisen, much like control of our movements generated consciousness. Current events are partially dominated by the movement of people (Cresswell 2006, 2010; Cresswell and Merriman 2004; Goldin et al. 2011; Millman 1997; Sheller and Urry 2006; Urry 2007), most dramatically around the Mediterranean Sea (Fabre and Sant Cassia 2007; Hamilakis 2016) and at the American-Mexican border (De León 2015; Zubiaurre 2019). "Globalization is tied to the dreams and desires of the kinetic elite who inhabit the luxurious space of flows, and who need the kinetic underclass to service it. There are no *tourists* without *vagabonds*" (Cresswell 2006:256). Our humanity and being in the world have ultimately been defined by our ancestors evolving and learning to ever more carefully control increasingly complex movements.

Acknowledgments

I would like to express my sincere thanks to my undergraduate and graduate students, for allowing me to discuss the above subjects *ad nauseam* and to Megan Daniels, for her insistence for me to partake in this project and write this chapter. Thanks are also due to three anonymous reviewers, the opinions of whom resulted in better phrasing and more unity in this chapter. Furthermore, I would like to thank Peter Biehl, Ran Boytner, Kym Faull, Efrain Kristal, and Steve Rosen, for their support, and Willeke Wendrich, for her unwavering encouragement.

Note

1. Their rather crude animation can be viewed at <www.youtube.com/watch?v=VTN-mLt7QX8E> (last accessed February 29, 2020).

References Cited

Adams, F. 1886 *The Genuine Works of Hippocrates: Volume 2: Translated from the Greek with a Preliminary Discourse and Annotations by Francis Adams, LL.D.* William Wood and Company, New York.

Al-Saedi, F. A. T., and A. H. Mohammed 2015 Design and Implementation of Chess-playing Robotic System. *International Journal of Computer Science Engineering and Technology* 5(5):90–98.

Altschul, J. H., K. W. Kintigh, T. H. Klein, W. H. Doelle, K. A. Hays-Gilpin, S. A. Herr, T. A. Kohler, B. J. Mills, L. M. Montgomery, M. C. Nelson, S. G. Ortman, J. N. Parker, M. A. Peeples, and J. A. Sabloff 2017 Fostering Synthesis in Archaeology to Advance Science and Benefit Society. *Proceedings of the National Academy of Sciences* 114(42):10999–11002. DOI:10.1073/pnas.1715950114.

Ambrose, S. H. 2001 Paleolithic Technology and Human Evolution. *Science* 291(5509):1748–1753.

Antón, S. C., R. Potts, and L. C. Aiello 2014 Evolution of Early *Homo*: An Integrated Biological Perspective. *Science* 344:1236828. DOI:10.1126/science.1236828.

Archibald, S., A. C. Staver, and S. A. Levin 2012 Evolution of Human-Driven Fire Regimes in Africa. *Proceedings of the National Academy of Sciences* 109(3):847–852. DOI:10.1073/pnas.1118648109.

Armitage, S. J., S. A. Jasim, A. E. Marks, A. G. Parker, V. I. Usik, and H.-P. Uerpmann 2011 The Southern Route "Out of Africa": Evidence for an Early Expansion of Modern Humans into Arabia. *Science* 331(6016):453–456. DOI:10.1126/science.1199113.

Arnold, J. E., A. P. Graesch, E. Ragazzini, and E. Ochs 2012 *Life at Home in the Twenty-First Century: 32 Families Open Their Doors*. Cotsen Institute of Archaeology Press, Los Angeles.

Babbitt, C. C., L. R. Warner, O. Fedrigo, C. E. Wall, and G. A. Wray 2010 Genomic Signatures of Diet-Related Shifts during Human Origins. *Proceedings of the Royal Society B: Biological Sciences* 278(1708):961–969. DOI:10.1098/rspb.2010.2433.

Baines, J. 1985 Color Terminology and Color Classification: Ancient Egyptian Color Terminology and Polychromy. *American Anthropologist, New Series* 87(2):282–297.

Barnard, H., and K. Duistermaat (eds.) 2012 *The History of the Peoples of the Eastern Desert*. Cotsen Institute of Archaeology Press, Los Angeles.

Barnard, H., and W. Z. Wendrich (eds.) 2008 *The Archaeology of Mobility: Old World and New World Nomadism*. Cotsen Institute of Archaeology Press, Los Angeles.

Barnes, J., M. Dove, M. Lahsen, A. Mathews, P. McElwee, R. McIntosh, F. Moore, J. O'Reilly, B. Orlove, R. Puri, H. Weiss, and K. Yager 2013 Contribution of Anthropology to the Study of Climate Change. *Nature Climate Change* 3:541–544. DOI:10.1002/wcc.219.

Barnes, J. 1991 *The Complete Works of Aristotle: The Revised Oxford Translation, Volume 1: Physics*. Revised edition of the 1912 original. Princeton University Press, Princeton.

Bateson, G. 2000 *Steps to an Ecology of Mind: Collected Essays in Anthropology, Psychiatry, Evolution, and Epistemology*. New edition of the 1972 original with a foreword by Mary Catherine Bateson. University of Chicago Press, Chicago.

Becker-Asano, C., N. Riesterer, J. Hué, and B. Nebel 2015 Embodiment, Emotion, and Chess: A System Description. In *4th International Symposium on New Frontiers in Human-Robot Interaction,* edited by M. Salem, A. Weiss, P. Baxter, and K. Dautenhahn, 74–80. Published by the editors, Canterbury.

Bennett, J. 2010 *Vibrant Matter: A Political Ecology of Things.* Duke University Press, Durham and London.

Bentham, J. 1907 *An Introduction to the Principles of Morals and Legislation.* Originally printed in 1780 and first published in 1789. Clarendon Press, Oxford.

Beyin, A. 2006 The Bab al Mandab vs the Nile-Levant: An Appraisal of the Two Dispersal Routes for Early Modern Humans Out of Africa. *African Archaeological Review* 23(1):5–30.

Boivin, N., D. Q. Fuller, and A. Crowther 2012 Old World Globalization and the Columbian Exchange: Comparison and Contrast. *World Archaeology* 44(3):452–469. DOI:10.1080/00438243.2012.729404.

Boroditsky, L., O. Fuhrman, and K. McCormick 2011 Do English and Mandarin Speakers Think About Time Differently? *Cognition* 118(1):123–129. DOI: 10.1016/j.cognition.2010.09.010.

Bosch, T. C. G., and M. J. McFall-Ngai 2011 Metaorganisms as the New Frontier. *Zoology* 114(4):185–190. DOI:10.1016/j.zool.2011.04.001.

Bovine Genome Sequencing and Analysis Consortium, C. G. Elsik, R. L. Tellam, and K. C. Worley 2009 The Genome Sequence of Taurine Cattle: A Window to Ruminant Biology and Evolution. *Science* 324(5926):522–528.

Bowman, A., and A. Wilson (eds.) 2009 *Quantifying the Roman Economy: Methods and Problems.* Oxford University Press, Oxford and New York.

Bowman, A., and A. Wilson (eds.) 2013 *The Roman Agricultural Economy: Organization, Investment, and Production.* Oxford University Press, Oxford and New York.

Boyd, R., and P. J. Richerson 2009a Culture and the Evolution of Human Cooperation. *Philosophical Transactions of the Royal Society B: Biological Sciences* 364(1533): 3281–3288.

Boyd, R., and P. J. Richerson 2009b Voting with Your Feet: Payoff Biased Migration and the Evolution of Group Beneficial Behavior. *Journal of Theoretical Biology* 257:331–339.

Boytner, R. 2004 Clothing the Social World. In *Andean Archaeology. Blackwell Studies in Global Archaeology 2,* edited by H. Silverman, pp. 130–145. Blackwell, Malden, Oxford, and Carlton.

Braje, T. J., J. M. Erlandson, C. M. Aikens, T. Beach, S. Fitzpatrick, S. Gonzalez, D. J. Kennett, P. V. Kirch, G.-A. Lee, K. G. Lightfoot, S. B. McClure, L. M. Panich, T. C. Rick, A. C. Roosevelt, T. D. Schneider, B. Smith, and M. A. Zeder 2014 An Anthropocene Without Archaeology: Should We Care? *The SAA Archaeological Record* 14(1):26–29.

Bramble, D. M., and D. E. Lieberman 2004 Endurance Running and the Evolution of *Homo. Nature* 432(7015):345–352.

Briuer, F. L. 1976 New Clues to Stone Tool Function: Plant and Animal Residues. *American Antiquity* 41(4):478–484.

Brooks, R. A. 1990 Elephants Don't Play Chess. *Robotics and Autonomous Systems* 6(1–2):3–15.

Brooks, R. A. 2001 The Relationship Between Matter and Life. *Nature* 409(6818):409–411.

Brown, K. A. 2014 Women on the Move: The DNA Evidence for Female Mobility and Exogamy in Prehistory. In *Past Mobilities: Archaeological Approaches to Movement and Mobility,* edited by J. Leary, pp. 155–173. Ashgate, Franham and Burlington.

Bruner, E., and M. Lozano 2014 Extended Mind and Visuo-spatial Integration: Three Hands for the Neanderthal Lineage. *Journal of Anthropological Sciences* 92:273–280. DOI:10.4436/JASS.92009.

Bruner, E., M. Lozano, and C. Lorenzo 2016 Visuospatial Integration and Human Evolution: The Fossil Evidence *Journal of Anthropological Sciences* 94:81–97.

Campbell, M., A. J. Hoane, and F. H. Hsu 2002 Deep Blue, *Artificial Intelligence* 134(1–2):57–83.

Carrigan, M. A., O. Uryasev, C. B. Frye, B. L. Eckman, C. R. Myers, T. D. Hurley, and S. A. Benne 2015 Hominids Adapted to Metabolize Ethanol Long Before Human-directed Fermentation. *Proceedings of the National Academy of Sciences* 112(2):458–463. DOI:10.1073/pnas.1404167111.

Cawthorne, N. 2007 *Serial Killers and Mass Murderers: Profiles of the World's Most Barbaric Criminals.* Ulysses Press, Berkeley.

Chaubey, G., Q. Ayub, N. Rai, S. Prakash, V. Mushrif-Tripathy, M. Mezzavilla, A. K. Pathak, R. Tamang, S. Firasat, M. Reidla, M. Karmin, D. S. Rani, A. G. Reddy, J. Parik, E. Metspalu, S. Rootsi, K. Dalal, S. Khaliq, S. Q. Mehdi, L. Singh, M. Metspalu, T. Kivisild, C. Tyler-Smith, R. Villems, and K. Thangaraj 2017 "Like Sugar in Milk": Reconstructing the Genetic History of the Parsi Population. *Genome Biology* 18(1):110. DOI:10.1186/s13059-017-1244-9.

Chen, J., H. Zheng, J.-X. Bei, L. Sun, W.-H. Jia, T. Li, F. Zhang, M. Seielstad, Y.-X. Zeng, X. Zhang, and J. Liu 2009 Genetic Structure of the Han Chinese Population Revealed by Genome-wide SNP Variation. *American Journal of Human Genetics* 85(6):775–785.

Cho, I., and M. J. Blaser 2012 The Human Microbiome: At the Interface of Health and Disease. *Nature Reviews: Genetics* 13(4):260–270. DOI:10.1038/nrg3182.

Clark, A., and D. Chalmers 1998 The Extended Mind. *Analysis* 58(1):7–19.

Clark, G. A. 2010 Should One Size Fit All? Some Observations on Killick and Goldberg. *The SAA Archaeological Record* 10(1):36, 39–42.

Coolidge, F. L., T. Wynn, K. A. Overmann, and J. M. Hicks 2015 Cognitive Archaeology and the Cognitive Sciences. In *Human Paleoneurology: Springer Series in Bio-Neuroinformatics 3*, edited by E. Bruner, pp. 177–206. Springer International, Cham.

Cresswell, T. 2006 *On the Move: Mobility in the Modern Western World.* Routledge, New York and Milton Park.

Cresswell, T. 2010 Towards a Politics of Mobility. *Environment and Planning D: Society and Space* 28(1):17–31. DOI:10.1068/d11407.

Cresswell, T., and P. Merriman (eds.) 2004 *Geographies of Mobilities: Practices, Spaces, Subjects.* Ashgate, Farnham and Burlington.

Crick, F. 1994 *The Astonishing Hypothesis: The Scientific Search for the Soul.* Scribner and Sons, New York.

Crompton, R. H., W. I. Sellers, and S. K. S. Thorpe 2010 Arboreality, Terrestriality and Bipedalism. *Philosophical Transactions of the Royal Society B: Biological Sciences* 365(1556):3301–3314. DOI:10.1098/rstb.2010.0035.

De León, J. 2015 *The Land of Open Graves: Living and Dying on the Sonoran Desert Migrant Trail.* University of California Press, Oakland.

de Saussure, F. 1959 *Course in General Linguistics.* Originally published in French in 1916, edited by C. Bally and A. Sechehaye. Translated by W. Baskin. Philosophical Library, New York.

Derricourt, R. 2005 Getting "Out of Africa": Sea Crossings, Land Crossings, and Culture in the Hominin Migrations. *Journal of World Prehistory* 19(2):119–132.

Diamond, J. M. 2000 Talk of Cannibalism. *Nature* 407(6800):25–26.

Diamond, J. M., and P. Bellwood 2003 Farmers and Their Languages: The First Expansions. *Science* 300(5619):597–603.

Diogo, R., B. G. Richmond, and B. Wood 2012 Evolution and Homologies of Primate and Modern Human Hand and Forearm Muscles, with Notes on Thumb Movements and Tool Use. *Journal of Human Evolution* 63(1):64–78. DOI:10.1016/j.jhevol.2012.04.001.

Downs, E. F., and J. M. Lowenstein 1996 Identification of Archaeological Blood Proteins: A Cautionary Note. *Journal of Archaeological Science* 22(1):11–16.

Dreyfus, H. L. 1972 *What Computers Can't Do: A Critique of Artificial Reason*. Harper and Row, New York.

Eerkens, J. E. 2005 GC-MS Analysis and Fatty Acid Ratios of Archaeological Potsherds from the Western Great Basin of North America. *Archaeometry* 47(1):83–102.

Effros, B., and G. Lai (eds.) 2018 *Unmasking Ideology in Imperial and Colonial Archaeology: Vocabulary, Symbols, and Legacy*. Cotsen Institute of Archaeology Press, Los Angeles.

Ehrlich, P., and M. Feldman 2003 Genes and Cultures: What Creates Our Behavioral Phenome? (with Comments and Reply). *Current Anthropology* 44(4):87–107.

Ensmenger, N. 2012 Is Chess the Drosophila of Artificial Intelligence? A Social History of an Algorithm. *Social Studies of Science* 42(1):5–30. DOI:10.1177/0306312711424596.

Erlandson, J. M., and T. J. Braje 2013 Archeology and the Anthropocene. *Anthropocene* 4(1):1–7. DOI:10.1016/j.ancene.2014.05.003.

Evershed, R. P. 2008 Organic Residue Analysis in Archaeology: The Archaeological Biomarker Revolution. *Archaeometry* 50(6):895–924.

Fabre, T., and P. Sant Cassia (eds.) 2007 *Between Europe and the Mediterranean: The Challenges and the Fears*. Palgrave MacMillan, Basingstoke and New York

Farrier, D. 2020 *Footprints: In Search of Future Fossils*. Farrar, Straus and Giroux, New York.

Ferm, O. (ed.) 2005 *Chess and Allegory in the Middle Ages: A Collection of Essays. Runica et Mediaevalia/Scripta Minora: Volume 12*. Sällskapet Runica et Mediaevalia, Stockholm.

Fiedel, S. 1996 Blood from Stones? Some Methodological and Interpretive Problems in Blood Residue Analysis. *Journal of Archaeological Science* 23(1):139–147.

Flegr, J. 2007 Effects of Toxoplasma on Human Behavior. *Schizophrenia Bulletin* 33(3):757–760.

Forrester, G. S., C. Quaresmini, D. A. Leavens, D. Mareschald, and M. S. C. Thomas 2013 Human Handedness: An Inherited Evolutionary Trait. *Behavioural Brain Research* 237:200–206. DOI:10.1016/j.bbr.2012.09.037.

Foster, M. L. 1994 Symbolism: The Foundation of Culture. In *Companion Encyclopedia of Anthropology*, edited by T. Ingold, pp. 366–395. Routledge, London and New York.

Frank, M. C., D. L. Everett, E. Fedorenko, and E. Gibson 2008 Number as a Cognitive Technology: Evidence from Pirahã Language and Cognition. *Cognition* 108(3):819–824.

Gallagher, S. 2005 *How the Body Shapes the Mind*. Clarendon Press, Oxford.

Gallese V. 2009 Mirror Neurons, Embodied Simulation, and the Neural Basis of Social Identification. *Psychoanalytic Dialogues* 19(5):519–536.

Gewin, V. 2012 Turning Point: Craig Bennett. *Nature* 490(4720):437. DOI:10.1038/nj7420-437a.

Gibney, E. 2016 Google Masters Go: Deep-learning Software Excels at Complex Ancient Board Game. *Nature* 529(7587):445–446. DOI:10.1038/nature16961.

Gilling, I. 2007 Clothing and Modern Human Behaviour: Prehistoric Tasmania as a Case Study. *Archaeology in Oceania* 42(3):102–111.

Goldin, I., G. Cameron, and M. Balarajan 2011 *Exceptional People: How Migration Shaped Our World and Will Define Our Future.* Princeton University Press, Princeton and Oxford.

Gordon, B. 2011 *Textiles: The Whole Story.* Thames and Hudson, London and New York.

Graves-Brown, P., R. Harrison, and A. Piccini (eds.) 2013 *The Oxford Handbook of the Archaeology of the Contemporary World.* Oxford University Press, Oxford.

Griffin, D. R., and G. B. Speck 2004 New Evidence of Animal Consciousness. *Animal Cognition* 7(1):5–18.

Gros, F. 2014 *A Philosophy of Walking.* Translated by J. Howe. Verso, London and New York.

Guerra-Doce, E. 2015 Psychoactive Substances in Prehistoric Times: Examining the Archaeological Evidence. *Time and Mind* 8(1):91–112. DOI:10.1080/1751696X.2014.993244.

Gurfinkel, D. M., and U. M. Franklin 1988 A Study of the Feasibility of Detecting Blood Residues on Artifacts. *Journal of Archaeological Science* 15(1):83–97.

Hambrick D. Z., F. L. Oswald, E. M. Altmann, E. J. Meinz, F. Gobet, and G. Campitelli 2014 Deliberate Practice: Is That All It Takes to Become an Expert? *Intelligence* 45(1):34–45. DOI:10.1016/j.intell.2013.04.001.

Hamilakis, Y. (ed.) 2016 Forum: Archaeologies of Forced and Undocumented Migration. *Journal of Contemporary Archaeology*, special thematic issue 3(2):121–293. DOI:10.1558/jca.32409.

Harrison, R., and J. Schofield (eds.) 2010 *After Modernity: Archaeological Approaches to the Contemporary Past.* Oxford University Press, Oxford.

Heider, F., and M. Simmel 1944 An Experimental Study of Apparent Behavior. *American Journal of Psychology* 57:243–259.

Held, R., Y. Ostrovsky, B. de Gelder, T. Gandhi, S. Ganesh, U. Mathur, and P. Sinha 2011 The Newly Sighted Fail to Match Seen with Felt. *Nature Neuroscience* 14(5):551–553. DOI:10.1038/nn.2795.

Henrich, J. 2016 *The Secret of Our Success: How Culture Is Driving Human Evolution, Domesticating Our Species, and Making Us Smarter.* Princeton University Press, Princeton.

Henrich, J., and R. McElreath 2003 The Evolution of Cultural Evolution. *Evolutionary Anthropology* 12(3):123–135.

Hensley, C., S. E. Tallichet, and E. L. Dutkiewicz 2009 Recurrent Childhood Animal Cruelty: Is There a Relationship to Adult Recurrent Interpersonal Violence? *Criminal Justice Review* 34(2):248–257.

Hockings, K. J., N. Bryson-Morrison, S. Carvalho, M. Fujisawa, T. Humle, W. C. McGrew, M. Nakamura, G. Ohashi, Y. Yamanashi, G. Yamakoshi, and T. Matsuzawa 2015 Tools to Tipple: Ethanol Ingestion by Wild Chimpanzees Using Leaf-sponges. *Royal Society Open Science* 2:150150. DOI:dx.doi.org/10.1098/rsos.150150.

Hodder, I. 2012 *Entangled: An Archaeology of the Relationships Between Humans and Things.* John Wiley and Sons, Chichester and Malden.

Hoffman, D. D., M. Singh, and C. Prakash 2015 The Interface Theory of Perception. *Psychonomic Bulletin and Review* 22(6):1480–1506. DOI:10.3758/s13423-015-0890-8.

Hughes, J. K., A. Haywood, S. J. Mithen, B. W. Sellwood, and P. J. Valdes 2007 Investigating Early Hominin Dispersal Patterns: Developing a Framework for Climate Data Integration. *Journal of Human Evolution* 53(5):465–474.

Hyland, D. C., J. M. Tersak, J. M. Adovasio, and M. I. Siegel 1990 Identification of the Species of Origin of Residual Blood on Lithic Material. *American Antiquity* 55(1):104–112.

Iacoboni, M. 2009 Imitation, Empathy, and Mirror Neurons. *Annual Review of Psychology* 60:653–670.

Ingold, T. 2011 *Being Alive: Essays on Movement, Knowledge, and Description*. Routledge, London and New York.

Ingold, T. 2013 *Making: Anthropology, Archaeology, Art and Architecture*. Routledge, London and New York.

Jameson, J. H., and S. Musteață (eds.) 2019 *Transforming Heritage Practice in the 21st Century: Contributions from Community Archaeology*. Springer, Cham.

Key, A. J. M., and C. J. Dunmore 2015 The Evolution of the Hominin Thumb and the Influence Exerted by the Non-dominant Hand During Stone Tool Production. *Journal of Human Evolution* 78(1):60–69. DOI:10.1016/j.jhevol.2014.08.006.

Killick, D., and P. Goldberg 2009 A Quiet Crisis in American Archaeology. *The SAA Archaeological Record* 9(1):6–10, 40.

Knick Harley, C., and N. F. R. Crafts 2000 Simulating the Two Views of the British Industrial Revolution. *Journal of Economic History* 60(3): 819–841.

Kok, B. E., and B. L. Fredrickson 2010 Upward Spirals of the Heart: Autonomic Flexibility, as Indexed by Vagal Tone, Reciprocally and Prospectively Predicts Positive Emotions and Social Connectedness. *Biological Psychology* 85(3):432–436. DOI:10.1016/j.biopsycho.2010.09.005.

Kooyman, B., M. E. Newman, and H. Ceri 1992 Verifying the Reliability of Blood Residue Analysis on Archaeological Tools. *Journal of Archaeological Science* 19(3):265–269.

Koyabu, D., I. Werneburg, N. Morimoto, C. P. E. Zollikofer, A. M. Forasiepi, H. Endo, J. Kimura, S. D. Ohdachi, N. T. Son, and M. R. Sánchez-Villagra 2014 Mammalian Skull Heterochrony Reveals Modular Evolution and a Link between Cranial Development and Brain Size. *Nature Communications* 5:3625. DOI:10.1038/ncomms4625.

Kozorovitskiy, Y., C. G. Gross, C. Kopil, L. Battaglia, M. McBreen, A. M. Stranahan, and E. Gould 2005 Experience Induces Structural and Biochemical Changes in the Adult Primate Brain. *Proceedings of the National Academy of Sciences* 102(48):17478–17482.

Krauss, W. 2015 Anthropology in the Anthropocene: Sustainable Development, Climate Change, and Interdisciplinary Research. In *Grounding Global Climate Change*, edited by H. Greschke, and J. Tischler, pp. 59–76. Springer Science and Business Media, Dordrecht.

Kuper, R., and S. Kröpelin 2006 Climate-Controlled Holocene Occupation in the Sahara: Motor of Africa's Evolution. *Science* 313(5788):803–807.

Lafferty, K. D. 2006 Can the Common Brain Parasite, *Toxoplasma gondii*, Influence Human Culture? *Proceedings of the Royal Society B: Biological Sciences* 273(1602):2749–2755.

Lambert, P. M., B. L. Leonard, B. R. Billman, R. A. Marlar, M. E. Newman, and K. J. Reinhard 2000 Response to Critique of the Claim of Cannibalism at Cowboy Wash. *American Antiquity* 65(2):397–406.

Lane, P. J. 2015 Archaeology in the Age of the Anthropocene: A Critical Assessment of Its Scope and Societal Contributions. *Journal of Field Archaeology* 40(5):485–498. DOI:10.1179/2042458215Y.0000000022.

Leach, H. M. 2003 Human Domestication Reconsidered (with Comments and Reply). *Current Anthropology* 44(3):349–368.

Leary, J. 2014 Past Mobilities: An introduction. In *Past Mobilities: Archaeological Approaches to Movement and Mobility*, edited by J. Leary, pp. 1–19. Ashgate, Franham and Burlington.

Lefebvre, L. 2012 Primate Encephalization. In *Progress in Brain Research: Volume 195*, edited by M. A. Hofman and D. Falk, pp. 393–412. Elsevier, Amsterdam, Oxford, and New York.

Lemire, B., and G. Riello 2008 East and West: Textiles and Fashion in Early Modern Europe. *Journal of Social History* 41(4): 887–916.

León, B., A. Morales, and J. Sancho-Bru (eds.) 2014 *From Robot to Human Grasping Simulation. Cognitive Systems Monographs (Cosmos): Volume 19*. Springer International Publishing, Cham.

Libby, W. F., E. C. Anderson, and J. R. Arnold 1949 Age Determination by Radiocarbon Content: World-wide Assay of Natural Radiocarbon. *Science* 109(2827):227–228.

Libet, B. 1985 Unconscious Cerebral Initiative and the Role of Conscious Will in Voluntary Action (with Comments and Reply). *The Behavioral and Brain Sciences* 8(4):529–566.

Link, T., K. Moeller, S. Huber, U. Fischer, and H.-C. Nuerk 2013 Walk the Numberline: An Embodied Training of Numerical Concepts. *Trends in Neuroscience and Education* 2(2):74–84. DOI:10.1016/j.tine.2013.06.005.

Lövheim, H. 2012 A New Three-dimensional Model for Emotions and Monoamine Neurotransmitters. *Medical Hypotheses* 78(2):341–348. DOI:10.1016/j.mehy.2011.11.016.

Loy, T. H. 1983 Prehistoric Blood Residues: Detection of Tool Surfaces and Identification of Species Origin. *Science* 220(4603):1269–1271.

Loy, T. H. 1993 The Artifact as Site: An Example of the Biomolecular Analysis of Organic Residues on Prehistoric Tools. *World Archaeology* 25(1):44–63.

Lyman, R. L., and T. L. VanPool 2009 Metric Data in Archaeology: A Study of Inter-analyst and Inter-analyst Variation. *American Antiquity* 74(3):485–504.

Malafouris, L. 2013 *How Things Shape the Mind: A Theory of Material Engagement*. Massachusetts Institute of Technology, Cambridge, Massachusetts, and London.

Malainey, M. E., P. Przybylski, and B. L. Sheriff 1999 The Fatty Acid Composition of Native Food Plants and Animals of Western Canada. *Journal of Archaeological Science* 26(1):83–94.

Mann, C. C. 2011 *1493: Uncovering the New World Columbus Created*. Alfred A. Knopf, New York.

Matuszek, C., B. Mayton, R. Aimi, M. P. Deisenroth, L. Bo, R. Chu, M. Kung, I, LeGrand, J. R. Smith, and D. Fox 2011 Gambit: An Autonomous Chess-Playing Robotic System. In *2011 Institute of Electrical and Electronics Engineers International Conference on Robotics and Automation (Shanghai, China)*, pp 4291–4297. DOI:10.1109/ICRA.2011.5980528.

McCorriston, J. 1997 The Fiber Revolution: Textile Extensification, Alienation, and Social Stratification in Ancient Mesopotamia (with Comments and Reply). *Current Anthropology* 38(4):517–535.

Medicus, G. 1992 The Inapplicability of the Biogenetic Rule to Behavioral Development. *Human Development* 35(1):1–8.

Millman, J. 1997 *The Other Americans: How Immigrants Renew Our Country, Our Economy, and Our Values*. Viking Penguin, New York.

Mirza, M. N., and D. B. Dungworth 1995 The Potential Misuse of Genetic Analyses and the Social Construction of "Race" and "Ethnicity." *Oxford Journal of Archaeology* 14(3):345–354.

Moroz, L. L. 2015 Convergent Evolution of Neural Systems in *Ctenophores*. *Journal of Experimental Biology* 218(4):598–611. DOI:10.1242/jeb.110692.

Morris, J. N., J. A. Heady, P. A. B. Raffle, C. G. Roberts, and J. W. Parks 1953a Coronary Heart-disease and Physical Activity of Work. *The Lancet* 265(6795):1053–1057.

Morris, J. N., J. A. Heady, P. A. B. Raffle, C. G. Roberts, and J. W. Parks 1953b Coronary Heart-disease and Physical Activity of Work. *The Lancet* 265(6796):1111–1120.

Moseley, M. E., D. J. Nash, P. R. Williams S. D. deFrance, A. Miranda, and M. Ruales 2005 Burning Down the Brewery: Establishing and Evacuating an Ancient Imperial Colony at Cerro Baúl, Peru. *Proceedings of the National Academy of Sciences* 102(48):17264–17271.

Mottram, H. R., S. N. Dudd, G. J. Lawrence, A. W. Stott, and R. P. Evershed 1999 New Chromatographic, Mass Spectrometric, and Stable Isotope Approaches to the Clarification of Degraded Animal Fats Preserved in Archaeological Pottery. *Journal of Chromatography A* 833:209–221.

Müller, M. 2002 Computer Go. *Artificial Intelligence* 134(1–2):145–179.

Nabokov, V. 1990 [1930] *The Defense*. Translated by V. Nabokov and M. Scammell. Random House, New York.

Nagel, T. 1974 What Is It Like to Be a Bat? *The Philosophical Review* 83(4):435–450.

Naya, D. E., H. Naya, and E. P. Lessa 2016 Brain Size and Thermoregulation During the Evolution of the Genus *Homo*. *Comparative Biochemistry and Physiology: Part A* 191:66–73. DOI:10.1016/j.cbpa.2015.09.017.

Newborn, M. 2000 Deep Blue's Contribution to AI. *Annals of Mathematics and Artificial Intelligence* 28(1–4):27–30.

Newman, M. E., and P. Julig 1989 The Identification of Protein Residues on Lithic Artifacts from a Stratified Boreal Forest Site. *Canadian Journal of Archaeology* 13:119–132.

Nigra, B. T., K. F. Faull, and H. Barnard 2015 Analytical Chemistry in Archaeological Research. *Analytical Chemistry* 87(1):3–18. DOI:10.1021/ac5029616.

Nunn, N., and N. Qian 2010 The Columbian Exchange: A History of Disease, Food, and Ideas. *Journal of Economic Perspectives* 24(2):163–188. DOI:10.1257/jep.24.2.163.

O'Sullivan, D. E. (ed.) 2012 *Chess in the Middle Ages and Early Modern Age: A Fundamental Thought Paradigm of the Premodern World. Fundamentals of Medieval and Early Modern Culture: Volume 10*. De Gruyter, Boston and Berlin.

Ocklenburg, S., C. Beste, L. Arning, J. Peterburs, and O. Güntürkün 2014 The Ontogenesis of Language Lateralization and its Relation to Handedness. *Neuroscience and Biobehavioral Reviews* 43:191–198. DOI:10.1016/j.neubiorev.2014.04.008.

Oppenheimer, S. 2009 The Great Arc of Dispersal of Modern Humans: Africa to Australia. *Quarterly International* 202(1–2):2–13.

Oppezzo, M., and D. L. Schwartz 2014 Give Your Ideas Some Legs: The Positive Effect of Walking on Creative Thinking. *Journal of Experimental Psychology: Learning, Memory, and Cognition* 40(4):1142–1115. DOI:10.1037/a0036577.

Oudemans, T. F. M., and J. J. Boon 1991 Molecular Archaeology: Analysis of Charred (Food) Remains from Prehistoric Pottery by Pyrolysis-Gas Chromatography/Mass Spectrometry. *Journal of Analytical and Applied Pyrolysis* 20:197–227.

Palsson, G., B. Szerszynski, S. Sörlin, J. Marks, B. Avril, C. Crumley, H. Hackmann, P. Holm, J. Ingram, A. Kirman, M. P. Buendíak, and R. Weehuizen 2013 Reconceptualizing the "Anthropos" in the Anthropocene: Integrating the Social Sciences and Humanities in Global Environmental Change Research. *Environmental Science and Policy* 28(1):3–13. DOI:10.1016/j.envsci.2012.11.004.

Passingham, D. E., J. B. Rowe, and K. Sakai 2013 Has Brain Imaging Discovered Anything New About How the Brain Works? *NeuroImage* 66:142–150. DOI:10.1016/j.neuroimage.2012.10.079.

Patrick, M. M. 1899 *Sextus Empiricus and Greek Scepticism*. Deighton Bell, Cambridge, and George Bell and Sons, London.

Pertea, M., and S. L. Salzberg 2010 Between a Chicken and a Grape: Estimating the Number of Human Genes. *Genome Biology* 11:206. DOI:10.1186/gb-2010-11-5-206.

Petraglia, M. D. 2003 The Lower Paleolithic of the Arabian Peninsula: Occupations, Adaptations, and Dispersals. *Journal of World Prehistory* 17(2):141–179.

Pétursdóttir, Þ. 2017 Climate Change? Archaeology and Anthropocene. *Archaeological Dialogues* 24(2):175–205. DOI:10.1017/S1380203817000216.

Pfeifer, R., and J. Bongard 2007 *How the Body Shapes the Way We Think: A New View of Intelligence.* Massachusetts Institute of Technology Press, Cambridge, Massachusetts, and London.

Pinhasi, R., J. Fort, and A. J. Ammerman 2005 Tracing the Origin and Spread of Agriculture in Europe. *Public Library of Science Biology* 3(12):e410. DOI:doi.org/10.1371/journal.pbio.0030410.

Pollard, A. M., and P. Bray 2007 A Bicycle Made for Two? The Integration of Scientific Techniques into Archaeological Interpretation. *Annual Review of Anthropology* 36(1):245–259.

Pompilio, L., A. Kacelnik, and S. T. Behmer 2006 State-dependent Learned Valuation Drives Choice in an Invertebrate. *Science* 311(5767):1613–1615.

Raichle, M. E. 2006 The Brain's Dark Energy. *Science* 314(5803):1249–1250.

Rainey, F., and E. K. Ralph 1966 Archeology and Its New Technology. *Science* 153(3743):1481–1491.

Randell, B. 1982 From Analytical Engine to Electronic Digital Computer: The Contributions of Ludgate, Torres, and Bush. *Annals of the History of Computing* 4(4):327–341.

Reed, E. S. 1982 Darwin's Earthworms: A Case Study in Evolutionary Psychology. *Behaviorism* 10(2):165–185.

Regier, T., and P. Kay 2009 Language, Thought, and Color: Whorf was Half Right. *Trends in Cognitive Sciences* 13(10):439–446.

Richerson, P. J., and R. Boyd 2005 *Not by Genes Alone: How Culture Transformed Human Evolution.* University of Chicago Press, Chicago.

Rightmire, G. P. 2004 Brain Size and Encephalization in Early to Mid-Pleistocene *Homo. American Journal of Physical Anthropology* 124(2):109–123.

Roberson, D., J. Davidoff, I. R. L. Davies, and L. R. Shapiro 2005 Color Categories: Evidence for the Cultural Relativity Hypothesis. *Cognitive Psychology* 50(4):378–411.

Rolfe, J. C. 1914 *Suetonius: Lives of the Caesars: Volume 2.* Macmillan, New York.

Roth, G., and U. Dicke 2012 Evolution of the Brain and Intelligence in Primates. In *Progress in Brain Research: Volume 195,* edited by M. A. Hofman and D. Falk, pp. 413–430. Elsevier, Amsterdam, Oxford, and New York.

Rowe, C., and S. D. Healy 2014 Measuring Variation in Cognition. *Behavioral Ecology* 25(6):1287–1292. DOI:10.1093/beheco/aru090.

Sapina, C. 2015 *Beyond Words: What Animals Think and Feel.* Henry Holt, New York.

Sasakura Y., K. Mita, Y. Ogura, and T. Horie 2012 *Ascidians* as Excellent Chordate Models for Studying the Development of the Nervous System During Embryogenesis and Metamorphosis. *Development, Growth and Differentiation* 54(3):420–437. DOI:10.1111/j.1440-169X.2012.01343.x.

Schmidt, P. R., I. Pikirayi (eds.) 2016 *Community Archaeology and Heritage in Africa: Decolonizing Practice.* Routledge, London and New York.

Schmitz, J., G. A. S. Metz, O. Güntürkün, and S. Ocklenburg 2017 Beyond the Genome: Towards an Epigenetic Understanding of Handedness Ontogenesis. *Progress in Neurobiology* 159:69–89. DOI:10.1016/j.pneurobio.2017.10.005.

Sears, P. B. 1973 Oxygen Isotope Analysis as a Means of Determining Season of Occupation of Prehistoric Midden Sites. *Archaeometry* 15(1):133–141.

Shackley, M. S. 2010 Is There Reliability and Validity in Portable X-ray Fluorescence Spectrometry (pXRF)? *The SAA Archaeological Record* 10(5):17–20, 44.

Shanks, O. C., M. Kornfield, and D. D. Hawk 1999 Protein Analysis of Bugas-Holding Tools: New Trends in Immunological Studies. *Journal of Archaeological Science* 26(9):1183–1191.

Sheets-Johnstone, M. 2011 *The Primacy of Movement: Expanded Second Edition. Advances in Consciousness Research 82.* John Benjamins, Amsterdam and Philadelphia.

Sheller, M., and J. Urry 2006 The New Mobility Paradigm. *Environment and Planning A* 38: 207–226.

Shermer, M. 2011 *The Believing Brain: From Ghosts and Gods to Politics and Conspiracies: How We Construct Beliefs and Reinforce Them.* Henry Holt, New York.

Shott, M. 2010 Crises and Solutions in American Archaeology. *The SAA Archaeological Record* 10(1):37–38.

Shusterman, R. 2012 *Thinking Through the Body: Essays in Somaesthetics.* Cambridge University Press, Cambridge.

Silver, D., A. Huang, C. J. Maddison, A. Guez, L. Sifr, G. van den Driessche, J. Schrittwieser, I. Antonoglou, V. Panneershelvam, M. Lanctot, S. Dieleman, D. Grewe, J. Nham, N. Kalchbrenner, I. Sutskever, T. Lillicrap, M. Leach, K. Kavukcuoglu, T. Graepel, and D. Hassabis 2016 Mastering the Game of Go with Deep Neural Networks and Tree Search. *Nature* 529(5787):484–489. DOI:10.1038/nature16961.

Sjödin, P., and O. François 2011 Wave-of-Advance Models of the Diffusion of the Y Chromosome Haplogroup R1b1b2 in Europe. *Public Library of Science* ONE 6(6):e21592. DOI:10.1371/journal.pone.0021592.

Smith, M. P., and D. A. T. Harper 2013 Causes of the Cambrian Explosion. *Science* 341(6152):1355–1356. DOI:10.1126/science.1239450.

Smith, P. R., and M. T. Wilson 1992 Blood Residues on Ancient Tool Surfaces: A Cautionary Note. *Journal of Archaeological Science* 19(3):237–244.

Solazzo, C., W. W. Fitzhugh, C. Rolando, and C. Tokarski 2008 Identification of Protein Remains in Archaeological Potsherds by Proteomics. *Analytical Chemistry* 80(12):4590–4597.

Sperry, R. W. 1952 Neurology and the Mind-brain Problem. *American Scientist* 40(2):291–312.

Suárez-Ruiz, F., X. Zhou, and Q. C. Pham 2018 Can Robots Assemble an IKEA Chair? *Science Robotics* 3:eaat6385. DOI:10.1126/scirobotics.aat6385.

Tallis, R. 2003 *The Hand: A Philosophical Inquiry into Human Being.* Edinburgh University Press, Edinburgh.

Temin, P. 1997 Two Views of the British Industrial Revolution. *Journal of Economic History* 57(1):63–82.

Thorpe, S. K. S., J. M. McClymont, and R. H. Crompton 2014 The Arboreal Origins of Human Bipedalism (with Comments and Reply). *Antiquity* 88(341):906–926. DOI:10.1017/S0003598X00050778.

Trestman, M. 2013 The Cambrian Explosion and the Origins of Embodied Cognition. *Biological Theory* 8(1):80–92. DOI:10.1007/s13752-013-0102-6.

Tuk, M. A., D. Trampe, and L. Warlop 2011 Inhibitory Spillover: Increased Urination Urgency Facilitates Impulse Control in Unrelated Domains. *Psychological Science* 22(5):627–633. DOI:10.1177/0956797611404901.

Tunstall, K. E. 2011 *Blindness and Enlightenment: An Essay.* Continuum, New York and London.

Turnbaugh, P. J., R. E. Ley, M. Hamady, C. M. Fraser-Liggett, R. Knight, and J. I. Gordon 2007 The Human Microbiome Project. *Nature* 449(7164):804–810.

Uexküll, J. von 1992 A Stroll through the Worlds of Animals and Men: A Picture Book of Invisible Worlds [originally published in German in 1934 and in English in 1957, translated by C. Schiller]. *Semiotica* 89(4):319–391.

Uomini, N. T. 2009 The Prehistory of Handedness: Archaeological Data and Comparative Ethology. *Journal of Human Evolution* 57(4):411–419.

Urry, J. 2007 *Mobilities*. Polity Press, Cambridge and Malden.

Vandervert L. R. 2009 The Appearance of the Child Prodigy 10,000 Years Ago: An Evolutionary and Developmental Explanation. *Journal of Mind and Behavior* 30(1–2):15–32.

Varki, A., D. H. Geschwind, and E. E. Eichler 2008 Explaining Human Uniqueness: Genome Interactions with Environment, Behaviour, and Culture. *Nature Reviews Genetics* 9(10):749–763.

Vermeersch, P. M. 2001 Out of Africa from an Egyptian Point of View. *Quarterly International* 75(1):103–112.

Wade, N. 2009 *The Faith Instinct: How Religion Evolved and Why It Endures*. The Penguin Press, New York.

Weinstein, L. B. 2007 Selected Genetic Disorders Affecting Ashkenazi Jewish Families. *Family and Community Health* 30(1):50–62.

Wen, B., H. Li, D. Lu, X. Song, F. Zhang, Y. He, F. Li, Y. Gao, X. Mao, L. Zhang, J. Qian, J. Tan, J. Jin, W. Huang, R. Deka, B. Su, R. Chakraborty, and L. Jin 2004 Genetic Evidence Supports Demic Diffusion of Han Culture. *Nature* 431(7006):302–305.

Wendrich, W. Z., and H. Barnard 2008 The Archaeology of Mobility: Definitions and Research Approaches. In *The Archaeology of Mobility: Old World and New World Nomadism*, edited by H. Barnard and W. Z. Wendrich, pp. 1–21. Cotsen Institute of Archaeology Press, Los Angeles.

Wilson, F. R. 1999 *The Hand: How Its Use Shapes the Brain, Language, and Human Culture*. Vintage Books, New York.

Winner, E. 1996 *Gifted Children: Myths and Realities*. Basic Books, New York.

Wnuk, E., and A. Majid 2014 Revisiting the Limits of Language: The Odor Lexicon of Maniq. *Cognition* 131(1):125–138. DOI:10.1016/j.cognition.2013.12.008.

Wolpert, D. M., Z. Ghahramani, and J. R. Flanagan 2001 Perspectives and Problems in Motor Learning. *Trends in Cognitive Sciences* 5(11):487–494.

Woolford, K., and S. Dunn 2014 Micro Mobilities and Affordances of Past Places. In *Past Mobilities: Archaeological Approaches to Movement and Mobility*, edited by J. Leary, pp. 113–128. Ashgate, Franham and Burlington.

Wrangham, R., and R. Carmody 2010 Human Adaptation to the Control of Fire. *Evolutionary Anthropology* 19(5):187–199. DOI:10.1002/evan.20275.

Zhang, D. D., P. Brecke, H. F. Lee, Y.-Q. He, and J. Zhang 2007 Global Climate Change, War, and Population Decline in Recent Human History. *Proceedings of the National Academy of Sciences* 104(49):19214–19219.

Zhao, Y.-B., Y. Zhang, Q.-C. Zhang, H.-J. Li, Y.-Q. Cui, Z. Xu, L. Jin, H. Zhou, and H. Zhu 2015 Ancient DNA Reveals that the Genetic Structure of the Northern Han Chinese was Shaped Prior to 3,000 Years Ago. *Public Library of Science ONE* 10(5):e0125676. DOI:10.1371/journal.pone.0125676.

Zilhão, J. 2007 The Emergence of Ornaments and Art: An Archaeological Perspective on the Origins of "Behavioral Modernity." *Journal of Archaeological Research* 15(1):1–54.

Zubiaurre, M. 2019 *Talking Trash: Cultural Uses of Waste*. Vanderbilt University Press, Nashville.

Contributors

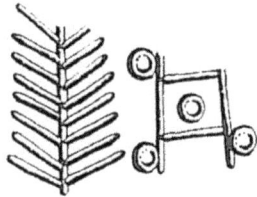

Megan Daniels, University of British Columbia
Kristian Kristiansen, University of Gothenburg
David W. Anthony, Hartwick College
Omer Gokcumen, SUNY-Buffalo
Franco De Angelis, University of British Columbia
Catherine M. Cameron, University of Colorado, Boulder
Elena Isayev, University of Exeter
Assaf Yasur-Landau, University of Haifa
Marc Vander Linden, Institute for the Modelling of Socio-Environmental Transitions, Bournemouth University
Cornelis Drost, Independent scholar
Jane Gaastra, Department of Archaeology, Durham University
Ivana Jovanović, Institute of Archaeology, University College London
Sébastien Manem, UMR 7055, Centre National de la Recherche Scientifique
Anne de Vareilles, Historic England
Thomas K. Harper, The Pennsylvania State University
Ezra B. W. Zubrow, SUNY-Buffalo
Aleksandr Diachenko, National Academy of Sciences of Ukraine, Institute of Archaeology
Jay Leavitt, Premata Funds LLC
Aurora E. Camaño, Simon Fraser University
Anne Porter, University of Toronto
Elizabeth S. Greene, Brock University
Justin Leidwanger, Stanford University
Thomas P. Leppard, Florida State University
Hans Barnard, University of California, Los Angeles

Index

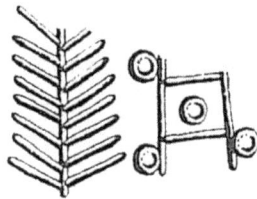

Figures in *italics;* n refers to note

abduction, female, 38, 39, 40
ABM. *See* agent-based model
acculturation, 8, 149
Acheulean industry, 297, 330
Adana, 233, 239
adaptation: to changing climate conditions, 155, 157; coastal, 286; cultural 319; to ecological conditions 175–78; evolutionary, 8; to forest environment, 38; high-altitude and high-latitude, 295; human, 11, 17, 19, 111; processes of, 5, 7; of societies, 14; technological, 294
adoptees, 121, 125, 126
Aegean, 83, *271*; Acheulean and Mousterian stone artifacts from the, 297–98; Dark Age of the, 99; geotectonic nature of the, 295, 297; immigrants in southern Levant from the, 154–55; Last Glacial Maximum (LGM), 303–306, *305*, 307–308; movement between eastern Mediterranean littoral and the, 271–72, 275
affiliation: cultural, 85; ethnic, 14, 85; networks based on 10; religious, 85; Roman and Italian, 139

agency, *323*; evolutionary, 301; human (political), 8, 11, 13–14, 33, 104; migrant, 232–34; migration studies and lack of, 10, 61, 231–32; in model of migration, 201, 216; of objects, 10, 322
agent-based model (ABM), 16, 157, 166, 167, 170, 173. *See also* Cultural Dissemination Model (CDM)
Akhurian River, 236, 239, 240
Akkad and Akkadian identity, 250, 252–53
AlphaGo, 328
Amenemhet II or III, 156
Amenhotep II, 156
Amenhotep III, 150–51
Amorrites, 250–53
Anatolia: farming colonization from, 36, 61, 63, 84; genetic studies of past and present, 84–87; Kura-Araxes (Red Black Burnished) Ware, 253–54, 263; Mediterranean coast of, *271*, 272; neolithic genetic variation of, 83–84; Old Assyrian trade network, 252–53, 261–63; paleography of 297, 305–306; plateau, 236; Uruk(-related) materials, *254*, 262–63

347

348   INDEX

Anavarsa, 233, 240, 241, *242*
ancestry: Amorrite, 253; Bell Beaker, 39–40, 70, 82–83, 124–25, 148; biological, 250, 253; correlation with nationality and culture, 14, 85, 155; Corded Ware, 14, 38, 39, 40, 58, 65–70, 82; from Danubian farmers, 66; as imagined pasts, 240–41; maternal (mtDNA), 63, 80–81, 124; mobility of DNA, 154; from Neolithic farmers of Europe, 61, 66, 70; paternal (Y-DNA), 63, 66, 80; steppe-derived (Yamnaya), 14, 40, 58, 65, 66–70, 82
Ani, 231, 239, 240
Anthropocene, 321, 333
antiquarianism, 4–5, 8
archaeogenetics and -genomics, 81–87, 148, 196
Aristotle, 4, 318
Armenia: Bagratid Kingdoms, 231, 236, 238–42, 243; Greater, 231, 238–39, 241; Kingdom of Cilicia, 231, 237, 238, 241–43; Rubenid, 233, 237, 240, 241–42; Western (Greater), 236, 238–39
Armenians, 85; Byzantine-led deportations of, 233; Cilician, 238; resettlement in Cilicia, 230–31, 233–34, 236–37, 239, 243
artificial intelligence, 318, 328–30
Ashdod, 155
Ashkelon, 155
Assur, 252–53, 261–63
Atapuerca hominins, 296, 306
Australia, 237, 295, 298

Bab-el-Mandeb Strait ("Gate of Tears"), 295–96, *296*, 302, 303
Baden culture, 57, 71, 186, 195. *See also* Coțofeni culture; Globular Amphorae culture
Bagaran, 239
Bagratid Kingdoms, 236, 243; capitals, 231, 239–41; dynasty of the, 238, 241; romanticized past of the, 242
Balabac Strait, 298, 303, 307

Balkan: Anatolian farming colonization into the, 36; Neolithic and Eneolithic cultures of the, 202–204; paleogeography of the, 297, 303, *305*, 306; premodern hominins and circum-, 300, 302, 303–304, 307; tell cultures of the, 38; western, 16, 167, 170
Bell Beaker: ancestry, 39–40, 70, 82–83, 124–25, 148; in Britain, 83; (pottery) culture, 40, 82; Iberian maritime, 40; Lech valley of southern Bavaria, 124–25; migrations, 37, 41; period, 69; warrior groups, 41
belonging: feeling of loss of, 233, 242; place-, 230; sense of, 135, 137, 232, 237, 240, 243
Belyj Kamen settlement, 218
Bet Yerah, 259–60
Bible, biblical worldview of, The, 4, 5, 6, 19
bilateral symmetric, 317, 326–27
bonobos (*Pan paniscus*), 319
Borneo, 298, 302, 304, 305, 307
brain, 321–25, 327, 331
Britain: Anglo-Saxon period wars and slave trade, 117, 120; Beaker culture, 83; early industrializer, 101
Bug: -Dniester culture, 186; region of Middle, 204. *See also* Southern Bug
Bulgaria: hominin fossils, 306; Yamnaya-culture traits in, 60, 63
Burgaz ("Old Knidos"), 276, 277, 279; central role in network, 281–83; eclipsed by Tekir, 286; harbors, 274–75, 281, 283; move of "Old Knidians" to Tekir, 272, 285; proximity to arable land, 274
burial(s): Alalakh, 154; Ashkelon, 155; Bell Beaker and Early Bronze Age Lech valley (southern Bavaria), 124; Corded Ware, 37, 69–70; cremation, 184; Dnieper-Donets culture, 189; informal, 45; inhumation, 184, 188; Late Tripolye, 188; rituals, 7, 40, 41, 66, 69, 253, 260; sex-age structure of, 188, 190; sex ratios in, 124, 190; stable isotope analysis of, 37, 63, 137, 154;

sub-floor, 263; Yamnaya, 63, *64*, 66–67, 69, 82. *See also* funerary practices; kurgan; mortuary practices

Caenorhabditis elegans, 319
Callao Cave (Luzon), 299, 300, 308
Cambrian explosion, 326–27
Canaan: cattle mobility, 156; zebu introduction, 155–57
Canaanites, 5, 154, 155
canid sacrifices, 67–68
carbon isotopic analysis: goat and donkey, Tell es-Safi/Gath, 156; Tell Abraq, Bronze Age tomb, 154
Carpathian Basin, 70, 175. *See also* Pannonian Basin
Cagayan Valley (Luzon), 300, 307
Carpathian Mountains, 66, 185, 204
cattle: Asiatic, 155; hump-backed (zebu), 155–57; mobility, 153, 156–57; Nordic Bronze Age Culture, 40; protein as limited threshold in migration model, 209; relative importance of (Neolithic Europe), 175–76; taurine, 155, 175; third millennium BC pastoral economy, 37
Caucasus: Armenian villages in South, 238–39; Kura-Araxes (Red Burnished) Ware, 253–54; present-day genetic variation of the, 85; southern Levant population related to Bronze Age, 154; steppes of the North, 65, 66
Cavalli-Sforza, Luigi, 61–63
CDM. *See* Cultural Dissemination Model
Celebes Sea, 303, 306, 307
Celts: migrations, 36, 38; language, 42, 67; slavery, 41
cemeteries: Ashkelon, 155; Corded Ware, 37; Dnieper-Donets culture, 188–89; of the Etruscan Volsinii, 137; Globular Amphorae people ancestral, 69; kurgan, 60, 61, 63, 66–67, 69–71, 189; Late Tripolye, 188; migrants within, 60, 62–63; outside ordinary, 45; Pontic-Caspian steppe, 66, 189; Roman (Isola Sacra), 137; Sidon, 153–54

^{14}C dating, 33, 39, 264, 318, 320–21; Corded Ware, 65; and Cultural Dissemination Model (CDM), 171, 173; of introduction of European farming, 61, 166, 171–72; Late Chalcolithic Uruk, 256; of Neo-Eneolithic Eastern Europe, 184; revolution, 31, 98, 112; summed probability distributions, 185; Yamnaya, 63, 65–66, 187
Chapaevka cemetery, 188
Chechelnitskaya group (Western Tripolyte Culture), 218, 219–21
chess, 318, 327–31
Chichirkozovka (Western Tripolyte Culture), 204, 220
chiefdom society and slave raiding, 39–40, 116
chimpanzees (*Pan troglodytes*), 319
chromosomes, 66, 80
Cicero (Tullius Cicero, Marcus), 139, 141n3
citizenship, 135, 262
climate: change, 2, 71, 148, 331; 5.9 ka event, 187; variability, 187
clothing, 125, 320, 332; toga, 139
cognition: bodily movement and, 325, 327; cognitive archaeology, 202, 222; cognitive complexity, 14, 17; cognitive parameters of archaic *Homo*, 300–301; cognitive process(es), 16, 294, 309, 324; cognitive psychology, 221; cultural landscapes and cognitive relationships, 235. *See also* consciousness
cohesion, social, 257, 258, 317
colonization: of the Americas and Australia by *Homo sapiens*, 295; Anatolian farming, 36; ancient, 10, 134; community-based farming, 31, 36, 39; conquest, 36–37, 38, 39; European, 6, 114–15; Greek, 97; of insular Aegean, 297–98, 303–306, 307; Iron Age, 42; island, 293, 308; Island Southeast Asia (ISEA), 298–300, 302–308;

350 INDEX

colonization *(continued)*
  maritime, 149; Near Eastern, 6; types of, 35, 39; Yamnaya, Corded Ware, and Bell Beaker groups, 41
"Columbian exchange," 332
Conibo, 116, 119
connectivity, 4, 104, 280, 283; human, 10; inter-, 10, 17; Mediterranean, 10, 17, 149, 270; Purcell and Horden's *The corrupting Sea*, 10, 104–105
conquest, 56, 134, 149, 250; colonization, 36–37, 38, 39; Gimbutas' model, 55, 57; migration, 5, 31, 37, 38, 39, 41
consciousness, 317–18, 321–26, 329, 333. *See also* cognition
Corded Ware culture: abduction of Neolithic women by males of the, 38, 40, 41; ancestry, 14, 38, 39, 40, 58, 65–70, 82; and Bell Beaker people, 40, 82; burial rites, 69–70; cemeteries, 37; economy, 69; migrations, 37, 41, 65, 70, 71; package, 68–70; Pastoral Mode of Production, 37; warrior sodalities, 41. *See also* Globular Amphorae culture
Coțofeni period, 71, 186
Crete, 297–98, 304, 307, 308
Cucuteni-Tripolye cultural complex (CTCC), 183, 185–86, 188–89, 196, 202, 204; cemeteries, 188–89; Eastern Tripolye Culture (ETC), 196, 204; Western Tripolyte Culture (WTC), 186, 196, 204, 212, 218–21
Cultural Dissemination Model (CDM), 167–78
cultural evolution, 318–20, 332
culture history approach, 6–8, 9, 11–12, 13, 15, 99
Cyprus, 99, 153, 154, 297

Danube: basin, 175; gorges, 173; prehistory of the, 7; region, 204; valley, 57, 60, 61, 63, 65–66, 71
Dark Age, 97, 98–99
Darwin, Charles, 6, 326; Darwinian biology, 43; Darwinian revolution, 31; social Darwinism, 6

Deep Blue, 327
deep change, 150
Delos, 139–40
deportations, mass, 229, 233
diaspora, 3, 233, 250; African, 114; Kura-Araxes, 258; Uruk, 258
diet, 37, 39, 40, 61, 69, 331–32
diffusionism and diffusion, 6–7, 12, 231; of elite funerary inscriptions and epitaphs (Italy), 138; of early farming in Europe, 166
displacements, 237; Anthropological studies of, 232, 234, 235–36, 240; conflict-induced, 134, 231, 234; disaster and, 2, 231, 249; fear of, 135; forced, 140–41, 233, 243; mass, 2, 16, 134, 135, 140–41, 230–34, 242–43; of Neolithic farmers, 38; and rebuilding legitimacy and identity, 240, 242; trauma of, 233, 236, 241, 242. *See also* relocation; resettlement
Dnieper-Donets culture, 189
Dnieper River, 184, 185, 187, 204; interfluve of Southern Bug and, 196, 204, 212, 218, 219; Rapids, 189; region of the Lower, 189
Dniester: Early and Middle Neolithic culture of Bug-, 186; interfluve of Southern Bug and, 204, 218, 221; region of Middle, 204; region of Prut-, 196
Dobrovody (Western Tripolye Culture), 204, 220
dogs, 68, 71
Drosophila melanogaster (fruit fly), 319

Eastern Tripolye Culture (ETC), 196, 204. *See also* Cucuteni-Tripolye cultural complex (CTCC)
ecology, 319; cultural, 8, 84; disaster, 249; economic and social interconnection with, 10, 39; ecosystems, 205; historical, 99, 104; niche, 172; numerical, 168; and over-water movement, 294; temporal and geographical adaptions to local, 175, 176–77
economy: agricultural, 258; backwardness of, 102–103; of the Dark Age, 97; early modern European, 101; of Globular

Amphorae and Baden culture, 71; institutional, 33–34; of mix farming with pastoralism (Yamnaya), 38, 40; mobile pastoralism, 250, 251–52, 254, 257–59, 260–61; pastoral (Mode of Production), 37, 38, 69; political, 34–35

Egypt: New Kingdom, 15, 150–53, 155–56; Viking slave trade, 117; zebu (hump-backed cattle), 155–57

Ekallatum, 252

Elam, *251*, 252

Emecik, 281, 283

emulation, 255–56

Emutbal mobile pastoralist group, 251–52

Enlightenment, 4, 6, 43

enslavement, 114, 117, 124. *See also* slavery

Escherichia coli (coliform bacterium), 319

ETC. *See* Eastern Tripolye Culture

ethnicity, 105; artifact assemblages (archaeological cultures) and, 7, 8, 11, 81–82, 112, 121, 253, 259; continuity and ethnic affiliation, 13; ethnic cleansing, 40, 113; and identity, 41–42, 85, 121, 250; kinship and, 121; language and, 11; Mesopotamian use of, 250–51, 252; relocation of ethnic minorities, 229–30, 233; scientific methods and, 12, 19, 82–83, 85–87, 121; of slaves and captives, 117, 121–22; social boundaries and, 122

Etruscans, 19n1, 96–97, 104, 105; backwardness of, 102–103; metallurgy, 102–103; cemeteries of the Volsinii, 137

evolution: biological, 6, 319–20, 327, 328; cultural, 319, 320, 332; genetic, 318, 319, 320; homophily and, 170–71; models of, 13–14; multilinear, 8; processes, 8–9, 308; roll of migration, 14, 166, 309; sociocultural, 6; unilinear, 6–7, 19

Ex Oriente Lux, 7, 96, 99

exaptation, 329

exogamy, 38, 39, 40, 124–25

farming: aDNA of early European communities engaged in, 63, 84, 86, 166; aDNA of Levantine communities engaged in early, 149; colonization of Europe, 36, 39; community-based, 31, 36; conquest, 36–37, 38, 39; European Bronze Age, 42; interaction between farmers and hunter-gatherers/foragers, 36, 39, 63, 173; spread of Neolithic, 3, 8, 12, 15, 61–63, 84, 165–67; pastoralism combined with mixed, 37, 38, 40; western Balkans and spread of early, 170–77

fertility, 193, 194, 204, 210

fetishism, Marx's concept of, 33–34

figurines, animal, 259, 260; bull-shaped, 275

Flores: island, 298–99, 300, 303, 307; Sea, 303, 305, 306, 307

fMRI. *See* functional magnetic resonance imaging

foragers: European, 63, 84, 166, 172, 173; West Asian Neolithic, 84. *See also* hunter-gatherers

forest, 36, 38, 41; pine, 303, 307; -steppe, 38, 186, 195–96, 204; tropical, 303

functional magnetic resonance imaging (fMRI), 325

funerary practices, 40, 41, 68, 69, 140, 142n11, 184, 263. *See also* burial(s); mortuary practices

gender: differences in adult age-at-death, 189–93; differences in Corded Ware and Yamnaya burials, 69; differences of Icelandic people, 117; differences in migration/mobility, 38–40, 70, 116–17, 119, 124–25, 154–55, 332; differences in mortuary populations in Ukraine, 190–93

genome sequencing, 79–81; Copenhagen National Museum laboratory, 65; of Early Neolithic farmers, 63, 84; Harvard Medical School laboratory, 63, 65; *Human Genome Project*, 319; of individuals from Ashkelon, 155; parental markers, 63, 66, 80–81, 124; of people belonging to Corded Ware culture, 65–66, 68, 70; of people belonging to Globular Amphorae culture, 68, 70; of people belonging to Neolithic Anatolia, 83–84; of people of present-day Turkey,

genome sequencing *(continued)*
  85–86; prehistoric (archaeogenomics), 31, 32, 63, 65, 83, 86; whole, 9, 12, 14, 17, 63; of Yamnaya, 14, 63, 65, 66–67, 69
Germe, 281, 283–84
Gibraltar Strait, 295–96, 302, 303
gift giving: of captives 116–17; cycles of, 122; depicted on the tomb of Nebamun (TT17), 156
Gimbutas, Marija, 14, 56–60, 65, 71
glacial-interglacial cycle, 295; the Aegean 297, 303–306, 308; glacial maxima, 303; Island Southeast Asia (ISEA) 298, 303, 304–306; Last Glacial Maximum (LGM), 303; the Mediterranean, 297, 303–304, 307, 308; Red Sea, 303; severe Middle Pleistocene glacial, 297; Sundaland, 298, 303, 304, 307; "Wallacea," 303, 306, 307
globalization, 3, 4, 10–11, 104, 333
Globular Amphorae culture, 57, 68, 69–70, 71. *See also* Corded Ware culture
goat, 156, 175, 176
Greece, 36, 56, 85, 97–98, 99, 104, 234
Greeks, 9, 96–98, 100, 102, 103, 105, 138
Gwembe Tonga, 235–36, 240

Hăbășești-Holm, 196
Habuba Kabira, 256, 263
Halikarnassos, 285, 286
Hammurabi, 253
"Hellenization," 97–98
Hippocrates, 321
histories: based on archaeogenomics, 65, 80, 83–84, 85–86; imagined, 235, 240–42; (individual) life, 83, 154; nationalist identities and common cultural, 6; oral, 61; political dismissal of multiple, 86; population, 81, 187; quantitative demographic, 183
Homo (H.) erectus, 202, 293–94, 307; Javan, 306
Homo (H.) floresiensis, 299–300, 308
H. heidelbergensis (neanderthalensis), 81, 293, 297, 307–308
Homo (H.) luzonensis, 300, 308
H. neanderthalensis (heidelbergensis), 81, 293, 297, 307–308
Homo sapiens, 17, 297–98
homophily, 167, 168, 170–71, 178
horticultural societies, 115, 118, 119
household(s): Alashian, 153; Archaic Greek, 42; chiefs, 42; of Assyrians at Kültepe, 262–63; intercultural, 154–55; of the Kura-Araxes expansion, 261; of the Uruk expansion, 257–58, 261
human genome, 63, 65, 79–80; *Human Genome Project*, 319
human grasp, 328–31
Hungary: Linear Bandkeramik (LBK) groups, 36, 38; Neo-Eneolithic human remains in, 189, 189t, 190; Yamnaya, 38, 57, 60, 63, 66, 70
Hutton, James, *Theory of the Earth*, 5, 18
hunter(s), 38; -gatherers, 20n8, 36, 39, 84, 194, 205; slave, *118*. *See also* foragers
Horden, Nicolas and Purcell, Peregrine, *The Corrupting Sea*, 9–10, 104
Hylobates muelleri (Bornean gibbon), 319

identity: Akkadian, 253; aDNA and, 12–13, 18–19, 84–85, 320; Assyrian, 262–63; Bantu, 148; biological, 250, 254, 260; of captives, 122–23; claims and attributions of, 250; collective, 41, 235; complex, 12, 42; construction of, 250, 253, 260; cultural, 37, 41, 42, 70, 230, 240–41, 254; essentialist approach to, 57; ethnic, 19, 41–42, 253; human-generated, 16; loss of, 240, 242, 243; maintenance, 237, 257, 260, 263–64; management, 236, 243; material, 41, 258; migrant, 61, 70, 113, 229, 235; monumental constructions and, 238, 242, 256–57; multigenerational notions of, 232; multiple, 121, 252; natal, 123, 257, 262; national, 5, 84–85; nationalists, 6, 7; negotiation, 121, 236; personal, 321; place-based, 230, 237, 240; practices of, 257, 259–60; psychosocial, 320; regional, 42,

285; religious, 263; role of ritual practices in construction of, 256, 257, 263; social, 9, 33, 126, 257–58

ideology, 97; built landscape as medium for expressing, 242; captives affecting local, 123; of ethnicity and identity, 12, 86; of male prestige, 115–16; and self-representation, 137; use of the past, 11

IKEA chair, 329

Indo-European speakers, 8; Anatolian farmers, 62; archaeogenomics and origins of, 83; common marriage practices, 37, 38, 42; Corded Ware culture, 82; Kurgan Culture migrations, 56–57; myths, 67–68; pastoral social organization of society, 38

Indonesian Throughflow (ITF), 306, 307

Industrial Revolution, 2, 101–102, 205, 332–33

infiltration, 56, 57

interconnectivity, 10, 17

interculturality, material, 255, 256, 258

invasion theory of migration, 8, 14, 56–57, 59, 71

Ionian Islands, *296*, 297, 302, 304, 307, 308; paleo-, 298, *305*

iron technology, 97, 98

Iroquios, 115, 117, 119, 120

Island Southeast Asia (ISEA): paleography, 298, 303, 304–306; slave trading, 116, 117; transmaritime dispersal of hominins, 298, *299*, 306–308

isotope analysis, 321; advances in, 3, 9, 11, 18, 111; animal mobility, 156; Bell Beaker and Early Bronze Age Lech valley (southern Bavaria) individuals, 124; carbon, 154, 156; challenges for archaeological theory, 148; identifying captive migration, 112, 123, 125, 126; identifying migration within regional population trends, 184; interpretating processes of migration, 15, 114, 124, 126, 149–50, 250; Megiddo Middle Bronze Age tomb, 154; oxygen, 62, 154, 156; providing data on personal mobility history, 17, 62, 114, 123, 154;

Roman cemeteries of Isola Sacra, 137; strontium, 62, 123, 124, 154, 156; Tell Abraq Bronze Age tomb, 154; use of data in tandem with historical and archaeological data, 150, 153, 154; of Yamnaya individuals, 63

Italians: forced displacement from Yugoslav territory, 141; living in Asia Minor, 138–39; living in the Eastern Mediterranean, 138; operating from Delos, 139–40; worshippers of Eastern deities, 140. *See also* Romans

Italy, 135; backwardness of, 95–103; Bay of Naples, 137; cave sites, 177; central, 104; hominin fossils, Pirro Nord, 306; role of Phoenicians and Greeks in the making of, 97–98; Roman cemeteries of Isola Sacra, 137; ties with sites around the Mediterranean, 137–40; Treaty of Paris, 141

ITF. *See* Indonesian Throughflow

Java: island, 298, 305; Sea, 304

Javan *erectus*, 306

Jebel Aruda, 256, 263

Kalinago of the Lesser Antilles, 116, 119

Kanesh (Kültepe), 261, 262, 263; Kanum, *150*

Karfitepe, 281, 282, 283

Kargı, 283

Kars: Bagratid capital, 239, 240; River, 239

karum, 261, 262, 263; Kanesh, *150*

Katıyalı, 283

Kefalonia, 297, 303

Kenamun (*also* Qenamun, TT162) tomb, 150–53, 155

Khirbet Kerak Ware, *255*, 259–60. *See also* Kura-Araxes, Ware

kispu ritual (mortuary ritual), 253, 260

Knidians, 272–74, 276, 283, 285

Knidos. *See* Burgaz ("Old Knidos"); Tekir ("New Knidos")

Körmen, 277, *277*, 283, 286

Kos, 272, 286
Kossinna, Gustaf, 7, 19, 81–82
Krasnosamarskoe, 67–68
Kudur-mabuk, 252
Kültepe (ancient Kanesh), *150*, 261, 262, 263
Kura-Araxes: expansion, 253–55, 258–61, 263; Khirbet Kerak Ware, *255*, 259–60; Ware (*also* Red Black Burnished Ware), 253, *255*
kurgan: Corded Ware, 69–70; Hungary, 63, 66; Gimbutas' Kurgan Culture migrations, 56_57, *58*, 60, 71; as proxy for migrant identity, 61; Tripolye ceramics in, 189; Volga-Ural steppes, 63; Yamnaya, 60, 63, *64*, 66–67, 69

labor: division of, 103; migrating, 223n3; mobilizing, 36; movement of free, 221; need for, 39–40, 205; practices, 209; slave, 121; specialization, 249; surplus, 34; value of, 33; women taken captive for, 40, 118, 119, 122
landscape archaeology, 229, 230, 235
Larsa, 252
Last Glacial Maximum (LGM), 303, 308
LBK. *See* Linear Bandkeramik
LDD. *See* Long Distance Dispersal
leapfrogging (*also* retarding lead), 63, 95, 101–102, 103
Lefkada/Leukas, *296*, 297, 303–304
legitimacy: and loss of social, 230, 242–43; role of historical memory and myth in reclaiming (political), 230, 235, 237, 241, 242–43
Lesser Sundas, 298, 306
Lesvos (Lesbos), 234, 297
Levant, the: animal mobility, 149, 152, 155–57; Bronze Age inland sites, 156; Bronze Age Southern, 154, 155; Canaanites, 5, 154, 155; complex societies of the 2nd millennium BC, 150–53; early farmers of, 83, 149; Iron I and II, southern, 155; Khirbet Kerak (Kura-Araxes) Ware, 253, 259–60; scientific revolution and the archaeology of, 15, 149
Levantine people: depicted in tomb of Kenamun, 151–52, 155; depicted in tomb of Nebamun, 156
LGM. *See* Last Glacial Maximum
life table, model, 190, *192*, 194, 196–97
Linear Bandkeramik (LBK) culture, 36, 38, 44–45n4, 62, 167, 175, 186
Linear Pottery culture. *See* Linear Bandkeramik
LLD. *See* Long Distance Dispersal
Lombok, 298; Strait, 298, 303, 306
Long Distance Dispersal (LDD, *also* sweepstakes dispersal and waif dispersal), 294, 301–302, 307–308, 309n4
Lower Paleolithic, 294, 297–98, *304*, *305*, 306, 309n2
Luzon: Cagayan Valley, 300, 307; Callao Cave, 299, 300, 308; *Homo (H.) luzonensis*, 300, 308

MacHack VI (chess algorithm), 330
Maidanetske (Tomashovskaya group), 204, 218–21
Makassar, 300; Strait, 298, 303, 306
Malay Peninsula, 298
Malthus, Thomas Robert. *See* neo-Malthusian population dynamics
Manzikert, Battle of, 85, 231
MARDU (*Amurru*, Amorrite), 250–52
Mari, 156, 252, 253
Marine Isotope Stage (MIS), 297, 303, 304, *305*
Marxist materialism, 33–34
mass displacement, 2, 16, 134, 135, 140–41, 230–34, 242–43
mating networks, 62, 65, 70; exogamy and female abduction, 38, 39, 40, 124–25; patrilocal residence, 38, 42, 124
Medinet Habu reliefs, 155
mega-sites of the Western Tripolye Culture, 184, 186–87, 196, 204, 218–21
Megiddo, 154

Mesopotamia: genomes of agriculturalists, 83–84; greater, 261; isotopic maps, 250; mobility of cattle 156; Old Assyrian traders from northern, 252–53, 261–63; southern, 253, 256–57, 259, 260; textual and linguistic evidence for micro-movements in, 250–51, 252. *See also* Kura-Araxes; Uruk
Messenian Salinity Crisis, 297
Mesudiye, 276, 283
metallurgy: Etruscan, 102–103; Iberian maritime Bell Beaker, 40
metalsmiths: Assyrian, 262; capture of skilled, 123
micro-mobilities, definition 249–50, 270
microregionalism, 103–104
Middle Paleolithic, 293–94, 297–98, *304, 305,* 306
migration, definitions, 18, 113, 135–36; forced, 113, 230–31; impelled, 229, 231; voluntary, 113–14, 231
migrationist theory, 6, 19, 71, 231
Migrations Period, 5, 41
Miletus, 270–71
militarized society, 36–37, 38, 39, 40
Mindoro Strait, 298, 302, 303, 307
MIS. *See* Marine Isotope Stage
Mississippi River, 117
Mithridates, 138
mitochondrial DNA (mtDNA), 63, 80–81, 124
Mode of Production, 34; Germanic, 36; Neolithic Corporate, 42; Pastoral, 37, 38
Moldova, 183–89, 194–95; life table, *191–92*
Molyneux problem, 329
monumentalization, 229, 236, 237–38, 241–42, 275
mortality: childhood, 188, 190, 194–95, 197; fertility and, 204, 210; mass-, 187; (preindustrial) profiles, 188, 190–91; (perceived) rates of, 193–96; slave raiding and village, 119
mortuary practice, 184, 264; Assyrian, 263; *kispu*, 253, 260. *See also* burial(s); funerary practices

motility, 318, 327
motor control, *323,* 330
Mousterian tradition, 297
Myous, 270–71, 285
myths: and belonging, 235; Indo-European, 57, 67–68; Kossinna's "Nordic," 7, 81–82; origin, 240–41; and reformation of identity, 230, 241, 243; Southeast Asian warrior, 116

nakharar (princely house), 238, 240
Naplanum, 251–52
nature versus nurture, 320
Naxos, 297
Neanderthal (*Homo neanderthalensis*), 81, 293, 297, 307–308
Nebamun tomb (TT17), 155–56
Nebelevka (Western Tripolye Culture), 196, 204
neo-Malthusian population dynamics, 16, 205, 221
neo-processual archaeology, 148–49
neoteny, 327
network(s): "affiliation," 10; approaches, 4, 10, 16, 105, 157, 209, 222, 276; captives and cultural, 15; Hellenistic, 272; of kinship, 41, 70; maritime, 42, 269; mating, 62, 65, 70; pastoral, 37; Plains tribes and European trade, 122; religious, 33; settlement, 239; of social relations, 33–34, 171, 257; transregional trade, 42, 97, 261. *See also* Social Network Analysis (SNA)
neutron activation analysis, 255
New Archaeology (processualism). *See* processual archaeology
New Guinea, 298
New Materialism in archaeology, 33
nomad(s), 331; conquest colonization, 36–39; identity, 252; Indo-European horse-riding pastoral, 57; large-scale movements of, 250; steppe, 39, 55, 62; Turkic-speaking, 85
North Africa, 2, 134, 154
North Pacific Rim, 115, 119
Northwest Coast of North America, 115, 116–17, 119, 120

nostalgia, 233, 241
Numha, 252

Old Assyrian trading empire, 252–53, 261–63
oral histories, 19n3, 61, 115
Orce, 306
Orientalization, 97, 99
out of Africa, 3, 80, 81, 201, 332
ovicaprids, 175, 176
oxygen isotopic analysis: goat and donkey at Tell es-Safi/Gath, 156; Linear Pottery culture, 62; Tell Abraq, Bronze Age tomb, 154

Palamutbükü Adası, 281, 283
Palawan, 298, 302, 307
Paleolithic: hunter-gatherers' growth rate, 194; Lower, 294, 297–98, *304*, *305*, 306, 309n2; Marxist theory since, 34; Middle, 293–94, 297–98, *304*, *305*, 306; "seafaring debate," 293–94
Pan paniscus (bonobos), 319
Pan troglodytes (chimpanzee), 319
Pannonian Basin (*also* Carpathian Basin), 70, 175
pastoralism: Corded Ware people, 69–70; Kura-Araxes culture, 254, 258–61; mixed farming combined with, 38, 40; mobile, 17, 70, 250, 251–52, 254, 257–59, 260–61; pastoral conquest, 36–39; Pastoral Mode of Production, 37, 38, 69; Yamnaya, 38, 65
Patras, Gulf of, 304, 307
patrilocality, 38, 42, 124
Pergamum, 138
phenotype, 319
Philippines: captured women in slave raiding chiefdoms, 116–17, 123; hominin infiltration, 300, 307; paleo-, 298, 306
Phoenicians: colonialist narrative, 96–97, 102, 105; Etruria and Sardinia, 103; trade network, 42
pigs *(sus domesticus)*, 175, 176
pilgrimage, 253, 317

Pit-Grave culture. *See* Yamnaya
Pithekoussai, 137–38
place attachment, 233, 235, 237–40, 243
place making, 231, 232, 236–38, 241–43
Plains: Great, 120, 122; High, 123; tribes, 117, 120, 122
Plakias region (Crete), 297, 298
Plautus (Titus Maccius Plautus), 134
PNI. *See* potential natural increase
Poland, 66, 69–70
Pontic: -Caspian steppes, 57, 60, 65, 66; Christians, 85; steppes, 14, 189
population genomics, 31, 184, 187, 196
post-processual archaeology, 8, 43, 149, 231; integrating processual and, 13–14, 157, 202, 210, 222, 243
potential natural increase (PNI) of a given population, 185, 187–88, 193–97
prestige: goods, 34, 255, 257; male, 70, 115–16, 119
primates, 301–302, 319, 325
processual archeology (New Archaeology): in the Anglophone world 7–8; culture history versus, 15, 87, 148; the "Great Divide," 9–11; integrating post-processual and, 13–14, 157, 202, 210, 222, 243; neo-, 148–49; postcolonial view and, 99; versus post-processual, 43; processual approach to migration, 55, 59–60, 66, 68, 71, 185, 232
production. *See* Mode of Production
Pueblo villages, 68, 117; people, 117, 123
push-pull models, 59–60, 71, 114, 222, 231; factors, 62, 256, 331

Qenamun. *See* Kenamun

radiocarbon dating. *See* ^{14}C dating
rage to master, 330
raiding: Indo-European myths of male war bands, 67–68; slave, 40–41, 112, 116–19; and trading, 38, 39, 40, 42, 122, 125; Viking, 38, 117–18, 119: of women (and children), 40, 41, 112, 116–20, 122, 125–26

Red Black Burnished Ware (also Kura-Araxes Ware), 253, *255*. *See also* Khirbet Kerak Ware
Red Sea, 296, 303, 332
refugee(s), 113, 149, 231, 241, 250, 255, 260; crisis, 202, 230; resettled, 230, 243; study of, 113, 232–35, 243
relocations, 3, 250; duration of, 113; forced, 136, 229–33, 241; landscapes of, 235, 236–37, 243; serial, 183; urban (*metoikesis* and *synoikesis*), 270–71, 272. *See also* displacement; resettlement
resettlement: forced, 230, 232–34, 236, 243; landscape of, 229, 235–36, 243; and material culture, 237–38, 240, 242; memory and, 232–33, 240; multigenerational process of, 230, 240, 243; of refugees, 229; societal impacts of, 16, 230. *See also* displacement; relocations
Rhodes, city of, 271–72, 285
Rodafnidia, 297
Romania, 60, 184, 185, 187, *188*, 195–96
Romanovka (Tomashovskaya group), 218–21
Romans, 9, 96, 97, 117, 138–39, 140. *See also* Italians
Rubenid dynasty, 233, 237, 241–42

Saccharomyces cerevisiae (baker's or brewer's yeast), 319
Sahul, 298, *299*, 308–309
Sakızyakası, 281, 283
Samara Valley Project, 63, 65, 67
Samsi-Addu (Shamshi-Addad), 252–53, 263; Upper Kingdom of, *251*, 252–53
Sardinia, 103, 104, 105, 154
Sardinians, 86
SARP model, 187, 195
scouts, 60, 66, 67–68
sedentism, 5, 17, 83–84, 249, 253, 260–61, 262
sentience, 17, 317, 323–27, 329, 331
Shamshi-Addad. *See* Samsi-Addu
sheep and goat (ovicaprids), 156, 175, 176

Shirakavan, 239–40
Sidon, 153, 154
Sinai Peninsula, 295, 332
Sis, 233, 240
Sivas, 231, 236
slavery: (farming) conquest expansion, 37, 39, 41; slave raiding, 39, 116, 117, 119; slave trade, 39–41, 116–18, 119, 122, 125, 333; of women and children, 40, 41, 112, 116–20, 122, 124–26; written records of, 114–15, 117–18, 120–21, 134, 136, 153
Slovakia, 66, 70
SNA. *See* Social Network Analysis
So'a Basin (Flores), 298, 308
Social Network Analysis (SNA), 278–80; visualizations, 270, 280–86
sodalities, 40, 41, 42
Southern Bug: and Dnieper interfluve, 184, 196, 204, 212, 218, 219; and Dniester interfluve, 204, 218, 221
status: of captives, 114, 121–22, 125; exotic goods to enhance, 255, 257; male, 70, 115–16, 119; migration and social, 15, 134, 136, 137, 140, 153; political, 241
Stélida (Naxos), 297
Stena I, IV (Chelchelnitskaya group), 218–21
steppe(s): -derived ancestry, 14, 58, 65, 66–67, 70, 82; forest-, 183, 186, 195–96, 204; Hungary, 38; "Neolithic," 189; North Caucasus, 65, 66; Pontic, 14, 189; Pontic-Caspian, 57, 60, 65, 66; Volga, 63, 65, 67–68; Volga-Ural, 63
strontium isotopic analysis, 32, 33, 35, 123; Bell Beaker complex and Early Bronze Age, Lech valley, 124; Corded Ware cemeteries, 37; goat and donkey at Tell es-Safi/Gath, 156; Linear Pottery culture, 62; Megiddo Middle Bronze Age tomb, 154; Tell Abraq Bronze Age tomb, 154
subsistence: practices, 254, 258, 259; resources, 204
Sulawesi, 298, 300, 302, 307
Sulu Sea, 303, 307
Sumatra, 117, 298, 304–305

Sundaland, 298, 303, 304, 307
Sun-Language thesis, 85
synoikism (also *sympoliteia*, amalgamation) 270–71, 272

Talepu site (Sulawesi), 299–300
Talianki, 204, 218–19
Tekir (Knidos or "New Knidos"), 272–75, 276, 281, 282–84, 285–86
Tell Abraq, 154
Tell es-Safi/Gath, 156
Tell Miqne/Ekron, 155
textiles, 151, 262, 332
Thebes (Egypt), 151, 156
Theropithecus gelada, 319
third spaces, 256, 257, 258
Thutmose III period, 156
Thutmose IV period, 151
Tigris River, 252, 261
Tomashovskaya group (Western Tripolye Culture), 196, 218–21
T'oros: church of, 241; Prince, 233
tourists, 333
trade: aDNA and stable isotope analysis, 149; in the ancient economy, 9; animal, 153, 156–57; Delos, Mediterranean trading hub, 139; and identity, 42; large-scale bulk, 152; maritime, 39, 42, 99, 149, 156; Old Assyrian, 252–53, 261–63; palatial, 249; between Plains tribes and Europeans, 122; in Plautus comedies, 134; private, 249; and raiding, 38, 39, 40, 42, 122, 125; slave, 39–41, 116–18, 119, 122, 125, 333; small-scale, 151; variability of objects and, 321; Uruk period, 255
traders: Bronze Age sodalities of warriors and, 42; Old Assyrian, 261–63; and pastoral conquest migrations, 37; Romano-Italian, 140; as scouts, 68; slave, 117
tribes, 39–40, 120; Germanic, 5, 117; Michigamea, 117; Pawnee, 117; (Great) Plains, 117, 122

Ugarit, 153
Umwelt, 322

Ur, Third Dynasty, 251–52
Urnfield expansion, 36, 39
Uruk expansion, 16, 253–61, 262–63

vagrancy, 136, 333
Vahram of Edessa, 241
Vasilkov, 220
Veselyj Kut, 169
Viking: expansions, 36, 39; raiding and trading, 38, 117–18, 119
Visual Basic for Applications (VBA), 202, 216
Vykhvatintsy cemetery, 188

wabartum, 261
waif dispersal (*also* Long Distance Dispersal (LDD) and sweepstakes dispersal), 294, 301–302, 307–308, 309n4
Wallace, Alfred Russel, 6, 298
Wallacea, 298–303, 306–308
Wallace-Huxley Line, 298–300, 307, 308
war bands, Indo-European male, 67–68
Warad-Sin, 252
warfare, 36; to achieve status for males, 115–16, 119; and captive taking, 112, 114–16, 118–19, 124–25; endemic, 39; people fleeing, 2, 113, 201; small-scale recurring violence, 42, 45n5. *See also* conquest, colonization; raiding
warrior(s): -based migration (male-dominated), 37, 38, 39; -based societies (patrilocal), 42; Bell Beaker, 41; Corded Ware, 41; elite of militarized, 40; Gimbutas' invasion of, 71; sodalities, 40, 41, 42; success based on captive taking, 115–17; Viking, 117
wašbūtum (residents who live permanently abroad), 261
wave of advance model, 61–63, 332
wéiqí (game of go), 327
Western Tripolye Culture (WTC), 196, 204, 212; Chechelnitskaya group: 218–21; mega-sites, 184, 186–87, 196, 204, 218–21; Tomashovskaya group sites, 204, 218–21. *See also* Cucuteni-Tripolye cultural complex (CTCC)
wolves, 68

WTC. *See* Western Tripolyle Culture

Yamnaya people: Corded Ware people genetically related to, 58, 65–66, 68–70, 82; genetic study of, 14, 63, 65–67; Gimbutas' Kurgan Culture, 56, 57, 58, 60, 71; kurgan burials, 60, 63, 64, 66–67, 69; Hungary, 38, 57, 60, 63, 66, 70; migration into the Danube valley, 57, 63, 71; Pastoral Mode of Production, 37; Ukraine west of the Dnieper River, 187; warrior-based type of migration, 37, 39

Yasmah-Addu, 252, 253

Y-DNA, 63, 66, 80

Yersinia pestis (plague), 44n3, 187

Zagros Mountains, 83, 154, 252

Zakynthos, 297, 303

www.ingramcontent.com/pod-product-compliance
Ingram Content Group UK Ltd.
Pitfield, Milton Keynes, MK11 3LW, UK
UKHW050544150426
5217IPUK00026B/2063

9 781438 488004